1-49

FIRE FROM THE ASHES

To Nora

One who knows
the boundless love
of a friend.

Thank you & yours.
Contained in this book
is a cause to which
I have dedicated my
life.

Nigel Hobina mashl
18.9.99

Fire From the Ashes

A Chronicle of the Revolution in Tigray, Ethiopia, 1975-1991

Jenny Hammond

The Red Sea Press, Inc.
Publishers & Distributors of Third World Books

The Red Sea Press, Inc.
Publishers & Distributors of Third World Books

First Printing 1999

Book design: Wanjiku Ngugi
Cover design: Jonathan Gullery

Library of Congress Cataloging-in-Publication Data

Hammond, Jenny.
Fire from the ashes : a chronicle of the revolution in Tigray, Ethiopia, 1975-1991 / by Jenny Hammond.
p. cm.
Includes bibliographical references and index.
ISBN 1-56902-086-8 (hc.). -- ISBN 1-56902-087-6 (pbk.)
1. Tigray Kifle Hager (Ethiopia)--History--Autonomy and independence movements. 2. Hezbawi wayane harenet Tegray--History. 3. Guerillas---Ethiopia--History--20th century. I. Title.
DT390. T5H36 1998
963'.4--dc21 98-44349
CIP

We never gave up. Now our children started again in 1975 what we started before. The flames of the first Weyane were quenched. But the embers were still burning and our children took fire from the ashes.

—Desta Abuy

Contents

Acronyms

ANDM	Amhara National Democratic Movement, the new name given to the EPDM after the end of the civil war
EDORM	Ethiopian Democratic Officers' Revolutionary Movement One of the member organizations of the EPRDF after 1989
EDU	Ethiopian Democratic Union, a feudal-monarchist party defeated by TPLF in the late 1970s
ELF	Eritrean Liberation Front
EPDM	Ethiopian People's Democratic Movement, a largely Amhara organization founded in 1981 to oppose the military dictatorship. In 1989 it formed a united front with the TPLF and thereby formed the coalition movement, EPRDF
EPLF	Eritrean People's Liberation Front
EPRDF	Ethiopian People's Revolutionary Democratic Front. A coalition of four organizations, TPLF, EPDM, EDORM and OPDO, formed in 1991. Since the end of the war it has expanded to include other organizations
EPRP	Ethiopian People's Revolutionary Party
ICRC	International Committee of the Red Cross
MLLT	Marxist-Leninist League of Tigray
OPDO	Oromo People's Democratic Organisation, one of the member organizations of the EPRDF

PMAC	Provisional Military Administrative Council or the Dergue
REST	The Relief Society of Tigray
TNO	Tigray National Organization
TPLF	Tigray People's Liberation Front, founded in February 1975
WAFT	Women's Association of the Fighters of Tigray
WPE	Workers' Party of Ethiopia, established in 1984 as the political wing of the military junta. It was responsible for carrying out many ofthe atrocities ordered by the Dergue

Glossary

Afars Minority nationality of pastoralist Muslims living in the eastern lowlands of Ethiopia. Since 1993 they have had a separate state under the federal structure of the Federal Democratic Republic of Ethiopia (FDRE).

Agazi One of the founder fighters of the TPLF, who was killed in the second year of the armed struggle. His name was given to the spectacular operation in February 1986 in which the TPLF released 1,800 Dergue prisoners from Mekelle prison.

Agew A minority nationality divided between Tigray and Wollo until their lands became part of the Amhara region under the federal structure introduced in 1993.

AK47 Semi-automatic rifle, supplied in the first place by the USSR to the Dergue army, but becoming the weapon of choice, through capture, of other armed movements in Ethiopia.

Amhara The nationality which has been politically dominant in Ethiopia since the nineteenth century until the EPRDF victory in 1991 forced them to relinquish power.

Amharic Language of the Amhara people and the national language of Ethiopia.

baito Elected local council in Tigray.

banda Clandestine groups of Tigrayan mercenaries trained by the Dergue to infiltrate dissident areas and perpetrate acts of terror.

birr Unit of Ethiopian currency.

Blatta Minor feudal title of respect.

Dejazmach Feudal title meaning "Commander of the gate."

Dergue Popular term for the military government of Ethiopia. Amharic for "committee."

Dergue towns The five main towns of Tigray which remained in government contronl until the Dergue was forced to evacuate them in 1989. They were Mekelle Adigrat, Axum, Adwa and Endaselassie.

ferenji White person.

field Field of revolutionary activity, the rural area.

First Weyane Peasant uprising against Emperor Haile Selassie in Tigray in 1943.

Fitaurary Feudal title meaning "Commander of the vanguard."

'Front' Shorthand reference in this text to TPLF/EPRDF.

gabi White traditional shawl made of four layers of hand-woven cotton, worn by both men and women.

Grazmach Feudal title meaning "Commander of the left wing."

Hamien Women who use their traditional poetic skills for begging.

hidmo Type of stone building with stone and turf roof.

himbasha Traditional Ethiopian bread baked in rounds on a griddle.

injera Fermented grain pancake, the staple food of Ethiopia.

kebelle Dergue urban association, retained after 1991 as the smallest unit of local administration.

Kegnazmach Feudal title, meaning "Commander of the right wing."

kushett Hamlet, part of a village, smallest unit of rural administration in Tigray.

mes/tej Tigrinya and Amharic names, respectively, for the traditional honey wine.

Mass Bureau	Department 08, the TPLF department responsible for administration and political relations with the rural people during the armed struggel.
melkes	Funeral oration, sometimes critical of the social and political system.
melkesti	Men or women poets skilled at delivering the *melkes* or funeral chant.
MiG	Soviet fighter plane, either MiG 21 or MiG 23, used for aerial bombardments by the Dergue.
Oromo	Majority nationality in central/southern Ethiopia.
Ras	Prince.
sewa/talla	Tigrinya and Amharic names, respectively, for a local beer fermented from sorghum or millet and herbs.
shemek	Trained contra-guerrillas of the Dergue.
Shewa	Ethiopian province, largely populated by the Amhara people.
shiro	Nutritious puree of chick pea flour, onions and spices.
sorghum	Grain crop (red or white) common in lowland areas of Ethiopia.
tabia	Village, usually comprising three or four kushettes.
taff/teff	Tigrinya and Amharic names, respectively, for the unique, indigenous grain crop, which is the preferred grain for injera.
Tigrinya	Language spoken in the highlands of Tigray and Eritrea.
'torch of the revolution'	Politically active member of a local community, given special training by TPLF/EPRDF to lead the local people.
wereda	Administrative district, comprising seven to fourteen tabia.
weyane	Tigrinya for "revolution" or "revolutionary."

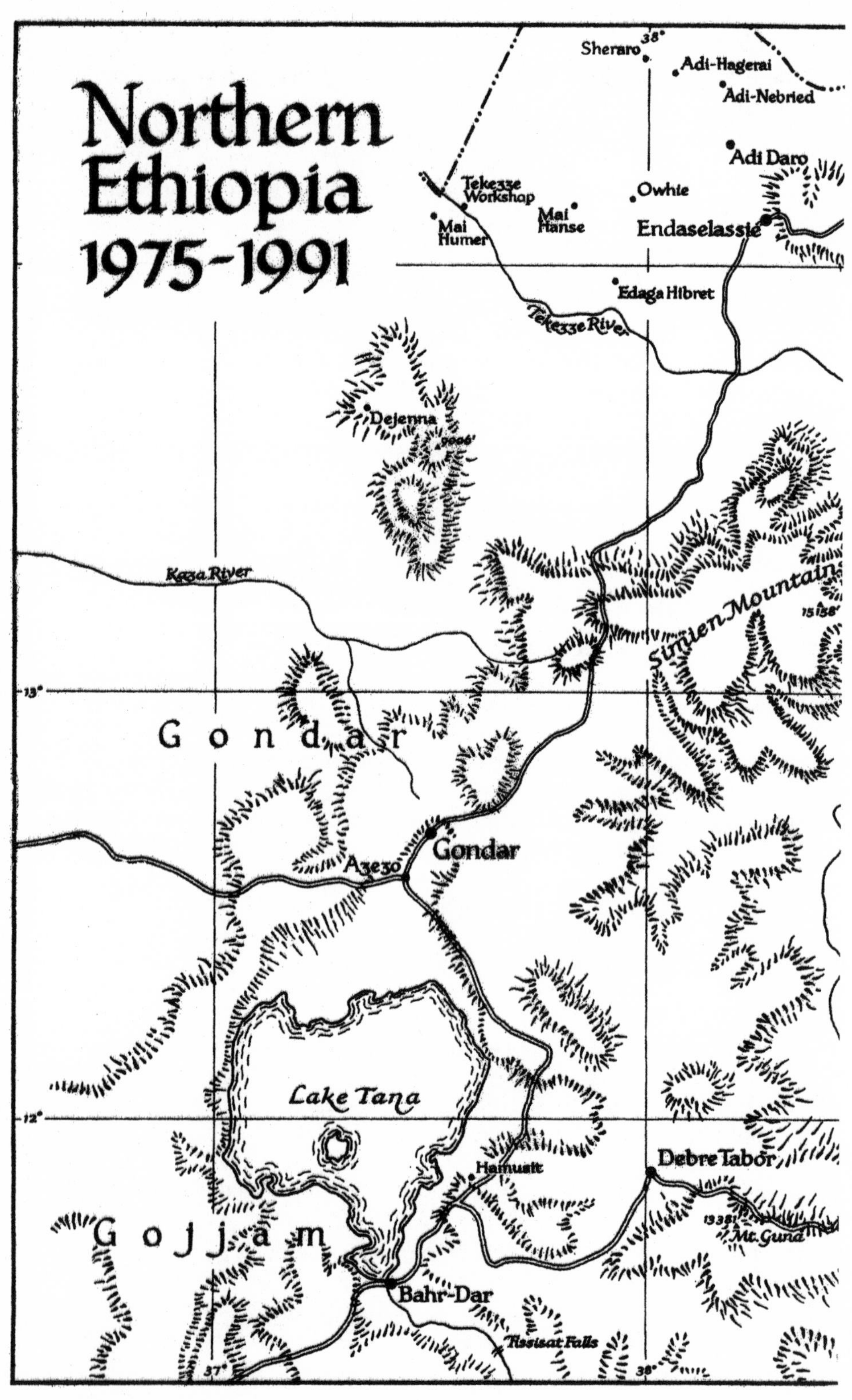

Northern Ethiopia 1975-1991
Sheraro
Adi-Hagerai
Adi-Nebried
Adi Daro
Tekezze Workshop
Owhie
Mai Hanse
Mai Humer
Endaselassie
Edaga Hibret
Tekezze River
Dejenna
Kaza River
Simien Mountains
Gondar
Gondar
Azezo
Lake Tana
Debre Tabor
Hamusit
Mt. Guna
Gojjam
Bahr-Dar
Tisisat Falls
13°
12°
37°
38°

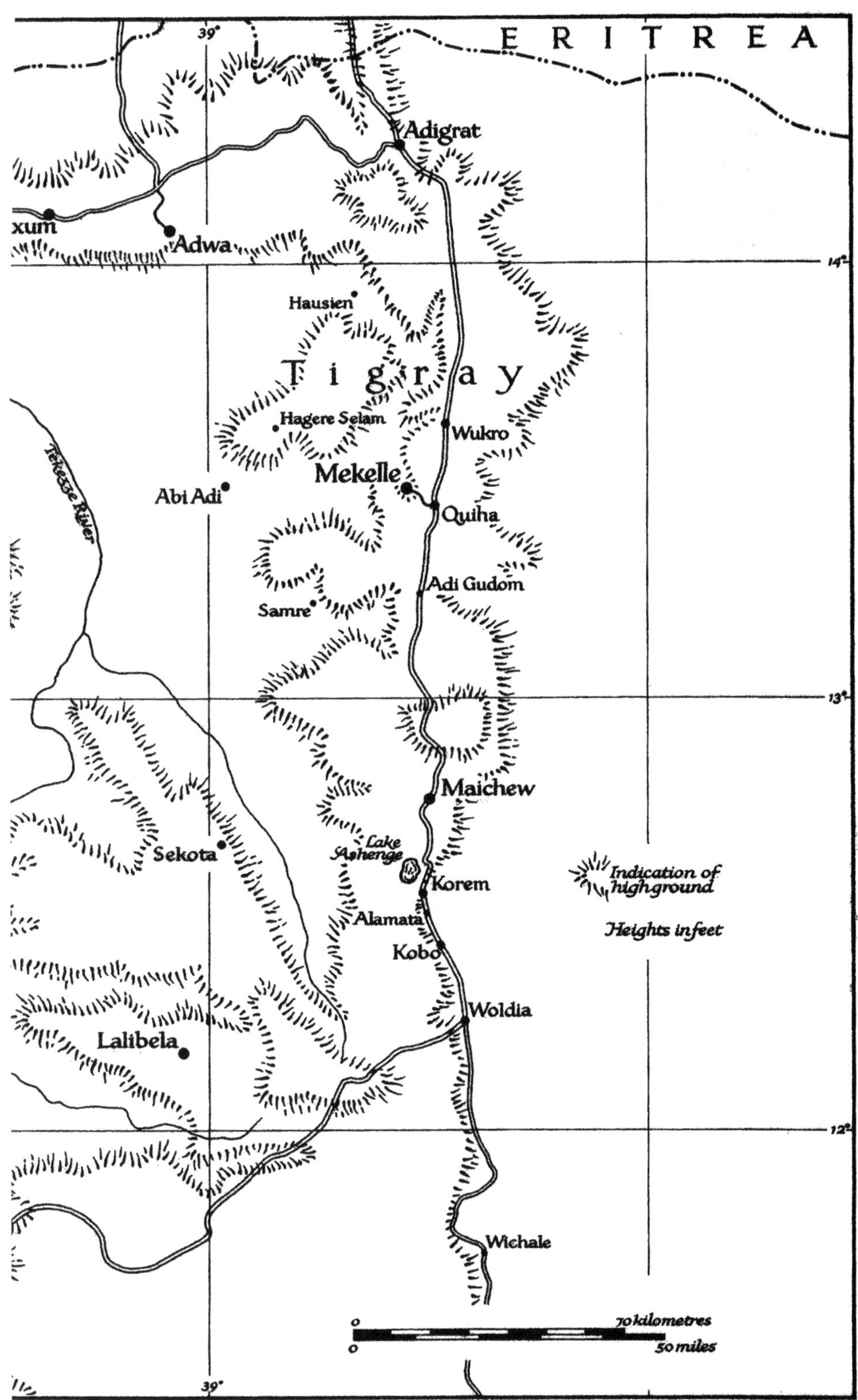
ERITREA
39°
Adigrat
xum
Adwa
14°
Hausien
Tigray
Hagere Selam
Wukro
Tekesse River
Mekelle
Abi Adi
Quiha
Adi Gudom
Samre
13°
Maichew
Lake Ashenge
Sekota
Korem
Indication of high ground
Alamata
Heights in feet
Kobo
Woldia
Lalibela
12°
Wichale
0
70 kilometres
0
50 miles
39°

Ethiopia and its Administrative Regions
Before 1991

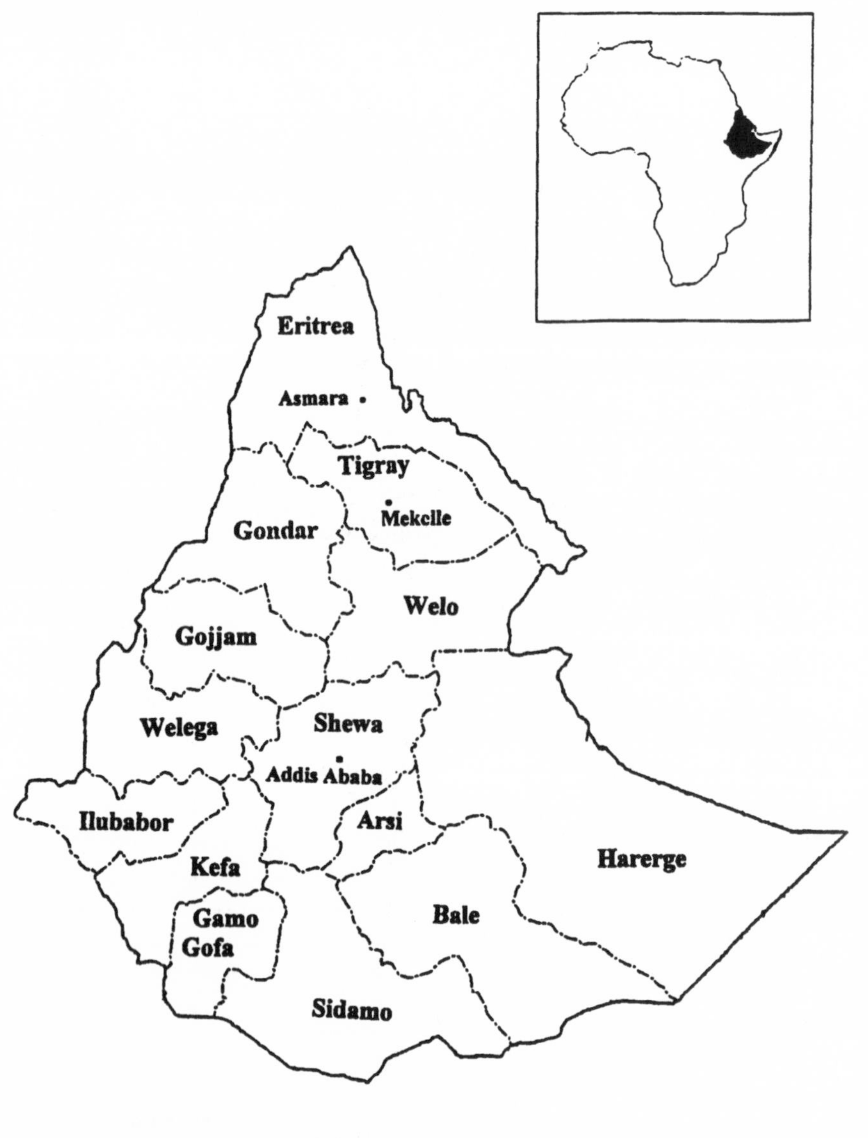

Ethiopia and its Administrative Regions
After the formation of the Federal Government in 1995

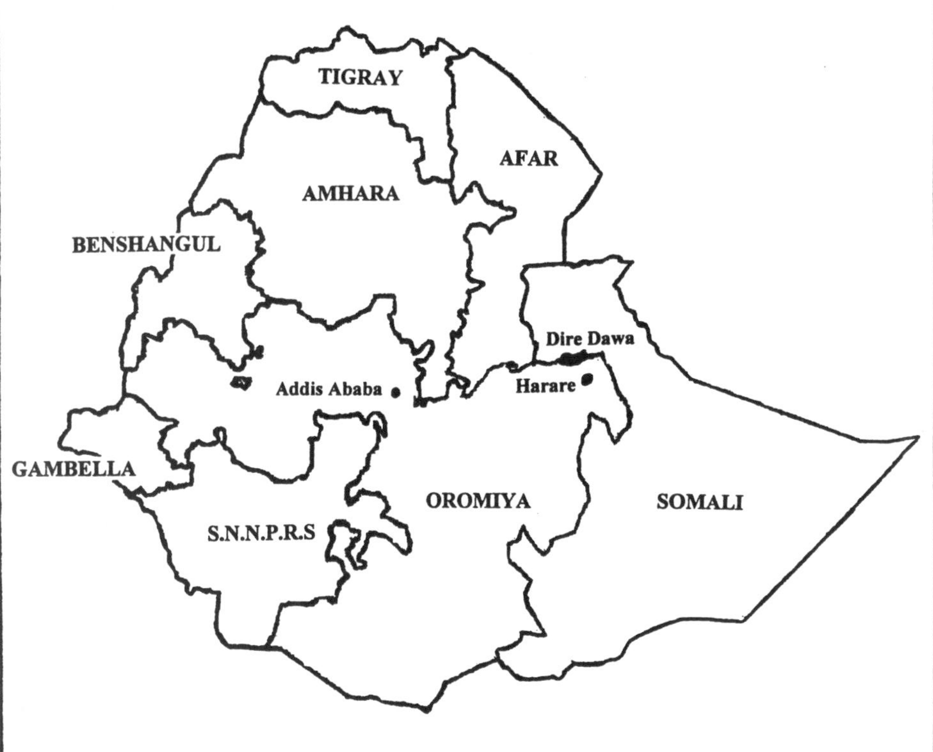

ACKNOWLEDGEMENTS

I would like to thank the following for their help with this book: the people of Ethiopia whose steadfastness, endurance, warmth and hospitality have become models to me of human behavior; the TPLF for facilitating my journeys and for giving me such freedom at a difficult time, without any attempt to censor my conclusions or accounts; the EPDM in the field (now ANDM) for its openness and cooperation; my guides and translators, Berhanu Abadi, Heshe Lemma, Mulugeta Berhe and Aklilu Tekemte for their energy and patience; Solomon Inquai for information and comments; Christian Aid for funding the first journey and for help with photographs; the Ethiopian Embassy in London for its help and cooperation; and of course to my family for encouraging me to take up all opportunities and for responding so wholeheartedly to all my experiences on my return.

Introduction

This book is the story of a revolution. In May 1991 the long civil war in Ethiopia came to an end. It was started in Tigray by a small group of students; in official terms, it was won by a coalition of liberation fronts (the Ethiopian People's Revolutionary Democratic Front); in practice it was won by the massive movement of peasant farmers who supported and fought with the fronts in the north. They were determined to tolerate no longer the repression, despotism and brutality of successive regimes. Political solutions since 1991 have grown directly out of the experience of dictatorship. Power has been decentralized to the regions and regional and local democratic elections have been conducted under international supervision. In 1995 national elections brought into power the first democratically elected government in Ethiopia's history.

It has been a hidden history, yet it is becoming increasingly important, not only because it makes visible the record of those now in power in Ethiopia, but because it provides an important and unusual, perhaps unique, example of people forced to take up arms in order to survive, determined to wrestle into being a more just and accountable political system—and succeeding. It is a very different story from the images of dependency and famine often associated with Ethiopia in the West and a reversal of the usual assumptions in the 'developed' world that the West is the provider and teacher and poor countries the receivers and learners in survival battles in the modern world.

I began monitoring the activities of the liberation fronts in Ethiopia from 1984, especially the Tigray People's Liberation Front (TPLF), and the book is based on my experiences in three protracted journeys in 1987, 1989 and 1991. It presents the process of change which started with ten young students going off into the wilds of Tigray in 1975 to start the revolution and ended with the successful taking of Addis Ababa in May 1991. I travelled widely throughout northern Ethiopia, talking to peasants and townspeople, at times living and travelling with guerrilla fighters, recurrently meeting and talking with the leadership of the Front in the caves and camouflaged strongholds of their base area. Their voices are included in the account, describing their own experiences and interpreting their own history. Their words do not always accord with the European view and often undermine the confidence with which European visitors, including myself, claim expertise or authority in understanding and interpreting what they are witnessing.

The account is divided into three sections, each corresponding to a different journey. All three accumulate into the more important and crucial 'journey' of Ethiopia itself from dictatorship to democracy. Each section has a different quality and illustrates a further stage in a dynamic process. The final one, told by fighters and a cross-section of Addis Ababa citizens, is the story of the capture of the capital, Addis Ababa, which brought the long civil war to an end.

Part One

First Journey

December 1986 to 1987

1

Air Raid

February 1987

The MiGs come at seven in the morning. Their distant rumble mixes with my dreams. Berhanu shouts. Techana, on guard, hurls himself into the tent. In the two seconds before the planes scream overhead, so low they must have bent the trees, I am out of my sleeping bag, grabbing my boots. The roar of engines is like a body blow. One. Two. Three MiGs.

"Quick! We go!" says Berhanu.

There is no time for laces, so I pull sandals onto feet raw with blisters. In a frozen moment, poised for flight at the tent flap, we wait to hear the planes disappear into the blue morning. Maybe it's a coincidence and they don't know we are here.

But they do know. The sound swells again. They are circling, coming back, and we are prisoners in the flimsy tent as the first MiG goes over. Then we are running, but we only make the cover of a bush and a bank before the second MiG screams overhead. I press my face into the dry soil under my shawl in case my whiteness shines. Under my cheek, in my flesh, the earth booms and judders as the bombs hit the ground. Then we are running again, across the open spaces between the sparse trees, before we throw ourselves under a patch of scrub as the next plane comes.

We run in crazy zigzags from clump to clump. The MiGs circle again and again, expelling their deadly burden. Under one low tree we crouch with peasants who had come for last night's celebrations and are now on their way home. "Selam" we say to one another and shake hands politely as the blast covers us with dust. Berhanu gives me a nudge and suddenly I see one of them is Leteberhan, the young "torch of the revolution" who made such an impression on me in Awhie, so many miles away.[1] She is smiling at me, but we have time only for a brief embrace before Berhanu urges us on, running, running.

My mind is clear and lucid. I think, I didn't know bombs sounded like that. Bombs thud and boom. These also crack and crackle like gunfire. Then I realize it is gunfire. The MiGs are not only dropping bombs. They are strafing the valley floor. I feel no fear. I even have time to make observations. Berhanu's heels, as he runs in front of me, pop up and down like two pale rabbit scuts. I am worried about my feet and how long I can keep this up. The breath in my throat roars louder than the planes and my chest feels too small to contain the compulsion of my heart.

The bombing and strafing continue for more than half an hour before the MiGs fly off into the heat haze. It seems like half a day. We run along a little gulley, which protects us from all but a direct hit. It leads to a camouflaged storehouse, dug like a cave into the hillside. We are safe. My companions moved urgently, swiftly, during the raid. Now it is over, they get on with the morning as if nothing has happened. Somewhere they find plastic sheets and blankets and lay them on the trodden earth. Two of the peasant women we briefly sheltered with earlier are brought in, their bodies filled with shrapnel. All day we hide among tools and spare parts, until we can leave the area in the safety of darkness.

In the long day that follows, I have plenty of time for reflection. My fingers need to crumble the dry, warm earth. My eyes taste the reality of spades and jerry-cans. I smell the sun outside and the sharp edges of life. A series of chances brought me to war-torn Ethiopia. Maybe only chance will take me home again. I think of my family, glad they do not know how I have spent this morning. They would make too much of it. Images of my four children shimmer in my mind, each frozen in some characteristic posture. I am curiously detached.

The woman moans. They have given her pain-killing drugs. She is wounded and in pain, but she is not dead. She knows this too and smiles at me in moments of wakefulness. What is sensational, exceptional, to me, yet leaves me unharmed, is to her a common occurrence. For the peasants and fighters in this valley, the air-raid is all in a day's work. For me it is a turning point. In some obscure way it turns me from an observer of a revolution into a participant. I understand for the first time in my bones, not just in my head, why every bomb that falls, every death, reinforces a passionate determination to compel the birth of a different future.

But what dictates the moment of ripeness? For hundreds of years Tigrayan peasants more or less accepted the normality of exploitation and poverty. What finally made them say "Enough?" What drives a people over the abyss from fatalistic acceptance of routine misery to armed struggle?

"There is no other way," I remember a combat fighter called Meley explaining a few weeks ago, as we crouched in a hot dusty gulley waiting for transport. "There is no democracy. We can only fight." There was a pause. Then he suddenly added, "We want to hear our children singing in school instead of hearing bombs. In fact we want peace."[2]

They have been engaged in this struggle for twelve years. I have been in Tigray for as many weeks. My reasons for coming are growing dim. I am already a different woman from the one who crossed the Sudanese border by night convoy more than two months ago.

2

Convoy

December 1986

"Goodbye Sudan." At last!

I left Gedaref[1] on a convoy of fifteen Mercedes trucks at three o'clock this morning. It has taken more than two weeks in the heat and sweat of Khartoum and Gedaref to get the necessary papers to cross the border into Ethiopia. There is no other way into the areas held by the Tigray People's Liberation Front.[2] If there were I would have taken it. It is not only the heat and dust that stifle in the Sudan; it is the bureaucracy, the photographs in triplicate, the endless queues for papers if you want to move from one town to another, the police checkpoints when you do.

Berhe woke me at two and drove me to the Workshop to join the convoy.[3] *The Workshop*, as it's always called, is a huge maintenance depot in the dunes outside Gedaref, from which all supplies and relief aid are taken by convoy into Tigray. It is run by the Relief Society of Tigray, REST for short.[4] Berhe supervises the Gedaref operation and also takes care of foreigners passing through the Sudan into Tigray. A heavy man, he eased himself out of the Toyota and disappeared into the darkness. I sat in the landcruiser waiting for something to happen. The sheds and repair shops were immobile and silent, lines of huge trucks outlined against a blaze of stars. We waited here for hours three nights ago and then I was taken back to my accommodation. There were no explanations.

Before three o'clock, dark forms began to move among the trucks. Yesterday evening, Berhe gave me a sack of tinned and dried food for emergencies. This and my backpack were loaded under the tarpaulins, mechanics checked from truck to truck, engines fired, headlights melted the dark and, at exactly three o'clock, the convoy of fifteen trucks moved off. I was in the cab of the tenth truck between the driver and a guard, two silent, anonymous figures, their heads muffled in shawls.

Towards six the sky began to lighten. The sun seemed to catapult above the horizon and my companions, who had not exchanged a word, cast off their wrappings, introduced themselves as Abadi and Bissrat and began to chat and laugh together. The truck bounced and strained over twisting dirt roads, which had been gouged into fissures set hard in the sun. The desert gave way to flat fields of sorghum and dryland grasses, then low wooded hills. As the convoy passed through villages, raising an immense cloud of dust, women stirring to collect wood and water, small boys driving oxen to the field, waved and smiled and the driver returned their salutations. In another hour or so we arrived at this transit camp, a short drive from the border. Bombing by Ethiopian government MiGs means that it is possible to travel only at night. We will wait here during the heat of the day and depart at dusk.

At nine in the morning it is already hot. I am writing my diary in the shade of a hut made from tree branches and grasses. The day is alive with noises. Tigrayan voices talking, shouting instructions. Grass walls crack and stir in the breeze and the sorghum fields make a continuous background rustle. Inappropriately, it reminds me of the sea noise near my sister's house in Cornwall. Birds are calling to one another from small trees twisting up the slopes.

A few feet away several sleeping forms are wrapped up like coccoons. The one in a sleeping bag, a Dutchman called Hans, travelling in the opposite direction out of Tigray to Gedaref, is tired and disgruntled after twenty four hours over "unbelievable" roads.

"And the food. *Injera* is OK once or twice, but morning, noon and night!"

He works as a mechanic for a relief agency, helping sort out problems with the convoy, wrecked by the roads even with a special reinforcement he has devised. I could not believe, I replied, the roads we had wriggled over that morning.

"This is the Sudan. In Tigray it is much worse. Sometimes it takes an hour to cover eight or nine kilometers."

At about five in the afternoon, a bustle of activity signals preparations for departure. The trucks have been dispersed all day in patches of shade. Engines are revving and now they are brought up into line in the big clearing. People emerge from scattered huts and the near-deserted settlement suddenly looks like market day. Crowds of passengers swarm up the sides of the trucks. If they are lucky, they will be riding into Tigray on top of the load, women with children and bundles, men who came to the Sudan to find work and are now going home, fighters for the Front posted from the Sudan back to "the field." Some of them are returning from the camps set up during the 1984 famine. For a year now thousands of refugees have been trekking back into Tigray on foot, hundreds at a time, organized by REST and guarded by fighters. Of these, only the sick, the old, the pregnant and the newly-delivered are sure of a place on convoys. The others are trying their luck.

A crowd has gathered by the trucks. Among them, a group of young men and women are talking and laughing together. They are wearing jeans and T-shirts, but they all have stripy shawls draped over their shoulders. They are fighters for the front. They turn, smiling and curious, and a slim young man surprises me by putting his arm around my shoulders. He strokes my cheek and draws me into the group. Only when he asks my name in stilted classroom English do I realize he is a woman. The hair is confusing. Northern Ethiopian women wear their hair in a beautiful and distinctive style, fine plaits drawn back from the brow and released at the nape of the neck into bushy curls. Women fighters, on the other hand, cut their hair short like men and wear the same clothes, instead of traditional dresses with tight bodices and full skirts.

Communicating is an uphill task. I can only say, "Hello, how are you?" in Tigrinya and count from one to ten. Two or three of them have a few English phrases, but they are not very relevant to the present situation. They practice them all the same and their companions fall about laughing. They carefully devise questions. Where do I come from? Why I am going to Tigray? Do I know about the struggle? But the only word they understand of my answers is "England." I come from a society where we understand the words, but the barriers are insuperable. Here, we don't have any words, but there seem to be no barriers at all.

They beckon to a young man standing on his own nearby and he comes over, smiling shyly. His name is Woldeselassie and he speaks English because he has been a teacher. His cheekbones arch over the hollows in his face and he has a melancholy expression until he smiles. Now we have an interpreter, the fighters listen seriously and ask me serious questions. They are interested that I know Tigrayans in London, that I know about their revolution.

"How do you know about our struggle? Do English people support us?"

I explain that over the last two or three years I have been researching and writing on the politics of famine.

"Your organization has invited me to come and see for myself, to investigate everything going on here."

"It is good that you come. Tell all the English people to come here and see, like you. When they see what our revolution has done for the people, they will support us. The Russians support the Dergue, who is very bad. Who will support us?'

I know already that "Dergue" is not a Tigrinya word, but Amharic, the official language of Ethiopia, the language of the Amhara people and the governing class. It means "committee," but the Tigrayans use it to mean the military government.[5]

I want to ask some questions too. Where do they come from? Did they want to be fighters or were they compelled? Why have they been in the Sudan? But the sun has slipped behind the hill. The convoy is ready to go. They disperse to climb on top of the trucks and a strange driver comes to tell me I am travelling with him.

I have a sudden urge to pee and, in case this is the last opportunity for some time, I indicate with a sweep of my arm that I am taking a walk to the sorghum field. The driver looks reasonably relaxed about it, but I feel self-conscious as I walk away to hide and the convoy waits. Crouched down in the forest of dry sorghum stems, I discover to my horror that I have started my period. Two weeks early. My tampons are in my backpack which is buried under one of the tarpaulins on one of the trucks. I don't even know which one. The driver looks disconcerted when I ask him to unload my backpack. Passengers climb down again to see what is going on; some drivers climb out of their cabs; I am the center of a circle of curious eyes. I half unpack and dig out my tampons in front of what seems a crowd of thousands.

I walk back again to the sorghum field, wondering why normal biological processes seem so unnatural. Or is it only female ones? The dry season has crazed the soil between the sorghum stalks into a network of cracks, some several inches wide. Trying to hurry, I slip into a fissure and turn my ankle. Come off it, I say to myself, as I limp back to the waiting convoy, you have come here to investigate a revolution. That should put a period into perspective.

An hour later we cross a wide shallow river and we are in Tigray. "Tigray, Tigray," says the driver, with a big smile and a big gesture at everything beyond the windscreen. As it is now pitch dark, I can't see anything beyond the headlights. The guard, on my right, fumbles under the seat. It takes a few seconds for me to realize he is now holding an AK47 ready at the open window. Ready for what? The road seems less bumpy than in the Sudan, but it throws up a fog of dust. Both men wrap their shawls around their heads, leaving slits for the eyes. I do the same with my heavy cotton scarf. Unbearably hot, but better than choking.

The road from the border, carved out of the earth by fighters, is only a few years old. It is only open in the dry season. Every summer the torrents of the rainy season wash it away and every October fighters put it together again before the huge Mercedes trucks of the convoy can use it again. This convoy is the lifeline of the revolution, transporting vital food aid, fuel, and spare parts into the liberated area. But if the rains don't fall, if they don't wash away the road, it is a worse catastrophe for the Tigrayan people than if they do.

For white travellers, the night convoy from the Sudan is more than an ascent from the boiling plain to the mountains. It is more than a journey into the "dark interior" of Africa. It is the beginning of a journey into their own interior, the start of an unravelling process of cultural assumptions constructed over hundreds of years. Is this why generations of explorers have insisted on exoticizing Africa into a continent of unfathomable mystery? Perhaps they are confusing it with the deconstruction of their own unconscious.

A kilometer or so further on, the convoy stops. The engines and headlights are turned off. The driver and the guard get out. After a few minutes I decide to do the same. I climb down from the high cab, waving my legs about to find a foothold in the pitch dark and stand by the truck, unsure what is happening, but conscious that I am standing on Ethiopian soil for the first time. As my eyes adjust, I can pick out the great hulks against the starlight and shadowy figures moving about, their heads swathed in shawls and Kalashnikovs slung on their backs. There is the flash of a torch here and there. It's very quiet.

Someone comes along beside my truck, flashing a torch in my eyes. He says something, but I am blinded and therefore can't seem to hear either. It turns out to be Wolde, who has come to see if I need anything.

"Come over here to the others. There is food."

Ahead, beside a truck, is an illuminated circle. One of many. Some of the fighters I met earlier are crouched around a dish of food. They smile a welcome and make room for us, but first Wolde tips a canteen of water for me to wash my right hand before we begin to eat. They tell me it is the first of their checkpoints. There are *banda* in the area, groups of Dergue "contras," so security is tight.[6] We must be quiet and show few lights. We are eating *injera* smeared with bean paste. *Injera* is a thin, fermented, grain pancake, the staple food of Ethiopia. This one is sour and sticky, made of wheat, but welcome all the same. The fighters apologize, laughing.

"Forgive you. This is picnic," says Hailu.

Wolde tells me sorghum injera is better, but the best is made of *teff,* a grain found only in the Ethiopian highlands.

"One day you will taste it." He looks even more melancholy. "One day perhaps I will taste it again."

"Why 'perhaps?' You are back in Tigray now."

The others, hearing the word *teff*, join in. Some bits I can understand—when they roll their eyes to heaven in ecstasy and kiss their fingers.

The Front's base area, says Wolde, is in the lowlands in the west, where only sorghum grows. Since he was released from prison a few months earlier, he has been working in their Propaganda Bureau. *Teff,* so unimaginably delicious, so nutritious, so rich in iron, only grows on the cool, high plateau of the central highlands.

"I have not tasted *teff* for nearly four years. In prison we were given rubbish to eat. But even the fighters working in the villages in the highlands do not eat *teff.* It is too expensive."

We make several stops during the night, to pee, to change tires, to allow the drivers to sleep for an hour. I have a torch, but unless I want to see something in detail I find I can sense things better without one. I get better at walking away from my truck and finding my way back to it again. On the second stop I begin to make my way off the road to pee. Someone calls out sharply. A fighter, the safety catch off his Kalashnikov, insists on accompanying me into the wood.

"*Abzi*!" he says, pointing to the ground.

He moves two yards away and politely turns his back. After that, Wolde appears at my side every time the convoy stops and calls a guard if I look like I'm wandering into the bushes.

At one point, the convoy halts for ten minutes and shuts down lights and engines. No one gets out. Everyone listens. When they start up again, they ease their way over the ruts and holes with agonizing slowness. Later, Wolde tells me it was a stretch of road which has been mined in the past. The only way to find out is for fighters to walk in front of the first truck. I have been put in the middle of the convoy because I am a visitor and it is safer there. I want to ask Wolde about prison, but the engines are starting up again. It is time to go.

About two in the morning, the convoy halts for a longer break. The drivers need a rest. Some in their cabs, some on the ground beside the road, they lie down to sleep on a blanket, swathed like corpses against mosquitos. My friends, after examining the ground by torchlight for stones and scorpions, invite me to lay my sleeping bag next to them on a plastic groundsheet. I'm too exhausted to sleep. Wolde wants to talk. He asks me about my work. I ask him about prison.

He had been a teacher in Mekelle, the capital of Tigray, when he was arrested and charged with being a member of the Tigray People's Liberation Front.

"In fact I was not. I had nothing to do with them and thought of myself as a loyal supporter of the Dergue."

For three years he was in prison and tortured continuously. He describes their main methods in graphic detail. He had been bound over a stick and hung upside down, while they beat his feet with thongs. Once they had ordered him to stretch his left leg out in front with the foot resting on a chair.

"Then they broke my leg with a big stake brought down with force. Look, I will show you."

He pulls up one trouser and his torch reveals a thin leg. Around the calf and shin the white scar where the leg was broken shines like a bracelet.

"They kept on insisting I was a guerrilla. They tortured me. It was too much, the suffering. When I confessed, then they stopped. I confessed and also incriminated others. I said everything what they wanted. But I was lying."

The Dergue, he says, controls the five main towns in Tigray and the roads connecting them to Gondar and Addis in the south, but the rural area belongs to the liberation forces. The February before, the fighters had made a daring raid on Mekelle prison. They had released eighteen hundred political prisoners, including himself, and taken them into the countryside.

"After that, I became their supporter. I didn't know much about them before. There is so much Dergue propaganda in the towns, you don't know what to believe. I have been given treatment for my leg and now I work in the TPLF Propaganda Bureau. In prison I wanted to die. I tried to kill myself. Now I am better."

He draws deeply on the cigarette he is smoking. Above us the stars are impossibly bright. At ground level beside the massive truck tires there is only the single moving point of Wolde's cigarette and sound of his voice in the darkness.

"I have just been to Khartoum to see relatives there. They did not know if I was alive or dead. In fact they thought I was dead."

This is what I have come to find out, but I have no pen or paper handy, no proper light, and if I were scribbling all the time maybe he wouldn't tell me so much. Troubled about my failure to be a proper journalist, I drift into fitful sleep while he is still talking.

The road into Tigray from the Sudanese border falls into three categories. All terrible.

First, the dust road. The light, thick topsoil with no plants to keep it in place, has turned to dust under the truck tires. It is not just *dusty*, it is two feet thick. The trucks in front whirl it into the air in an impenetrable cloud.

We go at a snail's pace. Sometimes, when visibility is zero, we have to stop altogether until it settles enough to go on. Sometimes, the truck wheels bog down in it like mud. It is too hot to keep the windows closed, but everyone is wrapped in shawls. Only their eyes show. The people riding on top of the trucks look as if they have fallen in a flour bin. Inside my shawl, inside my shirt, the dust has mixed with sweat and turned into a hot paste.

Second, the rutted road, the legacy of the rainy season. For long stretches the road is fissured with deep ruts, bumps and depressions, which in the dry season have set like concrete. The trucks maneuver over and round them, so that the massive vehicles themselves seem to ripple and bend. How do the axles stand it? I begin to understand the grumbles of Hans, the Dutch mechanic I met at the border post. Sometimes the rutted road and the dust road combine. On the front seat of the cab, between the driver and the guard, without seatbelts, with nothing to hold on to, I bounce about like a ball. Mesmerized by the space made by the headlights in the surrounding dark, lulled by exhaustion and the din of the engine, I fall asleep and bounce out of control. Once I land across the lap of the driver; another time my head hits the windscreen. I can't keep awake. Eventually, the guard grasps a handful of shirt behind my back and anchors me to the seat.

Third, the boulder road. Towards the end of the journey, when the road runs through rivers and over mountains, the road is made of small boulders. We ford many small rivers, tumbling with water over huge stones. In the last stretch we cross the wide, winding Kaza River again and again and in places the river itself becomes the road. The largest boulders have been cleared out of the way and their bulky forms waymark the route on each side, but even the ones remaining seem impossible obstacles to driving. The drivers patiently ease the protesting trucks over them, judder and stall, go on again. I find I am easing and stretching my stiff body, as if by mirroring the motion of the reluctant truck I can help it on its way.

We finally stop before it is light. We have been nearly twelve hours on the road. We lost our guard a few kilometers back, when he went to the aid of a truck with a burst tire. Now it seems as if we have lost the convoy too. The driver speaks to me and gets out. I don't understand. When I climb down, there are no other headlights, no other trucks. The pre-dawn air is sharp. I hear water, but I can't see anything. I am in a world of impenetrable blackness, intensified by torchlight. I don't know where I am. I don't know the rules. I don't speak Tigrinya. My exhaustion feels like illness. I want to go home. But home is the other side of a terrible journey and the Sudan. The driver comes round to my side of the truck and lays a blanket on the ground and gestures at it with his torch. It feels like we are the only people in the world. I huddle into my sleeping bag and feel astonishment when he lies down beside me. The absurdity strikes me suddenly. Here I am in a foreign country in the middle of the night lying down in the middle of nowhere with a complete stranger. I am shaking with laughter before I too sink into the darkness.

It is daylight when I wake. The Tigray I wake up in is a country of rivers and of water. In the dark of my sleeping bag I am first aware of water-sounds, gushing, rushing. I am beside the wheel of the truck, under an enormous tree twisted into loops and coils. Of course! Camouflage against the MiGs. There are other huge trees and sunlight. Nearby is a steep cliff like the side of a gorge, covered with bushes and tall grasses and everything is green and some birds are calling to each other with glorious flute-like sounds. The driver is nowhere to be seen. I am all alone. I resist the desire to skulk in my sleeping bag, my home, my snail-shell. In fact, it is not a practical proposition. It is laid on six inch round stones like a beach, which only the first flush of exhaustion will tolerate. It turns out to be the shore of the Kaza river.

I sit on my sleeping bag beside the truck, waiting for something to happen. A group of about a dozen or so women fighters walk by a few yards away. They are wrapped from head to foot in camouflaging shawls held over their mouths against the morning air. They stare at me curiously, but don't come near. They must be going down to the river to wash, because I hear their voices and laughing and splashing at the water's edge. Soon after, two men fighters arrive and indicate that I am to accompany them. When I start to wrap up my sleeping bag, they stop me peremptorily and gesture that I am to come at once and leave everything behind. Oh, I think, that means we are coming back in a minute or two, so I turn my back on my sleeping bag and my backpack and obediently follow them.

I bitterly regret it, as we walk several kilometers before coming to a fighters' camp and I don't see my belongings again until the evening. However, I am distracted by the beauty of the valley. It is early in the dry season so, although the grasses are brown, leaves are abundant on the trees and late flowers still adorn the tall shrubs. It is more like parkland than the wild forest. Wisps of mist still cling to the cliff top, but the morning sun illuminates the statuesque shapes of trees and boulders. It gets hotter by the minute and the fighters keep up a scorching pace in and out of trees, through thorn thickets and little glades. They look as if they are strolling, but I have to trot to keep up. By the time we see the encampment I am pouring with sweat.

They take me to a small hut of tree branches and black plastic, thatched with dried grasses. Above us are the arching trees, so we are well-camouflaged from the air. Inside, there are two couches made of rocks, like dry-stone walls. Their top surface is filled in with clay and spread with blankets. I spend the day on one of them, sleeping off the journey and having political conversations by turns.

"How do you like our Tigrayan beds? Too soft for you?" asks Teklai, an English-speaking fighter who has been assigned to look after me. He brings me food and asks me questions whenever he sees I'm awake.

Other young fighters, men and women, call in during the day to join the discussion, even if they don't speak English. This seems to be the pattern. Everyone I meet wants to talk politics. They ask what I think about their revolution and wonder why the revolution of the oppressed masses in Britain hasn't happened yet. What am I doing about it? I tell them I work for an organization campaigning on international issues.

"Why aren't you a Party?" they ask.

"Why do you work mainly with petit-bourgeois elements like students?"

"What are your relations with the workers? How are you going to organize them?"

"If you give the correct political education, then the workers and the people will certainly rise."

I feel stunned and stimulated together. I try to explain the situation in Britain. But how can I? How can these young people blazing with enthusiasm understand entrenched apathy? How can I convey the depth and subtlety of our kind of political education? Most people don't even see it as political education, but it instructs them that politics is for the professionals, that passionate concern by non-professionals is taboo, that the ultimate boredom is talking about it, that they are powerless to change their lives, that putting a cross on a voting slip every four or five years gives them a voice in decision-making even if their chosen candidate never gets elected.

Teklai is tolerant and kind. He evidently doesn't think I am committed enough, but he is also worrying that I am thirsty or hungry or still tired. He wants to chase everybody out. I'm OK, I say. Don't worry.

As the sun goes down, a fighter comes to take me to the reception center for foreign visitors, an hour's drive in a landcruiser down the valley. It is difficult to assess the distance, because the roughness of the track enforces a low speed, in some places not much above walking pace. There are other passengers in the vehicle, but their faces are concealed by shawls and darkness and no one speaks to me. By the time we halt it is pitch dark and we set off on foot for fifteen minutes through forest, downhill, across a river, up what seems to be a mountain, with the darkness barely diluted one step ahead. In the fitful swing of torches, I see that one of my companions has lost a leg and is on crutches. He swings across the river and negotiates the boulders and steep paths with ease. I am taken to a hut, brought some *injera,* which I feel too disoriented to eat by candlelight, and left to sleep.

I am shocked into wakefulness by voices only a few feet away, the other side of a partition. The strangeness of these voices. The unmistakable ringing tones of men speaking English. Why are their voices so loud? I feel like rapping sharply on the wall, but it is not solid enough. Now I realize the hut is spacious and divided into two rooms. It is made of tree branches, spaced a foot apart with the walls draped with groundsheets. The ceiling is lined with black plastic extending into an awning in front over a veranda and, when I peer outside, I see the whole roof is thatched with grasses for camouflage and coolness. The building is on the side of a hill, which curves round from the left so that I see similar huts fifty yards away on the incline facing mine, scattered among trees as big as plane trees. Perhaps they are plane trees.

In any new place the first necessity is locating the latrine. As I set off to explore, a loud male voice with a North American accent issues from one of the opposite huts.

"Look, boys. A woman!"

Appropriate put-downs occur to me too late, as I march down the path. I have got out of the way of those routine defensive tactics that become second nature in Europe. When I climb up to the hut again, my fellow-occupants are hovering on the veranda, waiting to introduce themselves. They are both English, although Chris is a male nurse working for an Australian agency. He is on his way out of Tigray, waiting for a convoy to the Sudan. Richard, however, is on his way into Tigray, a PhD student from Manchester University who is here to research land reform under the revolution. It turns out that I know his supervisor, so we are quickly on friendly terms. They are apologetic for the man opposite, who is Canadian and on his way out too, although he only arrived on the last convoy. Apparently, he got this far on false pretenses, with no proper credentials or mission, and is now being expelled.

We chat over breakfast. At least, they eat and I watch. I don't seem to be hungry. Also, they act like old hands, so they talk and I listen. Richard has been here three weeks, but Chris is at the end of his second or third visit to Tigray. His agency is one year into an ambitious well-boring program, which has run into technical and geological problems. He came here with his wife, another nurse, to run community health programs in conjunction with the wells to ensure their efficient use. He expresses dissatisfaction with the TPLF. Chris wants to work directly with the people and had expected that he and his fellow agency workers would control the project. The Front and REST, he says, insist on their own control of all health programs and reserve an enabling or training role for foreign personnel. This sounds reasonable to me. After all, it's their country and their priorities, but I am a new arrival and Chris feels aggrieved so I say nothing. Later, I discover from Richard that Chris has been asked to leave well before his term is up, that he too is being expelled.

All foreign aid workers come first to this station for discussions and briefing before dispersing to different parts of Tigray to do whatever work has brought them here. A man called Tekleweini is overall REST coordinator of relief and development work within Tigray. I will have to meet him before I can go any further. The conversation has now shifted to agency gossip. They refer to a Swiss worker for another agency, who has recently been expelled also. Goodness, I ask, is anybody ever allowed to stay?

"Well," says Chris. "They are very strict about cameras. You must always ask if you can take a photograph. They are especially touchy about skylines, any topography, which could lead to identification of their base area or a project and bring MiGs on their trail. They are worried about spies."

The Swiss had refused to abide by any constraints on his photography and finally his cameras and equipment had all been confiscated.

"They are fighting a war after all," says Richard.

Chris asks me why I have come to Tigray. When I tell him I have come to investigate the claims of the Front, he looks skeptical. Perhaps he thinks the project vague or self-indulgent compared with the priorities of aid workers.

"What's the matter?"

"You don't think you'll ever get a straight answer out of these people, do you? You say you want to talk to the peasants, but they'll never let you talk directly to the people. You'll never get past the fighters. Even if you do, they will be standing there with sub-machine guns on their backs and you won't be able to believe anything you hear."

This directly contradicts the impression of the people's support for the Front I have had from Haile Kiros, their London representative, but that evidence is not exactly impartial. Also, at my present stage of inexperience I accept the need for skepticism. Chris is equally cynical about Richard's area of research, the program of land redistribution to the peasants.

After breakfast, Richard offers to show me round the camp. There is no village here, just a newly-built transit camp for foreign visitors. There are about six huts already constructed and we watch the hillside being cleared of scrub and terraced between the trees for a seventh. Small shiny goats, surprisingly tame, are springing about between the workers as if the platform is a play area just for them. The ground slopes beyond the tree cover down to the river, which is wide and shallow and tumbling over stones. Huge smooth boulders each side testify to the force and volume of the flood in the rainy season. Immediately below the camp it widens into a pool deep enough for swimming. Now, three young men are standing up to their waists in the water, soaping themselves while their clothes dry on the rocks. I turn away before they see me. On flat land behind the rocks are two *tukuls,* the traditional round thatched African huts I saw everywhere in the Sudan and which are also characteristic of this part of Ethiopia. A cooling breeze plays in and out of the spaced branches of the walls. Two women are inside, cooking.

These are the first "real" Tigrayan women I have seen. Their hair is braided in a pattern of thin plaits tight to their heads until it billows out at the nape of the neck. They are wearing traditional tight-bodiced dresses in dark blue and dark green flowered cotton. One is chopping meat on a board. The other is pouring batter in decreasing circles to make a large *injera* pancake on an oiled bakestone above a wood fire. She covers it with a two foot wide clay lid and beckons us in, smiling. Richard leaves to write a letter for Chris to take out with him. There is no post in Tigray, only an informal courier service in the pockets of aid workers travelling to the Sudan and beyond. I stay for a few minutes to find out how *injera* is made, but the smell of fermented dough mingled with the pungency of garlic and onions turns suspicion about my unsettled stomach into certainty and I have to dash outside to throw up behind the rocks.

I spend the next hour at the latrine and the rest of the day in bed. I don't wake up until night, although I dimly remember a shadowy figure coming at intervals to check my temperature and pulse. Someone lights a kerosene lamp in the corner and its pale flicker helps to ward off the ugly pulsating terrors of fever dreams. Through the partition wall I become aware of voices. Chris and Richard and someone else are discussing Richard's research project into land reform. Chris is very disparaging.

"The TPLF are dividing the land between the people according to how many people are in the family. When the numbers reduce then they can take it away again. That's not much of an incentive, is it? Production is bound to fall. I mean, a farmer is not going to bother to develop his land, if in the end his investment goes to somebody else, is he?"

Two days later, feeling shaky and thin, I am nevertheless strong enough to sit up and drink some tea. Tekleweini comes to see me. He is small, wiry and dynamic, with wild hair. He is head of REST in the field. (They always call revolutionary Tigray "the field.") He is worried about my health. Am I strong enough for this mission? Worried whether the words "as a woman" are lurking in the margins, I insist on my robust health and ask when I can continue my journey. However, he knows little about my visit or my program.

"We have to make this distinction between the humanitarian and the political," he says. "It is a false distinction, because it is only through the revolution that our people have had a chance of an improved life. Nearly all our visitors are humanitarian ones from the agencies, so they all come here first because REST handles them all. You will be transferred to the care of the TPLF as soon as possible."

I ask him if, in the light of his comments, his relief organization is simply a branch of the Front in disguise.

"Oh no. Like other relief agencies, we have to work within the policies of the TPLF, as it is the de facto government in Tigray, but we are independent. We have disagreements sometimes and have to argue strongly for what we want."

One of the basic aims of the revolution, he says, is to transform the life of the people through the development of agriculture and the provision of health care and education. By channelling aid from outside Ethiopia to Tigray, the role of his organization is to assist this process. But real development can never be achieved without breaking the mold set by totalitarian dictatorship, without, in other words, military victory and a change of government.

The overthrow of a totalitarian dictatorship, supported by one of the largest and best equipped armies in Africa, financed and armed as it is by the Soviet Union? This seems so far-fetched, such a far cry from this moment under camouflage in the west of Tigray, that the intention lacks all credibility. I feel the hopelessness of it. The heat and my weakness make it seem an insuperable task at any time.

As if to reinforce the point, there is a thrumming in the air at the very edge of consciousness. Until Tekleweini leaps to his feet and moves to the door, I hardly register it. I follow him. Through the doorway I see a woman swiftly pluck a few drying garments from the bushes and jump into the shadows. The form of a man turns momentarily into bark as he presses himself into the trunk of a tree. No one else is to be seen. Then the MiG is overhead, flying low, and the landscape is silenced by the roar of the jet engines. Its huge noise is still reverberating among the rocks long after it has passed.

Tekleweini sits down again as if nothing has happened. In five minutes it has become clear to me in a practical way why no movement is allowed in daylight, why every hut is so carefully camouflaged, why I was instructed to bring dull-colored clothes, why I was requested to change my metal watch strap for a leather one. I knew it all before; now I understand. However, I follow Tekleweini's lead and nonchalantly we continue our discussion for another half hour. As he leaves, he tells me to spend the day resting, but to be ready to leave for the Propaganda Bureau early tomorrow.

3

Pillows of stone

Today I start my program. As the "no movement in daylight" rule is strictly enforced, I have to be ready to leave for the Propaganda Bureau at four a.m., so I can get there before daylight. Without an alarm clock, I doze through the night in case I don't wake in time. A fighter leads the way down the valley and across a little river to where Tekleweini is waiting in a pick-up. I am getting much better at moving in the dark along rocky tracks, but leaping across a river from one stepping stone to another while weighed down by a large backpack is another matter.

The slow drive, winding upwards over rough-hewn tracks, takes about an hour. I can see only the rocks and potholes immediately ahead. No one has given me any information about the Propaganda Bureau. I could have asked Tekleweini, but sickness has reduced my energy for asking questions. For a Westerner, *propaganda* has an unfortunate ring about it. The lies of the enemy. There is something naive about the openness with which these Tigrayans use the term. We are taught to associate it with the marketing strategies of the Third Reich or the rewriting of history by the Kremlin, never with truth-bending by Western governments. Perhaps I'm on my way to a *1984* Ministry of Truth.

Twice, we are called to halt by sentries. As the driver shows our papers, the headlights' glare exposes a row of fighters recumbent under a tree, each one rolled chrysalis-like in a blanket. It is very cold in the back of the pick-up. The one sweater I have brought is too thin for the nights. The track peters out in a little clearing, where we wait for another hour as the sky lightens and the exotic calls of unfamiliar birds celebrate the dawn. No one tells me why we are waiting or what for. I have to unpack my sleeping bag to keep from dying of cold. Then, from every side, fighters muffled in shawls and blankets start emerging from the bushes and trees, silently streaming across the glade and up the slope until they are swallowed by the forest.

A contingent arrives from the mountain to meet us. One of them is Amare Aregawi. Small and lean in a leather jacket, he is responsible for the Propaganda Bureau. He and Tekleweini greet each other Ethiopian-style, bowing their heads on each others' shoulders, first one side then the other, as they clasp hands and ask after each other's health. Amare greets me in good English, instructs a fighter to carry my large backpack, and leads the way upwards.

The path is in fact the course of a stream as it tumbles down the mountainside. Using the huge boulders as steps, Amare and the fighters go at a cracking pace. By now the early sun is brilliant on the strange eroded shapes of mountain peaks and, even in the valley, dawn light filters through the leaves of deciduous trees, exposing trunks twisted into sculptured forms. As the stream cascades from one level to another over boulders smoothed by countless winter rains, the arching trunks reflect the bubbling surface in a constant interplay of light between leaves and water.

Still weak from three days of sickness, I soon lag behind and wish I had not chosen to carry even my little backpack. Twisting and springing up the path of the waterfalls, up and up, we pass a meeting-place cleared from the mountainside like a stand in a football stadium. Its benches are carved out of the slope in tiers and shaded from the sun and the MiGs by a straw roof. Now men and women fighters are streaming past me, as I flag and stumble in their wake. The path twists up and round, with the mountain rising above us to the left now and the incline falling away through trees to the right, and then seems to wind beneath the mountain itself, between two pillars of rock like a vast portal. I feel cold moist air on my cheeks. We are passing behind a waterfall, which pours like molten steel down the face of the overhang above before it joins the water course we have just climbed.

Before us is a huge horizontal cleft in the rock face more than a hundred meters long, but low in proportion to its length, a gash oppressed by the weight of mountain above. In front, the cave is open to the air, but completely concealed by trees and pillars of rock. I hear the dull roar of a generator out of sight. The place is full of activity, full of fighters busy with the tasks of first light. Many of them are women. I have been told that about a third of the fighters are women, but so far I have seen only a few. Here, they seem in the majority. They stare at me as we pass. Tentatively I say 'Selam' and they break into smiles.

"It is rare to see a *ferenji,* a foreigner, here," says Amare. "You are almost the first. That is why they look at you. They are surprised."

Some women are chopping onions and garlic for a huge pot on an open fire. Behind them, all along the mouth of the cave, other fighters are wedging slim poles between the rock floor and the roof. They seem to be draping from one to another lengths of white cotton fabric, which have huge Tigrinya letters painted on them. Elsewhere, the work is finished and I realize they are dividing the whole space into cubicles, whose walls are made of several lengths of cotton sheeting, each about three feet wide. Amare tells me they are recycled TPLF banners.

"Nothing is ever wasted here. It is not like the West."

His gesture takes in the cave, the valley.

"Two months ago the Bureau was down in the valley. We had built many strong, stone buildings, all camouflaged, as well as huts for our less important activities. But three MiGs came and bombed the whole valley and forced us to retreat here. As you see, we are still getting settled."

The publishing and printing departments are already operating from caves deeper under the mountain. Now they are setting up offices and some sleeping spaces for the permanent staff of fighters, although most of the fighters I have seen are here temporarily for political education courses and sleep out under the trees.

The floor of the cave sweeps out and up beyond the overhanging rock to a flat rim on which are set some chairs. From here, the mountain slopes steeply through trees to the valley below. Women fighters bring hot sweet black tea to us in battered enamel cups and a plate of *himbasha,* a traditional wheat bread baked in large rounds.

"Why is it unusual to see a foreigner here?" I ask Amare.

"Almost all the foreigners who come to Tigray are humanitarian visitors," he replies. "They are looked after by REST, not by the Front."

As individuals, he continues, they might be interested in the struggle, but their organizations usually debar them from any involvement in political issues. In Tigray, it is not possible to make such a distinction between the humanitarian and the political. The revolution is a struggle for survival. The people have been forced to take up arms because there have been no democratic channels through which to change society, but the military struggle is only one aspect. The other is the struggle for a self-reliant agriculture, the struggle against disease and ignorance.

"The second is not possible without the first. The people now have their own land. They administer themselves in local councils. They help organize schools and clinics. None of this would be possible without the protection of the armed struggle."

One reason I am here is to investigate the truth of reports, which have filtered through to Britain of this process of social transformation. We spend some minutes discussing my work. It turns out that Amare knows England himself. He spent three years at school there in the late sixties and his memories of the friendly family he lived with, their children close to him in age, are still green. No wonder his English is so good.

"You are a very unusual visitor," says Amare, "because you are interested in our entire revolution. But now you must excuse me as I have work to do. First I will show you where you can rest. We will have plenty of time to talk later."

He shows me to one of the banner-walled cubicles, where a camp bed, a chair and a small desk share the bumpy space. My backpack is propped against the desk. Fighters in the neighboring cubicles cast their shadows on the thin fabric. The generator is thundering somewhere in the distance. Tigrinya voices talk and laugh, or shout above the generator. The chains of lightbulbs pinned across the cave roof to light the gloom are permanently on. Suddenly I feel very tired. I know I have been using sleep as a place of retreat against strangeness; I know also from experience that Ethiopian culture associates sleep with tiredness or heat, never with quiet. Peace, quiet and privacy are found within the space of an enshrouding shawl, not beyond it. My sleeping-bag is the only place I can call my own. The day is warming up. I take off my shoes and sweater and retire beneath my sheet sleeping bag, just to rest my eyes. Perhaps, like the games of children, when distinct domains are not only suggested by sticks and a blanket, but take on reality, I begin to feel secure in my little room. The clamor distracts me from fears and loneliness and I sink into sleep after all.

Halfway through the morning, Amare comes to collect me for a tour of the Propaganda Bureau. He introduces me to so many fighters as we go along that my hand aches and I don't remember any names. Some cubicles are living quarters, some are offices for typing and duplicating. I notice that the typewriters have Tigrinya type and that the duplicating technology is very old-fashioned. Leaving aside power supply and cost, mechanical equipment is more reliable and easier to maintain and repair in these conditions. In a nearby cave is the repair shop and a training place for all the separate skills useful to the work here. Suddenly, in the distance, beyond the cave mouth, I am aware of the sound of drums and singing, but as we go deeper into the main cave to the binding and collating station, the noise of the generator seems to be caught and intensified by the pockets of rock and it is hard to hear ourselves speak.

In the collating room, piles of printed sheets are set out on big tables illuminated by necklaces of lightbulbs. The tables, chairs, shelving, everything, have been made by the workers here, all of whom, to judge by the ones I see in front of me, seem by their dress to be fighters. There are half a dozen of them at the moment, collating by hand at different tables. Others are working at binding machines and stacking up copies of texts. I take photographs of the whole process—the offices, the stores, the typing, proof-reading, collating and binding sections, and an area where two fighters are writing material.

They are simple, cheap and functional texts. Examining some copies, I wish I could read Tigrinya. One is a medical text on cholera, another a health manual, a third the History of Tigray, Part One. The title pages have a printed date, 1979. They are not old texts. The ancient Ethiopian calendar calculates the birth of Christ eight years later than the Gregorian calendar, so Ethiopian 1979 is European 1987, which it will be by the time these books are distributed. All the texts encouraged by the Front and circulated throughout Tigray are printed here. I see stacks of literacy leaflets, books for schools, manuals for clinics and hospitals, political magazines for fighters, stories, and poems. Most of it seems to be propagation of information, rather than the propaganda of my dawn fears. The technology may be primitive, but this is a large and complex publishing operation, most of it not political, except in the sense that any education can have political consequences for a deprived population.

I ask Amare how many Tigrayans can read. He replies that at the beginning of the revolution in 1975 there was about ninety-five per cent illiteracy in the province as a whole and that most of the literate people were in the five main towns, which are still under the control of the Dergue.

"The only functioning schools were in these towns. There were no schools in the rural area. Education was not considered necessary for farmers."

"Didn't any farmers living near the big towns send their children to school?"

"Richer peasants living near the towns might consider sending their sons to school in the town. Poor peasants would have found it impossible to pay for books and pencils. And the girls would rarely be sent to school."

"Why not?"

"Because women and girls were servants in our culture, second-class, especially in the countryside, scarcely above the animals. Their parents would pay someone a dowry to marry them at about eight or nine-years-old."

My immediate concern is to find out how they run their publishing operation, not to talk about something completely different, but I privately resolve to put the position of women at the top of my list of priorities for later investigation.

After the tour, we walk down to the meeting place we had passed on our dawn ascent. The session is in full swing. There are now about two hundred fighters ranged up the tiers of seats. Heads turn as we approach, but when I smile, curiosity turns to friendliness. The fighters make room for us and we sit down fairly near the top. One of them takes the flat stone he has been sitting on and politely offers it to me.

Below, facing the tiers of seats, is a table at which two older fighters are sitting, talking through a microphone to the assembly. As I don't understand a word, I sneak a look at my companions. They are all young, eighteen to twenty at a guess. Twisted round their heads are the shawls most fighters seem to wear, in patterns of green, purple and earth colors. Many of them have their Kalashnikovs slung behind their backs. Men are definitely in the majority, although women fighters are scattered through the crowd, not sitting separately or in any obvious groups. As they dress the same, it is not always easy to identify them from the back. Many of them are sitting with their arms around each other's shoulders, men and men, women and men, women and women. No distinction. It looks good. It looks different from any soldiers I have ever seen. They seem to be listening intently.

In Britain the term "political education" is a negative concept, like "propaganda," with overtones of indoctrination by a totalitarian power. What does it mean here? I will try to find out later and then put what I find out to the test. Amare starts explaining in an undertone what is going on. They have recently circulated in draft a new text, in a series called *Struggle,* on conditions of life for fighters. These sessions involve going over this text, all the young fighters together, discussing and challenging the more controversial sections, as part of a process towards making it a policy document. When a modified version is eventually drafted, it will be debated by fighters again, before it takes its final form. Similar meetings apparently are going on all over Tigray.

After half an hour or so the session breaks for an interval of music and singing. This must be what I could hear before from the cave. Two young men, long drums slung under their left arms, beat out the rhythm in a kind of dialog between drums. They leap high in the air as they circle round each other and the audience clap in time and roar out a well-known song.

One of the songs is sung unaccompanied. The cultural group stands still and straight. There is no clapping and the faces of the assembled fighters, as they sing, are intent and serious. It is one of the early songs of the revolution. Amare whispers an off-the-cuff translation:

> *There is no mountain we cannot climb;*
> *There is no river we cannot cross.*

It is a song about the harshness and dedication of a fighter's life. In spite of deprivations, their strength is drawn from the support of the people and from their refusal to submit to injustice. One line, *Our pillow is a stone; a cave is our home*, could be written for the present situation. It sticks in my mind.

After this, a short play devised by the cultural group at the camp tells the story of a poor peasant family oppressed by years of hunger and toil sending their son off to be a fighter as the only hope of a better life.

"We use songs and plays to teach the fighters why they are fighting," says Amare. "A fighter can only be strong if he understands what the whole struggle is about and believes that what he is doing is right."

"Or she."

"Or she," he corrects himself, smiling.

It is time for lunch. We climb up again to the cave. In the spaces between the trees, the heat beats off the rocks. As we walk back to the chairs above the slope where earlier we had drunk tea, a woman approaches us, carrying a baby. She has very short hair and an open, engaging expression. Instead of the trousers or shorts that most women fighters wear, she has tied her shawl around her waist as an elegant skirt.

"Hello, you are Jenny, I think? I am Harnet." She holds out her hand. "And this is Niat."

She sits down with us and Amare leans forward and takes the child, who must be about three months old. As Ethiopian men tend to cuddle or play with every child they meet, I think nothing of this, until he says,

"Well, what do you think of my daughter? Don't you think she is beautiful?"

At this point a tray of *injera* and *shiro,* a paste of ground chick peas and spices, is brought to us and a jug of water for washing our hands before we put them in the common pot. I feel hungry for the first time for days, but my stomach is still delicate.

"Eat, eat," says Amare. "You must eat or you will not be able to climb our mountains. You will get ill."

We chat. I wonder whether it is difficult to bring up a baby in these conditions.

"No, we are used to it," says Harnet. "In our traditional society, women help each other in their families. Here, my comrades help me look after the baby. They are my family."

Harnet and Amare find out I have four children of my own, well grown by now. Their astonishment and admiration takes me by surprise. I certainly don't get this kind of recognition in England.

"You see," says Harnet, "In our culture women have many children, but they are never expected to do anything else. It is very unusual for them to be political or to travel."

"What about women fighters? They have a job to do. They have to be fairly mobile."

"We have only just started having babies," she says, smiling. "We are still learning."

They tell me that for the first ten years of the struggle marriage for fighters was strictly forbidden. I work it out. The revolution began in 1975, so the laws must have been relaxed about a year ago. As the conversation continues I realize that by "marriage" they mean sexual relationships. The life of a mobile fighter in the early years was very harsh and involved many sacrifices. Dedication to the revolution meant first of all the sacrifice of a personal family life. Even more important was for fighters to establish a different identity for themselves in the eyes of the peasants from the rapacity and violence which bitter experience had associated with incursions of soldiers. Peasants had to be convinced that fighters could be trusted and that included trusting them with their women.

How do you enforce such sexual prohibitions, I ask. Discipline was very strict, Harnet replies. In fact, after ten years, many women fighters did not agree with relaxing the marriage laws, because they felt threatened with relegation to a second-class domestic position. Freedom from child marriage had liberated them in so many ways. So there were fierce debates. What tipped the scales finally was the close relationship between the Front and the people.

"The peasants could not understand this unnatural way of life," Amare adds. "They love the fighters. They have given their children to the organization. 'You must have your own children,' they told us, 'revolutionary children.' Children are the most important thing to Tigrayan people."

He lifts Niat high in the air, making her laugh.

"Even now, we cannot live a normal life," Harnet continues, "because we have our work. We have time off before and after the birth of the child and of course we stay close to our children while we are breastfeeding, but we will not be able to live together as a family until after victory."

Beyond the shade of rocks and trees, the heat is intense. The meal ends with a cup of sweet black tea and we go to rest. I was sleeping until eleven this morning and now I am not tired. The private time is more important than sleep. I write in my diary. I lie on my camp bed, looking at the patterns made by the cracks and crevices in the cave roof and reflecting on the sacrifices necessary to make a successful revolution.

Later in the afternoon I discuss my program with Amare so that he can make the necessary arrangements for transport and a guide. I have come to investigate the achievements of the revolution, particularly the claims that it is not a minority imposing its will, but "a people's struggle." In Britain what little media coverage there has been has suggested that the "rebels" are separate from the people, that the war with the government is an imposition of unnecessary hardship and suffering on an innocent and passive populace caught between two sides each as bad as the other. The Front's representatives in London, on the other hand, deny this interpretation. They have been forced to take to arms, they say, as the only way out of an absolute poverty and oppression imposed on them first by the feudal dictatorship of Emperor Haile Selassie and his forbears, and continued since 1974 under the savage regime of Mengistu Haile Mariam.[1] The people fully support the revolution, because it has already brought them benefits they have never experienced before. They say they have started a social transformation at the grassroots. This is what I want to investigate.

In fact, there are certain difficulties. For a start I cannot proceed independently. The Front has invited me here to conduct an independent investigation, but I cannot go anywhere without their support. I am in a war zone where security is tight, so for my own safety I have to be accompanied by guards. I cannot yet speak the language, so I must be provided with an interpreter. I am also hampered by ignorance. They have invited me to write my own program, which they have promised to fulfill as far as they can, but I can only put on my program what I already know at second hand, not what I know nothing about. I have a feeling I shall know the questions I should have asked when it is time to go home.

Some of this I say to Amare. He laughs and tells me not to worry, dismisses my doubts with a wave of his hand. Perhaps I have already broken the first rule of independence.

"We will help you to be independent," he says. (This *must* be a contradiction in terms.) "We are confident in our revolution. We have nothing to hide. It is in our interest that your reports are independent and credible, although from my experience of the British media they may not be ready, for their own reasons, to hear what you say."

"How can you help me?"

I can do what I like, he tells me, as long as it will not endanger my safety —it would not be safe to go to the front line at the moment, for example. I should not have too tight a program of interviewing; I should discuss and learn at every opportunity and add things to my program as I go along. Some interviews will have to be planned, but I should also talk to people I meet by chance to cross-check my information and impressions.

"OK," I say. "It's a deal."

I don't add that media coverage about Tigrayan revolutionaries has also dismissed them as Marxists, extremists, communists, or that, although at home I prided myself on my independent analysis, I now find lurking within me some of the indoctrinated skepticisms and prejudices of the average Westerner.

"We know your work," Amare adds, as if he had read my thoughts. "We trust you. We think of you as a comrade."

He then tells me I can start at once. Seven Agazi comrades are already waiting to talk to me about their experiences. I go to collect my tape recorder and notebook.

4

Escaping the Dergue

I know the name *Agazi* already. He was one of the founders of the revolution who was killed early on in the struggle and is revered as a hero.[1] The Front's spectacular release last February of eighteen hundred prisoners from Mekelle prison was named after him. Now I am to have the opportunity of adding to the information I gleaned about the Agazi Operation from Woldeselassie on the convoy, although when I arrive at the cubicle allotted for our meeting Wolde is not there and only six people are quietly sitting waiting for me.

In common with all the educated minority in Ethiopia, these men speak good English. I want to know what were their circumstances at the time of their arrests, whether they were supporting the Dergue or the liberation struggle, what was alleged against them. Only Sahle and Berhanu were supporters, caught up in the radical student movement, which has been the focus of such continuous and determined opposition to the dictatorships of both Emperor Haile Selassie and his successor, President Mengistu. The other four men are older, mid to late thirties I would guess. They were all government officials. Mulugeta was responsible for political activities in a Farmers' Training Center in the south, Haile promoted from teacher to a desk job in the Ministry of Education, Assefa a teacher and also the chairman of the *kebelle* or local administration, and Tesfai employed in the Ministry of Culture. These four assert very firmly that they were entirely loyal to the central government of the Dergue and that their only crime was to be Tigrayan.

"The whole aim of that purge in 1983 to 1984," says Haile, "was to eliminate Tigrayans, especially intellectuals and those holding posts under the Dergue."

"Why was that?"

"Because organized opposition was growing stronger all the time and the

Dergue could do nothing about it. They were forming their Party at that time, the Workers' Party of Ethiopia, and the Dergue was making sure that no Tigrayans would be in it. They didn't regard the Tigrayans as human beings. We were under suspicion all the time."

Except for Tesfai, who spent only five months in prison, all these men had been incarcerated for over two years and Berhanu for six years, when they were released in February 1986. They had been accused of membership of the TPLF and repeatedly tortured to get them first to confess and then to name their fellow conspirators. That is how all of them came to be arrested in the first place.

"It was in October," says Sahle, "when they came to my dormitory in Addis and took me to the Dergue office. They tortured me. I denied I was a member of the underground. They took me to Mekelle and there I found a previous friend of mine who had given my name because he was tortured. He was not a member either, but he gave my name and that of other friends. I then confessed because the torture was so bad."

The others tell similar stories.

"I was so confident the truth could not be hidden," says Haile. "I thought I would explain all my work for the Dergue and then be released. I still thought the Dergue meant justice. I became highly vexed, but they dismissed my words. They said they had found all the leading members of the underground "so you can't cheat us!" and they sent me to the torture."

"They started to torture me," says Assefa, "And I couldn't stand the torture. I decided if they refused to accept I was not a traitor, then I would become a member of that forbidden organization, starting from now.

'Who else?' they said.

'No one. I was a member all alone.'

'Give us the names of all the others, of your comrades.'

I told them so many times, but they tortured me again and I gave them the names of all my friends."

As the appalling stories pile one upon another, remorselessly captured by the spinning capstan of my tape recorder, ironically I find some refreshment in their openness. They describe the succession of betrayal and counter betrayal with honesty, without false heroics or false remorse, as if the corruption of the time has its own logic and its own imperatives, as evident to the listener as to themselves. The methods were effective. Confessions were inevitable and bore fruit. Thousands more were rounded up and subjected to the same processes in an endless chain of fear, suffering, and self-preservation.

And it is not over. It is going on, even as they speak, in all the prisons in all the towns under Dergue control throughout Ethiopia. The paranoia of the

Ethiopian state is an ironic acknowledgment of the injustices and brutality through which it maintains its power. The prison system is sustained by lies and fantasies, but it gets results. Its self-fulfilling processes produce the "evidence" of betrayal by conspirators and saboteurs. It is the only efficient operation of the Ethiopian state. Agricultural production is falling, the economy is in ruins, the largest army in Africa is failing to contain rebellions in Eritrea and Tigray, but the prison system is flourishing. In fact the lies, the restrictions, the double-speak, the fear of friends, have seeped through the prison walls like bad air to contaminate the world outside.

The Central Investigation Department handles the newly-arrested prisoners and is responsible for the charges, the torture, the securing of confessions. I discover there are grades of development and underdevelopment even in the art of inflicting intolerable pain and extracting false confessions. In Ethiopia, where electricity is not available to ninety per cent of the population and electronics a rare acquisition in the capital, torture is a mechanical, physical, brutal, face to face affair. Not for them the sophistications, which spring from a more advanced technological base. The different tortures are given numbers, which seem to indicate different methods of suspension over and from sticks and ropes for varying periods of time, while different parts of the body are beaten or broken.

The session usually begins with a barrel of water. Haile describes it for me:

"First they bring a big barrel of water and they push in your head. You cannot breathe and your belly gets filled with water, beyond its capacity. You vomit in the barrel. You are asked to confess. You deny. Then they put in your head again. Then they give you number six or eight, then the barrel again. Then another person is pushed into that barrel, already full of vomit. You can see how many diseases can be communicated in this way. He will name fifty or sixty persons, all Tigrayans, and they will be rounded up."

From the CID they are taken to the main prison. Mulugeta recalls the conditions in Mekelle prison and the others nod or add details. Twenty eight cells, four by five meters in size, contained eighteen hundred to two thousand prisoners, sometimes more. There were usually about sixty-five or seventy people in each cell. There was no room to lie down at night or even to sit.

"In the cell, especially at night, there was no room to defecate," says Berhanu. His soft voice is almost obliterated by a cock crowing so lustily a few yards away that Sahle slips out to chase it away. "There was a small jar for maybe eighty people. To get there, you had to walk across the bodies of the others to urinate. If someone had cholera he had to defecate there. If someone had a bad stomach and diarrhea he had to defecate there. When you wake up in the morning you see somebody dying. There is nothing to be done. If he has no money he cannot even go to the clinic. You just watch him die. The food was so bad, there was no resistance to cholera, to typhoid, to relapsing fever. Sometimes twenty or thirty prisoners would die at a time. In fact, the government wants the prisoners to die. They never admit to killing anybody. They say, 'He died of typhus. He died of malaria.'"

The prison was a microcosm of the world outside. Money counted. Money could buy certain privileges and bribery was a way of life. The guards made most of their income out of the prisoners and the prisoners' families. Those prisoners whose families brought food or paid for medication and clinic visits had a better chance of survival. The peasants had least chance of all. The period these men were describing covered the great famine of 1984-5. Families were migrating to the Sudan. They were too weak, starving and impoverished to make the journey to Mekelle to succor imprisoned relatives. Furthermore, most of the countryside was then in the liberated area and peasants travelling to a Dergue town ran the risk of being arrested also.

In all this dismal catalog there is one amusing interlude. I decide to move the discussion on to the story of their release. Mulugeta has just been talking about the confession document they have to sign, that its final sentence contains the statement "without any force I have given my word." The irony amuses everyone. Yes, this is the moment to move on.

"Tell me the story of your release," I say. "Maybe that's a better bit."

"A better bit? Suddenly everyone is laughing. Instead of moving the discussion on, my intervention has stopped it altogether.

"What?" says Mulugeta. "What did you say?"

It turns out that "A better bit" sounds like an Amharic expression and refers directly to a prison incident they had witnessed.

"A better bit means 'Give us justice' in Amharic!" Mulugeta explains. In October 1984, a rumor circulated that Chairman Mengistu was going to visit the prison. About a thousand prisoners decided to organize a protest inside the prison, to bark like dogs, "Abeit abeit," to demand justice from their Comrade Chairman.

"Mengistu ignored us," Mulugeta continues, "but the Vice Administrator came, Desta Maj. I was one of the representatives. We told him frankly we were not members of the rebel organization. But nothing was done and things became much worse. People began to be shot in front of us."

Before that, many prisoners had been called out for execution, five, eight, ten at a time, but they were always taken away from the prison. Now things changed and this added to the chronic anxiety of the prisoners. As witnesses to atrocities without even a pretense at judicial process, would they too not have to be exterminated?

Two particular incidents stand out in the tales that follow. Haile describes the arrival at the prison of fifteen prisoners from Tembien. They were farmers and they came in shackles. Despite the restrictions on fresh air, the prison governor assembled everyone together and began describing the complicity and crimes of the fifteen peasants.

"Ten of them were given their sentences—ten years, fifteen years, and so on. At last he came to the five remaining men. "They are reactionaries. They are counter-revolutionaries. They are members of the TPLF. We will execute them now!" The five prisoners were on a sort of stage. Immediately after, he said the words they started firing and they were shot dead in front of us, in front of fifteen hundred or more prisoners. We were paralyzed. We couldn't eat. We couldn't sleep. Those people were calling on God before their death — "Oh God, we are innocent, we are innocent."

Mulugeta recounts the second incident. It is most vivid in his own words. Like most Ethiopians telling a story, he falls naturally into the direct speech of the participants, so a little drama comes alive in front of us.

"One day there were about eight people to be executed. It was in 1985, about five in the afternoon. One of them was called Haile Berhe. He was charged with being a spy of the TPLF. Then, there was his namesake, another Haile Berhe, who was accused of abducting a lady. The police came and called out the list of people to be executed. The first Haile Berhe was not around, so they seized the innocent Haile Berhe, who was awaiting trial."

'I am not that Haile Berhe. My charge is not political. I am simply accused of abduction. I am waiting for my trial date. The case has not gone to court yet, so there is nothing to make me executed.'

'You have no right to speak! Go!'

"He was screaming and struggling. While they were tying him they broke his shoulder. They threw him in the car and took him and executed him. You know, later, after it was all over, they found the other Haile Berhe."

'What is your name?' they said, taking hold of him.

'My name is Haile Berhe.'

'What is your charge?'

'I am accused of being a spy for the TPLF.'

'Your case is very simple. You are sentenced to ten years.'

"They put the shackles on him, but after one month they called him and they executed him. For one case, they killed two people. This is the corrupted administration of the Dergue."

At this moment a young fighter comes in with a vacuum flask of hot water and some cups. He makes us tea, pouring a strong elixir through a strainer of tea leaves, then topping it up with water. I add a lot of sugar. I seem to need it here and sugar so far has not been available in any other form, like fruit or vegetables. We sit and stir, flicking ants out as they float to the surface. Mulugeta's last words had been delivered with a ringing emphasis. Yet he and three of his companions, as also Woldeselassie whom I will see again tomorrow, were employees of the Dergue for years. What were they required to do during their term of office to prove their loyalty?

There are many questions I would like to ask, a long path to travel before I understand the pressures and fears, which have been for these people the stuff of everyday normality. Nearly two hours have passed. The day has darkened beyond the riffling banner walls. I forget at this latitude darkness comes swiftly at twelve hour intervals. Activity in the caves seems to be hushed, the generator to be muted. The cockerels, which have been strutting in uncomplicated rivalry at the cave mouth and drowning out with crowing the softer tones of Berhanu seem to have gone to roost. The men sit quietly for a few moments, reflective, remembering, stirring their tea. The slightly-swinging naked lightbulbs give the lean jawlines and hollowed cheeks a harsh beauty.

"In fact, it is very terrible to live in the prison," Berhanu's thoughtful voice begins again. "It is a different moral order. You are always hearing the sounds of the prisoners, always knowing prisoners are being executed. If our mothers and fathers came to the prison on Sundays, they felt for us. You see, after coming to the prison for so many years, they understood our situation and there were problems for the whole family, not only for the prisoners, especially in the year of the famine. Some of the wives, they cling to their husbands: 'I haven't enough food to feed the children so what can I do? Shall I sell my bed or shall I sell the stove?' and so on. In November and December of 1985, just before the February Agazi operation, there was a different condition in the prison from the past. They executed so many prisoners within a week, two weeks, a month. Most prisoners were being tortured with a savage kind of torture. At this critical moment the Agazi operation happened."

The mood changes as they begin describing the events of that night. Beyond the perimeter walls, the military presence in Mekelle appeared to outnumber the civilians. The town had a huge garrison, as well as about two hundred heavily armed prison guards. The prison governor would mock the prisoners from time to time by inviting them to escape, "Go ahead. Try. There is nowhere you can go." What the prisoners had no way of knowing was that, by a series of strategic diversions elsewhere, the Front had lured the garrison out of the town, leaving only a skeleton force behind. The firing started about midnight. The prisoners had no idea who it could be. Their first assumption was that they would be shot.

Berhanu was asleep when the first gun was fired.

"I woke up immediately and the gunshots continued. Somewhere there must be war I thought. Whether it was the Dergue or the TPLF I didn't know, but I decided to put on my clothes. There was one prisoner beside me: 'What are you doing? Please, don't wear your clothes. What's happening? What's happening?' "No, it's better to be prepared for whatever happens. Then after fifteen minutes, they came to my cell and they opened my cell first, so I was the first person to get out of that circle of the prison."

Haile's brother was also a prisoner. They were both expecting to be shot at any moment. Just at that moment, he says, he was imagining his mother's grief at losing her two sons, when the door was broken open by fighters.

'Come on, brothers. Hurry, hurry.'

Some prisoners were trying to gather together their meager possessions.

"For myself," says Mulugeta, "I didn't even take my sheet. I just stepped forward as I was at that minute."

Most of the prisoners expected to start running in all directions outside the main gate of the prison. Those who had supported the Dergue up to the time of their arrest had no reason to expect leniency from the guerrillas. All they knew about them was government propaganda that they were all long-haired illiterate peasants or a kind of wild men of the woods with guns.

"But it was not like that," says Mulugeta. "The fighters were very calm. They said, 'Be cool, be calm.' We said, 'Let's get out of here. The Dergue will come. The military will come and kill us.' They were smiling. 'No problem. Don't worry,' they said. And we were gathered together, organized, and marched out of the town like a military operation, eighteen hundred of us. 'Just walk easily, just walk slowly,' they said. But everybody was in a dream, not believing. He would ask his friend, 'By the way, is it an illusion or is it actually happening?'"

They stopped outside the town and one of the fighters made a speech. Berhanu says he will never forget that speech for the rest of his life and repeats it to us. The others listen and their faces are shining.

"We have come to release you and this is what we have done. Whatever happens now, whatever force comes, they will never take you from us. Now you are free. The one thing we need from you is discipline. Try to obey our orders for the sake of your lives and for the sake of your freedom."

The first few days were difficult, however. Everyone was weak. Some had bare feet. They had to walk all day long, often up steep hillsides.

"But there was good help," says Haile. "Some fighters carried prisoners, even their goods. They gave good support, there was good morale and there was good medical treatment. On the way, those of us who didn't have shoes were given shoes. Those of us who didn't have clothes were given clothes."

"There was no problem except sometimes in dreams we woke and thought we were captured by the police."

The first night they walked for six hours. It was all uphill. A terrible experience. The next day, fifteen or twenty kilometers from Mekelle, they stayed hidden from aircraft attacks during daylight. The second night the fighters guiding them doubled back to within thirteen kilometers of Mekelle. The prisoners could see the lights and, still scarred by the irrational logic of psychological torture and betrayal, wondered if they were being taken back again. After that they went straight, but the military continued bombarding in the first direction. The spies of the Dergue were always two steps behind. After three days the military got information that the escapees were in the towns of Gijet and Samre, but by the time the helicopters came to bombard the town, they had departed.

Berhanu is the only ex-prisoner in this group who was well-informed about the Tigrayan revolution. For the Dergue supporters, this long journey into the relative safety of the liberated area was also a journey of a different sort. They were Tigrayans, but had also been employees of the government. They had no information to counter the propaganda that the rebels were weak, a few ruffians who had not won the support of the people.

"In the places we passed through from the prison we saw so many things," says Assefa. "We were in the liberated area. We saw so many fighters. We saw so many schools. We saw so many clinics opened by the TPLF. No one expected it, but we took an understanding from that, that it was a progressive organization."

"I was doing political work for the Dergue," adds Mulugeta, "and what I was seeing here was quite different. People from their own hearts, from their own feelings were welcoming us. All the people were politicized. I started understanding the work of the revolution from the moment I began talking to the peasants. They were telling us the nature of the Dergue and of their struggle."

"I want to add about the bright face of the people of Tigray," Haile breaks in. "When we were released it was an unexpected face. It was highly smiling and highly pitying us for the things we had suffered. Every house was ours. We had hospitality in every farm."

Mulugeta was expecting reprisals, or "hardship" as he expresses it, for having supported the Dergue, but in Samre the assembled ex-prisoners were addressed by a leader of the Front, who assured them they would not be asked to justify any previous stand. In the three months of political education that followed, they had the opportunity of getting an understanding of the aims, political base and achievements so far of the revolution. Haile and Mulugeta make no secret of the arguments and discussions they had during this time. It was difficult to give up old attitudes and loyalties and they refused to consider joining the organization out of gratitude. They gradually became convinced, not least because they realized that the democratic discussions they were able to have here would have been impossible under the Dergue.

At the end of this period the ex-prisoners were given four choices: to become fighters, to go as refugees to the Sudan or elsewhere abroad, to live in the liberated area as a merchant, farmer or teacher, or to return to the Dergue. So far, they tell me, smiling, no one has returned to the Dergue. These men have all opted to be fighters, which in their case, as intellectuals, means desk jobs in this department. Whatever their past, their testimony is told now from the point of view of TPLF supporters. I have no way of knowing at this point the choices of their fellow prisoners.

It is three hours later when I emerge from interviewing. The world is black beyond the dim and fitful radiance of the strings of lights. I feel the need for wild and mindless exercise to purge the tension of the stories I have heard, but nothing is possible in this darkness. Beyond the cave mouth I sense the invisible forest and the ground falling away down the steep and dangerous water course. Two figures emerge into the dim light to stand by me. One is Harnet, Amare's wife. Her companion is another woman, heavily pregnant, whose cropped hair shows her to be a fighter also. Her name is Leila. They take me to where a tray of *injera* is waiting for me and, when we have eaten, ask me if I would like a bath. They laugh when I look surprised.

"Not a bath like in Europe," says Harnet. "No bathrooms here."

"We will show you the bath of the Tigrayan countryside," says Leila. "The bath of women fighters, when we have a chance."

I am getting used to being sweaty and dusty, to lying down in my clothes, to washing when opportunity permits rather than habit dictates. The only parts that are automatically washed are the hands before meals. Now the word "bath" conjures up a delicious image, not so much of cleanliness, as of self-indulgence and relaxation. Yes. Oh yes.

"Go get a towel and clean clothes."

When I return, they lead me to just beyond the edge of the circle of light to where two chairs are already waiting with a large plastic water carrier. They have planned this for me in advance. Harnet finds a large flat stone, tips water on it to wash it clean and puts it in front of one of the chairs. "For your feet," she explains.

"Now undress and put your clothes here," indicating the second chair.

What? Take all my clothes off? Out in the open like this? I look around.

There seem to be fighters everywhere within the lighted area in front of the cave, walking, sitting, hurrying, chatting. A few yards away.

Too proud not to rise to the challenge, but feeling like a reluctant child, I fling my clothes off and sit naked on the chair in what I feel to be full view of the entire camp. But all the men seem to have mysteriously disappeared and nobody even glances in our direction. Harnet and Leila don't let me do a thing. I gradually relax as they trickle warm water from a cup and soap me all over like a child. They massage my head and body, pour water to rinse off the soap and help me to dry and dress. I not only feel relaxed and clean, but cherished in a way I have never felt before. I try to thank them.

"We always do like this for each other," says Leila, smiling. "You are like fighter. You leave your own country, your children. You come so far to see and appreciate our struggle. You are our sister."

Over tea, we sit and chat and find out more about each other. Leila was eighteen when she became a fighter ten years ago in 1977. Harnet joined a year later at seventeen. They had both been school students in Mekelle. Mekelle and the other four larger Tigrayan towns, Adwa, Axum, Endeselassie, and Adigrat are still in government hands, so they have been separated from their families for all those years. In that time they have seen the liberation of most of the rural area of Tigray. Now only the five main towns, the roads connecting them to each other and to Dessie and Addis Ababa further south, and small areas round Humera in the west and in Raya in southern Tigray remain under Dergue control. Now they both work in the Propaganda Bureau, Leila in the Personnel Department and Harnet as a newscaster for the radio station.

There are so many things I want to ask them, but my eyes seem to have a will of their own and my brain is going on strike. I have been up since before four. It has been a long day. I seem to have been through so many experiences since I arrived here, I can scarcely believe it was only this morning. They accompany me to bed, each holding a hand, but I think I was already asleep. I don't remember unlacing my boots. Perhaps Harnet and Leila did it for me, because when I wake I am without my boots, but in all my clothes and wrapped in a fighter's shawl.

The camp is stirring before six the next morning and I wake full of energy. The cockerels are at it again. In my other life I keep chickens myself, so I feel very comfortable. Wrapped in the shawl over my sweater, I take my notes, diary and tapes out to the chairs at the cave's edge to take advantage of the lightening sky. This is not a high altitude by Ethiopian standards, but the blue air is as sharp as a blade. A few minutes later a fighter arrives silently with tea and a wedge of *himbasha.* I spend the next two hours listening to yesterday's tapes and adding to my notes, the only company a goat tethered to a nearby sapling. It will be in the pot later in the day and every few minutes it raises its head and yells to its herd to come to the rescue. I have two milkers in kid at home so I speak the language. I start to wonder whether I'll be back before my own goats kid and how the family is coping, but this is not a constructive direction to take and I concentrate hard on my work.

The experiences of the Agazi prisoners certainly put lesser deprivations into perspective. At the end of yesterday's session I asked some of them informally whether they had been able to contact their families. They told me that lists of names of all prisoners released in the Agazi Operation had been distributed throughout the liberated area and where possible in Dergue-occupied areas. After deciding to become fighters, they had been sent to a fighters' training school for three months, but when that was over they had another three months leave to travel to their home villages. In government-controlled areas, underground networks had helped make contact with families, some of whom had managed to travel as peasants or traders into the nearby liberated area to embrace relatives believed long dead or whose survival they had despaired of.

I meditate over this for some time. What basis is there in my own experience for understanding what that can be like? I am educated; I have travelled; I live in a developed country. Yet the skills and achievements adulated in the West fail to respect what is common knowledge here. In this countryside I am an illiterate. I have no survival strategies; I lack stamina for long climbs; I dehydrate too easily. More important, how would I survive the scattering of my family? How long could I withstand torture? What do I know at all of the limits of my strength?

This work is beginning to take the form of stories within stories, like those Russian dolls, which hold within them ever-diminishing facsimiles of themselves. They are different stories and the same story. Paranoia, oppression, suffering, endurance. History as accumulated experience. The history I was taught was all about power from the point of view of the rich and powerful. This is about power as seen from below, collective experience as multiple and coagulant as frogspawn, rather than a history linear and coherent like a chain of beads. Don't the weak and enslaved know more about the nature of power than the mighty, because they spend their lives trying to mitigate its effects? Where is their voice? How have the historians at Addis University been recording the dictatorships of Emperors Menelik and Haile Selassie and President Mengistu Haile Mariam? Nothing to their detriment, presumably, or historians would be packing out the prisons too. What rulers deny to history is perhaps more telling than what they crow about.

I recall the terrible famine in northern Ethiopia in the early seventies in which millions died. Haile Selassie denied it was happening and suppressed all publicity about it. In the end this was one of the factors, which toppled him. Mengistu still does not publicly admit the existence of the TPLF or of the civil war in the north.

My reverie is interrupted by Amare, who comes to fix my program for the day. He joins me as the sunlight begins to filter through trees and rocks and touch my papers with unbearable brilliance. It is eight o'clock. How am I? How did the interviews go yesterday? When would I like to talk to Harnet and Leila? I ask him if I could talk to the Agazi comrades again, not about their prison experiences, but about conditions in Mengistu's Ethiopia. He is full of energy, this Amare. He listens to the BBC World Service every day and is well-informed about affairs in Britain. He seems particularly interested in how dissent is handled in a "bourgeois democracy," how the British people have been persuaded to accept restrictions on their democratic and civil rights under the Thatcher government. He has closely followed the miners' strike and has been impressed by the organized support of women in the mining communities and the challenge to the government from the women at Greenham Common.

"In Ethiopia, we have never had any democratic channels for expressing our grievances or bringing about change. This and the terrible oppression of our people has forced us to take up armed struggle."

The concept of nonviolent civil disobedience, he says, may be appropriate in a Western country, but not in Ethiopia.

"In your kind of democracy the main strategy is to put pressure on the government by influencing public opinion, but in this country it would play into the hands of Mengistu who is looking for opportunities to annihilate us. If we were to lie down in front of their tanks and trucks they would ride over us with pleasure."

Breakfast is brought. Tea, *himbasha* and omelette fried with onions and rings of green chillies.

"But what have they achieved, these people in Britain?" continues Amare. "The newsmedia mostly support the Conservative Party and the Right. They create the climate of opinion, so it is difficult for dissidents to communicate their ideas. Eventually, they are worn out. Freedom to strike, to demonstrate and protest have become channels to dissipate the energy of opposition, not to change anything."

"Don't you believe in these freedoms then?"

"Yes, they are important, but they do not bring about change on their own. The people themselves must be able to participate in the administration of their own affairs on a local and daily basis and their representatives must be genuinely accountable to them."

"Is this what you want to introduce," I ask, "if you win the war?"

Smiling, he stands up to depart. "We are not waiting for that. We are doing it already."

I spend the morning with the Agazi comrades and the afternoon touring the valley with a guide. It is not idle exercise. Sahle points out the buildings of the Propaganda Bureau, abandoned after repeated bombings had made it evident that its existence had been exposed to the Dergue. Some have suffered direct hits. We stand on the edges of craters fifty to eighty feet across. Sahle points out bits of shrapnel and large bomb cases. I take photographs, but feel I ought to know more than I do about weapons and explosive power. Some of the surviving buildings are substantial stone structures with traditional stone and thatch roofs. Now empty. Perhaps peasants will come along and live in them. Except that this area, so beautiful and fertile, is so infested with malaria mosquitos that people are reluctant to live here.

Sahle refuses the water I offer him and I finish the bottle before long. I have noticed the Tigrayans do not drink nearly as much as I seem to need. By the time we climb back to the caves at about three in the afternoon I feel dizzy and dehydrated and no matter how much I drink during the afternoon, collapsed on my bed, nothing will alleviate my insatiable thirst.

By the early evening I feel more refreshed, in time to tape a conversation with Harnet and Leila. Harnet has the baby with her, but she sits peacefully on her mother's lap. I want to ask them about women's role in the revolution. I already have some theoretical knowledge of the condition of women under the feudal system, which began to topple with the demise of Haile Selassie in 1974 and they add to my information. Under a system, which condemned the rural majority to extreme poverty, women were at the greatest disadvantage. Girls were commonly married between seven and twelve and had no rights even within the family. They could not own land or play a part in public affairs and were often treated little better than animals. The dowry tradition meant that the birth of a girl baby was a curse, whereas a boy was seen as a productive member of the family.

"Even now," says Leila, "the custom is that when a boy is born the women of the family ululate seven times. For a girl baby they only ululate three times."

Women had no role outside the family and within the family their duty was to bear children, sons if possible, to obey their husbands and to serve the needs of the family. Wife-beating was not only commonplace, but often regarded as a duty of the husband to enforce compliance and good behavior. A young girl was supposed to be trained by the age of seven in all the household duties, both to help her mother and in readiness for her own marriage. The most exhausting of her duties were fetching wood and water, often over long distances, and the long hours spent grinding grain on a primitive grindstone.

Listening to this, it is difficult for me to see how it is possible for women, coming from so far behind, to contribute in a mere twelve years to the revolution. I remember the young woman fighter on the convoy who had slipped an arm round my shoulders. She had been chatting and laughing as an equal with the male fighters. The women fighters here in the caves seem calmly self-assured. How is it possible?

Women fighters like Leila and Harnet fled from the towns to the strongholds of the Front during the Red Terror purges of 1977 and 1978 and have completed twelfth grade education, but the majority of fighters of both sexes are illiterate peasants when they join. It will take more than twelve years to change such a deep-rooted culture.

"Women are half of society," says Harnet. Niat has begun to mutter and she pulls up her tee-shirt and begins to feed her. "If we want our revolution to be victorious, the participation of women is necessary. This is what our organization believes."

"There are different ways women can participate," says Leila. "She doesn't have to become a fighter. She can work for the revolution in her village."

"Have you fought in the front line yourselves?"

What I really want to ask is have they been under fire as guerrillas, have they killed people? But the question sounds a bit crude.

"Yes, of course. In the beginning every fighter was in the front line. Now we have so many fighters we do many different jobs, according to our education and how we can contribute. We fight against the Dergue in the army, we teach in school, we work as physicians and pharmacists, we work in propaganda. Harnet works in the radio station."

As we talk I slowly begin to realize that their concept of "fighter" is different from my own preconception. Uncritically, I've been thinking of a fighter as an armed guerrilla and the images in my mind have them leaping down from rocks upon government convoys or taking potshots from the trees at unwary troop detachments. However, Harnet and Leila see the whole revolution as a struggle to shift the population from one state of being to another. It includes a military war, but as important is the struggle against feudal mentality, against disease, against superstition and ignorance, against the conditioned powerlessness of women. It is about galvanizing a whole people to believe in their own power to change their lives and to work for it.

And die for it. Fighters are those who leave the village and dedicate their lives to this struggle, doing whatever their skills fit them for.

It sounds like a religious vocation. When I remember that until recently marriage among fighters was forbidden, it begins even more to resemble a monastic ideal. Are these women expressing the ideal? Are they describing what they would like to happen or is it the reality? I will have a lot to corroborate and cross-check on my journey.

I try not to let my skepticism show, but some of it must show through my surprise at the extent of the enterprise.

"You are looking like the women in the villages when we first went to teach them about the struggle," says Harnet, laughing.

"At first," says Leila, "they say, 'How can you come to fight? How can you move about freely with male comrades? Our place is only in the kitchen.'

'Yes.' They said to us, 'You are not a woman. How can a woman hold a gun? You must be a man.' Our appearance shocked them, wearing trousers, with short hair, with no decoration, carrying guns. To show them we are women we even had to show them our breasts. Then they believed us. But they didn't believe all women could struggle, all women could fight and go to the field. They thought we were exceptions."

"It was a very important work in the beginning, teaching the women in the villages," Leila goes on. "We told them the only difference between us was that we were conscious of our oppression and that forced us to fight. It forced us to struggle. We told them they would be like us after a while. But they didn't believe it. 'We kill the troops of the Dergue,' we said. They only laughed and said, 'Maybe your comrades leave you at home when they go to the front line.'"

"We told them, some comrades have children and have left them with their families, because it is necessary at this time, because we are blind. It's as if we are blind, because women have no rights, no right to learn, no right to teach or to go anywhere because she is a woman. Then we taught them individually or in groups and in meetings. Gradually, they became conscious. Now all over Tigray women become fighters and also administrators, cadres and so on."

They make it sound so easy. I know it could not have been. I want to know exactly how they persuaded these hordes of women. I want to learn from them. I want to go into the towns and villages of England and persuade women everywhere to demand their rights, so that husbands, brothers, sons, bosses and governments cannot withstand the pressure.

Harnet is standing up, with Niat in her arms. Somewhere out there among these escarpments is a hidden radio station and she has to go back to work.

We say goodbye and she goes off with several companions, one of them carrying the baby. I hope I see her again.

My thirst is bothering me again and Leila goes off to ask for tea. She says I need sugar and not just water. My thoughts are still preoccupied with our discussion, with the similarity of problems experienced by women all over the world beneath the apparent differences of wealth and lifestyle. In my own "developed" country I reflect on how undeveloped the economic status of most women is.

When Leila comes back, I ask her how men respond to them as women and as fighters and how long it will take to change men's fundamental perceptions of women as inferior. She agrees it is a long struggle and a long way from being over. The fighters are a vanguard in this as in so many things, because comradeship and political education introduce both men and women to the "woman question." Most fighters join when they are young and open to new ideas. They are working alongside each other, separated from traditional communities.

"As you say, even in your country it is a big problem. Ours is more, because it is a very backward society. It is easier for us fighters to understand these issues than for other women, because we are living together. We work out political questions together. We believe in process, a long process. We discuss and argue every point."

Western feminism, she says, is not the way forward. Men are also victims within an oppressive system and making them the enemy will not change that system. Men and women must work together to understand the problems and change their perceptions. If men and women are divided against each other, they can never win the larger revolutionary struggle and the oppressive forces will maintain their power. Yet, within the class struggle, women must have their own organizations where they can discuss their difficulties and gain confidence and support to struggle for change.

Leila is equating feminism with what I would call radical or separatist feminism and I try to explain that there are many strands of feminism in the West that have encouraged women to become conscious of their secondary place in society. Many of these women have male partners.

"Yes, exactly. You are divided among yourselves. And it is a middle-class movement, isn't it? What has it to offer working-class women? Isn't it ignoring their fundamental economic problems? How can these be solved except as part of a much wider revolutionary struggle?"

It all looks much simpler from a few thousand miles away. The idea of working for a better society with intelligent and sensitive male comrades is certainly appealing, but they seem pretty thin on the ground where I come from.

Our discussion is brought to a close by the arrival of supper. The second meal of goat in the day. This must be the one I heard hollering at first light. I know fighters live very simply, so it is probably on the menu in my honor. Ethiopian hospitality respects meat and despises vegetables, so they assume rich Europeans expect meat three meals a day. I am grateful and I also need to build my strength, so I tuck in. It is more difficult to persuade Leila to eat her share, out of hospitable anxiety, I suspect, lest I might be able to eat it all.

Late at night Amare interrupts my diary writing to say I am to leave at four tomorrow morning. He has discussed my program (with whom?) and I am to go next to the base camp of the Central Committee of the Front to talk to the leaders and to those having overall responsibility for health, agriculture and political education. I am sorry to be going. I feel as if I have been here at least a week. I am not the same person who struggled up the water course two days ago. Yet a part of me, shrinking but still alert, thinks that not for nothing was the Propaganda Bureau so named.

5

Mountain Stronghold

There are too many mountains in this story. There are too many journeys. It is all Up, Up, for lung-searing stretches of time—or the bone-ache of Down, Down. What do I include? What can I leave out? In between the journeys, there are too many meetings, too many partings. But the mountains are part of the story of this revolution. The people are mountain people, tough and resilient, with a long warrior tradition. This is a mountain war.

Another mountain fortress, full of fighters. The headquarters of the Front. It is not a combat unit, although everyone is armed. It is the Central Committee's base camp in a place called Dejenna, a mountainous area jutting into the western lowlands, but the first time I go there I don't know that.[1] Tents are perched all over the steep slopes on little terraces under the trees, connected by a warren of rabbit paths, dusty, narrow and difficult to negotiate. Everywhere you go is someone's home, above or below or along a bit. It is a problem finding somewhere to pee in the middle of the night.

I left the Propaganda Bureau at four in the morning with a dozen or more fighters. I didn't know who they were in the dark and, in any case, their heads were completely shawled against mosquitos and the night air. I knew one of them must be the guide Amare promised to provide. It took four fighters to carry the boxes of food and my backpack. I have given up the struggle to carry my personal luggage. Sickness and weeks of waiting around have drained away all my physical fitness.

Most of the fighters didn't have torches and didn't seem to need them. We moved fast in the pitch dark down the course of the stream, leaping from boulder to boulder, twisting and turning along little paths beneath overhanging trees, which blocked the stars, the only sound the rattle of water. At the bottom we waited nearly an hour in perfect silence before a landcruiser arrived. Picking up extra fighters and leaving others behind, jammed with people and luggage, we bumped and jerked and staggered over the rough road, up and up, snaking and circling, until dawn suffused the sky with pink and orange. We were high in a range of mountains, more than three thousand meters above sea level. Far below, a series of valleys receded into mist, like troughs between seawaves frozen in mid-flow. These were still in black shade, although the fantastic eroded forms of peaks, plateaux and escarpments were glowing with sunlight.

In the landcruiser I felt the tension. It was daylight—late to be exposed in the open. The passengers scanned the sky. Once, following a whispered command, the driver stopped and switched off the engine. Everyone listened intently for a few seconds before we went on again. We finally stopped at the top of a steep escarpment, eased ourselves into the chill air and unloaded the gear. Only then, when the car drove off to find cover, did I discover my guide was the same Berhanu I'd already met, an Agazi comrade, the one who suffered six years in Mekelle prison. No one told me who had been selected. I'm beginning to realize this is the pattern. There was scarcely time to exchange smiles, before the fighters took off like deer down the mountain side.

We plunged downwards for about a mile, down treacherous paths of loose gravel, which slid like ball bearings under foot, before the ground flattened into tableland. There was rock and low scrub, but little tree cover if a MiG came and there was no sign of a settlement in the treeless landscape. Fighters with Kalashnikovs seemed to materialize out of nowhere to scrutinize our passes, even those of fighters they must have known. Then they melted away again, their earth-colored uniforms and stripy shawls indistinguishable from the shadows. In the distance I could see where the flat land terminated in a drop to a lower level, one of a series of shelves to the valley floor, thousands of feet below. Even the near landscape was deceiving for, concealed until the last minute by a ridge, a ravine opened out almost beneath our feet, running from the cliff and filled with a tangle of low trees. In the shade of the trees, perched on the sides of the incline, were scattered tents and benders.

My new home is a dark green tent erected on a terrace scarcely bigger than itself, halfway down the gorge side. Within, two rock sleeping platforms have been built, one piled with my luggage and Berhanu's bag. This bag is about the size of a school satchel and contains his personal needs for the next couple of months. I feel uncomfortably conscious of the contrast. I remember the accounts of Burton and Bruce and other white travellers to Africa, the enormous quantities of kit and equipment and sometimes the travellers themselves that had to be carried by Africans. I thought I was travelling light. In fact, with one backpack and a day bag, I am, by European standards. I realized in the Sudan that I had brought too much and left there all except one change of clothes and innumerable pairs of pants. The rest is recording equipment, cassettes, batteries, notebooks, health kit and washing stuff. As long as the big towns remain government garrisons and out of bounds, visitors have to arrive with everything they need for their entire stay. Toilet rolls are the biggest problem. Even flattened and without their cardboard centers, they take up an inordinate amount of space.

Berhanu comes in, followed by a young woman fighter with a thermos flask and some bright orange plastic mugs. He unclips his ammunition belt and adds it with his Kalashnikov to the pile. I gesture towards the mass of goods.

"Berhanu, why do we need so much food?"

His manner towards me is formal and reserved, but a flicker of a smile passes over his face. I wonder how old he is.

"Don't you want to eat?"

"Yes, but so many tins, milk powder, packets of tea, onions."[2]

"It's not only for us. We will have fighters to guard us, sometimes a driver. We have to pick up more supplies here. Oil and sugar."

He passes me a mug of tea. He stirs his own, thoughtfully. Everything he does looks thoughtful.

"Can't we pick up food as we go along?"

"We have a fighters' code. Never take so much as a needle from the people without their permission and without paying a good price."[3]

"But I thought the people supported you."

"Now they do, but at first they didn't trust us. They had learned never to trust strangers, especially if they had guns. However little they had, outsiders always came to take it from them. Sometimes, these were bandits, sometimes officials.[4] I was a student then, but I was working underground for the Front, so I had some contact with fighters."

"Doesn't the Addis press refer to the TPLF as *bandits*?"

Berhanu gives a little laugh.

"The Addis newspapers are government newspapers. Yes, the Dergue pretends there is no revolution in Tigray—that we are just bandits."

Perhaps bandits are the reason why, outside guerrilla encampments, I am never allowed to go off for a pee without an armed guard in attendance!

No, says Berhanu, bandits used to be a serious problem here but not any more, although they still exist in other parts of Ethiopia. The injustices and poverty of feudalism generated lawlessness and there was no system of effective justice for the poor. The early fighters looked like bandits with their rags and long hair, but in fact the first thing they did was to eliminate banditry. This made a deep impression on the people.

"It is because of *banda* that we don't want you to go without guards in the countryside. They are the Dergue contra-guerrillas. They creep into the liberated areas and commit atrocities in the villages and then say it was the work of fighters."

The trees outside and the dark green canvas make the tent dim even with its flaps open and I begin to feel the effects of the early start. A boy appears at the opening and says something in Tigrinya to Berhanu. One of the leaders, someone called Meles, will be ready to talk to me in a few minutes. Berhanu tells me I will also be talking to Gebru, Tedros, Aregash and Roman. My equipment is already unpacked. I am getting used to being prepared for instant summonses.

The sun is well up and has warmed the chill from the air. We thread our way up the rabbit paths through the trees to the top of the ravine. I am not sure at what altitude the heart and lungs begin to register discomfort, but even this short climb sets my pulse racing. My legs feel like butter. We cross the flat land and plunge over the edge of another cliff, down another steep path cut into the face between tufts and scrub. The thought of having to climb up again, let alone make the eventual climb back up the mountain to the road above, already makes me panicky, raising my pulse rate further.

After an initial descent, the path levels out and takes us round the side of a horse-shoe escarpment. The scree is covered with bushes and small trees, under which tents and huts are huddled for camouflage in tiny terraces dug into the steep slope. Above them, the rampart soars into the sky. A waterfall, cascading down this cliff, partially conceals a ribbon of huts built along the shelf of rock and tucked into the concave foot of the rampart. From a distance they would be invisible.

"Those are the offices of the Central Committee."

To a MiG pilot, flying overhead this would be one more deserted mountainside, one more inhospitable abyss.

I am not accustomed to being summoned for discussions with important people. I feel nervous, but it may be the altitude playing with my pulse. Who are these leaders? If they were to win this war one day, as they seem so confident of doing, then presumably they would be involved in a future government of Ethiopia. As it is, they are the de facto government of most of Tigray. Yet, it is not easy to find out the identity of the leadership. Other revolutions have been associated with charismatic leaders or influential thinkers, populist orators of one kind and another, the Lenins and Che Guevaras of their place and time. Yet, in the London office I never heard responsibility for this revolution ascribed to any named person or persons, just the organizational name, "the TPLF had done this" or "the TPLF has decided that," again and again, as if the TPLF were a living organism.

"Is Meles head of the TPLF?" I ask Berhanu.

"No, he is not. The Chairman is somebody else."

"Is it Gebru or Tedros?"

"No, it is not."

He does not seem very communicative. I try again.

"Who is the chairman, then?"

"His name is Sebhat."[5]

I have never heard this name. I wonder whether the reticence has to do with their sensitivity about spies, although government intelligence must know the names of the leading members of the Front. Perhaps reticence becomes ingrained and extends to all kinds of communication by force of habit.

"They are not their real names; they are field names. At first, fighters adopted new names to protect their families from Dergue reprisals. Now we don't usually bother—too many thousands are joining us."

We wait in a tent a few yards down the scree until Meles is ready for us. He has only just woken up, Berhanu explains. Meles is famous for working all night and only snatching a few hours sleep before mid-morning. There is an admiring note in his voice. The same boy who brought the message from Meles earlier, now brings tea. Tea covers every hiccup, all the moments of waiting. He leaves the strainer and thermos of hot water in case I want more. Berhanu disappears. He has left his Kalashnikov on the end of the rock couch. The ammunition belt, thrown casually on top, drapes itself in a casual loop around the flask and the orange mugs. Like a still life. Sub-machine guns and tea. It strikes me suddenly as emblematic and I take a photograph just as Berhanu enters the tent. He gives me a strange look and takes them with him when he goes out again.

I go over the questions I have prepared. I already have some information from a multitude of sources on the background and principles of the Front, but I need to check it out. It is deposited in my imagination like a Hollywood movie, infinitely watchable but not very believable. It comes in chunks and the continuity is not very convincing.

"On the eighteenth of February, 1975, ten Tigrayan students from the University of Addis Ababa, inspired by the wrongs done to their people by the Amhara dictatorships, went off to the forests of Tigray to start the revolution."

"They sent the feudal lords packing and divided the land among the people."

"Women, who before were married at eight or nine years old with no rights of any kind, are now protected from child marriage, can plow their own land and be elected to the Council."

"The concept of illegitimacy is abolished."

"The people administer themselves in democratic local councils."

"Through a network of local clinics and schools, the people are experiencing their first taste of education and health care."

This morning I had another heroic soundbite from Berhanu. "We have a fighters' code. Never take so much as a needle from the people without their permission and without paying a good price."

It sounds too good to be true, but it has nevertheless grabbed my imagination. I come from a world steeped in cynicism about revolution and the corruptibility of idealists, where selfishness and materialism can be excused as long as you are not an idealist in the first place, where idealism itself is seen as a romantic dream. This cynicism has touched me too. I want to believe in the possibility that people can change their lives for the better through disinterested and collective effort, so I am particularly distrustful of myself.

I go on jotting down a list of all the information I can remember about Tigray under the Front and look at it. The items are theoretical only in the sense of being second-hand and as yet unconfirmed by personal investigation. They are all rooted in the practical life of people and there is no reference to leaders. Interesting. There must be another side.

A shadow blocks the light.

"It is time," says Berhanu.

The Magnificent Ten

Once upon a time (in February 1975 in fact) ten Tigrayan students with five outdated guns left Addis Ababa to start a revolution in Tigray. They left because it was not possible to mount an effective opposition in the capital. The military junta had abolished every democratic right, and opponents of the regime and those whom the regime imagined to be opponents were every day being killed on the streets or dragged off to prison and tortured. They made for a wild and desolate area in the western lowlands called Dedebit, where the dust in the dry season blows continuously between a tangle of thorn bushes and in the wet season turns into a sea of thick soft mud.

Nearly all these first fighters were from cities and towns. They liked to talk about the countryside, but had never had to make their living from the soil. Dedebit seemed a good idea because in this wilderness they could hide and plan, but on the other hand its very wildness made survival difficult. Wild animals, malarial mosquitos, unbearable heat or torrential rains. All these had to be endured. It was no wonder that, despite the fertility of the soil, few peasants cared to farm there.

It is difficult to discover who these fighters were. However, one of them was called Meles. He had given up medical school to go to Dedebit and was reputed to be an intellectual. Another fighter, called Asgede, was famous for his memory. He was not a student and had never been to Addis, but had trained as a health worker and a soldier in the Ethiopian army. Recently he had been cultivating farmland in the Dedebit area. He had hated the slave-relationship of the army and he hated the feudal lords for their treatment of his parents. When, through a friend, he came in contact with Tigrayans who were preparing for revolution, he decided to join them.

Asgede's words help to fill the space between the mythology and the real experience. Practical and down-to-earth, he was astonished that these intellectuals who could command high salaries in the capital, had come to the field. "When I saw the difficulties they had in adapting to the rough life, to the hours of walking, I was even more inspired," he said. "It made me realize how much these intellectuals had sacrificed. I had sacrificed little by comparison. Their comradeship changed my entire life. I loved my comrades and admired them. My life as a fighter became like steel."

The plan was to start armed struggle by rousing the peasants against their traditional oppressors, the feudal landowners and the government. The government had seventy thousand soldiers and mechanized units, tanks and planes and helicopter gunships. The ten fighters had five old guns.

"But they had big sacks of books, Marxist books," said Asgede. "They would spend twenty-four hours reading, discussing and debating what were the political differences between us and the junta, between us and other opposition groups. They would talk for hours about how they should approach the people and organize the people. This was their daily work—politics! It was not a simple matter for me to cope with this, to be with them throughout the day."

They were constantly mobile to elude capture, but their presence could not be concealed from herdsmen and shepherd boys bringing their beasts to the forest. Word spread among local peasants that fighters had come to liberate the people. One afternoon they put their baggage down beside a little stream and sat down to rest. Then, absorbed in conversation, they moved along the bank. By degrees they moved further and further away. The peasants were following their trail and first came upon the baggage. Then they heard voices laughing. Finally, they came upon them and they were very angry. "Do you want to throw away your lives? You came here to fight for people, but you are throwing away your lives by laughing, by sitting by the stream where everybody can see you. You must drink water, but if you want to sit and talk, you must move far away from the streams."

Such hints and rebukes accumulated into a sort of training given in the first few months by the peasants to the fighters on how to survive in the forest. They saw them as young people who, although feeble in terms of survival, had good ideas and needed seasoning. They brought them game animals for food. Their advice was practical and useful. They taught them how to get cool water in the heat of the day, how to identify edible or useful roots and plants, how to keep a distance from the stream and watch, because eventually all animals and people have to come there for water. There were, said Meles, a lot of things they had to learn from them—how to identify the different animals, for example.

"You identify a cheetah from the way it walks at night, its sound in the dried grass. If you shoot, it will go for you, but if you shine a light in its face, it will go away."

Survival in the forest depended on mutual support and learning from each other. Respect for the peasants overturned whatever preconceptions the first fighters had of being the givers in the revolution. Most of them were highly educated in Ethiopian terms, but in the forest it was the peasant who had the wisdom of life and experience. "When you are in real armed struggle," added Meles, "that wisdom is perhaps more important than some far-fetched theory you might have had."

That first summer was a terrible time. Animals were not the only danger. The rains were exceptionally heavy. Rivers and streams were in flood. Mud made it almost impossible to move around, but move they must to avoid detection. They couldn't make shelters. They got sick. Meles fell seriously ill with what was probably typhoid. The only privilege a sick person had was to sleep in temporary shelters built here and there by the peasants. They could have retreated to the villages, but that would endanger the peasants at a time they could not defend them and, besides, there was the temptation to prove that they also were capable of hardship and survival. They were still very young and their fervor was high.

The following summer, they were in villages and small towns, mixing more with the peasants. The hardships were never to be so severe again. Or never in the same way.[6]

My interview with Meles took place in one of the rooms built into the crevice at the bottom of the rock face.[7] Berhanu brought me to the door and then left us alone. The falling stream fanned the air outside and the room felt pleasantly dim and cool after the day's hot brilliance. There was a simple table, one chair and a rock bed spread with patchwork quilts.

Meles was friendly and welcoming. We shook hands Western-style and I sat on the bed. It was his eyes I remembered. He has large, widely-spaced eyes in a heart-shaped face. He set me at ease at once, asking about the journey, my health, my family, my work. When I asked his full name, he said 'Meles' would do and that he was a member of the Central Committee of the Tigray People's Liberation Front and responsible for political education. His English was exact and idiomatic and he was happy to have the conversation taped.

For over two hours we talked about the aims and political development of the Front and particularly its successful creation of a mass base among the rural population over the last twelve years. I wanted to know how this had been achieved.

One of the first strategies, he said, was to unite the people under a minimum common program, which reflected their immediate interests.

"The TPLF describes itself as a democratic Front, but our democracy has its own limitations. We believe that democracy must mean anti-feudalism, which means we have to crush feudalism; then our democracy does not include the right of exploitation by external powers. If they don't stop that—and we know they won't stop that peacefully—we are ready to deny them the democratic right of oppressing us and exploiting us."

The minimum aims, he said, also included the right of Tigrayans to free themselves from the national oppression, which they have suffered under the Amhara ruling class this century.

"This is the democratic right of any people. We fight for the right of self-determination, but not for secession. We believe that secession is one means of exercising this right, but not the best means."[8]

This assertion, straight from the top, was important. The British press had repeatedly described the Front as secessionist and newspaper reports had blurred the distinction between secession and self-determination. They had also been branded as Maoist. Meles rejected both labels and also denied that the Front's program was Marxist. There was a Marxist-Leninist Party, he said, quite distinct from the Front, but which also had to accept the minimum common program of the TPLF. The Front itself had to unite the people against their common enemies across a broad spectrum of opinion.

"We believe," he said, "that every Tigrayan democrat has to fight, for our cause to be successful. The TPLF has the widest possibility of appeal to the Tigrayan people. It would be self-defeating to narrow that circle of appeal."

Meles's voice was quiet and he did not wave his hands about. He combined a quality of physical stillness with a sense of concentrated mental energy.

"What do you say?" he said. "the proof of the pudding is in the eating? Well, the proof of the politics is in the practice."

I had not expected this emphasis from a member of the Central Committee. I had expected political theory, even political dogma. There was theory of course, but it was not abstract. It enshrined the importance of the support of the people and the relevance of the revolution to the practical realities of their daily lives.

"If we try to force anything on the peasants," Meles went on, "and at the same time fight the Dergue, then we are stuck. So we let the peasants go their own way. We try to convince them through practice. Once they hold it through this protracted process, then they hold it fast."

I learned that the strategy of the Front had been to liberate one area at a time through defeating the feudal forces and then to supervise the election of a council in each area, through which the people could govern local affairs. The importance of learning through experience, through responsibility, through mistakes, seemed to be a basic tenet of their theory of people's participation. They saw it as a part of political education. The decisions of the social revolution, such as the division of the land among the people or the advances made in the position of women, the very factors that had drawn me to investigate Tigray, had on the face of it been made not by the Front but by these councils. There must be a lot to look into here. People who have been for centuries kept in feudal subjection, don't easily get together in democratic councils and make wise decisions. I determined to find out their methods and to learn about some of the mistakes.

"We believe that for people to fight for victory they have to be able to see what victory will mean," he went on. "We don't want to promise them any paradise, because we can't give them paradise."

What interested me, if this was true, was that the people had not been called on to lay down their lives for the revolution on the basis of promises for the future. They received tangible benefits as each area was liberated—a share of the land and the power to determine their affairs in the council. The councils and the Front collaborated in health and education schemes, minimal at first, gradually becoming more elaborate. The participation of the people in decision-making, Meles said, was fundamental to the revolution; a society must be "built by the people, not for the people by somebody else. Any system that is given in charity can be taken away at any time."

This was a fundamental change and much of the impetus to support the Front in the military war must have been to defend these social and political gains. But how much did the people really participate in running their own affairs? How effective were these new structures in changing their lives for the better, within the terrible constraints of poverty and the war economy? These were the things I was hoping to find out over the coming weeks.

In the evening I lie on my rock bed in the dim glare of a single light bulb listening to my day's work through earphones. Berhanu has his own accommodation elsewhere, but now he is sitting on the other bed, writing in his notebook. The tapes I made at the Propaganda Bureau were punctuated by the amazing din of cockerels. Today's tapes too have captured a texture of sounds, none of which I noticed at the time. Meles's voice, steady and articulate, is the dominant thread against a cacophony of calling voices, bird songs, buzz of flies, the gurgle of pouring liquid, and incessant stirring of tin cups. It is curious that the ability of the brain to select out whatever it has not chosen to hear does not transfer to the secondary experience on tape. If I were to tape a conversation with Berhanu now, it would give equal importance to the thump of the generator and the whine of mosquitos.

"Was Meles one of the original ten fighters, Berhanu?"

"I'm not sure. Why do you want to know?"

I find the question surprisingly difficult to answer. Why *do* I want to know? I had heard the story of the ten students with four out-dated guns in England from Bissrat, a woman fighter for a time representing the Front in London.[9] It sounded so dramatic. I find myself replaying the scenario.

"Five guns," says Berhanu.

"What?"

"I said five guns."

"Oh. How do you know?"

He suddenly laughs.

"I just heard. Like you. But you're right. How do I know? I wasn't there."

"Do all the fighters know the story of the founding of the TPLF?"

"Yes."

"So why can't you tell me whether Meles was one of them?"

I am convinced he is holding out on me for some reason. He is so serious. It is so difficult to get him to open up—but then, why should he, to me? He stops writing in his notebook and stares at the tent wall for a moment.

"We know the story, but we don't know the names. In fact, some fighters do because they joined the struggle early on. Some of us know one or two or guess others. They weren't all students for a start—Subhat was one of them and he was director of a school and Suhul was in his forties and a member of the Parliament under Haile Selassie. But what does it matter? The individuals are not important. All sorts of people have made an important contribution, whenever they joined the TPLF."

I feel rebuked. I've grown attached to the idea of a band of idealistic students and I find them hard to renounce. I am obviously a Western individualist. Just when I thought I was getting out of the habit.

The boy peeps into the tent and says something in Tigrinya. I have discovered his name is Wode-Asmara (or Asmara Boy). He has a radiant smile. Berhanu goes out after him. Then he sticks his head back into the tent.

"Eleven." he says, grinning. "I think there were eleven."

"Eleven what?"

"Fighters. Eleven fighters."

His face disappears. More words drift back to me as he climbs away from the tent.

"That's if you don't count the other forty-five."

Berhanu obviously knows more about the founding of the Front than I do and I resolve to pin him down at the earliest possible moment.

The distant generator hiccups and slows down; my light bulb blinks and goes out. The experience of trying to find my torch a few times in unexpected darkness has taught me always to have an alternative within arm's stretch. As I light the candle, I remember Meles referring to the constant work of research and learning needed to back up this revolution, that its constantly evolving political philosophy has depended on continuous intellectual endeavor and a continuing critique of the achievements and mistakes of other revolutions. How were they able to keep it up in the wilderness after they fled the vengeance of the Dergue? The first fighters had neither generators nor light bulbs. It must have been a major hazard securing even torch batteries or candles from towns filled with government troops and spies. By comparison, these camps now, with hundreds of fighters backing up thousands more at the front, must seem luxurious. Yet sophistication brings sophisticated problems. The liberated areas depend on a complicated and dangerous infrastructure for penetrating Dergue towns and garrisons for some necessities and for organizing the system of cross-border convoys from the Sudan for others. By what route have these generators and these light bulbs arrived on this mountain?

The candle flame flickers wildly as the tent flap is drawn back. It is Wode-Asmara coming in with supper. Berhanu is standing behind him waiting to trickle water over my hands, but the boy insists on taking the jug from him and pouring for both of us. He is one of several teen-age boys in the camp who, orphaned or separated from their families by the war, have been adopted by the fighters. I invite him to join us in the meal, but only when

Berhanu indicates his permission does he shyly, out of politeness, wash his own hand and take one mouthful of *injera.* Nothing will persuade him to take more.

"*Tsegibe, tsegibe,*" he repeats. "I am satified, I am satisfied."

I am beginning to disbelieve the *"Tsegibe"* formula, which they use to suggest they have already eaten, but they are such a polite people it is difficult to tell. Berhanu also refuses to take more than a mouthful. There is not much food on the tray. The *injera* are poor quality—the wet, soggy wheat kind—and merely smeared with a few lentils and a dusting of *berbere*, the hot pepper, which accompanies every meal. I eat about half and steadfastly refuse more. "*Tsegibe, tsegibe,*" I repeat. Outside, a few minutes later, I hear their low voices as they squat together around the tray to finish the remains.

Several other boys arrive with the tea. First, they peep curiously under the flap at this strange visitor, but before long we are sitting on the rock beds in two companionable rows with tea cups between our feet. Berhanu, who was a teacher before he was arrested, is a stern disciplinarian when they shout with laughter at some joke I can't understand. They want me to teach them English. Solomon has already learned a few words in the camp school. He keeps repeating, "My name is Solomon" and "I am a boy." We make a bargain. I want some Tigrinya phrases in exchange for English. Soon they can all write their names and say "I am a boy." They insist that I don't call myself a woman, but a fighter. OK. "Tegadalit eeyay." I am a fighter.

I put my cup back on the floor between the rows of feet in fighters' sandals made of truck tires and plastic grain sacks. A small black scorpion is marching confidently down the middle, its sting erect over its back. In response to my squeak, Solomon swiftly stamps on it and throws it out of the tent. They laugh at my reaction and Wode-Asmara pats me reassuringly. Some fighter, I think to myself. After this, I find myself scouring not only the floor, but the walls and the roof of the tent in case one should drop on me in the night.

In the morning, breakfast is later than usual. I'm hungry, but there is only a very small piece of *himbasha,* although there's also a dollop of delicious honey, very yellow and thick. Perhaps it's from wild bees. I put out feelers about whether there is any more bread, but the look of alarm on Wode-Asmara's face makes me quickly retract. Under their code of hospitality, I can imagine them depriving some fighter of food in order to satisfy the ravenous demands of a guest. Later, Berhanu admits that the camp has run out of food and last night they ran out of diesel. They are waiting for a convoy. He has had nothing to eat today (nothing presumably since my leftovers yesterday evening). He laughs and shrugs his shoulders as if it is a regular experience. But why not use the provisions we have brought with us? Then I realize they would not be enough for the camp and he would not feed himself alone or use up stores intended for our journey. We use our own sugar, however, and he puts extra in his tea.

Yesterday evening I should have talked to Aregash and Roman, two senior women fighters, but they did not come. This morning, they still have not arrived in Dejenna and the prohibition on travelling in daylight means they cannot be here before the evening. I spend the morning talking to Gebru and Tedros, two Central Committee members, about economic, health, and agricultural policies. Afterwards, two other senior fighters, Jamaica and Seyoum, invite me to drink *sewa* with them. It is dark brown and opaque and sour. A sip at a time, I manage to get down half a mug. They both work in the Department of Foreign Affairs and know London well. In fact, over the last few years they have spent more time in London and Washington than in Tigray. They beam with pleasure at coming home, at drinking their local beer.

"But the best thing about coming to the field," says Seyoum thoughtfully, "is the freedom to speak our thoughts, to say what we like—that is not possible in the West."

Now, the most important thing for me is washing my clothes, but when I ask Berhanu to explain the system he disappears with my bag.

"We will go for a walk," he says a few minutes later. "I will show you the pool where you can wash your clothes."

On the plateau at the top of the ravine, the crazy shapes of the mountain still tower above us, like participants in the drama. Yet, we are high enough for the valleys below us to open out from one another in diminishing levels and the peaks shift themselves in layers of greys and purples. Between stunted trees and bushes the grass is a brilliant gold under the blue sky. I would like to record the dramatic topography on film but that is forbidden. The idiosyncratic forms could identify the location of the camp.

"Soon everything will be dry and dusty, even here," Berhanu says. "I like the rainy season best. It is difficult to move around because of the mud and water, but everything is fresh and green. There are so many flowers and there is not so much danger from MiGs. The Dergue cannot see us through the clouds."

I ask him what he meant yesterday evening by "the other forty-five," his parting shot in our conversation about the ten (or was it eleven?) founder fighters.

"Well," he says, "I'm not sure of the actual numbers, but some members of the TNO went to Dedebit and twenty or thirty others went to Eritrea to be trained by the EPLF."

"So it isn't even the original eleven then. It's more like the original forty!"

"More than that. There were members who stayed in the towns to work underground. Some of them went backwards and forwards from Dedebit. Numbers are not the point. I don't think they stayed constant. The TNO..."

"Yes, what's the TNO? I don't know about the TNO."

I'm beginning to realize that talking politics here depends on juggling acronyms. They seem to be multiplying by the minute.

"The Tigrayan National Organization. Under Haile Selassie there was so much prejudice and discrimination against Tigrayans. The governing class was mostly drawn from the Amhara nationality in central Ethiopia. Tigrayans had to get higher marks than Amhara students to be admitted to college and they couldn't get jobs. They were also angry because of the lack of development in Tigray. There is still not a single factory here. After Haile Selassie was overthrown Amhara domination and oppression became even worse under the Dergue. We were forbidden to write our language. We could be reported to the police for asking for a Tigrinya song to be played in a bar. On the streets we would be insulted or beaten. The TNO was a way of getting together to discuss these problems."

Berhanu's factual version fills out the mythology and pins it to the earth. It is even more gripping.

"Does the TNO still exist?" I ask him.

"It became the TPLF. The Dergue tried to diffuse student opposition in November 1974 by shutting down colleges and schools and sending the youth on a campaign to the countryside. Those who boycotted the campaign were being hunted down, so they decided to start armed struggle in the countryside."

"Were you involved then?"

"I was in school in Mekelle. We were protesting against the bad conditions in schools and then I was sent on the campaign."

This sounds too interesting for casual conversation. Berhanu promises to let me record his story on tape when we have enough time.

In the distance we see a peasant family; father, mother and child, stalking silently and separately one behind the other through the bushes. The man walks with both arms hooked over a long staff laid across both shoulders. The woman, wearing long black clothes, carries a large black umbrella against the sun. The child trots behind. I have heard so much about the importance of the peasants from leaders, from fighters, but so far I have hardly seen any. Berhanu says it's all right to take a photograph as long as I keep the camera low and don't catch the skyline. I move fast to catch them before they disappear. The child sees me and howls. The family freezes and he hugs his mother's knees. I laugh, but I remember too at the Propaganda Bureau holding out my hand to a child about four-years-old, who took one look at the strange white being and screamed in terror. I must be more careful.

We climb through the rocks to where the stream courses down the mountain a quarter of a mile from the top of the overhang. Several fighters, all men, are washing clothes in a pool. One of them smiles at me. Suddenly, I recognize my own clothes! He is washing my clothes! I feel real embarrassment at the thought of a fighter, man or woman, washing my dirty underwear. I try to pull them away, but he won't let go and Berhanu is really laughing now. At Kaza, I washed them in the river, but since then it has been difficult. The days have been filled with hard work and little rest and then at night we rush off to the next place. It is hard to take on, in addition, new ways of laundry, finding the way to the right pool, making sure things dry before the next unexpected move. Now, all my things are dirty at once and I get myself in this position! He wrenches the wet garment away from me and humorously retreats to the other side of the pool.

The other fighters have stopped to watch, but after a few minutes I decide to quit a tussle that does nothing for my dignity and we squat at the edge of the pool to exchange names and chat while they work. I tell them I am surprised and impressed to see men washing their own clothes, let alone mine. Berhanu translates.

"In a revolution it's all struggle," replies the fighter, his face perfectly straight.

"I heard in England that the fighters are the vanguard of the revolution, that they give an example to the people. But I didn't believe that men could change in these fundamental things in so short a time; now I know it's true."

They are all laughing when Berhanu translates, but I am taking it seriously. I take a few pictures of social revolution in practice. It is difficult to stop them standing to attention. The one with my clothes points to my T-shirt and makes a remark. It is very grubby with sweat marks under the arms and spills down the front. He shouts up the next tier of the waterfall, eight feet up, and a young woman peers down and then beckons me up between the rocks. Up above is another pool where women fighters are washing themselves, each other and their clothes. They throw my remaining clothes over the edge and when I have been washed all over, wind me in a shawl until they dry, less than an hour later. After days of meetings, it is a fine way to pass an afternoon.

It does not look as if Aregash and Roman are coming. As usual there are no explanations. Berhanu tells me they were among the first women to join the Front. Aregash is the only woman on Central Committee. The more I learn about the status of women in the traditional culture, the more extraordinary it seems that any women became fighters at all. I feel disappointed. "Don't worry," Berhanu says, "You are sure to meet before long."

We are moving on at twilight. "We are going to the people," says Berhanu. The people. Do they really exist? This is a world made up of fighters and mountains, in which everyone talks obsessively about 'the people," but you never see any. The escarpment towers above us. Somehow I have to get up it. Somewhere over the other side the people are waiting. The topography of this country is rearranging itself in my imagination into an image of rings of mountains, circles within defensive circles. In the middle are the people. Before I can get to them, I have to scale the ramparts like an initiation test I might fail.

"No," says Berhanu when I make a sour comment along these lines. "It is not like that. It is the opposite. The *center* of Ethiopia is mountainous with lowlands round the edge. The villages where we are going are in the lowlands."

He doesn't understand.

"Don't worry about climbing the mountain," he adds kindly. "We know foreigners are always weak. You can have as many rests as you like."

At five, Berhanu and I join a group of fighters setting off up the mountain to the road. First of all, the gradient is shallow over the apparently flat table-land, then rises steeply in zig-zag paths. In some places, rocks form deep steps. Even the first shallow gradient makes me out of breath. I start to feel I can't go on, my body won't do it. My lungs will not cooperate. I'll have a heart attack. Yet this is only the beginning. After a rest, it becomes easier for a while, but then becomes impossible again. It feels as if my whole body's shaking. Climbing up and up with no end in sight.

I need repeated rests. Berhanu waits. Gradually the whole column overtakes us. One of the women fighters smiles at me. She is mature, perhaps in her thirties, with a beautiful face.

"In the beginning I was like you," she murmurs in good English as she climbs past with slow strides, smiling, "We were all like you when we first came to the field."

Her words make me stronger. I discover a new way of walking. You don't look up. It scares you too much. You disconnect your head and turn your body into a machine in which the only moving parts are the legs. On the outbreath you gradually empty the whole of the upper body. The tension drains out of the brain, down the shoulders, out of the back and abdomen, into the legs. The arms are floppy. You are a rag doll being borne up the mountain by an engine in the lower half. But you can't keep it up. You start thinking and all the muscles in your upper body contract, your pulse becomes uncontrollable, you panic. Your face is scarlet, your body bursting. You have to rest.

It takes practice. The only sound you hear is the soft pad pad of sandals, the roll of a stone, and the thrum of blood inside your skull becomes the rhythm of the march, the rhythm of the other fighters in unison with the chafing between your legs, the chafing of the pack on your back, the sore places on your feet. One rhythm driving me on. The mind floats free and seems to hover above the snake of climbing forms. Images arise from the past, disconnected and unreal. Images arise of women fighters marching, carrying heavy loads, struggling for acceptance. Sisters, marching, marching. Lemlem has told me.

Lemlem's story

I was one of the first woman fighters to join the TPLF. Marta was already in the field and there might have been one or two others. But we were very far apart, working in different areas.

Can you imagine?—coming from the town to those shoes fighters wear! I had a very acute problem with my legs for a long time. My feet were swollen all the time, with pus coming out. I was famous for my foot-problems! My shoes would come on top of my feet while I was walking. You see, when I did my training it was the winter, the rainy season. We had no shelter of any kind and only one piece of clothing made of something, not cotton, which was neither warm in winter, nor cool in summer. We were always on the move and had no household items, so when we got flour we could only make one kind of lowest level bread, always the same. The guns were very heavy—there were no Kalashnikovs then as the Soviets had not started to support the Dergue.[10] *We carried these old rifles and, since the guns were more important than life itself, we used our clothes, not for us, but to protect the guns. I used to carry one of the heavy guns. At every step it banged my calf muscles. But with all the hunger, without enough clothes, with so many difficulties, you could not believe the comradeship there was between us. We were always kind to each other; there was no grumbling, no complaints. It was what kept you going. And we didn't know each other —we were all from different parts of the country.*

There were hardly any women in the TPLF. Their acceptance of women was a long process. At first, all I knew was that the organization was reluctant to accept women fighters because the natural things that make us different from men were seen as an obstacle. The discussions went like this: "We are poor. We often have to do without food. We have to travel fast. How can we provide such things as panties or pads for menstruation? Even if pads cannot be provided, there have to be clean clothes and this is not possible. If people are starving, how can an organization provide pads, when we have not even enough clothes to cover ourselves from the rain?" I don't believe they were saying women have no role to play, but at that early stage of organization it seemed a great problem. It took a long time—in fact it has remained a problem, it has never been solved completely. It has been one of the biggest problems of women fighters.

Every unit had a physician or a person responsible for health and medical equipment. We were supposed to tell him if we had our periods and if the towns were not far away then someone was supposed to buy what we needed. So, at times we did get supplies of pads or tampons; at other times we didn't. We were in a war situation and constantly on the move. It wasn't possible to keep a stock and it wasn't a priority. But the TPLF had a clear policy that if a woman told the medical officer that she was menstruating then she didn't have to fight. This meant we never told him until later because we didn't want to be excluded. Even today the organization hasn't resolved problems like this.

After they accepted and trained the first group of us, including Aregash, there was a long period when they didn't accept any more women into the TPLF. We had to prove ourselves so as not to be excluded, especially physically. There is a policy that a woman does not have to carry so many rounds of ammunition as a male fighter. We fought that vigorously. It is easier to prove our equality to the men physically than mentally, so we refused to carry less than the men. There were very few of us, widely scattered, but if we met, the first things we gave each other were words of encouragement: "Never show you're tired. Don't let them make you carry less." We not only helped each other physically, but gave each other moral support as well. There is no way you can stay behind in war. Even if men had to stay behind for some reason, we were in every battle. In addition to our own guns, women fighters always helped with the heavy guns. During our periods of rest we were always doing something, teaching our fellow fighters to read and write, never just sitting still. If we were staying in a house, we would always share the woman's work. We wanted to teach her everything we knew and learn from her. In fact, we did more than the men did.[11]

Lemlem, Bissrat, Zafu, Harnet, and Leila were the friendly woman fighters on the convoy. Thoughts of these women I have met, whose watchword is "struggle," yet who shrug off the hardships of their past, push me up the mountain. Lemlem, now in a wheelchair, trying to construct a future for herself. I think of Roman and Aregash whom I will meet soon. If they could do it, who am I to whine? The woman who spoke to me just now—she threw out a rope and hanging on to it I haul myself upwards.

Of course, the impossible happens—I reach the road. In fact I could have taken more time over the climb. There was no hurry at all, for the truck has not arrived. After a rest, the climb seems less than it was. I have beaten this mountain and I'm ready to take on all the rest. Simple, really. But looking over the edge in the gathering dusk, I notice we can look down on mountains whose shape and color, towering above us, I pointed out to Berhanu earlier in the day. While we are waiting, I talk to the fighter who smiled. Her name is Kudusan and she is a Zone Secretary for the Front.[12] In her area, she tells me, they are organizing a Zone Congress of the people to decide new laws for the redistribution of land.

The truck bears down on us in a cloud of dust. We have to separate. As a visitor, I travel with Berhanu in the cab. The fighters, talking and laughing, swarm up the sides and lie on top of the load. The truck will not be taking us all the way. The road is still under construction, so we will have to climb down the far side of the mountains on foot, down into the valley of Min Minay, down into the lowlands on the other side. The throaty sound of a horn. Headlamps like eyes peering into the gloom. Another journey. This time we are going to the people.

6

The Land is Our Blood

It took us four days to reach Adi-Hagerai. The truck took us to where the dirt road disintegrated into mounds of sand and rocks. Ahead, the roadmakers were at work in the dark. A huge earth-mover, newly emerged from its daytime hibernation, was roaring away in a dust cloud with headlights blazing, like the dragon in a medieval tale. As it lurched back and forth we could just make out in the fitful glare toiling shapes of construction workers. The Transport Department of the Front uses fighters, prisoners of war and sometimes peasants paid in food to carry out its road-building program. When this section is completed, there will be continuous road for the first time from the Sudan through the Front's base area to the towns and villages of western Tigray and the convoys will be able to truck in essential supplies in half the time. At the moment, they have to be transported from the end of the road into central Tigray by camel train, mules, and even donkeys.

We walked for most of the first night, sleeping on the ground for the two hours before dawn somewhere in the long valley of Min-Minay, but the second night we managed to catch a truck to the hot dusty convoy depot of Mai Humer. We spent the hot days hidden in huts or gulleys, talking or dozing away the hours in preparation for the night's exertions. It turned out not to be time wasted. Our enforced daytime halts were at junction points where other travellers were also awaiting the safety of night. They were friendly and open, keen to ask me questions about my homeland, my mission and my politics, and I had opportunities for unscheduled interviews and conversations.

Resting through the daytime in Min-Minay, we coincided with a party of teachers. They were sitting on the ground around a bright blue plastic globe of the world. They had just finished a year's teacher training and were on their way to a new school for fighters, a day's journey away. They told me that, as most fighters were peasants who had had no opportunity for education and as it was a tenet of the Front that all fighters should be educated, they would concentrate on the basic academic subjects, including English, for a two and a half year course. These teachers wore the uniform, multicolored shawls and the truck-tire sandals of fighters, but most of them had never been in combat, although they had basic military training and all carried Kalashnikovs. They were an example of the Front's policy of making the best use of available skills as much for the social revolution as in battle. Listening to them talk, I rearranged yet again my ideas of the Front. The Education Department, the Transport Department, the Agriculture Department, the Health Department—this didn't sound like any guerrilla movement I had ever heard of before.[1]

"Yes of course," said Berhanu, when I shared my thoughts with him. "The TPLF is the state in Tigray. The state in Addis Ababa has not done anything for the Tigrayan people."

Later on, one teacher fetched his homemade *krar* and he and Berhanu took turns playing and singing revolutionary songs. The five-stringed *krar,* like the guitar in Western culture, is played informally everywhere, although it is not played the same way and often looks more like the back of a kitchen chair with a sound-box at the bottom. Magnetized by the music, more people crowded into the hut, encouraging the performers to play and sing until a truck arrived past two in the morning. In the light of a kerosene lamp, the branches of the hut walls, spaced about six inches apart for breeze, threw strange shadows over the company. Bats, swooping in and out as I dozed and listened and dozed again, seemed to flit in and out of the strings and wavering music of the *krar*.

The second day in Mai Humer was intolerably hot. Overrun by ants and assaulted by flies, we hid in a gulley, ten foot deep and fifteen wide, but so slung with fallen tree trunks and muscular roots that we were invisible from a few meters away, let alone from the air. Nothing moved by day in the truck depot and trucks and equipment were wrapped in nets and tarpaulins and carefully disposed under larger trees. Sometimes we heard the noise of a plane, usually an airliner on its way to Addis. "Civilian," Berhanu said, almost before I had consciously registered the sound.

Daytime delays gave me a chance to get to know my companions. There were six of us in the gulley. Travelling with Kudusan was a young woman called Weini, whom I had already met in Khartoum where she was working at the REST office. Wearing stylish Western clothes and a plaited hairstyle, she was evidently not a fighter and was on her way to visit relatives in the countryside.

Berhanu and I had also acquired two fighters as guards. Techana was compact and wiry, a seasoned fighter against the Dergue from the time of the Red Star Campaign.[2] Hagos was a huge eighteen year old, well over six feet, and very shy and quiet. Most of the fighters and drivers in Dejenna and here in Mai Humer seemed to wear flares and Michael Jackson T-shirts, but Techana and Hagos wore their uniform—very short shorts with an ammunition belt and grenades slung round the hips, a slim-fitting khaki shirt, shin guards above fighter's sandals and a purple and green shawl wound turban-like around their heads. Techana looked not old exactly, but gnarled by experience. Nothing could shock him. I asked him in halting Tigrinya where his uniform had come from. He looked at me with a glint in his eye and said he had fetched it himself.

"He means," said Berhanu, with a laugh, 'that it came from a raid. Everything we have—uniforms, weapons, equipment, even exercise books, we capture from the enemy. If the Front needs something we go and get it."

Techana kept the camp in apple-pie order, boiling water for tea, cooking for the six of us, singing songs of the revolution under his breath. Hagos was still a boy in a huge and beautiful body, surprised by everything. He stared at me when he thought I wasn't looking. He watched in amazement when I limbered up with yoga stretches at first light. Most of the time he was on sentry duty with his M14 rifle, but in odd moments of waiting he took out a bamboo flute and played the haunting murmuring music of shepherd boys.

Berhanu himself was changing, loosening up. He looked happier. He said he was happy because he was going to the people.

"All the fighters are happiest when they are working with the people," he said. "They inspire you. They show you your aim. But we have to work where we can most help our organization."

This was the first time he had been away from the Front's base area since his release from Mekelle prison eleven months before. He had spent most of that time researching and writing in the Propaganda Bureau.

To while away the hours in the gulley, especially when Kudusan and Weini were sleeping, Berhanu started to teach me Tigrinya script. I learned there were about thirty-five letters, but as each one has seven forms with the addition of an integral vowel, through which the letter often lost all resemblance to its base form, I saw it as an alphabet of well over two hundred letters. It had four sounds for "k," made in different places in the throat. I couldn't hear the difference between them, let alone make the sounds. Learning Tigrinya was going to be a struggle.

He also told me about Ethiopian time. I knew already that their calendar calculated the birth of Christ seven or so years later than the European one, complicated further by a new year starting in September. I now discovered that there was also a seven-day difference in counting the days of the year. For example, the much-celebrated anniversary of the founding of the Front on February 18th (as I thought) is actually observed here as February 11th. Ethiopian Christmas, on the twenty-ninth of December is for Europeans the seventh of January and so on. Even telling the time is different here. As in the West, before the advent of the twenty-four hour clock, the day is divided into two blocks of twelve hours, but here they correspond logically with the near equal division of darkness and light. Darkness falls soon after six; it lasts for about twelve hours and varies over the year only by about an hour. These cycles of darkness and light dictate Ethiopian time-keeping. The first hour of the day begins at six o'clock in the morning and Ethiopian twelve o'clock is six p.m. European time.

Anxious to adapt culturally, I rewound my watch to Ethiopian time and spent the next few days in total confusion. I never knew whether it was time to eat or to sleep, never knew the time of day or night and felt upset and disoriented. In the past I had fancied myself a critic of timebound Western ways and I was even more discomforted to find myself enslaved. I discovered I had completely internalized Western time. The phrase "body clock" had new meaning. The situation was not helped by the fact that Ethiopian time was being eroded in the cities by European time so that educated people tend to operate both systems. I learned to check every arrangement, every appointment, with the question "Ethiopian time or European time?" And I humbly rewound my watch a second time.

If I am in a camp or settled for a few days, I wake at dawn to make best use of the morning. As the temperature rises and energy declines, the afternoon becomes the time for rest. But as the day cools and turns to dusk, night is the time for revolutionary activity. Many meetings and conferences take place after dark. In the dry season when bombings are more frequent the villages and small towns hold their markets in the evenings. Journeys take place at night to elude government surveillance and make more difficult the work of spies. I never know exactly when I am starting a journey; I never know exactly where I am going. I go to bed not knowing whether I will be sleeping until six o'clock (twelve o'clock Ethiopian time), or if I will be roused at two or three or four, depending on the length of the journey. I get used to being packed and ready to leave at a moment's notice. A moment is about four minutes. Berhanu places a light hand on my sleeping bag. "We go in four minutes," he whispers. It's lucky I've always been a light sleeper. He is proud of me. "You are like a fighter," he says.

Darkness descends swiftly. Outside the five main towns, still government-controlled, there is no electricity, but in some of the larger fighters' camps the generator starts thumping at dusk until the small hours. Strings of lightbulbs are threaded through the trees to some tents—to those whose job requires reading or writing after dark. Sometimes I am lucky enough to have one. Writing up my notes or diary and preparing for the next day's program mostly have to be done at night. A single light bulb swinging at the apex of a tent is diffused gloom rather than illumination. Everything seems more of an effort in a dim light, as if intellectual illumination needs literal illumination for sharp focus. In small camps, on the road and in villages, I have to work by candle or torchlight and then a light bulb seems an unimaginable luxury. For the millions of peasants with few means of illumination available to them, the darkness must be a block to be worked round, an obstacle that always has to be taken into consideration. Yet, to the Front, darkness is both a respite from air attacks and an opportunity for action against the enemy.

I learn to feel at home in the darkness. I tramp in the middle of a column of fighters, my footprint in their footprints, silent in the strange sounds of the night, without torches for the most part, a kind of radar developing in my feet, sense of ache and sweat suppressed by the mesmerism of the shared march. At twilight, looking out over countryside already invisible, without a single point of light anywhere to be seen except for the first stars emerging above the black and jagged profile of the mountains we have crossed, I am conscious of the softness and self-indulgence of life at home. How much I have taken for granted at the flick of a switch.

We reach Adi-Hagerai at seven in the morning. The dawn reveals a brown landscape of round undulating hills, like dunes, stretching to the horizon. The few trees look like dead twigs. The gulches are dry. It is quite different from Kaza or Dejenna. Yet it is a mistake to equate aridity with infertility. It is the dry season. Here the trees lose their leaves to protect themselves from heat and, on closer inspection, the dry poverty-stricken hills are not all dust and rocks, but here and there are covered with a down of dried grasses or the flattened stalks of harvested sorghum. Nevertheless it must be a bitter labor wresting a crop from this hard and stony soil. This is part of the first area, which was liberated ten years ago. On the way here last night we travelled through Dedebit where the revolution started. In the darkness I was only aware of flat bare ground and dense thickets of thorn bushes and incense trees. The absurdity of passing through Dedebit without being able to stop and explore struck me in a dim sort of way but at the time I was too tired to care.

The Rescue of Musie

The first operation of the fledgeling Front was the rescue of Musie. The first fighters had gone to Dedebit in February and this happened in July. Musie had been a fighter for the Eritrean People's Liberation Front, although his father was Tigrayan. He was the contact who arranged for the training of the new fighters in Eritrea. By May, they were returning and the numbers in Dedebit had swelled to forty or more. Musie meanwhile had transferred to the TPLF. He persuaded his friend Jamaica, another Eritrean fighter with a Tigrayan father, also to join the struggle in Tigray. The experience of these two friends was invaluable to the new Front.

Musie, Jamaica, and others were organizing an underground network in the towns, raising support and funding for the revolution. They travelled to Gondar and Addis and the main Tigrayan towns. Once, when Musie was trying to escape from security agents in Gondar, his bus was stopped at a checkpoint and he had to run for his life. In July, he set off with Jamaica and Seyoum on a mission to Eritrea. They had one pistol between them. They had only got as far as Adi Daro when Musie went into a bar to buy some cigarettes. It was about seven-thirty at night. In spite of his disguise he was immediately under suspicion—all outsiders were under surveillance because the formation of the TPLF had been sensationalized in the area. A Dergue militia in the bar drew a gun and put Musie under arrest. Outside, Jamaica and Seyoum saw him being taken away to the district town of Shire.[3]

Seyoum took the pistol and went off with some sympathizers to a point on the road where the police party could be ambushed, but in fact they took another route. Jamaica ran back to Dedebit to tell their comrades what had happened. But he couldn't find them. They were constantly on the move and he didn't yet know his way around Dedebit. He was lost in the wild forest for over two days. It was the rainy season and he had to wade through rivers and struggle through mud. He had new shoes on. His feet were all blistered and he could scarcely walk. He was starving hungry. In the end he bumped into his comrades by accident. His first words were "Food! Food!" When he had told the story of Musie's capture, they gave him kitcha, the simplest form of unleavened bread. He was so happy he laid the kitcha on his chest and slept. He didn't eat it until later.

Jamaica's companions were deeply shocked to hear of Musie's capture. He was an experienced leader and knew all the secrets of the organization. They decided they were prepared to pay any price, even death, to get him out. Seven of them went to attack the Shire garrison—Seyoum, Asgede, Kelbet, Heluf, Tekele, Berihu and Suhul. It was the Front's first operation.

They had three grenades, one Kalashnikov, one Simonov, one French gun, one carbine and a pistol. The fighters were nervous and inexperienced, for Musie himself was the pillar of the organization. They walked for five days with very little food. There was heavy and continuous rain. The rivers were all in flood. Crossing one river in the dark, Suhul was swept away with his gun. Mourning, the others continued on their way. They knew he couldn't swim. In fact, he saved himself by hanging onto a branch, but his gun went to the bottom. The loss of a gun at that time was a disaster.

Meanwhile the authorities were boasting that they had caught 'the leader," the "one from Eritrea." The Head of Security in Mekelle phoned through a message to Shire that Musie should be transferred at once to Mekelle, but the administrators in Shire decided he should stay there one more night for interrogation. The fighters knew nothing of this. There was a problem of timing because so much was unpredictable and, after they entered the town, they had to operate in small units so communication became difficult. They were short of essential information. How long would he stay in Shire? Would he be transferred by road or by helicopter?

The first task was to find Musie. There were three possibilities. Disguised as a peasant, Seyoum went first to the mayor's house as a beggar, then to the District Administrator's office with papers like an appellant, then to the police station with more papers as if he were taking a case to the police. Passing through the compound and into the main door, he glimpsed Musie through a door to an inner room. Musie looked up and saw him. He was shackled to the wall. Seyoum stayed long enough to study the numbers and movements of police before a guard became suspicious. To put him off the scent, Seyoum had to walk round the town, buying from shops the sort of things a peasant would buy.

Five of them were in the house of a very old nun. Her next door neighbor was the Head of Police; opposite was a militia's house. They stayed there a night and a day. They couldn't go out, even to shit—they had to use a water jar. At eight in the evening, they met at a prearranged spot outside the town. By chance Agazi had arrived on a mission from other towns in Tigray and he was roped into the operation. His job was to monitor the security of the nun's house, to ensure the safety of the fighters and agents within. Together, they discussed a detailed plan of attack and even an escape route. Agazi was to stay at the meeting-place as a guard.

The raid was over in minutes. Heluf, Asgede, Seyoum and Berihu went to the police station. There were two police guards, one on either side of the gate. They had a grenade for each. They flung open the door, firing the Kalashnikov and crying, "Everyone lie down!" As they had no key they wrenched the chains from the wall and carried off Musie with all his shackles into the countryside.

The rescue of Musie was good news for the new Front. Until this point the only information was the bare fact of its founding. It was a landmark in the popular imagination and launched the TPLF as an organization.[4]

The moment we arrive in Adi Hagerai we are surrounded by children. Although it is still early in the morning, they pour out of every door and alleyway and surge around us in a dense grinning crowd. They are soon joined by several men and women who stare at me, curious and unsmiling. They smile at Kudusan, however, and embrace her, one after another. This is her homebase, the center of her zone. She is radiant. She is so happy to be here. She turns to me and takes my hand.

"Jenny, I must say goodbye. I have many things to do. We will meet tomorrow at the Congress."

I remember that the Zone Congress on the redistribution of land is to start sometime soon, but this is the first clue I've been given about the precise day.[5]

As soon as she has gone, the crowd of children presses closer. Some of the adults rebuke or cuff them, but they don't take any notice. I feel little fingers poking experimentally in my back and stroking my bare forearm to see what my skin feels like. Berhanu's teacherly persona comes to the fore and he clears a path through the crowd and into a house where I subside onto a rock bed to sleep off the journey until lunch time.

It is impossible to sleep for more than an hour or two in daylight. I am woken by a loud squawking noise outside. A chicken is being slaughtered in the yard. I go out there and meet a woman called Zafu who is now plucking the chicken in a kitchen of tree branches. Before the revolution, women were thought to be too weak to kill animals and now they proudly claim this role as a sign of their new equality. When Berhanu comes in to help with interpreting I learn more about Zafu than I could on my own. She has two sons in their teens and a daughter of about a year, but she also helps run the Women's Association here and is on the executive of the *baito* or local council.

After four, we walk around the town and visit the school and the clinic. Immediately, we are surrounded by children. They are cheeky and intrusive and amusing. Berhanu and Hagos try unsuccessfully to chase them off, but it is like swatting flies. They rise in a swarm and immediately settle again, chattering and laughing. The younger girls compete to hold my hands, until I have three or four of them hanging off each arm. It is too hot to hold hands.

It is supposedly beginning to cool down, but the bright white lowland heat still slices the eyes.

Berhanu tells me that Adi-Hagerai is a town, although to me it looks and feels like a village. The Tigrinya word for "village" (*tabia*) means a collection of scattered farms within a specific area, rather than a number of dwellings all in one place. This town looks as if it has grown up out of the earth in which it is imbedded. The single story houses are made of local wood or stone, plastered over with local clay, cracked, and scabbed. The people wear clothes in the same traditional patterns they must have been wearing for hundreds of years, the women mostly in long dresses of handwoven unbleached cotton, now as brown as the houses and the soil in the dry brown fields. As if to make a point, persistent gusts of wind blow the dirt road in swirls around our ears and into the open doorways of the houses. Everything is brown.

When we get to the school, the pupils are streaming out. About a hundred and fifty of them squat in a crowd in the shady side of the building and the young teacher invites me to talk to them. I feel unexpectedly shy and unprepared, but I ask a few questions and look at some books, feeling unpleasantly like a badly-trained royal. Most of them are not children at all and the teacher, Tsegai Gebreselassie, explains that shortage of teachers and resources forced them to give up teaching children in favor of young people between the ages of twelve and twenty-eight.

"Most people with teaching skills are in the Dergue towns," he says. "First, we have to educate a generation of teachers, people whose skills can be passed on to society as quickly as possible."

What bitter choices are dictated by scanty resources! The problems, apart from constant fear of air-raids, are all of shortages of essential equipment. The curriculum division of the Education Department provides text books, but exercise books or paper, pens and pencils have to be provided by the students and even these are beyond the reach of many families.

"Why are there so few women?"

"Because they leave to marry. Twelve years ago, girls were married about nine years old. The minimum marriage age was then raised to thirteen or fourteen by the *baito*. Recently it has been raised again to fifteen."

"Why do they have to stop school when they marry?"

"They don't have to, but they have so many duties in the house and then they stop coming to school. We are fighting these old traditions, which keep women illiterate and ignorant, but it is very slow."

Yes, I say to myself, it is the same everywhere. Educational provision is only one factor. Social attitudes and the burden of women's work have to change before women can take advantage of education.

The area was liberated about ten years ago and the school was reopened four years after that. It had been founded in the last years of Haile Selassie, then closed down by the Dergue. The Adi-Hagerai *baito* requested that the school be reopened and provides the building and the teachers' food and accommodation. Tsegai, self-effacing and polite, is director. He and the other six teachers are fighters and receive no salary. They are fighters, he explains, because they are working to transform Tigray into a free and just society, but they are not combat fighters. Their weapons are literacy and knowledge. As I talk to him, I begin to glimpse what they are up against in trying to change a traditional rural society—the superstitions, the ingrained gender roles. I begin to see the young women who make up a third of the student body as an encouraging stage in a long process, as a triumph, rather than a defeat.

"We also have a literacy program," Tsegai explains, "that is more popular with many women. Many of the children who were educated before the policy was changed to educating adults, are now old enough to be recruited for this program."

In government schools, education was conducted in Amharic; now these students can study their own language, Tigrinya, and the second language is English. I am impressed by the relevance of the curriculum to the students' lives. Science includes soil erosion, soil conservation and terracing, as well as egg and chicken production. History includes the history of Tigray (suppressed in government schools in favor of an Amhara version), and of the Front. I begin to understand why it is a part of the political education course.

Up the road is the clinic. It is housed in a typical single-story building, surrounded by a low wooden fence. A number of patients, mostly women with babies on their backs, are waiting for attention. Like the school, it is a partnership between the Front and the *baito*. The physician is really a dresser trained on a number of very short courses to diagnose and treat the main epidemic diseases of the countryside, such as gastrointestinal complaints and malaria, and to recognize and refer complicated diseases such as tuberculosis to the regional hospital. The service is free, except for a small charge for medicines and bandages. The emphasis, as Gebru told me at Dejenna, is on preventive health care through health education and a growing band of community health workers. On the wall is a long Tigrinya message, recalling the expensive private pharmacy that was the only official health care before the revolution, well beyond the means of poor peasants. "Today, even the poorest can receive treatment and the payment is regulated. Health and revolution are one!"

Half a Story

My name is Tekebach Murubi, but now they often call me Adey Woyanit (mother of the revolution). When I was a child I was married to a farmer. I was seven years old and he was twenty. Both our families were rich. As a reward for my marriage I was given ten cattle and one mule. Because I was rich I had no problem. At the age of sixteen I gave birth to my first child, a son. Continuously after that I gave birth to seven children. The gap between the first two was two years and after that every three years.

At the age of thirty-four I started my "sickness." There was a woman called Desta who was a zar.[6] *Before I was sick I was not interested to go to that* zar, *because it was forbidden and because I believed very much in God. Then a man came to my home. He wanted his son to marry my daughter. I wanted it too, but my husband opposed me so she was given to another. But he was a* debtera[7] *and because we rejected his plan and were not interested in giving our daughter to his son, our cattle started to die. One night two died. Then people started to come to us and suggest, "Why are you longing to lose all your wealth? Why don't you go to Desta? She knows everything—why human beings die and why cattle die." But we said no and all our cattle died, except one ox.*

Now we were not able to plow, so we made arrangements to borrow an ox, but our last ox started to get sick. A week later, he died. Then again people started to ask, "Why are you waiting to die yourself? Why not go to Desta for the solution?" So we went to her house. We came late and there were other patients waiting to see her, but as we drew near the house, we heard this Desta saying, "Please leave me in peace because a very big owlia[8] *is coming." Then out of respect for the new* owlia, *she prepared coffee for me, her guest.*

"That sorcerer, because you didn't give your daughter, kept a medium in your house, a very big zar. *There are three important things. The first is the sorcerer; second, there is a* zar *in your house and he has not had his share of blood so he drank of your dead cattle; third, you are pregnant and that baby is going to be changed into bones." These are the three things that Desta told me as a solution.*

"There is another wizard in Abi Adi, a Muslim.[9] You go to Abi Adi and get a spell or a charm from him and hang it round your neck."

I still feel within me a child of bone. Seven years ago I felt it too.

My husband went to Abi Adi and bought the charms and when I put the kitab[10] on, my period started and I couldn't control the flow of my blood. I desired to eat it back again because it was too much. My only chance to have blood was to drink the blood of my chickens. I had a foreign breed of cockerel. After that our relatives began to say, "If the blood is not enough, your children might die, so we ought to get a sheep so she can drink more blood." Then after I drank the blood of the sheep I was a bit healthier.

Then one day I was returning from visiting a relative, when I saw the huge roots of a plant upturned in the field by the plowing. I felt dizzy when I saw it and a spirit I couldn't understand came to me and said, "take it, take it to your house. It's a medicine." So I took it to my house. Then day and night I started to dance a special zar *dance. Day and night I was like this and when I danced sick people came who liked to dance with me and the spirit ordered me to give medicines for the sick, even the quantity and quality of the medicine, and they started to be well and free from their sickness.*

Then rumors started to spread in the villages that I had become a witch, a full zar *by myself. If I took a part of those roots that I found, then the spirit ordered me the right type of medicine for those who were unable to urinate, or whose stomachs were swollen and other kinds of medicine also.*

Then in a place called Gijet is a very big fukera *who is head of the* owlias. *So some months afterwards I went to him. I was ordered by the spirit to go there and kneel down to that chief and he was pleased and said I was approved as a queen. They were very pleased with me and my coronation song was like this [making certain movements of the head].*

I returned to my village and a few months later the organization started. Fighters started to come to my home. Meskel, the feast of the Cross, is the time for harvest, the time for gathering wood for a bonfire.[11] *There is a dance that is always danced at that time. So every year I was queen of the dance and in every village those who respected me would come to me for the sake of the dancing. But at that time, fighters were coming and there were rumors of the fighters being around us in the forests. So when the villagers came to me I thanked them and said it was not the time. The next morning fighters were in every house.*[12]

After supper Berhanu has arranged for me to meet representatives of the three main mass associations—for women, farmers, and youth. Whereas, the *baitos,* the administrative councils, are elected by the people and independent of the TPLF, these associations are political organizations within the Front. They are their chief means of educating the people and thereby influencing the decisions of the *baito.* I am interested that, although preferring a class analysis to anything resembling a feminist analysis of women's oppression, they still encourage women to organize separately within the struggle.

We walk round to a nearby house, followed as usual by Hagos. The wooden shutters are closed. The moonlight cannot penetrate and the small room is inky black at the edges. I sit with Berhanu behind a table on which an oil-lamp illuminates our faces for them, but leaves theirs only vague shapes in the darkness. Peering, I make out about a dozen people in the room, half of them women. Only in the silence after Berhanu's brief introduction, do I realize I am expected to make a speech. Unprepared, I explain that I have been invited here to find out about their revolution, that already I am discovering an Ethiopia no one knows about in my own country. In Britain, the popular image of Ethiopia is of people dying of famine, helplessly waiting for aid from the West. I am discovering a people who are strong and doing things for themselves, who have problems of poverty and drought, but whose poverty and hunger have been mainly caused by politics, by the exploitation and injustice of governments and people in powerful positions. Most important of all, the people are changing things by their own efforts. This has been a revelation to me.

Berhanu translates sentence by sentence and a burst of ululation follows. Then, I ask some questions of each association in turn. The speaker for the Women's Association is called Ametetsion. It was founded ten years ago, when Adi Hagerai was first liberated. At first, she admits, they were not keen to start the association or organize themselves. They closed their doors when fighters approached, but gradually the persistence of the women fighters won them over.

"Before that, we accepted our position. We were never able to sit with men and discuss things. It was forbidden."

Although membership is voluntary, they now have three hundred and seventy members—only twenty-five or thirty of the oldest village women do not attend.

"What kinds of things do you discuss at your meetings?"

"We have come to realize that women can struggle too, that we can participate in the revolution, so we discuss our progress, we discuss our problems, the source of women's oppression and how to struggle against it. The situation for women has changed over the last ten years. We have land. Now we have the right to discuss issues and be elected to any position. And we are being elected."

"At the school there are twice as many men as women. Is this a problem for you to tackle?"

"It is because of marriage. We want to raise the minimum age of marriage from fifteen to eighteen to relieve the burden of women in the home."

The men from the Farmers' Association speak movingly of feudal conditions under Haile Selassie, how the landlords took most of the crop, leaving too little for them to survive until the next harvest.

"When we tried to free ourselves, they became even more brutal and imposed bribes as a punishment."

"What part did the TPLF play?"

"They agitated us. They helped us to understand the politics. There was a very big uprising of the peasants armed by the TPLF. Then we smashed the feudal lords. The feudal lords' party, the EDU,[13] was very strong around here, but we smashed them."

I am still brought up short when a word like *agitate* (or *propaganda* or *mobilize)* is used approvingly as a straightforward political term. In Britain, our political education has taught us to avoid and distrust this language. Here these words are relevant. They mean something. But I am caught in the revolutionspeak of Berhanu's language. Although I know enough Tigrinya to trust the integrity of his interpreting, I won't ever know enough to gauge the values of the words the peasants use.

The talk switches to land. They say all the peasants own land now.

"Has this improved the standard of living?"

"The land is our blood. Before, we were landless, now we have our own land. But there have been problems of drought and famine."

I ask them also what goes on in their meetings and it emerges that their association is also the place where they talk about strategies for combating drought and underdevelopment, where they discuss improved techniques of plowing, soil and water conservation, reafforestation, how to spread the skills and knowledge of the most active farmers. Their definition of politics incorporates every priority of their daily lives. Underdevelopment in Ethiopia is man-made and here are men and women fighting back in appropriate ways.

The young people are shy. Their speaker makes a few politically correct statements and then describes interestingly the work of the Youth Association through their cultural group, using music, theatre and dance to politicize their peers. Finally, we stand up to go and Ametetsion presents me with a handwoven and embroidered shawl. The women gather round me and drape it over my head and shoulders so that the embroidered border is shown to advantage.

"They are smiling," says Berhanu, "because you told them you have four children and this is the shawl of a bride."

Walking back to the office, I wonder aloud where this notion of the simple peasant comes from.

"You are right," says Berhanu. "They are not simple at all. They have a very correct idea of their interests. This has helped us to politicize them."

Even with a moon, it is impossible to see his face, but his voice is relaxed. Since crossing the mountains, his face has lost some of the stress lines that were so marked when I first met him with his Agazi comrades. Perhaps this is like a holiday for him, after the long years in Mekelle prison and his intellectual work at the Propaganda Bureau. Even Hagos is smiling more, not looking so often into the distance towards mild-eyed oxen and absent fields. Perhaps a posting to the mountain camps we have left behind is for these fighters another kind of exile.

Early the next morning, before either the sun or questing MiGs appear in the dawn sky, the three of us set off on foot again for the Congress. To guide us, one of the fighters who is "working with the people" in the town comes with us, although there are plenty of other men and women streaming along the paths in the same direction. I had thought the meeeting-place was in Adi-Hagerai itself, but to get there we have to walk fast for an hour and a half over the brown hills. I am much fitter now, but before we reach our destination the sun is well up and I feel thirsty and overheated.

At the end of the walk, our guide takes us to a peasant's house on top of a hill for a drink and a rest. It is built of stone in the traditional *hidmo* style with thick walls and a roof of stone slabs across tree trunks, all overlaid with turves. We enter through a simple veranda, providing shade for the open doorways. The balustrade of stone and branches is hung with goat skins drying in the sun. It is delightfully cool inside. The room is large with benches against the walls but very little else. From continuous sprinkling and sweeping, the clay floor has the dull shine of stone.

A young woman brings us a drink of *sewa,* the local beer, in long gourds. She is dressed in the tight-bodiced, full-skirted traditional flowered dress, calf length, of the style that seems to be favored by younger women. They seem to come in dark blue and dark green. This one is blue. Through the doorway I see other women of the house in the homespun and embroidered heavy cotton long clothes of older women. One of them is her mother and she comes to greet us, shyly, bowing low to the floor, her shawl pressed against her lips. The fighter smiles and says something in a low voice to Berhanu.

"He is saying they are trying to discourage these old-style manners from feudal times. They are not good for the people. But old people cannot change."

The manners of the daughter are certainly very different. Her posture is upright. Her clear intelligent eyes meet ours directly, with polite friendliness.

"How do you like our *sewa*?" asks Berhanu. "It is good here in the countryside."

In fact I'm not at all sure about it. I tried a more refined version in Dejenna, when my stomach was still delicate and I decided it had a similar acidity to vomit. This home brew is thick and mud-colored with bits of leaf and twig floating in it. But now my stomach is sound and thirst helps me to persevere. By the time I have emptied the gourd I am almost developing a taste for it.

From the top of the hill outside, I can see no sign of the Congress venue, just an undifferentiated landscape of round brown hills to the horizon, like a child's drawing. However, when we walk down the slope and between two hills, there it is in front of me, half as big as a football pitch, like a flat haystack spreading up the hill—the Hall of the Congress. Within is a simple amphitheatre of shallow bench seats in tiers carved out of the hillside, but so well camouflaged with a thatch of dried grasses on roof and walls that from a short distance away the whole structure melts into the golden brown of the hillside. From outside, it looks too low to stand up in, but it must be an optical illusion, because inside it appears spacious, the roof upheld by slender trunks at least seven feet high. It is already filled with people and the cool dappled light is bright with yellow and red banners and long white cotton strips a meter high covered with Tigrinya slogans. Facing the assembly, Kudusan and another fighter ("that is Seyweon," whispers Berhanu) are sitting behind a table.

The proceedings open with a cultural show. To the beating of drums a makeshift curtain threaded on a wire is drawn back to reveal a double rank of singers who provide a chorus to the solo voice of the lead singer in front. The audience takes tremendous pleasure in these songs, joining in the rhythmic clapping of the chorus singers and, when the message is particularly rousing, leaving their seats to embrace the singer or dance alongside. Meantime I look around the hall. There are a few scattered fighters, but most of the assembly of a hundred or so people are elected delegates from villages throughout the zone. I am disappointed not to see more women, although when I do a rough count they account for about a quarter of the numbers, which seems reasonable for this stage of the revolution.

Seyweon introduces the three-day program. The main agenda of the Congress is to discuss the necessity of redistributing land, to make new laws for the redistribution (how to do it), and to nominate a committee to undertake the task. First, the legality of the meeting has to be checked. A hundred and twenty-six *baito* members are qualified to attend, making eighty a quorum. In fact, a hundred and four are present.

"Others are on their way," whispers Berhanu. "Some people have to come on foot from many miles away."

Kudusan then briefs the delegates on the background and necessity for land reform. She surveys the history of the Tigrayan people as a history of oppression under the feudal landowners and a government of the Amhara ruling class, under a succession of colonial rulers, the Egyptians, the Turks, the Italians. But it is also a history of resistance, a history of struggle. She reminds them particularly of the First Revolution against Haile Selassie in 1943—she calls it the *Weyane.*

"This, our second *Weyane,* started in 1975 and this time we shall not fail. Already, we have so many victories and the most important has been the right to land. First, we shared the land so that the poor peasant owned land for the first time and could control his produce without handing it over to the landowner. Now, the time has come for a second distribution to improve the productivity of the land and to construct a war economy."

Kudusan ends her speech with the slogan *Awat na hafash*, the main slogan of the revolution. "Victory to the people" the assembly echoes, with fists raised.

The morning passes in discussion by different delegates. Several of them are women. Then Berhanu nudges me to stand up. "Now you will speak to the people," he says.

There is no time to wallow in horror. I am already being propelled down the aisle. Why wasn't I told in advance? However, I remind myself I have faced plenty of audiences in my time and that stands me in good stead. I tell them why I have come and that I am particularly interested in the democratic structures evolving in Tigray, that after centuries of systematic impoverishment, without rights of any kind, they are now running their own affairs. This is impressive and, indeed, I have been impressed by the level of organization and debate. Glancing at my paper to check the words, I end with *Awat na hafash.* The roof goes up with the enthusiastic roar of their response, melting into the high poignant wail of women ululating. Berhanu indicates we should go. He is smiling. My bash at revolutionary slogans may not have done much for my boasted independence, but it has been a triumph of public relations.

Outside, the hot light is like a blow to the face. We walk back to the same cottage where we drank the *sewa* earlier. Hagos, his heavy M14 rifle over his shoulder, stalks behind.

"They feel so happy to hear you speak their language," Berhanu says, "they never expect a *ferenji*, a foreigner, to be interested. They are very sensitive on this issue—for so many years the Amhara government was forbidding us to use Tigrinya, only Amharic."

A new gourd of sour local beer tastes good. This time, the daughter of the house stays to talk. She tells us she wanted to become a fighter, but the Front rejected her. Too many young people wanted to be fighters, they said. They would only take so many from each family, because it was important not to leave parents without hands on the farms.

"Also, they told me working to support the revolution in my community was just as important, so I went away for training and now I am a *shig woyanit*."

I look enquiringly at Berhanu.

"A torch of the revolution," he says, "not a battery torch, you understand. A torch with fire. They help teach the people about their interests and mobilize them to struggle."

Kudusan soon joins us. The congress will break until the day begins to cool off. She praises my speech.

"They responded especially," she says, "when you said the words, "I am from a rich country, but I come to learn from you."

Berhanu is discouraging me from attending the rest of the congress. He says it will be too boring for me—lots of discussion and argument in a language I can't yet understand. In fact, I was thinking the same thing, but I want to know the decisions and the main problem areas. Kudusan says this is the highest level congress, which decides the laws for the zone.[14] The problems will emerge when the laws have to be implemented at the district level. Why don't I attend the Sheraro district *baito* in a few weeks time and sit in on some of the debates? Meanwhile, she suggests I could come back at the end of three days and find out directly from the peasants themselves what has been decided.

The three of us, Berhanu, Hagos, and I start the long march back over sunbaked hills at the hottest time of day to Adi Hagerai where we have been invited to a meal by one of the members of the *baito*.

"These people are rich, I think," murmurs Berhanu, as we heartily tuck in to a dish of sorghum *injera* and goatmeat. "Have you seen her jewelry?"

The daughter of the house, a young woman newly married called Mulu Takere, has gold earrings glinting in her ears and a gold cross hanging on purple threads around her neck. It would not have occurred to me to use the word "rich" for such a simple house with a dirt floor and a few sticks of furniture, but when I look around I notice Mulu has a pretty white dress on in our honor and on the walls there are embroidered hangings praising the Front and basketwork bound with brightly colored threads.

Mulu herself is sweet and smiling and, when we have eaten, she says she wants to henna my hands out of friendship. She shows me her own palms, which are greenish black. I know that women fighters reject all decoration, clip their hair short and wear clothes indistinguishable from men. If I have hennaed hands will I lose all credibility with progressive women here? These are the same puritanisms that I find myself struggling with in Britain. Are hennaed hands in Tigray the local equivalent of high heels and pancake make-up?

In the end, I settle for the fingers of one hand. Mulu binds the henna mixture, like a thick paste of marsh slime, onto my finger tips with strips of rag. Then unexpectedly Hagos speaks up. He is usually so quiet. He is asking to have it done also, just the little finger nail on one hand. Only then do I discover it should stay on several hours "to set."

"Don't worry," says Berhanu. "You can sleep here while it's hot. She is doing you honor. I'll come back later."

So Hagos and I, looking like wounded soldiers, sleep away the afternoon —I on the bed, he on the bench—until it is time for our bandages to be taken off. My finger tips have turned brown and the nails a burnt orange.

I was quite wrong to worry about it. When Berhanu returns he is impressed and all the women fighters I meet are full of admiration. From now on my nails are the first thing peasant women notice when I meet them. They sieze my hand, scrutinize the finger tips and ask who did it. Like my slogan at the congress, it gives them pleasure that I am sharing in their culture. The stain wears off my skin in a matter of weeks, but the indelible orange nails take months to grow out. They give me pleasure too, reminding me of Mulu and women in Tigray long after I return home, although, ironically, in the English cultural context, they provoke comments about smoking sixty cigarettes a day.

Mulu's house adjoins the market place and the market is in full swing as we make our way across it, followed by the usual crowd of children. The square is packed with people, but there is not much to sell. Barely recovered from famine and cut off as they are in the liberated area from the five government-held towns, poor peasants sell their scanty surpluses to each other for the few necessaries they cannot produce themselves, like cooking oil or bars of soap as seamed with cracks as the dry earth. The traders sit on the ground under black umbrellas with their pathetic wares displayed on rags or sacks in front of them—a kilo of lentils, a cup of chick peas. Most of them seem to be women, thin and ragged, the harsh light accentuating the edges of their cheek bones and the sharp angle of their jaws. Berhanu was right. We have been eating in the house of rich peasants.

Late in the evening, we leave Adi-Hagerai to talk to farmers in the remote countryside. A Toyota will take us part of the way. Our driver is a young fighter called Hailemariam, his head shaven as a last resort against lice infestation. Techana has rejoined us and Hagos, as the most junior, folds his long length into the back between the boxes and bags. It is brilliant moonlight, although the moon is not yet full. Techana and Berhanu seem to get on well. They are always singing songs of the revolution, especially on journeys, and now the lilting music, is beginning to reveal variations and subtleties I could not at first perceive. Some songs are even becoming familiar so I can hum along and Berhanu has promised to teach me the words of one or two. He says some of them are beautiful poems in their own right.

The mountains scrape the sky
But we can climb them.
The rivers boil in flood
But we can cross them.
Our strength is in our people and our politics
And we will not submit.

To the sun's scorch or the lash of hail
We are indifferent.
We dry with thirst or drown in marsh—
We do not care.
Our pillow is a stone; a cave is our home.
Our strength is in our people and our politics
And we will not submit.

I am woken from a doze by a sharp command to halt from Berhanu.

"Come!" he says in his peremptory way. "Where is your tape recorder?"

It is not an emergency, but a wedding party of peasants winding between the hills in the moonlight. The bride, veiled like a ghost from head to foot, is seated on a mule with a young man behind her, holding her on. I assume he is the groom, but later discover he is probably his *arci* or best man. About twenty-five peasants are literally dancing attendance on her—men, women, children, and a band of musicians. As he walks along, the lead musician is playing the traditional Ethiopian *tchirra*, a kind of single-string violin played with a bow. At once, they pause in their journey to form a dancing circle and draw us into it. A women takes my new shawl from my shoulders and wraps it round my head and body like the other women and guides me in a dignified shuffle to the exquisite music of the *tchira*, while half the group stand and clap in time, watched by the invisible bride. Berhanu, his shawl wrapped round his waist in the male fashion, dances backwards in front of the *tchira* player holding out the tape recorder with a beatific expression on his face. Techana is dancing. Hagos is dancing. After ten minutes, we play back some of the recording for them and shake hands round the circle. Then, the bride drifts off into the spectral light and we go our way again. In the car, everyone is immensely happy. As we jolt along through the white night, they start once more their passionate singing. Only now, they are singing love songs.

Three days later, we returned late at night to Adi Hagerai. The congress had just finished, but two farmers, Haftom Gebremichael and Yakob Tesfai, both *baito* representatives from the Adi Hagerai district, had stayed on to talk to us before walking back through the night to their village. In a candle-lit room we talked until well after midnight. They were youngish men, perhaps in their thirties, intelligent, dignified, articulate. As always, after dark, their heads and upper bodies were wrapped in thick white *gabis*. They looked tired and still had to walk back through the night to their villages, but they were also enthusiastic about the new laws.

Land, they said, would be given to people who had come of age since the last land distribution and the age of eligibility had been lowered from eighteen to fifteen for women and from twenty-five to twenty-two for men.

"Youth has power and energy," Haftom said, shadows dancing on his face. "They know how to plow and are a valuable productive force. By giving them land we can increase production."

"Why is it different for men and women?"

"Because twenty two for men and fifteen for women are the minimum legal ages of marriage, decided by the *baito* in this area. Women used to be married as children. The *baito* has made this illegal. We would like to raise the age for women to sixteen or even eighteen, but it is not possible at this time. But if a woman is old enough to be married and look after a home, then she is old enough to have her share of land."

This sounded pretty advanced to me. Few women in Britain have their own viable economic base as wives and mothers, independent of fathers and husbands. It was astonishing that after centuries without land rights, this age difference amounted to positive discrimination in favor of women.

One-third of the land was to be set aside for a cattle pasture and the upper slopes earmarked for reafforestation. These would be under the control of the *baito*, who would impose stiff penalties for illegal felling or for grazing animals in protected areas.

"The people know the advantages of forests," Haftom continued. "Our society is built on forests—our tools, our houses, our fires. We know the value of trees from our daily experience and we know our climate has changed because some people have destroyed the forests. We discussed which trees we should use, which one can withstand dryness, which can regenerate after it is cut for tools, and which supply us with fruit."

Yakob told me the names of the selected trees and all their characteristics.

"Where will you get the seedlings from?"

"Our organization, the TPLF, has an agriculture department. They have done the research and will distribute the seedlings."

The land set aside for cattle grazing and tree-planting would be under the control of the *baito*, who would also be responsible for its rotation. Both the *baito* and the Mass Associations would be allotted land to provide them with the income they needed for their work.

The rest of the land would be shared according to a policy of "standardization" at the level of the standard of living and agricultural expertise of the "middle peasant."[15] The amount varied according to household size and any other income from trading or handicrafts. The fields would be studied by a special committee and split into three grades of fertility. If possible, each household would get land from each category; if not, then land would be distributed at the rate of one unit of the most fertile land to one and a half of medium to two of poor. A unit was defined as the area that could be plowed by a team of oxen over a specific period of time.

Land, said Yakob, can never be mortgaged, rented or sold. It is the resource of the people and must never be allowed to accumulate again in the hands of a few individuals.

"Won't this be a disincentive to farmers improving the land?"

"No," said Haftom. "Excellent farmers will not be discouraged, because they will keep the same land from year-to-year. If they improve a piece of land they don't own, they will be given a piece of land elsewhere as a reward. The best farmers are a model for everyone else to follow."

Discussion had been heated. Opposition had been from individuals who had large shares of land already and from old men whose minds it was difficult to change. The drafting committee had circulated the proposals widely beforehand, so they had already been argued in the Farmers Associations. Some differences had been resolved through amendments, others by discussion. Final decisions were made by majority vote.

"The revolution is not going smoothly," said Yakob. "We face some problems; there is some opposition but the majority know we have to distribute the land. If we want to build a new society and be free of exploitation, we have to build a strong economy."

The door opened and a man stood there in a shaft of moonlight. He spoke to Haftom. Other figures stood behind him, wrapped to the eyes in white. They were Haftom and Yakob's village delegation, waiting for them all this time. I looked at my watch. It was long gone midnight and their day would start soon after four. They smiled at my anxiety and Haftom said he was proud that someone had come from so far to talk to them about their revolution. I felt proud just to have shared two hours of their time. We embraced and they turned and walked off towards the hills.

We were ourselves to leave before dawn. Berhanu left me to rest for three hours, but I couldn't sleep. At length, I got up and went outside. The moon was not quite full, but its light was brilliant enough to do many daytime tasks. I sat on the threshold leaning against the door, staring up at its face, so strangely on its back. My mind was filled with darkness. Every day packed with information, packed with more discoveries. Yet, with every day that passed I felt less confident of ever making a synthesis of all this experience in a way that would not distort it. The wellsprings of this revolution were in their history, perhaps over hundreds of years. An hour's conversation with peasants revealed how inseparable in their consciousness was the present from the past. I had not begun to scratch the surface. Moreover, their methods of organizing this revolution were interconnected with their culture. How could I, a *ferenji,* hope to have a proper understanding of what they were achieving without knowing deeply where they had come from?

I was miscast for the role of explorer, even more for the role of journalist. The foreign correspondent often seemed to me like the old imperialist traveller, updated but still dishing up the same old missionary stew of secondhand information and prejudice to serve the turn of economic expansion. Travellers had exoticized Africa into a land of mystery, of darkness. The darkness was in their own heads. There was no mystery for the people who lived here. It was just the place where they lived, the everyday, where they struggled to get along, like people anywhere.

7

Very Good At Digging Wells

There is a particular kind of rivalry in the air when aid workers get together. It is hard to tell whether it is the competitiveness of individuals or of organizations. When they stride in at the end of the day, sweating and covered with dust, they have a special look which says, here I am sweating and covered with dust from this important work of saving the world. They sit around tables talking in loud voices of their own projects. Their strong hands look as if they should be nursing glasses of strong liquor. But, in Mai Hanse they make do with water from the bucket in the corner and the odd bottle of Italian beer smuggled from Eritrea.[1]

Mai Hanse is a REST station for foreign visitors. It is not much more than a single story, L-shaped building. The long arm holds two rooms, each with three beds, and the short arm is a sitting room where meals are served. For security, the building itself forms one side of a compound with openings only on the inner walls. The fourth "wall" of the compound is a deep dry gulch opposite, connected to the house by palisades of branches. There is usually an armed fighter at the gate and at night another sits on the roof. Trees provide plenty of cover and over much of the compound a lattice of branches, threaded through at this season with the dry bones of a vine, offers both shade from the sun and camouflage for drying wash. Outside the compound are scattered thatched huts among the trees, housing Tigrayan REST workers and a few fighters.

This simple whitewashed building seems the height of luxury after weeks of sleeping on mats on the ground or on rock sleeping platforms. For one thing there are real beds with whinning springs and foam mattresses. Then, up the hill, a hundred yards away, is a stonebuilt shower and a latrine, back to back. Instead of a roof, a couple of beams hold up an oil drum with a tap at the bottom. Every morning at sunrise, a boy comes with a donkey, its panniers filled with water to replenish the *ferenjis*' shower. On the ground beneath the tap is a large flat stone to stand on out of the mud and a cavity has even been left in the wall for soap or shampoo. A stretch, a flick of the tap—and bliss.

As usual, I arrive in the middle of the night and spend the next morning washing myself, my hair, my clothes. I have a rash around my waist and my hair is stiff and itching. There is no one about, so I wrap myself in a shawl and wash everything I possess. By ten in the morning it is too hot for such exertions and by eleven everything is dry. Soon after twelve there are sounds of vehicles approaching, car doors slamming and unmistakable tones of men speaking English.

When I go into the dining room the three men there don't look up. They are all talking with their mouths full about their morning's work and my pleasure at the prospect of talking to compatriots is a little dashed. These are the first Europeans I have seen since Kaza and they don't bother to introduce themselves. It is unpleasant eating out of a common pot with strangers, so I ask their names. One, Ian Robinson, excuses himself almost at once to work. The others are Richard, an Englishman working on a well-digging project for an Australian agency, and Steve, who works for a European development consortium. No one asks what I do.

We only meet at meal times. Sometimes there are different faces around the table for a few hours, foreigners passing through on their way to the center or on their way out to Kaza and the convoy. The cooks make an effort to produce food more acceptable to a *ferenji* palate: omelette, rice boiled in meat stock, spaghetti with tomato sauce. In fact, it all tastes bland to me. I miss Techana's food—an anonymous tin (the labels have long since worn off), usually mackerel, cooked up with onions and garlic, lots of tomato paste and a fiery dose of chilli powder. Yet although I'm not conscious of feeling deprived in any way I have started to dream about food. Guinness in a variety of English settings, apples, and muesli with fresh milk. I wake up, crying with frustration, just before the first bite, the first sip.

After supper, my companions spend hours talking about their projects in a "technical problem needs a technical solution" sort of way. Some of it is quite interesting. Richard also spends a lot of time grumbling about his Tigrayan workers for laziness and inefficiency and about REST for not prioritizing his project in the way he thinks appropriate. They all grumble about the Front for having priorities, which seem to be at odds with REST or which exclude their projects altogether and for requisitioning agency cars for its own purposes. I begin to wonder whose Toyotas I have been riding in lately. It is a different world from the one I have been sharing with Tigrayan people over the last few weeks.

Richard's dismissive attitudes about the revolution don't match my own impressions of the effectiveness with which the Front has been working with the people to improve the basic quality of life here. He doesn't seem to know, or want to know, about clinics and schools and the *baito* system. Of course how one judges these achievements depends on how much one knows of the feudal conditions of life under Haile Selassie before the revolution started. I am discovering that many Westerners, in Africa, start from their own unexamined cultural assumptions which are so remote from conditions here that they seem unable to see that a process of change, albeit a gradual one, is underway. What do they see when they look at peasants? Perhaps just an unimaginable, undifferentiated and poverty-stricken way of life. It makes me wonder what attracts these men to this life. Is it a nineteenth century philanthropic impulse or is it a chance to have adventures? Certainly some of their attitudes seem to combine the zeal of boy scouts with the arrogance of old-style white hunters in pith helmets.

Sometimes, when Letif brings in the tray of food, Richard makes comments about her shape and other unacceptable remarks. One day, he is even worse than usual—so much so that I mention it to Haile.

"We don't worry about it," he says, smiling sweetly. "Those things are secondary. He is a hard worker and he is very good at digging wells."

On reflection, I decide Haile is right. It is the job that is important, not the shortcomings of individuals. They are all enthusiastic about their work and about policies, which give priority to long-term development projects, rather than disaster relief. Nor is their ignorance about the wider political and social context here entirely their fault. Both REST workers and fighters regard them as "humanitarians." Tigrayan suspicion of an attitude, which distinguishes nutrition, education and health as worthy priorities and at the same time questions the validity of the military struggle, means that aid workers tend to be ghettoized into development work and, even if they are sympathetic, have very limited access to any information or experience outside it.

Mai Hanse is a convenient point for me to visit a number of places. The Tekezze Workshop is within driving distance; the regional hospital is nearby. Berhanu thinks it should be possible to find a vehicle here, so less walking will be necessary. For two or three days, however, while he makes arrangements, I am left to my own devices. For the first day, it is pleasant to have time for washing, to catch up on my diary, to catalog my tapes; then it begins to pall. Berhanu, Techana and Hagos, even the driver Hailemariam who has not been with us very long, are beginning to feel like family. I miss their jokes, their songs, their concern if I am quiet from fatigue or a headache. Now they have all disappeared.

It's as if this is a no go area for Tigrayans. Except for the guards and the boy with the donkey, the only ones I see are Haile, the Tigrayan coordinator of REST in Mai Hanse, and the women who prepare the food. One afternoon when there seems to be no one about, I slip into my cassette player the tape of the wedding music we recorded recently near Adi Hagerai and turn up the volume. Almost at once people start emerging from gateways, from trees and shadows—young fighters, REST workers, women from the kitchen—about nine or ten of them. Some men knot shawls round their waists and start to dance. Others lean against the wall, gazing into their memories. Some are smiling, all are moved. When the tape comes to an end, they ask me to start it again. Later, I tell Berhanu.

"It is that music," he says, looking as if he is about to slip into a reverie himself. "The music of the *tchirra*. It is our traditional music, for weddings and important occasions. We don't get much opportunity to hear this music. When we do—you know, it reminds us of the families we have lost. It moves our hearts."

As soon as fewer foreigners are around, Tigrayans appear and the barriers built into this foreigners' hostel start to crumble. During the afternoon, Berhanu comes to keep me company and other fighters join us, hoping to hear the wedding music. I still have lots of batteries left, so a group of them take my cassette player and the tape and listen to it again and again with the same thoughtful expressions on their faces as before.

Perhaps the music has its effect on Berhanu too. He begins to talk about his family and his early life in Quiha, a small town not far from Mekelle, the capital of Tigray. These are both still in government-held areas, so it must be seven or eight years since he saw them. He talks of the student protest movement and how it politicized him. He talks too of a special friend from that time, a girl, whose memory has stayed with him through the years of torture in Mekelle prison and through his escape to the liberated area.

Berhanu's Story

I started to be involved in politics in 1973 when I was an eighth grade student. There was a student movement in Ethiopian schools opposing the Haile Selassie regime and in Tigray we were resisting the domination of the Amhara ruling class.

We had many uprisings in the schools. Once, we shut the schools for two months and in 1974 for the whole year. Even the teachers decided not to teach. Mass protest movements were starting. Even the military started to oppose Haile Selassie in different parts of Ethiopia and Eritrea. At last in 1974, he was forced from power.

At once, the Dergue proclaimed a Zemacha,[2] *a campaign for students above tenth grade to go into the countryside to teach the peasants what the new regime wanted them to learn. The politically conscious students in the university opposed it, but most of us weren't so aware. I had a very close friend at school. He was very inspiring. He knew much more about politics than I did. We were both sent to Korem and he shared all his experience and information with me so that I became involved in politics consciously.*

When we started to oppose the campaign openly, they arrested thirty-six of us and took us by truck to Addis Ababa where they threw us into an underground prison with nearly two hundred other students. Really, we suffered a lot. They flogged us, they tortured us. Then on May Day 1975 there was a big student demonstration in Addis. One of the demands was "Release the imprisoned students." So, a week after this demonstration we were released and I was transferred to southern Ethiopia.

I was one of six Tigrayan students. We linked up with Oromo students, who had the same problem of domination by the Amhara ruling class. The Amhara students would try to insult us because we were Tigrayan. One evening, a meeting was called to celebrate the first anniversary of the campaign. When we were all in the hall, they suddenly brought out clubs and started to beat us. There were six of us and sixty of them. We knew we could not survive there. Four of us climbed the fence and ran towards the town. But the other two had been so severely beaten that in the end they sent them to the clinic by stretcher.

The head of the campaign transferred us to the Harar province. Opposition to the Dergue was increasing. Students all over Ethiopia were leaving the campaign and returning to their homes, but our homes were three or four days journey from Harar and we had no money for transport or passports. So we made links with other like-minded students. Then we heard of an organization called the TPLF, which had started armed struggle in the countryside in Tigray. We heard something about its programs and from that moment we began sympathizing with them.

The following year, also on May Day, there was a student demonstration against the fascist government. We six Tigrayans joined the other students. Workers and peasants also joined in. The officials of the campaign fired at us, killing one worker and one peasant, and the police tried to crush the demonstration. All the local people were against the campaign, so we decided that under these conditions we couldn't stay there.

I went home at the end of 1976 and I decided to make contact with the TPLF. In fact, they were my old friends who had been in Tigray during most of the campaign. When we were students we had similar political views. They knew my background and that we had been in prison in Addis. So I started propaganda work, writing slogans on walls, distributing leaflets. The Front was well-organized. There were communication links with the field and with their public relations workers. They smuggled leaflets into the towns, even cassettes with revolutionary songs. We tried to send back information about military secrets.

The next year, in Addis Ababa, the Dergue started a big operation against the opposition movement, called the Red Terror. Many students and youths were executed and thrown into the streets. Families were even forced to buy back their bodies for burial, paying more than a hundred birr [Ethiopian dollars]. It was a very terrible situation. The following year, when I was nineteen, it spread to Mekelle and in March, I was arrested.

When I entered Mekelle prison, really, it was very hard to believe what I saw. There was not enough room for all the five hundred prisoners, so most of them were lying on the ground. More than half were being tortured and you were forced to hear their screams of pain. I passed the night there. It was a problem to find a place to lie down. The cadres ordered me to confess everything about my work with the TPLF, but I denied it and then they tortured me.

First, they flogged me. Then, with a rope through my mouth, they tied my legs and hands behind my back. They threw me from the roof to the ground and then threw me outside. My friends and comrades were there and they tried to treat me. After that they tortured me three times. At one point, they executed four sets of people. First, they named fifteen persons, members of the TPLF and and other opposition groups. They killed them at the back of the wall behind the prison. We were listening. We could hear the noise of the gunshots. The next day we heard them sell the bodies in the streets.

They executed thirty-two prisoners, also from the main prison and threw them in the streets. It's very terrible to remember. Some of the mothers searched out their children and fell down upon their bodies. I remember one mother—she had only one son. He was a student and I knew him. His name was Muchakos. Really, he loved his mother. He was the only person to help her as his father was dead. They killed him. Really, his mother ...she goes up to him, she drinks his blood ... terrible to remember.

The third time, they killed twenty-six prisoners, including two women. Then, after two months and two weeks of imprisonment, they let us go, more than a hundred prisoners. Most of the students by that time were terrorized by the Red Terror so they tried to keep out of politics. Some of them started to support the Dergue out of fear and were even recruited as cadres and military officers. Only a few youths continued to support the

TPLF. After six months, I again started to work underground, but after only six weeks, in February 1980, there was a mass arrest and I was again sent to prison, this time for six years.[3]

Full moon. Really. At last. Whether it is the light flooding in the doorway or irritation at the narrow perspectives of my compatriots, once again I can't sleep. I long for the distraction of a book, but there is no electricity here and my torch seems to be on the blink. At length, when everyone is asleep but the guards, I get up and sit out on the bench wrapped in a shawl. This degree of nonconformity is quite difficult to achieve. First, the guard wakes up some poor woman to approach me, probably thinking I need company on a toilet trip. We can't understand one another and she goes away again. Then, at the various points of activity over the next two hours (because all movements from place to place have to be at night), fighters come to see if I'm all right. I give up about two thirty and I'm sound asleep at three thirty when Berhanu comes to wake me for a trip to the Workshop at Tekezze, leaving as usual in four minutes.

The journey takes about three hours. I share the Toyota with Steve who wants to report back on technical equipment, which his consortium has supplied to the Workshop. However, when we get there the Director is away. The difficulties of finding transport, the distances, the absence of good roads and telephones, mean breakdowns in arrangements happen all the time. His subordinates assure us he will be back at any moment, so we go down to the Tekezze River and laze away most of the day listening to music in the shade.

At this time of year the huge Tekezze River is only a third of its full width, but is still an impressive force of water. It is one of the tributaries of the Nile and has a reputation for flushing down to Egypt every year its population of crocodiles. Behind us are the great trees of the Tekezze Valley, which provide the camouflage for the Workshop and many more projects of the Front. On the opposite bank, the small twisted trees demonstrate the progress of the dry season—on the higher ground they are already leafless, although the ones near the water's edge are still green. When it gets too hot we go to bathe, Berhanu, Techana, Hagos and Steve's guide downriver, I upriver on my own. From my solitude behind rocks I hear the others laughing and splashing. I see no crocodiles. The water is cool and delicious.

After four, two department heads start to show us round the Workshop until Haddish, the Director, arrives. The Workshop is primarily a training school. It is part of the Front's overall concept of self-sufficiency in support of the war and it aims to provide workers skilled in a range of technologies. "Fairly low technologies," adds Haddish, "as is appropriate to our stage of development."

Its physical aspect is similar to other installations here, scattered camouflaged buildings and huts under the forest cover, equipment, and vehicles disguised with nets and branches to fool the spying planes, the general lackadaisical air of an outdoor encampment. There are several departments: a woodwork shop, a machine shop, a metalwork shop, mechanics, electrics, welding and forging sections, and a truck repair shop for maintenance of the convoy which works in concert with the Workshop in the Sudan where I joined the convoy, so many weeks ago. Haddish clears the camouflage wraps from two landcruisers awaiting repair. The windscreen of one is smashed and they have as many holes in the bodywork as a colander.

"Helicopter gunship!" is his terse comment.

At the moment, he says, shortage of tools is the main problem, but eventually they hope to make both tools and spare parts on site, when the machine shop, recently captured from the Dergue, is fully operational. The courses last six months and include theoretical as well as practical training. There are forty students taking carpentry training, for example, fifteen of whom are women. Forty percent is the average for women carpentry students, slightly higher than for other skills. In a shed we see the students' work stacked eight feet high—simple pine tables, chairs, and benches awaiting distribution in the district. We watch the students, all fighters, doing their practical work and distract the instructors with questions.

In the evening, we drive back to Mai Hanse in time for a late supper. Afterwards, dawdling over tea in the dining room, I have an interesting conversation with Ian Robinson. Inexplicably, he decides to be friendly, which means on the whole giving me the benefit of his advice and considerable knowledge of rural agriculture here. Perhaps I misjudged him. Perhaps it is unwise to generalize about aid workers in the way I have been doing. He has been a free-lance consultant on semi-arid zones and is now based at Bangor University, but he still spends up to ten months of each year abroad. About fifty, stocky and sun-tanned, he is resting up at the moment after hurting his back in a fall from a mule.

I learn a lot, especially about the subtle (and less subtle) difficulties a Westerner finds himself in—so far they all seem to be men—when they come here to do a practical or technical project. These difficulties, he says, seem to be based on a difference of perception between the limited perspective of a foreigner with his own assumptions about finding an efficient solution to a technical problem and the logistical imperatives of a Front juggling all the priorities of a guerrilla war with very limited resources. Hence, the "borrowing" of agency landcruisers.

Ian pays tribute to the understanding and skills of poor farmers in the central highlands within the limitations of their backward technology. He has been impressed by the way the Front's Agricultural Department has been working, rejecting as counterproductive the imposition of alien technologies on the people and preferring to improve and extend traditional methods of soil and water conservation. He cites the Shawata agricultural project as an example of their approach. I have heard of Shawata many times before and had been hoping I would get a chance to see it. Ian describes it for me. An ambitious water conservation project in the highlands, it is a collaborative venture by a number of agencies whose literature often includes photographs and descriptions of it. A complicated system of stone terraces, weirs, sluice gates, and channels carry rainwater where it is needed and in the volume required, demonstrating that, with effective water retention, three to five times the normal crop yields are possible. However, according to the Front's Agriculture Department, this costly endeavor is not cost-effective, because it has made a handful of farmers extremely rich and dependent on Western expertise, instead of raising the general standard of production and efficiency in ways farmers can understand and carry out themselves.

This example of clashing aid priorities I find interesting and revealing. The agencies are interested, rightly, in promoting long-term development as opposed to using food aid to mop up disasters, which might have been prevented. They also need a number of neat projects, explicable in Western terms, to put in their brochures to demonstrate their usefulness and thereby attract a continuous flow of funds. The Front, although desperately short of resources for improving conditions in the areas under its control and needing the agencies' help, has a different diagnosis and a different cure. Its priorities are small-scale schemes throughout Tigray, which will involve local farmers and councils from the beginning in the introduction of new techniques and improved tools and encourage a more self-sufficient and responsible attitude towards their own future.

"In time, perhaps, the Shawata techniques may be more widely adopted," Ian concludes. "They are suitable for communal agriculture and if they choose to move to more cooperative, communal development then they may have a place."

He sees endemic poverty and hardness of life as the fundamental obstacle to the Front's strategies for increasing production and improving the standard of living of the people.

"Most of the people live in the central highlands. Just getting about, you know, is so impossible. There are no roads. Each hamlet is divided from the next by a series of deep gorges. To get anywhere you have to go up and down montains along precipitous and dangerous paths. Yet the markets are the vital means of exchange for basic necessities and variety of diet, so from before dawn peasants stream along these paths to markets eight or ten hours walk away. I have seen children about ten years old carrying their own weight on their heads or shoulders up paths I find it extremely difficult to climb unencumbered."

He pauses, gazing somberly at the floor. His sympathy and respect for the people he describes is evident. He sighs.

"How can this be changed quickly?" he adds at last.

The next morning Berhanu wakes me at four. He has managed to get transport to the Regional Hospital. We arrive just after dawn and sleep for an hour on the ground until a fighter turns up to guide us for an hour's tramp across country to a forested ravine. Techana is on form as usual, but Hagos doesn't look too well. We are shown to a camouflaged hut, one of many among the trees. For security reasons they won't tell me where we are, even the name of the locality. The Director here, Dr. Samuel Zemariam, comes to greet us with a cup of tea and then leaves me to sleep the rest of the morning. Meanwhile, Hagos has collapsed on a bed in the adjoining room. He has malaria and a few minutes later a fighter brings him chloroquine tablets for treatment.

After lunch Dr. Samuel shows me round the hospital. Although he receives us calmly and makes me welcome, I have come at a difficult time. They moved to this site only two weeks ago, after lack of water drove them to evacuate their previous site. In fact, this valley was their home until four years ago, when the presence of the Regional Hospital was discovered by the Dergue and a series of MiG raids forced them to move out in a hurry. Most of the buildings from that time are unusable, but the fruit garden they planted then has flourished and is now bearing a good crop.

There are three departments, surgical, medical, and maternity. The operating theater and the wards for intensive care or for very sick and surgical patients are strongly built *hidmo* constructions of stone and clay, built into the sides of the ravine and cool from stone and turf roofs. Most of these are drying out after construction and are still empty. Convalescent wards and dwellings are lighter constructions of timber and thatch. Instead of the usual mud plaster, the operating theater and laboratories are rendered with cement—the first and only cement I see during this visit to Tigray—and in addition the operating theater has a linoleum floor covering. Until the main pharmacy is ready, the pharmaceutical supplies are piled up on the ground at the bottom of the ravine in a hill of boxes and containers and a few yards away an autoclave bubbles away on a charcoal fire.

All patients who are well enough and mobile have gone to a political education meeting on the same text, *Struggle,* about conditions of life for fighters, which I saw discussed at the Propaganda Bureau.

"Does this mean all your patients are fighters?" I ask Samuel.

"Most of them. Only about twenty percent are from the people, although we accept all referrals from the clinics. Our people are not yet used to medical care. If they are working adults they only go as a last resort. Sometimes they leave it too late."

This is confirmed when we visit the TB ward where most of the patients are peasants, in a very bad way. The meningitis ward too is crowded with seriously ill patients, but as I have taken no prophylaxis against it Dr. Samuel refuses to allow me inside.

However, the maternity and children's sections are real counter-propaganda for the images of famine that filled western television screens until recently. Peasant women stay about a month here with their babies; women fighters up to a year, before they go back to their jobs in the Front. So, apart from the newborn babies, there are some dumplings of children several months old. A dozen or so older children, discovering our presence by accident, are now following us around. They are orphans of the famine, looking bright and healthy, but their headshapes and scars indicate their past experience. Eventually, they will move to REST's orphanage somewhere near Kaza.

In the irrigated fruit and vegetable garden, banana and papaya trees are laden with ripe fruit; citrus trees are laden with green fruit. My eyes are popping out of my head. I have eaten no fresh fruit since the Sudan. The nearest I have gotten is pineapple chunks when Techana opens one of the anonymous tins and finds pineapple instead of mackerel. They have planted chili peppers and herbs so far and plan potatoes, tomatoes, cabbage, and peppers. A well is half dug to help with irrigation in the dry season. Dr. Samuel lays great stress on the new health education policy of prevention as the best way forward and a balanced diet high in fruit and vegetables is an important part of the strategy of healing here.

This is a much more radical emphasis than it sounds.

"Traditionally, our people despise vegetables as food for animals, not human beings," he says. "You only eat vegetables here if you are too poor to eat meat. Then, you are ashamed. We are training our health workers to educate the people to grow vegetables as well as grains and legumes."

"More vegetables are eaten now in the towns," adds Berhanu. "The influence of the Italians is felt in the bigger towns, especially the influence of Eritrea, which has been colonized by the Italians for sixty years. But in the countryside of Tigray there is a saying, "If your neighbor offers you vegetables, then throw the food on the ground." He has insulted you and you never go there again."

"The famine was a great setback for us," says Samuel. "If we are going to win this war, we have to improve the health and nutrition of the people. Nutrition, agriculture, health, self-reliance—these are all necessary and a part of our political education."

We return to the hut for tea and bananas and to record a formal interview. The bananas are unlike any I have tasted before. They are small and stumpy and green with black smudges. They are firm and perfumed and flavorsome with a lemony tang. By comparison, the fat yellow unblemished bananas of British supermarkets taste like potatoes. I want to write an ode to these bananas. At the very least I want to record on tape their characteristics, their horticultural needs, and their bright revolutionary future. Samuel laughs at my enthusiasm. He takes his bananas for granted and there are other things he wants to tell me.

There are only six or seven fully trained surgeon-doctors in the liberated area in Tigray—for four or five million people. Two of them are in this hospital, Samuel and another surgeon, Dr. Kahsai Mekonnen. Samuel was trained in Gondar Health College in western Ethiopia and was working there until he decided to become a fighter.

"I became a fighter because I understood the oppression of the people," he says simply.

In addition, there are six nurses, who have been trained in the Central Hospital in Kaza. The Front has divided Tigray into three regions, Region One is the west, Region Two the central highlands, Region Three the eastern highlands and Afar lowlands of the Danakil. There is a hospital like this for each region and a fourth "central" hospital, which handles training, research, and difficult cases.

I ask about health care first under Haile Selassie and then the Dergue. There were a few clinics in the towns, he says, and nothing at all for the majority of people in the countryside. The private clinics were beyond the means of most people, even if they lived near a town, and the state provision was inadequate. He has seen real improvement under the Front, because there are many clinics throughout the liberated area and they are also trying to teach people about the causes of ill-health and how to prevent the worst epidemic diseases.

"Yet, even now the material base of the people is not enough, even for prevention, but there is an improvement. Now, not so many people are dying of malaria as before because they can get chloroquine at the clinics. Listen to what the people say. Ask them."

We return late at night to Mai Hanse. We give some fighters a lift in our Toyota. One of them is a young woman pharmacist. To make room, Techana and Hagos go in the back on top of the baggage. There is more of Hagos than anyone else, but he always has the least comfortable places and the worst jobs—because he is the most junior fighter, I suppose. He has made a startling recovery during the day from his malaria. Berhanu says there are different strains and it's not so severe if you treat it early.

The woman is on her way to a clinic near Mai Hanse. She sits next to me and, like many women before, takes no notice of the men in the group, but puts her arms round my shoulders, strokes my hair and leans her cheek against mine. This powerful physical connection between women, a part of the culture here, cheers me up whenever I meet it and fortifies me against the loneliness of being so far from home and travelling so much with men. Twelve years ago, I reflect, in the time of Haile Selassie, a young woman like this, aged twenty and from the countryside, would already have been at least ten years married with several children. The pursuit of socially useful skills would have been unthinkable. For the rest of the journey we talk together about the simple facts of our lives, as much as my Tigrinya will allow.

Back at Mai Hanse, I discover Ian is moving off to the Sudan in the early hours of the morning so I stay up even later writing a letter to my family for him to post in England. In the morning, I learn that Steve left yesterday while I was visiting the hospital and Richard is moving out of the REST House today to a separate hut he will share with an Australian geologist and his wife whom he is expecting to arrive at any moment. By the time I wake up he has gone off to the well-digging site and the compound is deserted. A quiet day to work is just what I need. But first I need to do more washing. I am beginning to suspect I have headlice and the rash round my waist is spreading down my stomach. Itching is driving me mad. Perhaps I ought to shave my head like Hailemariam.

The next morning, I meet three German journalists from Heidelburg who arrived during the night. All three of them are well over six feet tall and this makes such an impact on me that for a few hours I fail to register anything else. Dieter, a journalist for a scientific and ecological magazine called *Nature*, is travelling with his partner, Christina, and a friend called Dorotea, who works for the REST Support Committee in Heidelburg. Their interpreter is a Tigrayan called Mebratu who also works for REST and apparently is often in London, although I have not met him before. They have been in Tigray for three weeks walking into the highlands to Abi Adi, crossing under cover of darkness the dangerous government-held road to Gondar.

They spend the morning washing themselves and their clothes. For about an hour Dorotea stands in the shade minutely scrutinizing garments. It turns out she is hunting body lice. She shows me what they look like, where they hide in seams and waistbands, and how to crack them in half with my thumb nail. If they are well gorged, they are dark with blood and easy to spot. I join the hunt and find several in my own clothes. Then I wash everything all over again and spread my clothes and sleeping bag out in the full sun at the hottest time of the day. Dorotea tells me that hot sun makes even the most robust louse pops its clogs. Unfortunately, although my clothes are camouflage colors, my sleeping bag is blue and a fighter tells me sharply to take it inside as it can be easily spotted by MiGs. Half an hour later two MiGs fly over, low, slow, hunting. We hunt lice and the MiGs hunt us.

In the afternoon, we all drive out to look at Richard's well-site. The new well, only half dug, is part of a long term project to construct about eighty wells in western Tigray. Originally, the proposal was for a hundred and thirty wells, but geological problems have made that unrealistic. When we arrive they are lowering a concrete ring into the cavity. Richard's Tigrayan trainees keep it steady as, suspended by a pulley from a tripod of tree branches, it slowly disappears into the pit. I peer over the edge. It looks about two and a half to three meters deep. They found water at one and a half meters and a diesel pump drains it off into the other well.

"The ultimate depth will be six meters," says Richard, his face under his red hair flaming from heat and enthusiasm. "We use a bosun's chair for lowering the diggers to the floor of the well and for removing the soil. The rings protect them from a cave-in and line the cavity."

The topmost ring will eventually project above ground and protect the water supply from animals. Contamination of water by animal and human feces is a major cause of gastro-intestinal complaints here. Both the cement and the metal mold, two meters in diameter and about half a meter deep, for casting the concrete rings, are imported, but sand and gravel for mixing the concrete are excavated only a hundred meters away.

The site is next to a dried river bed where local villagers have already bored a hole to get at the ground water, reinforcing the edges of the two foot square opening with tree branches. Although we are right out in the countryside, the place has the air of a market day. Women are standing in line easing round-bellied pottery water jars from their backs. Boys are bringing up donkeys, some slung with goatskin panniers, others with large plastic containers plugged with leaves. Dieter is busy taking photographs with very professional-looking cameras. Mebratu is explaining something to Christina and Dorotea. There are lines of camels—I have never seen so many camels in one place—padding softly one behind the other with supercilious grace. As I watch the women heaving the full water jars onto their backs, tying the cords in front and then, bent at an angle of forty five degrees, setting off for a village perhaps three hours walk away, I realize that most women I see on the road are bent double like this, under a child, a water jar, a load of wood, or a huge cloth-wrapped bundle. Children, too, I often see carrying large loads; men rarely. Men usually have donkeys to carry their goods. Women's daily labor seems as hard as it ever was. Does this mean the opportunities of the revolution, by extending women's roles, have thereby increased, rather than reduced, their burdens?

The sun is setting as we leave for the REST house. Berhanu melts away as soon as the Europeans arrive. Mebratu does not. He is not a fighter, but a visitor like us and he sleeps and eats in the same house. He has been educated at Western universities and lives in Germany. Supper is served soon after our return and afterwards we sip tea and swap stories.

Mebratu loves telling stories. He tells us tales of TPLF history, fast becoming legend, and amusing personal anecdotes. Forty years ago he was a shepherd boy in the countryside, but Haile Selassie had a policy of removing promising children from their parents in the countryside to go to school in the towns and Mebratu was whisked away to Adwa. Later, he won a scholarship to McGill University in Canada, trained as a social worker in Kent in England and is now working for REST in Heidelburg. He would like to return to Tigray, he tells us, to farm a plot of land, but educated Tigrayans are in such short supply that he can make a greater contribution to the revolution in Europe than in his homeland.

"I must admit," he says, "in the beginning I was skeptical of the TPLF, but now that I have seen what they have done for the people, I am convinced."

His last visit here was eight years ago and he remarks on the change in the demeanor of the people from dourness to cheerfulness.

"I noticed it particularly through a change of attitude towards myself. Formerly, as an obviously privileged class, I was treated with distrust and reservation. I was aligned with the feudals and the oppressing class. Now, the people's confidence has increased so much, in themselves, in the revolution, that they make me the target of their witticisms."

He turns humorously to Christina and Dorotea.

"Do you remember, when I fell off the back of the donkey climbing up that path? There were a lot of comments at my expense—about my being too fat. That would never have happened before."

Mebratu's Story of Deseligne the Mule

In the early days of the TPLF there were very few fighters. They had little food and no money, but they did have one advantage, a mule whose name was Deseligne. He was a fighter himself and a steadfast believer in the revolution. When the fighters were engaged in forays and assaults, they had to walk in the night over steep and rocky paths without a sound.

Deseligne too would place his hooves without disturbing a stone or cracking a twig. He carried heavy burdens over long distances without complaining and would never call to his comrades in the silence of the night.

But now the fighters were hungry. They were without food and without money. What were they to do? They were reluctant to ask the peasants for food, for often the people did not have enough to eat themselves. The long years of feudalism had led to a deep distrust of strangers among the peasants, whether Feudals, soldiers, merchants, or officials. From long and bitter experience they were convinced that all who approached them were after something, either taxes or grain, labor or goods. It was not easy for the fighters to gain the trust and confidence of the people. At that time, too, bandits were the scourge of the countryside and the farmers could not tell the difference between them and the shabby fighters who had recently been sighted in the wild and lonely forest.

They were not far from Axum, an ancient and holy city, which attracted many visitors from elsewhere in Ethiopia and other countries. It was richer than other towns. So, they decided to rob the bank. It would be difficult because it was still within the first year of the revolution and not only the town, but also the surrounding countryside, were under the control of the Dergue.

Seven fighters approached the town. Pretending to be the family of a pregnant woman in urgent need of treatment, they telephoned for an ambulance. When it arrived, they overpowered the driver. Half of them went on foot to the police station to create a diversion. The others went to the Bank in the ambulance. They said, "We are the TPLF. This is a political, not a criminal act. Hand over to us the money." The staff of the Bank handed over to them a sum totalling 170,000 birr. In return the fighters gave a receipt stamped with the official seal of the TPLF.

The money was then loaded on the back of the waiting Deseligne, but, before leaving the city, the fighters returned the ambulance to the driver at the spot from where they had taken it. They wrote a declaration that they were a combat force of the TPLF engaged in a struggle to free their country and that the driver was in no way involved. Then the seven fighters left the city with Deseligne carrying the great weight of 170,000 birr.

It was the rainy season. They were on foot and the going was slow. It grew dark. They managed to evade pursuit until they reached a great river in flood, but the soldiers and militia of the Dergue were not far behind. They plunged into the swirling waters and after a great struggle with the current the fighters crawled out on the far bank. But Deseligne, weighed down by the money, was swept away into the darkness. His comrades ran from place to place along the river bank, calling his name, but they could hear only the rushing of the torrent and the racket of the wind. Giving him up for lost, they retreated sadly into the hills. There they found a cave and slept.

In the darkest point of the night, they were disturbed by a curious sound, like heavy breathing. Thinking it was the enemy they grabbed their guns and peered out of the mouth of the cave. There was Deseligne, wet through, exhausted, but triumphant. He had tracked his comrades for many miles and now he was rumbling quietly through his nostrils to tell them that he had escaped the river and that the 170,000 birr was safe.[4]

I enjoy talking to Mebratu and the Germans. They are journalists, not "humanitarians." They see how the politics of food and pure water fit into the larger politics of armed struggle for survival. They are interested in the progress of this revolution, struck by an exceptional quality. The leadership's concern for the problems of the people and the massive support given in return have caught their imagination. They are to be the only journalists I come across during these months in Tigray. Unlike most journalists, they are prepared to spend the time travelling by convoy from the Sudan and to risk their personal safety in a war zone to get accurate information about conditions under the Front. The alternative is to fly into Addis Ababa and listen to the gossip of other journalists and the propaganda of the Dergue.

Our paths are soon to diverge, however. Two days later, they leave for Sheraro, where I will follow them in a week or so. Perhaps by then they will have moved on. Meanwhile, I leave at twilight with Berhanu, Techana, Hagos, and the driver, Hailemariam, to visit the Front's agricultural projects in the Tekezze valley.

8

Fighting Famine

We travel from Mai Hanse to a small town called Edaga Hibret. A truck drops us at eleven at night. We sleep on the ground in an outbuilding and I wake up dirty and tired. The barn is on the outskirts of the town at one end of its one wide street, lined with poor and rickety dwellings, behind which are huddles of huts. Over a wall in the yard, we overlook what in the half light of dawn seems a huge brown plain, but as the sun comes up it emerges as bank upon bank of rolling treeless hills slightly lower than this one.

I have come to this area to talk to peasants about the famine. Tigray was one of the worst-hit regions, along with Eritrea and Wello, and it seems sensible to find out, if I can, how a random sample of communities were affected and what strategies are being adopted to prevent a repetition in the future. I have not been thinking much about famine lately. The rains were good last summer and when I first arrived the rivers were full and the streams cascading down the mountainsides. It was hard to believe in the reality of drought. Now, the streams are shrinking before my eyes, but that's as it should be. As long as the rains start falling again in June, the harvests should be there in October. *As long as* the rains start falling in June....

The rains are crucial, but they are not the only factor. It is a common error in the developed world to confuse famine with drought. If that were true there would be famine every year in Australia or, in the summer of 1976, even in the south-west of England. It takes politics to turn a drought into famine. In the last hundred years, there have been many famines in northern Ethiopia, most of them "green" famines, not associated with drought at all, but with troop movements and with war. In the terrible famine in the early seventies, the cover-up of which helped to topple Haile Selassie from his throne, agricultural production in Ethiopia, as a whole, was scarcely diminished. What was lacking in the government was the political will to distribute grain from areas of surplus to areas of drought, which happened to be the areas of political opposition. What was lacking among the poor peasants was any entitlement (such as money) to the food that was there.

In 1984, history repeated itself. Haile Selassie's government had been replaced by the military junta, the Dergue, who called themselves Marxist-Leninist and after 1977 were supported by the USSR instead of the USA, but in other respects little had changed for northern Ethiopians. On the whole, Tigrayans saw the change merely as a palace revolution, leaving the government still largely Amhara with little motivation to bring development to Tigray. Even before the drought incessant bombardments and military campaigns at sowing and harvest times had made food provision marginal here. Mengistu saw the drought as an opportunity to intensify his manipulation of food as a weapon of war. Although this information was widespread among aid workers, it failed to make much impact in the Western media. In Britain, relief workers, who had become the main informants on the famine, were gagged by charity laws, which forbade their making political statements and few journalists made the difficult and dangerous journey behind rebel lines.

As with so many journalists, writers and aid workers, famine was the indirect cause of my coming here too. The research for a publication on the causes of famine in Sub-Saharan Africa had brought me into contact with many groups, including the TPLF. A year later, they invited me to visit Tigray on a fact-finding mission "to see for yourself what we have done and what needs to be done." As Haile Kiros, their London representative, said, "Why should you trust what we say? You must make your own independent assessment."

I sit on the wall above the view for an hour, until the sun drives me into the shade, making notes of facts I should like to check and possible points to raise in the day's discussions. I am getting better at interviewing, developing different techniques. I still carefully prepare questions for those in positions of responsibility, although I don't always stick to them. But, for other people, it is impossible to predict what they have to tell. A pre-determined line of questioning could deflect them from revealing astonishing experiences. My technique is absence of technique—or at least absence of intervention, tempered by an occasional prompt and an unfeigned absorption in what they have to tell me.

When Berhanu returns from making arrangements, the yard is already shimmering with heat. He walks through the door and stops dead, his head cocked to one side, listening. There is a hum in the air from behind the hill, gradually intensifying into a rhythmic beat. First I think it's a plane, then a generator.

"Helicopter!" says Berhanu.

Techana leaps into the building. Through the doorway I see people scattering to find cover. Then the sound fades away. We wait a few moments, rigid, listening. Nothing. Berhanu pokes his head outside the door, but the slope of the hill hides the westward landscape.

"Come!" commands Berhanu, at his most cryptic.

But I am not ready to go. What do I need to take? Do I change my shoes or take my shawl? Are we off for an eight hour hike or a ten minute stroll?

"Now!" says Berhanu, seeing me hesitate.

He disappears through the door. I follow, clutching my diary and glasses, but, feeling the sun's blast, I turn to pick up my shawl and by the time I run after them I am fifty yards behind. On the distant hill top are some farm buildings. In between is a huge sorghum field on a forty-five degree slope. The field seems entirely composed of quartz blocks and flattened in between, the remnants of the crop are as slippery as glass. Sandals are my undoing. It is all I can do to stay upright. Tripping and stumbling, slipping and sliding, my eyes stuck to my feet, I glimpse the distance between us growing wider all the time.

The noise of the helicopter again. Louder this time. The others have gained the shelter of the farm. I am half way—in the center of the field. The noise is getting louder. A huge beating, almost overhead. I can dimly hear shouting.

"Run, Jenny. You must run."

Then a remarkable thing happens. I grow wings. Where before I was stumbling, now I fly over the rocky surface without my feet touching the ground.

It's a non-story really. When I reach the farm, the noise of the helicopter recedes and finally fades away. It never even appeared over the crest of the hill, but it will be many months before I can hear a generator with peace of mind.

We crouch with the family for half an hour in their tiny living space and then, when the only sound is birdsong and the distant barking of dogs, we move on to a second farm across open hillside that now seems a threat in itself.

We rest in the farm store-room. Berhanu wants to change the plans. He proposes that peasants should come to talk to me here, rather than my going to them. Just for today; tomorrow we will go to them. He is very short when I scoff at his concern and insist on proceeding as planned.

"Your safety is my responsibility. It is not a personal thing. We have never lost a foreigner yet. It would be very bad publicity for us if you were killed or injured. Our enemies would exploit it."

I am silenced. He goes off to fix the new program, leaving Hagos to keep an eye on me. Techana goes to fetch the abandoned baggage.

The store-room is an education in itself. I sit on a mat next to a mound of sorghum, leaning against a six-foot high grain store of basketwork lined with clay. There are pottery grain-jars of beautiful shape, bundles of dried rushes, and a heap of large gourds waiting to be made into milking buckets. The only people at home are the son and daughter of the family. The son, Tesfay, is seventeen and already a farmer alongside his father. His sister is called Abeba ("flower"). She has been married for five years and has two boys of three years and eight months, although the baby, typically, looks only two or three months old. Abeba tells me he is sick. She is delicately beautiful, but very thin, and when she opens her bodice for the child to feed, her breast does not look as if she is getting enough nourishment to feed a baby. Her brother, Tesfai looks strong and well-fed. Perhaps the men still take precedence at meals over the women.

Abeba has work to do. She slings the baby onto her back, securing him with the traditional baby-carrier made of soft goatskin decorated with cowrie shells. A single-story stone house is at one end of the yard which is separated from the surrounding field by a fence of entwined branches. This outbuilding—our temporary home—is at the other end, also stone-built for the cool storage of grain. Next door is another "room" at a distance from the house, reserved for grinding grain and cooking *injera*. Meat and legumes would be cooked on the small portable charcoal stove either there or out in the yard under a canopy of thatch erected on four twisted tree trunks.

First, she finishes off the grinding, which the helicopter and our arrival have interrupted. She is finishing the second stage of the process. The raw grain has already been coarsely ground by the large grindstone in its sloping stone channel and now has to be reduced to a fine flour by the smaller one. Grinding of a reasonable amount can take up to eight hours. After that, in the shade of the canopy in the yard she fashions out of wet red clay a domed lid for the *mogogo*, the large built-in bakestone with a fire beneath for baking *injera*. Halfway through the morning she brings *sewa* for Hagos and me to drink in goblets made of gourds and, when I try to find out why they look so different from those I have picked recently from a wild vine, teaches me how to cut and clean and smoke them over a fire until they resemble old leather.

Berhanu returns after an hour or so and soon after that peasants start to arrive in ones and twos. It would be impossible and too lengthy to reproduce even a fraction of the conversations I have over the next few days, here and at other farms in the area. There are gnarled old men leaning on their staves. Women come, the long-married as well as young women with babies in leather pouches on their backs. There are the widowed and the newly married; young TPLF activists still in their teens; Muslim men and Christian priests.

I call them my "famine interviews" because I am hoping to learn from them about that time, but they are much more than this. The peasants tell me also about conditions in Haile Selassie's time—their exploitation by the landlords and the miseries of taxation; they describe the changes brought about by liberation and life under "our organization," as they call the Front. They each see the improvements in their own terms. For one woman, it is the absence of rape, bringing her a new freedom of movement; for another that she is now allowed to plow and as a widow can feed her family; for yet another that she has learned to read and write.

"We could not even look at men," says Kidan Gebretensai. "We would have to hide if we saw them coming. We could not go to meetings or make any decisions or suggestions."

Mohammed Wasse Salih, a Muslim, tells me how Muslims were similarly discriminated against. There was a saying "that a Muslim has no land as the sky has no pillar." Now, he says, Christians and Muslims are equal. Muslims own land for the first time and he no longer goes in constant fear of being robbed. Other men in the room, non-Muslims, nod sagely and confirm his allegations with anecdotes about the bad old days, as if relieved to be released from the burden of antagonism.

This area was liberated in the late seventies and the people have had their own land since 1979. It is unlikely that deep-rooted cultural attitudes against women, muslims, and minority nationalities could have changed in so few years. But a start has been made. Their words suggest that the climate of ideas is different and discrimination is no longer underpinned by the economic realities. The most significant aspect of all, the Front's strategies is that they have not imposed the changes on a reluctant populace. First of all, the new policies relating to equality have been debated and mapped out in a congress attended by representatives from every area, to become law only when passed by each local council.

However, the precarious nature of the struggle for subsistence is everywhere apparent. They describe the quality of life at any one time in terms of food availability and their relative wealth in terms of animals they own, particularly plow oxen.

"Before the famine we had enough," says Gebrehiwet Woldu, a patriarch of sixty who looks at least ten years older. "Our babies could drink milk and on holidays we had meat. Our grain was sufficient from year-to-year and we could prepare weddings."

Before the famine he had twenty cattle, thirty goats, and two donkeys. Now he has none.

Famine is not a sudden event, but a long-drawn out process and their personal stories illustrate its every stage. They are divided on its causes and the divisions point to different levels of political awareness. Some suggest the obvious—shortage of water or strong winds. Older people refer to the superstitions of god's anger, but as if they belong to the past. They are more aware of cite underdevelopment and deforestation as factors in decreasing rainfall. The political activists, as translated by Berhanu anyway, couch their assessment in revolutionary language.

"The cause of the famine was the arrogance of the reactionary state," says Deste Welde.

This assessment is borne out by repeated stories of Dergue bombardments, especially at sowing and harvest times.

"In May 1985," says Gebrehiwet, "the Dergue came and burned our homes and anything that was left."

Some of the scandals about Mengistu's use of food deprivation as a weapon of war have broken briefly in the international media and have been well documented by aid agencies. That May would have been after eight or nine months of desperate famine, just when those who had not fled to the Sudan would have been plowing in readiness for the next rains.

The stories pile up, corroborating each other with minor variants, although several speakers are anxious to tell me that their area was not so hard-hit as the central highlands. The earlier stages of famine are like a disease spreading beneath the skin. The moment of visibility is when animals begin to turn up for sale in large numbers in the market places. There is never so much meat available so cheaply as at a certain stage of drought.

"It was bad," says a middle-aged woman called Beriha. "It is painful to remember. Our crops were useless and were eaten by the animals. I started to sell my goats. The price of goats was low and the price of grain was high. For one goat I got only two or three cups of grain."

Soon, there was no food whatsoever. People began to eat roots and leaves. Some were poisonous and people died. It was time for the great trek westwards.

The part played by the Front and REST in the massive migration to the Sudan is a revelation to me. In the Western media, it came across as a spontaneous movement of suffering people. Now, from these peasants, I discover for the first time it was an astonishing and well-organized bid to save the lives of the Tigrayan people. Each community was organized to travel together in groups. Each group was provided with food for the journey and medical care. Fighters accompanied them as guides and to guard them from attack. Many of the weakest still died on the grueling journey. On the way, they say, they were bombed by Dergue MiGs.

Some people stayed behind.

"We were ready to go to the Sudan," says one, "but my wife was sick. The organization gave me food for the trip, but we didn't go so we ate the food instead. This saved our lives."

Others who were too sick to walk were also too weak to get to aid distribution points.

"The main problem was communication," a young woman explains, "transport was impossible so aid couldn't be brought here. Some people brought flour on their donkeys. Others could only bring a little, but they shared it out. Our friends saved us. They gave us flour or maize. The aid saved us from starvation."

The famine sabotaged not only food provision, but most of the development policies of the revolution. Health care, schools, the councils, and the people's associations all disappeared. But by the time the next rains fell the long process of rehabilitation had begun. The strongest made their way from the Sudan to be ready to sow. They could not risk another season without a harvest. The richest peasants, of course, could ride the famine or even profit from it, but up to a point it seems to have been a leveler of wealth. The following year REST organized aid agency support to provide farmers with fifty *birr* for seed and money towards an ox, so that they could share plow animals and begin to rebuild their lives. But, it was not always so simple, as Desta Welde explains.

"Because the TPLF gave us fifty *birr* I spent it all on seed without putting any aside. Fortunately, I got a good crop. I had to borrow a hundred and seventy-five *birr* to rent an ox to plow my land. The TPLF gave me a hundred and fifty *birr* to buy a half-share in an ox, but I had to use it to pay back the loan. The price of grain is very low now, so we can't get enough from selling the surplus to buy an ox because the price has gone up. If we could take the crop to a Dergue town, there the price is high, but we are too far away. But maybe this year or next we can buy an ox."

It's the way the poverty trap works in Britain too.

Berhanu has organized transport to come and take us to Mai Hanse. I am beginning to suss out their methods of communication. Some of the time the Front communicates through a radio network; otherwise there is a constant traffic of courier-born letters. Paper is in very short supply and I never see an envelope. Instead, these little missives pass from hand to hand, every inch covered in tiny writing before they are folded to the size of a large stamp and stapled together. I tease Berhanu that the real Leader, the real Power behind the revolution, is the Man sitting on top of some mountain holding the Stapler.

We walk down to Edaga Hibret in the early evening to drink tea and *mes* (honey wine) in one of the houses while we are waiting for the transport to arrive. It never does, but we have a great evening swapping stories, drinking *mes* and laughing with fighters and people of the town. Apparently, the five big towns, still controlled by the Dergue, have many bars—places of ill-repute frequented by the troops, in which the serving women are always prostitutes. I have seen no such bars in the little towns of the liberated area, but many families survive financially by selling home-made beer, mead, and tea in a simple room like this, where women can also come without damage to their reputation.

Before long, a group of young women and girls congregate in the doorway, peeping at me curiously, and then slide onto the benches to listen. Two or three of them are *shig woyenti* and have attended March Eight Women's School. The whole group ends up by giving us a concert of revolutionary songs, which I record on tape. When they disagree noisily about which song to sing next and then burst into hilarious laughter whenever they make a mistake, the teacher in Berhanu shows itself at once. He takes them in hand like a conductor, the microphone his baton. He re-records one song three times until he considers it good enough.

"No! No good! Off it!" he says to me and "Start again. All over again!" to the girls, some of whom, not at all intimidated, are paralyzed with giggles. When I play it later, I am quite relieved to hear that the spontaneity and the odd giggle or two have escaped censorship.

At eleven at night a truck arrives. Immediately, it is surrounded by crowds of people with bundles hoping to get a lift. Berhanu is one of them. Lots of talking and haggling. There is no commercial transport at all in the liberated area. All the trucks are the product of aid and in the service of REST, but people everywhere are allowed to ride from place to place on top of the load. In fact, the driver is too tired to drive anywhere and we trail back to the barn where we stayed the first night and sleep on the ground again for a couple of hours. We wake at some harsh hour, climb onto the truck and jolt and lurch and bump over the ruts and reach Mai Hanse before dawn.

In my absence, two Australian geologists, Graham and Liz, have arrived, a middle-aged husband and wife team who are intrepid Africa veterans. They have moved with Richard into the newly-built hut for the well-digging team. A man from Oxfam, UK is also here and a Swiss and a Frenchman from the

International Committee of the Red Cross. These three are moving westwards tonight. I also move on tonight to a place called Owhie. There are no roads to Owhie, but Graham and Liz, who have an agency landcruiser agree to drop us as near as they can on their way to Adi Hagerai.

Owhie is a resettlement area, where the Front and REST have given support to families willing to leave the overcrowded highlands for the fertile, underpopulated, but malarial west. "Resettlement" has a bad name in Europe, since the terrible stories of forced deportations by the government to the south began to emerge in the mid-eighties. People were rounded up at gunpoint, it was alleged, from market places and feeding camps, mostly in disaffected areas. According to testimony gathered by *Survival International*, peasants were sent in unpressurized planes and many were dead on arrival.[1] The survivors were given a little grain and told to settle in a region different in climate, vegetation and health risks from the cool highlands of the north. Moreover the land was not empty. It was populated by other peoples with different languages and cultures, who had a natural hostility to the intruders. Some of these were also disaffected by long-term Amhara colonization and were fighting their own liberation struggles. Testimonies of survivors allege high mortality rates. Of those who survived the journey, many died of unfamiliar diseases. In desperation, some escaped, but few managed to make their way back to Tigray.

The Dergue claimed its resettlement policy was a humanitarian solution to the problems of overcrowding, environmental degradation, and drought in the highlands; the liberation fronts in Tigray and Eritrea condemned it as enforced deportation aimed at weakening and demoralizing support for opposition to the Government.

"It is better that you do not use the word *resettlement* for what the Dergue is doing," Berhanu chided me. The people are taken against their will. Many have died. They are like the Nazis in Germany. Fascists. It is a part of their war strategy, but they are getting humanitarian aid for it from the European Community. It will be harder for them if your words make it clear."

Their Words Make it Clearer

My name is Lemlem Hagos. I am twenty-five years old and I come from Wajirat. My husband is a farmer.

One day, in June 1985, I went to the market in Raya with my husband, leaving my two children at home with my sister. The way was long, and the market was already busy when we arrived. Soon after we got there, soldiers came and herded everyone into some waiting lorries. I was fright-

ened. I didn't understand what was going on. All I could think about was my children.

We were driven to Mekelle and put in a huge tent. We stayed there for one month without ever being allowed to go outside except to the latrine, and even then we were followed by guards. We lived on kitcha, a kind of unleavened bread.

More and more people arrived. The ones who tried to escape were always caught. When this happened our guards were doubled. After one month, we were taken by plane to Gambella in south west Ethiopia and put in a Resettlement Camp. My husband and I were assigned to a grass hut. Single people shared one hut between two. We were given fifty kilos of flour and some salt. This was supposed to last eight people for a month. To make the food more palatable, we bought pepper with the money, which we had taken with us to the market, and which the soldiers had never taken away from us after our capture.

The place where we were living was surrounded by jungle. There weren't even any visible paths. At night we weren't guarded—presumably because the soldiers never thought we would be able to run away. But after two weeks, six hundred and fifty of us escaped after dark to make our way back to Tigray. We had no idea which direction to take, so we just watched the sky. We ate fruits and leaves and kept going in this way for several days. Eventually, we got to a river[2] *and for the first time since we had left the camp came across some people.*[3] *They were quite black, and weren't wearing any clothes. I had never seen people like them before and I couldn't understand what they were saying. By chance, one member of our party had been to this area some years ago and could speak a few words of their language. He asked them if they would help us to cross the river in their boats. They agreed, but asked us for money and clothes, which we gave them. They seemed a bit frightened of us, perhaps because we were so many in number. But when they had taken about half of us across to the far bank, they refused to take any more and started pushing those who still had to cross into the water. There was nothing we could do to help them and we had to go on. I don't know if any of them survived.*

I was still with my husband. As we went along, we frequently met other groups of black people. They terrorized us, then killed some of the men and took several of the women away. We were powerless to stop them, for they were armed with bows and arrows. We went on like this for a month, and then one day myself and two of my friends were captured and taken to a village, where we were put into three neighboring houses and made to cook for the families who lived there. The man who had taken me had seven wives.

I stayed with one of them for most of the time, and I think this is what saved me from being raped. My two friends were not so lucky.

Our clothes were taken away from us and we were made to go around naked, just as they were. We felt ashamed and I cried continually. But whenever I was caught in tears I was beaten, so I hid myself away. We stayed in the village for three years, by which time we had learned to speak their language. One day we overheard one of the men saying that on the far side of a mountain on the horizon "brown" people were living. It was then that we decided to try and escape.

Twice we were caught. The second time, one of my friends was so badly beaten that she died. But at the third attempt the two of us who were left managed to get away in the middle of the night. We made for the mountain, and after travelling for two days we reached a road—the first we had seen since leaving Mekelle. By that time we were so hungry and tired, but also so relieved, thinking that now at last we would find people who would help us, that we stretched ourselves out where we could be seen by anyone passing by and slept. A car came along and stopped. The man looked very surprised to see us, especially as we were not wearing any clothes, and started to speak to us in Oromo. We replied in Tigrinya and immediately he said, in our own language, "What are you doing here?" When we told him what had happened his eyes filled with tears. "Hurry up and get in the car," he said and took us to an OLF[4] *camp at Tasha Begi district, where we were given soap, food, and clothes. Everyone took care of us. They were horrified when they heard our story.*

The next day they took us to Fashmi, where there were two white women and some other Oromo people. The women gave us clothes and shoes, and we stayed with them for eight days. Then they took us to Gedaref in their car and a white man took us to Khartoum the following day. The Sudanese authorities took charge of us and after a further eight days, we were visited by the TPLF and went to stay with them until we had recovered from our ordeal.

We are now working for Sudanese families in their homes, but I am hoping to go back to Tigray shortly to find my children. Perhaps my husband will be there too.[5]

A guide called Gebremeskel has joined Berhanu and Techana for this trip. Hagos is not with us—he has malaria again. We leave about seven in the evening and drive for about two hours before we are dropped off in the pitch dark to walk the rest of the way. The cloud-cover, which has raised the temperature and humidity to intolerable levels during the day, now hides the stars. I walk second in the single file behind the guide, Gebre Mescal, who walks fast but, as long as I don't think too much, my feet follow his unerringly between thorn bushes and rocks, up and down the low hills. Every mile or so we are stopped by armed sentries, local militia appointed by each community to guard the villages against incursions of Dergue *banda*. Each guard carefully inspects Berhanu's papers by torchlight.

We do a lot of walking over the next few days. The families we have come to talk to live in scattered farmsteads on the tops of hills and we walk from one to the other through thorn scrub and dried-up sorghum fields. Their stories reinforce each other. REST invited them to register for resettlement in the early eighties and those families who chose to move started trekking westwards with REST support in 1982. The Owhie clinic was built in the same year and provided with two health workers. To help them over the first few months they were loaned a supply of grain; they were given the tools through overseas aid. The rains fell and the grain was repaid out of the first year's harvests. Then the rains stopped. Their accounts of the famine years echoed the stories I had heard in Edaga Hibret. Most of the casualities were among old people and children, but information filtering through from the central highlands brought tales of worse suffering in their homeland—of neighbors and friends who had refused to move, whose families had not survived—and this helped reconcile them to their new home. Their hardest task was learning to trust one another, "to learn how to make a community out of strangers," as one woman expressed it. Although many families had moved from the same district of Egela in the highlands, it took several seasons of weddings and births and feast-day gatherings to weave them together.

One afternoon, when the sun is just beginning to lose its bite, we arrive at a cluster of round *tukuls*. We have grown into quite a little band by now. Besides Berhanu and Techana and myself there is not only Gebremeskel, our guide to the area, but also a local leader called Woldegabriel who is introducing us to each family. We sit in the shade inside the stockade of laced branches drinking *sewa* and watching Gebremeskel who has, unaccountably, started washing two of the children all over. The younger one is howling every time a cup of water is poured over him.

"You know," Berhanu says to me quietly, "I met a woman of the Irop nationality who had become a TPLF fighter.[6] 'Why did you become a fighter?' I asked. 'Ah,' she replied, 'it was when I saw how the fighters behaved when they came to our village. They picked up the children and kissed them. They played with them and washed their bodies. They looked for their lice. That is what made me so interested.'"

However, the mother of the family does not seem at all interested. She does not speak and when we refuse more beer she goes away with the empty plastic bottles and does not return. The father is absent and the speaker for the family is a young woman called Leteberhan. She is twenty-one and the fourth of ten children. An older brother comes to sit with us, but he makes only occasional comments; the younger ones come to stare at us, get bored, wander off. The silence of the afternoon is broken by the occasional plaintive calls of young calves who are picking over a litter of stalks in the corner of the yard. The family came to Owhie in the early eighties, she tells us, but under their own steam, without registering, because they had relatives in the area. After initial difficulties, they are doing well. They have a surplus of production over their needs, ten cattle, including calves, and other animals besides, although they still do not have the stock they had before the famine. Her parents are not politically active, but she herself is a *shig woyanit.*

After a while, I ask if the mother could be persuaded to talk to us. I don't want to hear just from the politically engaged. But when she comes, reluctantly, she winds her shawl to hide most of her face and her monosyllabic replies merely echo the views of her daughter. She looks an old woman to me, like someone in her seventies. Her body is lean and stringy, but her face collapses with shyness into a thousand wrinkles. She would have been married in Haile Selassie's time—perhaps at eight or nine or ten years old, when feudalism was alive and well, many years before this revolution changed the minimum age of marriage. If her oldest child is twenty-seven, allowing a few years for puberty before she became pregnant, she could be as young as forty or not much older. Her youngest is only five. She could be younger than I am.

This simple arithmetic makes a deep impression on me. I continue recording answers, asking the occasional question, cross-checking the odd point with Berhanu, but all the time, on a parallel track, I am thinking *she could be younger than I am.* This woman's face has taught me more in a moment about the hardness of life for women in this country than any amount of straight information has done. She has probably given birth to more children. These ten are the survivors. I know all their ages. The closest gap is two years, but other children are three and even four years apart. I wonder why she is so shy and inarticulate and then remember the oppressive traditions that forbade women to talk in public, to show themselves before strange men.

Leteberhan, on the other hand, is the new woman. Calm, intelligent, confident, she gives clear explanations of her family's experience in Owhie, their economic position, her own political views, and reasons for supporting the revolution. Her gaze meets mine, clear and direct. She is beautiful. She has had her own land from an earlier age than her brothers and she has plowed it herself. Yet, she has so far chosen not to marry, in a society in which marriage has traditionally been seen as the only possibility for women.

The conversation is interrupted by throaty bellowing, matched by the frantic and noisy efforts of the calves to penetrate the fence. Two girls about nine or ten are bringing the cows back from the field and suddenly we are surrounded by huge pale beasts, their fearsome horns and humps belied by their mild eyes. The mother, Webet, goes to milk them where they stand, while the little girls wave their sticks and chase the calves away from the mothers until the best of the milk has been drawn off.

As we set out on the long march to a point where we can find a truck, the images of Leteberhan and Webet hang in my mind, the one bowed and hiding her face, the other clear-eyed, upright, and articulate. I will meet other women while I'm here whose experience is commensurate with Webet's, but who are more confident and outspoken; I will meet other young women who are shy and silent. Nevertheless, the contrast between this mother and this daughter becomes for me emblematic of the new opportunities available to women in Tigray.

Halfway to Mai Hanse we change trucks. I don't know why. Techana stays in the first truck and he has the only torch. When we are dropped at three o'clock in the morning, the sliver of moon has set and we stagger about in the dark, totally confused by the maze of approaches to the Mai Hanse valley. Sa'adu, a friendly truck driver, comes to our rescue with his torch and guides us down to the bottom of the cleft. It is pitch black under the trees. Even with his help we keep falling over roots and stones. Laughing doesn't help.

At the bottom we hear a noise above us and instantly freeze. There is a flicker half way up the opposite slope and an eerie wavering sound floats down to us. Suddenly, Berhanu and Sa'adu start to laugh. They are laughing themselves sick, so it is a few moments before I can discover what is going on. It is Techana, lost, frightened, and disorientated. He is calling on his comrades the trees to come to his aid and show him the way. The "gallant fighter" of the Red Star Campaign won't hear the end of this for a long time. Today, the fighters here are rolling about addressing trees and bushes and asking them favors. Techana, a wit himself, seems to be taking it in good part.

A day or two later it was not so easy to get from Mai Hanse to Tekezze. More problems with transport. We caught a truck to Mai Humer, but then had to wait there through the night and a scorching day until Berhanu could negotiate a Toyota to take us to our destination. Instead of the gulley where we had waited before, we passed the day in a nearby farm. The word soon spread and children came running from all the scattered homes in the area to have a look. Most of them were girls and homed in on me because I was female and because I looked strange. First, they peered at me through the slats of the hut, fixed and fascinated, only shifting their position when I moved, to keep their eyes on my face. Then, in the afternoon, the bravest gradually edged to the doorway, then into the hut, and finally onto the blanket.

Two of the girls were sisters, eight and six years old, who were particularly lively and intelligent. Techana and other fighters tried to shoo them away, but it was hopeless. They loved our music. They looked at themselves in my tiny mirror. They grew bold and cheeky. When Techana came back with a water carrier, the older sister, Owuru, showed me a pile of rocks where there was enough privacy to wash. She poured the water over me according to custom, wanted to smell my few toiletries and was charmed when I dabbed cologne behind her ears. These chance encounters hang in my memory like precious bubbles, unable to burst, with nowhere to go.

We arrived late at night at the headquarters of the Tekezze Horticultural Project, where a warm welcome was waiting for us. The two-room office-dwelling of the Director, Belai Gebremedhin, was built into the hillside, its entrance concealed by trees and bushes. Belai was a quiet, dignified man, perhaps in his early forties. He kept us company with several other fighters while we tucked into a delicious meal of *injera* and fresh vegetables. They had been expecting us for three days, but that's what Tigray-time is like, nothing to do with people, everything to do with transport. Their only concern was in case the hand of bananas they had buried underground pending our arrival would not be in peak condition. Then we had drinks of papaya crush and easy talk until well after midnight.

"This is for you," Belai said, waving towards a sleeping platform in the corner. "Feel at ease here. Worry about nothing. I will be working at my desk next door for a couple of hours yet, if there is anything you need."

And I fell asleep at once in the unfamiliar bed with Belai's lantern casting a glow through the archway like a nightlight.

After a breakfast of rice and bananas, we walked down to the Tekezze River to see the pump and irrigation system on which the whole project depended. A pool had been dug out like a reservoir below the steep bank. Now it was low, like this vast river, still flowing with a considerable volume of water around sandbanks and dry patches not exposed before. On the bank above, concealed by bushy evergreen trees was a generator and an electric pump. The water was piped into an aqueduct and thence into plastic-lined irrigation channels, which carried it into every part of an extensive vegetable and fruit garden.

In the main vegetable gardens I photographed healthy plots of onions, tomatoes, chard (which Belai called cabbage), courgettes, sweet potatoes, and peppers. The plants were growing on the sides of steep furrows which contained the water at pumping times. As we walked, Belai explained the history of the project. A garden was first started in 1980 at a site near Sheraro with the aim of teaching horticultural principles, agronomy, and veterinary science to fighters, agricultural cadres, and peasants. When the Front moved its base area to Tekezze two years later, the garden moved here. First of all, a large area was cultivated so that vegetables could be distributed widely throughout the districts of Shire and Wolqait, as part of a nutritional strategy to teach the people about vitamins and to persuade them to include vegetables in their diet. Recently, the Front changed its policy because district *baitos* are beginning to teach farmers more effectively through local demonstration fields and fruit and vegetable gardens in collaboration with the Agriculture Department. So, from this year, the main aim of this project has been to produce and distribute seeds and seedlings, rather than vegetables. These are sent out with trained cadres into the communities. Fighters and cadres are trained in horticultural theory at one of two agricultural schools and then come here for practical experience.

Belai's words echo what Dr. Samuel had told me at the Regional Hospital a few days before, of the difficulty of persuading people to eat vegetables.

"We try to teach them about the role of vitamins in resistance to disease. We say, 'during the wet season your cattle eat grass. They get fat and give you milk. But in the dry season they grow weak and get diseases.' We say they should learn from this that vegetables can make them strong. When they sow their crops we encourage them to grow a small area of vegetables near the house, especially if there is a water source nearby."

Until recently, Belai explained, they imported seeds, but these would only yield with large amounts of expensive fertilizer and were susceptible to molds.

"Now, the Department studies which seeds best suit this climate and which are resistant to pests and diseases. We are working towards a self-reliant agriculture and are trying to develop appropriate strains and distribute them through the people's councils for the people to grow themselves."

They were also growing tree seedlings both for fruit gardens and for reafforestation. We walked on to the fruit garden, although "garden" is hardly the word I would choose. It was an exotic dreamtime forest. There were plantations of banana, papaya, groves of orange, lemon, and grapefruit, and some young date palms. The papaya were in full fruit, great lush green fruit the size of coconuts. There is often only one male tree to a large papaya grove of female fruit-bearing trees, but here there were several, festooned with hanging strings of blooms, pale yellow and cream. The larger banana plantations formed cool dim tunnels between great columns whose leaves met overhead. A stem, once fruited, never fruits again. It is cut down to ground level and a new fruiting stem grows more than twenty feet in a season. We passed into grapefruit groves, their unripe fruit huge and heavy and green; then orange groves, so healthy-looking with their compact habit and glossy dark green foliage, beside the paler small-leaved lemon trees.

On our right was a cliff and, until Belai pointed them out, I failed to see the camouflaged huts built into caves and crevices at its base. These were the retreats for workers at times of attack. There have been many MiG attacks on this area and also three ground assaults in 1983 and 1985 by Dergue troops who slashed and cut the trees and tried to destroy the garden.

"These banana trees are our comrades," said Berhanu. "They have withstood three campaigns—like our people!"

His face was so serious I looked around with new respect.

"Look!" he said, starting to laugh, "look how they are standing at attention to salute us."

"Awat na banana!" murmured Techana dryly behind us. "Victory to bananas."

A few minutes later we passed a massive bomb crater in an empty glade between the trees, missing the plots completely. There were more jokes about MiG pilots searching for a hole in the trees to pop a bomb into, never hitting anything. It seemed a paradox that these fighters should always be so lighthearted, that there should be so much laughter from those who had known so much suffering and bereavement.

One morning, a day or two later, I drift into wakefulness to the sound of sweeping. A woman is sprinkling the dirt floor and brushing it to a marble shine. She has thrown incense crystals onto the coals of a tiny stove and the breeze through the open door brings to my corner swirls of calming fragrance. It is a quarter past six. As I peep out of my sleeping bag a patter of soil trickles onto my head from the branch and turf roof overhead. I am getting used to rats and mice running around the roofs. Sometimes ceilings are lined with sheeting or grain sacks sown together. "Mice. Only mice," Tigrayan hosts laugh, when I can clearly see the prints of four feet running over the cloth with a span of at least ten inches between front and back. Here there is no lining and I hide my head to avoid another drizzle of dust. Time to get up.

After breakfast, Berhanu and I sit in the cool hut writing in our notebooks. I have discovered he writes stories and poems, some of which have been published in the Front's magazines. We are joined by Solomon, a young boy who has adopted the fighters and lives here most of the time. He looks like a bright four year old, but is probably six or seven. He is drawing pictures and practicing writing his name on paper I have given him. He draws a spidery *tegadalai*, a male fighter, and nudges me to take notice.

"Now a *tegadalit*," he murmurs.

"But how can you tell it's a woman fighter?" asks Berhanu.

"But they look the same in everything—hair, clothes, everything," the boy replies, wrinkling his face as he considers the problem. After a few moments he adds a little circle to the middle of the woman fighter and looks round proudly.

Solomon's father is a *shig weyane* in a nearby hamlet. The family are too poor to feed him, so he spends most of his time here. Two nights ago, he had so many bad dreams that last night he curled up with Berhanu. Today, the child is following him around like a little dog. He has a cheeky smile and in fact *is* very cheeky to the fighters in the games of mutual insult and assault they have developed, but they are gentle and loving with him.

Outside, sitting on a wall of rocks, two women fighters and three male fighters are having a heated discussion about the problem of petty-bourgeois elements in fighters themselves.

"How do these elements show themselves?" I whisper to Berhanu.

"By wanting private things, by selfishness, by working for personal advantage," he mutters back.

He starts to take notes of the conversation and I concentrate hard to see what Tigrinya I can pick up for myself.

While we are writing and listening, sand and gravel continues to drift down with an occasional rattle in the corner over the sleeping platform. The rats or mice who cause the disturbance always make me look up. As I do so for the dozenth time, a small black snake falls onto the bed with a plop and streaks out of sight into the folds of my sleeping bag. Instantly, three or four men I had hardly realized were there leap forward with sticks, sort the snake out of the folds onto the floor and beat it into fragments. It was a black mamba, one of the most venomous of African snakes and the only one which attacks without provocation.

The women fighters, attracted by the scuffle, put their arms round me and draw me outside to sit with them. It is a good excuse to join in their discussion, with Berhanu to mediate. Apparently, the earlier references to petty-bourgeois elements were made in the context of a discussion of the year-old law allowing fighters to marry. The women fighters are deeply critical of the ways in which some male fighters are behaving—staying faithful for only two or three months, then swapping partners. Sex between fighters is not disapproved of, they say; there is no need to marry for mere sexual need. Berhanu agrees. There is nothing to prevent a full exploration, including a sexual relationship, of an agreeable partner's character and personality before deciding on marriage.

I suggest that after ten years of unnatural prohibition, no matter how good the reasons, it will take time for sexual relations to develop a healthy balance. They agree with this, but assert that it may never happen if women do not criticize and expose what is going on. The men defend themselves. The women are assertive, but good-humored. The conversation leads on to questions about sexual relations, women's issues and feminism in Britain. Tigrayan women often have an unrealistic and inaccurate optimism about gender relations in a "developed" society. These women are no exception. They see appropriate technological development at village level as crucial to solving the problems of women's work here, work which keeps women oppressed irrespective of their hard-won "equalities." I explain that in the West it is the problems of women's psychological dependency and low self-esteem that are the hardest to eradicate, no matter how many machines they have in the home.

"Yes, I see that" says Werknesh. "Our women's associations and our two women's schools are places where women improve their confidence and skills, but if they return to their houses and still have to spend hours at the grindstone or fetching water, how can they practice their new knowledge?"

The Tekezze project also includes a farm at Tsebri, several kilometers away. Belai drove us there after dark by tractor. The old model only had one seat and the four of us perched on the metal rims above the wheels, clinging on like mad for the two hour journey while the tractor lurched over the ruts and sank into the potholes like a crazy mule at a rodeo. We were met about midnight by an old woman called Belainesh who gave us tea in an underground office. She was in her late sixties and immensely proud of being the oldest woman fighter in the Front.

The following morning, before breakfast, I talked to her and other farm workers filling out my conversations with facts and figures from Belai. In this country, where women have been so oppressed, this peasant woman insisted on being a fighter. She was so pushy that the Front could not withstand the force of her will. Although she had two children of her own, a son in Addis and a daughter nearby supporting the revolution, she called the fighters her sons and daughters. Belai said she has trained many women agricultural cadres to plow. Berhanu said she is unusual, perhaps unique. There are militia of her age supporting the Front, but she is the first woman fighter he has come across with white hair. She posed for the camera, very erect, with her ancient carbine slung across her shoulders.

After breakfast we spent several hours touring the farm, which specialized in researching drought-resistant varieties of white sorghum and improved varieties of red sorghum. Except for a few dessicated stalks, the huge flat fields were empty and the ground crazed and dry, but I could see at a glance the fertile black soil, which makes the west so productive even in drought years. On the eastern skyline the first mountains leading to the central highlands rose straight out of the flat land in a purple haze. The threat of malaria has kept this land relatively empty and the Front has farmed parts of it to feed its fighters since 1979.

We were in time to watch the later stages of harvesting. Sorghum grows in large sprays nearly thirty centimeters long. These had been heaped in high stacks according to type, red or white, to await threshing. The white is less tasty, but its proven drought-resistant qualities make it an important element in the Front's strategies for food security. Nearby, a ring of thorn branches defined the threshing floor. Within the circle a small herd of cattle was being driven round and round trampling the sorghum seeds from the twigs. In the milling pool of heads and horns one set of horns reared high above the rest, more huge than any I had ever seen or imagined.

"Do you see the Raya bull?"

Berhanu's voice was full of admiration. A town boy, an intellectual, yet interested in everything rural, he is getting as much as I am out of this expedition. Raya is an *awraja* (county) in south-eastern Tigray with its own distinctive culture. Raya bulls, Belai told us, their gentleness belying their fearsome appearance, make the herd more manageable.

Despite the six tractors on the farm, the tools and general methods seemed to be traditional. Within another thorn circle a dozen workers were methodically raking threshed debris away from the seeds with two-pronged forks which were no more than carefully selected and trimmed tree branches. Not far away, a group of workers were tossing the grain high into the air, the chaff streaming away in the light wind. Others were shovelling heaps of white sorghum into sacks with pointed spades. These were imported, Belai said, and were a vital form of development aid all over Tigray. Sacks heaped on platforms of tree branches were waiting for camel trains to collect them. Every *baito* was then responsible for distributing the seed to local farmers through its agriculture committee.

Workers come from all over Tigray to earn extra money on these farms during plowing and harvesting, but at this late stage of the season all the workers were fighters.

"Fighters should be workers and teachers, as well as fighters," said Belai. "They should produce with their left hand and fight and educate with their right hand. But they must work for the people. Before, we had a mistaken policy. Our skills and resources were centerd on the Front. We had to change it. We decided that all the TPLF's skills and resources should be used for the benefit of the people, to improve their agriculture and their standard of living."

By this time, we had been out for several hours and walked several miles. The sun was directly overhead and underneath my wraps my skin was prickling and trickling with heat. My water bottle was empty. On our way back we discussed the superstitions and cultural attitudes, which had been obstacles to production before the revolution. Women were forbidden to plow and were restricted to menial tasks like weeding. They were thought to curse the plow if they touched it and to blight the harvest if they approached the fields at certain times of year. If they were bringing food to their menfolk in the fields, they would have to pause a certain distance away and shout. During the terrible famine, in the early eighties, the priests had pointed the finger at women. It had been their fault, they declared, for interfering with the land. God was angry and had sent the drought as a punishment.

Now, Belai said, most priests in the countryside supported the Front, although it had been hard work to win their confidence. One of the problems had been the number of holy days in the year.

"The priests said it was a sin to work on holy days. It was a specially big problem during the rainy season, when there were two week-long holidays in June and one week in July. These are the main plowing times."

"What did you do?"

"We held a conference of priests and explained our point of view and discussed everything with them. After that the holidays were reduced, but in some places there were still problems. Snow is rare here and when it snowed people thought God was angry, that it was a punishment for working on holy days. So we took fridges to the priests and told them to put water inside. We showed them that snow and ice were formed from cold, that it was a scientific phenomenon, not a religious problem."

Too tired, thirsty, and hot to talk, I walked the last kilometer in silence, but Berhanu and Techana still had enough energy to turn everything to laughter. Back in the cool underground rooms, Belainesh had prepared *injera* with hot pepper and curds from the farm's cows, the first dairy product I had seen here. Then the delicious sensation of limbs sinking, sliding into sleep on a rock bed. I seem to have multiplied the opportunities for sensuous gratification since I came here. It is the little things that delight. Cool shade at mid-day. Fresh curd cheese after weeks without milk. The sweetness of bananas. Clean feet.

We were meant to return to Mai Hanse last night. We went by tractor to Mai Humer, but the truck would only take us back to the Tekezze garden. So here we are again. Back to eating bananas and papaya. What's more, Belai has insisted on exchanging sleeping places, mistakenly believing that I am scared of snakes. Surely, I persuaded myself, snakes never strike in the same place twice. Today, as we walked back from bathing in the river, we came across another deadly snake. Two fighters beat it to death.

I am reluctant to leave this place. I will miss the sense of stability and closeness to the earth that gardens give me and (worst of all) I will miss eating vegetables and fruit three times a day. After supper, we walk to meet another truck. We are now torchless, but a third of a moon gives enough brilliance to walk by. The path takes us between rocks and trees and through the garden. We walk silently and in single file through alternate patches of cool moon and thick darkness until I feel a change in the air on my face, a freshness whispering of all the good things of gardens.

9

"Can an Elephant be Killed if it is Guarded by Lions?"

The story of Sheraro is mixed up in my mind with the stories of the women who went from there to join the struggle. Bits and pieces of the same story. When I first went there I hadn't even met most of them. They told me their stories over the next five years, as their confidence in me grew. Now, I can't remember what it was like not to know all that; I can't put myself in Sheraro without their presence. Of course, Sheraro has its own independent story too. But for me it's mixed up with the history of Aregash and Roman and Tsehaitu and Laflaf.

On my first visit, Sheraro looked like a slightly enlarged version of other tiny Tigrayan towns—dusty and unkempt overgrown villages—except that here, there were some trees in the streets, even more children and a few parked camels chewing in the shade. Berhanu and Techana had been dying to get to Sheraro for some time as if it were the promised land. Their expectations gave me expectations, so I was not so much disappointed as surprised to find the same accumulation of shabby one-story buildings in a web of dirt roads, where inedible succulents in odd corners expanded their tongues of fleshy greenery and the same wind blew the hot dust into our faces in the afternoon. It's hard to put my finger on when I changed my mind and Sheraro became special for me too, hard to define in what precisely its special character lay. The people? Of course—but isn't that the case everywhere?

We made all the basic visits that first time—the clinic, the school, the executive of the *baito*, the handloom weavers—all the institutions they were proud of. We were lucky enough to coincide with a cultural festival and the women, sitting separately from the men in their associations according to age, led me out to the dance. We even paid a visit to "the only industry in

Tigray" (Berhanu's words), which proved to be a sesame grinding mill, its one worker a lone camel padding an interminable circle through the heat of the day. ("My joke," said Berhanu. "A bitter joke!") The *baito* was the first to be established in liberated Tigray. I was interested to find that both the chairman and vice-chairman of the executive were Muslims—objective evidence, like the women members, of improving conditions for the most oppressed sectors of society. The *baito* established the clinic in 1980 and the school two years later with the help of the Front.

Everywhere we went, Berhanu met "Agazi comrades," people who were in Mekelle Prison with him and had been released in the Agazi operation. The director of the school, Ashebir Zeleke, was one of these.

"Did you know Berhanu ran a school in Mekelle prison?" he asked.

I didn't know. He was very cagey about his achievements.

"Yes. More than sixty students and about twenty prison guards were studying from third to fifth grades. He was accused of teaching politics and tortured, but still kept it going."

Ashebir was an Amhara and had taught for twenty-one years in Addis before he joined the Front, the first of many Amharas I was to meet over the next few years, driven by consciousness of injustice to fight with the Tigrayans. He was unable to use the purpose-built schoolhouse because its tin roof and isolated position on the edge of the town made it an easy target for MiGs, so the school was semi-mobile in whatever buildings they could find.

"But it's not the schoolhouse that's a problem, so much as the air-raids," Ashebir remarked. "They make it impossible to teach freely."

As we spoke, a MiG thundered over our heads and we huddled breathlessly for the next hour while planes repeatedly skimmed the rooftops. No bombs were dropped; it was only harassment.

"Why is it called March 28 School?" I asked Berhanu when the MiGs had given up for the day and we were walking across the exposed expanse of square again.

"It is in memory of the war between the TPLF and the EDU."

This area had been the center of confrontation between the Front and the organization of feudal landowners called, inappropriately, the Ethiopian Democratic Union. It was led, and still is, by the Prince of Tigray, Ras Mengesha Seyoum. Berhanu, Meles, other leaders—all Tigrayans who speak English in fact—always refer to these landowners collectively as "the feudals." Many of the early fighters had died in fierce battles, "martyrs" as the Front prefers to call them, before this privileged class had been overwhelmed and sent packing to Dergue areas or to the Sudan. Support for the

Front is so rock solid now that it is hard to imagine a time when different political groups were competing for the people's support.

"Yes, the peasants had a feudal mentality," said Berhanu. "The feudals were a powerful force around here. It was two years before we defeated them and drove them out. There were Ethiopian, Eritrean, and other Tigrayan revolutionary groups too—all fighting us and each other and at the same time trying to impress the people."

This early history is very confusing—so many radical groups and so many acronyms. What comes across loud and strong from that time is the discontent of the people and the bubbling revolutionary fervor for political change at any cost. And it was happening only ten years ago. Despite the MiGs and despite endemic poverty, there is an air of stability and confidence in Sheraro now that traps me into thinking this history is at least fifty years old. The revolutionary fervor is still there, but instead of a confusion of rival politics, it is channeled and disciplined into a single cause. What was it about this Front that had caught and retained the people's favor?

Berhanu was pursuing his own line of thought.

"And it was not only the feudals—the Dergue was sending soldiers to suppress discontent and paying people to be its spies. We had so many enemies. You can't imagine .... When we were fighting against these organizations, our fighters never ate dinner where they ate lunch. They never slept where they ate dinner. So after dinner, when the peasants were asleep they had to walk three or four hours to avoid encirclement in the night."

We were nearly back at the place we were staying. In every direction, at the end of every street, the stony dust of the road merged with the endless brown hills. Had they really been the site of so much stress, conflict, death? We passed through the patch of cool archway into the courtyard. Strands of dessicated vine crackled in the fire of the afternoon. The shadows were resonant with flies. I found myself projecting somnolence and stability onto the landscape and thence to the people. It was the lazy time of day. Difficult to imagine the rattle of gunfire or the sinister and inexorable tanks of the Dergue rolling across the square.

Yet, in every conversation, in every encounter with people in Sheraro I had been getting messages about this past. In the house of the *baito,* where I had talked to the Executive Committee one day, I had been very taken with a huge banner hanging on the wall. Each half was divided into five horizontal sections and each of the ten sections represented a different year in the history of the Front, like elongated frames in a comic. The story-telling technique was an interesting blend of imagery and captions, which I needed help to understand. A huge python (the Dergue) almost filled one frame; a mountain denoted an important battle. The frame for 1977 showed the Front (symbolized by a whirlwind) caught between the double onslaught of the feudals (a locust) and the Dergue (a raza bird). 1979 ("after three years of bitter campaigns," said Berhanu) showed the Front organizing its first Congress. A worker held a massive loud-hailer out of which boomed a balloon —"You masses, be conscious, be organized, arm yourselves!" The 1983 frame recalled the Red Star Campaign of the Dergue (in which Techana was a fighter). MiG 21s and MiG 23s made devastating raids on the liberated towns. Sheraro was there in the right hand corner—in flames.

Now, as I sit writing this account, the image of the banner returns as an analog of what I am doing with words. But I am not painting; I am stitching. I feel my words are the stitches of an enormous tapestry, intricate with events and with colors—a touch of purple, a hint of green, a tide of red, a stitch here, a stitch there. Every detail tells a story. Still too many blank spaces. It could almost be a banner like the one in Sheraro—the making of a revolution.

Every house has an air-raid shelter like a large rabbit hole dug out of the road in front, its roof supported by tree branches. I have never seen them fenced or covered. It must be easy to fall down them in the dark. On the edge of the market square a chunky masonry monument looks down on market stalls sparsely stocked with hanks of bright colored threads and bars of harsh soap. But the people need no reminders of the day in 1983 when MiGs killed thirty-one people, injured sixty-one more, destroyed thirty-five houses and slaughtered many animals. The raid was in retaliation for five or six days of heavy fighting around Sheraro after which the fighters pushed the Dergue troops right back. It was not the first MiG air-raid, nor the last, but it was the worst. The shelters have been been built since then and the early warning system has grown more sophisticated, both through spies and advance intelligence radioed from the Front.

After that the Dergue brought in reinforcements from Eritrea, including forty tanks. The Front retreated and the Dergue invaded the town. The townsfolk immediately decamped into the hills ("Sheraro in the Hills" they still call it), taking their shops, their school, and the clinic with them, and carried on as usual—and the troops occupied an almost empty town for twelve months. The only ones left were fifty or so old people who were too weak to travel. After the troops left, it took another month for the fighters to clear the rings of mines around the town. But the Dergue had the worst of it, so the story goes. They could not get out and no food could get in. Completely encircled by the liberated area under the control of the Front, they were in a prison of their own making.

Aregash and Roman, the two senior women fighters I had just missed at the Front's headquarters in the mountains, finally catch up with me on my third visit to Sheraro. Coming back home one night, I find them waiting for me. They are a contrasting pair, perhaps in their mid-thirties. Aregash is small and round, the only woman on the Front's Central Committee. Roman is tall and thin. She works in the Mass Bureau and is the secretary of the Women Fighters' Association (WAFT). We sit in the little courtyard around a lantern. Over our heads the papery remnants of a vine trail from a horizontal trellis and a slight breeze brushes seedpods against our hair.

So these were among the very first women fighters of the revolution. I study their faces for signs of particular heroism or toughness, but they just look like women—relaxed, together women perhaps, but ordinary women all the same. It is appropriate we should meet here, Aregash says, because they were working together in Sheraro during the first year of the struggle and it was from here that they went to the field in the summer of 1976.

I want them to give me an account of the revolution from their point of view, to talk with as little direction from me as possible about the position and the contribution of women. In fact, they start where all Tigrayans start —with feudalism, insisting that without an understanding of what life was like under feudalism, it is impossible for a foreigner to understand why they are fighting or what they have achieved since the revolution started. But, they move on quickly to the particular oppressions of women. Much of this overlaps with my conversation with Harnet and Leila at the Propaganda Bureau a few weeks ago—the depressing catalog of child marriage and a life restricted to back-breaking work in the home with its legacy of ill-health, high maternal mortality and low life expectancy, a life of exclusion from decision-making, from land rights, from education.

But, I learn for the first time how restrictions on women's lives made them a prey to sorcery and superstitious practices. Many of these were associated with the *budda*—men and women who were thought to harness spirit forces to avenge offenses or injuries. Their power was thought to wound the victim through the eye like an arrow. Blacksmiths particularly, but also other artisans like potters, were commonly held to have these powers and so, as a group, they were both despised and feared. According to Roman and Aregash, the power of superstition is fading now that women have more power and a greater stake in their communities. I wonder how they can be so sure of that?

It has been a long struggle, they tell me, since the time when the early fighters first went into peasant homes to persuade the women to see their oppression. Now, women both own land and can plow it themselves. No wonder they seem so supportive of this revolution. Women make up about thirty percent of fighters and over twenty percent of *baito* members.

"We want women to be free," says Aregash, "free from oppression of all kinds, politically, socially, economically, culturally free. We want them to participate in activities that are useful to society. We aim to make them equal with men and be able to do all the things that men can do."

She stops for a moment. Pulled up short perhaps by the loftiness of these aims. They are fine aims. Nothing like them had been achieved anywhere in the world. They are smiling and talking to each other in Tigrinya.

"But at the same time, you have to be flexible and understanding about the pace at which women can contradict the habits of so many years," she adds. "It's still a new thing for a woman to go to a council meeting and talk about politics or even about their oppression."

They are happier talking about feudalism and Tigrayan women in general than about themselves, but once again the thing that interests me most is how these two women first came to be involved in politics, how they managed to make the break with a mainstream society which had such a restrictive view of women's role and potential.

"Yes, you are right," Aregash says,"our society discourages women from doing anything but marriage. My friends were often forced to leave school to get married."

"What made you so different?"

She thinks for a moment.

"My mother was a handicrafts teacher and encouraged me, but from five years old I lived with my aunt in Adwa. She brought me up to be courageous in my studies. 'Do not distract your attention by marrying,' she said to me. "That can come later—after your studies are finished."

So, this is also the story of women behind the scenes, the invisible women who were determined that their daughters' lives would not be as restricted as their own. This is their success story also.

"I was at university in Addis Ababa until 1972. I was interested in maths and science, but we had to list our top ten preferences from the courses available and I was forced to take social work, my tenth and last choice."

"Why didn't you want to do social work?"

"Social work socializes people to be submissive and I was not interested in people staying as poor and problematic as they are, but I had to do it. Then, I became involved in the student movement against the Haile Selassie regime, but when it became a party I disagreed with their policy on nationality so I left it and joined an underground Tigrayan organization instead.[1] At the beginning of 1975, they went to the field to start the armed struggle. I was worrying I would be too late. Three of my best women friends had joined the struggle in Eritrea and I was left behind."

"What brought you from Addis to Sheraro?"

"I wanted to get to know the countryside before I joined the struggle, so I worked here for nine months in a development project. The project's administration was critical of the government and in favor of accepting people who were political. The feudals opposed us because we were politicizing the people and demanding health centers. Soon afterwards, the administrator, Dr. Assefa, was arrested and imprisoned in Addis."

Roman, too, was a student during the period of continuous uprisings against Haile Selassie's government. After she finished twelfth grade in Tigray, she went to Addis to look for work. By then, the Dergue was in power and Roman, still out of a job, was press-ganged into joining the government *Zemacha* campaign in the south. I remembered Berhanu describing the bitter politicizing effects of that experience.

"We tried to give land to the peasants and we disarmed the feudals. But, the Dergue did not mean us to do it, so they harassed and imprisoned some of us. The feudals even killed some friends who were with us, burned them by fire when they were asleep in the tent. We escaped to our homeland, to Tigray. The national question was a hot issue in Tigray, so I joined the struggle."

For nearly a year in Sheraro, Roman and Aregash worked for the project. This work went hand-in-hand with their underground work for the newborn revolution.

"What kind of things did you do?"

"There were other women working there—and Roman of course. We were members of a section dealing with women. We tried to contact peasant women. We tried to ask them why women were poor, why women were dying at childbirth, to show them the necessity of struggle."

"We were going from house to house," says Roman, "teaching people. The women make special celebrations for the feast days of the angels and saints, St. Mikael and St. Mary, and so on. They prepare beer and bread. We'd go there and discuss with them their problems. They'd talk about how they were going to dance in their group. We'd do the same even if we didn't know how to. Then at the end we'd throw in something about the struggle, our aims."

"We tried to wear the same clothes and adjust our way of talking and our lifestyle to that of the peasants," continues Aregash. "Women with trousers and shoes could not build the confidence of peasant women at that time. Men were afraid that women would rebel against them. We tried to convince the men that the problems of women were the problems of society, but the feudals were undermining our efforts to politicize women. They distorted everything to the peasants," suddenly she starts to laugh, "saying that we wanted to take their husbands because we couldn't find husbands for ourselves in the towns, that because we were educated we could manage houses better."

Roman is grinning too.

"That year, in Sheraro, was important for us. It taught us a lot. Some men, especially feudals, thought we were organizing threats to the family and marriage. They thought women should be subservient and so they spread distortions about us and our movement. The women were trying to close their doors against us. Some even left the area altogether."

I find I am hanging onto every word. This seems the real world, closer to the skepticism and distrust I have met in my own.

Despite the setbacks, Aragesh and Roman and their companions didn't give up.

"From day-to-day we tried to contact the women individually, in churches, in ceremonies, gathering together, and drinking *sewa*. They experience that we had no interest in finding husbands. We told them our life history—we were students; we wanted to share their problems, help with their children, with the grinding, to discuss all the issues of their lives."

Roman says, "We began to realize opposition is not simple. Even a non-feudal man can support the idea of feudals; therefore, we realized the struggle would not be simple."

"Yes," says Aregash, "we realized that women are fearful of educated women and women influence their husbands. We tried to raise issues appropriate to their lives. Gradually, they became deeply involved in what we spoke and enthusiastic about expressing their views. Our knowledge was scanty. They expressed themselves in very concrete ways, their actual problems, so we were educated by their lives and their descriptions of life. It encouraged us to continue the struggle with more strength."

From Sheraro, they "went to the field," revolutionary jargon for "joining the struggle," which is revolutionary jargon for leaving the safe world of privileged education and paid work for the unsafe one of mobile fighters, hunted not only by the army and local police, but by rival revolutionary movements. I too find myself rolling these phrases off my tongue. They are no longer jargon; they have meaning. To escape arrest, all the women and men project workers left together. One of the servants, a peasant woman they called Laflaf, also went with them. They were not the first women to join the struggle, but almost the first. Marta and Lemlem had joined some months before. There were now about thirteen women altogether.

We go on talking for most of the night, about personal things, about family, about the condition of women in Britain, about the struggle for equality, even within the Front itself.

"It's tough to change the mentality of the male," says Aregash at one point, with a laugh.

Then, just before they leave—it is the darkest time of the night and we have been talking about lighter things and they are already winding their shawls around their heads and shouldering their Kalashnikovs—she turns to me seriously.

"You know, you cannot convince any individual or oppressed sector of society through theoretical discussion. You cannot convince men of the equality of women through political argument. If women are to be accepted as equal, if society is to build confidence in them, they have to show their participation in practical ways. Only practice can show women's capability, their talents, their contribution."

Laflaf Becomes a Fighter

I come from Zana, but I never knew my father and my mother died when I was thirteen. I started to work as a servant when I was eleven years old. When I heard my mother was sick I went back to my home in Zana and after she died I stayed with my young brother for a while, then went to Asmara to work. In Asmara, the political atmosphere was very hot. The towns were very hot. There were lots of rumors about fighters, about the Eritrean struggle. I bought clothes for my brother with the money I earned and went back with them to Zana, but because of our poverty, I decided to go to the Sudan.

I only got as far as Sheraro when I heard rumors about bandits in Tekezze raping women, so I decided to stay in Sheraro as a servant. One of my jobs was for an agent of the feudal organization, the EDU. Their members came to the house, so, as I was a servant and they were feudals, they even asked me to wash their legs every day when they rested! My fourth job was for seven people working for a government development project. It was a bit better paid and more secure. Two of them supported the Eritrean struggle and the other five, including Aregash and Roman, were interested in the TPLF.

I heard stories about Tigrayan fighters and I kept asking Aregash, Roman, and the others what it meant, but they shut me up because it was secret. One day, at the beginning of June, I saw a fighter nearby in camouflage. Suhul, Geday, and Siye were also around, so I knew something was going on. My seven employers wanted to invite the fighters to the house, but I had been grumbling that there were too many for me to feed and look after. They knew if more people came I would be sure to reject the extra work, so they decided to tell me they were fighters. I didn't believe them. Because they knew my interest in the revolution, they said, "Go out and see." So I went outside and recognized Geday. I was very happy and said they must come home.

After this, things became very difficult. There were threats from the feudals, from the government, and from an Eritrean political group. The workers decided to withdraw to the field. On June 5th, Geday and Negash had come to stay. They were both in disguise and Negash was hiding in the house. One morning, when Geday went out, leaving Negash in the house with me, he started telling me about the organization.

"Are there women fighters participating in the struggle?" I asked. "Peasant women?"

"One. Her name is Marta."

In the middle of June, the other three servants were paid off and went back to Shire, but when the workers wanted to leave me behind in Sheraro, because I'd had this discussion with Negash, I wouldn't allow it. They kept trying different means of persuasion, but I rejected them all. They disagreed with each other over what to do with me. On June 25, Berhe, a senior worker for the project and also an undercover agent for the TPLF, was talking with Geday in English with a little bit of Tigrinya mixed in, because they didn't want me to know what they were saying. I was very curious. I was removing bran from the flour and stayed nearby, listening to everything. The five women project workers, Aregash, Roman, Herit, Ybralef and Genet, were all going to the field. Twenty days before, I'd asked Negash if I could join and he'd said yes and I made him swear on oath to take me. I met Mekonnen and caught him by the hand: "I must go with these women, otherwise I'll die!" Now, I forced them and they took me.

In the end, taking most of the organization's materials, including Toyotas and medicines, they drove to the base area to join the armed struggle and I went with them.

We went for training at the end of June. They were still trying to persuade me to turn back, even from there, but, because I knew what they were doing, I immediately cut my hair and changed into very unsuitable clothes for a woman, shorts and shirt. I didn't even want to stay with the other five women, but I joined the male fighters and started training. The trainer, Walta, put pressure on me to go back whether I'd cut my hair or not. So I said:

"First, I was told not so long ago that there is a peasant fighter called Marta—that must be a lie. Second, this is an elitist organization. Aregash is an intellectual. You are rejecting me because I am not an intellectual, but a peasant. I will never be a servant or a civilian again."

Walta went on a mission. Everyone discussed it and disagreed. Finally, they let it drop. I stayed and started training.

Although I was accepted as a fighter, I was not convinced they accepted me as a peasant. Sebhat and Abai tried to convince me, but it was not easy for me to accept their answer, but when I saw so many intellectual women not allowed to come to the field, I began to see they had no choice but to accept Aregash and the other women, because they were in danger of arrest. I came to see the truth of their arguments through practical experience and saw that it was not because I was a peasant.

By that time, there had begun to be a differentiation of tasks into separate departments. I was assigned to Supplies (food and ammunition). I opposed this job because I wanted to go to the forces. I had a very strong argument with people like Aregash. When we finished training, even intellectual men were assigned to the army, but all the women were left behind, so even women like Roman were demanding to go. So I said, "What they are doing is bad. You are not putting enough pressure on them. Why don't you challenge it? It's your weakness. You could force them to accept you to go to the army." I took training a little earlier than Aregash because I started immediately, "Therefore," I said, "there is no problem. I would like to go to the army." Eventually, they said I could go in the second batch.

But, they didn't even send me in the second batch. By this time there were problems of male chauvinism. Male fighters were saying that women's nature is like a handicap. Different political education was given to men and women. We did most of our military and political training with men, but for a whole month there was a discussion for women alone. They wanted us to concentrate on the Woman Question, to know in depth the role of women in primitive communal society, then capitalism and oppression developing the role of mother, and so on. They wanted the women to know about this very deeply. I opposed this also. I was not interested in this. I said, "Why are you not pressurizing them to send us to the units?" But, men were mocking and teasing, "You are handicapped. That's why you are left behind, because you are not fit to be a fighter."

At last, they accepted my application and sent me to the forces. I was sent to Force Forty-One in October 1976, one month after the Battle in which Musie was martyred. We were assigned to western Tigray to fight the feudals. There were battles in Adi Nebried and Adi Daro. We were very mobile throughout the west. I had no problems. I had been a slave and now I was liberated. I was happier than anybody. I had no illusions, nothing else in my head but to work with enthusiasm.

When I was in Force Forty-One, I was the only woman among fifty or sixty men. Although I was a lone woman, the social life of the fighters prevented me from ever having a feeling of loneliness. We shared all our problems. They used to carry water for me to wash my clothes and pants. When I had my period, they used to carry my gun and ammunition. If there was a forced march when I had my period and I found it hard, they tried to give me every privilege. It was as if we were all male fighters, with no loneliness or shame. This is what I shall remember all my life—their comradeship and support.

Once, there was a very bad battle with the feudals in Tekezze. It was very hot. We had been walking for many hours and days. My period started and all my trousers were soaked in blood. Then my comrade, Asekhe (now martyred), took off his trousers and gave them to me to wear. He wore his shawl like a skirt.

One of the great problems was thirst. You couldn't talk even in a whisper, because your throat was all closed up. My state was the worst, so they offered me their urine to drink, but I said I would drink my own. But even to give me their urine—I remember that. Another problem was head-lice. We all picked lice off each other. There was no sexual harassment—sex did not play a part when I remember life in the forces. The commitment, the sacrificing yourself for your comrade, to decide to die first—these things are all strong in my memory. No one was afraid to die, but preferred to be in front to protect his comrade.

The only thing that was bothering me in the struggle was that I was illiterate. I didn't want to work in the departments with the intellectuals. All I wanted was to struggle with my Kalashnikov. But, I was sent to the Revolutionary school, an academic school, and I stayed there from 1983 to 1987 for nearly five years until I had completed fifth grade. This was my key problem, so when it was decided I was very happy. My pressure to go was equal to my desire to be a fighter, at first. They were saying, "How can you get on with these little kids? You will never tolerate it. You will never have the patience." After I had completed third grade, the TPLF encouraged me to go on. I was happy, but after 5th grade, because of the urgency of the time, I had to stop and be assigned to work. The small kids were calling me "mother." Genet was a small kid in that school. Now she has become a mother before I have become a mother!

Earlier, I worked with the mass in Agame, then as Director of March Eight School, now I am working with the people again. I was a peasant like them. That was my problem. I know their feelings, I know their difficulties in understanding. I love this work very much.[2]

The following day, I have been invited to sit in on the weekly political education meeting of the women's association. After breakfast, we walk across the town, past the ruins of a monument to the Front's defeat of the EDU. Dergue tanks twice destroyed it earlier in the eighties and now the people think it is a more effective monument broken than repaired.

A large crowd of women are sitting in the dust, in the shade of a three-sided barn. There must be about two hundred of them. At one end, the leader, in a white traditional dress, is sitting on a stool on a grain scale, reading from a book. I have met her before. She's on the executive of the *baito* and her name is Medhin.

A low bench is brought for us and we squeeze into the shade. Nobody takes any notice of our arrival. They seem to be listening intently, but in an inconsequential and non-reverential sort of way—some with their backs half or fully turned, some staring up at the roof or into the mind's eye perhaps. No one talks. The Tigrinya is too fast for me and I can look around. Many have children either at the breast or little humps under shawls on their backs. There seem to be a large proportion of old and older women among them, but then I see that a number of these are carrying infants. Women bear children into middle age, but even when they are younger, the harshness of their lives is etched into their cheekbones and their eyes. I remember the mother of Leteberhan in Owhie, how old she looked, how relatively young she was in years. I remember Abeba in Edaga Hibret, still young, but so thin and hardworking.

Medhin is a "Torch of the Revolution" and the chair of the Sheraro Women's Association. She appears to be giving a question and answer session. She is reading from a text, part of the curriculum prepared by the Mass Bureau for the mass associations. The theme is "Prison." Berhanu starts taking notes and whispering in my ear at the same time, so I get a succession of disjointed sentences, but enough to get the idea.

"The purpose of prison is to control the operation of oppressed classes."

"When there is oppression, there is also struggle."

"When there is struggle, there is also prison."

"Prisons are found all around the world and also in Ethiopia."

The expansion of the prison system, she says, begun under Menelik II at the beginning of the century with the construction of two new prisons in Addis Ababa, was continued by Haile Selassie, especially the development of the torture system for political prisoners. An electric chair was imported from the USA, even though Ethiopia had not the electric power to make it work. But, the assault on human and political rights has been worst under the Dergue:

"According to the Dergue, even a Tigrayan baby, even in its mother's womb, is a revolutionary, is in struggle, because it might support the Front in the future."

After half an hour she finishes expounding the text and women from the floor take up the theme. This is the most interesting part of the meeting for me—and the most revealing. It is really an exchange of memories. One woman after another rises to drop her experiences or those of grandfathers, fathers, husbands, and brothers into the common pool of false accusations, brutality, and pain. As a strategy for mobilizing resistance, for transferring experience from the powerless individual sphere to the powerful consciousness of shared oppression, it seems unequalled. The women are dignified and quiet. I am near tears.

One of the last speakers changes tack. In a few sentences, she refers to the simple issues of daily life for women, the time spent fetching water and wood, and grinding grain. The prison is not just in Mekelle or in Addis. There are also chains in the head. If they are to change their own lives, she says, they have to break these also.

"Speak to the women themselves," Roman had advised. "Talk to women in Sheraro. See what they have to say."

Often, I discard formal interviews. Although there is no way I can melt into the background in a community, which rarely sees white people and whose language I am just beginning to get the feel of, everything is relative and I try to put myself in situations where I can sit with women informally, where the common experiences of women—family life, childbirth, domestic tasks—can be the currency of conversational exchange. These sessions are quiet, almost desultory, never intense. If they can afford it, they make coffee. The women don't feel the need to talk all the time; people come in and out; babies cry and are fed or passed around; children fall and are comforted; the woman of the house peels onions and garlic for the *wat*, the *injera* sauce. Their companionship nourishes me. I forget what I hoped to learn. It feels like taking a rest and only much later I realize I absorbed more through sitting around, not trying.

They want to know about my husband. How has he "allowed" me to leave home for so long? They look sympathetic over my three daughters and only one son, even more so when they learn that a fifth child, my firstborn son, died in infancy. Why don't I have more? they ask. Next time, it might be a son. Four children is too little. They all seem to have lost children—to malaria and other diseases, to the floods of the rainy season. Many of the older women have sons and daughters who are fighters. Some they know have died in battle. Sometimes, they are waiting for definite news. In every village where I have arrived, I remember the faces of women crowding around the trucks and landcruisers, waiting for messages, asking fighters to read letters, hoping for news of long-silent children.

On one occasion, I meet a woman called Dahab. Eight of her nine children are fighters.

"When I see all these developments, it's all worthwhile," she said, "even if my children have to die."

I reread Dahab's words so often in my notes that I get to know them by heart. For days after that, my own children would interrupt my dreams. If anything happened to them in my absence, how would I reassess my time here?

"For me, there are more things than the days of my daughters and sons to disturb me. I have seen many heroes who died in front of me. I knew all the old fighters and most of them are no longer with us. Their vision always knocks my mind. Death is not new, unique or strange for me."

At the end of one afternoon, we walk home in the twilight. In the market place a few twinkling lights in the shadows announce that the market is getting under way. It is mid-February. The eighteenth will be the twelfth anniversary of the founding of the revolution and around this time MiG harassment and bombings become more frequent. Markets take place at night; security becomes much tighter. As a further precaution, anniversary celebrations, held in every town and village in the liberated area, are always held at night and never on the actual day, but staggered over a period of three weeks until the beginning of March.

The spice and pepper sellers and the salt traders from the Afar lowlands sit together; those selling the ingredients for *sewa*, or grains, or onions and garlic are each grouped in their own area of the market square. On the stalls are imported goods, such as batteries, soap, pens, sweets, chinese teacups (for coffee), the brightly-colored yarns used for binding basket-work or embroidering banners. The craftsmen take up one whole side of the market place—potters surrounded by coffee pots and clay bowls, blacksmiths behind rows of plowshares, sandal-makers cutting up truck tires and plastic sacks.

It is a lovely time of day, no longer hot. Our faces are fanned by gentle warm air so that the dusk feels like velvet. As the darkness gathering in corners begins to reach into more open spaces, little oil lamps multiply on market stalls, casting a soft light, soft shapes floating on shadows. There is nothing harsh to the senses. This light, this air, must have lulled generations of tourists and travellers in Africa into complacency and sleep. But, if you are awake, there are other things to notice. Many of the traders have no stalls. They spread out their wares on sacks on the ground. Many of them are women. In a night market these have no lamps and no torches. They can't afford them. I would trip over them in the dark if my companions did not steer me carefully between the rows. Most of these peasants have travelled long distances to sell a handful of the same narrow range of grains. How marginal must be their way of life, if selling so little makes a difference.

Bending to examine a row of plowshares in the light of Berhanu's torch and next to them some stoves adapted from large Oxfam biscuit tins, I recall Roman's words about the superstitious links between blacksmiths (the *budda*) and supernatural powers. In some areas, metalworkers are predominantly drawn from the *Falasha* people—Jews reputed to be descendants of the Israelites who supposedly kept the first Menelik company when he was sent back to Ethiopia from Israel. As the son of King Solomon of Israel and Sheba, the Ethiopian Queen, Menelik is believed to have established the Solomonic line, so important to the heredity of the Ethiopian royal house and also to the historical ties between the Ethiopian Orthodox Church and Judaism.[3]

So why have metal workers been credited with special powers? Does it date back to the first discoveries of smelting and the suspicion of new and mysterious technologies? Is it a racist response to the "otherness" of certain groups of artisans like the *Falashas*? Is it something else altogether? In the torchlight, these gaunt peasants are indistinguishable from any other. The barrier of surface appearances is impenetrable. I can't see the signs, let alone read them. Today, I feel like a deaf woman, surrounded by a babble of sound; I am good at lip-reading, but I don't have an interpreter. On other days, it is more like looking at an interior reflected in a mirror, forever out of reach, and in any case my own head blocks the view.

One afternoon, two of Berhanu's Agazi friends call around while we are still resting off the heat. We all walk around to the house of Adey Tsehaitu to drink coffee. *Adey* means "mother" and is a term of respect for older or particularly wise women. She is a staunch supporter of the revolution. We are conducted through the house to a little detached room in the yard. Sacking has been thrown over the grindstone in the corner and the stone benches covered with rush matting to sit on. There is a yard-square mat of fresh evergreen leaves on the floor and on this Tsehaitu places a stool bearing three thimble cups. She is preparing the coffee ceremony. Ethiopia is the original home of arabica coffee. It is a part of Ethiopian culture and coffee-making is an inseparable part of women's culture. Never casual, often protracted, it is the way women honor each other and show respect for men and visitors.

First the beans, a pallid green, are roasted on a charcoal stove. When they are glistening black, Tsehaitu shakes the smoking pan for each of us in turn, while we fan the smoke towards our faces the better to savor the aroma. Then they are pounded in a mortar with a thick steel rod before being tipped into the narrow-necked coffeepot and put on the fire. Three times, the overflowing liquid is quenched with a cup of cold water before it is stoppered with a bundle of threads and is ready to serve. The serving of coffee is not only ceremonial; it is also hierarchical. The grounds are boiled up with fresh water three times, each serving diminishing in strength and quality. The best of each serving goes to the most honored person in the room, according to the laws of hospitality. A foreign visitor comes first; unfamiliar visitors supersede familiar ones; men count more than women, visitors more than family, the maker least of all. You need a very good reason for refusing the required three cups, one from each brew. On this occasion, the three cups are handed to me and Berhanu's friends. Not until I have had three and Tesfay two, do Berhanu and Hagos consent to have one each.

We sip the strong sweet first cup and comment on its deliciousness. Tsehaitu accepts our commendation with an impassive inclination of her head, but I have noticed how Tigrayans never appear to take food and drink for granted and always compliment the cook or coffee maker. Sometimes, I get distracted and Berhanu has to remind me. Tsehaitu says something rapidly to Berhanu. He translates.

"She says she has had many years experience of making coffee. She had a small house on the Humera road when the revolution first started where she used to make a living from selling coffee, tea, and *sewa*."

I ask what she had made of the first fighters and how she had come in contact with them.

"I was born when the Italians first invaded Tigray. That was in 1936. I have lived in many places before I came to Sheraro, fourteen years ago. I had been in Eritrea where there had already been a long struggle, so I had a spirit of supporting fighters. When I heard there were fighters near here I was interested. It gave me a very good feeling to hear that Tigray had its own fighters."[4]

She sets a few hot coals from the stove in an incense burner and sprinkles them with incense crystals. The draft from the open door blows the fragrance into the room where it mingles with the aroma of the coffee.

"What first drew me to them was the information that fighters did not take even a cup of water that was not theirs. They always paid for everything they needed, whereas those bandits fighting for the feudals beat people with thorn twigs and took everything by force."

"But how did you first meet them?"

"One day, Meles and Berihu were going nearby dressed like peasants on their way to Dedebit. They ate food and paid for it. They asked for bread and spice to take with them. I didn't know why they wanted it, so I refused. I didn't realize they were fighters and facing a seven or eight hours walk to Dedebit. In May 1975, Berihu came to explain who they were and later I contacted them to pass on secret information, which proved to be correct and I started working closely with them."

She pauses to pour a second cup of coffee. By Ethiopian standards, she is elderly, but her face is smooth and she is still handsome. She has only a strand or two of grey in her hair. She had been divorced at the end of the sixties, when her third child was only a year old. I wonder whether this had given her greater freedom to join the struggle.

"My sympathies grew out of my own interests. I was very poor and had never lived a settled life. The first thing I liked was their discipline. Fighters respected the dignity of others. Their concern for justice and equality appealed to me. In 1976, when I saw them in Sheraro, you could see from their attitudes and their way of living that they didn't go socializing, never taking anything unless you gave it yourself—just talking to the people, that's all. If the people reported wrongs done to them, then they gave justice and punishment."

She hesitated and smiled. The three fighters are listening intently. They were only boys at this early stage of the struggle and have never heard this before.

"I don't like to talk about my own work ... but as you asked ... when the feudals controlled Sheraro for nine or ten months, I was persuading their members to defect to the TPLF."

Had she known Aregash then?

"I knew there was a government project here, but I didn't know anything about it. Aregash was here and then Roman came. I was close to Aregash. Sometimes, she came with Genet to stay the night with me."

After the feudals were defeated, Tsehaitu had been a member of the committee of twelve who ran Sheraro until the first *baito* had been elected in 1980, the first in Tigray. She has been involved in the administration of the area ever since and has been repeatedly elected as a representative to congresses of the Front. She fills in more details for us on the repeated assaults by the Dergue on Sheraro. I am full of admiration. When Berhanu communicates this to her, she looks at me sharply.

"I was not an exception. It was not a matter of a few people in the beginning. When an organization comes along and saves you from pain, relieves you from heavy taxes and oppression, then the support for it is massive from the first."

Later in the evening Berhanu finds a *krar* somewhere and sits in the corner of the courtyard playing and singing. Techana, Hagos, and a small crowd join him, contributing suggestions for songs and accompanying him with traditional rhythmic clapping. He sings several times one particularly haunting song.

"Berhanu, what's that song? I haven't heard it before."

"This song I am singing for Sheraro," he says. "It could be written for them—for the lions of Sheraro."

Later, he translates it for me. The first half of the poem recreates the violence of war made vivid with the details of a peasant farm.

Our beautiful bull has been slaughtered;
Our plow has been turned to ash;
Our faces burned with soot and smoke;
With bombs instead of seeds our yard is sown,
Our hay washed away to dam the flooded river.

But the women, whose voices we hear in the song, fight back. They have given their children to the revolution and their children are like lions who don't shrink from death. The last line rings into the night—*Yet can an elephant be killed if it is guarded by lions?*

That must be what is special about Sheraro. You can't see it or touch it, but you can sniff it everywhere—the spirit of resistance.

10

A Tale of Two Martas (and other tales)

Women are more than half this revolution, Berhanu says. They have had to come from further back; they have had more to gain. They will have more to lose if it all comes to nothing.

A woman came up to me this morning, as I was coming back from the river with Saba. She shook my hand, looked hard into my face, saying something briefly in Tigrinya.

"This is Kebbedesh," Saba said, "one of our teachers. She wants to tell you her story. She has had a very interesting life."

"I would be happy to listen," I said.

"You are lucky," said Saba as we continued along the path. "Kebbedesh does not tell her story to everyone."

In the early evening, Roman turns up. She arrives at Marta School on foot with other women fighters. This network of wooded valleys of the Kaza River basin is the Front's base area and includes political schools, army training camps, the music department, the main teaching hospital, and an orphanage, as well as the two special women's schools, March Eight and Marta. They all seem to be within walking distance of each other—not European walking distance of course.

"I've come from just up the road," says Roman, in response to my question, "only four hours walking."

Marta is named after a woman hero and March Eight after International Women's Day.[1] We have left it too late to see March Eight in action. We called there on the way here and discovered that, as half its students are peasant women activists, the terms are determined by the pressures of the agricultural year. We were only in time for the graduation ceremony.

We all eat together in Saba's hut. Kebbedesh is there and another woman called Genet who arrived with us last night. We were unloading baggage from the landcruiser with several other shawled and shadowy figures, when there were cries of joy in the darkness and Berhanu and this woman were laughing and embracing and talking together. They had both been prisoners in Mekelle prison and had not seen each other since. Genet had been released a good three years before Berhanu, but fearing rearrest had fled to Italy.

"She was only fourteen when she was arrested," said Berhanu, his voice cracking with emotion. "You must hear her story. It is really amazing."

Marta is stuffed full of stories. So many women gathered together, unpacking their lives. Marta herself is a story. Ever since I arrived, I've heard vague references to her life and her death. But, Saba has told me there were two Martas. The first was an activist in the radical student movement against the misrule of Emperor Haile Selassie in Addis in the early seventies. She was captured and executed with other students in 1972, after they had unsuccessfully tried to hijack a plane. The second Marta was the first woman to join the Front in its second year. In fact, her name was Kasu, but her comrades renamed her in memory of the first Marta. She was from a peasant family, but poverty forced her to find a job in a factory in Asmara, in Eritrea. There, she came in contact with women fighters in the Eritrean Front, then over ten years old, who put her in touch with the new revolutionary movement in Tigray. Although she was killed, in battle, in 1980 (Saba uses the word "martyred"), she has lived on ever since as a hero for both men and women fighters.

The small hut buzzes with conversation. People are crammed onto the benches round the walls and on the rock bed, their faces reflecting the glow of two candles. Berhanu and Genet are sitting with their arms around each other's shoulders, exchanging their life stories since they last met. Saba and Roman, old comrades, old friends, are deep in conversation. Roman, through her twin roles in the Women Fighters Association and in the Mass Bureau, plays a coordinating role in the Front's strategies for increasing women's participation; Saba has been Director of Marta since it was founded in 1983 after a congress of the Front decided women needed extra help to turn their paper equality into reality. Now they work closely together.

Kebbedesh crosses the room to sit by me. Berhanu stops talking and joins us. The time for story-telling has come.

Kebbedesh's Story

My family were peasants. I never knew my father—he was murdered by outlaws when my mother was pregnant with me. My mother faced many problems after his death. She was shocked and her health was not good. Because of her troubles she called me Kebbedesh, "a heavy burden."

After a while, my mother remarried. She left for another village but I went to live with my aunts. When I was seven, my aunts arranged for me to be married to a wealthy neighbor. He was rich and he was huge, with a beard. My uncles told him not to have sex with me. They made him promise in front of a priest that he would wait until I was mature, but this did not work.

I saw him for the first time inside his house. He was like a giant, like something that makes you afraid. At that time, I didn't know what marriage, being husband and wife, meant. After three terrible nights, I escaped back to my aunt's house. My family insulted me, shouted at me, "Why did you come back, you stupid girl?" They forced me to return.

After some weeks, I escaped again, this time to the forest. I passed several very difficult days. I was hungry and thirsty, and I wanted to die. I fainted and a peasant found me and took me back to his house. He knew me and knew my family were angry, so he kept me in his house. He gave me milk because I couldn't eat injera. After a few days, he took me back to my home. My family took me in, but then they tried to persuade me to return to my husband. They said he was rich and owned many cattle. They wanted me to go and live with him again.

They took me to him for the third time. I lived there for some months, maybe a year, but then I escaped again. I felt it was too difficult to live in the world. I took a rope and went to the forest to hang myself. A neighboring peasant who was tending his cattle in the forest found me standing under a tree. He was surprised and asked me what I was doing there with a rope. I told him I was collecting wood. He didn't believe me and tried to take me back to my husband. I refused to go—I said I was looking for wood.

After two days in the forest, I became so hungry that I returned to a neighbor's house. They tried to reconcile me to my family. When I was eight, one year after I was married, they made me return to the man they called my husband. He forced me to have sex when I was eight years old. I was sick for many days after that. I just didn't know what to do or how to help myself. All paths seemed closed. All the people in the area were against me. They said I should stay with my husband because he was rich. They couldn't see it from my point of view—they thought it was natural.

I continued like this until I was eleven, escaping and being returned by my family. At last, my mother learned what was happening to me. She came back to the village, divorced me from that man and took me away with her to her village.

But, once I was there I faced another problem. The people there insulted me. Because I didn't know my father, they said I was undisciplined. They said I was rubbish because I had been brought up by a woman. They said a woman could not bring up a child properly and that I was undisciplined to divorce my husband. They teased and insulted me. Things weren't easy for my mother either. She also felt shamed because I had left my husband. So, I decided to go to Asmara. A friend had come to visit us from Asmara, so I begged her to take me away with her. I was fifteen at that time.

But, when I reached Asmara I didn't like it. There was nothing for me there. After a miserable time, I went to Tessenei near the Sudanese border and got a job in a bar. In the bar, I was badly treated—men came and kicked me, spat in my face. They could do whatever they wanted. The bar owner was also cruel. She wouldn't pay me if I broke a glass. I worked there for two years but wasn't able even to buy any clothes. The male customers cheated me. They said they would give me money to pass the night with me, but after they slept they would leave without paying.

At last, some women came to the bar from Sudan. They had jewelery and good clothes, so I asked them about their life in the Sudan. They encouraged me to go there with them, saying I could have a good life. So I went to Sudan, after two years in Tessenei. I lived there for ten years. I rented a room and worked as a prostitute for ten miserable years. The life of prostitution is clear to you, so I don't need to explain it.

In 1977, TPLF members were trying to agitate the people in Sudan and to establish underground movements wherever there were Tigrayans. I became interested in this news. TPLF didn't need to politicize me—I had led a terrible life. No one knew more about women's oppression than I did. I became an active participant in TPLF activities and worked for two years with them. I learned sewing and then, in 1980, I decided to come to the field as a fighter. After I finished training, I was assigned to the workshop as a tailor. Then, three years ago, I was assigned here to Marta School. I am a student and I teach sewing. I am also a fighter.[2]

Kebbedesh finishes speaking. There is complete silence in the hut. She has been speaking in a low voice and Berhanu has been translating for me quietly line by line, but gradually all the other voices have died away until everyone is listening, although most of them know the story already.

Tea has just arrived. Roman takes a cup off the tray and presents it with great respect to Kebbedesh.

What does she think of Marta school, I ask.

"I feel proud and happy to be here. We are many women with different miserable experiences. We discuss our past lives all the time. This gives me a very special feeling. It makes me happy that I came both to learn and to teach. I feel happy to be teaching my sisters. They are illiterate and backward and they cannot yet understand their oppression."

She grows serious.

"In your country too I'm sure there are women like this."

She pauses to pass cups of tea along the row from the tray near the door, then looks up at me.

"So you and your comrades must struggle against this backwardness to politicize the people. You must make the people able to participate in the struggle."

Fortunately, the circulation of tea and the minor bustle of sugar and stirring makes an answer unnecessary. Conversation in Tigrinya resumes and gives me a chance to digest what I have heard. People here are not used to talking about themselves and this is particularly true of women. They have no habit of valuing their experiences or their emotions. Their stories are factual, terse, spare, lacking embroidery, or rhetorical contrivance. It is easy to miss the resonance. Yet, the more I reflect on it, the more Kebbedesh's account of her life gathers meaning.

Later that night, sleepless, I will offload my reflections into my diary:

Kebbedesh has shown me what life under feudalism was like, her father's death and how widespread bandits used to be here before the Front came. Lawlessness in an unjust and unequal society is another means to survival. What is the difference between armed bandits and the armed struggle? Both would give survival as their justification. The difference must lie in their practice. From the Dergue's point of view, Eritrean and Tigrayan fighters are "bandits" because all opposition to the government is "lawless."

"The bitter dilemmas of poverty become preserved in cultural practice. Sons were productive members of the family and through marriage could bring wealth into the household in the shape of oxen or goats. A girl was another mouth to feed and upon marriage would take wealth out of the family in the shape of a dowry. Marriage or prostitution? In both, women were commodities for sale or barter. Banditry and prostitution—the more

visible economic effects of an exploitative social and economic system. How much has this changed?

Here they see K. as a triumph of women's strength and as a model for fighters. In her story, a clear pattern emerges of refusal to submit to a life she doesn't want (although she's not clear about an alternative—how can she be?). A series of choices led to her seeking out the TPLF and becoming a fighter. A story about women, not one woman. It's also about her mother, perhaps barely out of childhood herself, widowed when K. was too young to remember. The poignancy of her name. No mention of siblings. If K. is an only child, that supports the theory of her mother's youth. Then, there are the aunts, turned into instruments of social pressure by an extra mouth to feed, by a society, which measured husbands in terms of the oxen they could provide, and by public opinion which regarded a child brought up by a single mother as "rubbish." In fact the prostitutes are the nearest we get to independent women—with their jewelery and "good clothes" and freedom to travel.

But sitting on Saba's bed, looking up to see the faces of women fighters shiny in the glow of candles, I am also aware of a context. Kebbedesh's story doesn't exist in isolation. She is telling it here in Marta school, on this bench in this hut, surrounded by women who have rejected the twin oppressions of marriage and prostitution and are working for ways of constructing more equal lives for women.

During my conversation with Kebbedesh, a package on the floor has been getting in the way of my feet. A plastic bag is knocking against my calves and everyone laughs when I look inside and find a football and a pair of trainers.

"It's Genet's," says Berhanu, "Genet's prize possession. Football is her passion. She even managed to find a team to play for in Rome!"

Genet takes the bag and stows it under her own feet. She looks different from the other women. It is easy to tell at a glance Tigrayans fresh from abroad—they are always much fatter. The stylish cut of her jeans and bomber jacket and her mop of wild hair make her stand out even more from the bone-thin women fighters. Several of them, including Saba, have heard Genet's story earlier in the day. Now they urge her to tell it again.

"Can I Have My Ball Back?"

I was always a good football player because I used to play at a Catholic mission. The trouble started about 1980 when the kebelle *Youth Organization*[3] *wanted me to go to meetings. From the beginning I didn't like it. I was thirteen—I told them I was too young but the guards forced me to go. At the meeting, there was a discussion about football teams and they elected me onto the women's team. When they forced me to give a payment, I gave them twenty-five cents as an insult. The next day they came to my home and arrested me. They took me and flogged me with a stick on my back, my knees, and arms. My parents tried to visit me but the guards refused to let them because I had scars. They were in tears. After two weeks, my elder sister begged them to release me, which they did.*

After they released me, I started playing football again because I liked it so much. I forgot about everything else and just played football. Then, the kebelle *asked me to carry water to the kebelle garden to help grow produce for the state. But, they had taken the land by force from my neighbor and he used to come to our house and complain to my parents. I knew it was his means of income, not extra land and I told the kebelle I would never take water to that garden.*

One day, when I was going to the well to get water, the kebelle guards saw me and stamped on my bucket, so I went home crying. Then, they came to my house and stole my football. This devastated me. They confiscated my football! The next day, I went to ask for it, but they insulted me and beat me and threw me in prison for four days. From that day, I declared war on the kebelle. I insulted them whenever I saw them. I would shout "you bastards" at them in the street. I refused to go to any meetings or to pay the subscription. That year, my eldest brother was taken forcibly from school to a training center for troops in Addis. I was beside myself with anger.

Two months after that, they arrested my uncle. He worked in Asmara for the Telecom Department; then he transferred to Mekelle. They accused a friend of his of supporting the Eritrean revolt. Under torture, this man named my uncle, so he was arrested. After a month, both men were executed. I went with my family to ask about him, to find out if he was still alive, but the guards said he had been taken somewhere else. This was how we learned he had been executed.

After that, my protest against the Dergue grew. One time, I deliberately quarrelled with the chairman of the Youth Association. He kicked a stone into my forehead, so I went to his house and threw stones through his window and kicked him. Then, they arrested me. They flogged and beat me again. My sister, who is ten years older than me, went and bribed the guards to get me released. She was my eldest sister, her name is Letensae.

I started my own protest movement, even more openly. Some of my family came from Samre, a TPLF area, so I had some idea about them. They tried to politicize me, telling me about the women fighters, their courage and their feeling for the people. I begged them to take me to Samre, but they said I was too young and told me to stay at home.

I started to write slogans against the Dergue and distribute them. The secretary of the kebelle was a neighbor of mine, and he looked after the kebelle seal. I went to his house and stole the seal and a pass paper. I stamped the pass paper and kept it. Then I wrote two slogan-papers and stamped them and then returned the seal to his house. I decided to distribute these slogans and then escape to the TPLF area. I went to the meeting with the slogans in my pocket. My plan was to ask to leave the meeting, then drop the papers and leave. I asked to go to the toilet. I asked a particularly brutal cadre, called Kebede, who killed many people in the Red Terror. He refused and told me to sit down and not to interrupt the meeting. I asked again, but he refused so I asked him if he couldn't even give me a potty, "The Red Cross have helped you so much with food and medicine. Why haven't they given you a potty to use?" This made him very angry. He hit me two or three times and then let me leave.

When I was outside, I put the two slogans by the gate and left. I went home and got ready to leave. I took a traditional manure sack, so I could deceive the guards. But, before I could leave, the meeting finished. The cadres found the papers and asked some children who had put them there. They told the cadres it was me and they went after me. When I knew they were following me, I went home and bolted the door. They demanded that I open the door, but I refused.

Then, my younger sister came back with a bucket of water. She asked me to open the door, but I wouldn't. She climbed over the fence and came in the back door. Then the military police came—they arrest people and are notorious killers and executioners. They came in their red helmets, broke down the door, and took me to the Central Investigation Department. This was in May 1981, and I was fourteen.

They asked me whose paper it was. I told them I didn't know, that I wasn't even a kebelle member so I had no access to the seal. They told me to tell the truth and confess, but I refused. So they tied my legs and hands together behind my back by a rope, which was tied through my mouth and around my head. I think they electrocuted me and I became unconscious.

The next day, I woke up to find my feet were swollen, my hands were scarred and my mouth was cut. The Lieutenant, called Habtemariam Ateye, a notorious torturer, came. He stood on my foot purposely. I could not bear it. This made my feet so painful. He made me suffer so much. After three days they took me and tortured me again. At the second time, there were three investigators. Their names were Tarekegne, Legesse, Teshome. When they were beating me, they kicked me in the head and made me unconscious. After that, they lowered me to the ground and put me outside. I lay there from ten in the morning until three. My clothes were covered in blood, and stuck to my neck. I didn't know what was wrong. There was blood on my ear. I asked the soldiers what had happened and they said I had internal bleeding because I'd been kicked in the head.

In the afternoon, the investigators found me and realized I had internal bleeding. This made them scared and they took me to the health center outside the prison. A physician checked me over, washed my ear, and gave me eardrops. I was escorted back to CID with four guards. When I returned, my mother was queueing outside waiting to give food to me. When she saw me, she was shocked and ran out to hug me. But, the guards hit her with a stick and pushed her back into the queue. We were both crying.

When I was back in prison, they asked me again to confess. I refused, and they waited to torture me again. I was afraid because of my ear, and my foot was in agony. So, I confessed that I was a member of the TPLF, although I wasn't, and that I'd written the slogans. But, I said the secretary of the kebelle and the chairman of the Youth Association had given me the seal on purpose [laughs]. They were taken and severely tortured for two weeks. I could hear their cries. Eventually, I felt guilty and told the guards that they were innocent, that I did it myself, I stole the seal. I wanted to show these two people the real nature of the Dergue, that was why I accused them. I told the investigators I had named them out of revenge, not because they were members of the TPLF, so they were released. Because I did this the investigators beat me.

I confessed I was working for the TPLF and I wanted to kill the Party Chairman and administration of Tigray. They said, "How could you do this? You are not militarily trained." I said, "Oh yes I am. I have a gun, and have been training in Kelaymino, five kilometers away. If you want we can go there." This made them very happy. Lieutenant Moftemariam and the Chief of CID, and Captain Fissehatsion, Head of State and Public Security (Secret Police) for Tigray came. They took me by car.

My plan was for them to take me outside Mekelle in the hope that I could escape and the officials would be arrested by the TPLF. Unfortunately, there were no fighters there. They said to me, "Where is the gun you have hidden?" I told them where to dig, but of course there was no gun. They accused me of trying to get them captured, but I said that since my arrest, fighters must have come and taken the gun. They beat me for this.

Then, they wrote everything on a statement: that I was in the TPLF, I had a gun, I tried to kill the Party Secretary and that I was signing of my own free will. Then they forced me to sign it. It was a very great crime, which I hadn't done. After I had signed the statement, the Head of the Tigrayan Police, Colonel Tilahun came. "You donkey, how do you dare to kill these people?" "You are the donkey not me," I replied. [laughs]. He was an Amhara and this is a traditional insult by Tigrayans against Amharas, but I meant it only against him; I said this in Tigrinya and he couldn't understand, but a Tigrayan official told him what I'd said. He was furious. He wrote that I was a very dangerous member of the TPLF and should be executed. Then, he signed the paper and left.

I was sent to the main prison, in Mekelle. I could not walk properly or sit because of the torture. I had to squat because of my back. I suffered for six months. I went to the clinic, but they didn't treat me. My ear was still bleeding and discharging but they didn't treat me. So my sister Letensae brought drugs from a pharmacy and smuggled them into the prison. I really thought the Dergue would kill me, so I didn't use the medicine. I thought it was useless. I just passed the time in pain. Psychologically, I had real problems. The investigators used to come at night, so I had bad nightmares. I would scream in my sleep, which worried the other prisoners.

My sister tried her best to get me released. She went to the CID Chief and other officials and tried to convince them I was innocent, that I was too young to be involved in politics. They went with my sister to the prison. They called me from my cell to ask me to tell the truth. I replied, "I did it. I am in the TPLF. I did it for the true line. Don't try to trick me, leave me alone." [laughs]

My sister was very shocked. She had begged for my release. She expected me to say I'd been tortured. In prison, I used to insult the guards and say whatever I believed. After that, my sister went to Addis Ababa, even though she was married. She spent three months there trying to get me released. She gave them bribes and did whatever they asked. After three months they said I would be released and that she should go back to Tigray.

They released me and took me to the Tigray administrator. This was after two years. I stood in front of the Administrator with my family. He said they were releasing me because I was so young. They wrote a statement saying if I did the same thing again, I would be killed. They made my father sign this instead of me. I said, "OK, but you have tortured me so severely I still have a head injury, you must write a statement on that, and say I will never go to your kebelle again."

After I was released, I had many problems. Spies were following me everywhere and I had severe headaches. Eventually physicians referred me to the psychiatric Hospital in Asmara. I went there and then returned to Tigray. My sister went to Rome to find a job. She sent me a document to enable me to get a passport, but it was confiscated when I tried to get a pass paper to leave. So, I went to Addis and bought a forged passport. I went to Rome—my sister paid for the flight.

In Rome, I had two months treatment for my head and body injuries and then I started working for the TPLF. Now, I have come back to Tigray. I have decided to train to be a fighter.[4]

I expect them to give admiration and praise, but Roman, although she smiles at Genet, has been shaking her head in rueful disapproval as she listens. Saba looks equally doubtful. They admire her bravery, but for them it is an example of spontaneous revolt without "political consciousness or organization." It is the same criticism they make of the *First Weyane*, the widespread peasant uprising against Haile Selassie in the nineteen forties. Genet's one-girl rebellion brought pain to her and suffering to her family, but achieved nothing for the revolution.

"We have had to make too many necessary sacrifices for the struggle," says Roman. "Not a single unnecessary sacrifice can be justified."

That the fighters' response to Genet's story is markedly different from their reaction to Kebbedesh is to be an important lesson for me in revolutionary consciousness. Individualism is not much help to a revolution. This comes home to me slowly, however. At first, I feel too overwhelmed by the story itself to take it in. Just as Kebbedesh's experience was about life under feudalism, so Genet's history gives a vivid picture of life in the Dergue towns. The many references to her sister, Letensae, ten years older but still so young, so unflagging in her efforts to free her little sister, are sparse on detail, but keep knocking at my imagination. I suspect they encode information well-known to Tigrayans.

"What do you make of the sister?" I ask Berhanu afterwards. "What does *even though she was married* mean? —and *She gave them bribes and did whatever they liked*?"

"It means she had to give her body to officials to get them to agree to release her sister. You know, many women have done this, in order to save their husbands or their fathers or their brothers. It is common under the Dergue."

"If it is common, does this mean their husbands will be understanding?"

Berhanu looks uncomfortable.

"I don't think so. Traditionally, men don't want to touch their wives after another man has.... Even if a woman is raped, she is usually rejected. We are trying to change this."

Later, going over the transcription, I realize I didn't need to ask the question—the answer was in Genet's story all the time. Why else would Letensae have left her family and gone to Rome? Once she was there, how else could she have paid for Genet's flight from Ethiopia?

Berhanu and Genet exchange some reminiscences about the time they were together in Mekelle prison, which reminds me of an encounter we had on our journey here. Waiting for transport with brigades of fighters fresh from the eastern front, we discovered they had been involved in the Agazi operation a year ago. It was my first opportunity to get an insight into the Front's military activities. Two commanders, whose field names were Meley and Anbessa, gave us the information and now we pass it on in a muddle of English and Tigrinya to the women in the hut.[5] Even Berhanu, himself one of the released prisoners, had not known the other side of the story and the women fighters here, knowing only the bare bones, are riveted by the details.

Preparation for the operation began many weeks beforehand. The Front knew from their underground informants in Mekelle the size and location of the garrison and that the feared 119th brigade were stationed there. Fighters in disguise were sent into the town as spies, even into the prison as visitors on Sundays. Two forces (about two hundred fighters) were sent into a remote area for training. It was heavily guarded. No one was allowed in and nobody was allowed to leave. First, they built an adobe replica of the prison, complete with cells and towers, the locations of the lights, the types of guns and their positions. They knew which gates and turrets were heavily guarded, where the fence would be cut and the exact timing and method of getting the prisoners out.

"We practiced every day," said Anbessa, "and every day we improved the operation. After a month we were ready."

The plan included a number of diversionary tactics in order to avoid the casualties of direct military confrontation. The main diversion was at a Dergue garrison about twenty kilometers from Mekelle, where there was a fortified trench built by the Italians. Meley's force destroyed several guardposts with artillery and, as forecast, the 119th Brigade was immediately dispatched from Mekelle. Then Meley's brigade, stationed at a strategic point, let the 119th pass and then blocked the road to prevent their return.

Meanwhile, the two commando forces were about to penetrate the outer defenses of Mekelle. These were the only fighters who knew that the real target was the prison. The guardposts were barely a hundred meters apart. It took an hour-and-a-half for the fighters to creep or crouch-walk, silently and one at a time in the darkness (I show them how Anbessa demonstrated this for us). By the time they had slid through, undetected, two separate forces were attacking the airport (up on the plateau above Mekelle) and a truck depot inside the town, destroying a hundred trucks. The commando fighters penetrated from the north and the force against the truck depot from the south. A further battalion was just outside the town, awaiting the first shot and staged an artillery attack on the 16th Division, which was still in the barracks in Mekelle. The Dergue forces were in total confusion.

There was a wall and a trench around the prison. When grenades had dispatched the guards in the four watchtowers, a few fighters scaled the wall and opened the main gate for their companions.

"The prisoners didn't understand what was happening," said Anbessa. "They thought it was the Dergue executioners. They were in a dream state."

The prisoners who had been supporters of the Dergue were caught between fear of the Dergue and fear of the Front.

"We surrounded the whole prison. They tried to run in all directions, but we got them together in one place outside the prison. We told them about the operation and that they would be safe with us, that no one would take them from us. Then we took them in two columns, guarded all the way along for security, into the liberated area. Some were unable to walk because of the torture or old age. Many were barefoot and could not be given shoes until we reached Samre, many hours walk away."

At Wajirat, meanwhile, Meley's brigade were still distracting the attention of the enemy.

"We wanted to make a dent in the 119th Brigade," he explained. "Some were killed and we took some prisoners and captured military equipment. There were very few casualties, even less than we expected. Then all the forces involved met together at Samre with the prisoners."

They made only two mistakes. The prisoners had dug a new shit pit outside the prison wall. The leader of one unit fell into it with a radio. Someone was left to get him out, but he didn't take any further part in the operation. The second mistake was more serious. Although they released fifteen hundred prisoners, in the rush of events one prison hut was overlooked, its doors never unlocked, its inmates forgotten. Meley and Anbessa tell me about the first, but not the second. It is two or three years before I discover it.

Early the next morning, Saba takes me down to the river to wash. We walk down through dried grasses glinting yellow in the early sun. Dotted among the trees and up the slopes are huts thatched with the same grasses and women moving between them, bent on serious tasks. Camouflage is doubly important at this time of year for the foliage cover is becoming sparse and dry leaves crackle under foot. At the bottom the water course is turbulent with boulders worn into wierd smooth curves, devoid of all vegetation, although the river itself is diminished to a tumbling stream forming occasional pools.

Saba is strict about washing at a distance from the river itself. She carries water in an old milk powder tin to a place in the rocks where the run-off will trickle away from the stream. Women fighters here are trained never to pollute the water source. I remember the shrinking pools, thick with dirt and soap, at the Front's headquarters at Dejenna and the accumulation of dead batteries, plastic and empty tins behind the tents. The fighters there, where you would most expect it, had not seemed conscious of pollution.

Saba shows me how to wash my clothes on a convex rock using trickles of water from the container. While we work we talk. I tell Saba about my work and my family; she tells me about her life as a fighter and about the school. The policy here is to train women fighters in self-reliance and in skills they can pass on to women in the villages.

"Men believe they are the only ones who can build houses or do agriculture. So we teach the women that they can live without men—they can build, make tools, plow the land themselves. Women can do anything men can do. Here, they learn it in practice. They build their own houses, kitchens, clinics, and stores. Some students weave shawls for other fighters. Weaving is a male skill in our culture as it is a productive activity. Women only cook and look after children."[6]

When Marta School was founded in 1983, the first intake of peasant fighters were all illiterate. It has taken four years to educate them to fifth or sixth grade. But now, there are other means for fighters to receive elementary education, so from this year they are switching to intensive one year courses and only admitting students who have already reached fifth grade.

"We have two aims," says Saba. "To produce skilled women fighters and send them to the mass. Rural women were dominated by feudal values. They have come to know their oppression, they want to struggle, but they need skills—home economics, rural science, health care, mother and child care, agriculture."

This approach challenges the direction taken by the women's movement in the West, which has been largely devoted to theoretical or political ends; only rarely has attention been given to providing the mass of women, as well as the middle classes, with the practical tools they need—hence the irrelevance of feminism to the lives of most women. Yet, here the central tenet of political analysis is class struggle, not the struggle against patriarchy.

"In Britain, as well as other places," I comment, "this argument is used by men and organizations on the Left to say that women have no need to organize separately. They say if you join the class struggle, the woman question will be solved with no extra attention."

"We do not agree with that—you must give special attention to women. In the class society we lag behind culturally, economically, in every aspect, so we have to balance that by organizing women in a special way to participate fully in society and in the struggle."

The lowland heat is shimmering off the rocks. Our clothes are dry enough to pull on and we start walking up the slope.

"Our second aim is to make women fighters more politically conscious, so they will understand their oppression and struggle consciously. They must know their question deeply and scientifically."

We spend the rest of the morning watching classes in action. The main teaching area is a wide dry river bed covered with pebbles and shaded by tall trees, the river bank providing tiered seating for the students. Four classes are in session: sex education, science, home economics, and rural development science. At other times, they also learn agriculture and nutrition, plowing, soil and water conservation, politics and the woman question, psychology and human relations, Tigrinya and poetry.

"The main aim," says Saba in my ear, as we stand at the back of the sex education class, "is to teach women to understand their bodies. In our culture, men considered menstruation as abnormal. Women would try to hide it. They are still not allowed to enter church at that time. We try to teach them it is normal and something to be proud of. They also learn all about conception and pregnancy and birth control. We also emphasize hygiene and preventive measures against disease."

Lack of resources means that the only birth control method available to the general population is the safe period and that is what they are learning here, although contraceptives are given to fighters. The courses are designed to be relevant to the conditions of life in the villages and to emphasize the development and improvement of rural life within the practical resources available and in keeping with local culture. Home economics is not about cooking, so much as managing resources. The Front is trying to dissuade the peasants from extravagance after harvest and on feast days or at weddings and to teach them if possible how to eke out their grain until the next harvest.

At the end of the morning, we return to Saba's hut. A young fighter is sitting on a rock outside cleaning her Kalashnikov. After a few minutes, she invites me to sit with my back against her knees and patiently goes through my hair strand by strand picking out lice. She has noticed me scratching.

After *injera* at lunch time, we sit drinking tea in Saba's hut. It is oppressively hot and my eyelids are sagging, so that I barely register an unknown fighter who comes in and takes her place beside me. Then, alerted by silence, I realize everyone is looking at me. Their eyes flicker, smiling, from me to my neighbor.

"Don't you want us to introduce you, Jenny, to this new fighter?" Saba asks.

I look quickly at the stranger and it is a second or two before I recognize Genet. She is so changed. Her wild hair is clipped short. She is wearing the fighters' uniform of sand-colored trousers and slimline shirt. She looks neat and disciplined.

"Genet!"

The other women burst out laughing. They think my failure to recognize her a great joke and so does she. This is the first stage of her transformation into a fighter. She departs tonight for the training camp. I forget to ask whether she will take her football with her. I hope she keeps some of her free spirit.

Most afternoons, about four or five, women stream along the tracks to an assembly in the school hall—the usual tiers of earth "benches" hidden from the sky with thatch and open to the sunlight at the lower end. They have talks and debates here, and question and answer sessions to check their absorption of their lessons. One afternoon, I watch Roman leading a session on women's health. She uses as a teaching aid diagrams of the uterine area made out of colored cloth in the fashion of a banner. Paper and card are difficult to find and in any case would not survive the rainy season. The women are leaping from their seats in their enthusiasm to answer her questions. At the end of the session, they ask me to address the students myself. I talk about the things I have learned since I arrived in Tigray. I talk to them particularly about the young woman, Leteberhan, who impressed me in Owhie and how the contrast between her confidence and her mother's careworn shyness had been a vivid image of the changing times for women.

Everywhere I go, I am asked political questions and become involved in political discussions. Marta School is no exception. The questioners are always friendly. They seem consumed with interest in the world they have never seen, as if their growth of political consciousness through their revolution has been also a growth in every kind of awareness, as if the existence of an outside world has only just come home to them. One day Saba asks me if I will come to the hall for a "conversation" with the students—a rather daunting prospect as there are more than three hundred of them. The session starts off slowly and gathers momentum. They are bursting with questions of such huge significance that it is difficult to know how to answer them at all:

"What is the nature of your struggle?"

"What is your relation with the proletariat?"

"What are the aims and character of the women's struggle?"

"Who is leader of the revolution in Britain?"

I have been asked versions of these questions before, but it is easier to deal with them one-to-one or in small groups and easier then to trim your words to the understanding of the questioner. It is not simple to explain how power operates in a Western parliamentary democracy, the existence of forces much more powerful than democratically elected representatives, the lack of accountability of those representatives, the lack of participation of the electorate in decision-making. So, what are we doing about it, they ask. This leads on to the divisions in the working class and the multiple strands of the women's movement. So, what are you doing about it, they ask.

"Tell them about Greenham Common[7]," says Berhanu, to whom I have told some of my experiences earlier in the eighties.

"Yes, tell us about Greenham Common," say Saba and Roman, who listen to the BBC World Service.

So, I tell them about Cruise Missiles and the women's camps and dancing on the silos. I tell them about the new ways of resistance evolved by women, effective in a Western democracy, but not in a dictatorship like Ethiopia— ways of subverting, through ridicule, authority that is abusing its power. I explain the effectiveness of the strategies of non-violence against supposedly democratic but in fact non-accountable and militaristic Western powers—the women's use of song and dance and laughter to provoke the police and the military. Instead of Kalashnikovs, I said, the women had bolt-cutters and no threats or punishments could stop them breaking into the base. On one occasion, the women secured the main gates of the camp with a heavy-duty unbreakable lock (locking the missiles and the army *in*!) and then filmed the police trying to break into the gates themselves with ever-larger bolt cutters, while chains of women danced and sang their mockery. Another time I was present at a court hearing when the women defendants sang all their replies like a comic opera with their supporters acting as the chorus, so that the trial had to be abandoned. If they were sent to court, they ridiculed the proceedings because they did not accept its authority. If they were fined, they would not pay and had no money anyway. If they were sent to prison, they staged roof-top protests and politicized their fellow prisoners.

I explain how we were organized in small "affinity" groups who trained together. Once we were up before High Wycombe Magistrate's Court on my birthday and my affinity group organized a birthday party inside the courtroom. All the supporters carried bouquets. The police and the Bench had been instructed to be relaxed. They decided to accept the flowers, so every policeman had a daffodil in his buttonhole and there were potplants all along the bench. When it was my turn to be sentenced, a cake full of lighted candles began to wobble its way from the back of the courtroom.

"Remove that woman from the court!" cried the magistrate. Margaret was hustled out, but not before she had passed the cake to Sian.

"Remove that cake from the court!" screamed the magistrate.

It nearly reached me that time. Then, in the confusion, my daughter slipped past them up to the dock and gave me a huge brown envelope. I opened it and held it up before the court. It was an enormous photograph of the birthday cake. Even the officials were laughing. I was sent to the cells for contempt.

Finally, Roman and Saba, Berhanu, the assembled students and I too, are all so convulsed with laughter that the meeting is forced to break up. We go back to Saba's hut to drink tea while I ask myself how I could indulge in an exercise so inappropriate to a serious armed struggle in a country with no respect for human rights. Next morning, Berhanu joins me at breakfast and his shoulders start to shake so that the spoon chatters in the tin cup.

"I have slept very badly," he said. "I was so tired, but I kept thinking about your stories and laughing all over again."

11

Singing their Own Songs

My stay in Ethiopia is nearing its end. Suddenly, I am restless to see my family. My colleagues at work must be restless to see me, but as there are no phones and no post in rural Tigray, I can only guess. It is also nearly the end of February. February 18th, the twelfth anniversary of the revolution has come and gone, marked by some smuggled Italian beer and a few songs. There has been no sign of implementing Meles's promise (made on a recent visit to Dejenna) that I could "go to the people" and celebrate the anniversary with them. Berhanu is not to be drawn on this score. I stay on at Marta school for a few days longer. Roman goes away; then we go away. In this country, in these wartime conditions, whether you meet people by chance or you meet people by design, you touch hands fleetingly and are whirled away, unsure whether chance or design will ever bring you together again.

But a few days later, after visiting the central training hospital and interviewing wounded prisoners of war, we return again to Marta. Unexpectedly Roman comes back on the same day. It feels like a homecoming. In the evening I start talking to Roman about the nationalities issue. This is perhaps the most fundamental and obdurate problem facing Ethiopia.

For some time, it has been niggling at the corners of my mind that I have not been getting to grips with this "nationality question." It is not so much that I have not been getting the information as that I have been ignoring it. In a *baito* meeting I attended in Sheraro, on land reform, there was a fierce debate on the Kunama people, one of the four minority nationalities in Tigray, the Tigrinya nationality being the majority. The question was whether to exclude Kunama land from redistribution on the grounds that Tigrinya landholders had already eaten up most of their traditional lands. The *baito* finally voted to accept that reparation must be made to the Kunama, but not before heated arguments had exposed some of the divisions within the community. Although I was present for these discussions, at the time I had not seen their significance.

Ethiopia has over eighty distinct ethnic and language groups. No one seems to know exactly how many. A final count has never been made. Since the Tigrayan Emperor Yohannes was succeeded at the end of the last century by Menelik, the Amhara King of Shewa, who annexed the territories south of Abyssinia and so created the modern boundaries of Ethiopia, the Amhara nationality has dominated the ruling elite. They "solved" the problems of multiple nationalities by enforcing an official unity on the different regions. Amharic has been the official language ever since and other languages and cultures have been downgraded or suppressed, at least for all administrative, legal, or official purposes. In particular, their fear of Tigray, so I have been told, has led to a punitive attitude to Tigrayan development, particularly since the uprising against Haile Selassie in 1943. As a result, Tigray is one of the most economically backward provinces of Ethiopia. The military coup in 1974, through which the so-called Marxist-Leninist regime of the Dergue succeeded the dictatorship of the Emperor, did not alter the pattern of domination and repression. Tigrayans seem to regard that as merely a "palace" revolution.

Nationality is an issue, even within Tigray. Not only is the "national oppression" of the Tigrayans by the central government a major issue in this civil war, but the Tigrinya speakers themselves have a history of dominating and exploiting the four minority nationalities in Tigray, the Afar in the east, the Kunama in the north west, the Irop in the north east and the Agew in the south.[1] In Sheraro, close to the traditional Kunama homelands, long-term Tigrayan oppression of the Kunama people is a hot topic. The Front is trying to persuade the population that if they are justified in fighting for freedom from Amhara domination, then they should be critical of their own history of discrimination against the Kunama, a people with a traditional culture very different from the Tigrinya-speakers. Hence, the debate in the *baito*.

Eritrea further complicates the issue. The long struggle for independence, which began after its illegal annexation by Haile Selassie in 1962, is represented by the Amhara elite in Addis Ababa as an issue of Ethiopian unity. It is domino theory. To allow the right of secession of Eritrea, they argue, is to risk the total disintegration of a country composed of so many different nationalities. Where would it stop? In addition, they say, how could they continue their economic life, landlocked, without access to the Red Sea?

The Front, on the other hand, supports the right of the Eritrean people to determine their own future and a twenty-five year old war first against the Emperor and then against the Dergue seems to suggest quite a degree of determination. The Western media tend to reflect Addis Ababa opinion, which brands the TPLF also as secessionist (this allegation is regularly stated as fact on the BBC World Service), although the members of Central Committee I talked to in Dejenna, as well as their representatives in London, all deny this. In conversations with me, they make a distinction between secession and self-determination. They say that every nationality, in Ethiopia, has a right to self-determination *up to and including secession*, but they are convinced that, if repressed nationalities were to be granted cultural freedom and relative regional autonomy, they would not see secession as in their interest. I know the theoretical position, but I don't know enough about the different cultures to understand and weigh the problems, which would face any future government willing to relax the repression.

On our way here, we changed to a truck at Tekezze crammed with a brigade of fighters straight from the front line in eastern Tigray. During one of the stops, a fighter called Adam came to talk to me. He was on his way to the Propaganda Bureau where apparently I had met his brother, Hassan. (Berhanu: "He has saluted you three times—why can't you remember?") Charming and interesting, he described his work in Afar territory, the slow persuasive strategy and how it appeared to be working. The nomadic Afar culture, he said, is so distinctive, so different from the culture of Tigrinya speakers, that it represents the strongest challenge.

"Why should you want to change their culture?"

"In fact we don't, if it is possible. Our aims include self-determination for all the Ethiopian nationalities and their cultures. We believe this is the right of the people and they fight more strongly if their resistance to domination is based on their culture. But, we also want to end hunger and exploitation and some cultural traditions are not helpful for this. But, it takes a long time to build this political consciousness. They must decide for themselves to change. Nothing lasts that is done by force."

I asked for examples of things the Front would like to change. The Afar people, he said, were among the most affected by the recent famine and thousands had died of starvation. The Front was trying to persuade them to introduce limited land cultivation alongside their nomadic stock-grazing traditions so they would be less vulnerable to droughts. The second aspect of their culture that could not be accommodated was their attitude to and treatment of women.

Roman promises to give me a briefing. Her job in the Mass Bureau gives her some responsibility for nationality issues, especially aspects relevant to women. She doesn't appear until late at night when I have already given her up.

"We do so much of our work at night," she apologizes. "There are long meetings. It's often the only time for planning—or for discussion and self-criticism. We all have our other duties in the day."

She catches me in a yawn.

"Are you too tired? Do you want tea? You know, we women must struggle —or nothing will be achieved, nothing will change."

This word *struggle.* I've heard it often from women in Tigray. Again and again village women tell me, "the only solution is *struggle*" or urge me to describe the *struggle* in my own country. It's inspiring when you're tough and strong and on top; but when you're dog tired or sick and discouraged... I strenuously deny I am tired.

I want to hear about the Kunama and the Afar peoples, the largest of the minority nationalities in Tigray. How different are they, I ask, from the Tigrinya-speakers and from each other? I've heard that the Kunama culture is matriarchal—is that true?

"The Kunama nationality have remnants of the primitive society in their culture and their marriage customs. It's different from the Highland culture of the Tigrayans. For example, they don't mind if they give birth to a boy or a girl. They see both of them equally. But, among the Tigrinya speakers, if a baby is a girl they know they have to give a dowry when she gets married. Before the revolution, they assumed her to be a problem and we still have remnants of this attitude now.

"The age of marriage among Tigrinya-speaking people before the revolution was eight, nine, ten, but among the Kunama it was different. If a girl is fifteen or she has started menstruating, the mother builds her a house in their compound, meaning that she is an adult, she can stand by herself. So, after the appearance of menstruation, she goes to her house and youngsters, young men, come there and dance every night. After the dancing, she can choose one of the youngsters and have him with her. If she wants it to last, to marry him, the boy will stay till early in the morning. When the mother goes to check and finds somebody, she knows her daughter has chosen a partner. If she doesn't want him, she will send him away early in the morning before the mother comes. So, this is very different from Tigrinya speakers."

The candle sputters and needs to be renewed. The cassette is nearing the end, so I change it anyway. After the break, we start to talk about female circumcision. Clitoridectomy, Roman says, has been widely practiced throughout Tigray, although the Front has tried to discourage it. It has been condemned in the *baito*, but no punishment had been set as yet; they are trying to change it through education, not compulsion.

"Conscious people are no longer doing it," she adds.

The Afar are a different matter. They practice pharaonic (or total) circumcision.

"When a girl is born, her vagina has to be sewn up. This is to control her when she goes to tend the cattle when she is a little kid in order to avoid kidnapping or rape, although it does not in fact control these things. When they marry, the man is forced to tear the sewed part. It is a problem for men too, but their culture teaches that it shows the man is strong. They accept it and even the women see it as a good thing. Even after her marriage, she has to be sewn up again and when she gives birth it is going to be torn again. Some of the Afar girl children suffer from infections. Some of them die from infections."

"What can you do about it, Roman?"

"First," she says, talking quietly into the candle flame, "we have to convince the Afar that the Front is a positive force. We work to gain the confidence of men by discussing their aims and their program; we work on distributing the land. Only after do the women, following the example of the fighters, want to go and talk about their problems."

"So, what have you managed to achieve?"

"Now, we are at the stage when we can gather women separately and teach them something in general about society. We've got a constitution. At their conferences and in their meetings they condemn infibulation and circumcision. Some people are not practicing it now. But, some of them, especially the older women, are not accustomed to going without sewing their vagina. They feel something is wrong with them. The men said at their conference that it was a real problem for them, the fear that penetration might take three days or longer—it is very hard for them too."

She stops and looks towards the door. We hear steps outside. A woman looks in to tell Roman her transport has come. She stands up.

"One last thing: most Afar women are attracted to our cause because they see women have got land by the struggle, they have got some freedom. The age of marriage is now fifteen, like in the rest of Tigray, instead of nine or ten, and when a woman is divorced she gets a hundred and fifty dollars. Before, she got only fifteen dollars. Especially the meetings and the age of marriage—these things attract them."

Eysa's Story

Afar culture is a problem for women. When we are children they sew our labia together and then tie our legs together with a rope. This happens when we are seven or eight days old or if the girl is very small after forty days.

The most important thing is the culture of marriage. Most Afar women marry between eleven and fourteen. If someone wants to marry, they have to give money to the woman's family. We are treated like commodities—first they buy a bride with money and then they have to buy her jewelry and clothes.

Before the wedding time, the bride is forced to enter a room full of smoke. She cannot breathe but she has to sit there because it is meant to make her beautiful. She sits there for a month without moving, allowed only to go to the latrine. She cannot even use her hands to eat, someone has to feed her with a spoon. This makes her very thin and pale. Her bones become frail. Her nails grow very long. All this is thought to be a sign of beauty.

Our dark night begins on the wedding night. It's very difficult for me to talk about it. They decorate our nails with a kind of ring, which goes around the nails in a spiral. When we fight with our husbands on the wedding night we are afraid our nails will be broken and we will lose our beauty. So, we submit. Also, the smoke makes the bride very weak and unable to fight. It is very hard for the men too; if they cannot penetrate they are ridiculed. It may take a month and all this time it is torture for the girls; all this time they fight. They don't know anything about sex, why this is happening to them.

Before the revolution, young women discussed these things, especially about marriage and the wedding night. They had some idea about this and the problems in the house, overwork and so on. Some of them tried to escape to foreign countries, like Saudi Arabia, or join the Eritrean Liberation Front. Some committed suicide even before they were married. Others decided never to marry, but they were forced.

A middle-aged woman is also in a very bad situation. Whenever she bears a child, it makes her vagina wider and it has to be stitched again each time. They discuss these things, but they have no political analysis; they only see it as natural. Old women accept it as cultural law and as legal. If they hear younger women complaining they say, "Why are you complaining? We've been through this, and so must you."

Another thing is eating. The woman has no right even to drink water in front of her husband. If they go to a wedding ceremony, she cannot eat or drink while he is there. If he leaves, she tries to eat while he's gone. Even in her own home she has to cover her face with a shawl when she takes him food or pours him water to wash his hands. If he wants, he can leave her some food. If not, he finishes it all up. She cannot eat alone, so if she is hungry she has to go to a neighbor's or invite a neighbor to her house to eat.

Another problem is that women have to play the major role in creating the family wealth. We have to carry water on our backs for very long distances. In our village, it may take four hours, on average, to get water. We have to go to market to buy everything, even our husband's cigarettes! Most of the markets are in the central highlands so we have to travel one or two days. Then there is a house we use called senan ari, made of mud. Women have to make these houses. Men don't do any labor. They just come at ten for a cup of tea, then at lunch, and again at tea. We look after the cattle, fetch water, cook food. The men just comb their hair, clean their teeth, and wear good clothes. They do not work at all.

The wealth of the household is built by the women. But, women have no right to divorce. Only the husband, or occasionally the bride's family, can call for divorce. If the two families quarrel, they may make the couple divorce, whether they want to or not. At the time of divorce, a woman can take only her clothes and the goat or cow her father gave her on her wedding night. The father gives her husband double the amount of cattle at the wedding time, but even if they breed she can take only the same number she herself was given. Her husband gives her only fifteen birr.

One reason we joined the TPLF was because of all these things. We realized we would have to face the same things as our sisters and mothers. When I first saw fighters around my home I was surprised. When I saw women with the men fighters I was more surprised! I had never seen women fighters before. The fighters were not able to speak Afar so I can't say they gave us deep political education about their aim, but I understood from their behavior that the women were equal with the men. The men cooked their food; the women cooked their food. Men spoke at the associations and so did women equally. The men had guns; so did the women fighters.

I am the eldest daughter of four. My family is middle class. Their stand towards the TPLF was uncertain because my homeland was newly liberated. In our land, women are seen as half humans. Afar women had not even the right to see their husbands fully. We had to cover our faces. When I saw women fighting for their liberation I felt inspired.

There were five of us who decided to fight. I didn't tell anyone. The fighters were nearby, but we couldn't express our feeling because of the language barrier. We went to the maize farm and stayed for several days keeping the birds away. Two fighters, Iyassu and Adam, made contact with us. We discussed everything and they agreed that if we wanted to struggle, we should. They said we would have to go that night. So that night, we got up silently and made it look as if someone was sleeping in our beds. Then, we crept away. I was thirteen when I left home in 1981.[2]

The next afternoon, when the sun is low but there is still brightness in the sky, we set out on foot for the music department. It is somewhere in the Kaza River basin, three or four hours walk away on the flat. I am sad to leave Saba and the women at Marta School, but the blow is softened somewhat when a group of students insist on accompanying us to make sure we don't get lost. What's more, they insist on carrying all the baggage. Berhanu reluctantly gives in after losing a tug of war over my backpack primarily because he is incapacitated by laughter. They have never seen a backpack before. They try various ways of carrying it, but prefer, in the end, to carry it on their heads.

The walk passes too quickly, filled with jokes and laughter. The countryside slips into twilight and darkness; a huge moon slides up the sky. They start singing the rousing March Eight women's song and other songs of the revolution. As soon as one song ends, someone starts up another. Suddenly, in a moment between songs, we hear distant sounds of music and drums mixing with the chirp of tree frogs over the warm still air. It is strengthening at the end of a long walk; it feels like a welcome. In fact, it is a rehearsal by a cultural troupe and by the time we have covered the last kilometer and jumped the stepping stones across a confluence of streams, it is already breaking up. Our companions must return at once and after warm goodbyes they turn to cross the river again. I stand with Berhanu at the water's edge watching people streaming through the trees, but the dim deceiving moonlight filtered through leaves makes identification difficult. I forget that I am easy to see, that I glow in the dark.

"Jenny!" calls a voice. "Where have you been? We've been expecting you for two days."

It is Iyassu. He comes out of the trees with Jon and Cathy. Why didn't I see them before? They glow in the dark too. Hugs and handshaking all round.

"The car didn't arrive yesterday, so we walked tonight."

Iyassu is head of the Cultural Department. Jon and Cathy are English musicians, who are working for six months with the main cultural troupe, teaching musical notation and techniques for playing instruments like keyboards and electric guitars. I met them recently at the March Eight graduation ceremony where the cultural group had put on a show. It is good to meet up again.

"The EPDM[3] cultural troupe is here," Iyassu says. "We are having a special concert tomorrow night. I was worried you would miss it."

I had forgotten the impact of his personality. It is not just that he is exceptionally tall; it's as if he gives off a continuous vibration of energy.

Ahead of us is a high steep hillside, almost a cliff, shrouded by immensely tall trees with dappled trunks. In between, a river flows over stones and boulders, wide and strong for the time of year. It is crossed precariously by a combination of stones and slim saplings, but I have just that degree of tiredness where the conscious mind is in abeyance and I am perfectly coordinated. We climb the path to Jon and Cathy's house, where I am to stay. It has been specially built for them on a shelf carved out of the incline. As we drink tea, sounds of the *krar* and the *tchirra* drift through the open doorway. It feels different from anywhere else I have been in Tigray. I catch a sense of openness and freedom.

Iyassu is telling me about the visiting cultural troupe. EPDM is the Ethiopian People's Democratic Movement. They are an Amhara liberation struggle operating south of Tigray in Wello and Gondar. Their democratic aims and program of social rehabilitation are so similar to those of the Tigrayan Front that I asked Meles when I passed through Dejenna recently whether they had or were considering a united front with EPDM. He said they were as close as it was possible to be without having a united front; there remained some small points of difference, so not at this stage, maybe in the future.

Still influenced by media allegations of Tigrayan "secessionism" and "narrow nationalism," I ask Iyassu whether the Amhara performers meet with prejudice in Tigray because of their nationality. I also remember Genet using "donkey" in her story as a traditional Tigrayan insult for Amharas.

"Formerly," Iyassu replies, "we considered all Amharas our enemies. Our people used to say even the poorest Amhara, although he is poor, his heart is dangerous. But we don't now—we believe only the exploiters are our enemies. So, now we sing in Amharic; we dance Amhara dances. This is an important preparation for when we move outside Tigray to Wello and Gondar, and especially when we take captives. When we are explaining our program to them, we need Amhara revolutionary songs."

"But how do you teach the mass of the people that there is a difference between the Amhara ruling class and a poor Amhara?"

"It's included in all our political education for the mass and for the fighters—in schools and in the mass associations. Also, through our cultural work."

This is what I have come here to learn. At our first meeting at March Eight, Iyassu started to explain the fundamental importance of this cultural work to the process of the revolution, but we were interrupted. Now, again, this social gathering proves not to be the right moment to pursue a serious topic.

In fact, I want a chance to get to know Jon and Cathy better. There is a feeling of wonderful refreshment at the prospect of talking to compatriots after a long stay in a foreign country where you are inevitably on the outside. But I am more cautious now. Ironically, the only place I have felt loneliness in Tigray was at Mai Hanse where my experience of the aid workers there was so different from my expectations. Jon and Cathy seem straightforward, friendly, and without self-importance. They have only been here three or four weeks and will leave before the rainy season cuts off access to the border, at the end of June. Cathy has developed a teasing jokey relationship with Iyassu. It is obvious they all get on well with each other. She rallies him about how hard they have to work—long hours teaching classes under the trees followed by practical instrumental sessions until late into the night. Iyassu sprawls his long legs in front of him and smiles lazily. But, I too have been astonished at how hard the fighters work, with so few breaks.

"They expect the same from us, I suppose, as from themselves."

"Exactly," says Iyassu.

The conversation swiftly passes from classes to music, to Iyassu's poetry, to the importance of preserving traditional instruments against the invasion of Western culture.

"What do you think, Jenny?" Iyassu asks.

I confess to being totally addicted to the *tchirra* and to dreading the obliteration of unique Ethiopian musical cultures in the tide of cultural imperialism.

Everybody laughs.

"No, she is right," says Iyassu kindly. "I agree in fact. But, all our young fighters listen when they can to Addis radio. Even on our mountains, far away from towns, our musicians are influenced by the popular culture of the West. They want to play electric guitar instead of *krar*, keyboards instead of *tchirra*, and Western drums instead of our traditional drums. So, we encourage both together."

He turns to me with a serious expression.

"Do you know, Jenny—we were so happy when we made our cassette of revolutionary songs. We distributed it widely to all the fighters. Do you know what they did with this cassette?"

His voice rises to a humorous squeak.

"...They taped over it Amharic love songs off the radio!"

I tell them about the last time I broke my journey at the Front's headquarters in the mountains. The four of us—Berhanu, Techana, Hagos, and I—were clambering down steep paths by the light of half a moon. All sight and sounds of the camp were blocked by the rocky buttress of the mountainside, until the moment the path turned a corner and we were suddenly confronted by a bizarre scene. Two hundred meters down the slope, a huge cinema screen was blinking away in front of a silent audience of several hundred fighters. On the screen, singers in sophisticated Western dress were singing Amharic love songs in exotic flowery locations in Addis Ababa.

They held the audience rapt. We picked our way over legs and feet and sat down among them for a few minutes. The Addis on the screen looked so untouched by war, so twentieth century, so Western. I resented it. Nobody else did. They loved it. After a while Berhanu and I went on to the camp, leaving Hagos and Techana mesmerized by the moving image.

"But it is a problem, you know," says Iyassu. "So many fighters are joining us. They miss their families, their wives, their children. We must provide entertainment and relaxation—in the middle of nowhere, in the mountains!"

The next morning, we are jerked awake by shocks and vibrations through the hut.

"Those bloody monkeys!" Cathy's voice growls from the depths of her sleeping bag.

Apparently, the local monkeys regularly pelt the intruders with rocks and stones. There is shouting. Above us, I hear the trees swaying and creaking as if in a high wind. Then, there is a loud report followed by total silence.

"Oh no, they haven't shot them?"

Cathy leaps off her bed, pulls on her jeans and rushes out of the hut. I hear her haranguing someone. She is furious.

"It's against the rules," Jon says sleepily. "They're not allowed to fire at any old thing. Besides, it's a waste of ammo."

I've heard about the monkeys in Kaza, but these are the first I've met. Curiosity drives me out of bed.

Outside, Cathy is taking to task a knot of fighters. One or two look slightly downcast, the others amused. The body of a large grey monkey is huddled on the ground nearby. Its companions are nowhere to be seen. I get a strong impression of confrontation between two cultures. I remember once, in London, sitting with a group of Tigrayans talking about British political culture.

"In England, they've only got as far as the Animal Liberation Front!" one had commented.

The others all fell about laughing. I had found it funny too.

Cathy is warm and extrovert. By contrast Jon is so relaxed, he scarcely seems to have bones in his body. They are both very attractive. I admire Cathy because she stands up for her own wishes without losing a sense of humor. She refuses, for example, to let the fighters blow their noses through their fingers onto the floor of her hut, rubbing it into the dust with their sandals. I realize I have become inured to this over the months and no longer notice it.

However, over breakfast, it emerges that their experience of Tigray is confined to music and personal relations in this department, that they know little of the aims and practice of the revolution and nobody has thought to inform them. I noticed this before with aid workers. Both REST and the Front tend to put *ferenjis* in categories and then confine them to the categories, whereas visitors would be much more sympathetic if they were given the opportunity of seeing more widely and judging for themselves. I have taken this up more than once with Central Committee members:

"You take such trouble with your prisoners of war," I said, "treating them humanely, teaching them all your aims, allowing your practice to speak for itself—because you know they will be your best ambassadors. Why don't you give foreign visitors a chance to be ambassadors? If they understand the context, maybe they will be able to see in perspective the occasional requisitioning of their cars."

I give Cathy and Jon an idea of some of the things I have seen and learned, the working of the *baitos*, changes in the position of women, health clinics, and so on. Cathy lists some possibilities to add to their program. They are particularly interested in my interviews with Dergue prisoners of war, a few days ago.

"The start of their political education seems to be knowing who is your friend and who is your enemy. They teach not only their own fighters but even Dergue soldiers that the enemy is the elite, not the poor peasant."

Comradeship and respect for Amharas with similar problems or objectives have been confirmed by Jon and Cathy's experiences here with the Amhara cultural group. Yet, I have been doubtful about some of these claims. I was told, in London, that fighters only kill their adversaries if they have to; that they give first water, medical aid, and food to wounded prisoners of war, before their own fighters; that after three months of political education on the objectives of the revolution, they release the prisoners and give them three choices: to return to the Dergue areas, to go as refugees to the Sudan, or to stay and fight with the Front.

"Can you blame me for being skeptical?"

Experience now inclines me to believe that the Front has a genuinely humane policy—perhaps, like so many of their policies, the result of enlightened self-interest—but I still find it hard to believe in its implementation. Yet, I have met Amhara and Oromo fighters, here, who were originally captured soldiers and have been told there are many more. In the hospital, the prisoners were side-by-side in the same wards with wounded fighters. They seemed relaxed and friendly, but could of course have been making politic statements. None of the prisoners I interviewed wanted to fight for the Front, although one or two said they might in the future. They were all young, had all been forcibly recruited from schools and market places and to a man they wanted to go back to their farms in the Dergue-controlled areas to see their mums.

Cathy and Jon go off to their "classrooms" beneath the trees. I spend the morning interviewing Iyassu and other musicians. From the first, the Front believed that to fight successfully, to have their hearts in the struggle, the people had to recover their self-respect lost through long oppression. They had to reclaim their cultural identity, use their language with pride, sing their own songs as part of their fight for liberation. The cultural group has provided encouragement and example. Each musician I talk to has arrived at this point by a different path. Gedamo is a peasant and weaves into his plowing songs the warbling calls and whistles which farmers use to their oxen. Others have been shepherd boys and play the bamboo flute. Tartarow came to music in his earliest childhood through liturgical songs, because his father was a priest in Axum. He is one of the Front's most respected poets and also the creator of one of my favorite songs, a poignant expression of exile and longing for home of the famine refugees in the Sudan. Accompanying himself on the *krar*, he sings it for me in his gravelly voice, caused by a bullet in the throat, eight years ago.

I will go back to my home
And grow wheat.
Another's country will never be
As your country.
Another soil will never be
As your soil.
Famine has parted me from my country
For too long.
How can you spend your life
In another's homeland?
How can you, sound of body,
Be a parasite?
We are forced to live against our will
By another person's gift.
Famine has confused the intelligent
And made blind those who can see.[4]

Iyassu himself comes from the provincial capital, Mekelle. It is still under Dergue control, so it is many years since he has seen his family. Like many families in the towns, they are politically divided—some support the Front, others the Dergue. Reticent about his own background, he prefers to tell me about the importance of culture to the struggle for liberation, illustrating his story every few moments with bursts of song.

Iyassu

Even before the revolution, there was a hidden culture of resistance. Even if a society can't read and write, it does not mean it doesn't have literature. It has an oral literature: a lot of sayings, a lot of poetry. There were resistance songs even against the big feudal lords. There was a very big prince here in Tigray called Ras Mengesha and before him his father, Ras Seyoum. Ras Seyoum was leading a war against he Italians in Eritrea. In the valleys between Ethiopia and Eritrea, there is a big river called the Mereb and when they reached the Mereb the warrior Tigrayans wanted to continue into Eritrea, but, without telling them, Seyoum turned back to his castle. The Tigrayans, assuming that their leader was with them, fought on and there were a lot of casualties. When they heard that Ras Seyoum had retreated long ago, then they made their own song:

What big shoulders, Ras Seyoum!
Because he was afraid,
He left us in the middle of the river,
In the middle of the fight.

The people of Tigray knew the character of their princes. Imagine this, before the revolution! Even then, students were mobilizing peasants to sing songs. You can really identify people by the songs they like. You can understand the real feelings of the people, not from the songs sung for the feudals, but when you hear the peasant behind his door. Then, you really know what's going on.

Then, we began to hear the revolutionary songs of our revolution. People were singing:

She is red, she is very red,
She is down in Hazemo, the red lady.

You can understand that "red" means revolution. "She is down in Hazemo" means the revolutionary sons of the people are down there starting a revolution. It's a kind of code. The people have two types of speaking; one is the normal kind, the second is called kinea, *a word with two meanings. It seems to be about a lady, but when you "open" it, the whole thing is about the revolution. When you "open" the words, they insult the exploiters—we have a lot of words like that.*

We were very few in the revolution at first. We were all in the cultural troupe then, because everybody was interested to sing Tigrinya. You had to walk ten hours a day with only one drink even in the hottest areas. You did not have a chance to wash yourself for a month or to cut your hair. We were almost naked. We had lice. But, that was the time when we felt very happy and very free in our free nation. When we reached somewhere, we sang songs. There were only a hundred or so of us then, with very old fashioned guns, but everybody was happy. We really understood the meaning of culture and what part it plays in the revolution.

To teach people new ideas, it's very hard. They have to use their own culture, their own language. They don't know anything about what struggle means by itself. In our culture, if someone has a gun and stands against the government, he is called a bandit. They don't know the difference between banditry and revolution. The people having power has never been seen before in Tigrayan society. So, when we tell them that we are going to overthrow the Dergue's government and have power in our own hands, power of the people, they can't imagine it. They had an expression, "Each morning, a new sun is our sun." It means "If a king or a prince comes, no matter who comes to power, it's all the same for us. Nothing we can do will change anything."

If you tried to tell them something directly about the revolution, they wouldn't believe it, because a peasant, no matter what you want him to approve, has already learned the opposite from his experience. So, when we taught them about the tactics of guerrilla fighting, we told them it's like the dog and the flea. The flea jumps on the dog's back. The dog starts scratching. Then the flea jumps to another place. Soon, everywhere there are fleas. They suck his blood and the dog becomes skinny and in the end, it will die. In the end, it's only because they see the revolution is very powerful that they join and feel that it's "their" revolution.

So, one of the first departments was the cultural department. At first we didn't have a single instrument, no amplification, nothing, only people. Then a group of them wrote a song and asked a local bamboo flute player to play with them, and they accompanied him on the mogogo*—the griddle we cook* injera *on. And so we made a cassette of our first song,* Dewel tede wilu:

The bell is ringing
For the Revolution.
The big bell is ringing.
Rise up, all you people!
Stand up for your rights!
Take up your arms and fight
Against the oppressors.

And we had some other songs, too. All sung by the fighters and the peasants were playing the bamboo flute. Marta, the first woman fighter, sang a story about women and the revolution, her first song:

Women! Get up off your knees;
We knelt beneath the feudals' rule;
We were only speaking tools.
Now we as well as men have guns
And one day we'll be free.

This was the first time the Tigrayan people had a cassette of their own music. Meanwhile, the Dergue were importing Western films and fashions. They didn't want the students to be politicized or to participate in the revolution. But, although the towns were under the Dergue, the TPLF were working underground. So, everybody was roaming here and there to get hold of our cassette, just so he could hear something about his nation and his struggle. The national sentiment is very strong. It's our music, already in our blood, under our skin. Though the political meaning is there, it's the music itself...it hurts. It breaks down your heart.[5]

There is a football match in the afternoon, but I am struck down by a headache so severe that, when two doses of painkillers have failed to shift it, I convince myself I have meningitis. I have been taking my health for granted, so it's a bit of a let-down. From time to time, figures come into the shadowy hut to take my temperature and study my symptoms in case it is malaria. Iyassu comes and holds my hands in his.

"Jenny, what can we do for you? You must be better for tonight!"

Eventually, I sleep and feel better and the cool darkness after nightfall restores me even more, so I get up and go to the concert after all. I am not quite myself, however. This time, crossing the river to the arena clearing, I keep falling off the stepping stones into the water.

An evening of songs and dances brings me back to life. The best dancers and musicians from the cultural groups of the Tigrayan and Amhara Fronts have come together for this concert. It is my first experience of Amhara dancers' astonishing technique of rhythmic shaking of shoulders and breasts and the leaps and twirls of the Kunama dancers, athletic in the manner of breakdancing, could not be more different from the restrained and dignified Tigrinya style.

The songs that have become familiar on journeys with Berhanu and Techana I now hear sung by well-known singers with full instrumental accompaniment. The audience, roused to admiration and tears by little plays and mini-operas, show their appreciation by going up to the performers. Without money to tuck into their clothing, they wind scarves round their necks or stick biros in their hair. They embrace and kiss them, while the singers try to keep their balance and look unmoved.

In the middle of the program, Iyassu comes to the microphone and makes a speech in Tigrinya. Suddenly I hear my name. Then Berhanu is prodding me to my feet and I go to the stage to receive from him a present of traditional embroidered women's clothes and a *tchirra*, their national instrument.

"These are the clothes worn by our old mothers," he says, first in English and then in Tigrinya. "We have great respect for our old mothers in Tigray. They are foremost in supporting our revolution and we call them *adey woyenti*, mothers of the revolution. You have come to our country from a distant place to see our struggle with an open mind. You have shared our difficulties and our dangers. This is how we think of you, *adey woyanit*."

I don't remember what I said in reply, something no doubt about my impressions and experiences and I mentioned Leteberhan again, the "new woman" I met in Owhie. But, I do know that in the overwhelming moment I forgot to say thank you for the presents.

"Tonight, we leave," says Berhanu, on our way back through the trees.

"Oh? Where are we going?"

I had been hoping to have longer discussions with Iyassu about subversive peasant songs.

"We are going to celebrate the revolution with the people."

"Berhanu! So it's on!"

I had assumed the celebrations were already over, that for mysterious reasons I was not allowed to attend.

"But I told you, we stagger the celebrations in different places over two or three weeks to confuse the spies of the Dergue."

"But I've made arrangements to talk to Iyassu tomorrow."

Berhanu tells me that Iyassu and the cultural group will be going to the celebrations too.

"Where are they being held? How far do we have to go?"

"That I can't tell you."

But it's over the mountains again anyway. While we wait unsuccessfully for transport in Mai Humer, Berhanu goes down with malaria again. So I leave him in the truck depot office to come on later by car with the gear when the chloroquine has begun to take effect. I set off on foot in the baking afternoon for the Tekezze River with a Spanish journalist, his guide and others going to the celebrations. The truck-tire sandals I am wearing soon rub my feet into blisters. The river is only half-an-hour away, but we walk another tantalizing half hour along its bank, sizzling and dripping with sweat, before finding a place to bathe, I upriver from the others as usual. They must have forgotten about me, because, wallowing blissfully in a foot of water, I suddenly see they are nearly dressed and they set off across the river before I can pull my clothes on. Rushing after them, limping and angry, I am soon twice as hot as before. Typical male behavior, I tell myself sourly. Berhanu's courtesy, which I have come to take for granted, must be the exception. Perhaps, I am ready to go home.

Still not sure of our destination, I begin to suspect we are drawing near to the celebration site itself. We have left behind the shrubby scrubby vegetation of the river bank for a region of tall trees, the space beneath their arching branches as cool as a nave. As we go deeper into the forest, unusual numbers of people are making their way through avenues of trunks. Now, we come upon banks of *injera* stoves pulsating heat under thatched awnings and peasant women in flowered dresses and carefully braided hair pouring out creamy batter. Towers of finished pancakes are already stacked on trays, ready for the rush. Peering into oil drums three rows deep, I inhale the heady smell of local beer.

Our share of delicious food is brought to us in the hut appointed for visitors. Marco, the Spaniard, is having trouble with his stomach; I am trying without much success to doctor my blistered feet. How feeble we Europeans are! But, at least we have prophylaxis against malaria, I tell myself, when Berhanu joins us after dark, looking weak and pale.

When it is nearly time for the celebrations to begin, we walk a quarter mile to a huge amphitheatre under the trees. Thousands of people are already crowding the terraces and, above side screens of woven grass and banners, chains of lightbulbs send flickering shadows across the mass of faces, punctuated by the vertical strokes of Kalashnikovs and farmers' staves. We squeeze in to join Cathy and Jon, about a third of the way up. They have a note for me from Iyassu who cannot be here after all. In front of the stage, I recognize members of the cultural group who are warming up the audience with Western keyboards and electric guitars before the speeches begin.

The speeches begin. One representative after another comes up to the microphone, from political organizations, from nationality groups like the Kunama, from mass associations. There are solidarity messages from supportive Tigrayans in exile and from sympathetic foreign organizations. I notice that the Amhara front are given a prominent place in the speeches after Tigrayan organizations, but that the Eritrean front appears to be absent. I had heard that relations are strained. Unfortunately, my Tigrinya is not good enough to understand much of the speeches and Berhanu can give only the barest outline. My concentration is also affected by nervousness, for Berhanu has warned me that I also will be expected to speak, but, when my turn comes, I take inspiration from the unselfconsciousness of all the other speakers. I suspect that for the Front, the substance of the evening is over with the speeches, but for me the highpoint is the program of songs, dances, and plays. When the visiting EPDM cultural group demonstrate their songs and dances the audience explode with clapping and ululation. Then, at two o'clock in the morning we go back through the black night to the hut to sleep.

But, Dergue spies have done their work. Soon after dawn three MiGs fly low overhead. Like vultures, they circle and return. For half-an-hour they bomb and strafe the Tekezze valley. Leaping into action straight from sleep, running, dodging and weaving, pausing to hide only when the planes are immediately overhead, I follow Berhanu to a dug-out where we stay for the rest of the day.

Half-an-hour or so after we arrive, a fighter clears a space among the spades and sacks and makes a bed of blankets on top of plastic sheeting. Four more fighters arrive, supporting between them two village women, wounded by shrapnel. One of them is Leteberhan from Owhie. In a curious coincidence, we had met earlier, crouched together with a party of peasants under a tree, while the MiGs roared over our heads and bombs rocked the ground. I had run on, but the blast had caught them where they sheltered. The fighters from the medical team dress their wounds and give them hot sweet tea and painkilling injections. They will wait here until nightfall makes it safe to transport them to the hospital.

Leteberhan opens her eyes and smiles at me. I remember the beauty and clarity of her expression on our first meeting. Now, she just looks exhausted.

How is she feeling? (Oh, the uselessness of words.)

"*Dehan*," she says. "Well."

I have made this woman special, turned her into a symbol, spoken of her three times to large audiences, making her and her mother representative of the aims and progress of the revolution. Now, events have twisted our paths together again, first under the bushes, now during this long day of pain and reflection. The reality and mystery of her presence defies the use I have made of her.

I spend the long day thinking and writing. I wonder how my companions of yesterday reacted. Marco left already in the night and would have been out of range. Berhanu comes to tell me that John and Cathy had a narrow escape. They survived, but all their belongings were caught in a direct hit. I have been under fire. I have run away from bombs. For Western readers, this experience will validate my time here. If I were writing a book, I could start with this sensational and vivid event. It would engage the reader, confirm all the usual expectations about revolutions—the brutal interchange of war, passive populations victimized by the lust of warring factions for aggrandizement. What a distortion.

These bombs are curiously irrelevant. They don't change anything. Neither fighters nor peasants pay them more than incidental regard. I get a sense of the necessity of the military war as a facilitator of change, but the real revolution is elsewhere. It is constituted, not in cataclysmic moments, but in an infinite series of small steps effected first in the hearts and minds of the peasants and then taking shape in the decisions of the *baitos*, in land reform, in anti-discrimination laws, in local health centers, and literacy schemes. It has taken years to persuade the peasants to redraw their vision of the future. Now, they seem to be pursuing it with wholehearted determination. The importance lies there.

The older woman's wounds are less serious. Her name is Awatash. She comes from Adi Abo and knows Kudusan and is Leteberhan's companion only through this accident of war. She encourages the younger woman.

"Be cheerful," she says, "men and women can only die. What is that? If the struggle is to be successful, we must make sacrifices. We must be prepared to sacrifice ourselves."

Disconcerted by the difference between her words and the kinds of mealy-mouthed reassurance I would have given in her place, I realize that for them, this is a common occurrence. Leteberhan shivers, perhaps from shock, perhaps because it is dank and cool in the dug-out. I am powerless. Why them and not me? All I can do is add my shawl from Iyassu to her own thin blood-stained robe to help keep her warm and murmur *Awat na hafash* as I leave.

Later in the day, we move to Haddish's house nearby in the Tekezze Workshop. He lays blankets on the floor for us to rest. For two nights, we have had little sleep; this morning was emotionally and physically exhausting and tonight we will have to climb up the mountain of Min Minay again as the first stage to my catching the convoy back to the Sudan. We wake every hour or so, look willing and then keel over, asleep again. We're all in the same state. Berhanu and Hagos are as tired as I am. Techana has disappeared.

There is only one car, so when it comes, late as usual, we relinquish it to the two injured women and a third casualty with head injuries. Now, we can relax. Haddish comes to talk to us. He is a man who would stand out in any crowd, not only because he is unusually tall, but because of an intelligent sensibility in his face and bearing, which is borne out in conversation. He greeted me last night at the celebrations, remembering my name from my visit to the workshop some weeks ago. What did I think of the morning? he asks. I try to express my sense of sharing, of pain, that so sensational an experience for me is routine suffering for them, but I am hampered by the inadequacy of words to convey without pretentiousness things that feel momentous. He shrugs his shoulders.

"It is our common experience. It becomes clear that Tekezze is one of the most routinely bombed areas. Nothing is damaged. They drop the bombs at random. They know it is a strategic area, but they don't know accurately where anything is. They nearly always miss. There are three casualties this time, no deaths. It makes no difference. We get on with our work. It is the work that is important. The bombing, the oppression, just strengthens the spirit of the people."

Haddish questions me about my experiences and says they should be collected into a book. The only Western writers who have commented on the revolution have their information from the Dergue side and have never been to Tigray.

"We want a book that gives the history," he says, "and a real insight into the condition of the people. Written from life. What it is like for the people and what you feel about what you have seen."

Would I like to go to a meeting? he asks. What sort of a meeting? I'm not too keen, but the habit of work is too strong. It turns out to be one of the best decisions I have made. We walk through the pitch dark up and down rugged paths back to the arena of the celebrations, now bereft of banners, slogans and decorations. Last night, it was crammed with fighters and peasant representatives, with the cultural group and formal speeches, an official celebration. Tonight, it is the peasants' own part in the anniversary celebrations. The men wear a variety of hats of cloth or straw, or new-washed *gabis* round their heads. They carry curved crooks of polished pale hardwood, the badge of their life on the land. The women are in their best clothes, mostly ragged and worn, their hair new-braided. Gold-colored ornaments and bunches of threads adorn their ears and necks and their babies are a bump beneath their shawls.

Fighter electricians are fixing up an amplification system for the *tchirra*. The seats are filling up. As they come in, unpretentious but dignified, it's hard to believe the peasants ever accepted such oppression. Their look of contained calm suggests to my romantic imagination, overworking since the drama of the morning, a nature tempered like the rock that makes up most of Tigray, which, jagged and fragmented, makes even working their fields a routine hardship. The evening starts with poems and speeches. These are short and to the point. Yesterday, representatives from the districts nominated a drafting committee. Their suggestions are now read to the assembly before being taken back to the villages for discussion and amendment. They are resolutions to strengthen the *baitos* and the militia, to support the Front by building a war economy, to implement the new land laws. Finally, I notice with interest, they pledge to support "our organizations's call for a united front," presumably with the Amhara movement, the EPDM. If this happens, it will be a significant political move and suggests the Tigrayans are anticipating the expansion of the revolutionary struggle beyond Tigray into Amhara areas.

The dancing begins. No Western instruments tonight. The *tchirra* has pride of place, then the *krar* and the bamboo flute. Each district has its own dance, all similar to the uninitiated eye, and each subtly shuffling circle has its own leader and the leaping drummers keep the beat for the whole assembly to clap to. This is dance as community ritual. It is impossible to describe because it eschews extravagant movements or virtuoso gyrations. Its effect depends on a sense of energy repressed, of a kind of dignified passion beating beneath the skin and barely kept in check. Or is its power in the sound, the strange haunting notes of the *tchirra* and the undecorated, unchanging, heartbeat resonance of the drums? However difficult it may be to record, it is easy to enjoy and makes a fitting send-off.

At midnight, we leave them dancing to hitch a lift on a truck to Min Minay. Three days later, I cross the border to the Sudan.

Part Two

Second Journey

May to July 1989

12

Walking on Eggshells

> Mekelle has been like an egg. The shell has been so hard to break through, but there is life inside.

It was not an easy matter to get back to Tigray. There is no room for bystanders in a war zone and the difficult journey over the Sudanese border precluded anyone from going in who did not have a pretty good reason. I began to accept the probability that I might never return unless there was something definite I could contribute. I would have to be content with watching events in Ethiopia from the sidelines, as much as poor communications and minimal press coverage would allow.

I had left Tigray with much of my ingrained skepticism overcome by the sheer weight of their conviction that they would win the war. In the colder light of England, this began to seem a rosy-tinted improbability. The Front's press releases, which reached me from time-to-time, had slogans stamped across them—*Victory is ours!* or *Victory is certain!* My own uncertainty grew by the day. Ethiopians, in London, who had never been behind the lines charged me with bias when I reported what I had witnessed. English people were reluctant to accept perceptions of Ethiopian people, which contradicted the images of famine they had been fed by the media. Once, I was accused of "celebrating violence." Media coverage, too, reflected Western cynicism about revolution and social change along with a preoccupation with stereotyped perceptions of Ethiopia and Africa, which conflicted with my own experience.

However, although everything I wrote or said about Ethiopia seemed to be against the grain of mainstream opinion, I received support from colleagues and from those agencies who regularly sent their representatives into Tigray to work in the liberated area with REST. I had travelled out of Tigray to Khartoum with Stephen King of the Catholic agency, CAFOD, a sensitive and perceptive man who respected the efforts made to improve the lot of the peasants. He was impressed by the material I showed him and hoped it would be published. Aid workers from Christian Aid and Oxfam, although occasionally troubled by the Front's revolutionary rhetoric, had also been impressed by the practical social changes in Tigray and REST's concern for the welfare of the people.

Some of my work had appeared as articles, but much of the best material —life stories of women like Kebbedesh and Genet recorded at Marta School —remained unpublished. I began to sort it out for a book focusing on Tigrayan women, not as a matter of feminist principle, but as an investigative tool. Women had been the most disadvantaged and oppressed sector of Ethiopian society under feudalism, so listening to their views was one way of finding out whether the claims of the Front to be changing conditions for the mass of the people had any substance. Colleagues supported the idea and in 1989, when it was nearly completed, I returned to Tigray to fill in gaps and gather updated material before publication in the autumn.

I had arranged with the REST office, in London, to leave in midwinter. There were delays. "The military situation. It's not safe," said Habtom, REST's representative in London. As usual, there were few explanations. The news over the last few months had been mixed. During 1988, the Front had begun to put serious pressure on Mengistu's forces. They had even gained control of some of the main towns like Axum, Adwa, and Adigrat, but withdrew from most of them when MiG bombardments made their tenure more of a punishment for the people than a release. At the same time, there was publicity of drought, locust swarms, infestations of army worm and impending famine. More recently, however, there had been reports that a series of battles had made real inroads into the Dergue's remaining power-base in Tigray. With equipment assembled and backpack packed, I waited through January and February and wrote the history chapter for the book.

In January, I received the news I had been expecting for over a year. The Tigrayan and Amhara liberation fronts (TPLF and EPDM) had at last formed a united front. The new Front was called the Ethiopian People's Revolutionary Democratic Front (EPRDF). More acronyms. I groaned at the thought of the extra difficulties this would create for anyone attempting to communicate Ethiopian politics to the West. News consumption depends on being able to serve up the info in small palatable soundbites. "Palatable" means no acronyms and confirming rather than challenging the existing prejudices in the public mind. How could I say, "The EPRDF is a coalition of four organizations—TPLF, EPDM, OPDO, and EDORM?" Oh, the yawns of editors, let alone readers. The new coalition *was* composed of four organizations, in fact, two of which I had not heard of before. One was an organization of the Oromo people, the largest nationality in Ethiopia in the southern half of the country; the other an association of former officers of the Dergue army, mostly captured in battle, now working with the opposition forces to bring down the Mengistu dictatorship.

This news was a vital turning point. It finally gave the lie to persistent allegations that the TPLF was secessionist or nationalist in a narrow sense. It challenged also my own slide into skepticism. Here were Tigrayans, Amharas, and Oromos working together in a multinational organization for a democratic Ethiopia. Outside the new coalition, however, were what seemed countless factions of Tigrayans, Amharas, and Oromos, all giving different diagnoses of Ethiopia's ills, counseling different remedies and offering counter interpretations of latest events.

During February, the stories began to trickle in. The Dergue was being forced out of more and more towns. The list of victories was accompanied by chilling statistics of dead, wounded, and captured, although according to custom the Front gave no figures of their own casualties. Then, in nine days of engagements from February 19, the huge garrison at Endeselassie was wiped out and the 604 Army Corps and several divisions, some thirty thousand strong, were destroyed with massive taking of prisoners. On the 27th, the Dergue abandoned the capital Mekelle and retreated from Tigray altogether. The Front had achieved the impossible. They were now in complete control of Tigray.

I finally flew to the Sudan in May. The journey over the border was easier in some respects than before; in some ways, more difficult. The blow to Dergue power of the loss of Tigray had brought about a temporary lull in MiG surveillance, so although the convoys were still going by night, the drivers were more casual about driving in daylight at each end of the day and, once they reached the central highlands, they could now join the all-weather roads built by the Italians in the thirties to connect the major towns. The only trouble was that it was now so late in the season that the early rains had already fallen in western Tigray and the huge trucks kept getting bogged down in several feet of mud and had to be towed out by the even huger Russian trucks, which accompanied the convoy for the purpose. The main rains were due to start in June. How I would ever get out again? Would I, like several aid workers I had heard of, be cut off by mud until October?

Nevertheless, there was a tremendous sense of relief, security, even celebration, on the convoy. Tigrayan exiles from the Sudan and Saudi were already streaming back home to restart their lives in towns now free of the Dergue. One of them was a friend of some years standing, Solomon Inquai, an Ethiopian academic in Britain who had not been back to his birthplace in Tigray for some eighteen years, since in fact the last years of Emperor Haile Selassie. He would be visiting his family, in Axum, and touring Tigray for a month, assessing the main aid priorities for REST, the Tigrayan relief organization. After the convoy, we shared transport as far as Mekelle. Our first stop was at a fighters' training camp at Atsrega to talk about our different requirements with Gebru Asrat, whom I had met before at the Front's headquarters in Dejenna and who was now Commander in Tigray. He promised to facilitate my program and gave me a briefing on recent developments.

Solomon's presence was a real bonus. He became interpreter for useful interviews on the way, introduced me to his family and old friends, once we reached the towns and was a constant source of information. But, his despondency was increasing daily and in Axum it reached a peak. Axum was the ancient capital of the Axumite Empire and is still the sacred city of the Ethiopian Orthodox Church, the seat, according to believers, of the true Ark of the Covenant. Even for non-believers it is a treasure house of archaeological remains and priceless manuscripts and paintings. For Solomon, it was the place where he grew up and the present home of his brother's family. This, his first chance to return for eighteen years, was a devastating experience.

"It's gone back to ancient days!" he cried.

Although no supporter of Haile Selassie, Solomon was overwhelmed by the contrast with Axum as he remembered it. Its deterioration became an image of the days of the Dergue. The houses were decayed, the roads broken up and he saw in the people's failure to maintain or whitewash their houses an indicator of their demoralization. Axum had been famous for its goldsmiths and gold filigree work, for the variety of its handweaving. There was nothing left. Solomon seemed despairing and suddenly uncertain of the Front's ability to reverse the economic situation.

The Tigray of this visit seemed a different country from before. The townspeople, economically dependent for so long on food and supplies flown in by the Dergue, had developed a psychology of dependency, in contrast to the self-reliance I had encountered among peasants in the countryside. Most of the salaried workers, like teachers, civil servants and medical staff, had fled with the Dergue. Many of those remaining showed symptoms of psychological disarray from their long experience of forced passivity under state terror and their continuing sense of powerlessness. In interviews, people showed, on the one hand, genuine relief to be free of the constant threat of brutality in the streets or torture in prison; on the other, they saw no reason to trust the

Front and were deeply imprinted with Dergue propaganda. They were used to the yawning gap between the benign rhetoric of the Dergue and the brutal practice. Why should the new authorities be any different? The main anxiety of many I talked to seemed to be to placate the new masters. Apathy was a way of life. With dull eyes, the people waited for the fighters to feed them and tell them what to do. The months I had spent with peasants and fighters in the countryside two years earlier began to seem a golden dream.

I learned most about life under the Dergue from interviewing prostitutes.

"The troops were out of control," Berhan, the laundrywoman at the hotel, told me. She was in her mid-forties, an old woman by Ethiopian standards, and as wrinkled as a springtime apple.

"They went around the town and knocked at every house for sexual need. Even myself—they knocked at my door and when I refused, they beat me."[1]

Disorderly troops in these garrison towns had forced many women into prostitution as their only means of survival after rape. It was the same story in all the towns, but in Endeselassie, where the largest garrison was stationed and the problem most acute, it was hard to find a woman who had not been forced at some time and, as traditional culture decreed that a woman who had been interfered with sexually, even involuntarily, would be rejected both by her husband and the community, prostitution had often become the only means of support for these women and their children. Wives whose husbands had joined up as fighters or were absent Dergue soldiers were particular targets, but according to women I talked to no woman or girl was safe.

Others did not get off so lightly as Berhan.

"They did terrible things," Yomar told me. "My friend was selling *sewa* one day. A soldier came over and asked her to meet him. She refused, so he returned later and threw a grenade into her house. She was killed and her mother was wounded."[2]

Yomar and Rahma came to see me together. One was sixteen, the other twenty. Both had been married at thirteen; both had a child. They were dressed discreetly, their heads covered by traditional shawls and their eyes downcast. They had many similar stories to tell, confirmed and duplicated by the many other women I interviewed.

"One day, a soldier came to this woman's house and asked her to spend the night with him. He gave her twenty birr, so she slept with him. After that, he gagged her mouth and shot her with his pistol and took her tape recorder and jewelry."

"They would arrest your brother," said Yomar, "and when you went to visit him in prison they would ask you to sleep with them. To get your brother released or stop his murder you had to choose whether or not to give your body."

Many women acquiesced to secure the release of family members and their continued compliance was ensured by threats of rearrest. I remembered the story of Genet, the football player, that I had recorded at Marta School and how her sister had eventually obtained her release at the cost of her own marriage. I thought also of the months I had spent two years before, travelling with men, sleeping side-by-side with men, free of sexual harrassment or even considerations of gender, liberated into comradeship. My own sense of pleasure and freedom, compared with Europe, had been echoed by peasant women who were experiencing freedom of movement for the first time in their lives. Was this the same country? I had heard reports, but never had them confirmed, that the Front, unwilling to risk any disruption of trust between peasants and fighters, had used summary execution of offenders to enforce this disciplinary code. Baffled by contrasts, I cast out my earlier uncritical assumption that Tigrayans were not as other men.

Women were reluctant to admit they worked as prostitutes. Their stories always applied to friends and neighbors, never themselves. I didn't think Yomar and Rahama were prostitutes; Heshe, my new guide, disagreed. They wanted their photographs taken. When they returned a day later with their friends, I hardly recognized them. Adorned for the camera without shawls, with straightened hair, shiny short dresses and plastic earrings, I realized in this Tigrayan context Heshe was right.

At the hotel, a woman called Abrahet worked in the bar. She had the elegant features and erect posture characteristic of northern Ethiopian people and her beauty was emphasized by a reserved and dignified manner. I learned she had only been working in the hotel for a month, so I wondered how she had got by before. When she was making the coffee ceremony for Heshe and me, I asked about her life under occupation and, although reluctant to talk at the hotel, she invited us to her house for coffee the following day. I had been told that all bar women could safely be assumed to be prostitutes, but again I found it hard to believe, which no doubt was more revealing of me than Abrahet.[2]

I arrived before Heshe and had time to look around while she prepared coffee and *injera*. The room was small with a bed and two chairs, apart from the little stool on which Abrahet sat to cook. I sat on the bed and played with her two year old daughter, Rosina. There were photographs on the wall, which would never be seen in conventional households, of men in heart-shaped frames and two hand-colored drawings of hearts pierced with pencils. There were several banners with Tigrinya inscriptions I couldn't read, but two in English read "Love is the salt of life" and "Truth and Love are one," together with religious decorations and Westernized Christian emblems such as the Sacred Heart. Four or five other women were also living with their children in similar rooms around the courtyard. They kept popping in to say hello or to borrow or return knives and other implements. These women, whose way of life debarred them from conventional society, were joining forces for mutual support.

One day, I went with Solomon up into the hills around Endeselassie where last February's battle had raged, the battle that, taking the long view, turned out to be the turning point of the civil war. As we approached the area, we came across increasing numbers of military vehicles randomly stranded on and near the road, some blocking the way so completely we had to bump over the stony fissured ground to avoid them. Most showed signs of fire; some were blackened and burned into mere hulks. Tanks littered the fields and hillsides. Like sinister wounded beasts, they were abandoned at odd angles or tipped backwards into gulleys with their gun barrels pointing at the sky.

The Dergue had ordered nine brigades out of Endeselassie to move on the TPLF who were still hanging on in Axum. But, at the point in the hills when they were strung out over a wide area, they had been ambushed by the Front. The detritus of the battle extended over several kilometers and we drove from one point to another, getting out several times to take photographs. We had to watch our feet because of unexploded shells and bullets sprayed over the ground. We walked about in the quiet sunshine from tank to burned-out truck. It was a curiously sanitized experience, like viewing the skeletons of dinosaurs in a vast open air museum. Missing were the bodies, the blood, the stench, the screams of the wounded.

The Dergue had inflicted maximum damage on the towns before their evacuation, destroying the electricity-generating and water-pumping stations. In Adigrat, they had set fire to the clinic and in Endeselassie they destroyed—deliberately, I was told—an ammunition store absurdly sited next to a clinic full of their own wounded soldiers. I walked with Heshe through the dusty run-down streets to see what remained of this atrocity.

On the left hand, two ruined and roofless buildings faced one another across a huge yard. A litter of metal debris from a depth of a few inches to three feet stretched right across the yard and out onto the access road to our feet. It was the mangled remains of thousands of weapons and ammunition —shells, anti-aircaft bullets, metal ammunition cannisters for AK47s, grenades, bullets of all kinds, some still unexploded.

"Watch your step," said Heshe.

But we couldn't watch our step. There was nowhere else to put our feet, so we shuffled through this sinister parody of autumn leaves. To reinforce the point, leafless trees stood next to the path, charred and topless trees lined up in grim attention, all the more sinister for the desperate attempt of one or two to put forth a green sprout.

Both buildings were blasted open to the sky and in front of the one, which had been a clinic, was a pile of twisted stretcher frames, hubs of truck wheels and spare parts for tanks. To the right, was a building still intact, its windows blown out and framed with scorch marks and its blue-washed walls pockmarked by thousands of exploding bullets This was the annex to the clinic and had contained wards full of the seriously wounded. As we entered from the road, a huge triumvirate of Marx, Engels, and Lenin stared down at us and inside there they were again gazing impassively at debris of a different kind, dirty tangles of wadding from torn mattresses, blackened bed linen on which bloodstains were still distinguishable from the dirt. The earth floor of one room was heaped halfway to the ceiling over a mass grave and through the doorway, fringed by the fresh green grass of the first rains and beneath the shade of acacia trees, I glimpsed the long mounds of the main mass graves in which the Front had buried the dead.

It was an emotional moment, driving for the first time with Solomon into the Tigrayan capital, Mekelle. Tigrayans placed so much symbolic value on its liberation even if it was not their own home town. This would be my base for a week or two, but Solomon's program would take him repeatedly into the countryside. Our paths were diverging and it was no longer possible to share transport. It was time to say goodbye, for the moment.

I stayed in the Green Hotel, so called because in Haile Selassie's time the dusty broken space before its entrance had been filled with gardens and fountains beneath lofty eucalyptus trees. Only the trees were still there, as dusty and tired as the ground, browsed free of its few stalks by wandering cows and goats. The two women who ran the day-to-day affairs of the hotel blamed it all on the Dergue, but exactly how the Dergue had destroyed the garden was never explained.

The hotel belonged to a family called Gebrekristos. The owner's son was a well-known fighter in the Front's Foreign Affairs department. When I asked his name I realized I had met him with Seyoum and Jamaica in London. Other sons and daughters were also fighters and perhaps because of this connection or perhaps because they felt uneasy in the grander Castle Hotel, fighters and Front members would often use the dining room for meetings. The rooms were small and dark, the latrines smelly and the arrangements casual, but the atmosphere was extremely pleasant, which helped to bridge the gap between my first experience of Tigray—of sleeping in caves and huts or under the stars—and the strange luxury of staying in a hotel at all. Guests at a loose end would sit on the wall outside their rooms and in no time be chatting to townsfolk, stray fighters or each other. One evening, a young man waiting for a meeting to start described to me his life as part of the underground force working for the Front during the occupation.

"Mekelle has been like an egg," he said. "The shell has been so hard to break through, but there is life inside."

Several people described, in emotional terms the coming of the fighters.

"After six hours the TPLF came," said Askale, a mother of two young children, whose husband was away in the Dergue army. "They came through the castle at about six in the evening in a single line. The light was getting dim. Everybody came out of their houses and showed their joy, and they were ululating. They came down, men and women fighters together, and went off to different parts of the town. 'Everyone be calm,' they said, 'be settled. We are here now. Be glad.'"[4]

Askale took her crying four year old on her lap. "From that instant," she added, "we believed that the TPLF could destroy the thieves and agents of the Dergue and build up the towns again."

I was not so confident of this support, the less so because I discovered Askale was a supporter of the Front. I knew others who did not agree.

I went to see Tadelle, the new TPLF administrator of Mekelle, to discover the Front's view of the situation.[5] I found him in a little office in a small house previously occupied by a Dergue official. His list of problems was formidable. There was no electricity and, without power, no water. The hospital was virtually paralyzed by lack of staff and its building and equipment had been vandalized; there were no teachers to run the school; all the humanitarian organizations had left with the Dergue except the SOS School and the Catholic Mission, leaving large numbers of orphans and war disabled to join the mass of those newly without income and dependent on relief. These included massive numbers of prostitutes who had lost their clientele. In addition, the list of dead and injured from the multiple rings of mines around the town was growing longer by the day.

But Tadelle was surprisingly optimistic.

"It took many years of bitter struggle to establish the revolution in the rural area," he said. "But here, the people have known the cruelty of the Dergue for fifteen years. They can already feel the difference. It won't take us long."

The problems were economic ones, including prostitution. The Front's approach, he said, approximated to the method they had tried and tested in the countryside and in which they were now very experienced. Essentially, it was that the people must solve the problems for themselves; the Front would have an enabling role. They had already set up a loans system to enable merchants to band together to buy trucks for the importing of essential goods from the Sudan or to provide transport between towns. Only two months after the departure of the Dergue, many of these were already on the road.

Their main strategy would be to set up an elected *baito* to take over the decision-making. Initially, it would be a temporary council, whose brief would include setting up a permanent elected body.

"We believe the *baito* itself should be a means of rebellion and struggle," said Tadelle.

The similarity to the strategy used in the countryside was clear. Through a participatory system of decision-making and involvement at every level of problem-solving, the peasants had not only gained confidence in their own abilities but also increased their political consciousness and their determination to protect their gains. But could it work here? Tadelle not only believed it could, but that the transition to self-administration and support for the war against the Dergue would happen much more quickly than in the villages.

"In the towns," he said, "the general level of education is higher."

"But better education can increase the desire for status and private gain, can't it?"

"It can. But here, now, the people hate the enemy. Their life was very tortuous in the Dergue's time. They were restricted even in movements from place to place. They couldn't see their relatives. They had no right of protest or any other democratic right. They all have their own bad experience of the state and the occupation, so their concern was to be liberated from the enemy, no matter what the problems might be. They want a peaceful and democratic life."

"You mean in the long term."

"Yes. But not too long. They have come also to realize that the Dergue is in a state of breaking and falling down. They want to destroy the enemy completely and expect him soon to be destroyed. The existing social and economic problems they say they can tolerate if the Dergue is destroyed as soon as possible. They also want to know how they can help in destroying the Dergue and everyone wants to be involved, but they don't know how to do it and are demanding direction from us."

There was no way of knowing, at this point, whether his optimism was misplaced. Certainly, the Front had a long experience of mobilizing recalcitrant and conservative people, but I was aware of a much more varied range of opinions than his homogeneous description suggested. I was also beginning to realize that the relative sophistication of the townspeople compared with their traditionally-dressed country neighbors was largely illusory. For all their Western dress or straightened hair, they were confused and ignorant, blown about by conflicting winds of fear and hope. In the countryside, I had come to take for granted the political awareness of peasants whose appearance would not have looked out of place in the Middle Ages or Old Testament times. It now seemed so astonishing I even cross-checked in the old diaries I had brought with me for reference that I really did have the sophisticated conversations I remembered. Of course, the peasants were not uniform any more than town dwellers, but I had recorded an awful lot of them.

At this time, there were meetings in all the large towns. The Front called the people together in the local stadium or some large open space where they could answer questions, invite participation or communicate plans. REST also used these meetings to register for relief those who needed it. It was at one of these, in Mekelle, that I saw peasants from the villages taking the stand to chastise the populace. Ethiopians, even more than their European counterparts, presuppose the superiority of townsfolk over bumpkins from the country. At this meeting, although appearances supported this prejudice, the substance of the exchange overturned it completely. I couldn't get a complete transcript, but the substance of the peasants' message was "Look you lot—take control of your lives, get off your arses and sort out the problems here. If you don't, who should? And the only way to make sure this freedom lasts is to join forces against the Dergue." This challenging oratory was backed by cogent arguments of self and collective interest and those sitting on the ground around me, listening intently, seemed both stimulated and stirred. This evidence of successful politicization seemed to astonish even Tadelle and other fighters.

Meanwhile, Heshe and I were becoming more comfortable with one another. He was not a fighter, but a guide and interpreter for REST, the Tigrayan relief organization, which worked closely with the Front's Agriculture, Education and Health Departments on long-term development projects. He came to find me in the Green Hotel one morning.

"I've brought a friend of yours to say hello to you," he said.

It was Genet, the football player. We hugged each other and exchanged news over several glasses of tea. She had trained, first as a fighter, then as a teacher, and now she was teaching in Adi Awalla, in the area where I had first investigated land reform. She, too, had come to Mekelle to see her parents, her first visit since the Dergue's evacuation and so her first since her release from Mekelle prison. I asked after her sister, Letensae, who had sacrificed her own marriage and happiness to secure Genet's release from prison. She was now in Canada, Genet told me, and a firm supporter of the TPLF.[6]

"I still play football," she said, laughing. "I play with my students and train them in football and volleyball. We have matches with other teams in the area."

Meeting up with Genet made me think about Berhanu, my guide of two years ago. As soon as I arrived in Mekelle I had inquired about his whereabouts. It was not difficult—as an Agazi comrade he was well-known to fighters—but I was disappointed to learn he had been in Mekelle a day or two before my arrival on his way back from a reunion with his family in the nearby small town of Quiha. All fighters from the newly-liberated towns were being released from their duties to make contact with families who often did not know whether they were still alive. Although I had just missed Berhanu, I learned he was still working for the Propaganda Bureau, but his job had changed. Now, he was an announcer for Tigray Free radio, the Front's radio station, working presumably with Harnet, Amare's wife. The Propaganda Bureau, the women's schools, the training hospital, had all moved with the Front's base area to the Simien mountains, so it was most unlikely that I would see Berhanu, Saba, Iyassu, and many other old friends on this trip.

Thoughts of Berhanu reminded me of his six years imprisonment in Mekelle prison. All the harrowing stories of its brutal regime came back to me. I still had not seen it. A letter from Tadelle secured permission for Heshe and me to go a couple of days later. It had been empty since the Dergue troops left in February, freeing the prisoners as they went, to add to the chaos. On the edge of the town, the prison was a complex of crude single story buildings within a series of concentric outer walls. The gate in the second wall was partially bricked up and, despite our consciousness of the grisly history of the place, or perhaps because of it, the irony of having to climb in with some difficulty struck us as very funny. Through the next gate was the dusty compound where relatives were admitted to bring food and medicines and within that was the prisoners' compound, the heart of the prison.

Several long stone buildings lay in parallel in a small yard. Each building was divided into large cells about five meters square with a single unglazed window high in the roof. Then, I remembered that seventy or eighty prisoners had been crammed into each one and decided they were not large after all. Nothing had been disturbed. The cells were filled with the detritus of the miserable lives spent in them, piles of disgusting rags and filthy mats and mattresses, tin cans, rubbish of every kind left in the casual swirls in which the prisoners had abandoned them. The walls were lined with greasy shadows where countless prisoners had leaned their backs, as if their wretched ghosts were watching us in mute appeal. I wondered which one was Berhanu's. I remembered his recalling one dreadful night of stifling humidity before the rainy season, the heat of many bodies crushed together, his illness, the breathing problems, which dated from that time, the respiratory illness, which more recently had sent him for five months to the Sudan. Feeling myself suffocating, I could not stay there long.

Nothing stands still in a revolution. There had been two Congresses since my last visit, one of the Front as a whole and the other of the Women Fighters' Association. I had heard there had been a number of important policy changes. I heard rumors that the numbers of women fighters, about thirty percent of the combat force, were being reduced and that women were no longer being taught to plow. These two factors—women's visibility as fighters and their right to plow, formerly the sole prerogative of men—had not only practical but immense symbolic value especially for peasant women and, for them, testified to the integrity of the Front's declared support for the equality of women. I was alarmed. At home, I had defended them more than once against the common allegation that revolutions opportunistically espouse the cause of women's equality, only to drop it again on attaining power. So far, the Front had attained power only in Tigray, but were the cracks already showing?

These questions demanded answers from the top and I contacted Gebru about a meeting with the leadership. Since our last meeting near Dejenna in the western mountains, the location of the Front's base area headquarters had changed to somewhere in the remote and mountainous region of Simien. There had been other changes too. Meles Zenawi was now Chairman of the TPLF. I was told the early rains had already made some rivers impassable and I could not go to Simien, but a few days later, a message arrived from Meles to say he was camped with Aregash (still the only woman on Central Committee) and a few other fighters only half a night's journey from Mekelle. The place was called "Beloved Sand," beloved also by women fighters, so Aregash later told me, as the location of the first women fighters' congress at the end of the seventies.

It was a relief to get out of Mekelle and into the countryside again, even if it meant bumping over rough tracks and losing a night's sleep. We arrived as dawn was breaking. The green camouflaged tents were erected under trees among dry sandy gulches, which looked as if they hadn't seen rain in a long while, despite the stream bubbling nearby. The welcome was as warm as ever. While Heshe went off to discover the schedule, I sat on a log and young fighters brought me tea in the same old battered enamel cups. Then two young women took me to a tent and helped to bathe me in warm water and, after breakfast, suggested that I sleep for a couple of hours. The tensions and confusion of the towns fell away and I slept better than I had since my arrival in Tigray.

I talked with Meles for the remainder of the morning and to Aragesh in the afternoon. They were characteristically generous with their time. My questions were all directed to understanding the changes over the last two years, including strategies for solving the economic problems of the towns. The most important development, Meles said, was the "rising tide of revolution all over Ethiopia." Groups beyond Tigray were approaching the Front, asking to be organized and armed to fight the Dergue. The new multi-national Front (the EPRDF) had been formed to take the struggle for a democratic Ethiopia beyond Tigray and he expected the revolution to spread much faster than before. Within Tigray, they had extended democratic structures by establishing the *baito* or local council at the lowest level of social organization, the *qushette* or hamlet, so that now the people were self-governing at the hamlet, village, and district levels. Their recent victories he attributed to a wholesale rethinking of military policy after a period of stagnation in the mid-eighties. One of the main aims of these policies, it seemed to me, was to increase the peasants' involvement in the armed struggle and thereby their sense of responsibility for its outcome.

Meles on the New Military Policies

In the last three years, we have made a fundamental review of our tactics and strategy.

You know, in a way, one of our advantages is that we have very strong enemies. If you want to fight with only primitive means, a strong army backed by powerful supporters, you have to be able to create a force that is stronger and of a different kind. You have to be able to mobilize the initiative of the ordinary fighter—the sense of duty, the sense of conviction of the ordinary fighter and of the ordinary peasant and of the ordinary woman. The only way is to confront it with a strong will. And, the only way to create a strong will is to convince each other, to discuss things together and come to a conclusion. Our fighters have the will to fight because they are convinced that they have a just cause.

We had a lot of democratic discussions among the people and inside the organization to thrash things out, to analyze the situation in Ethiopia and to spread the word beyond Tigray. We started to act in the past year.

In the past, the people were more or less passive sympathizers, except those who joined the army or the militia. They provided materials for the army in terms of food and clothing; they took care of wounded fighters and so on. It was not thought possible or correct to involve them right up to the battle front. Then, we realized that this was not the best way of doing it. All the people have to be involved in the armed struggle in a direct sense. The only efficient way is the way that convinces the mass to fight to have conditions that in the end will be better. That is the shortest way, and the surest way....It might take more time, demand lengthy debates and so on, but in the final analysis, paradoxically, it's the shortest path.

The tactic now is to disperse the army, not to crush it completely. The target is the disintegration of the command system, because only the commanders want to fight us. So, the first thing to do is to remove the control of the officers by cutting the army into smaller units. The snag is, you have to penetrate deep inside to dismantle the core without ever attacking the outlying areas. This brings the risk of being encircled, so it demands a lot of personal courage and organization. But we've proved that it is possible.

The battle is conducted in a political way. Soldiers in the enemy army do not have the will to fight, because the TPLF is not the enemy. If they are dispersed, they have no will to resist and they can be mopped up by all the people, ordinary women without any guns, even shepherds. Once an enemy soldier disintegrates, he's an ordinary peasant whom you can try to convince to give up his arms. He will be hungry and tired and you can ask him to come into your house and give him some water and some food. Maybe, he will sleep and you can easily pick up his arms or maybe you can convince him that he can run nowhere and he should give up his arms. This is less bloody and more effective.

One of the most difficult things about these military tactics is convincing the people that those who are burning their huts are not the enemy. One thing we did—we sent captured soldiers, who were convinced that what they were doing was criminal, although they had been forced to do it, around the villages to spread the message. They would go to a village and say, "We have burned your huts. We have also our own huts in our own village. We have been forced out of them. We came here. We were given guns and ordered to shoot you and to burn your houses. If we didn't, we would die. Of course we could have died without burning your houses, but after all, it's human to try to save your life. So, in order to save our lives we had to burn your huts. That's very bad and criminal and we regret it. But that's a fact."

A simple statement like this would immediately change the outlook of the peasants from hostility to a feeling of sympathy for the plight of the ordinary soldier—for the fact that he had been forced to leave his wife and his children and his family, taken to a place he had never seen before, and forced to fight.

However, some priests were not helpful because of the burning of churches, saying whoever burned churches was a messenger of Satan and should be treated like Satan. Some priests even threatened to excommunicate any peasant who cared for a wounded enemy soldier. It wasn't easy to convince them that the soldiers who had burned their churches were not alien. First, we convinced the peasants and then came back to the priests.

Also, some of our TPLF leaders resisted the idea that military tactics and strategy were not some mysterious field of knowledge acquired from military books. They wanted to continue in the traditional way. They said it was too risky to penetrate deep inside the enemy's territory without clearing the ground; that paralyzing the command structure was stupid because the army also consisted of other ranks; that trying to involve the ordinary peasant in actual combat would be pointless because unarmed people could not conduct battles. Some were prominent members. One was a vice-chairman of the TPLF and another one was a commander of the army of the TPLF. But, if you convince the people, then any individual who is not convinced just remains an individual who doesn't support the agreed policy. We let them go, but they left alone.

The strategy has proved successful. Those who were skeptical in the past said, "Well, it looks fine in theory, lets see it in practice." Now, everyone is convinced that it works.[7]

In the afternoon, the green dimness of the tent providing the illusion of cool, Aragesh echoed the same concerns as Meles, but from a different perspective.[8]

"We are trying to keep the ties between fighters and society very close. There is a danger in any country involved in combat. They become uprooted from the active life of society. They form their own groups and sections. This is very dangerous."

No wonder they were anxious. The history of Ethiopia was a history of warlords and dictators, of oppression by armies. The ancient feudal right of the armies of the Emperor to live off peasants as they travelled over the country was cited by villagers more often than drought as a cause of misery and famine. The private armies of feudal landlords, the Soviet-backed war machine of the Dergue—all made up of peasants indistinguishable from those whose grain they consumed, whose daughters they raped, whose houses they torched—the central mystery of the poor taking orders from the oppressor to do what as individuals they could not condone. As in all dictatorships, the instrument of power and oppression was the army.

"We are trying to handle it very consciously," said Aregash, "with the fighters always discussing and contributing to solving the problems of society, involving themselves in constructing society along with the peasants. The struggle must be handled by everyone, so eventually the fighters are prepared to involve themselves in building a new Ethiopia, and will be farmers or factory workers if necessary."

This was an interesting glimpse of the forward planning of the Front. Not only looking ahead to victory in this civil war, they were identifying potential dangers and trying to defuse them before they happened, a sort of political preventive healthcare.

This has only become fascinating with hindsight. At the time, I was more absorbed by the problems of women and with wanting to challenge Aregash to provide some answers on what seemed to be a diminution of women's gains under the revolution. She admitted they had made mistakes, but not by reversing the policy of encouraging women to plow, but by allowing themselves to be carried away by the tide of women's enthusiasm in the first place. The right to plow carried a symbolic glamor and became an icon of women's equality, when, in fact, it detracted from it by contributing to their already unreasonable burden of work. It came down to the same old problems of poverty—the labor of the grindstone, the unavailability of fuel and water. Women already worked longer hours than men. I asked Aregash how it was possible for them to take over men's work before their traditional burdens had been eased.

"Some of the towns, Sheraro, Adi Daro, Adi Nebried, have grinding mills, but most of the villages are far from these towns and most women do the grinding themselves. We are working with some development organizations to have wells dug nearer the village and on simplifying the grinding with simple powered mills. We have some information on simple machines in use in India."

Graduates of Marta School were also working with women in the villages to ease their way of life, but although a start had been made, real progress would only be possible with economic development and this would only come with the end of the war.

They had similarly reassessed their policy on women fighters.

"The revolution is made powerful," said Aregash, "through the people, both men and women, using their capabilities as effectively as possible. Most women are not as fit for combat as men, although those who are fit should still be involved."

They had even concluded that too great an emphasis on combat roles could adversely affect women's general involvement in society and therefore their political and economic advancement—it was better for a woman to be involved in the local *baito* than in battle. In fact, the non-combat opportunities for women fighters were expanding since the liberation of the towns, particularly in health care, but, because the largest number of rural recruits had been to combat roles, the overall proportion of women would be slightly reduced from the thirty percent it had been before. However, women fighters who were illiterate could no longer be accepted as health workers, teachers or agricultural cadres. From now on they had to be educated at least to fifth grade.

"What was the response from women fighters?" I asked.

Aregash smiled ruefully.

"At first, there was resistance from women comrades. They were furious. Especially peasant women—because being a fighter has been such a liberation for them. They feel resentment and we have, ourselves, created those feelings through the way we have conducted the revolution."

Bumping along in the landcruiser back to Mekelle through the dark, I tried to free my judgement from my prejudices. The twin images of women either behind Kalashnikovs or the plow had been powerful for me too. It was too easy, ironically, to make of these women fighters a vicarious compensation for the freedoms not available to Western women. Another subtle variant of the imperialist project. For us, the ikon of the woman in fatigues with an AK 47 on her shoulder; for them, death or injury, loss of friends in battle, the alternative of constant child-bearing and back-breaking labor on an impoverished farm. I had to accept the hard realities behind Aragesh's arguments.

There wasn't enough political work done, in the beginning, to convince the people that women should plow so it wasn't universally accepted. There has to be a lot of change in men's ideas, as well as in women's.

There are not so many women plowing these days. Those who had training can plow if they want to. No one will stop them. But, with so much cooking and childcare it adds to the hardship of our lives.[9]

As we jolted over the ruts and potholes and I struggled not to doze off, the voices of women combat fighters I had interviewed wove themselves into the growl of the engine and the clamor of Tigrinya songs from the cassette player. Then, when I got back to the Green Hotel I was wide awake, so I looked over my notes and played back tapes of interviews I had not pondered at the time. Eventually, I fell asleep and their earnest faces jumbled with their voices into dreams.

Women with children cannot be combat fighters any longer. Personally, I don't want to have children because I believe that it hinders my activity.

Before the adoption of the new policy I was very strongly opposed to women not being combat fighters. There's only about five or six in my unit now.[10]

They organized themselves in their associations and came in huge numbers and joined in the battle. They provided food, bullets, and took away wounded comrades. Some of them picked up Kalashnikovs and joined in the battle, taking prisoners or catching soldiers running away in disarray.[11]

My days in Tigray were numbered if I were not to be trapped by the rains. We had been caught more than once by sudden cloudbursts, unbelievable stair-rod stuff virtually out of a clear sky. Once, there were hailstones as big as hens' eggs. I had wanted to go to Hausien, where last summer on market day Dergue MiGs and helicopters had attacked the little town and massacred fifteen hundred or more people, but I couldn't find transport. Oh well, I'd had my fill of atrocities. I could take no more. It was time to go. Then, unexpectedly, I was offered a landcruiser for one day.

We set off early in the morning, northwards on the Adigrat road and three hours later we were in Hausien. To get to it, we had to leave the main road at Sinkata and cross a wide plain. In the distance, spiky mountains shimmered in a mauve haze. This is one of the harshest regions in Tigray, yet today it looked benign and comfortable. The recent bursts of rain, although inadequate for the needs of agriculture, were already turning the pastures to green in contrast to the brown furrows of fields plowed ready for sowing and as we approached the little town, the huddle of stone buildings shone white in the sunlight. We parked the car on the outskirts and turned off the engine. The plain lay peaceful. Green, blue, gold, silver. The only sound was birds.

Hausien stands at a junction of four "counties," Agame, Adwa, Enderta, and Kilte Awalalo, and its market attracted traders and buyers from a wide area. The day of the bombing, Wednesday, June 22, 1988, was market day and the population of the town was swelled by the huge weekly influx of visitors. No one expected a bombardment, because there was no reason for it. Maybe this was foolhardy. There had, after all, been eight or nine air attacks since the beginning of March, but the area had no military significance, was not controlled by the TPLF, and most of the traders came from areas controlled by the government. There were no fighters or people with guns in the town and the people felt safe enough to hold their market in daylight, unlike markets in the liberated areas. The market square was packed, not only with people, but also with oxen, sheep, goats, and donkeys. These factors made for difficulties in the recovery operation and there is disagreement about the numbers who were killed. The official figures were eighteen hundred dead, but although about thirteen hundred were lost from Hausien itself, the presence of so many from outside and the fragmentation and mingling of both human and animal remains meant that no exact count could ever be made. The mayor thought a more accurate estimate would be two and a half thousand.

The bombers had used high explosives and cluster bombs. The helicopters used machine guns and rockets. The survivors described a "burning liquid," which fell from the planes onto people and cattle and which would not stop burning. This has been identified as either napalm or phosphorus. Cluster bombs are a battlefield weapon, each one designed to eject at a predetermined height a range of sub-munitions, including shrapnel and anti-personnel mines, which in turn can explode in the air or on the ground, the huge blast penetrating human bodies with multiple fragments and causing extensive damage to buildings. They are one of that class of weapons that can be used to cause massive wounding rather than instant death, on the assumption that on the battlefield nothing can be done for the dead, but the wounded distract their comrades from the battle. When the victims reach the field hospital, they are more difficult to treat. In Hausien, of course, there was neither hospital nor medical care. Cluster bomb technology originated in the USA; it has been alleged and never disproved that they were supplied to the Ethiopian airforce by Israel; they were dropped by Soviet-supplied MiG 23s on an entirely civilian target.

From close to, it was clear that not much of the town was left standing. What from a distance looked like buildings were piles of rubble. Not a soul was to be seen. A deserted village. Then, two figures emerged from somewhere or other and began to walk towards us across the open space. One was the mayor who took us first for a tour of the town. We photographed ruin after ruin, some reduced to rubble, some roofless, others partially demolished. Here and there a house stood miraculously intact, next to a shell; a few buildings showed signs of repair and reconstruction.

In the school yard lay an unexploded, but defused, cluster bomb.

There were more people still living in Hausien than I first thought. They emerged out of half-built dwellings as we passed; children ran out of the alleyways, shrieking and waving at the novelty of a white visitor. They didn't dare follow us into the mayor's house when we went in for coffee and *sewa*, but they clustered on the threshold, their big eyes peering curiously round the door posts to see what was going on in the gloomy interior. Men and women slowly gathered in the room until the benches around the walls were crammed with people. The first to speak was Berihu Deress, a man of fifty-five, whose large two-story house in the market place became a refuge for over sixty people. They thought it was indestructible because it was made of cement.

The Massacre at Hausien

My house is in the market, the two floor house, but I wasn't in it, but in a house nearer here. I was drinking sewa *when I heard two MiGs approaching. They began to circle around, but I didn't expect bombardments because it was market day and no fighters were here.*

After a few minutes, the planes returned and began bombing us. Even the house where I was drinking sewa *was bombed. I was sitting near the door and the roof fell in and the walls. I was injured. I was buried from the waist down under the rubble. The air was filled with smoke. There was no pure air and we were fainting. Then people came and freed me. First, I was fainting and after a little I revived with purer air. I didn't expect to live. I expected to die. My wife and three children were dead in the market place.*

It started at eleven thirty and went on until six in the evening. There were four MiGs, flying two-by-two. They were bombing in the town, but two helicopters were circling the town and if people tried to run away the machine guns on the helicopters killed them.

In June, all the farmers come to Hausien to buy seed, so the market is very crowded. Everyone was running in different directions, turning and running back in confusion. Some houses were destroyed. People were crashing into one another, trying to find shelter, but the houses were crushed and the doors were broken. People were scattering in all directions. We didn't know what was a man, what was a woman, what was an ox. All the bits were mixed up. One person had no face, one person had no leg. We gathered together from the houses and went to the church.

Even now, when we dig in the rubble to rebuild, we find bodies and parts of bodies. At that time, on the school side of town, from Debagai, there were fires and a lot of people from Sinkata, Wukro, Adigrat. They said, "Our families are dead" and they came and started to dig. In my house, after digging, we found, out of sixty people, only two alive. So many people ran into the house from the market because it was a strong two-storied house and they thought it would protect them. But, the MiGs saw and bombed it over and over again. It had eight rooms, four on the first floor, and they were all crowded with people and only two survived.

In the house where I was, three people were dead and next door on the left, where four families lived, five people were dead there. One was Haimanot Seyoum. In my house, in the market, there were sixty-six people and only two survived. In the house of Haile Selassie Berhe, fourteen people died, including Haile Selassie Berhe himself, with his sons, his wife, and his family, who had come from their village because it was market day. Almaz Gerezighier, her house was near the market place and eight people died in it. Now, all her family have moved away. In another home, Alemayo Desta's, they were all dead.

My wife's name was Haddas Asfaw. My three children who died were Berikti Berihu, Tukaw Berihu, and Tesfay Berihu. I have two other children who were not here at the time. They had stayed in the countryside. My boy is now in Asmara and my daughter is now married.

After the bombing, the MiGs even came the next morning, without bombing, just circling. But, they expected all the houses to be burned and no-one was here—everyone went. Everyone was strong for TPLF. This government is no use to us. Only with TPLF will peace come.[12]

Berihu finished speaking. No one broke the silence. It throbbed against my temples, like the heat. The Mayor's wife came over to top up with *sewa* the gourd next to my feet. Flies, ignored, crawled on every surface, every rim.

There may have been more than four MiGs, more than two helicopters. The people only know they returned in pairs. Four MiGs would not have been able to maintain an aerial bombardment for so long. They must have meticulously planned a series of sorties from Asmara, a succession of MiGs and helicopters to assault this little town in a series of coordinated shifts for six or seven hours.

A soft wind blew through the doorway. We flapped the flies from the *sewa*. An old woman called Kidan began to speak again. Her father had been in the big building in the market-place. She had dug him out and he had survived. He was eighty-six.

"After the bombs stopped, I went automatically to that house. There were hundreds of people underneath. They were calling out, 'Please help me, please help me.' I saw only the fingers of my father, but I recognized them and dug him out of the ground. We couldn't see anything, only hear the sound of voices crying, 'Please help me' and after a while there was silence."

Negisti was in the market. She was pregnant and when she heard the MiGs she ran to her house, which was so packed with people that she was crushed and began to bleed from her mouth.

"All the dead animals and people," she said, "We didn't know which was which. Hands, legs, all mixed up. The hyenas were attracted by the terrible smell, so we had to collect all the bits together and burn them."

"Even the birds," added Ababa. "After that, we didn't see any birds for two days. They were killed not by the MiGs, but by the helicopters."

I asked her where she had been during the bombing.

"I was in my shop near the market. The roof blew off in the blast and we ran to the right hand side. I ran to my home, where we had dug a shelter in case Dergue soldiers came. My whole family went into the hole. Again the roof was blown off by the blast. There was intense heat. We were melting like butter or like a very hot dish sizzling in cold water."

The words recorded in my notebooks and cassettes are a poor expression of the pain these people communicated. In the spaces between words, in their small and sparing gestures, a hand to the head here, a blank contemplation there, were conveyed the trauma of a whole community barely scabbed over by a year's passing. Berihu estimated at least two thousand five hundred died, including thirteen hundred from Hausien itself. He thought there were roughly five thousand, two hundred left in the town.

After about four hours in Hausien, we drove back to Mekelle.

Two days later, we left Mekelle again and followed the same road north, past the turn-off to Hausien, to Adigrat and then westwards over the mountains to Adwa, Axum, Endeselassie to the Sudan, travelling by night, interviewing where possible during the day. Our driver was an old fighter called Wodi-Saba'a ("son of seventy"), famous for his loyalty to the Front from its earliest days and for having several wives. He asked us if we'd mind giving a lift to two women, Askaria and Askale, who were going with their children to the Sudan to find their husbands.

They were grateful for the transport. They waited patiently when Heshe and I went off to work, sometimes for a day or two. I needed to go into the countryside to reacquaint myself with the longer-liberated areas, to check I had not deceived myself about their political sophistication and support for the TPLF. We went to Adi Hagerai and to Adi Nebried. I talked to women on the executive of the *baitos* about their work and spent a day with Neriya, an ex-student of Marta School, who remembered me from my visit there two years before. She was now working with women on scattered farms, building demonstration stoves to the new Marta fuel-saving design and demonstration gardens to persuade them to grow and eat more vegetables. After the towns, it was a time of spiritual refeshment, like a holiday.

One of the detours Heshe and I made on this long slow journey to the border, was a visit to Atsrega training camp. There had been massive recruitment since the Dergue's retreat began to convince the people that victory was possible. A wave of euphoria had brought young people streaming to the camps. The Front had always been proud of never resorting to forcible recruitment, but the psychological pressure brought to bear on young people must have been intense.

I went there to talk to Gebru, but as we coincided with a performance from the Cultural Troupe, the visit became a reunion with Iyassu and old friends. We arrived in the early evening as hundreds of young fighters, organized in their units and singing songs, were making their way through the trees and across open ground to take their places on a hillside, which soared like an immense amphitheater above the performance area. At our last meeting, Iyassu had confided his idea for a musical drama. It will be like an opera, he said. It will be based on the ancient songs of the people. It will move the heart. For the last few years, the Cultural Troupe had been researching and collecting traditional songs from the remote countryside. They were really sung poems, which had been passed on orally from one generation to another and ranged from odes of praise to powerful feudals to bitter laments at the injustices and poverty of peasant life. The musical drama used these songs to make a powerful evocation of conditions in the countryside and to propagandize deliverance from oppression by the Front, mostly through land reform.

The simple story of a mother at her grindstone, the father at the plow, and the son (who eventually becomes a fighter) wielding his sling against the birds who threaten the crop, certainly moved the heart. There must have been several thousand fighters on that hillside, but there was not a rustle to be heard and when I turned to scrutinize the ones sitting beside and behind me I saw their faces were wet with tears.

In the end we stayed several days with the Cultural Troupe while they generously shared their researches with me. Iyassu explained and translated on tape all the different categories of songs and poems and the leading singers spent hours singing them over while I made recordings. There were wedding songs, funeral orations, poems of praise to feudal lords, songs associated with the different seasons, and procedures of the agricultural year. One singer was a daughter of a *hamien* family, a people who earn a living through complimentary poetry, which turns to foul insult if they are denied money or grain. She dramatized a typical doorstep encounter, asking me to play the lady of the house who first gives generously and then refuses to give anything at all. But, in almost every category, except perhaps the wedding songs, there were some poems, which gave voice to the peasants' consciousness and resentment of oppression. These were the poems, which most interested me. Some proceeded from deep resentment at grinding poverty; other poets were social critics, observing and judging exploitative or cowardly behavior of the feudals. They were protorevolutionary in the sense of preparing the ground for rebellion, rather than suggesting a political analysis or calling for organized resistance.

This was an unexpected haul—voices sounding from the past where before there had been only silence. Ethiopia is no exception to the general rule that recorded history in any country is controlled by the educated elite in the service of the rich and powerful, but its illiteracy rate of over ninety percent contributes to the silence and invisibility of the lives of the majority of its people. Iyassu and his companions were fascinated too. They had not suspected, Iyassu said, the existence of this material before. Yet, most of the cultural group came from a peasant background themselves. This suggested, on the one hand, a gulf between the more educated townspeople and rural culture, even when they had relatives in common, and, on the other, the coexistence of different pockets of cultural practice in the countryside, unaware of each other.

Endaselassie was the last big town before the final day's run to the convoy departure point. We said goodbye and picked up our patient passengers. Then, we were in the sweltering lowlands on the way to the Sudan, beyond all towns, waiting in gulleys to join the convoy. We would be travelling with Wodi-Saba in the landcruiser along with the convoy trucks as security regulations forbade vehicles to go alone. By this time, the route to Gedaref was impassable. We would have to go north through Eritrea to Kassala, with consequent delays while Eritrean fighters, as well as Sudanese border police, scrutinized our passpapers. We passed the daylight hours crouched under scrub in the dry treeless landscape, dozing, exchanging stories, trying to distract ourselves from heat and thirst.

These days in the countryside had been a partial palliative to the experience of the towns, but Askaria and Askale embodied all the confusion and anxieties I thought I had left behind. Using the new freedom of movement brought by liberation to leave Tigray, they hoped to go with their husbands to Canada where they each had relatives. They preferred a future as refugees rather than to test the promises of the Front. Their need for security, as well as their susceptibility to the material blandishments of the West, were completely understandable, yet I found myself contrasting their brand of self-interest with that of the peasants, which showed itself as a self-reliant determination to refashion Tigray so their communities had a better chance of survival.

"Before I was married, when I was a sixth grade student," said Askaria, "I was a contact for the TPLF in Abi Adi for three years until 1978. I was arrested and sent to prison there. Seven of my friends from school were killed. The Dergue used to come to the market-place and kill people."

So, it is impossible to avoid. The memories swirl around us. We are carrying them in the landcruiser. They greet us where we stop.

"Look at these scars on my feet," said Askaria at another stopping point. "I was bleeding. Then after being tied with a wire, they beat me until I bled more and more."

But the children seemed unscarred. The oldest was six. Constantly playing and laughing, they absorbed me into their family, told me stories I only half understood, scribbled all over my pads and lost my pens.

Jenny Hammond

Kudusan Nega at the Adi Hagerai Land Redistribution Congress (Ch. 6)

Jenny Hammond

Women are always bent at an angle of forty-five degrees (Ch. 7)

Jenny Hammond

Wells reduce women's work (Ch. 7)

Jenny Hammond

A Woman ploughing near Awhie (Ch. 7)

Jenny Hammond

A rural "ambulance" arriving in the town

Jenny Hammond

Woman carrying water near Mai Hanse (Ch. 7)

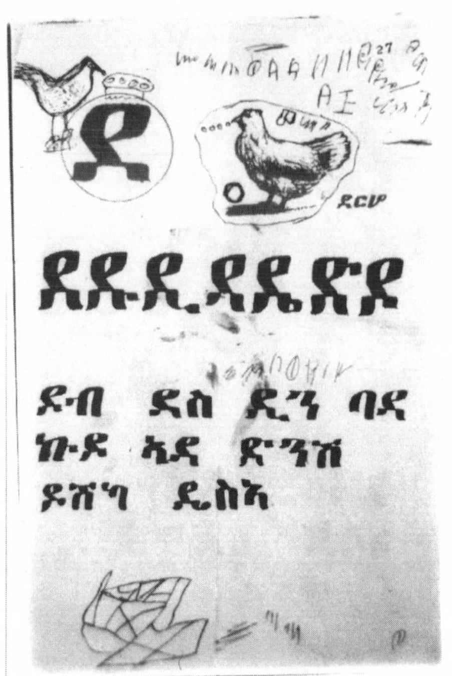

The letter "d", a literacy leaflet, complete with doodles from Sheraro (Ch. 9)

Jenny Hammond

Women speak out in a women's association meeting in Sheraro (Ch. 9)

Jenny Hammond

"I have seen children ten years of age carrying their own weight on their head." (Ch. 7)

Jenny Hammond

Children in Axum (Ch. 12)

Jenny Hammond

Making lunch at the Green Hotel, Mekelle (Ch. 12)

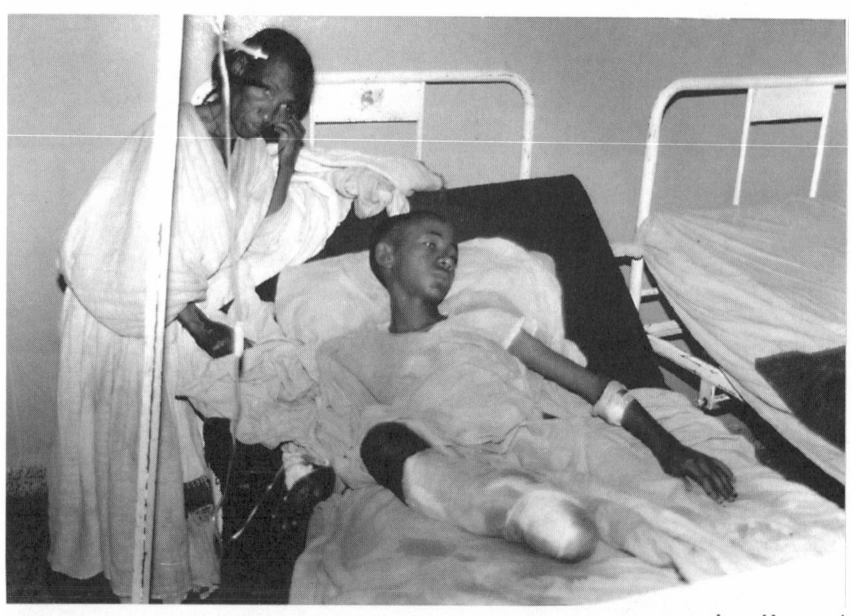

Jenny Hammond

A casualty of Dergue mines with his mother, Adigrat Hospital, 1989 (Ch. 12)

Jenny Hammond

A woman laboratory technician testing for malaria, Mekelle Hospital (Ch. 12)

Jenny Hammond

Kyros Aberra, veteran of the First Weyane, Mekelle (Ch. 14)

Jenny Hammond

Veterans of the First Weyane, Adi Gudom (Ch. 14)

Jenny Hammond

Shops built in Mekelle market-place after the First Weyane (Ch. 14)

Jenny Hammond

Aklilu with farmers from Sobeya. From left to right: Aklilu, Haleqa Embaye, Desta Kidane and Mebratu Adhanom (Ch.15)

Jenny Hammond

Agazi and his family (Ch. 15)

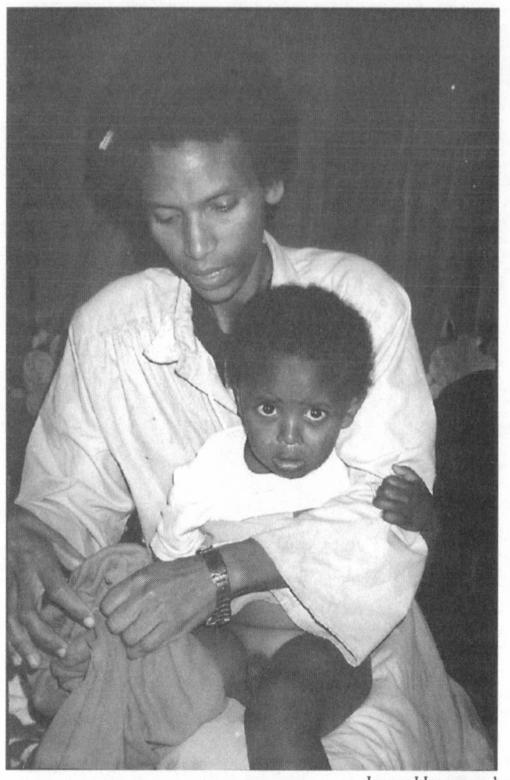

Jenny Hammond

Roman with Tekiye (Ch. 17)

Jenny Hammond

Making Plowshares in the new metal workshops in the old Mekelle Prison (Ch. 17)

Jenny Hammond

Metal working in the old Mekelle prison (Ch. 17)

Jenny Hammond

Swords into plowshares in the old Mekelle prison (Ch. 17)

Jenny Hammond

Roman, Aregash and Mebrat, three of the first women fighters (Ch. 17)

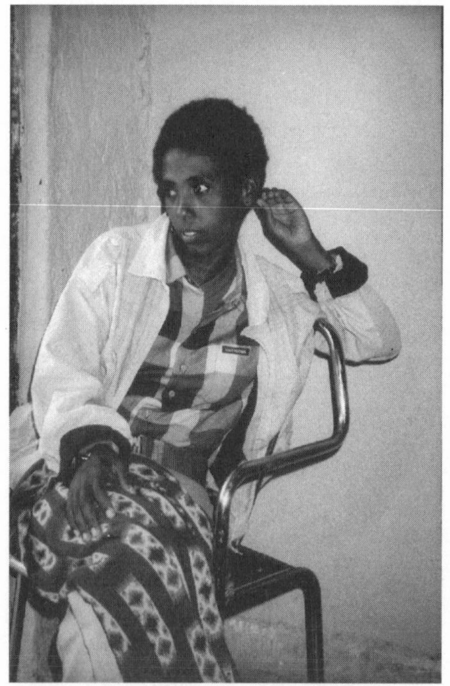

Jenny Hammond

Zewdu Ayelew, woman fighter and Commander of a Division (Ch. 18)

Jenny Hammond

EPRDF fighters guarding Dergue bombs on the runway of Bahr-Dar airport (Ch. 18)

Jenny Hammond

Mengistu's bombs stacked for loading at Bahr-Dar airport (Ch. 18)

Jenny Hammond

The mine store of the 603 Army Corps near Bahr-Dar (Ch. 18)

Jenny Hammond

Land reform celebrations in Woldia, Wello (Ch. 20)

Jenny Hammond

Mengistu's effigy awaiting burning at the land reform celebrations Woldia, Wello (Ch. 20)

Jenny Hammond

The crowd carries an effigy of Mengistu at the land reform in Woldia, Wello (Ch. 20)

Jenny Hammond

Villagers terracing the hillside to conserve soil and rainfall, March 1991 (Ch. 21)

Jenny Hammond

The whole community works to terrace the slopes (Ch. 21)

Jenny Hammond

Terracing the slopes against the flood of the rainy season (Ch. 21)

Jenny Hammond

Taking the palace in Addis Ababa, May 1991 (Ch. 22)

Part Three

Third Journey

January to May 1991

13

The Beginning of the End

January 1991

Nothing ever begins.

There is no first moment, no single word or place from which the story of this revolution springs. I should have known better than to expect it.

The threads can always be traced back to some earlier event and then to events that preceded it. It is all process. Yet I go on asking the questions: Where did it begin? What was the cause? What were the roots of conflict?

On my previous journeys I was absorbed in understanding the revolution as a contemporary phenomenon. Now, I've started asking different questions. How did it all start? When did it all start? Why did the revolution begin when it did in February 1975? What were the causes of the uprising? My answer—too slick by far—has been *oppression.* But, mere survival absorbs all the energy of the poor. If their anger and frustration erupt into occasional and spontaneous outbursts of violence, they bring down on their heads even more extreme forms of punishment and repression. Repression works. It is the *lack* of human capacity for rebellion that astonishes me. Instead, they show a stoic capacity for adjusting their idea of normality to daily experience and so accept a daily experience of suffering and deprivation.

At one moment, from the outside at least, it looks like acceptance, even apathy, nothing doing; the next, it all explodes and there is uproar. Enough is enough, the people cry. It is this crack, this gap between passivity and action, which is too little explored. A mere hair's breadth, barely visible, yet something is going on, out of sight, below the surface, under the skin. What is the catalyst? What dictates the moment of ripeness?

In the autumn of 1990, I started making plans to return to Ethiopia to find the answer to these questions. If I could. It would be a historical quest, but with no single objective. I expected answers to be multiple, explanations to be contradictory, and perceptions of the past to come in as many versions as there were people to offer them. I felt convinced, however, that the answers might be important for other people far from Ethiopia who were interested in the possibilities of freeing themselves from unjust and repressive regimes, and taking their destiny into their own hands.

I finally left England in mid-January, travelling with another woman, a musician called Lesley, who was going to Tigray to research into Northern Ethiopian music. It was an absurd time for us to go. Gulf War fever was at its height. There had been a tense few days in which the media had intensified their war-mongering rhetoric following threats to the security of the "British travelling public" from Abu Nidal and Co. Access to revolutionary Ethiopia was still only through the Sudan, but the Sudanese military government had lined up on the side of Iraq. European airline companies were cancelling all flights to Khartoum. At the last moment we had to switch to Sudan Airways to make sure of getting there, but Sudan Air flights suddenly became unpredictable because Egypt had aligned itself with the West and planes had to be rerouted to refuel in Athens to avoid Cairo. We finally made it to Heathrow on the eve of the deadline to Saddam Hussein. Tanks were dotted, at intervals, around the perimeter of the airport and inside the terminal building policemen with sub-machine guns were walking meaningfully up and down. Could this be England?

Our troubles were not over once we were on the plane. Officials at Khartoum airport were hostile and only timely intervention by Tigrayans who knew the ropes prevented our deportation. They moved us on swiftly to Kassala, but there we had a long wait for papers to cross the border, probably because we were unwilling to pay bribes. In Kassala, a bastion of fundamentalism, a brisk trade in framed portraits of Saddam Hussein had replaced fruit and vegetables on many of the market stalls. We were advised to keep our heads down, but on the one occasion when we visited the town center, voices in the crowd called out "Israeli!" and stones were thrown at us in the market-place.

Here in Adwa, two weeks later, the impact of the everyday overwhelms the politics of the future or the call of the past. My last visit here, just after the towns had been evacuated by the Dergue, was a depressing experience. The people had seemed anxious and confused, bruised from their experience of the Dergue, suspicious of the liberators. Every afternoon, MiGs would fly over the town and make them stupid with terror. Every morning, I was tired from catching bedbugs in the night. I had had an upset stomach. I hadn't realized for a while there was a separate lavatory for the hotel residents and had used the unlit and stinking public latrine on the ground floor where huge cockroaches waved their antennae on the fringes of the torchlight. I never did solve the problem of how to hold a torch and keep my clothes from touching the floor with only two hands.

This doesn't seem the same town. It's hard to put your finger on the details, the objective evidence—the whole atmosphere has changed. For a start, it feels so peaceful, so different from the Sudan, or England in the grip of war fever. Here, the war has passed south. It's still a reality—mothers still crowd around trucks and landrovers in case they carry letters; desperate for word of their children, they still seek out fighters newly arrived from the front—but it's a more distant reality. The Soviet Union is on its last legs and as a result, the Dergue is strapped for weapons and for cash. MiGs no longer come hunting in the afternoon and on market days. Their activities are more or less confined to the southern front. The people on the streets walk more confidently and look you in the eye. Lesley and I can stay in a REST house now and Letish, whom I remember from Mai Hanse, cooks for a growing stream of foreign aid workers.

I have come to forage into the past, but since my arrival, contradictorily, I have been aware of being borne forward, not backwards in time, of being on the crest of a wave of change as this movement propels a new Ethiopia into being. Yet, what is happening now has grown out of the past as a great river meeting the sea still depends on the numberless springs and tributaries, which have accumulated its volume up in the hills. It is always hard to recognize the present moment as a part of history. It is too confused with last night's headache, the slowness of waiting for time to pass until arrangements can be made, the hotchpotch of trivia that masks the significance of events as they unfold. Yet, although I want to unravel the past as far as I am able, I am beginning to realize the importance of recording present events as I witness them. They are the future past after all. And, I begin to be distracted from speculations about first causes and where it all began, by a growing awareness that I am witnessing the beginning of the end.

"They mean to strike fast and they mean to strike soon," says Tekleweini.

"You mean the final strike on Addis?"

"Yes."

"The end of the war?"

"Yes."

Adwa in January. Beyond the purple canopy of bougainvillaea the mid-morning sun strikes white. Underneath, it is twilight, cool. In a patch of shade in the corner of the yard, Letish is banging washing in a sawn-off section of oil drum. It is hard to make sense of the words. War has become a way of life in Ethiopia. What would peace feel like?

"The people need peace." Tekleweini is saying, as if hearing my thoughts. "They are longing for peace."

"Are you talking weeks—or months?"

"Hard to say." (Won't say, more like.) He grins at me. "Months rather than weeks. But not many."

Then he adds, "After victory—that's when our struggle will really start. Compared to that struggle to come, all our sacrifices, all our achievements up to this point are nothing."

The two weeks I was stuck in Kassala, battling with the Sudanese authorities for a permit to cross into Ethiopia have delayed me just enough to miss an important EPRDF Congress. Tekleweini has been briefing me on its decisions. In time, there will be an English translation, but for now I make do with an ad hoc translation from the Tigrinya. Tekleweini's appearance should have warned me of changes in the offing. He looks respectable. His wild hair is tamed, his clothes quite stylish.

The new EPRDF program inscribes Tekleweini's prophecy in another form—it sounds like the manifesto of a party destined for power.[1] It deals with the whole of Ethiopia, not just the liberated area. It sets out the ideals and intentions of the coalition Front in separate sections devoted to political, economic, agricultural, social, and foreign affairs policies. Most important of all, it responds to their perception of oppression over the last hundred years by a fundamental restructuring of Ethiopia's administrative regions and law and order provision, designed to prevent the recurrence of centralized dictatorship. It recommends the realignment of provincial boundaries to coincide more closely with ethnic settlement in order to facilitate self-determination for hitherto subjugated nationalities and thereby federal autonomy. It announces the intention of replacing the huge national standing army with a small central force and a system of regional locally-accountable militias. By recognizing the right of minority nationalities to self-determination, even to secession (if a referendum proves it to be the will of the people), the program projects a vision of an Ethiopia composed of diverse elements, united on a voluntary basis in mutual respect.

It looks to me like a time bomb for the ruling establishment in Addis Ababa.

Meanwhile, Tekleweini is beaming. I go on scribbling down details of democratic and judicial rights, but I can't take it in all at once. I spend the afternoon digesting my notes and reflecting on the fast-moving situation here. A lot has happened since I left Tigray eighteen months ago. In the second half of 1989, the Front had launched an initiative for bringing the war to an end through the formation of a provisional government formed from all concerned political organizations, including the Dergue's party, the notorious and feared WPE, the Workers Party of Ethiopia. Jimmy Carter had volunteered to be an observer of the negotiations. The Dergue played along with the idea, gaining time, in fact, for preparations for a massive offensive in Tigray, Wello, and Gondar. Government forces were in place by the end of August, but rebel forces were ready with a counter offensive. I remember the last months of 1989. Hardly a day passed without a military communique or a press release coming through the door. It seemed as if the Front could not put a foot wrong. They had long shown themselves to be able strategists and tacticians. Now, since the battle of Endeselassie the year before, they had tanks and heavy weapons and had learned how to use them. One of the four organizations in the coalition front was EDORM,[2] an organization of military officers who had defected from the Dergue to fight with the EPRDF. These had proved invaluable instructors in the use of military hardware. Furthermore, the main towns of Tigray, controlled by the Front since early 1989 and containing the only functioning secondary schools, had supplied a flood of recruits educated to twelfth grade who were capable of receiving the instruction.

The list of towns and villages they controlled grew day by day—Maichew, Korem, Alamata, Kobo, Lalibela, Sekota, Woldia, Wichale, Borena, Debre Tabor, Mekane Selam. I marked each military engagement with a felt tip on the map, red for the EPRDF, blue for the Dergue. They showed a steady expansion of the liberated area southward towards Dessie and westwards to Gojam and Gondar.

At the same time, I was compiling a parallel list of aerial atrocities. If the Front showed its superiority on the ground, the government had the advantage in the air, especially against defenseless civilian targets. Most towns and villages had dug air-raid shelters and the damage to buildings and animals was more extensive than the loss of life, often in single figures; occasionally, as in Hausien in 1988 and She'eb in Eritrea in 1989, there was a massacre. Both lists, of government defeats and government bombardments continued to grow through the months of 1990. In January, the Oromo Liberation Front launched its largest military campaign, to date, in Wellega, a province in western Ethiopia, and the government abandoned the battered north to batter its own people in Wellega in a series of bombardments. But, the rebel front from the north continued its inexorable progress southward and by June their divisions were within sixty miles of Addis Ababa.

Meanwhile, drought and food shortages continue and I wonder whether they will have an effect on strategy and timing. Last year, the Joint Relief Partnership (JRP), a consortium of Ethiopian church agencies, negotiated an agreement with the TPLF and the Dergue for free passage of aid convoys along a predetermined route into the drought-afflicted liberated areas in the north. The Front has been advocating free passage for some years, but it is the first time such an agreement has been wrung from the Dergue. However, there have been continuous reports of government sabotage of the scheme, including recent reports of intimidation and arrests of Tigrayan drivers. Would food shortages delay the final push to Addis? Apparently not. In fact, it is becoming obvious that, far from delaying the final push into Addis, the urgency of the food situation is propelling the Front to a speedy conclusion, as the only way of saving the people from famine.

From my first contacts with the Front, skepticism has outrun conviction, so they have generally taken me by surprise. Despite acknowledging the right to secession, they have always denied that this is their aim, whereas independence is the avowed aim of Eritrea. Nevertheless, I was prepared for a resurgence of narrow nationalism once they achieved control of the whole of Tigray. It didn't happen. Instead, they redoubled their efforts to educate the people to respect the "ordinary" Amhara and formed the EPRDF, a united front with Amhara and Oromo organizations espousing democratic principles. Now, they are doing it again. In fact, there is nothing in this program that is inconsistent with the theory and practice as they have expressed it to me in the past. It is just that my Western training leads me to expect less of them.

The political program does not surprise me. It expresses the intention of spreading throughout Ethiopia the participatory grass-roots model of democracy already tested in the liberated area—the *baito* system down to hamlet level and the prohibition against discrimination on the basis of gender, nationality or religion. Less predictable is their intention of introducing a mixed economy and, except for key sectors like financial institutions and energy, the explicit encouragement of private capital, particularly Ethiopian capital, to boost the war-devastated economy. Once again, I am more influenced than I like to admit by a Western media that insists on the doctrinaire far-left leanings of the Front. The media, in their turn, are too influenced by the Addis intelligentsia, who insist that no matter how bad the Mengistu dictatorship might appear, the "rebels" pose a far worse threat to peace and stability. Many evenings, on the World Service I hear cynical analyses based on Addis sources of the sinister intentions of the Eritrean and Ethiopian Fronts from "expert" analysts and journalists who have never been behind the lines and which bear no relation to my experience over the last few years.

A few days later, a contact in MLLT, the Marxist-Leninist Party here, gives me even more surprising information. They have had a conference also, in which they have voted not to set themselves up as a party of power in a forthcoming democratic Ethiopia, but to work as a pressure group behind the scenes "to safeguard the rights of the people."[3]

"Unfortunately," says my informant, "the Dergue, with its fascist policies, with its brutalities, has given a bad name to Marxism-Leninism. The people have a terrible hatred of these names because of what they have experienced. It is sad. Look at Eastern Europe, at what is happening there. Now they are saying communism and socialism are dead. But socialism has never been practiced—neither here in Ethiopia nor in the Soviet Union."[4]

A day or two later Tekleweini discusses my program with me. First, he says, I must talk with Meles. But Tigrayan time moves slowly and while messages are flitting back and forth in mysterious ways, I have a few days to get to know this new Adwa, to practice my rusty Tigrinya and discover the prevailing orthodoxies of the relief agencies. It's pleasant, too, to have a woman companion. After breakfast, Lesley and I generally wander about the town while it is still cool. I had forgotten, up on this central highland plateau, that the weather is balmy and mild at both ends of the day, like the Mediterranean, and at night cool, even chilly. In the Sudan, the sun was the enemy; here, it bathes with a golden glamor the cracked and shabby buildings and the crowd sauntering between them. The architecture in the center of the town shows the influence of the five years of Italian occupation after 1936 and make it even harder to believe we are in the tropics.

A woman fighter, stationed in London, has given me letters and photographs for her family here. I sit drinking coffee in their house near the grinding mill on the market square. Outside, the market is crammed with traders and buyers and a much greater variety of goods and vegetables than I have seen in any market on earlier visits. The restoration of town links with the countryside and with the Sudan has had its effect in improving trade and the local economy. Yet, how many of the country people can afford to buy anything? After two years of drought, harvests have been poor and foodstocks are low, and some areas are already totally dependent on aid convoys.

Poverty is blatant in the countryside; in the town, the concentration of goods to serve the needs of a greater range of incomes gives an impression of plenty, which is relative and deceptive. All the information is there, however, if you can read the code. Tins of powdered milk from the USA and food-aid grain in the original sacks are becoming more plentiful in the markets. This is not necessarily a corrupt use of aid, a black-market wheeler-dealing—families need to sell a proportion of what they receive in aid to purchase other essentials, like oil, and circulation of a certain amount provides a boost for the local economy, but as the effects of drought bite deeper and food supplies dwindle, desperate families begin to sell whatever they can, while prices plummet. In one area of the market square, the abundance of animals for sale, goats, donkeys, and oxen is a disquieting testimony of the shortage of fodder. Famines are not so much about lack of food in an absolute sense, at least in the towns, as about lack of entitlement to what is there. For those with money to buy, there is plenty of everything and, like anywhere else, plenty of profit to be made by merchants who buy the animals for a song and withhold their grain stocks until the prices soar.

On the way back one morning, Lesley and I unexpectedly bump into old friends, Negash and Mehret, two senior fighters who do organizational work for the Front in Europe. Although I have known them both for several years, only recently have I discovered they are married, as fighters are very discreet about personal relationships and the impositions of the war mean they have to spend most of their time apart. This is a happy meeting and exchange of news. Mehret is expecting their first baby; there is peace in Tigray; they have had a joyful reunion with their families; they are more or less on holiday and together in their homeland—what could be better? ("Except victory of course," adds Negash.) They are on their way to their old school for old time's sake, but also to greet the cultural group, which is preparing for some musical event.

"Why don't you join us?" says Negash. "You might meet old friends."

You could say that Adwa School has played its part in the revolution. Many of the first fighters went there, including Aregash, Sebhat, the last Chairman of the TPLF (as a teacher), and Meles, the present one. It would be interesting to see it, although when we get there the students are not there and the cluster of long low empty huts around a yard divulges no revolutionary secrets. The cultural group is there, however, and it is not an Adwa group, as I expected, but the Front's main cultural troupe, many of whom I met eighteen months ago.

"Where is Iyassu?" is my first question when greetings are over.

Iyassu is not here. His main concern, they tell me, is launching the newly-formed cultural troupe of the coalition Front, the EPRDF, involving musicians and performers of many different nationalities. Now that the main military focus is in central Ethiopia, it is important that cultural activity does not seem biased towards Tigray. Here, we are in Tigray and the emphasis is on Tigrayan songs and dances and we pass the next two hours enjoying an impromptu show. Even better—it's a party, for we can request our favorite songs and join in the dancing.

In the late afternoon, over the wall of the REST house, Lesley and I hear songs and the beating of drums and we run out of the gate to investigate. Bands of young people are coming up the slope of the main road, waving leafy branches and garlands of bourgainvillea. Three elderly musicians go before, producing a wierd and beautiful music from long metal flutes. They are accompanied by girls in white dresses with brightly-colored baskets on their heads like brides. Crowds are swarming towards the hill. All of them are singing. Everyone is joyful. Old women are clapping. They smile and laugh and welcome us. Without the slightest idea what is going on, we rush back for our cameras, but by the time we get back, the sun is down and it's too late for good shots.

Wave after wave of young people are coming up the hill. Some are just singing; some have drummers leaping in their midst; others come with musicians. All are accompanied by groups of young women and girls in their best clothes and by friends and families, making for a clearing in the trees at the top of the hill. We rush around like crazed tourists, taking poor pictures, until a young fighter called Abraha takes us under his wing. He has twelfth grade English, he tells us, so he can explain everything. First, it is a send-off party for the latest recruits to the Front, who are off to the training camp tomorrow. Each group is from a different *kebelle* or neighborhood association. Then I see Teklai, one of the lead singers from the cultural troupe, finishing a sound check behind the microphone. So, this is the musical event they have come for!

A few short speeches precede a program of music and songs, little dramas and new poems. As each soloist takes the mike, young people surge forward to present marks of appreciation—dollars, shawls, biros—which they wind round the singers' necks or stick in their hair. Teklai is like a pop star here. When he sings *The Mount of Guna*, recalling a recent devastating battle with the Dergue, a great mob of teenagers surrounds him, dancing, singing, and clowning. Fighters in the crowd tut disapprovingly. Despite the fighter who walks up and down with a rod in front of the first row of fighters' toes to remind them of their discipline, a few do manage to escape and join the throng in the arena.

"If too many go down it creates a disturbance," says Abraha. "It spoils the joy and blocks the view for everyone else."

The crowd, numbering at least five thousand, is also slowly edging forward in spite of exhortations from the microphone. But the mood is so joyful and their pleasure so spontaneous, it is hard to see what can be done about it.

Our own pleasure is dented by the thorns and pebbles we are sitting on, until our attentive companions find large flat stones for us. Their zeal to practice their English must be making more than a dent in their enjoyment of the music. Abraha and his friends want to talk about the West, which they think is the next thing to paradise. They look disconcerted when I mention poverty, hunger, ill-health and every kind of inequality, which co-exist with wealth in these the richest countries in the world.

"You mean, like Ethiopia?" says Abraha. "But they are not like Ethiopia—they are democracies. The people can express their opinions and participate. How is this possible?"

"It is a question of who holds the power and how it is operated," I say. "The power to influence decisions is very limited in my country, even for our elected representatives. The power is often in the hands of non-elected bodies and decisions are taken in secret."

I am beginning to think, with all its poverty and backwardness, Tigray has a more genuinely democratic system in the making than anything the West has known. But, it is a province of some four million people. How would this system of participatory democracy translate to a country like Britain of more than fifty million people? If they ever do get as far as introducing this democracy to the whole of Ethiopia (which, coincidentally, also has a population of some fifty million), they will have a thing or two to teach the West.

After a couple of hours, stressed knee joints and hips begin to distract us from the entertainment—unlike our companions, we have not been brought up to squatting on the ground for long periods—so we thank our new friends and leave the show long before it is ended. Sounds of music and the beat of drums, of ululation and applause, pursue us through the quiet streets and into our house. There, Letish, perturbed by our absence, greets me with a message from Tekleweini that I should be ready to leave for Tembien this evening. That time has already arrived and I have barely managed to swallow a few mouthfuls of supper, when the Toyota arrives. Fortunately, the fighter habit of being prepared to leave at a moment's notice has stayed with me since my first journey and in minutes I am setting out on the bumpy six-hour drive to Tembien.

The Front's headquarters have moved yet again. It is now in the central highlands about sixty kilometers from Mekelle, although I don't discover this until later. As usual, nobody tells me where we are going, but I keep my eyes skinned and notice we come to a halt a few minutes after passing through a little mountain town called Hagere Salam. We have climbed up and up a winding track high in the montains and when we get out of the land cruiser, the air is sharp and our breath comes in clouds. We are on top of the world under a great bowl of stars. By their light and a sliver of moon, I half see and half sense the land falling slowly away in front of us.

We have stopped at a guard post, a military tent huddled under a stone wall against the prevailing wind, and here we wait, nodding off and chatting by turns, as another hour of the night yawns by. I have a temporary guide from REST called Abebe, a colleague of my last guide, Heshe.

"How far is it?" I ask him, when at length the final security clearance arrives and we set off behind a band of fighters.

"Only a short walk—five minutes."

I should have known better than to ask. It takes a lot longer than five minutes. The path follows a gentle slope for half a mile before it plunges down the mountain side between rocky outcrops, twisting, turning, flattening out, plunging down again. In front of me, I feel a great space of air and dimly see in the starlight, so much brighter than in Europe, black deeps far below out of which rise layer upon layer of mountain ranges. Scrambling down behind Abebe I feel in danger of falling off the wall into the gulf, but it is all an illusion of strangeness and dim light. The next morning, I am ashamed at the fancy when I look at the easy angle of the slope and the land below which does not fall away sheer, but in a series of shallow steps, some of which are big enough to support villages.

The main offices ("Meles's house" Abebe calls it) are tucked into caves at the foot of a cliff, as they were in Dejenna four years ago. A narrow path connecting the buildings runs along the top of the screen—more than this I cannot see in the darkness, but when Abebe leaves me in a room to wait for Meles, I notice at once how much more strongly and permanently built this camp is than the one in Dejenna. The construction is of brick with tin roofs, even within the cave. Sturdy jointed wooden frames line the doors and windows; the floors are of concrete and all the windows on the open side have shutters. Camp beds have replaced the sleeping platforms of mud and stone, but the simple furnishings of patchwork quilts, wooden table, and chair are still the same. If they are serious in their prognosis of a speedy end to the war, then they must have designed this camp as a future place of pilgrimage.

Meles comes in after half an hour, not only looking as chipper as he always does in the middle of the night, but also very smart. Instead of fatigues, he is wearing a black leather jacket over a striped shirt and grey flannels. (Could this too be preparation for life after victory?)

Courteously he asks after my husband and children. Long ago, I told Aregash how much support my family has given me for my journeys and the news seems to have travelled. Meles does not seem to regard me as a questing individual so much as the front person for a clan, all interested in this emergent Ethiopia. My absences seem to have strengthened my bonds with my family, rather than the reverse. That is something Tigrayan people know all about—absences, separations, partings, migrations, exile, roving in search of seasonal work, children as servants of the better-off, girl children farmed out in forced marriages, death from hunger, death from disease, death from bombardments, and in battles. The effects of poverty and continual conflict. You would expect the complete erosion of the family, but family ties are a much more integral part of Tigrayan culture than they are in Europe. For me, it is muddled up with their sense of land and nation. Tigrayan exiles in Europe or the Sudan hearken back to their homeland, by which they mean, not Tigray, but their home village. Branches of families long moved to towns often think of the family farm as home. In the absence of any other type of security, families absorb displaced relatives so that it becomes impossible to distinguish between near and distant family members.

Fighters, of course, are separated from their families voluntarily. Do choosing and knowing why make separation any easier? In 1989, when the Dergue evacuated from Tigray, the war seemed almost suspended for a few weeks, while fighters trekked to the towns for reunions with long-separated families. Married fighters, even those with children, are separated by their jobs. They rarely experience family life—and how can bonds be strengthened by absence if they have not been formed first of all by day-to-day experience?

All these thoughts are running through my head as I give the latest news of my family and ask after Meles's wife and daughter.

"This time, I've brought a photograph of us all together," I say to Meles. It had been taken on my birthday a few months before.

"I admire your family," he says, studying it carefully, "and I think they are not typical."

Meles has a little daughter about two years old. She is called Samhal, after a small shrub whose fragrant leaves are prized for decorating houses on feast days or for part of the leafy mat for the coffee ceremony. I met his wife once, before I knew of the relationship. She was working in the Propaganda Bureau when I first visited it four years ago, although I have not met her since. Now, she works in the Press Office an hour or two from here by car.

In fact, it is an unusual honor to know anything at all about the personal lives of fighters. However important private life is to individuals, in this war individuals are less important than the common cause (this is so unfashionable in the West that it would be barely comprehensible there) and we pass on to what is now more important for both of us, the EPRDF's new program.

Meles confirms that the end of the war is imminent and that the program is a statement of intent "after victory," but he will not be drawn on more precise time-scales. In fact, they have had strategies worked out for a long time. In March 1989, just after the Tigrayan Front took over the whole of Tigray, they publicized peace proposals to the Dergue, which included the formation of a provisional government constituted from all political organizations, including the present government. A year later, the successor coalition Front republished this program "for the smooth and peaceful transition of power in Ethiopia" in a more strongly-worded and detailed statement in which an ultimatum to the Dergue withdrew the offer of participation in a provisional government if they rejected the chance of a peaceful solution and had to be removed by force. Now, nine months after that, they are committing themselves to a detailed democratic manifesto for a peaceful Ethiopia.

In advocating a very democratic program, says Meles, they are adapting to the needs of the time in both Tigray and Ethiopia. People have an intense hatred of Marxism-Leninism; they crave democracy, freedom, peace.[5]

"What kind of democracy?" I ask. "How will you preserve the advances already made in the revolution—in land reform and women's equality, for example?"

"The most important thing is to trust that the people, with the right guidance, will safeguard their own interests. We do not accept that the achievements of the revolution can only be safeguarded by a controlling or a repressive system. The people have to be free, but really free, to know their own interest and not be manipulated or exploited, which means they must have a proper political consciousness or education."

I can't help feeling skeptical. They have worked for many years to instill political consciousness in the Tigrayan peasants—with considerable success. In Tigray those words "with the right guidance," ominous to Western ears, has meant the circulation for discussion in draft during the setting-up of the *baito* of a suggested framework of laws to establish, among other things, the economic and social equality of women and minorities. That process in the towns is still under way. But in Tigray, they have been helped by national feelings and long experience of national oppression. How will the education necessary to underpin the kind of democratic system he is describing come about in the huge tracts of southern Ethiopia?

Meles says that the Tigrayan role will be a supportive one south of the border—*is* in fact already, as the process has already begun. The Amhara and the Oromo wings of the coalition Front are working directly with their own people further south and already several smaller nationalities, like the Beni Shangul, have applied for membership of the EPRDF and their fitness for inclusion is being examined.

"What are the criteria for inclusion?"

"That they are genuinely democratic. This is the one thing we have to be very sure of. If we, or any group in our name, try to force anything on a reluctant people, it won't last. We will merely be hearing our own echo."

"Does that mean that in your own organizations you are constantly monitoring the democratic practice right down to individuals?"

"You have to be confident that they are consistent in their democratic practice before you accept organizations into the united front. The TPLF and the EPDM had a long time to get to know each other and to build confidence in each other's practice. The new ones we have to see in practice how they go about their daily business."

"Which means that the whole method of training and consciousness-raising is crucial as well, because the leadership might have the right ideas but it might not filter down. Among the oppressed nationalities there must be strains of hostility to the Amhara, which are difficult to eradicate. This is understandable—a legitimate hatred—but how do you deal with it?"

"That is how we treat it, whereas chauvinism has no legitimacy. It starts from a feeling of superiority and a right to rule over others, whereas this is defensive. The hatred, the suspicion, that some of the fighters have of the Amhara, is based on the experience they have had. It's wrong to have a bias against the Amhara as a people, but it has to be handled in a different way. It comes from a people who have been on the receiving end of oppression. It must not be shouted down. The roots of this suspicion must be explained. You don't overcome suspicion by saying the oppressed Amhara is your friend. You have to show him how the process of oppression works, the role the oppressed Amhara plays in this and what suffering in different ways the Amhara has gone through because of the class structure. You have to show him, once the Oromo gets organized, once we do away with the established order, things will work out in a totally different way. A new relationship between Amhara and Oromo will be possible. The best way to undo the past is to undo the structures and to replace it with a new relationship based on equality and respect."[6]

The next morning, I wake early despite my short night and go outside. From the top path I take a steep fork, which winds down the slope above the roof of the latrine. It is much more extensive than the mere shit pits I've encountered in other fighters' camps—not so much a latrine as a bath house. Although there is no running water, a proper ceramic latrine cover to squat on is set in a concrete floor with a bucket of water and scoop next to it and a couple of yards away a separate shower tray with its own bucket, soap and toilet rolls within reach. What luxury!

Scrubbed and virtuous and trying to warm up again in sweater and shawls, I explore along the path the way we came last night. The sun has risen behind the mountain. The caves, the path and the whole scree are still in deep shadow. The caves are all filled in with neat little dwellings to which there are a number of entrances off the path. One of them has a satellite dish fixed to the rock outside it, camouflaged by a shawl. At the end of the path I climb up a few yards to get an idea of our route in the dark. The mountain slopes are covered with boulders with paths winding between. Now I can see what were invisible at night—camouflaged dwellings dug deep into the hillside, their roofs inclined with the slope and indistinguishable from the rocky ground, a door and window slit barely visible from the lip of an access "area" dug out in front like a basement flat in London.

I am away most of the morning until Meles wakes, sitting on a boulder outside the cave, writing my diary and going over my program proposal. The camp is very high. To the west I can see right over intervening mountains to the plain we crossed last night and beyond that, range upon range of ridges out of which, on the horizon, project the wierd distinguishing shapes of the peaks of Adwa. Stomach cramps bring me down to earth. I need breakfast. There seem very few people around. Perhaps Meles's nocturnal habits have spread to the whole camp. Occasionally, a fighter walks along the path and looks at me curiously. At length, one of them returns with tea and *himbasha* and omelette. It only takes a mouthful or two to force me to acknowledge a certain weakness this morning, a shakiness of the limbs, a certain disinclination for food. Could it be altitude sickness? How high is Hagere Salam?

At the end of the morning, a fighter comes to say Meles is ready. His entrance is the one with a satellite dish, but we sit outside in a little niche in the rock. He listens carefully to my proposal to research into the history and causes of the revolution. He agrees it is important.

"If it is so important, you should be recording this history yourselves."

"Yes, but unfortunately we have no time now. There are other more important things to be done."

Yes, to bring this whole struggle to a successful conclusion. But, after it is over (at some point I seem to have taken on board their conviction that this will happen soon) they will be even thinner on the ground with even more to do. What did Tekleweini say about the hardest struggle being in the future? My research is bound by all the constraints and limitations of being an outsider and a Westerner. It will be a version wholly different from theirs, but in a war zone the Front has to facilitate the project to enable it to be done at all. A leadership notoriously opposed to cults of personality and reserved about even the identities of the first fighters will have to give me access to this information and to those who have survived. I also need a guide who will understand the nature of the project and be able to open doors. This is why I have been sent to Meles.

We discuss the whole project, which seems to be growing a hundred hydra-heads even as we talk. This is the work of years, not a few months. A young fighter comes along the path with a message for Meles. It is covered with handwriting, folded small, and stapled. We may be sitting underneath a satellite dish on the top of a mountain, but some things have not changed. Despite these sophistications, at least the postal service is the same. The Man with the Stapler still rules.

The message, whatever it is, brings a change of mood. Meles has to go, but he courteously asks if I have anything else to say.

"I would like to talk also to the other EPRDF leaders."

"That is easy. They are here—did you know?"

I didn't know. No one had told me.

"This is the headquarters of the EPRDF, not just the TPLF. Tigray is now more secure than elsewhere in Ethiopia."

"I think you also need to go to the front," adds Meles, sliding off the ledge of rock. "I will make the arrangements. Come back and talk to us when you return."

14

Fire From the Ashes

I am to stay in Mekelle until I go to the front. Days? Weeks? I don't know. Until they tell me to go, I suppose, probably with four minutes notice. But, I sense something in the offing. Something is about to happen, a new strategy, a new breakthrough, a new campaign. I definitely sniff something in the wind. The forces of the Front are on the march to Addis, but what is the plan? What is the path?

While they are on the march to Addis, however, I am going to be marching back in time. My historical quest is to begin at once and not one, but two, interpreters are to help me. I meet them first in the Castle Hotel, which is rather smarter than the Green. Until the Dergue evacuation two years ago, it was the exclusive domain of higher-ranking army officers and officials. We sit in the bar and discuss my proposal. The two men are physical opposites. Aklilu Tekemte is taller and very thin. His wrists and the ankles, which protrude from his jeans look astonishingly fragile. But, it is his voice, which makes the immediate impact. It is high pitched, but hoarse and gravelly at the same time. He works with Meles in the caves at Hagere Salam as some sort of secretary.

Mulugeta Berhe is smaller and rounder. Like Aklilu, he is rarely to be seen without his peaked cap and, curiously, he is also the son of a priest in Axum. At least, perhaps it isn't so curious. Perhaps there is a hidden logic to their common background and their presence here; priests, especially those in Axum, the historical center of the Ethiopian orthodox church, are more highly educated, like the clergy in medieval Europe, and therefore value education more highly for their sons. The few schools in Tigray in Haile Selassie's time were so inadequate that Mulugeta was sent as a child to live with a relative in Addis Ababa to get an education. At the University, he majored in history for two years until the poverty of his family forced him to find a job "because my brothers and sisters had no one to help them." He was active in the student movement, which helped topple Haile Selassie and then, when so many young people were imprisoned and killed in the Dergue purges known as the Red Terror, he managed to get a scholarship to study in the USSR. The Soviet Union was by then arming and supporting the military junta, so it was at great personal risk that he began working underground in Europe for the young TPLF.

In fact, these details I learn gradually over the next few weeks. Our first meetings are spent summarizing the history of Tigray from ancient times. Mulugeta is to organize my immediate program of research into the times of the Emperors Haile Selassie and Menelik II; Aklilu will take over from the founding of the TPLF and accompany me to the war front. Mulugeta is fascinated by this history. He has already done a considerable amount of research and within a few days has set up the first interviews, no easy feat in the absence of telephones and predictable transport.

So, my days are spent talking about old times to the elders and the storytellers in the villages. Sometimes, they come to me at the Green Hotel in Mekelle; sometimes I go to them. I prefer to go to them. They should tell their history in their own places—places that have survived the vengeance of governments and the shock of bombs, from where the women watched them depart first for the *gareb* and then for the battle, with their staves across their shoulders and their rifles on their backs.

These aren't just any stories; these aren't just any tellers. These aren't just excuses for nostalgia, loose memories spiralling up into the roof space with the smoke from the charcoal stove and the fumes of *sewa*. These are historians who take their responsibilities to their communities and to future generations seriously. They always come in twos and threes, sometimes more. They fill in gaps for each other and argue about details. This is a different history, never written down.

Official written history is a tool of power. If all history is versions of the past, the version that has most chance of becoming confused with "truth" is the one that legitimates the ruling élite. Nowhere is this more the case than in Ethiopia, a largely illiterate society, riven by conflict, whose tiny educated elite, dominated by one nationality since the end of the nineteenth century, has marketed the achievements of autocratic empire and dictatorship. Meanwhile, for hundreds of years the huge rural population have acted out their lives in silence.

Yet, within these rural communities the voices have been loud and persistent. Oral history has its own strengths and its own difficulties. Its strength is its defiance of the simple syntheses and complacent expertise of conventional historians or the orthodoxies of academia, which prize documentary and inanimate evidence and despise testimony. Its weakness is its invisibility in the wider world. The problem for the investigator is its multiplicity.

So, I have my own methods of cross-checking. One of them is to take the same questions to different places. Each community has a local bias, telling the past from the point of view of their own experience, their own alliances, but except for these differences of emphasis, wherever I go the story is roughly the same.

Telling the past is the obligation of the old to the young. The old people are respected. They are never short of an audience, although some times are better than others. As it happens, now is the right time, the dry season, before the small rains, when there is no plowing, when the harvest is gathered in and there is no work—at least no work of that sort. It is the time of consolidation, of building. And, not only of terraces and dams and fences. If the rains have fallen the year before and there is a reasonable crop, it is the only time of year when you can be sure of something to eat. It is the time for building communities also, the time of weddings and the time of *kusmi* or gatherings. If the church has its saint's day even the people of neighboring villages come to join the celebration. The women prepare *injera* and *sewa* and there are plays and songs and stories.

The old people sit in the shade and talk to each other. They have had their years of work. Now, they play draughts and swap memories. As the sun sets, they hear the hoarse notes of the flute. The young boys are bringing the cattle back from the field—most of the older boys have gone off to join the Front. There are no books, no electricity, no television. In the twilight, as the oxen pick about in the straw, young people come up and ask questions. This is the best time for stories. Each village remembers in a different way. The old people each remember in a different way, but not everyone has the same skill. There are known and respected story-tellers ("I'm no good at telling stories. He's better than me—ask him! He's a very talkative man, so ... let him talk!"). One starts, the other adds something, a third remembers a poem made at the time and it extends into a bright bracelet, a chain of evidence.

In Wajirat, a district in eastern Tigray, they still have rituals for transferring exploits from the individual to the collective memory. It is called *sebr-gumarey.* Now, it is somewhat changed, but formerly it was used to celebrate new battles and after that, at celebrations and festivals, the victories of the past. Warriors lined up on one side, facing the people of the village on the other. In a rigorous order, the minor achievers first of all and the greatest at the end, the warriors came forward one at a time to declare the number of the enemy he had killed, how many arms he had siezed and the particular circumstances of the action. The story was told, with many rhetorical devices for suspense and excitement, in a loud and special voice with a semi-musical delivery, like a chant.

"It was early in the morning and the Italians came to start the fight...."

And the people all cried out together. "Y-e-es ...!"

There were (and perhaps still are) safeguards against exaggeration or dishonesty and severe penalties for breaking the code. Each warrior had to call witnesses.

"Are you not here, my friend Gebreselassie?"

"Are you not there, the son of my friend? Didn't your father tell you this story when you were only eight years old?"

He was not telling his own history, but the history of the village and the community have to confirm it.

"Is this not right?"

"Ye-es!" the assembly would shout and the women would ululate "Lililili..." and maybe one would come forward and lay her wide sash, the *netsela*, on the ground for the warrior to walk on. But if any man jumped the queue or pretended to exploits not his own he would immediately be shot, irrespective of his social status.[1]

There are no such rituals involved in the interviews I am engaged in. These old men come with their gnarled faces and worn jackets, their white *gabis* wrapping their heads and shoulders. Tadesse Ayele and Gebrehiwot Kiros in Adi Gudom carry ancient 1930s rifles. From Quiha come Desta Abuy and Mulaw Wores, very dignified, leaning on their staves, but as they talk their voices become young and springy like their memories and their posture becomes upright and heroic. This is what I see at this time. I am so busy directing the questions, looking out for gaps, cross-checking, monitoring the translation, scribbling and taping, that the information itself becomes a tangle of alliances and rivalries, of treacheries and commitment, of battles and bombardments. For a while, the only clarity I am left with is the sharp images of the tellers themselves.

I have come to ask them about the 1943 *Weyane* or revolution, a peasant uprising against Haile Selassie in eastern Tigray, especially the districts of Enderta and Wajirat. Mekelle and its environs were the heart of the rebellion. I cannot pretend to much detective work in finding this out. They tell you about it all the time. They see the First *Weyane* as the direct precursor of the present revolution. It lacked organization and political consciousness, they say. Otherwise, they would have won. It also taught them important lessons.

The mainspring of the uprising was Blatta Haile Mariam, still alive but out of reach in southern Ethiopia, where he was exiled nearly fifty years ago.[2] Nevertheless, there are other surviving leaders living in this area, as well as countless participants and supporters. One day, in early February, we go to talk to two *Weyane* veterans who live in Quiha, a small town on the plateau above Mekelle. Desta Abuy, now sixty-eight, was one of the leaders; he was twenty in 1943. Balambaras Mulaw Wores (both *Balambaras* and *Blatta* are minor feudal titles) is related to Haile Mariam and also his brother-in-law. He seems young for his seventy-seven years.

They sit facing me on one side of the table, Mulugeta on the side between us on my left. Mulugeta is as absorbed as I am. He is an invaluable source of information himself as he has been collecting data on the history of Tigray for several years already, and has a reputation as the unofficial historian of these turbulent times. Sometimes, he suggests new or more fruitful ways of questioning or points out opportunities for cross-checking controversial material. He has tremendous respect for the peasants and knows how to talk to them. He tells them my name and why I have come.

"She is investigating the history of the revolution. The First *Weyane* is a part of this history—so we have come to you."

The sense of ceremonial is catching. This is not the place for familiarity and jokes. I begin by thanking them for sparing the time to talk to me. It might take as long as two or three days. I appreciate their generosity. Mulaw inclines his head.

"She is our guest," he replies to Mulugeta. "She has come to our country from a long way. It is she who should be thanked, not us. We have survived the First *Weyane*. We had a few victories, many defeats; we lost many lives and saw many atrocities, but we have seen not only the First *Weyane*, but also the second revolution—and the first led to the second. That is a victory and it is another victory that our friends from the outside are now coming to speak to us."

But, it turns out not to be so simple to get answers straight off about the First *Weyane*. That's not where the veterans want to start. They want to explain their own need to rebel. This involves not only a discussion of the abortive attempt between 1936 and 1941 by the Italian dictator, Mussolini, to colonize Ethiopia, but a detailed account of the conditions before that, under Emperors Menelik II and Haile Selassie. It's becoming clear that my quest for causes will have to go back much further than the 1943 uprising.

Most of the old warriors I talk to were among the Patriots, as they call them, who fought fiercely against the Italians and had to flee into Afar territory during the five-year occupation. A few of them fought with the Italians, either in support of a feudal lord who, nursing some grievance against Haile

Selassie, fancied the Italians would be better masters or because they had been in Eritrea (an Italian colony since the end of the nineteenth century) and coerced them into the army. They seem to bear no grudges against each other and compare notes from different sides.

What is more astonishing is that, despite references to the resistance, to napalm attacks and to the atrocities of Graziani and other Italian generals, they don't seem to bear grudges against the Italians either, although they do bear a heavy grudge against Ras Seyoum, the chief Tigrayan prince of the time, and many stories, songs and poems refer to his cowardice and betrayal of his people. They also bear a grudge against Haile Selassie—first because he lost valuable time by delaying before bringing his troops to Tigray to fight the Italians; second, for skipping the country and leaving his people to face the music. Above all, they resent the Amhara version of events, which they say, leaves out the part played by the Tigrayan people in the front line of defense against the invaders.

Ironically, many people old enough to remember talk of the Italian occupation as a kind of golden age.

"The market was set up by the Italians," Assefa tells me. "Even the water system was introduced by the Italians. We had never seen anything like it before. They introduced *piazzas* with good two-story buildings. They built the football stadium. Then, they took all the land of Mekelle and distributed it to the people. Anyone who wanted to build a house was given land freely. Some rich people built houses and then sold them. It was a new thing to build a modern house. They constructed modern roads and established the city plan of Mekelle."[3]

It was the abolition of feudal taxation that really won them over. The Italians substituted a low cash tax dependent on land and income, so the poorest did not pay at all. No doubt, the Italian administrators would in time have increased taxation; no doubt the investment in infrastructure was made to facilitate their control, but five years was not long enough to reveal the dark face of colonial power. Instead, this glimpse of a different life showed the Tigrayan people the dark reality of feudal power. In 1941, the British restored Haile Selassie to his throne and with him returned the burden of feudal taxation and the obligation to provide for feudal armies wherever they marched.

Asrat the Merchant

I came from Gondar. My father was a peasant and a soldier. I was a soldier of Prince Iyassu, Prince of Wello. He was originally from Wello, but, al-

though he was the legitimate heir of Emperor Menelik, the Shewan ruling class did not accept Iyassu. Therefore, he rebelled against the regime. The lords of Gojjam supported Iyassu, but he was defeated. I participated in that battle.

When I was young, I was a slave trader. I bought slaves from the western part of Wellega and the slaves I bought were confiscated by the government. During the slave trade, the rich slavers killed one or two to intimidate the others. They traded in children and young ones. The lowest age was ten. They were sold for domestic work, both male and female. When we were selling the children, it was quite bad. We lived in poverty because we were cursed for carrying on the slave trade. I will not go to heaven, because of that one time when I traded in slaves and they were confiscated. Haile Selassie's good quality is that he stopped the slave trade, but that was the only good quality he had.

I became a merchant by accident. I came here by accident too. I came to Mekelle when I was thirty years old, in 1934, about a year before the Italian invasions. I was on my way to be a soldier in Tripoli. I set off to go to Tripoli, but Ras Seyoum was guarding the border to Eritrea and didn't allow me to cross the border to Asmara, so I had to come back. So, before the Italian invasion I began to trade in flax with Eritrea. During the Italian occupation, trade was flourishing. The Italians introduced bed sheets and I began trading in cloth. The time of the Italians was a time of plenty and you could earn a lot of money. We had mead and wine—we never drank water. The Italians were colonialists here and were settled.

Under the Italians, they were throwing "mangiamo" [bread] about, but after that they had no bread at all. When the British came, poverty came too. They took the property of the Italians, even from the army camps, and that flourishing trade ended. This town was built by the Italians, but the British took the telephone wires. They were quite hungry after the British took over. The British brought us Haile Selassie and he brought us poverty. I don't exactly understand it, but from the moment the Italians left, poverty reigned in our land.

I was still selling cloth as well as trading in cattle, mules, salt, and pepper. Some rich Italians bought salt, but we merchants remained poor. It was because of the system. Bribery was rampant. Judges were corrupt. Wealth became concentrated in the hands of a few. The rest of us remained poor. Unless you gave one or two hundred birr to the judge, you could not have land. So, some became very rich. Everything became corrupt. Even the poor plaintiff could be bribed and this system oppressed the poor. There was no justice.

The Weyane was started by Blatta Haile Mariam, but it caused in the end, even greater poverty, because it brought here the Amhara army from Shewa and they took my goats. They confiscated my harvest from my farmland and they wanted to take my donkeys. The Shewans took all the property. They even took my gabi. *If I had new clothes they took them before I had a chance to put them on. During that feudal age, the strong feudals used to come and loot the property of the people and, once it was looted, it never raised its head again. But, in Tigray there was a persistent resistance from the Tigrayan people. Several times, they resisted the domination of the Shewan Amhara.*

The Shewans looted every area and now it is the turn of the Tigrayans. During the time of Yohannes 1V the Tigrayans looted the property outside Tigray and during the time of the Shewans they did it back and now it is the time of the Tigrayans again.[4]

There is a saying in the Tigrayan countryside: *Every dawn a new sun*, which exactly catches the attitude of the peasants to their feudal leaders. The succession of leaders is as inevitable as the sun rising in the morning. It's a new day, but the same old sun. He might look like a new lord, but it's the same old power, the same old rivalries, the same old wars, the same old taxes with fancy names. The feudal class had its origin and identity in warfare. Even the feudal titles—*Dejazmach, Fitaurary, Grazmach, Kegnazmach,* and so on—denote positions on the battlefield in relation to the tent of the *ras* or the king.[5] But the cause of the lord is not necessarily the cause of the poor peasant. What difference does it make to the peasant struggling to scratch a living from soil not even his own, even if he takes his military service for granted? He knows he bears the brunt of it all. It's an attitude apparently philosophical, but in fact borne of bitter experience and expressive of total powerlessness to change his lot. Yet, anything that intensified his problems would be noted and recorded; anything that alleviated his lot, no matter by how little, would be tried. In Gojjam, in 1938, the Italian Commander-in-chief, General Cavallero, saw the people flocking to the forts to pay respect to the colonizers and misconstrued as submission what was merely deference paid to the stronger master, a means of buying time. As soon as the Italian troops left, the locals joined the Patriot resistance again.[6]

Behind the shoulder-shrugging acceptance of continuing misery and hunger, behind the deference, behind the mask, I have glimpsed the implacable face of the peasants. Deeper than misery and hunger, deeper than resentment, is their commitment to memory of resentment, to the recording of common experience of injustice, without hope of redress or change. It is an invisible, inaudible record—or at least inaccessible not only to outsiders like myself, but also to Ethiopian outsiders who are hopelessly divided by education and fear of poverty from the culture of the countryside. Without the help of Iyassu, who leads the Front's Cultural Department, I would not have suspected that the silence of peasants already dead could become a roar.

The evidence, this commentary on peasant experience, is stored in their poems and songs, but as these are composed and shared and remembered orally, their existence is unsuspected by townspeople. Even for Iyassu who was brought up in Mekelle, a small town preserving many links with the countryside, the discovery of this hidden culture was a revelation. There are songs for every function, like weddings and funerals, and for every season and activity of the agricultural year, that celebrate the cycles of nature and the partnership of the peasant. There are also songs, which show the hardness of the farmer's life and for what?—for the feudal's family. One of the traditional grinding songs, which Iyassu adapted for a musical play records the isolation and unhappiness of women in the struggle against poverty:

I can open my heart to no one near,
Whether they are home or the house is empty,
No one speaks to me.
My priest is a hen and my friend a grindstone.

In another the plowman talks to the oxen drawing the plow, but they are not his own:

If you were mine, my ox,
I could fill all my house
With the fruits
Of this harvest...
Yet I am not allowed
To taste the grain
I get from my labor.
Yet it is the straw
That comes to us
And the grain to the feudals.
Let us go and be hermits,
My ox, you and I together.
This land is not our land.

The funeral poems, the *melkes,* are the most interesting group. They could be conventional tributes or, because the *melkesti* who composed and recited them were traditionally protected from reprisals, they could be stinging political poems against feudal arrogance and mistreatment. Some contain coded messages and double meanings, so that although they sound like a song of praise, they are recognized by their peasant listeners as highly critical.[7]

One day, three veteran warriors of Mekelle come to talk to me about the times before the First *Weyane.*[8] They give their account, factual and unadorned, of the twenties and thirties, describing the feudal rivalries which preceded the Italian invasions, lists of different taxes that made people's lives a misery and the looting and exploitation of the feudal armies, which impoverished the peasants and caused lasting resentment wherever they went. Their faces are placid. Even their descriptions of the wretchedness of the peasants sound objective and dispassionate.

"What are your feelings about the pressures of those times?" I ask, curious, not sure whether I'm breaking cultural rules. "Did you accept the lot of the peasant? Did you feel resentment and anger?"

They express their bitterness in various ways.

"There was no chance of anything different. We couldn't rebel. They lived on the shoulders of the peasants," says Asefa Gebremariam.

Kiros Abera, at seventy-eight, the most senior and to whom the others defer, is silent and thoughtful. Then he begins to speak.

He chooses to reply not in his own words, but in a poem, perfectly remembered. The poem is a *melkes*, composed Mulugeta thinks about 1922 by a famous *melkesit*, a woman funeral orator. It is a compressed, elliptical, oral form, in this case as long as a sonnet, and packing a political punch. The original occasion was the funeral of a wealthy feudal, Belai Abai, but the place was the house of his princely relative, Ras Guxa, who was also the target of the savage critique of feudal exploitation, which is the object of the poem. It is almost impossible to translate, not only because the elliptical possibilities of Tigrinya make English expression wordy and long, but because every line is so dense with cultural and historical reference, that it needs a paragraph of explanation. The poet recalls a past occasion when she had made Ras Gugsa a present of a *gofala,* the huge basketwork jar-shaped table for *injera* in the homes of the better-off, and also a *gabi,* the multi-layered warm shawl, spun and woven by hand, but he had refused them and sent her away.

"*O Gugsa, that Belai your servant with his gofala belly,*" is the opening line. Only the richest feudals in this country of the bone-thin could achieve such a belly and only through devouring the produce of the poor. Gugsa's soldiers, it goes on, are good for nothing except scaring birds and vandals from the crops; he himself is only concerned with saving his own skin in the thick of the battle. Finally she says:

If they ask you who I am
Say, I don't know, I don't know.

For Kiros, this story of feudal arrogance and betrayal is a perfect answer to my question.

At last, we are getting to the point where we can talk about the First *Weyane*. Every group I talk to agrees that the immediate trigger for the uprising was the harsh treatment of the Tigrayan people by Haile Selassie. Italian defeats in the second world war had forced the Italians to evacuate Ethiopia and the British masterminded the return of the Emperor from exile in 1941. These old men insist that, in fear of the independent spirit of Tigrayans, Tigray was singled out as if for punishment. The Tigrayan prince, Ras Seyoum, was confined to Addis, and Amhara governors were installed as administrators. Having a gun was illegal and heavy fines were imposed to assist the disarming of the peasants. An array of taxes was reimposed, which further impoverished farmers already constrained to hand over a large proportion of their crops to feudal landlords.

But, everywhere I go it is memory of the behavior of soldiers that still arouses indignation. Not only did the Tigrayan district governors have their own unsalaried armies, but for the first time Haile Selassie established a central government force and set up garrisons of barely-paid soldiers in the major Tigrayan towns. These troops were a scourge of the people, encouraged, according to my informants, by both Amhara and Tigrayan authorities.

"The peasants in the villages were ordered to prepare food, beer and meat. They had a very bad time because the troops grabbed and stole and robbed. If you went to a judge, he was himself a feudal and acted as if you were insulting him by accusing his soldiers."

"But what made you begin to organize?"

"The people were unhappy," says Desta Abuy with characteristic Tigrayan understatement. "As we said earlier, there was injustice. There were also girls and women raped by the troops. People were being beaten like donkeys. They didn't treat people like human beings. When they came to your house, they didn't ask for a goat but just grabbed it. There were such heavy taxes also. The people couldn't stand it and began to rebel against the government. There were some people who rebelled before the *Weyane*, like Blatta Haile Mariam, and in other places too, so the government was always accusing villagers of giving sanctuary to bandits. This is the reason the government always sent troops. The people couldn't bear it any longer and secretly, from one village to another, from one district to another, they began to contact each other."

Despite the accusation of disorganization, the uprising was much more organized than I had expected, not "spontaneous" at all. In every district, they gathered to talk on river banks and *gareb*, the local word for this meeting-place, became the name of the meeting itself—*the place-of-the-meeting-beside-the-river-under-the-big-tree*. In every village, the people elected their own leaders and sent them to the *gareb*. Plunging a big knife into the earth, each delegate took an oath of loyalty—"If I betray the *Weyane,* then let this knife cut my throat." Every *gareb* formed its resolutions and sent them with representatives to a central *gareb* at Hintalo and it was here that they made a final declaration.

The democratic nature of the organization was reflected in the resolutions, which rejected Amhara administration in favor of electing their own local administrators. Less democratic was the decision that everyone, including local bandits, must join the uprising or take the consequences—"...especially the youngsters. Anyone who doesn't, will be dressed in women's clothing and displayed in the market-place." A chain of bonfires would signal from hill to hill the approach of government forces.

The first battle against the district governor and other powerful feudals was in Wajirat in May 1943, before the final *gareb* assembled. A *Weyane* victory, it was a huge boost to morale. Later, in the summer, there were also victories at Wukro, Quiha and Mekelle, where new administrations were established. Some feudals threw in their lot with the rebels. Even priests supported with food and water and, says Mulaw Wores, in some places "the priests even participated in the battle. They came dressed in their vestments and carried the big crosses of the church and held up St. Mikael's and St. Mary's pictures and other saints, carrying them against their chests and ringing small handbells and so, holding all these, they came from Dandera to Quiha."

A large army sent by Haile Selassie, finally met the rebel forces between Korem and Maichew in southern Tigray at the Aleji plateau. The *Weyane* forces had won every battle and victory seemed almost within their grasp this time also, but Haile Selassie had appealed for British aid. Royal Air Force planes sent from Aden bombed Mekelle, Quiha, and many other places, including the battle area and much of the countryside between there and Mekelle. Thousands of *Weyane* troops were slaughtered as they dispersed in alarm to their homes.

Kindaya Natu, a tailor in Mekelle, was also a part-time policeman at the time under the *Weyane* administration. On the day of the bombing, the market was in full swing.

"The market was as crowded, as it is today. Before the bombardment they dropped pamphlets. The people went towards the bombs. They were glittering in the sun and they thought these were pamphlets too and they ran towards them to catch them."

He stops and ruminates for a moment or two.

"We don't know how many people died. There were so many. People came to the market to take the bodies of their relatives away for burial, but nobody knew who was who, because there were just fragments of bodies, arms and legs and bits and pieces. Many never found their relatives because they could never be identified. I had to bury eight bodies. I dug three graves for them. I even remember the place where I buried them—I can show you, if you like. There was a bad smell for weeks in the market place, so everyone had to cover up their noses and mouths with their shawls. We were instructed by the *Weyane* leaders to gather all the bits of bodies together. We never knew whether they were Christian or Muslim and we buried them together in one grave."

We break for lunch. In the afternoon, before we start work again, I walk with Mulugeta to the market place. Even now it is impossible to dig in the dirt without coming across bones. According to Mulugeta, shops were built above the main mass graves to mark the spot. I want to have another look while the words are fresh in my mind, but when we get there, my imagination is defeated by the bodies surging in the narrow paths between the stalls, the smells of rubber tires and diesel, of rotting bananas and hot pepper, cow-dung and urine, of untanned goatskin and live goat, the forlorn cries of animals outdone by the irritable shouts of the sellers at the retinue of shrieking children behind me calling out "Cuba! Cuba!" or "Italienne!" or " *Ferenji*!" or "Money, money!" as they knock pots off the stalls or fall into the little heaps of grain or garlic. Most of the stall-holders are women. Some have umbrellas, but most of them sit unprotected, their skulls beneath the thin layer of baked skin exposed with shocking clarity in the harsh sunlight, their disintegrated clothing shimmering in the yellow heat. The air vibrates with flies, which settle on every inch of bare flesh and cluster in the eyes of children. My throat is dry, my brain frying. The reality of people's lives laid bare in all its harshness to the light of the afternoon stares back at me like an open wound. I look up at the unforgiving sky and try to imagine the glittering cascade of British bombs and thin hungry ragged people like these running to catch them.

I have been to the market several times without remarking the curious line of shops built half across the market place. Now, from a distance I pick them out at once, constructed as a single story, each shop in the row tall and thin. There is nothing unusual about the shop-keepers. In one doorway, a tailor is treddling away at his sewing machine; another dim interior is filled with bolts of brightly-colored cloth; next door is crammed with disparate but mundane necessaries like toilet rolls, biros, cigarettes, and washing powder. At this time of day, they cast a narrow shade, which is crowded with somnolent donkeys. I would never have guessed the memorial intent of these shops, but they certainly don't look like any others I have seen in Tigray. They have curious hooded semi-circular roofs—like the tombs that cluster around Tigrayan churches within the grove of sacred trees.

It was after the bombing that the cracks became apparent. The loose organization of the First *Weyane* under local leaders gave opportunity for conflicting responses and fragmentation, exploited by secret initiatives of Haile Selassie, who allegedly bought off the Wajirati people with promises of autonomy. Fired by grievances but without an appropriate political analysis, the peasants still had a feudal outlook and could be swayed by their affiliations to feudal lords who were themselves caught up in rivalries encouraged by Haile Selassie's divisive tactics. Some said that Kifletsion, son of one of the Tigrayan princes, should be king; others that Blatta Haile Mariam should be governor of Tigray. Even now, there is disagreement about the honorable or self-interested nature of the role played by Blatta Haile Mariam. Finally and perhaps most important, there was no central body of objectives or vision of the future strong enough to withstand the bombings and hold the peasants together. So the rebels began to disperse.

Government troops marched not only on Mekelle and Quiha, but even into the rural areas. They burned the houses, killing people and cattle; they set fire to crops either in the stack or ready in the fields for the reapers; they even raped the wives of the priests. Whole villages were destroyed and people who escaped killing were flogged or had hands or legs amputated. Many people fled from the highlands to the lowlands of the Afar and Agew peoples. Desta fled to Afar territory, where Blatta Haile Mariam held out for three years with members of his dedicated mobile force. But, the reprisals continued under the new Amhara governor, the War Minister, Ras Abebe.

Desta's Postscript

Ras Abebe told his people to bring him Haile Mariam alive, otherwise he would destroy all the people and all the cattle. Blatta Haile Mariam said, "I do not want my people to be destroyed, so I will give myself up to Ras Abebe." The people said, "We will ask Ras Abebe only to imprison you and not to kill you." The peasants went to Ras Abebe. Then Ras Abebe swore on oath not to kill Blatta Haile Mariam. The peasants said to Ras Abebe how the oldest son of Ras Seyoum, Kassa Byelak, had been taken to Addis and killed: "You took Ras Mengesha Yohannes and imprisoned him in Shewa and he was killed there. You took Dejazmach Abraha Araya and imprisoned him and he never returned to Tigray. So, now you will take Blatta Haile Mariam and the same will happen to him. When you took them you swore an oath, but you didn't keep your word. That is the story of the Tigrayan people. So, you Amhara are going to repeat this deed. This is bad for the Amharas and for relations with the Tigrayan people. So, we give you Blatta Haile Mariam, but you have sworn an oath only to punish and imprison him."

So, he was imprisoned for thirty years until the fall of Haile Selassie. The Dergue set him free and he came to Tigray. He is still alive. He came to Tigray and lived for one year here. Then he returned to Addis where he had children. Now, he is in Southern Ethiopia.

Jamaica's Postscript

In November 1975, we established our first base in Marwa in Eastern Tigray. Wherever we went we were welcomed. The month before, we had formed two units, travelling continuously around Tigray for two months to introduce the ideas of our liberation movement to the people. Each unit had fifteen to eighteen people in it. I was coordinating the units. Meles was engaged in this work. Siye and Hyelom were also. In the two months they travelled to Wukro, Adwa district, Tembien, Tsegerede and then turned back.

One day, when we were in the Asbi area, a truck came by. We stopped it. There were some villagers in the truck and three policemen whose guns we confiscated. On that day we also captured Blatta Haile Mariam, who had been put in charge of the militia in Tigray. He was an old man. We released him and the policemen with him, only taking the guns. This was in early November. We discussed with him and he was so happy. I knew his name from history and thought him a great man. I hadn't realized he was still alive. We asked his advice. He said, "Go on with the struggle. I wish I could join you." He was in his early seventies. He is still alive now. Two of his sons were with him at the time, but I don't know which ones they were. One of them later joined the TPLF but he left. He couldn't make it.[9]

It becomes more and more obvious in these conversations that the present revolution I am witnessing is rooted in events nearly five decades old. These ancient warriors are convinced of it. Nothing ever begins. As I said before, the threads always take you back to an earlier event. But, they also take you forward.

At the end of one session in Quiha, the eloquent Desta sums it up:

"We never regret what we did because we did it for the noble cause of the Tigrayan people. We were repressed and we rebelled. We had to do it. There were many people, our compatriots, who fled to Eritrea because they did not want to see the face of the Amhara. You know, although we were dispersed by the bombs of the British, our hearts were so staunch that some day we knew we would try again. We never gave up in our hearts."

His fellow veterans murmur agreement and then there is silence again. The room is dark. His posture, outlined by the light from the single open shutter, is very still and erect. Through the window, great banks of clouds are rolling up from behind the mountains.

"You know we were dispersed because we didn't have good organization at that time. During the Italian invasions, we saw how the Italian soldiers behaved during their advance, burning and killing, and when the British bombed us we didn't know how to defend ourselves. We knew only our experience of the Italians, who had destroyed us with napalm bombs. We didn't have education; we had no shelters, so we dispersed. But, we didn't submit in our hearts. Never, never! We never lost the thought that one day we would retaliate. We told our children every day of the atrocities done to the Tigrayan people. We told them the Amharas were victorious, how children were killed, cattle were destroyed. We never gave up. Now our children started again in 1975 what we started before. The flames of the First *Weyane* were quenched, but the embers were still burning and our children took fire from the ashes."

15

Spies and Heroes

The hillsides around Adigrat are covered with the prickly pear cactus. The peasants use them for hedging and plant them round their houses for animal feed when there is nothing else. You can see them creeping up the cliffs, clinging to the bare rock. At some times of year they are the only green in the landscape, an unlikely green, carrying the distant promise of fertility. Close to their fleshy fans covered in spines claw upwards like crowds of calloused hands supplicating the sky. Even their fruits carry contradictory messages. The vivid display of yellow flowers turn in June and July to a harvest of sweet fruit, yet so guarded with finest hairlike thorns, which on contact break off and lodge in the skin that they repel advances. Late in the season, when the rains have started, when they are beyond eating, they fall to the ground of their own accord and the horny carapace splits to reveal the pink soft flesh within, bursting with seed. In Tigray they are called *beles*.

Agame, the district of which Adigrat is the chief town, is one of the harshest and most poverty-stricken areas of the Tigrayan highlands. Travelling northwards from Mekelle, the old Italian road twists higher and higher through the inhospitable landscape. In many places, the bare white rock is exposed, like patches of snow. Yet, it is the pockets of thin topsoil—of brown or green, according to the season—which look to me as evanescent as snow resisting the onset of spring.

How do people scratch a living from this rock?

In the old days, before the eighties, the people depended on a handful of rich and powerful feudal lords. Fitaurary Dori was one of the most famous (or infamous) who owned all the most fertile land, leaving the poor to survive on tiny and unproductive plots only after they had labored in his fields.

Another was Bashai Bissrat. Eventually, most of the feudals left the area. One is still here. His name is Zewdu Dori, who quarrelled with all his brothers because he sided with the revolution.

The peasants are all poor in Agame. The proportion of the harvest they had to hand over to the landlord varied. If a peasant had his own oxen, his own seed, tools and materials, then he could retain half his production. If he had nothing but his labor and depended on the landlord providing the means of production, he would get only a quarter of the harvest. This amounted to between one and two quintals of grain, barely enough for two months. Even half the harvest, ready in October, would only be enough to feed a small family for three or four months. By the end of January, all the grain would be finished and farmers would have to look to other means to feed their families until the next harvest. The best times were not good enough to provide any margin against disaster; in bad years, in times of drought, there would be no harvest the following October. Starvation was routine. Worst off of all were the Saho Muslims, a minority nationality dominated and oppressed by the Christian highlanders and not allowed to own land. They scraped an impoverished existence herding other people's goats or bee-keeping for the feudals.

Migration was a fact of life in Agame, even in good years. Some survived the dry season by preparing charcoal for the towns. Many farmers worked as day laborers in Asmara, in Eritrea; others went to Humera in the far west to do the weeding and threshing on big farms. In Massawa, on the Red Sea coast, they collected and transported salt. But the mainstay of the dry season economy was *beles*. The prickly pear fruits were picked in Agame and sold in Asmara. No Eritrean would do this. It would be shameful. The very word *Agame* is an insult in Eritrea. There is an old saying, "Are you an Agame or are you a human being?" The Tigrayan itinerants would not be called by name in their places of 'work' across the border—*dirty Agame* would do.

In Agame, there is an unusual root called *ku'enti*. It is small and wild and shaped like an onion. In other parts of Tigray, it is shame to eat it; in some places it is even forbidden. But the Agame peasants have learned to dig it from the ground as a way of surviving hard times. *Arai ku'enti* is an insult; *wodi arai ku'enti* or "son of a *ku'enti* digger" is a worse insult. In the dry season, older boys would seek work with fathers or uncles and older girls were sent away to be servants. The half-dead villages were peopled by women, the old, and the very young. Old women could be seen bent double in the wild places, digging for *ku'enti*. In Marwa they tell a story of a feudal lord who killed a number of poor women digging for roots.

"Why did you do this?" he was asked.

"Oh," he said, "I thought they were just tortoises."[1]

Agame was the first area selected by the Front for working directly with the people. It was in 1975. They were still in their first year. The early months in Dedebit were an apprenticeship, a time of consolidation. They had cut their teeth in two important operations, the first to rescue Musie, one of the leaders, from the hands of the police; the second to combat their paralyzing poverty by robbing the bank at Axum. From Axum, they moved eastwards, close to the Eritrean border. The great gain was that they now could afford to absorb new recruits. In May, in Dedebit, there were about forty fighters. At the time of the Axum operation in early September, they were about sixty. By October, numbers had doubled to a hundred and twenty. In November, they established a base at Marwa in Agame.

They chose Agame for a number of reasons. Unlike lowland Dedebit, Agame's mountains provided cover for safe areas and guerrilla operations. Then, there were a number of other revolutionary organizations in the east. The TPLF hoped to make contact with them with a view to forming a united front. But, perhaps the most important factor was the character of the Agame people themselves.

"The Agame people," said Aklilu, who had taken over from Mulugeta for this expedition, "are very cooperative, very hardworking, very aggressive. They have had to do all the dirty jobs to survive."

Half a day later, a farmer called Halefom in Marwa would give his own version of the Agame special quality:

"The drought of '84 was even more severe in Agame, but an Agame is used to drought and famine. For the people of Raya, further south, it was very catastrophic. The effect here was completely different. For us, the experience of famine and starvation was not new. In Raya, a land of plenty, they could not cope with the difference."[2]

The Agame people moreover had a history of what Aklilu calls "anti-feudal sentiment." They are bone thin, tough, tenacious. They migrate to survive, but return to plow their patch of land before the next rains. Like the *beles* cactus, they are rooted in the craggy rocks of their homeland.

After a few weeks in Marwa, the first fighters moved at the end of December to a village called Dima, strategically placed close to the Eritrean border and for security, even higher and more remote in the mountains.

"We felt extraordinarily safe in Agame," said Sebhat, one of the founder fighters and the chairman of the Front before Meles. "The main reason was our good acceptance by the people. They had problems of security, of land, of justice. We acted fast. We had no experience of any sort in town or country of providing services of justice, security, land distribution, but we were highly motivated. It was easy for us. We instinctively reflected the sentiments of the people."[3]

"Our first real base was in Dima," said Jamaica, "and we were there for our first anniversary. Our base and beds were there. We would buy grain from the local peasants. Wherever we went we were welcome."[4]

In Marwa, they had formed two units of fifteen to eighteen fighters to travel continuously around Tigray to introduce the organization to the people. Jamaica coordinated this operation. Meles, Siye, and Hyelom were also involved.

"At first, when we arrived in an area, the villagers didn't know whether we were bandits or the Dergue. We chose a very strategic house, easy to defend if necessary. We called the elders together and asked them to summon the people from the area. Every person from every house brought food of some sort. So we ate; we talked; they gave us their point of view. We said, 'We are your sons and daughters. We come to liberate you from oppression.'"

About December time, Marta, the first woman fighter, joined them. "We were very happy," said Jamaica,"because theoretically, we thought the participation of women was fundamental to the struggle."

This aspiration remained theoretical for some time. It was to be six months before Roman and Aregash came to the field. In the meantime, except for Sebhat, the fighters were young and had much to learn about effective training, about communicating with peasants, about administering justice, about land distribution, about themselves.

The most testing time came when Marta was still a newcomer. Iyassu talked about it and Sebhat added some details.

Spy Story

We had a bad experience of spying. A spy came to Dima to study our movements in Marwa and Dima. His name was Amare Manjus. He was very young, maybe sixteen or seventeen. He was from Shire, but had been working in Asmara. He applied to join the TPLF, but we were strict, so we believed in making a few tests first. So, he was told to come back at a later date. This was an initial test of commitment.

So, this boy returned to the base camp. He was very curious and very dynamic, but in fact when he returned he had been recruited by the Dergue as a spy. We were very few, not more than a hundred or a hundred and twenty and we were scattered. In Dima, there were even fewer, only thirty or forty staff. On the way to Marwa, he rested in a supporter's house in Sarsit, who was called Father Shifare. These people knew everything about the fighters; they shared everything with us, even though the countryside was suffering from drought and they were poverty-stricken. This Amare Manjus had poisons with him. He left them on a shelf and he went on to Marwa, where he started his training.

There was a very gallant fighter training for the TPLF, called Ahferom. He was very human in his way of treating people and very good at assessing people's characters. Ahferom started to study this boy and began to suspect him of being a spy. The others had no experience of traitors, spies or prison. We lived in a very open way, all together, with comradeship. It was the only way of living we knew, sharing everything, never suspecting spies. But he created suspicion between us. Ahferom and Sebhat challenged him and he started to admit he was a spy, but he also accused Marta of being a spy also.

"I came with a mission and she's now against you."

This started a real suspicion because she came from Asmara too. Two days later, another comrade was accused; every day another ardent and strong fighter was accused. Finally, he accused Father Shifare of being against us and to prove it, he alleged that he had poison in his house.

At night, his house was checked. The spy found the medicine and the old man was taken to prison. We had no experience at interrogating people. Physical pressure was absolutely forbidden, only democratic methods, but, in fact, we beat them and Marta and the peasant. They all denied it, saying, "We are not afraid. We support you. You know, there is something not right in our organization. If you realize it, it is a victory."

Then the strong words of the prisoners like Marta gave us doubts. Especially impressive was Father Shifare.

"We are being tortured," he said, "but we accept it, because it is rectifying our organization."

Even the old man was beaten. He told the truth about the spy coming for just one night. In the end, we turned on the spy and he was the one who broke and the others didn't. At last, in front of all of them, he was killed.

The biggest lesson was the strength of those fighters. TPLF was very near to dissolution, without morale, without strength. From then on, the organization began to be alert to spies. From then on, we began to appreciate the nature of a fighter. Marta, especially, was appreciated.[5]

It was also during these early months that other members were making contact with rival organizations in the area to assess what they had in common, in the hope of coordinating resistance to the Dergue. This was much less successful than forging relationships with the peasants. (Acronym-haters had better leap over the next two paragraphs.) The issue the organizations disagreed about was the importance of the "national question." On the one hand the older and more established Ethiopian People's Revolutionary Party (EPRP) rejected all considerations of national oppression as "narrow nationalism" and contended that class struggle alone could solve problems of long-term discrimination against non-Amhara nationalities. At the other extreme, the main platform of the Tigray Liberation Front (TLF) was nationalist. They argued that Tigray was a country colonized by the Amhara and its people must fight for independence. The position of the new Front, TPLF, was that the Tigrayan people's experience of discrimination for over a hundred years made the national question of primary importance, but there were many other nationalities in Ethiopia experiencing similar oppression, or even worse. Narrow nationalism was not the answer. What was needed was a reconstructed Ethiopia in which all nationalities could enjoy self-determination within a democratic constitution. They were insistent that the people whose support they sought should not have to wait for some unspecified point in the future, when the Dergue would be defeated, to start benefiting from armed struggle. The benefits as well as the sacrifices should start at once, and the most important of these was the opportunity to share democratically in determining their own future.

Neither of the rival organizations seemed interested in democratic processes. The TLF, riven with internal disagreements, had recourse to violent solutions and within weeks had torn itself apart. There was also dissension within the ranks of the EPRP, perhaps fomented by discussions with the TPLF, because the points at issue were the same, the national question and democracy. Neither was the Party interested in a united front. They were, they said, the senior organization and multi-national, so the Tigrayan front must accept their authority. By this time, the Front was engaged in the west against the feudals' party, EDU, and had too few forces to fight elsewhere. When the EPRP attacked their base area they were compelled to counter attack near Adwa to mask their defensive weakness and, although they could not destroy it as an organization, they could and did eject it from Tigray. At the beginning of the eighties, the democratic strands within this group split off to form a separate Amhara liberation movement (the EPDM), which was eventually to form a united front with the TPLF in 1989.

The call to the front still has not come. I don't mind. The call of the past is strong at the moment and my investigations into the 1943 "first revolution" in the Mekelle area has turned me on to the next stage of the drama, the founding of the "second revolution," still in mid-process. I have collected a fair amount of material on the early years of this revolution on earlier trips. In the west, around Sheraro, I spent a lot of time talking to peasants and townsfolk about the past, but my information about the period after the fighters moved eastwards to establish their first real base area in Agame has come mostly from the first fighters. I need to balance it with evidence from the peasants themselves. How did they perceive the small bands of scruffy young men who started to infiltrate their localities after 1975? How did they view the effort to mobilize them? How was it done?

For me, the central riddle about revolution has always been how you mobilize, organize, and unite the diverse multitude of individuals into a mass movement. Confronted every day here by the established fact, the answer still eludes me. I thought perhaps I would find it in Agame.

Adigrat is three hours drive north from Mekelle, not far from the Eritrean border. Mulugeta has some assignment or other. Anyway, he has disappeared and Aklilu has reappeared. Travelling with us in the Toyota is a woman called Mebrat on her way back to Axum, where she owns a hotel. Her son was in Aklilu's class at school and through their conversation I discover that one of Aklilu's brothers was killed in the Red Terror and another has been in prison for seven years in Addis Ababa. Speaking in English, which she doesn't understand, he tells me her son was killed several years ago.

"After Axum was liberated, her husband came to see me. I think he realized their son was dead. He was very strong. He told me his wife was searching for me. She knew I was his classmate and would know everyone from Axum. So, I made sure I didn't meet her. I didn't want to tell her. I feel very bad in cases like that. Now she does not ask me—she knows he has disappeared. I think she is beginning to suspect he is dead."

Her youngest daughter, says Mebrat, has just started training to be a fighter.

Aklilu is silent. He became a fighter in 1976, before either of his brothers were taken by the Dergue. Perhaps he feels they were persecuted on his account, because he suddenly bursts out:

"My brother was in prison with Sebhat's younger brother! He was shot! On account of Sebhat!"

He gives a long list of mothers, fathers, brothers, sisters, mostly killed, sometimes only imprisoned and tortured, in revenge for the revolutionary activities of their children or siblings.

The only sound after that is the din of the engine. Aklilu stares out of the window. Beside the road giant euphorbia cacti spike the sky with huge candelabra arms. In the distance, a tiny church almost concealed by its grove of sacred trees balances on top of a high conical crag.

The first day in Adigrat I hardly see Aklilu. He is busy setting up interviews. We meet in the middle of the day in a little restaurant he knows, where Mebrat, who has not yet found a place in a truck to take her on to Axum, has ordered an Agame speciality, called *tuhulo,* as a thank you for her lift here. It is quite a party. There is a fighter-nurse who came with us from Mekelle and another man we bump into in the restaurant who is Director of the SOS School for orphans in Mekelle. His name is Haile Selassie and it turns out he was imprisoned for ten years in Addis Ababa with two of Aklilu's brothers.

Like the coffee ceremony, *tuhulo* is more than a meal—it is a ritual. The major crop in these lofty highlands is barley and this dish is a celebration of the barley harvest. Barley grain is first roasted in a dry pan before being ground into flour and then worked with water into a large ball of dough. At our table a young woman pulls the dough off in little balls and throws them onto a tray in the middle of which is a steaming pottery bowl of sauce, rich and spicy with tomatoes and hot pepper, striped with white swirls of creamy local cheese. We spear the barley balls with the special *tuhulo* forks, carved out of wood, and whirl them in the hot sauce. It is washed down with glasses of *mes,* mead made from famed Adigrat honey, followed by rich black Ethiopian coffee. When I return to the car, there is a little parcel of *tuhulo* forks, a present from Haile Selassie to remind me of an occasion I enjoyed so much.

What an irony. When I think of Adigrat I think of *tuhulo* and honey wine. I think of the good life, in Ethiopian terms. Yet Adigrat is the center of the most impoverished and deprived corner of Tigray, maybe of Ethiopia. Lying on my bed that night I remember Amartya Sen's writings on famine. His work shows that in many famines, including the terrible famine in Ethiopia in the early seventies, the overall food production hardly decreased. Once more, the problem is not only one of distribution and lack of political will, but of entitlement to what is there. There is always food for those with money.

In 1975, the first year of the revolution, Aklilu was sixteen, living with his parents in Axum and a student at the local school. He had recently been recruited as an underground member of the organization and watched the Axum Bank operation from the sidelines. He did not go to the field until after the base area in Agame had been abandoned; he only knows about this period through stories current among fighters, so he is as keen as I am to hear what these peasants have to say. We decide to concentrate on two communities: Marwa, the first base area in Agame, and Sobeya, the first village in which the fighters started land reform. They are a few hours walk north and east from Adigrat, remote outposts beyond a series of rocky gorges. It is hard to imagine at this point fifteen or so years later, when support for the Front seems virtually total in Tigray, what it must have been like before the fighters had proved themselves or built up the bedrock of support they later enjoyed. Over the next few days, we talk to small groups of farmers from each village and slowly begin to put together a picture of the early stages of the revolution from their point of view.

These farmers want to tell us first about their lives under the feudal landlords and the special harshness of survival in Agame. How else, they say, can I understand why they gave their support so swiftly to the first fighters? They had nothing to lose. Mebratu Adhanom in Sobeya tells us, "Even before the arrival of the TPLF we decided to organize ourselves and ask the Eritreans for guns to fight against the feudals."[6]

Not only did landlords, landlessness and food shortages make their lives a misery; poverty made the poor prey upon each other.

"Thieves and bandits were everywhere," says Keshi Beraki Woldu, a priest from a hamlet near Marwa. "They slaughtered cattle from the field. If someone had a gun he went and demanded whatever he wanted in the night. There were robberies on the roadway. They even took your clothing."[7]

"What worked was money and whose family you were from," adds Halefom Tekelu, a Marwa farmer. "If you were from a rich family, you could commit any crime and get away with it. Bribes were an essential part of the system of justice. Bribery started with the guard standing outside the office door, to make contact with the judge. You'd take something to the judge by night—honey or a goat or perhaps money. If your opponent had given more than this then you'd have no hope of winning anyway."[8]

The first fighters did not look very different from bandits themselves. They were living rough, continually on the move and often undernourished. From the start, a part of their discipline was that their behavior had to distinguish them from other outcasts in a society in which a rigidly enforced political and social system and the prohibition of dissent created many outcasts. A part of the government's propaganda program from then until now has been always to class political opposition as banditry and when forced to acknowledge the activities of liberation movements to dismiss them as *shiftas* or bandits. Sometimes, they use the term *weyane* as a similarly pejorative term, whereas in Tigray it is approving, used for veterans of the 1943 uprising or for the Front's peasant militia. Moreover, these farmers have been referring to *banda,* sometimes as if they were bandits and sometimes as if they were Dergue soldiers. It's all very confusing.

I ask Aklilu to explain.

"A *banda* is a traitor. They are not the same as soldiers in the regular army—more like an irregular army. It is a word we use for Tigrayan mercenaries paid by the Dergue to cause chaos and terror. They are like terrorists. They attack and kill civilians in the villages and try to blame it on us."

Shiftas on the other hand, he says, are just bandits, bands of thieves, criminal outlaws who used to terrorize villages in a particular territory. They have virtually died out in Tigray as the Front increased its control, but the Dergue continues to refer to fighters as *shiftas* as part of its tactic of denial that a liberation movement has established an effective opposition in Tigray. In fact, to add to the confusion, there have been two kinds of outlaws. Those who posed a challenge to established authority were often forced to take refuge in the bush to save their lives. These political outlaws were sometimes called *weyane,* and, helped by government propaganda, the distinction between revolutionaries and bandits became blurred within the general criminalization of dissent.

"You know, there is one more," says Aklilu with a laugh. "There is an Amharic word *shemek,* which you will hear more of if you go to central Ethiopia. These are the Dergue's trained contra-guerrillas who commit atrocities against civilians as well as acting against our guerrilla forces. They also operate in small bands, infiltrating over borders and into communities."

In Agame the fighters' reputation for dispensing effective justice spread from one village to another. Problems of basic security were always the first to be brought by the peasants to the fighters, more immediate even than land.

"There were very famous bandits," says Keshi Beraki, "like Berhane Asgedom, who killed hundreds and raped lots of women. Beyene Kidanu was another, and Tadesse Bissrat. Five times, my personal clothes were stolen. The last time, they just carried them all away in the box. I hadn't met the fighters. When I heard they were people of justice and for the poor, I went to Marwa to see them. They wrote down his name—it was Tadesse Bissrat— and imprisoned him. The news spread very fast. People even began to come from far areas to tell their problems to these fighters. Those who were justices before were reported for taking bribes and immediately imprisoned. Even the church materials were all returned to the churches."

When the fighters arrived in the area, they would talk first to the elders and ask them to assemble the people together and tell them about their aims. According to Keshi, they had five aims: land redistribution, justice, the preservation of the rights of the individual (including the right to speak and write in Tigrinya), equal access to health and education, and, finally, agricultural development.

"They told us our society would be developed and one day we would work with tractors and modern methods." He adds, "I didn't believe that one, but the first four aims were the actual problems of myself and everybody I knew."

Mebratu tells us how twelve fighters came the first time to Sobeya.

"The whole village was in church. Afterwards, they gathered us around the church and told us their aims and what they wanted to do. They asked everybody what were their immediate and burning problems. Everybody cried out, 'We want land.' The fighters replied, 'So far we have not distributed land anywhere before. But, if this is your question, if this is your issue, then so be it. Elect your committee and we will discuss with them how to do it. We will study land distribution here in Sobeya.' So, from this moment I decided to work with them, live with them, to love them."

"At that time, we were building a new church," says Desta Kidane. "The whole community were carrying stones from one kilometer away. The fighters stayed with us a whole day, carrying stones. This impressed us very much."[9]

"The first fighters were very good at making people accept their ideas," says Halefom, in Marwa. "When there was a problem about land they were very practical. When we had a problem with bandits they brought a solution. When you saw them dying for you, when they could have been living a comfortable life...."

He hesitates for a moment, peering into his memories.

"Their ideas were gold. But sometimes I felt frustrated.... How could only twenty people overcome so much? I liked to work with them. They spoke our language and were trying to solve our very crucial problems, but it was very hard for me to believe they would be victorious."

"We supported them because they stood for our reality," Keshi reminds him. "The five aims have germinated. I have seen them bearing fruit...."

"Yes, when I see all this success at this stage, my happiness is boundless, but at first ... at first, when they told us their aim, we knew it was noble. The problem was not in understanding it, but in knowing how it could be achieved."

In Sobeya, they say much the same.

"The enemy was surrounding us," says Haleqa, "all coming like rat and cat from four or five directions. So, all the time we were concerned. Where would our fighters sleep? Where would they eat? Where would they stop? Our fighters were our eyes, so we could not lose them. We had to guard them and watch over them."

Mebratu adds that he was one of those in Sobeya who collected food for the fighters from house to house.

"Also, we knew the best strategic places from which to survey the area. We used to show them how to go and where, to lead them during the night, because they could never sleep where they had been during the day."

They thank me for this opportunity to indulge their memories, to capture a past they see as noble. Of their own contribution, they are modest.

"It's not good to speak about our role," says Desta to Aklilu. "In our culture you don't speak good of yourselves. You fighters know what we have done. There was nothing we didn't participate in."

It is getting too dark to see faces. Their voices glow in the dark. Haleqa, who has left the room, now returns with a lantern, which makes us blink like owls, dispersing our thoughts as well as the darkness. Then Desta's calm voice continues.

"Then we were no different from the fighters. We knew every secret. We had no private life. The fighters were mobile, so we hid their property. If there was extra ammunition, we guarded it. In our houses, we made no distinction between our brothers and our fighters. When we hugged them to our hearts, its effect was very great on the other villages in Agame."

He pauses. A wind has come up and the draft makes the lantern flicker. The shadows bounce from the corners of the room.

"Nowadays, we are less important. There are many fighters we don't know...."

They are right. Things have changed. How could they not? From small idealistic beginnings, this has grown into a mass movement. I look around the zonal committee room, which we are using for this particular meeting. This is the local fighters' office. Pinned to the wall are some battered postards of American pop stars and some sexy stills from Western films. On the back of the door the message *I want to kiss you* is chalked in English. I recall accounts of the strict discipline of the early years, including celibacy. It is hard to imagine it now. Fighters, they say, are not what they were.

As their stories unfold, they mention the names of particular fighters. They remember Abai, Sebhat, and Iyassu. These are fighters I know. They also recall fighters like Suhul and Agazi, who are martyrs. I know them too because they are heroes. They remember Laflaf, one of the very first famous woman fighters, a peasant like themselves, who is alive and well in Wukro and they speak of the death in their village of another woman fighter, wounded in battle nearby. They even remember the date, September 9, 1976.

"We were carrying her. 'Comrades, I am making a problem for you,' she said to us. 'Don't carry me. Why don't you just kill me?' When we reached this area, she died."

It is refreshing to hear these early supporters speak with veneration of the early fighters, both the dead and the living. The Front is so wary of personality cults they never talk about the achievements of the living, except in the mass; only the dead are heroes. It is very difficult to persuade fighters to talk personally about their lives. On my first visit, I could never even discover the identities of the first fighters and only now that I have permission from the leadership to investigate the history are some of the doors opening. A fighter only achieves heroic status by dying for the struggle. Agazi is one of the big heroes, shot down in this area in one of the early battles. He was responsible for recruiting Halefom, the first supporter in Marwa and is very much alive in Halefom's story of their first meeting. Yet he remains elusive and the story raises as many questions as it answers.

Agazi in Marwa

At the very beginning, fighters were monitoring the security situation in the village. Agazi came to my house dressed in a gabi. He said to me:

"I am from Mekelle. My sister's son has left home to become a fighter. I heard that there are others around here. Can you put me in contact with them so that I can reassure my sister?"

This was about one month after they came to our area. It was a test of our loyalty to see if we would reveal their whereabouts to the enemy. Even I had no information about who these people were. I had heard the news. Sometimes, I would catch sight of them on my way somewhere—but no more than that. I said I didn't know anything.

"If you come from a long way, stay and take some sewa and some food."

He tried to persuade me.

"My sister is suffering because of her son. She cannot walk. I said I would come and find out how he is."

I thought there was a possibility he might be a fighter, but that was all. When he refused to eat or drink even though he had come from Mekelle and walked all the way from Edaga Hamus, I said to him, "Why aren't you hungry? Why don't you drink?"

It was my turn to be host for my religious group, providing food and drink during our discussion.[10] *When Agazi saw the members of the group, he decided to come in and see their mood and discuss with them. Leaving him outside, I went indoors and said to everyone, "We have a guest. Don't say anything about the fighters!" So I locked their mouths.*

I invited Agazi to enter and gave him a cup of sewa. *He tasted it, but stayed silent. When the gathering was over, I went out with the other peasants to say goodnight, leaving Agazi inside with my wife and my mother. They had heard me warning my companions not to reveal anything, so when Agazi started asking them the same question about his sister's son, my mother said she knew nothing and closed the matter. Agazi ate a little injera, but left the drink. He had money and offered to pay for the food he had eaten, saying, "Thank you for your hospitality. I was unable to bring any food with me, but I must pay for what I've had."*

My mother accepted the money. When I saw the money in her hand, I told her off.

"Why did you accept the money? This is not something for sale. Do you not want to go to heaven? We cook this food for God. Give back the money."

Agazi became very angry. The money he had given to her was fifty dollars. When it was discovered he said, "You are suspicious of me because I have given you so much money, so only take two dollars instead." He just threw it at us. Then he asked me to walk with him part of the way. When we were a short distance from the house, he suggested we sit down and talk things over. He took out a notebook and he also had a small machine gun. He asked me my name and I replied, "Halefom Tekelu."

"Why did you just hide me? Are you suspicious of me? From now on, don't be suspicious. We like people like you, who are strong and solid."

He gave me a sealed paper and introduced himself as Agazi. At this particular time they were in Dima, so he said by showing this paper and saying his name I could come at any time to see him. From that time on, I became a member of the organization.[11]

Today is a feast day. In the morning, I rise early and splash my face and clean my teeth with a cupful of water from the water bottle. The sky is light, but the sun filtering between the haystacks has as yet little heat. The two sons come from behind the house. The elder drags a little goat by a cord tied to a foreleg, so it hops to its execution on three legs. Perhaps this three-legged walk demands concentration, because it has stopped its cries and hops along in silence, reluctant, dragging. The younger brother, walking behind, carries two large knives and a metal tray.

They stop under a small tree, almost leafless from drought, whose jagged stumps show signs of constant lopping with blunt tools. At once, the goat sets up its dismal wail, nostrils dilating. The elder son, in one swift and practiced movement, with his left hand grasps the horns and bends the head right back upon the spine, exposing the throat, which, at the same moment as his lips form the customary blessing, his right hand slits from side to side. The wail becomes a scream, a bubbling shriek from a new mouth. The legs instantaneously collapse, but the young man holds the head erect as the blood flows out in a tide from the small body. It lingers for a few moments like a scarlet lake with depth and substance and then, as if changing its mind, sinks into the thirsty dust.

The eyes stare, unseeing. The pink nostrils still quiver. The tongue lolls. Without blood or brain, the body still has energy to twist and lunge. It shivers even as it hangs by the cord head down from the tree branch. One son begins to cut the hide away around the horns; the other opens the hide from throat to tail like unbuttoning a coat. Beneath the hide, the skin is red. They work like tailors, complicit but business-like. They lop the hooves and throw them to one side and begin to eviscerate the animal. The hide hangs from a branch; the organs are collected on the tray; the useless parts are kicked into the dust collecting early flies. The dogs lurk in the margins, awaiting their moment.

The brothers have learned their speed from their father, but now the old man's actions are slow. He watches from the doorway of a hut. His occasional comments are directive, to remind his sons of his authority. Tomorrow, he says, the remaining goats will go to market to be sold before the price drops further. Last year, the rains were patchy. Fodder is scarce. Now the price of grain is rising; the price of animals falling. He has seen many seasons, many droughts. Now, is the right time.

Land reform began in Sobeya, a month after the fighters arrived in the village. Ironically, it was also in the interest of the new military government to displace the power of the feudals and to this end they sent agents to the area to distribute the land.

"The question was," Desta tells us, "should we leave it to them?"

The villagers suggested that those among them who were already associated with government agents should do it. They decided that the measurement of land would be done by the government committee, but that a new committee would work side-by-side with them and be responsible for grading the fertility of the land. The feudal landlords tried to sabotage the scheme, a few even using their private armies to mount a challenge in open warfare. The EPRP were also working against land distribution, but, as Mebratu says, "the emotion for land was so intense and volatile." they could do nothing. So, for the first time land was redistributed and it was distributed without discrimination on the grounds of gender or religion.

"Even now," says Desta, "it is taken as a model of real, correct distribution, not like Marwa."

Yet, whatever the satisfaction at the time, they acknowledge that the second round of land reform in the early eighties was an improvement. By that time the *baito*, the elected local Council, had been set up along with the *sirit*, or body of law. Child marriage had been abolished and a new minimum marriage age established, of seventeen for women and twenty-three for men. Both women and men could claim land from that age.

In Marwa, things did not go so smoothly. For a start, there was much tougher opposition from large landowners, who were particularly powerful in Marwa, until Bashai Bissrat, the most intransigent, was killed by a squad led by Marta, the first woman fighter. Moreover, the first ones elected to distribute the land clung to old ways. Some accepted bribes and allotted unequal plots, so they were arrested and imprisoned. They were brought from prison and exposed before the whole village who voted to replace them, so one year after the first distribution, the land had to be distributed all over again.

"The first distribution was not right, that's why it had to be redone," explains Keshi. "If someone complained they said, 'You had nothing before, so be satisfied with what you've got.' They tried to placate the rich by giving more. Women got very bad shares, but not only women—the poor peasants too. It was not as it should be. The injustice was very much on women, not only in size of plot, but also in soil fertility."

He pauses and looks around his companions.

"The second round was good in every way."

Halefom and Tamrat nod their agreement.

One year after the second distribution, the Dergue won control of these areas again and the decisions on land shares were revised once more.

"Everything went back to the same ways as under Haile Selassie," Keshi continues, "bribes and inequalities."

Although the area was not completely liberated until 1988, fighters were constantly coming and going in the villages. The authorities were well aware of the revolutionary mood in Agame. Dima, Marwa, and Sobeya were continuously under surveillance and the villagers routinely harassed by Dergue soldiers.

"One day," says Desta, "the enemy came from Edaga Hamus. They always came from three or four directions. The fighters went to confront them at Edaga Hamus and left all their secret documents and radio communications for all Agame, as well as their radio, in my home. They were fighting all day and five or six comrades were martyred. Meanwhile, another army unit from Senafe, in Eritrea, came to Sobeya. I had a very big problem because all the fighters' materials were in my house. I took all their bags and hid them under the *beles* plants and, carrying the radio, I fled from the house. I came upon fighters retreating from Edaga Hamus. They were very worried about the documents left behind, which held all the names of clandestine members in the towns, all the codes, everything."

Peasant leaders like Halefom and Mebratu were wanted men as much as fighters were. Like the fighters, they depended on the tight-lipped loyalty of their communities to hide and protect them. The biggest danger was spies. Extreme poverty made some elements open to exploitation as informers. Some say that poor Agame people were even recruited in Eritrea and trained by the Dergue to inform on their own people for a few birr.

More Spy Stories

At that time, says Keshi, the justice system was carried out mostly in the night time. We had codes we used if we saw bandas in the distance. We shouted to someone, "The cattle with horns are coming! Go away!" to alert the fighters that they must hide themselves. Even when it was not really a liberated area, the fighters were working among us and the work of justice was very clean. Even people in Adigrat and from a long way away would come if they had a case to be solved. Even around the towns, even in areas not totally controlled by the TPLF, the militia would go and arrest those who gave or took bribes and imprison them. These people coming from enemy areas to tell their cases to the TPLF we later opposed, because we said they might be betraying us, the baito members and the fighters, to the Dergue.

An example of this danger, says Tamrat, was this woman who had just given birth. The father of the child was working in the towns, but they had quarrelled. I was a judge at that time because there were not enough fighters, so she brought her problems to me. We decided he must pay three hundred dollars, but he must bring someone responsible as a guarantor until the money had been paid to the woman. He asked for time to bring the money from the town—he was a builder—and we appointed a responsible person to bring him by a fixed date, November 4th. But, in Adigrat, he told the authorities his sentence and that the judges were the bandits.

He said, "If I am wrong, I commit myself to be killed, so just come and we'll get the bandits." The place of judgement was not a fixed place. It was always changing. We checked every area to make sure it was clean. We never went before the appointed hour and we assigned certain peasants to make sure the judgement place was safe. So, we were very alert, not to be surprised.

He came with soldiers all muffled up in gabis. The eighteen bandas, led by Major Mikael, were camouflaged as if they were going to a local holy day. They encircled the area and siezed innocent peasants who had nothing to do with the judgement. I had assigned one woman who was a nun to cover the area. She was sitting on a hill. When the nun saw them catching the people, she called out to my wife, Haddas, "Tell the ox he should go to the field and bring your calf and come to me." The nun shouting from the hill saved my life.

I was a member of the baito *then, says Halefom. Many spies were coming to the area. The army was coming too, to capture the fighters who were working with us. There were constant surprise attacks. I never slept in my house, always elsewhere.*

One day my house was encircled. We came to the village first and we saw the soldiers on the hills around the village. I left my house and fled and my wife managed to get away to safety with our two oxen, two cows, a calf, and our sheep. She saw what was happening from afar. As to my crops, I only kept enough for immediate consumption in my house; the rest I had hidden in other safer places.

The spy, who had studied the whole area, led them to my house which was encircled. When my wife ran out, she locked the door with a key. My mother who was blind was sitting outside. She had on a new shawl, a new white one. They brought an axe from a neighbor's and broke down the door. There was no food, but they took all our clothes—my wife's outfit, two sets of clothes of mine and a blanket. They didn't even leave a spoon—they even took the small rope we had for tying the calf. They stripped my blind mother except for a small shabby undergarment and left her virtually naked.

I decided to leave the village altogether and went away from the area to start a new life nearer to the Eritrean border, about an hour's walk away—on the edge of the forest where the enemy couldn't take us by surprise. But I went over to my old village to plow my land, and one day I was surrounded when I was plowing. They caught me easily.

My name is Halefom Tekelu, but the spy had written it down as Halefom Tefari. I told them I was a peaceful person, but they beat me with a stick.

"What is my crime?" I asked.

The one in command asked my name.

"Halefom Tekelu."

"Aren't you Halefom Tefari?"

But I peered at his notebook and saw he had the wrong name.

"No I am not. What's his job?"

"He is a baito *member. How far is Halefom Tefari's house?"*

"It's very far away—more than two hours. You'd better forget it!"

They had come with a whole lot of soldiers. The spy had pointed me out to the commander and then gone away to hide his identity. They only sent four soldiers to arrest me and only the spy could identify me. When they got back, the spy told them they had been tricked, that the name on the paper had been wrong, not the person.

This is how life went on until we were finally liberated, in 1988. We always had problems, but the fighters were with us all the time, giving us support.

We never stayed in the same place two nights running, says Keshi. I can give you another example of how they used to loot our homes. It was my own house. The things that were mobile or portable like cattle, we hid a long way away, but this time we had to run away, leaving our unthreshed crops behind. This time, they divided the crop into five parts, made the villagers thresh it and took it all away wrapped in sheets. It was fifteen quintals. It was the entire harvest of the entire family, my own, my father's, my brother Heshe's, the whole family. Our annual food was all gone in one go. Nine goats had also been left with a neighbor, but someone gave it away, so they were taken too. We had put one cow somewhere else, but a spy even knew about this. The neighbor swore it was his own, but they took it all the same and slaughtered it in Adigrat.

The whole community supported us and the fighters, but there were one or two individuals who knew the area and were tempted—spies were paid in money or grain. Their first targets were militia, fighters, and baito members. If a spy was found out, it was the decision of the whole village to imprison him. When a spy brought many soldiers to the area, the whole village was affected and the whole community became the victim, not just the individual fighter. The cattle were slaughtered and the houses burned and they beat the women and children.

"Where are the fighters? They were here yesterday. Where have they gone to?"

The village was tortured and very frightened, so when they discovered a spy they were very severe. We didn't see him being killed, but he was taken away by the organization and never returned.

There was one time when the enemy recruited a spy in the town. His name was Kassa, a militia of the junta. They gave him a mission and promised him a reward for his courage. He pretended to be fleeing to the countryside and became very close to the fighters. One day, a fighter who trusted him was walking in front and Kassa shot him in the back. The villagers saw the whole thing. Immediately afterwards, he started running, but in his efforts to escape he ran into a very rough area and was soon surrounded by the people. As it became dark, the circle closed around him and when it got light in the morning he was captured. Fighters took him and brought him before the assembled people and asked them what sentence he deserved. They were very angry.

"Why do you ask us this question? Why do you bring this criminal before us? He has killed a fighter who was fighting to liberate us. It won't bother us even if you cut him up into small pieces. We don't want to see his face. This killer is a blood relation, but, according to our principles, the fighter who died is closer to us."

They took him away and we never saw his body.

A spy is a sort of inverted hero, an individual remembered for an antisocial act. In a civil war, I suppose for the other side, he could be a hero. Immersed as I am in one side, it is difficult to imagine. The word *hero* presupposes an individual, but an individual with some greatness of soul, and that is why recognition has to be preceded by death, because this revolution is built upon the notion of collective action for the common good. I am drawn to the idea of all the unsung heroes who play small roles. Like that nun sitting on the hill shouting, "Tell the ox he should go to the field and bring your calf and come to me." In fact, I have been grumbling that, left to himself, Aklilu only arranges interviews with men.

"Where are the women in this revolution?" I complained. "It's all very well to talk about the benefits the Front has brought to women, to quote statistics about women's participation, to *say* how important women are—half the sky, half the struggle and so on—but why don't I ever talk to any?"

His face acquired the blank look of extreme annoyance restrained by politeness.

"Or are women working so hard, so busy being doubly oppressed, that no one imagines they can spare the time to talk to me?"

The upshot of this exchange, after an initial coolness, is that from Adigrat we set off southwards to Wukro, a dusty little town on the Mekelle road where Aklilu thinks there is a chance of a meeting with Agazi's mother.

For all his heroic status I know little more about Agazi than that he had a military operation named after him. If there is such a thing as a hero at all, I incline to the view that they are not born, but made, nudged in that direction by a multitude of factors. Mothers must be among the more important, so I am also interested in Agazi's mother on her own account, not only as a channel of intimate information about her son. Two young women fighters show us where to find her house in one of the back streets.

My first impression is that she is very ancient, but after a few minutes her erect posture and the humorous quizzical expression in her eyes make her seem much younger than her sixty-seven years. Her name is Kiros Kassa. She wears her grey hair cut very short like a fighter, instead of the traditional plaiting close to the head, and sits neatly on the edge of a bed with her hands folded in her lap, waiting to be addressed. Aklilu evidently knows her well and a few minutes pass exchanging recent news.

She has had her share of the disadvantages common to women in feudal times. Like so many older women I have talked to here, she was married at seven years old.

"You can't imagine," she says, with a sense of times irrevocably changed, "I hadn't even lost my first teeth! In fact, during the time I stayed indoors after my wedding, that was when I lost them."

After ten years, she was rejected for infertility by her husband, a secretary of Prince Mengesha Seyoum. He took up with another woman.

"And still he didn't have a child. It was all his fault!"

She recounts with some glee that she became pregnant at once when she married the father of Agazi, although this marriage too ended in divorce when her husband became so sick his parents took him to Addis Ababa for medical care. Perhaps it was three children and economic necessity, which drove her in Haile Selassie's time to become one of the few policewomen in Mekelle; there was certainly an intrepid quality in her determination.

"One day, I saw some women prisoners being escorted by male soldiers. I was so annoyed I decided a women's police force should be organized. There was a notice that women could apply to the police force and, because my previous husband had been Mengesha's secretary, they said it was possible. Twenty-one was too young to qualify, so I gave my age as twenty-eight. I enjoyed it. The trouble was," she stops to laugh, "the retirement age was fifty-five, so I was retired seven years early."

She talks cheerfully about her own life, but when she moves on to Agazi, the tears start to trickle down her cheeks. Neither Aklilu nor the young fighters make any attempt to comfort her. We sit quietly until she is recovered enough to go on. His last year at school was in Asmara, in the house of a paternal aunt and it was there that he was exposed to revolutionary ideas because in Eritrea the war had begun many years earlier. From there, he went to university and then to the field, to Dedebit, to start the revolution in Tigray.

"He came back from Dedebit after four months and stayed three days at home in Wukro, even though the government was here and I was in the police. I went to buy clothes for him and then travelled with him all the way back to Shire in the west. His older brother Mulugeta came with me. That was the last time I saw him."

"He was killed before I joined the revolution," says Aklilu in a low voice, "only ten or eleven months after it started. It was about fifteen kilometers from Axum in a small town also called Wukro. He was on a mission with Suhul. Suhul managed to escape, but Agazi was killed in an exchange of fire."

The interview more or less breaks down after that. Agazi remains as mysterious as ever and his mother wants to talk about his sister.

"Although I am crying ... I am his mother...and I am happy he is loved, that he lay down his life for his organization. I am crying more for my daughter. She was killed in Axum, for nothing, in the Red Terror. This is why I am crying. They killed her and threw her in the street. Her name was Tsedal."

She points to a collection of photographs on the wall. Aklilu gets up and lifts one down. Three photographs in the same frame. The first is a studio portrait of Agazi's father cutting a dash as a fine upstanding soldier. He is in uniform, a pistol suspended from his belt. In the second, a younger version of the woman before us is standing with her arm round the shoulders of a young girl, perhaps ten or eleven years old. They are both wearing the traditional white Tigrayan dress for holidays and celebrations. The photo has a certain formality about it, but it is not a studio portrait. They are standing outside on a patch of stony soil spiked with dried grasses. It looks like the dry season. Perhaps, it is the bright light that makes the child stare into the camera with a slightly wrinkled brow, a look both solemn and puzzled.

"She was sixteen years old. There was a Dergue cadre in Axum. His girlfriend shot her in her house. She was reporting repeatedly to the police that this woman was threatening to kill her. The cadres were playing with her, trying to use her sexually, but she refused. She tried three times to escape, to join the TPLF, but each time they caught her. They were watching her because she was Agazi's sister."

Aklilu's face is wet. I cannot stop my tears and neither can the two young women fighters who are listening with us. She tells us jerky little bits in stops and starts and we all sit there, crying.

The third photograph is of Agazi himself. It must be the photo of a photo, perhaps out of a magazine, because the contrasts are too marked. It lacks the reality of the other photographs. The hair and eyes and shadows are too black, the forehead and cheekbones and shirt too white for the day-to-day. The eyes are very large and the impact of the photo is in the intensity of the gaze. By some trick of technique, there is a radiance behind the head and it resembles nothing so much as the iconographic paintings of the great and the good, which stare down from the walls and ceilings of Ethiopian churches.

16

Tigers

The meeting with Agazi's mother seems to have restored Aklilu's equanimity and by the evening, he is cheerfully rearranging my program to include more meetings with women.

It would be easy to assume a passive role for women in the first years of the revolution, even of hostility to the prospect of change. After all, in Britain, women have remained a conservative force and doorstep polls still reveal many women as dependent on their husbands for their views on a range of issues. No doubt, this was also true of the majority of women in Tigray at the beginning of the revolution and the tremendous effort, which the Front have put into building the confidence of women through consciousness-raising in the mass associations, through literacy schemes, and the special women's schools, show they take account of the psychological effects of centuries of child marriage, absence of economic rights, and general discrimination.

Yet some women not only seem to have survived with their identity intact, but to have grasped with both hands the opportunities presented by the revolution to become activists in the process of change. A number of older women, like Mother Tsehaitu whom I met in Sheraro on my first visit, gave crucial support to the first fighters, who still pay tribute to their strength and steadfastness and call them "mothers of the revolution."

"They were like tigers," says Aklilu.

The only problem is that they live far from Agame in lowland villages in the west where the revolution first started. Nevertheless (in the absence of a summons to the front line in Central Ethiopia), we make plans to go west as soon as possible.

Aklilu is particularly cheerful because he has managed to arrange for his wife and new baby to join us. I have only just learned of their existence.

Genet, with three month old Semira in her arms, is accompanied by her close friend, Elsa, also the mother of a baby daughter of two months called Samhal, and Lemlem, another friend who will help out with the babies. All three women are fighters and have leave to visit their families who live in the countryside near Adwa and Axum. I find it refreshing to have the priorities of my historical quest slightly skewed by the presence of babies in the back of the car, although their mothers never make any demands on our schedule and the babies themselves seem trouble free and contented.

We set off in the pick-up after breakfast, with Aklilu driving and the three women fighters and two babies sitting in the seats behind us. The open back of the pick-up is crammed with fighters who want a lift to Adwa or Axum. Aklilu insists that since the front line has moved south, it is safe to drive in the middle of the day, so for the first time, I have the opportunity to see the landscape in daylight. So far, the places I have spent my time have been divided from each other by long dark tunnels of night travel. Aklilu seems confident that the Ethiopian airforce is engaged elsewhere and that no MiGs will be available to hunt us down. Presumably, he has access to intelligence reports from his work in Hagere Salam about the activities of the other side; perhaps the Front has some sort of hot line to the plans of the Ethiopian Military Command, assisted by the network of contacts of the ex-Dergue officers' organization now working for the Front. Nevertheless, I am nervous and agoraphobic. I have lost the habit of daylight driving.

The countryside to the west of Adigrat is spectacular. The Italian road winds over mountains with a birds' eye view of gorges far below. As we climb the series of upland plateaux, each higher then the last, it is clear that even those river beds that look like threads are themselves as high as mountains. Every curve in the road brings a new and breathtaking panorama of strange shapes and vivid colors and multiple dimensions of space and distance. If I sound like a tourist brochure, it is because I feel like a tourist in Ethiopia for the first time. But, unused to such exposure, I feel like a small nocturnal animal must feel at noon in the middle of a field, waiting for the rush of wind and the grip of talons in the neck.

On the way, Aklilu points out sites of historic interest. Against the skyline to the north we make out two monasteries high on their inaccessible flat-topped mountains. They are two of those founded by the nine saints who according to Church history, helped to establish Christianity, which spread gradually in Tigray from the third century. One of the nine, Abuna Aregawi, a prince who gave up the throne to become a hermit, wanted to found a community in which to pursue a scholarly and spiritual life remote from the distractions and temptations of the world. The story goes that, unable to find the right mountain, he was praying at the foot of a great cliff when a huge python lowered itself from the clifftop, siezed him in its coils and bore him to the top where he established the celebrated monastery of Debre Damo. This is one of the foundation legends of the Ethiopian Church and celebrated in paintings, even in small churches. Some of these early monasteries still survive with communities of monks and even now the only access is in a basket lowered from the rim. (As women are strictly forbidden within monastery precincts, I am unlikely to pursue this line of research). Nearer to Axum, we pass the route to the ancient settlement of Yeha, with its archaeological remains of palaces and temples.

Aklilu also indicates sites of early battles between the Front and the feudal organization, the EDU, and recounts many stories, but the road is too bumpy to take notes and the engine too noisy to make recordings, so I retain little more than a jumble of possibilities for future investigation. On the top of one high ridge, which feels too high and too remote for human habitation, we see a large gathering of peasants a couple of hundred yards from the road, some sitting, some squatting on the stony ground. From the road we can see the gesticulations of the speaker. I leap out to discover what it is about and take a photo, trotting towards them to save time. At once the fighters on the edge of the group run forward in alarm, at the same time raising their machine guns ready to fire.

"It's OK. It's OK," Aklilu cries out in Tigrinya behind me.

I learn two lessons: first, never to run unless it is an emergency; second, that it is much less secure in Tigray since the expulsion of the Dergue than it feels. The people are always on the look-out for *banda* and other infiltrators.

The meeting is about the soil and water conservation program, which in the two years since it was started by the Front's Agriculture Department and REST, has been spreading slowly to every district. In most places, it is already possible to see the difference made by local council prohibitions on indiscriminate tree felling, which have led to startling greening of affected hillsides through natural regeneration. Where a start has been made on new kinds of catchment terracing to prevent run-off of rainfall and soil erosion, the peasants seem to be reconstructing the very mountain sides. The program is about to be launched in this area.

Our route is through Adwa, Axum, Endaselassie, and on to our destination, Adi Nebried, a small town in the western lowlands. We stop overnight in Adwa and in Axum we break our journey for a few days because it is a town of such historic import for Tigray and Ethiopia that Aklilu judges it essential study. In any case, it is the destination for Genet, Elsa, and Lemlem. Axum is Aklilu's home town and as we get nearer his thoughts turn towards his family.

"We never talk about the past," he says.

Since the meeting in Adigrat with Haile Selassie, the Director of the Mekelle SOS School, who had been in prison for so long with his brother, Aklilu's thoughts seems to be returning restlessly and often to Axum. His parents are dead and all the large family scattered, some dead, some tortured and imprisoned.

"My sister is the only one who stayed," he remarks. "She said, 'Who is to stay in this house and keep the family home if I do not?' So she is there."

He concentrates on avoiding the potholes in the road. The presence of Genet and Elsa and the babies in the back seems to make no difference to his conversations, which are always in English, which they do not understand.

"But so many young people went to fight from Axum. When I went back after Axum was liberated, everyone was coming out of the houses. They were crying. They were asking me about their children."

He cannot bear it, he says. After that, when he had to stop over in Axum, he would stay in the house of a Muslim family who didn't know him and didn't ask him questions. Gradually, over the last two years, they found out that he was Aklilu.

"Now, nothing is too much for them to do for me."

Even now, he adds, he stops only for a few minutes at his sister's house. Nevertheless, he takes Genet and Semira to stay with his family and Elsa disappears with Samhal to her family home in the town. He suggests that I stay in the same hotel where I stayed the year before last, which turns out to be the one owned by Mebrat who treated us to *tuhulo* in Adigrat. On the way there I ask him about the incidence of traumatic illness among fighters or even civilians, especially after battles or dealing with Dergue atrocities and other extreme situations common to civil war. Aklilu, as head of the Front's health service for some years, must be the person to ask. Surprisingly, he denies that there are any such problems.

"Our fighters are conscious. They are prepared. They know why they are fighting and they want to fight."

We arrive in Axum at breakfast time. Halfway through the morning Aklilu reports meeting many obstacles in making arrangements—no cars are allowed to be driven in daylight, the monuments are closed because it is Sunday. We go to Mebrat's house for lunch. It is a single-story house luxuriously furnished, even by Tigrayan town standards, and in a style fashionable in Italy in the fifties. The sitting room opens onto a loggia festooned with orange and scarlet bourgainvillea and various plants in pots, another Italian touch unusual in Tigray. "This is Asmara!" Aklilu says. We are served the traditional dish of chicken and hard-boiled eggs in a rich peppery sauce, followed by the coffee ceremony. I always view delays as a blessing and take advantage of this one by returning to the hotel to bath and wash my hair. By three, all obstacles mysteriously removed, we set off to the monuments.

You see the TPLF insignia everywhere. It is incorporated into their official stamp and into posters and stickers. When you go into *baito* offices or into peasant houses, you see it embroidered onto banners hanging on the wall. In the center of a laurel wreath, there is a vertical column surmounted by a star. Towards its base it is crossed by a hammer and a gun. This column is one of the *stelae* or obelisks of Axum. It represents the proud and ancient history of Tigray.

Axum stands at the center of this history. It was the capital city of the ancient Axumite Empire, which in the first century BC grew into a powerhouse of influence and trade—with Egypt, Persia, Southern Arabia, Greece and Rome, and even as far as India—until its gradual decline and overthrow about 1000 AD. In the West, our own centers of learning have traditionally looked to Greece and Rome for the ancestry of our civilization. Although individual scholars have looked beyond the northern Mediterranean, their investigations have not filtered into our general cultural consciousness. Yet, Axum was well-known to Greece and Rome and rivalled their claims to greatness. The Axumite civilization, highly advanced for its time, has left a massive heritage of architectural remains, not only the colossal monolithic obelisks, but castles and palaces, temples, burial places and grottoes. Like Rome, Axum is built upon thick layers of a powerful past, most of it awaiting excavation.

Yet, unlike Britain, where our heritage of pre-Christian standing stones, tumuli, and long barrows has been diminished into quirky, semi-magical significance along with ley-lines and Camelot, not just scholars but even peasants seem imbued with consciousness and pride in this history, especially as represented by the *stelae.* I visited them first two years ago, just after Axum was finally evacuated by the Dergue; now, in a much more thorough investigation with an informed guide, I begin to wonder whether they too are a part of the history of this revolution. I have several times been disconcerted by the gap between the dignity and morale of peasant elders and the long experience of economic and social oppression they describe. Perhaps, this consciousness of past greatness, communicated century after century by generations of oral historians, has given them a sense of identity, which has kept their self respect from obliteration by poverty and oppression.

The group of obelisks rises from a stone terrace at one side of the town. Their age is disputed. Tigrayans assert they are at least three thousand years old, contemporary perhaps with the Queen of Sheba and King Solomon. Some European archaeologists argue a more recent origin, just preceding the introduction of Christianity in the third or fourth century AD. The tallest is lying prone in huge chunks. Intact, it would have reached thirty-one meters into the sky. The story is that it was destroyed by Yodit, the queen of the Agew people who overthrew the Axumites. Another obelisk, twenty-four meters high, was taken by the Italians during their occupation and erected in the Piazza della Stagione in Rome. The highest of the survivors is twenty-one-and-a-half meters, which seems lofty enough to me, as I stare up at the massive monolith against the moving clouds, its top crescent-shaped, with crescent bites carved out of each side. The great column of stone is astonishingly well preserved, with curious fake doors and windows sharply incised up its length like a spoof of a multi-story tower.

There are many unsolved mysteries connected with the *stelae.* One is that, like Stonehenge, the granite monoliths do not originate from Axum and, like the pyramids, must have presented a problem of transportation; the second mystery asks what technology at the time of construction could have been capable of carving so precisely the architectural features on so hard a stone. Oral traditions relate that the stone was first melted and then cast, like bronze; other stories refer to a mysterious machine called an *amaz,* which cut the stone. Some of this Mulugeta told me in Mekelle. He said *amaz* was the Greek word for "diamond," which could be almost true, if it is interpreted as a corruption of *ad-amas,* the ancient Greek word for the hardest substance then known, later transferred to diamond. Certainly, *almaz* is the Tigrinya word for diamond. Greek was the lingua franca of the Near East and there were irrefutable connections with Greece in the Axumite period. There are Greek inscriptions on stone blocks in the Axum area and legends insist that Christianity was first brought here by two Greek boys, Frumentius and Odysseus, who were shipwrecked off Massawa.

Essentially, the mysteries remain unsolved.

For several days, I mine the past. We visit not only the obelisks, but burial chambers beneath them, the palaces of King Kaleb and of his son, Gebremeskel, and the palace of the Queen of Sheba and her swimming pool. The excavated palace of Queen Saba, as she is called in Ethiopia, lies in the bare fields to the west of the town. We spend an enjoyable half-day in the hot sun, wandering through little archaeological spaces whose uses have long been forgotten, "rooms" between low walls of red-gold stone and open to the sky. In all these ancient ruins, the quality of the masonry is superb; the stone blocks look as if they have been cut by machine and fit each other with minimally visible joints. The stonework I have so long admired in the highlands evidently has a long pedigree. On the other side of the road from Sheba's palace, is a field full of standing stones, reputed to be the tombs of her followers. One larger obelisk, lying on the ground, supposedly marks the tomb of the legendary queen herself. The tombs of Kings Kaleb and Gebremeskel are close by their palaces, guarded by the burial chambers of their followers, and under the hill of Axum we clamber into the bone-caves of other great ones. How are the mighty fallen.

The dimensions and its broad sweep of steps put Sheba's palace in a different league from any building I have seen in Tigray, even the palace of Yohannes IV, in Mekelle. Its excavation in Haile Selassie's time must have been an event of the first importance. Both the Ethiopian Church and the Ethiopian monarchy have looked to the Queen of Sheba to legitimate their claims to divine provenance. The Church rests its authority on the guardianship of the Ark of the Covenant and Haile Selassie claimed his divine right to rule lay in the allegedly unbroken chain for three thousand years of the Solomonic line of Ethiopian monarchs.

This is the story as it was first told me by a very ancient guide, called Berhane.

Queen Saba and King Solomon

Queen Saba, attracted by King Solomon's reputation for wisdom, decided to visit him and see for herself. He received her with great hospitality. After some time, she returned home and soon afterwards she gave birth to a son, whom she named Menelik.

When Menelik was a young man, his mother sent him to meet his father, Solomon, and he stayed for several years, in Jerusalem. One day he was seen out riding by the people of Jerusalem. They thought he was King Solomon.

"There is the King. He looks just like King Solomon. Let's bow low to him."

There was also a cattle owner in Jerusalem who allowed his cows to eat the crops of a certain farmer. Now, it was the rule in Israel that if a farmer found cattle eating his crop, no matter if there were a hundred or even a thousand of them, then he could claim them as his own. But, when his cattle were taken, their owner was indignant and wanted to appeal to the King's son, Menelik. So the King gave his consent.

"OK, go and hear his judgement. Let's hear what he has to say."

Menelik asked how many cattle were confiscated, their value and the value of the crops consumed.

"Two or three cows are enough to compensate you for the harvest you have lost," he told the farmer.

The farmer was angry at Menelik's judgement and the cattle owner was pleased. Then the people were stirred up against Menelik and wanted him to return to Ethiopia.

"Send this man away," they said to the King, "before he causes trouble among us."

King Solomon agreed to send Menelik home, but he said, "If I am to send away my firstborn son, then he must be accompanied by the firstborn son of each of you."

So twelve hundred Israelites, the firstborn sons of every family accompanied Menelik. One from every house—of priests, of judges, farmers, goldsmiths, weavers, and musicians—set out for Ethiopia. King Solomon commanded that a replica of the Ark of the Covenant, containing the tablets of stone revealed to Moses, be given to Menelik, whereupon Menelik substituted the real Ark of the Covenant for the false and took it with him to Axum and there it has stayed until now. We say God wanted it so, wherefore we call it the Ancient Holy City, the second Jerusalem.

"What happened to them all, the twelve hundred Israelites?" I ask Aklilu's friend, Tesfay.

"They settled in Tigray. According to our oral history, the Falashas, the Ethiopian Jews, are the descendants of those people. In fact, historians also give other explanations for the Falashas—that they are descendants of escaped Iraeli slaves in Egypt under the Pharoahs or that they were converted by Yemeni Jews from southern Arabia in pre-Christian Axumite times. That is the most likely explanation, because the Falashas look Ethiopian, Tigrayan Falashas like Tigrayans, Amhara Falashas like Amharas and so on. But our people still believe they were the companions of Menelik."

"And is the Ark of the Covenant still here then?"

"Of course."

"Where is it?"

"It is kept in a sanctuary in the precincts of the Church of St. Mariam. It is looked after by a special guardian, who from the time of his appointment never leaves the sanctuary, until death. When he is near death, he chooses a successor."

"How many people have seen this Ark of the Covenant, or, even better, seen inside it?"

"No one except the guardian. No one is allowed to see it except him."

"Not even other priests?"

"No one."

"How do you know it exists, or that there is anything inside it? How do you know it is the real Ark?"

Tesfay looks shocked. I have breached the rules. Aklilu is silent. The Front has sponsored complete religious freedom to both Christians and Muslims. Many fighters are skeptical, but know better than to antagonize pious people or powerful priests. I decide to abandon the question in favor of another, only slightly less provocative.

"Tell me, Tesfay, about Queen Saba's palace. How do you know it is hers?"

"They found a stone carving of her head when she was a young woman. It is kept in the Treasury, near the Sanctuary of the Ark of the Covenant."

One reason I am being so annoying is that I am very annoyed myself. I had foolishly imagined that the Front, with its progressive ideas and administrative influence, would be able to bypass on my behalf the Church's prohibition against women entering the Church of St. Mariam, the most important place of worship in the Orthodox Church. No such luck. Neither can I enter the precincts of the Sanctuary to visit the Treasury, which contains some of the most important art objects in Ethiopia. I find it infuriating that any little jumped-up male tourist can be admitted to these secrets, while I, after years of patient investigation in Tigray, am to be denied it just because I am a woman. No wonder women are said to be more than half this revolution. They have so much to gain, so far to go. Yet, the strange thing is I have not heard them protesting against the Orthodox Church.

My complaints, however, do not fit well with the warmth and generosity of their hospitality code. I never know to what lengths I have pushed Tesfay and Aklilu or what strings they have to pull on my behalf, but the next day they arrive at breakfast time looking pleased with themselves. Tesfay announces that, although the prohibitions on my entry cannot be broken, concessions have been made. If I stand outside the iron railings of the precincts, the guardian priests will bring out of the Treasury whatever I want to see. It is difficult to make a list, I explain, if I don't know what the collection includes. Nevetheless, it is better than nothing. I have to be content.

So, later the same day, we peer through the railings as two old priests bear out to us one after the other a succession of objects. They forbid me to take photographs or to write, so much of what they show us is subject to the vagaries of memory. I remember a procession of imperial crowns—of King Fasil, Yohannes IV, Menelik II, and Haile Selassie's crown as the Crown Prince Ras Tafari in 1910. They are covered with gold, yet glinting in the sun they look like so many tawdry theatrical props. The sacred texts, beautifully illuminated as I have heard, are denied me. Finally, at my special request, they bring out the female head found at Queen Saba's palace and cited by Tesfay as evidence for its authenticity. On a piece of polished stone is incised the relief of a child-like female head. She is in profile, looking to the left. The head is poised lightly on the neck and slightly lifted as if surging forward, sighting the horizon or sniffing the breeze, which seems to be blowing back her hair—hair which is not curly but straight. They say she is three thousand years old. Whether she is the Queen of Sheba or not or how they know, I cannot tell, but I find her exquisitely beautiful.

The guardian priest has not allowed me to photograph the treasures, but he jumps at the chance of being photographed himself. He thinks his dusty black garments are too workaday for a portrait and disappears for a few minutes to change. He stands stiffly in his grand robe, puffed with consciousness of his portentous role, as I poke the lens through his prison bars.

There are other investigations I want to make in Axum. It was here in the first year of the revolution that the early fighters turned the tide of their fortunes by robbing the bank. It was recounted to me, as I have already told you, as the story of Deseligne the Mule. Now that I'm on the spot, I want a demythologized version, the facts. I know it's naive of me to think such things exist. I know history is versions and that this will be no exception, that the fighters will have a different version from the townsfolk, from the bank staff, from the police, from the Dergue. But, if I can get an unadorned account, even from a participant or an eye-witness (mules excluded), it would be something.

"Oh, you need to talk to Asgede," says Aklilu, as if that will solve everything, "and you are lucky. He is working around here somewhere."

Asgede, it turns out, is one of the founder fighters. He is renowned for his memory, for his recall of the smallest details, but although he does work in this area, he is away at the moment.

We are pulling away from the office where we had been making the inquiries, when Aklilu exclaims and abruptly stops the car. A man is leaning against a wall on the other side of the street. They look at each other for a moment. The man is smiling, but he does not move. Then he turns his head away.

"He was a fighter," Aklilu says, as we drive on slowly across the square and around the line of water jars waiting at the pump. "Now, he is mad. He was in the battle of Guna, but he couldn't cope and he had to leave. I liked him very much. He was my school mate."

After that, he is preoccupied and I stay silent. But, so much for his insistence that traumatic illness does not exist in Tigray.

"Now, we go on to Adi Nebried," he says. "We leave at dawn tomorrow. We can catch Asgede on our way back."

Our instructions to be woken at four are forgotten. Fortunately, I wake at six, alarmed that it is already light, so when Aklilu appears fifteen minutes later, I am ready to go. This area is so bad for air-raids that no driving is allowed in the daytime. Nevertheless, we drive the whole way in daylight, continuously downhill into the lowlands. For a change no one is with us, not even a guard. Aklilu is silent, as if not properly woken up and I have a cold and don't feel like talking anyway. By eight o'clock, we are driving into Adi Nebried. Fighters, standing at the barrier, tap their watches meaningfully and shake their heads in disapproval. There was an air-raid here yesterday so perhaps that has kept us safe today. If a MiG had come, there would have been no protection in this treeless landscape and the road is so pitted it would have been impossible to dodge about.

Surrounded by the usual crowd of children, we make our way to the Front's office and wait for something to happen. By eleven o'clock, Aklilu, who it turns out is sick and unwell, is asleep on a bed in the corner and I am catching up with my diary in the intervals between blowing my nose. We are back onto country fare—always an object lesson in the social disparities between town and countryside. For breakfast, we were given sour and sticky *injera* with salt and red pepper as a dry dip washed down with very boiled, very strong tea, very unlike the usual pale translucent liquid.

"Looks like coffee," growls Aklilu disapprovingly.

Writing my notes in a sort of limbo, my thoughts turn to my family. I look around the room and try to see it with their eyes. There are so many things I take for granted here—like the four machine guns against the wall—and no longer see, but which would be the first details they would notice if they could see me here. Ammunition belts on the hook on the wall, plastic sandals, a pile of yellow packets of that characteristic Sudanese tea, those heavy wooden ammunition boxes with iron latches, which they use for seats. On the table is a blue kerosene lamp, an indicator we are again beyond the reach of electricity. Everything is normal and familiar, even the rubbish on the floor, the dirty pock-marked walls, the tin roof, the birds scrabbling on the other side of it. The only unfamiliar thing in this landscape is myself. I get a shock when I see my own white face now—not that there's much opportunity for that, even in towns. There are no shop windows, few mirrors. I don't need a mirror to reflect my strangeness. I see it reflected in the eyes of every passerby and especially in the crowds of staring children, especially in the countryside.

Adi Nebried is one of the staunch longest-liberated rural communities. Its battered houses and the ragged garments of its people are the color of the brown dry-season earth. From the earliest years of the revolution, they have defended with grim determination and terrible sacrifices the gains liberation brought them and the possibilities of a better life it promised. Among these early supporters were some remarkable women.

The woman called Dahab comes about midday, accompanied by her daughter. While we are waiting for her to arrive, we interview a *weyane* or member of the local militia, also an activist from the early years, who has been waiting to talk to us for some time. It is not so much an interview as a series of oratorical pronouncements, of slogans strung together into a demonstration of solidarity and faith in the organization. Afterwards, he strikes a series of deliberately comic heroic poses for the camera, a wit and a humorist as well as a fighter for the cause, but I learn nothing new.

Dahab is in her mid-fifties with an energetic air and a diffident and modest way of speaking. She is not a tall woman and her slightness makes her history of determined rebellion even more remarkable. Or, maybe it is only astonishing to me, coming as I do from the cozy bourgeois modernity of the West, where we have lost the warrior mentality. Yet, it has a strange distant familiarity about it. Perhaps, I recognize it from the pages of Beowulf, Norse sagas or the epics and plays of ancient Greece—although the people here have their own ancient history in their blood, constantly reminded of a heroic past by the remnants of past greatness, by the Axum obelisks, by the stones of ruined palaces, the very ruins which at the same time signal not only the passing of time, but the transience of power.

Dahab's daughter makes coffee for us, while her mother and Aklilu chat over old times. Since I first started coming here, there has been such a shift in events and expectations, that this whole revolutionary stage is fast becoming old times even before it has been brought to a conclusion. It's because they have total confidence in the outcome. They might not know the timescale, but they have no doubt that they will win this war. I seem to have absorbed this confidence and, at least for the duration of my journeys, I don't see how such determination can fail.

Dahab Tesfay, Mother of the Revolution

I was brought up in Adi Nebried and I was married here in Adi Nebried. I was sister to the mother of Kelebet, one of the first fighters. I had nine children and eight are fighters—all except for the daughter here who made the coffee. I had twelve altogether, but the others died. My husband was also a fighter, in the militia, but he died fighting against the feudals.

I first became aware of the struggle when strangers in camouflage began to turn up at the house, invited by my husband after he had been recruited. At first, he didn't tell me what was happening, but after a few days they brought things to hide in the house, like bullets, so I came to realize they were fighters. I always felt very bad when I saw their problems, like a mother for her sons—their poverty, their simplicity. They never had a chance to wash their clothes. I cried for them and felt sorry for their condition. I felt a spiritual bond with them—they were so dedicated to their purpose.

My first son, Kafir, joined very early in 1976, when he was eighteen or twenty years old. The next two joined three years later—Gualdehab (nicknamed "Metro" because she is only one meter tall) became a junior nurse; the other was Abadi. After two more years, my daughter Mamit joined and later on four joined together.

For nine years, I was head of the Woman's Association for the whole area. I was first a member of the baito and then Chairperson of the baito. Now I am a judge for this district. I went to the Women's Conference in Dejenna and to March Eight School. I was at the founding conference of the Women Fighters' Association (WAFT) and the National Conference of Tigrayan representatives in Mekelle, when we first liberated Mekelle.

When our fighters were fighting in this area early in the struggle, just before they were defeated, I was preparing food for them and taking it to them in their bunker. I had already been head of the Women's Association. My husband was a militia working with the fighters, leading them in the night. I was giving them information on the situation. Suddenly, the EDU made an assault on our fighters. They fought for three days and the TPLF were forced to retreat for lack of ammunition.

When the feudal forces entered Adi Nebried, the fighters decided to take me with them. I had an eight month old baby. "If I go with you, I'll be a problem," I said. "Let me stay and face my own problems myself." My husband went with the fighters. EDU followers started to ransack our house, taking our clothes, our grain, the plates, everything we had. A few days later, when my husband was on a mission, he was intercepted by them and killed in an exchange of fire. Then, they came to Adi Nebried saying they had killed Yirgalem. They kept coming to the house boasting that they had killed my husband.

"So, what?" I said. "He died following his own choice, for doing what he believed."

So, they took my twelve oxen and left me with nothing. I followed to ask for them back, but when I found them they were all slaughtered and I was left with nothing. They came to arrest me, saying, "We have slaughtered your husband. We have slaughtered all your cattle. Now we will slaughter you." They not only took the twelve oxen, but all my sheep and goats, all my clothes, everything.

So I escaped to Adi Awalla. There was nothing to stay for in Adi Nebried. I was very badly sick at the time. I had sores in my hair and all over my body. I had nothing to eat. I was nearly dying. People came in the night to give debes *[funeral price]. I refused to let them in. I refused butter for my hair. They repeatedly summoned me to Adi Daro. Eventually, I went, but they only insulted me, "We have killed your husband. You are a supporter of the TPLF. You only eat rabbit." They tried to humiliate me. I never submitted. I gave them tough answers.*

Finally, when the feudals were defeated, fighters like Berihu and Walta came after that and felt very bad at my condition. They took me to the TPLF hospital where I stayed one month and two weeks. The fighters washed all my body. They fed me with milk and honey and in six weeks, it was all gone. After the defeat, the animals were irreplaceable. As for my clothes, Bissrat and Kelebat tracked down the thieves to a nearby village. The clothes were ruined by then, so the organization calculated they owed me seven hundred birr. They paid me and fighters brought me clothes and gradually I started a new life when the TPLF controlled the area.

In 1983, the Dergue's Seventh Offensive line was a few kilometers from here. I had nine goats by that time and when the enemy came, they slaughtered them again. Only this time, it was the Dergue.

People say it's sixteen years since the beginning. To me it scarcely seems a month. Four of my sons and daughters have just joined. When the others joined, they went to the organization's school and TPLF took responsibility for them. Even when I had two small children, I left them with neighbors because I was cooking for the fighters. I cannot express how much I like fighters, but nothing is too much and sixteen years is too little. I never ask the people of Adi Nebried to plow my land because I'm a mother of fighters or wife of a martyred fighter. For me, I have seen the fruit of the revolution now. I don't mind what happens to me. Now, I'm becoming old, but I want to go on working. I go with my niece. When I see all these developments it's all worthwhile, even if my children have to die.

My daughter's husband was also martyred in battle, in 1982. She lives nearby. She has three sons. The oldest went three years ago to join the revolutionary school. His mother doesn't know that he drowned in the flood.

My own son died in the flood in Kaza too. I know I must preserve this secret. The other two are still at home.

Life is changing, particularly for women. Before, you produced with your husband, you worked with your husband. Quite apart from the oppression of the feudals, let's look at the sex oppression. You had the baby on your back while you were working, but you were still being beaten by your husband. Women were the most oppressed of all. The change when I see it now, it's so great. Now, the life of the two partners is much more democratic. If you don't like each other, you leave. If you are divorced, the property is divided equally. You have your own land. It's become mutual—of mutual interest—and this is a very great development in the life of women.

I am a health worker, a teacher, in the baito, in the Women's Association. My rights are protected. I have the right to try criminals. I am equal in every case to talk, to argue. All this is the work of the revolution. Long live God. Long live TPLF. I am now free to go anywhere, any time. No one is raping me; no one disturbs me. There are no obstacles for me. I don't have land. I try to make enough selling sewa in my spare time.

What remains for women? Women must be organized nation-wide, at Tigray level and not just at district level. Being organized at this level is the next task. This is what we're starting to do now. As for the revolution, it is very important to finish off the enemy, to mobilize the youngsters to join the fight and to win complete victory as soon as possible.[1]

Later in the afternoon, Roman Ayenew arrives to talk to us. She is tall, erect and well-built, defying the label *old* in spite of her sixty-eight years. She has in her bearing that air of authority, which comes with feudal rank. She is the mother of Hyelom, one of the first fighters and now one of the top commanders of the Front's army. She and her husband, Dejazmach Araya, fought furiously against the Italians as patriots of the Tigrayan resistance. She was married at twelve years old, the year before the Italian invasion, so she must have been a young teenager when she accompanied him into battle.

"She was a hero of the five year Italian colonization," says Aklilu. "Her husband, Dejazmach Araya and his brothers, Fitaurary Kidane Mariam and Grazmach Haile Mariam—these three brothers went to the jungle when the Italians occupied Ethiopia. They stayed five years in the Dejenna area in Wolqait, fighting and making raids on the Italians until the Italians were driven out. They were heroes of the resistance against the Italians."

Despite her husband's rank of Dejazmach, one of the highest feudal ranks, their sons became fighters and the family became strong supporters of the Front. At intervals, Aklilu breaks into her story with memories of his own:

"Hyelom is a top commander, so whenever the enemy came to Adi Nebried, the first target was their house, there on the hill. It has been burned four times. It stands out because it is all by itself by a church. So, when the TPLF left to evade the enemy, she always accompanied them. This family always had terrible problems. Once, when Adi Nebried was under the control of the EDU for nine months, she stayed that nine months with us. She was like a fighter, gathering information, struggling, a real warrior. She fought with all her family, all her wealth—her life dedicated to the revolution."

At another moment he says, smiling at her:

"I remember when we were fighting here. Her reputation in the struggle was that, of the two, she was the Dejazmach—her husband was the weaker. She was organizing food for the fighters; she was looking after the wounded. I remember her standing on the mountain like a tiger woman. She was horrible."

Roman the Tiger

I was born in Asmara, but my father was from Axum and I went to live in Axum when I was nine years old. I married when I was twelve. I had eleven children. Hyelom was the second from last. That is his field name—his real name was Haddish. My father was imprisoned by Haile Selassie for eighteen years, but after Hyelom was born, my father was released, so we called the new baby Haddish Elem ["new world"] as a memory.

Hyelom was brought up with the son of his older sister, who became the fighter, Geranchel. I was a mother to both of them. They were like brothers, going to school together. They were going everywhere together all the time with their two shotguns and heard rumors of a Tigrayan movement starting. Unknown to me, they made contact and went to join the struggle. I thought they had gone to start farming. I didn't realize until they disappeared with their guns that they had left for the field.

When they first went, I didn't know a struggle had even started. There were some notorious bandits in that area. It was normal to hear about bandits with guns stopping cars and so on. I suspected that the two boys had joined them. I went in search of them in many places. Fekre, my oldest son, came to stay—he was living very far away in Gojjam then—and we walked all the way to Adigrat trying to find them. I met one of them and a few months later, when they passed near Adi Nebried, I saw both of them and I began to learn of the struggle in Tigray.

The main reason I began to support the TPLF was understanding my son's aim. We were well-to-do, we ate well, we had a very good life. We ate off the fat of the land. The day these kids left was a holy day. We had slaughtered an ox and a sheep. They didn't even eat it. They only ate shiro [bean sauce] like hermits. They were in a hurry to leave—I'll always remember that. For sixteen years I have lived their way. I decided to remain honest to their ideas. All that time I have not slept on a bed, but only on the floor. My husband was a very ardent supporter and sympathizer of everything I did. When there was a very fierce three-day battle against the EDU here, he said, "If I were thirty years old, I would be fighting these bandits myself."

The feudal armies had gained the reputation over many years for robbing and looting any property they liked as they moved across the country. In this area, all the shops were looted. All the ordinary people who wanted a chance to share in the scavenging flocked to join them when they moved into a new area, so they grew in numbers very fast. Most local feudals had joined the EDU much earlier—even the leaders were from round here. Fitaurary Mesfin from Adi Nebried, the son of my husband's brother, received a letter from Ras Mengesha that he was coming with thousands to Tigray. TPLF got the information and imprisoned him a few days before this battle.

We were fighting the whole day. The feudals were mounted on mules and their thousands of followers communicated with each other on horns. I brought the wounded to my house, which was on a hill and overlooked the whole area. One of them was a squad commander wounded in the jaw. I was trying to wash his mouth area and give him a fluid diet. We spent all night making splints. That particular night, a TPLF militia was wounded in the fighting. We tried to save him, but he died. We got a shovel and buried him. Nowadays, we are trying to identify the graves of everyone. The parents of this militia didn't know where he was buried, but I had protected a certain tree, which marked the grave. Recently, I was able to show his family the burial place. In that battle, a shortage of ammunition forced us to retreat. As we left our house after the third day, the mattresses were soaked with blood from these fighters. I burned them all to leave no sign behind for the EDU to find. I took the four children of Fekre with me, three sons and a daughter.

We left the house, driving all our cattle and sheep and went to Eritrea. My husband decided to stay in a village on the border, but I decided to take our herds to relatives inside Eritrea. The EDU were banking on living off our sheep and cattle for months, but they got nothing!

They burned Fekre's house and our house to the ground. Fekre stayed away with us for eight months, until TPLF captured the Adi Daro area. He was killed in the Red Terror and buried in a rubbish heap. When the TPLF captured Shire ten years later, I decided to bring his bones to this church for burial, but when the enemy captured Adi Nebried again, they made a point of digging up his bones and throwing them away. In this war, the enemy made me a constant target.

My youngest daughter, Almaz, was a teacher in Shire. She was wanted by the EDU and when they were trying to control the area, they searched her house. She bought peasant clothes from villagers for herself, her husband and her oldest brother, Hagos. She put a pistol in an injera *basket and they all escaped from Shire. In 1988 she was arrested in Shire by the Dergue and interrogated in Mekelle about Hyelom—his appearance, his height, his photo. Even now, they send death squads to kill him. She was in prison in Mekelle until the TPLF took control in 1989. She is back in Shire now, a member of the baito and a very strong supporter of the revolution.*

Eventually, the TPLF defeated the feudals, pushed them out of the country, and I was able to return. During the eight months the EDU were in command here, they sent me a letter granting me amnesty because I was from an influential family and trying to persuade me to come back and be on their side.

Whenever the Dergue came, I never stayed around. The Dergue was in Adi Daro, one and a half hours away, for a long time. From there, they frequently came here, encircling us, but they never managed to catch me. One day, just after my husband died, the area was surrounded. I was wearing black mourning clothes. The local people thought I would be easily identified as Roman, so they took off their white clothes and gave them to me to conceal my identity. I was in Addis for years and speak very perfect Amharic. This helped me to escape. When the major arrived, I cried and cried and said my father had just died in a Toyota accident. We chatted about Addis and this deceived him, because he did not expect me to know every detail about Addis. When he went away to arrest people, I escaped on a donkey, dressed in white clothes. They burned my house to the ground. We killed this major in the Adi Daro operation. He killed our supporters and after three days, he was killed. I wanted to wash my hands in his blood for revenge. My house was burned again in 1983. All this was twelve years or more ago.

My second escape from the enemy was in June 1985. They came from Shire and encircled my house. I heard shots. The fighters were firing. When I went out to see what was happening, soldiers were streaming into the area. I immediately left the house, called the militia to tell them where the soldiers were coming from and joined the fighters in the town to help them defend it from attack. The enemy had no time to burn my house this time. They were not a big force and were forced to run away.

In 1989, when the Dergue left Tigray for the last time, my house was burned to the ground for the fourth time. The enemy had advanced to Adwa from Mekelle and to Axum from Eritrea. They always attacked Adi Nebried from other towns they controlled and there was always danger from banda *because of the nearness to Eritrea. The Dergue sent bands of contra-guerrillas. These* shemek *attacked Adi Nebried to arrest me and Dahab. I was with my daughter in the clinic. I ran with the medicines and hid them in the latrine and then hid myself. Dahab was away from home and so she was saved. After a few days, the enemy came back with three divisions, a very huge army with mechanized units. The TPLF was an hour away on their defense line. I escaped eastward and they caught me in a little village where I had built a small house as a place to live when the enemy was threatening me in Adi Nebried.*

"Who are you?"

I replied in Amharic that I had a house there.

"She is the mother of the fighters. Kill her!" the major shouted.

"By God's will," I answered, "I am infertile. I am nobody's mother!"

While they were discussing me, I slipped out of the back without their noticing. This was when they burned my house for the fourth time and threw out the bones of my son from the churchyard.[2]

Roman strides away, her long stone-colored clothes sweeping the ground, her head wrapped against the dust, which gusts of wind send swirling along the alleyways between the low houses. Aklilu had addressed her with great respect. Now, when she is out of sight, he says thoughtfully:

"Influential individuals in the communities—like Roman, like Dahab—were even more at risk than the fighters. Dergue militia came with the soldiers to get them because they saw them as mobilizing the people. She was never frightened, because she has always been able to maneuver and outwit them and escape."

One of the old posters of the Front depicts a peasant woman who has broken the chains of her oppression. She is not only angry, she is enraged, furious, snarling. Her eyes crackle. Her mouth is wide with bared teeth. The wild locks of her hair are whipped by the wind so they mingle with the clouds of a turbulent sky. The broken chains, still clamped to her wrists, whip dangerously through the air as she raises one arm in a defiant clenched-fist salute; the other fist is tensed near her hip as if ready to throw a punch. I love it. I wanted it on the cover of my book, but in England, it was judged too wild for comfort. She was on the cover of the Turkish edition instead.

When I think of Roman, I forget her years, her weather-beaten face, her stately posture. I think of her as young, with wild hair like the woman in the poster. A tiger woman. The meetings with Dahab and Roman have tossed us out of the ancient world and back into the revolution. We climb slowly out of the sweltering lowlands to cooler Endeselassie, a semi-highland town and the only one of any size before the ascent back to Axum. For some reason, Tigrayans always call Endeselassie *Shire,* the name of the zone of which it is the chief town. By the time we arrive, it is dark and we stop on the edge of the town to set down a couple of young students who have hitched a lift. Aklilu's plan is to drop me off at a hotel and then try to find Asgede. As we lug the baggage off the pickup and into the courtyard, I hear him complaining irritably of my failure to pack my backpack properly.

"What do you mean? Of course I packed it properly!"

One glance is enough—the buckles are undone and the bottom zip compartment where I keep my interview cassettes, both used and blank, is gaping open. In the room, by the light of an oil lamp, I check through my collection. The only one I am sure is missing is the tape of Meles from my last visit to Hagere Salam.

"I will come back!" Aklilu says and disappears fast into the darkness.

Nearly three hours grind past before he returns. He throws two cassettes onto the bed. One is the Meles tape and the other a new one, still in its celophane, that I hadn't even missed.

"I have prisoned them!" he growls.

Unusually, we order whiskies from the bar and sit in the yard under the hibiscus trees, sipping slowly by candle light. We scarcely talk and he refuses to be drawn on the fate of the thieves.

The next day, he tracks down Asgede. He was one of the small band of ten or eleven fighters who had gone into the jungle of Dedebit to start the revolution. Unlike most of his companions, he was not a student, but a farmer who had been a soldier in the Ethiopian army. His rural, as well as his military skills, were invaluable in the first year of the struggle, as almost all the fighters were from an urban background.

Asgede's memory for detail really is prodigious and factual detail is a great demystifier. He not only remembers the number of old guns they took with them into the wilderness, but their names and the precise number of bullets that went with each one. He remembers the coincidence of accidents, which caused the day of departure (from Endeselassie, not Addis) to be February 18—February 11 in the Ethiopian calender—now celebrated throughout the liberated area as if it could have been no other. He takes me to the house of Suhul, a parliamentary representative in Haile Selassie's time and a senior fighter, from whose house the first revolutionaries left for Dedebit and who was martyred early on in the struggle. I spend a day with Suhul's wife, filling in some gaps.

The first operation of the new Front, as I have included in the account of my first journey, was the rescue of Musie from prison in Endeselassie. Asgede describes this in minute detail and then we go out into the town to see the police station where he was chained and to pace out the distances along the roads from the nun's house, from the crossroads to the police station, from the police station to where Agazi was on watch and so on. Then, off we go to Axum to do the same thing there.

Asgede's detailed account of the Axum Bank operation is not only of interest to students of Ethiopian history. It also provides a fascinating insight into the nature of guerrilla warfare and into the strategic and tactical preparations, which must be made if it is to be successful. Nothing was left to chance, although chance still produced the unexpected. At the same time we see the human, even comic, details that are generally lost to sight in the confrontations of great armies and the large events of history. Yet, this small event was of mighty consequence. It transformed the small group of aspirant revolutionaries into a viable organization, which from these small beginnings has gone on to overthrow one of the most powerful of African dictatorships and set Ethiopia on a new course.

The Axum Bank Operation

After the operation in Shire, we went to a remote jungle area called Widak about seven kilometers due north of Shire, almost on the Eritrean border. Fighters who had been training in Eritrea and those from Shire came together for discussions on a constitution and our future program. This was the first time we discussed the constitution of the organization in the field. We numbered about thirty-eight fighters altogether. We had severe economic problems—in other words, we had no money to run any sort of program. Central Committee decided that we should take a bank, either Axum or Adwa or Shire.

We made a study of the three banks, the security situation of each, which was the best bet financially. Fighters went to survey each area. We decided to target Axum. Axum was less secure. It was also the most politically influential of the three towns and one of the aims of the operation was to give publicity to the TPLF. Since the capture of Musie, Shire was full of arms and soldiers; Adwa, like Adigrat, was well-fortified, whereas there was only one military division in Axum. Also, Axum had an airport and attracted much more money.

We rescued Musie in the last week in July; the Axum operation was a month later. For five days, in the middle of August, six fighters went to Axum and studied every detail. Musie was one of the six. In addition, there were Awa'alom, Abai, Netsanet, Alamin, and Berihu. We selected nine others to carry out the operation, including me, Asgede. The nine of us were Asgede, Aferom, Geday, Geranchel, Seberom, Kokah, Nerey, Habtom, Kelebet. Six were to be armed, three unarmed. When we set out for Axum from the base area, there was no food there at all. Before the start of the operation we had spent two birr on raw maize to eat. We kept to the north of Axum along the river Mereb for a few days waiting for clothes to arrive from our town moles which would disguise us as students on the Dergue campaign. Then we moved to a village near to Axum, travelling in the daytime and singing the songs of the student campaigners and looking as unlike fighters as possible.

On the evening of the twenty-fourth of August, we travelled to Axum and went straight to the house of the two moles. The other six had finished their survey of the town. We had a mole inside the bank who gave us information of a lot of withdrawals that day, so we delayed for two more days, waiting for deposits to build up again. We had discussions with maps and plans, which the six had prepared of all the locations. On the morning of the twenty-seventh of August, we went a short distance along the Adwa road to a bridge where a small river goes under the road near the school. We pretended to be students washing our clothes and stayed there the whole day discussing the details of the operation.

The attack had to be made by car and there was only two cars in Axum, one in the hospital and one in the clinic. We sent two drivers, Nerey and Geranchel, one to each car, to beg to use the car for a dangerously ill patient. They discovered the hospital car had broken down. At the clinic, Nerey asked the health officer for the urgent use of a car.

"I have come from Addis. My sister has been in labor in a village near here. She has given birth to a still-born child and now is hemorrhaging. Please give us a car."

The Health officer refused, but Dr. Abadi, our agent, was a health worker in the clinic—some of the six fighters conducting the study had stayed in his house. He encouraged the administrator to lend the landrover, and he at last agreed. While Nerey was inside the clinic negotiating for the landrover, Netsanet was outside in disguise, pretending to have no connection, but in fact giving him cover in case anything went wrong.

Then Nerey, with a driver, a hospital worker called Arefaine, drove to the bridge, where the others were all waiting. They told him to stop at pistol point. He tried to resist, but there were too many there. He was told to get out and Geranchel, just back from the hospital, took his place as driver. Arefaine was very frightened and ran off into the countryside. We told him not to come back for a long time!

So nine got into the Landrover—Musie, Awa'alom, Berihu, Nerey, Geranchel, Kelibet, Seberom, Habtom, Kokah. The others had left earlier to take up their positions. Alamin, very short, a joker, disguised as a poor peasant, was a few meters from the bank. Geday, looking like the beggars you always see by the road, was in front of the police station near the guard. He had an Israeli machine gun. I was playing the part of a peasant taking a case to court. I was carrying papers, but no gun, and I went inside the police station to give the documents to the police and at the same time to investigate the situation. Hailu, who had been working with the six in Axum before the operation, stationed himself opposite the police station outside the Sugar Distribution Center, thirty meters away. He had a pistol that didn't work. Netsanet and Abai were assigned to the telecommunications office, which was further along from the police station at the bottom of the hill. They had one pistol that didn't work and one machete. Inside, there were only female operators and one was a relative of Abai's. He wrapped his head in his shawl so he wouldn't be recognized. When Abai started to cut the wires with the machete, they tried to struggle, but gave in as soon as Nerey showed them his pistol, so they very easily controlled the communications.

Meanwhile, the others drove from the bridge in the landrover and stopped outside the Bank. Berihu and Seberom jumped out. Alamin was already inside. A few meters further on where the road divides at a park, Aferom got out. It was his job to monitor with a French rifle all directions from that point in case an attack came.

Six people were still in the Landrover, which took the right fork to the police station, where they knew about forty police would be on duty. At three o'clock, all police had to report to sign the register. This was after three pm. At a quarter to four firing started. At that time, members of the junta were travelling from town to town to proclaim the aims of the Dergue's revolution. The six in the car were either wearing uniforms like these soldiers of the Dergue or were dressed as student campaigners. In many places, soldiers and campaigners worked together. When the landrover rolled up in front of the door, the police saluted them! They went into the police station, where they knew there was one room with ten carbines. They took charge of them and with them controlled the police. For the first time, the fighters were all armed. The fighters collected everyone together in two rooms at the back and locked them in. The only casualty was the captain of the police who opened fire. Musie shot and wounded him with a Kalashnikov and then Habtom killed him with a double-barrelled shotgun. That was the worst moment of all. All the others raised their hands and kept very quiet.

Then, all the arms were loaded onto the landrover, but unfortunately it had a shaky battery. If we started to push it ourselves, we could be shot at from behind. Behind the police station was a long-term prison. Kalibet went out the back to check for any attacks coming from that direction, then at gunpoint we took out of the two rooms ten or fifteen policemen and told them to load all the remaining guns and ammunition in the place onto the landrover and then to push it down the road.

Then, we went to the Bank. Aferom was still at the junction providing security cover in case police came from the airport or from the police station. At the Bank, they had one carbine and one pistol between three fighters. One was unarmed, but with his fist he disarmed the guard so then they were all armed. Earlier, they had taken big carrying sheets into the Bank with them. When the Bank Manager handed over the money to them, they gave him a receipt stamped with the official stamp of the TPLF. They were waiting for us with the bundles of money, but the car was so full of arms and ammunition that the money was too bulky to fit inside too, so we set off on foot with the money on our backs and the landrover going very slowly beside us.

The operation took fifty minutes from start to finish.

A Toyota and a truck full of peasants came towards us from the Adwa direction. We stopped both vehicles and loaded the money into the Toyota and the fighters climbed onto the truck with the peasants, whom we didn't allow to get off. We turned and drove off towards Adwa and well outside the town at the top of the long incline down to the Adwa plateau, we stopped and the peasants helped us unload all three vehicles. We asked the peasants to go with us and they carried the money, guns, and ammunition with us for five hours walk north towards the Eritrean border. We agitated them all the way and then we gave them money and sent them back again.

We captured 180,000 Ethiopian dollars, 50,000 US dollars, 6,000 pounds sterling and some Deutchmarks. Some currencies, like Italian Lire, were more difficult to change, so we left them behind in the Bank.

At the start, we had the following weapons: one Kalashnikov with one hundred and twenty bullets, one Ouzi (Israeli) with ninety bullets, two pistols (never fired), one Simonov with forty bullets, one carbine with forty-five bullets, one Mas with thirty bullets, and one double-barrelled shotgun with twelve bullets. At the end of the operation, we had seventy-two rifles, thirty thousand bullets, a hundred ammunition belts and two machine guns. After this operation, everybody was armed. Before, we used stones as grenades and shouted "bomba!" to make everybody lie flat. We had to pretend that sticks covered with cloth were weapons. Now, we were armed with automatic and semi-automatic weapons.

Sixteen fighters were involved in the operation, including Hailu from Addis. Six were armed and ten unarmed. Two of us, Asgede and Habtom, were slightly wounded, but could walk. The two moles whose house we stayed in during the operation were teachers. After that, they became fighters. They are still alive.

The impact of this operation was very big. Because Axum was a center of communication and was on the air route to Addis, news travelled very fast. People had dismissed the Shire operation, when we rescued Musie, as an Eritrean operation. But this didn't happen with the Axum operation because some of the fighters were from Axum. We had people working clandestinely in the town, and we distributed hundreds of pamphlets everywhere. They were called "The Armed" and were all written by hand! They were all stamped with the official TPLF seal of the Axum obelisk, the Kalashnikov, and the hammer. After that, the political work in the town expanded and our support grew very fast. Within a month, about thirty-one students came to the field from the towns. Our numbers were doubled. We thought ourselves a huge army and the problems of money were solved.

We were on the border of Eritrea and Tigray on the Mereb River. Two weeks after the operation there was a threat to our security because the enemy got information about where we were. We loaded the money onto Deseligne, the mule, to cross the Mereb. There was a lot of rain and in a flash flood Deseligne was swept away with all his load. I was with him and another fighter, Hadegai. We were swept five hundred meters down the river before we could get him to the bank. All the money was saved, but it was saturated and we had to dry it out in the sun! Then, we distributed it between our agents who took it to the Bank in Adwa and other places. We had a budget from then on and withdrew funds as we needed them.[3]

I have heard this story so many times and no two versions are exactly alike. The personal involvement and the mass of convincing detail suggest that Asgede's version might be the authentic one. The way certain details have been emphasized, while others have become marginalized or distorted, sheds light on the whole process of myth-making. In a country, which values storytelling, this is a movement high on the raw materials of myth: initiation in the wilderness, self-sacrifice, dedication, love of country, consciousness of noble cause, sense of national identity, sense of history, the mourning of dead heroes. All the elements of an epic are here, except a great poet with time on his hands. Once again, despite their encouragement, I am conscious they should be doing this themselves, not me.

"So where were you, Aklilu, while all this was going on?"

We have just come back from a tour of the town very different from our survey a few days ago of ancient Axum. We have walked every step of every relevant road, gawped at all the buildings: the bank, the police station, the telecommunications office, the monitoring spot at the junction of the two roads, even the bridge past the school on the edge of town where they did their washing and tidied the plans. The bank was all shut up behind the inadequate defenses of its railings, one broken window winking slyly as if at some secret joke. The banking system left Mekelle two years ago with the Dergue and cannot be restored until the end of the war. The police station is much as it was sixteen years ago, empty now that law and order is in the hands of the Front and the *baitos*—also until after the war, presumably. We walk along the long internal corridor, peering through the doors on each side into empty unswept offices, trying to imagine them full of police, our sense of the urgency and fear and seriousness overlaid by comedy as we imagine them helping to push the landrover full of guns and ammunition down the road. Not even the best laid plans can anticipate every eventuality.

"I was in the Library in the center of Axum," says Aklilu. "We were following all the events. People were running and some were firing. In a few minutes they had control of the police station, loaded guns onto the landrover and drove it back to collect the money and fighters from the Bank."

"Were you a member of the TPLF then?"

"I was a new recruit into the organization at that time. I was sixteen. Still at school. We were so happy at what was happening because our consciousness on the national question was rising and we had many political discussions."

He is really enjoying this excursion back into the heady days of youth. His voice cracks with enthusiasm.

"The huge amount of money really helped our operation. This money was our food. I joined as a fighter ten months later and it was still there. They could not possibly keep this amount of money with them so they later put it all back in the bank under agents' names...."

He laughs suddenly.

"... where they got six per cent interest!"

"And there really was a Deseligne the Mule!"

When I first heard the story, I was surprised that the tendency to mythologize had shown itself so soon after the event and so early in the movement and now I'm interested in the disparities between myth and the more factual version.

"Of course. He was bought for this operation. After many hardships, he saved the money from the flood. After that, we had many mules, but Deseligne was the first and most famous mule. All the fighters shared their food with him and honored him. Many fighters cried at his burial. It was about three years later, he died."

I tell him the Axum Bank story as I first heard it, with Deseligne playing the lead. He laughs.

"Yes, they tell it like that in the training camp. There are many stories about him. Deseligne would never accept any donkey going ahead of him. We were always mobile—every night, we climbed to a hilltop to sleep, but we always followed Deseligne in the dark because he always chose the best path."

So, there is more than one Axum. The Axum of ancient Empire and the Axum of the bank raid are in time-space layers separated from one another by hundreds of years, yet connected by patterns of meaning in oral tradition and collective memory. A third Axum is the one I've been experiencing inside people's homes. I've not only been several times to Mebrat's house, but I've also enjoyed warm hospitality and wonderful meals in the homes of Aklilu's relatives and Elsa's family. A fourth manifestation is of course that of the Orthodox Church, which shows itself in a new guise when we all attend the baptism service of Elsa's baby, Samhal.

The service starts soon after four in the morning and lasts for several hours. The many different stages, first in the baptistry of the Church of the Four Animals of God (as Elsa's brother translates it for me) and then in the Church itself. I remember past christenings in England, tense occasions overwhelmed by infant screams; now, the only time I hear a baby cry is when one is momentarily immersed in the water of the font. A restless child is immediately offered the breast and so both mothers and babies are completely peaceful.

The church is arranged as a square within a square. Only men are allowed in the central sanctum and we women walk to different sections of the outer ambulatory for different parts of the ritual and spend long periods sitting on the floor together while the dozen or so babies are annointed and prayed over, in turn. Aklilu has stayed away, despite his upbringing in a priest's family. Many fighters feel alienated from a church that has conspired with feudal authority to keep the mass of the population in miserable poverty.There is plenty of time for meditation. Habitual irritation at discrimination against women and the implications of Aklilu's absence turn my thoughts to all the other divisions of this divided land. There are divisions also within the Ethiopian Church. As in El Salvador or Nicaragua, the Church Establishment has been a reactionary force, closely identified with the monarchy and feudal power, but large numbers of poor rural priests have been strong supporters of the Front, with arguments similar to those of liberation theologians in Central America. The contrast between the religious freedom allowed by the Front and the repressive policies of the Dergue may, in time, win converts even from the upper ranks of the Church hierarchy. Axum, because of its central importance to the Ethiopian Christian Church, has been particularly repressive of Muslims, who have not been allowed to own land or property here. There are signs that this too is being slowly eroded by the anti-discriminatory influence of the Front, but as they work through persuasion rather than dictate, change happens slowly.

At one point, about two hours into the service, I am sitting among women in the outer corridor. Every inch of the walls and the barrel-vaulted ceilings are covered with paintings of biblical scenes and the lives of saints who stare down at me with big brown ikon-eyes. The scene in front of me is the harrowing of hell. At the top, God the Father, the Son, and the assembled saints look out of heaven with their transfixing glare; further down, the just are being sorted from the unjust by an assortment of fearsome devils, wielding four-pronged forks. The good souls fly upwards to everlasting tranquillity; the wicked are sent tumbling down into the flames of hell, which lick greedily, carnivorously, upwards from the bottom of the painting, crammed with souls whose faces writhe with pain and torment. After staring at these paintings for hours in different parts of the church, I notice something for the first time. God and the Just all have white faces; the Wicked and the devils all have black faces.

You don't have to be long in the Ethiopian highlands to become aware of distinctions based on skin color. At best, complexion is used as one means of identification, as we would say, "Oh, you mean the one with red hair"; at worst, it is an indicator of discrimination, which is indefensible, but deep-rooted. The favored complexion is fair (a golden brown, called "red" here), an important aspect of beauty in women. Dark complexions incur openly critical comments, although sometimes teasing or affectionate. The word *baria* (slave) is the word most often used to denote dark complexioned people and I have even heard fighters use the term of each other or of young children in the family. They seem not to have made the connection between a political consciousness, which outlaws discrimination against, for example, the Kunama people in northwest Tigray, and the skin color, which helps to identify them. I am shocked to find, in this church, that popular prejudice is underpinned by traditional images of a most powerful kind.

I take this up with Aklilu later, but it seems to be a new idea. At least, he doesn't seem to think images in wall paintings are politically important. "They've always been like that," he says, shrugging his shoulders. I suspect he doesn't want to think about it. He is worried about time. He wants to get me back to Mekelle and report back to Hagere Salam. I spend the afternoon with Genet and Elsa at the family home, celebrating the admission of Samhal into the congregation of the just. Aklilu is with the mechanics running some checks on the car. As the light dims at the end of the afternoon, we pile into the pick-up and set off for the return journey.

Before the dawn breaks the next morning, I am back in Mekelle.

17

Setback

For some time, I have not been well. It started in Hagere Salam. Climbing from the caves to the road, I had to rest every few yards, faint with weakness. First of all, I blamed my persistent nausea on the daily dose of bitter malaria pills, although a doctor from a European team in Mekelle rejected that theory, saying there was a lot of flu about. More recently, I grew worse in Adigrat, but improved on the expedition to Axum and Adi Nebried. Tigray, one of the poorest provinces of a poor country and suffering sixteen years of civil war, is not the best place to moan about personal afflictions, so I carried on with my work and the inspirational nature of the interviews even helped to distract me. Back in Mekelle, Aklilu returned to Hagere Salam, and Mulugeta reappeared. Gebru, my old friend on the Front's Central Committee and now Secretary for Tigray, arranged transport to the doctor and brought me curds to settle my stomach. He invited me to meet his family, and his ancient father, a wonderfully vital old merchant getting on for ninety, told me his story. But, their kindness didn't prevent my feeling steadily worse.

One morning, while interviewing in Mekelle, I develop a terrible headache, which no painkillers can touch. By lunchtime, the head pains are so severe I cannot stand up or bear light. The Dutch doctor from Médecins Sans Frontières diagnoses cerebral malaria.

A twilight time. Continuously queasy, constantly throwing up the bitter residues of an empty stomach, the added bitterness of medicine at regular intervals one more torture. My head expands. It is full of spaces, all the spaces filled with pain, pain so full of terror there is room for only one thought, the impossibility of surviving it, oblivion the only desire as long as it blots out sensation. Waves of heat blast my nerves and my brain flies free of a soaked and trembling body to wrestle with giant shadows. Sometimes, the shadows seem to be the doctor; sometimes Mulugeta or Gebru twisting into elongated and palpitating shapes, their heads on the ceiling. But, they are distant creatures, in some other world from the lonely spaces where I struggle with forces beyond my strength, forces that assume dimensions and density and strange shapes like the demons of old tales.

Water fills me with horror. It is impossible to keep it down. The doctor worries about dehydration and in more lucid moments, I hear him threatening hospital. I have visited the hospital, seen the effects of poor water supplies—dirty floors, the urine in corners, diseased patients sharing filthy mattresses. The eyes of anxious relatives pursue me now, their fly-covered food offerings pushed under the beds. He thinks I'm safer in this little hotel. I agree and force myself to take sips of water. But, in the long hours of the night when I'm alone my obsession is rabies. I never had the second jab. In the Sudan, I had nursed a child's puppy back to health after soldiers had stoned it. My head boils with hallucinations. The puppy, immense, its body obscenely white like a huge maggot, with lolling tongue and bulging eyeballs, lollops around my room.

The treatment begins to work. Bad dreams give way to periods of lucidity, which feel more like insanity than the delirium. In moments of quietness, the only certainty is death. For the first time, I wonder what I am doing in Ethiopia. How weak and fragile the human organism; the astonishing arrogance of my assumption of immunity; the rashness of exposure to untold dangers. If only I had perished under fire instead of in a squalid, maudlin and unheroic sickbed. I cry into my pillow because my family does not realize my suffering and by the time they do, it will be too late. I still can't bear light and noise burns my brain with physical pain. During the day they have taken to playing very loud Tigrayan pop music in the bar, a round thatched hut with a veranda fifty yards across the yard. The songs crackle with distortion on the old equipment. So, beyond my door life goes on, indifferent, selfish. I fail to understand it.

Mulugeta comes with a friend of his, Kassa, to sit with me. Only a few days ago Kassa, the keeper of ancient monuments for the Front, gave us a tour of the palace of Yohannes IV, the last Tigrayan emperor. Now, he sits wrapped in his *gabi* in lugubrious silence. Mulugeta is bored with nothing to do. He enlivens the dull room with flashes of wit. I begin to appreciate it, although I can't yet sustain a conversation. He has had malaria countless times. Once, he tells me, when the base area was in the Tekezze River basin, he fell asleep with exhaustion after hours of walking, leaving one foot exposed.

"I think every mosquito in Tekezze came to feast on my foot. In the morning, it was bleeding and twice the normal size."

One thought begins to dominate my afflicted brain with the force of revelation. How have they managed to organize a revolution at the same time as having malaria? How is it possible? Mulugeta laughs and shrugs it off, but the thought persists, entwined with guilt at my own feebleness. I am lucky. I have responded to treatment. Some malaria strains are resistant to drugs. Brain malaria is worst of all and often fatal. What am I moaning about?

Gebru comes and sits with me, bringing his sense of inner quietness. Foreigners, he tells me, have no immunity, so if they get it, they get it worse. After the first time, it is never so bad again.

"I remember clearly. When I first had malaria, it seemed preferable to die rather than to live."

His admission brings comfort. It's not so heroic. I no longer feel so alone and so pathetic. I begin to nibble just a few crumbs of the special *himbasha* that Geday or Kassetch bring me, the two women who run the hotel. Gebru often talks of his family, particularly his father, whom he loves. In the days of Dergue occupation, he would sometimes come to Mekelle on a mission for the TPLF. Disguised as a peasant, he would slip into the town with farmers coming to market and, at night, go about his business in the dark streets, perhaps past his family's house, unable to go near them for fear of putting them in danger.

The Dutch doctor comes every day to check on me. He is tall and thin and exceptionally reserved. He is also hostile to the Front, alleging that both sides are as bad as each other. He is bitter, cynical, and scathing. His views seem to be based on his experience within the hospital, although he shrugs off the hygiene problems, the feces in the yard, the unfamiliarity of latrines to peasants, which overwhelm many Europeans. He accuses the TPLF of discriminating between fighters and civilians. Fighters are not as disciplined as they make out, he says. How could they be, I reply.

"Sometimes fighters who are convalescent don't want to give up their beds, even though very sick civilians may be lying on the floor. Then, a peasant couple came to me recently and asked for contraceptives because they couldn't afford more children. I went to the TPLF administrator. He said they could not have contraceptives—only the fighters are allowed contraceptives. It is not right."

He exemplifies the clash of cultures. It is difficult to argue with him, because he only sees things in terms of individuals. I don't disagree with his examples. How could I? But, the basis of his information is as narrow as his experience, without any historical, sociological, or economic context. A hospital is an accumulation of negative experience anyway and with no other frame of reference, its catalog of mistakes can easily be seen as microcosmic indicators—as, to a certain extent, they are. The question is how to interpret them. He has scarcely travelled outside Mekelle, so he knows nothing about the changes introduced by the Front in the countryside. Presumably, even if he went into the villages, the apparently unchanging face of poverty and his ignorance of feudal culture and conditions would prevent him from seeing what had been achieved. He would be unlikely to ask the peasants their opinion.

"But there are no resources for universal contraception," I say, "so there has to be a policy. The TPLF has to discriminate. So, since the relaxation of the celibacy regulations for fighters in 1985, it discriminates in favor of women fighters because it is the military struggle that will bring an end to the civil war sooner and only then will real economic development become a possibility, including resources for family planning."

He has no faith in the nursing staff and he may be right. He cites examples of nurses forgetting to give post-operative antibiotics. But the context is gross underdevelopment crossed with the effects of civil war, which have left Tigray with six conventionally-trained doctors for more than four million people. The Front has given the countryside the first medical care they have known—but how did they staff these clinics? What do you do to raise the general level of health care for four million people with no resources? They recruited the most promising local personnel and gave them three-months training in diagnosis of the main epidemic diseases and simple treatment (chloroquine for malaria, injections, and dressings). More complicated needs were referred to one of the few field hospitals. Every year, these "physicians" receive a few weeks training to upgrade their knowledge and occasionally some are given extra training for specific tasks. For example, in 1986, MSF trained squads of these dressers to perform cataract operations for river-blindness, which Western surgeons would only be able to do after years of general and then specialized training. It is an ingenious and pragmatic approach to actual needs, but no one can pretend it is adequate.

When he has gone, I reflect on the sophisticated abstractions of modern medical treatments. Not many years ago, a young relative of mine returned to her local London GP complaining that the treatment of her little boy's earache had been ineffective. It turned out she had been pouring the antibiotic in his ear. A common-sense approach, if ignorant, I thought at the time, but not the risible stupidity suggested by the rest of the family. In Adwa, a few weeks ago, I enjoyed some conversations with an impressive Australian doctor who, although he had criticisms of the Front's medical training, especially their separation of theory and practice, saw clearly the context of a people emerging in a very short time from hundreds of years of superstitious health practices. My own theory is that it takes decades to internalize the understanding of the body on which modern health theory is based, particularly if it is invisible and therefore abstract. In the West, we have just about acquired a working knowledge of antibiotics, but although people *know* about the damaging effects of blue asbestos or radiation or chemicals or smoking, most of them haven't begun to *believe* it, otherwise unscrupulous companies would not be still getting away with risking lives.

There is no point in refuting the Dutchman's examples. The revolution would have to be perfect in every detail to deserve his respect. The discussion has to take place within a much wider frame of reference. Another day, I describe my researches into community health campaigns and the training of health workers in simple preventive medicine, in building latrines or instruction on the safe period. But, we both know the safe period is such a hit and miss approach to contraception that my voice trails off. He tells me he sometimes has to treat fighters with wounds from gunshot accidents "because they don't know how to handle weapons or grenades." This happens in the West too, I say, but the news rarely travels beyond the walls of military hospitals. In Britain, it is probably covered by the Official Secrets Act. I tell him about the split-second timing of the Agazi Operation; I ask him, "If the Front is so inefficient and hopeless how is it they have forced the Dergue out of Tigray and are now winning victories in Wello and Gondar?"

"Because government troops are demoralized and even less efficient," he replies, which coincides with my information as it happens, but which in this context sounds suspiciously like a racist dismissal of all African endeavors.

The conversations are doomed. He does not want to listen and I resent being pushed into a line of argument which suggests I am some sort of revolutionary groupie without any skepticism or critical sense. At the same time, my brain is coming back to life and it even crosses my mind that this cadaverous and dour Dutchman has my number and is indulging in some wierd form of therapy. He also orders me to walk as far as the bar and take a cup of tea before his next visit, to sit a few minutes in the sun. But, the following morning, when I wobble as far as the door, the bar looks a hundred miles away across a space of savage brilliance. A day later, however, I manage it all by myself and drink sweet tea at a metal table, trying to work up courage for the return trip while Geday flutters around me like a mother hen.

That night, about two in the morning the silence, usually broken only by the competitive howling of dogs, is disturbed by vehicles arriving in the yard and the sound of voices and movement in the room next door. In the morning, Mulugeta tells me they are German journalists on their way to the front in Gondar and if I had not fallen ill, I would be travelling south with them. It is a bitter blow and I shed more tears into my pillow. Later, the woman pops her head around the door and the couple turns out to be Dieter and Christina, whom I met in Mai Hanse in 1987. Christina is very sympathetic.

"I know what you need," she says. "Bouillon cubes. I never travel without them."

A few minutes later she brings back a steaming mug and I am surprised to find I can keep it down a sip at a time and it lines my stomach so that for the first time I can contemplate a return to normal life, say in two or three month's time. She also gives me a supply of little nightlights, which do much to keep at bay the terrors of darkness. Two days later, in the middle of the night, they leave for the south. Without me.

Every day I walk a little further, but I feel like some white subterranean creature, fearful of the sunlight, which makes my head ache. It is a struggle to ward off the depression, which keeps striking me down since Dieter and Christina's departure. I seem to have been out of the real world for a very long time, although it is not not much more than a week since the crisis began. Roman, Aregash, Mebrat, and Heriti all come at different times to cheer me up. They are some of the first women fighters and they have told me their experiences over the years. Illness makes me intensely sensitive to their sacrifices and their pains. They never indulge. Whatever strikes them down, they get up and get on with the business of the revolution. Gently, they rally me to get up and get on with it too.

Roman and Mebrat bring their little boys with them. Roman's son, called Tekie, is two years old. His name means "instead of," or perhaps "replacement," in remembrance both of her younger brother, a fighter killed in battle just before the baby's birth, and of the victims of the Dergue massacre at Hausien at about the same time. I remember going to Hausien, hearing survivors describe the market day on an August morning, in 1988, when more than two thousand people had been massacred by MiGs and helicopter gunships. Mebrat's son is now four. I first met her in Khartoum, when he was a few days old. He was named after Musie, one of the founder fighters of the revolution and a close friend of her husband, Jamaica. Musie was killed (they would say "martyred") in the early years of the struggle.

My brain still is not working properly. In this period of go-slow and recovery, it seems to see with devastating accuracy right to the problems at the heart of things, especially the thing called war. I cannot see solutions to anything. I cry a lot. Tekie and Musie, as well as the ebullient young teenagers who peddle cigarettes and matches around the Green Hotel, seem untouched by the suffering unexpressed in words but etched in adult faces. It is such a cliché to see children as the symbol of rebirth, the hope of the future, but that is exactly what they are. Tekie bounces on my bed convulsed with giggles and the shadows of dead fighters behind his back recede a little.

I am hoping that Roman, as Secretary of the Women Fighters' Association, will be able to distribute prints I've brought of photographs of women fighters I took on my last visit. When they come to the photo of Sophia (field name Gualnumeire), proudly sitting at the wheel of the landcruiser she drove for the Front, they pause and look mournful. They tell me she was trying to bring a supply of medicines from the Sudan at the beginning of the last rainy season. She was trying to cross a river in flood when the torrent turned the car over and she was drowned. They all say, "she was martyred."

It's time for a first trip out. Mulugeta, pleased at the prospect of returning to work, takes me to Mekelle prison. Last time I came here, the town was barely free of the Dergue and the empty prison was full of the ghosts of the tortured; now it has been turned into metal workshops. The compounds where relatives formerly queued with food for a chance to see their sons and daughters or husbands or brothers are now busy with a different activity. The air rings with the din of hammers on metal.

"See the raw materials?" Mulugeta says, pointing to a dump of old military vehicles captured from the Dergue and now past repair. Without his help, I would not have registered a couple of men stripping down a battered landcruiser; others are beating panels flat for recycling.

"We have no supply of metal here. They have to use whatever they can find."

Metalwork has traditionally been a low status occupation in Ethiopia. Artisans in general, but especially blacksmiths, have been a separate and despised class, but also feared as the *budda,* a sub-culture seen as having special powers to change the course of the future, to curse with the evil eye those who cross them. The Front has been working for some years to overcome the superstitions and discrimination associated with metal-working, by paying trainees from other social groups to acquire metal-working skills. The apparent success of the operation has less to do with a change of heart in the people than with their desperate need for work. Perhaps, nevertheless, by blurring the social divisions it will begin to erode the prejudices.

In different corners of the old prison, groups of workers are recycling the steel into basic and mundane necessities. In one place, they are stacking up cooking stoves; in another steel drums; in another buckets. In the forge, three men work as a team. One lifts the red-hot tongue of metal from the fire with pincers and holds it still on the anvil, while his companions rhythmically swing huge sledge-hammers over their heads and pound it into a plowshare. Outside, the gleaming finished tools are arranged in fans in the sand. It gives life to the old saying—swords into plowshares.

The next day is Sunday, the seventeenth of February, the day appointed to celebrate the sixteenth anniversary of the revolution. I spend the day with Roman and Tekie in Romanet, a village a few kilometers from Mekelle where she lives and has an office (the same room) from which she runs the Women Fighters' Association. Despite this full-time job, she is determined to bring up Tekie herself. Her husband is representing the Front in London and, although she sometimes looks very tired, she gets by with the support of other fighters. Today is a holiday, however, and very relaxed—chatting, eating omelettes, and watching the villagers singing and dancing through the village until the time comes to return to Mekelle for the official celebrations.

To avoid MiG attacks the celebrations, as usual, are in the evening, although since the USSR has withdrawn material support such attacks are less frequent. Two hours before the ceremony begins, people begin to assemble near the stadium. The Green Hotel, only a step away, is a good vantage point, while I am waiting for Roman and her friends to collect me. Sounds of clapping and drumming and singing mark the approach to the stadium of wave after wave of groups from the villages, of militia, women and fighters, skipping a slow skip and clapping as they go. I don't know what the selection process is for admission, but those who can't or don't want to go line the pavements and stand on little hills to watch them pass.

Within the stadium, the ceremonial parade takes a further two hours, first the people of Mekelle, then the organized groups—representatives from surrounding villages and from the *kebelles* of Mekelle, then priests, merchants, students, children, and veterans of the first *Weyane.* Each group carries garlands and appropriate emblems. The merchants walk behind a shop set up on a pick-up truck. The Front is represented by a procession, which traces the history of the struggle, beginning with the Dedebit story and then showing the technological progress of the Front. Ten fighters carrying very old-fashioned guns represent the first fighters. The packed stadium resounds with applause and ululations. Behind them, trundle old vehicles and fighters with AK 47s, followed by Toyotas and Mercedes trucks, then anti-aircraft guns. Heavy artillery and tanks coincide with the founding of the EPRDF. Finally, there is a float of the future. The coming of electrification to the villages is displayed on the back of a truck on which winking lightbulbs festoon refrigerators and electric stoves.

After the speeches, the evening ends with a sixteen-gun salute for the sixteen years of struggle—except that a number of fighters are carried away by the excitement and the popping of Kalashnikovs continues for longer than planned! Roman tuts with disapproval. I know the Front prides itself on its discipline, but they are reserved about their techniques of enforcement and I never find out what happens to the unruly few. As we leave, she gives me an idea of the content of the speeches, which is mostly the common rhetoric of official celebrations except in one respect.

"You know, they are saying this is the last February the Eighteenth celebrations of the war. Next February, we will be celebrating in Addis."

Although I still sag in the afternoons, my energy is gradually returning. It is time to get back to work, although for a time I restrict myself to working locally, which is less tiring and allows me to nap after lunch.

The Front seems to be making a determined effort to introduce a democratic culture here and last November the *baito* started functioning in Mekelle after several months of preparation. I interview members of the *baito* executive and make a detailed investigation into the processes of grass-roots education, consultation, and assembly, which preceded the elections and contributed to the making of the *baito* laws. It is a much more participatory process than I am used to in the West. Although fighters help guide the process and are represented on the committee, which drafts the laws, the draft is discussed and can be amended in each locality. Finally, it comes back for final discussion, amendment, and ratification before an assembly of elected representatives, which has absolute power. It is the power of this *baito* assembly which makes this process both more participatory and more democratic than other systems I have encountered.

The Mass Bureau, the department of the Front responsible for working directly with the people, has developed considerable skills over the years at politicizing and mobilizing the peasants and townspeople of Tigray. I would go so far as to say that these skills are the secret of their revolutionary success. Yet, these fighters can only guide and influence; they cannot dictate the end result. It is the Front, which has influenced the *baito* in every area to outlaw discrimination on the grounds of gender or religion, to raise the minimum age of marriage, and give women equal rights to land and property. Nevertheless, the final decisions are taken by particular *baito* assemblies, so there are variant decisions in different parts of Tigray. In some areas the minimum age of marriage for women is fifteen, in others sixteen; in some of the larger towns where there are better educational facilities, eighteen has been favored, to prevent marriage from disrupting schooling for young women up to twelfth grade.

In the interests of democracy, ironically, the Front has been encouraging the withholding of democratic rights to elect and be elected from "non-democratic elements" like recalcitrant feudals and old Dergue officials and Party members. In Mekelle, the *baito* assembly insisted on ignoring this advice and elected certain authority figures from the past. However, the regulations on accountability meant that when these individuals stood against the popular interest on such sensitive issues as land there were procedures, which enabled them to be replaced. "We learn from our mistakes," the vice-chairman says to me, spreading his hands in a rueful gesture.

It is not long before I am travelling further afield again. One day, as we are returning in the landcruiser from Adi Gudom to Mekelle, Mulugeta at an inconsequential moment makes an announcement of great consequence.

"The battle for Addis began yesterday."

The new front is nowhere near Addis in fact, but over in the western provinces of Gojjam and Gondar. He means that this is the beginning of the final campaign, which will end up with the taking of Addis.

They have called it Campaign Tewodros after the fiery nineteenth century Kassa who rose from relatively humble origins to become ruler of Gondar and then Emperor Tewodros. Through a combination of political adroitness and military skill, he united a fragmented country, controlled the territorial aspirations of the foremost feudal lords and restored the ascendancy of the Orthodox Church. Some commentators have seen him as laying the basis for the emergence of modern Ethiopia. His reign came to an end when he committed suicide after his defeat by a British force come to compel the release of European captives.

We are passing through rain-soaked fields across the high plain above Mekelle. The window winder is broken and the wind sends the rain lashing through the open window onto both of us and I snuff up the smell of wet earth on the parched land and lean out of the car the better for the pores of my parched skin to drink it in. For most of the journey, we seem about to drive beneath the central arch of a perfect rainbow. Through its two shimmering pillars we can clearly see the slope of the next hill, yet we never manage to catch it up and every curve of the track finds it still ahead of us transforming a new landscape with bands of color. This is the second day, not "of rain" unfortunately, but on which it has rained. Peasants say that they can predict from these "little rains" the quality of the big rains in June. Whether the rainbow is an augury of victory in Addis or of more better rain later I can't decide, but I am determined to make it an augury of something.

A day hanging around. No news. No Mulugeta. Nothing about Ethiopia on the World Service. They are obsessed instead with the Gulf War. A friend sends a *gabi* to keep me warm in the rainy weather. It is fresh from the loom in two halves, so I take it down to her house to be sewn together and stay for lunch. I read a book by Richard Pankhurst. He seems to be making the case that the people of the southern provinces at the turn of the century welcomed their forcible annexation by Emperor Menelik II. I feel I'm dying of frustration.

My next door neighbor in the Green Hotel is now Dr. Assefa. Today, even he is not around for an exchange of news and speculations and by the time I hear him through the wall, it is the small hours of the morning and I am already in bed.

I first met Assefa in the field four years ago. Since then, I have discovered he played a part in the early development of the revolution. In the mid-seventies he was appointed administrator of a development project in Sheraro. He was sympathetic to the cause of Tigrayan liberation and turned a blind eye when the project's employees, including Roman and Aregash, at the same time started working underground for the Front. After the flight of his personnel and dispersal of the assets of the organization, he was arrested by the Dergue and tortured and imprisoned in Addis Ababa for six years. Thence, he fled as a refugee to Britain. He was a founder member of the Tigray Development Association (TDA), channelling the goodwill, professional expertise and funds of Tigrayans in the West to development projects here.

The next day improves. News starts to filter in first thing in the morning. Anyone with a radio is stuck to it in the center of a little crowd. A stream of visitors comes to listen to my radio and give me a running commentary. Then Mulugeta comes with Fissaha, an old friend who is always very close to the center, and they stitch it all into a narrative.

Bahr-Dar on Lake Tana, the chief city of West Gojjam, was captured yesterday. The nearby hydro-electric power-station at Tisabai on the Blue Nile was taken over by the Front. The Fourth Mechanized Division of the Dergue was smashed at a place called Hamusit (between Bahr-Dar and Gondar) and tanks, lorries, and heavy artillery captured. Then the crowd around my radio burst into laughter. They are listening to Radio Addis. Apparently, President Mengistu is admitting there is a war in Raya in the south of Tigray.

"And he says the EPRDF are only the tools of *shabia*, the Eritrean Peoples's Liberation Front," says one.

They are talking about the larger coalition front of Tigrayan, Amhara and Oromo liberation groups. Beyond the boundaries of Tigray it is no longer valid to talk about the Tigrayan Front, who don't want to be seen as empire-building on their own account.

"He is saying his soldiers are gallantly defending Bahr-Dar. Even though it's already captured!"

"And that every Ethiopian, old and young, must defend their motherland against the Tigrayan bandits with...." He bends his ear to the radio again. "...your sickles, your spears, your shields..."

"But the Dergue has said this so often, the people are fed up. They don't want to listen."

Mulugeta tells me about some of the Front's preparatory strategies. They have prepared the ground for the final assault by three sets of radio broadcasts. First, the EPRDF appealed to all skilled workers—to workers in the factories, staff, and students in the hospitals, teachers in schools and higher education colleges—to protect their places of work from sabotage by Dergue troops and supporters. They learned their lesson two years ago when the Dergue destroyed all the power and water installations and some health stations in Mekelle and other towns before evacuating Tigray. Absence of basic facilities in the towns made the job of reassuring their populations so much more difficult for the Front.

"They are saying that these workplaces belong to the people," says Mulugeta, "and it is important to keep them going for the people without disruption. We have promised to go on paying their salaries."

A second series of broadcasts appeals to another liberation group, the Ethiopian People's Revolutionary Party (EPRP), which has a base area in western Gondar near the Sudanese border. This group is older than the TPLF and was very powerful in the late sixties and seventies. The TPLF defeated them in eastern Tigray in the seventies and their youthful membership was further devastated by the Dergue in the Red Terror. Now, they are much shrunken in size, with some influence in urban areas, but little following among the mass of the people. Over the radio, the Front has warned them not to oppose the Tewodros Campaign, assuring them that not only are they reluctant to wage war against any political force other than the Dergue, but they want the EPRP to join the Transitional Government they plan to establish at the end of the war.

"Are you saying the Central Committee are so sure of victory that they have already worked out their plans for afterwards?"

"Of course."

Of course they have. I remember Tekleweini's briefing in January on the future EPRDF program worked out in all the political, economic and social details. Stupid question.

"So who are being targeted in the third series of broadcasts?"

"The Dergue garrisons. Bahr-Dar has just been captured. Gondar city is encircled by our forces. The EPRDF doesn't want to shed unnecessary blood. We are saying put your hands up, surrender, there is no way you can win. The city is surrounded, there is no place to escape, give us your support.

This morning they were given a deadline of twenty-four hours, which will be up at seven o'clock tomorrow."

As soon as Assefa is up and around I relay all the news to him. He is very excited about the fall of Bahr-Dar and confirms that it is the beginning of the final push. Later in the morning, Mulugeta pops in to tell me unofficially that the Front's intelligence has picked up radio exchanges between the Dergue and the Gondar garrison. Mengistu is telling them to stay put; the troops are very nervy; the commanders are saying the soldiers are out of control and are asking for orders. In the afternoon, Assefa rushes in with the same news which he has got from Gebru and Aregash.

Lying on my bed in the Green Hotel late in the evening, I wonder what Dieter and Christina are doing at this very minute and resent the way my illness has deprived me of chances, which will never come again. There is a gentle tap at the door. It is Mulugeta. He has a message from Gebru. I must go south to the front as soon as possible. They are looking for a car for me, but they are widely scattered. If there is no car, I must go by bus as far as Woldia (due south in Wello province) and then work my way westwards. I must be ready.

Another day passes, drop by drop. At eight in the evening, Mulugeta comes by again. There is a car. At midnight, I am to leave for the south.

18

At the Front

I remember once in Adi Gudom a conversation about the atrocities of "the Amhara" taking a turn, which could with a little imagination almost be called heated. So I asked:

"What do you think now of fighting alongside Amhara people as comrades?"

"When we say *Amhara*," said Seyoum Gezai, at once removing the sting, "we don't mean ordinary Amhara. They are oppressed. We mean the Amhara administrators, the feudal system, the ruling class."

"When we send our children to Shewa," added Gebrehiwot Kiros, "it doesn't mean we are sending them to fight against the poor Amhara. We have a common enemy, Mengistu Haile Mariam, who is the oppressor of the people."

Tadesse Ayele also wanted to have his say:

"We are not against anybody. We are against oppression—we want to bury oppression. We are not against any nationality. Whoever is our enemy, we do not care. We fight for our liberation and that's why we send our people to Central Ethiopia."[1]

Now, here I was on the way to Central Ethiopia, south to the Amhara provinces, out of Tigray for the first time, *enemy territory*. I had asked the *Amhara question* in every interview to test the Front's claim to have educated the peasants away from nationalist prejudice. Now I discovered those prejudices in myself. "It's the ruling class we're fighting," I'd been told more than once, when I had used the word *Amhara* in some heedless generalization. In fact, one of the wings of the EPRDF was the Amhara liberation front, the EPDM, and the province of Wello, immediately south of Tigray, was the heart of their liberated area, so I was not going to enemy territory at all.

These thoughts jumbled together in my head as the landcruiser headed southwards through the darkness. The car was crammed with senior fighters on two benches facing each other, our knees touching, but we bumped along in complete silence. Assefa was among them. I saw Abai Tsehay, one of the founder fighters and a member of Central Committee. I recognized Dr. Kasu, a Guraghe, a member of the EPDM. I met him once in London. The others were unidentifiable in shawls. No one said hello. Perhaps it was protocol. This rejection of personal relations gave me the sense of being on some very serious and dangerous mission. Or, was it an aspect of culture? It was like the silence that comes over birds during the hours of darkness.

A full moon rose over the mountains, transforming the wild terrain into a luridly melodramatic landscape. The bare stone peaks shimmered and shifted in the surreal glow, losing all their substance. On the left, the earth yawned into an abyss that fell endlessly away to the eastern lowlands and, below us, rolls of cloud assumed the solidity of granite, like foothills in a land of dreams. It was cold in the landcruiser. We were all muffled up in *gabis*, nodding off one after another into an uncomfortable doze, jolted into half life by the bumps in the road. Beyond Korem, in the more mundane twilight of dawn, we began a nerve-tingling descent in a long series of hairpin bends. At every curl of the road, I held my breath to stop us tilting over the brink of the cliff, until at last we came down into slopes forested with a variety of deciduous trees and conifers and then down, down, down into the flat lowland plain of Alamata.

All this area from the highland town of Korem has shifted at different times from Tigray to Wello and back again, although its population is Tigrinya speaking. The border between the two provinces has been a victim of volatile political relationships between Tigrayan feudals and central government. It was also the scene of fierce fighting for ten days from August to September 1989, ending with the annihilation of the Dergue's 605th Army Corps and their Third Revolutionary Army front line command. The Front published the figures of dead, wounded, and captured on the government side, but as usual withheld the details of its own casualties. Now, driving across this flat treeless plane made me consider the implications of those battles for the first time. This string of little towns, Alamata, Waja, Kobo, Robit, Robiye, looking hot and dusty even at this time in the morning, all came into EPRDF control in that ten days. But at what cost? The fighters had to come down from the mountains, leave the protection of their guerrilla strongholds, to fight for the first time in the open. How many young men, almost boys, on both sides, must have died there? I thought of the recruitment celebrations, which Lesley and I had watched in Adwa when we first arrived this year, the young men dedicating themselves to the struggle. How many of them would survive this war?

With every kilometer, the temperature rose. *Gabis* were discarded and by the time we had crossed the interminable plain and ascended again to the semi-highlands of Woldia, it was nine o'clock and we were beginning to boil. There were compensations, however, for with daylight my companions became more sociable, even chatty, and by the time we reached Woldia I discovered that after rest and food they were going to continue westwards to Bahr-Dar. I was to stay behind, however, waiting for—I don't know what. I felt let down. Abai, who appeared to have seniority, was worried about my security in the newly liberated town of Bahr-Dar. Apparently, it was crammed with Dergue soldiers and WPE members who had gone into hiding with nowhere to go, because the town was encircled by the Front. He wanted to check it out before I got a bullet in the back. Disgruntled and powerless, I had no alternative but to kick my heels in Woldia and wonder why they thought it was so urgent for me to come at all.

I didn't have to wait long. Two young Ethiopian relief workers turned up and announced themselves my temporary guides. They found me a little hotel, showed me the town, and began to set up a program of interviews. I was still disgruntled enough to baulk at a back room above a latrine filled with about two million flies, so they moved me to the best hotel in the town. It was a one story building with a line of single rooms, each with a bed and a chair, around three sides of a dusty square with a non-functioning fountain in the middle and the usual dark holes of latrines and showers in one corner. There were facilities for running water, but the taps were dry because of the drought, although small quantities of water were usually available in a large drum replenished daily by small boys with donkeys. I had only slept there one night when, returning after a meeting the next morning, I was confronted with Aklilu Tekemte.

I hadn't seen Aklilu since before my illness. Now, here he was, as if dropped from the sky. He told me Meles had sent him with the one battered pick-up used for local trips around the HQ at Hagere Salam. He came with a driver and two young fighters. I was overjoyed. I felt like the rescued damsel in old tales, except that I was being freed into excitement and danger instead of security and boredom. What's more, I soon discovered Aklilu was a man who could make things happen.

He was as eager as I was to leave for Bahr-Dar as soon as possible. I interpreted that as after dark, but he meant after lunch. In daylight? I remembered his predilection for breaking night driving rules. I suspected he couldn't wait to see for himself a city so newly liberated, a city so much more developed and sophisticated than anything Tigray had to offer. One of the symptoms of the oppression the Tigrayans talk about so much is the absence in Tigray of any share of the industrial and educational developments, however limited, to be found in the rest of Ethiopia. This is most clearly seen in the contrast between the cities in the Amhara provinces and the main Tigrayan towns, which by comparison are little more than large villages.

So after lunch, we set off on the westward road towards Lake Tana and Gojjam and for the first time I had a chance to see something of the central Ethiopian landscape. We climbed higher and higher until we were driving along a lofty ridge, which seemed on top of the world. I was still nervous of daylight driving, especially as few fighters seemed as insouciant about it as Aklilu. Moreover, I had just been inspecting the bomb damage from recent MiG attacks on Woldia. However, not a MiG appeared in the blue breadth of sky, but it was a sensational drive. The Chinese-built gravel road ran for several hundred kilometers straight along the top of a high narrow spine of a plateau. Sometimes, it turned into lofty pastures dotted with villages and grazing herds; at others it narrowed to the width of a village and a field. In some places, we could see the land falling away to left and right at once, into gorges so far below that dry river beds looked a mere thread. At one point the plateau shrank to the width of the road itself and I was glad, after all, we were not driving in the dark. Then, as we descended a little, to our left rose the peak of Mount Guna, the site of a terrible battle with the Dergue the year before and celebrated in songs. We were so high already, it looked more like a hill than a mountain of well over four thousand meters. The long slow descent was interrupted by a night stop in a little town called Debre Tabor, which had come into the control of the Front a year ago. Although it was the chief town of East Gojjam, it seemed run down and depressed and the bed in the scruffy hotel was hopping with fleas so I scarcely slept. I was not sorry when we left before dawn to continue our journey.

A few kilometers from Bahr-Dar, we drove through the battle area of Hamusit. On either side of the road, the tanks of the Fourth Mechanized Division of the Ethiopian Army were abandoned to the donkeys and goats. The burned-out shells of armored vehicles littered the road, relics of one more government defeat a few days ago. Tanks lay in the middle of fields or tipped into gulleys, as inappropriate as space ships in the rural landscape. Then the huge expanse of Lake Tana spread before us sparkling in the early sun like an inland sea and within a few minutes we were rattling over a patched-up war-damaged bridge into Bahr-Dar. It was seven o'clock in the morning.

My experience in Tigray had not prepared me for Bahr-Dar. It was bigger than any town I had yet seen in Ethiopia, built on a scale large enough to be called a city with wide boulevards and tree-lined avenues, very different from the over-grown villages called towns in Wello and Tigray. It looked peaceful enough as we drove along and there seemed plenty of people on the streets going about their business and groups of peasants loaded with bundles or driving animals. There were manned tanks at strategic points and fighters in twos and threes at irregular intervals on the pavement with Kalashnikovs slung over their shoulders, but they looked relaxed and certainly it didn't seem as if anyone was skulking in fear of the occupiers.

"There are so many Dergue soldiers in hiding here," said Aklilu, contradicting my assessment, "and WPE members working underground. They are spreading Dergue lies and propaganda. It is not a good situation."

First, we tracked down Abai to discover where we should go and from there drove to a wooded area on the shores of Lake Tana where important officials and party members had lived in seclusion until a few days ago in smart bungalows among the trees. Now empty, their tenants fled, these houses had been taken over by the Front. We were directed to one, which had belonged to a commander of the Dergue Forces, a major-general, believed dead, and it was his double bed I shared with one and sometimes two women fighters. But, it was no longer smart or secluded. The house itself was crammed with senior fighters and one or two Central Committee members—officers, I suppose you could say, except the informality of their behavior did not resemble any other army officers I have ever known.

Outside, in the garden, were camped rank and file fighters in small self-sufficient units, sleeping and cooking together. Tents were dotted about among the trees and blankets and newly-washed clothes festooned lines slung from trunk to trunk. The ground was littered with debris, empty tins, scraps of *injera*, bits of paper. No doubt at a slightly greater distance you would have to pick your way among the turds, as you do on the periphery of most Ethiopian villages. I have the usual European revulsion for dirt and disorder, but I soon got used to it and even felt a sneaking pleasure at the thought of these guerrilla fighters who inflicted so resounding a defeat on the Dergue army so few days ago, now taking over the smart residence of the major-general in the only way they knew how. Most peasants know little of towns and less of latrines. Although fighters have usually been given a crash course in hygiene, circumstances don't always help them put it into practice. They washed themselves punctiliously in the lake every morning and pissed and crapped wherever they liked.

It was pretty messy in the house too. No one appeared to be doing any cleaning and as there was no running water the two toilets were indescribable, but people seemed to go on using them. I was not at all tempted to be school prefect, but I did take on the role of toilet-flusher for my own peace of mind and every day at dawn found me staggering up from the lake with buckets of water. This confirmed me in my view that modern sanitation systems, not working efficiently, are a worse health hazard than wandering into the undergrowth with a spade, or even without one. Although "officer" fighters were accommodated in the house, the fighters camped in the garden would come in and out at will and sit and chat in an easy way even with members of Central Committee. There was a certain amount of mobility and when new units arrived the fighters would wander into the house and look with wonder at the fridge and washing-machine, neither working, and shake their heads with disbelief at the pink-and-cream damask comfort of the divan bed, naked of any covering except my bedroll.

A day or two after our arrival Aklilu went shopping. He came back with a box of tinned vegetables of various kinds, which were as soggy and unpalatable as most tinned vegetables, but which he kindly thought I might find more to my taste than *injera*. He also brought a tin of porridge oats, which I pounced on with delight and a crate of bottled beer. The Front is always convinced that Europeans need alcohol. While discipline and limited resources make them abstemious, they do their best to keep guests happy. Every guide I have ever had has seemed able in the most adverse circumstances to produce bottled beer like a rabbit out of a top-hat. Circumstances in Bahr-Dar were adverse, but there were shops, so we had beer. The beer made us rather popular and I suspected I was the excuse for a little pleasure for many. I noticed with approval that if any young fighter—our guard, Fekre, for example—dropped in to report or to get instructions he would be offered a beer too.

Meanwhile, through a series of conversations, interviews and visits, I was trying to get a hold on the sequence of events leading to the taking of Bahr-Dar.

For some years, the Amhara wing of the EPRDF had been extending its influence and support from Wello into the rural areas of Gondar and Gojjam. In some areas, there had been land reform and elected councils had been set up. The Dergue, by now under no illusions about its vulnerability (whatever its propagandists might say) after more than two years of rebel victories, had concentrated the 603rd Army Corps in the area, including its crack mechanized and tank brigades, numerous garrisons of infantry brigades, and some heavyweight military hardware. The aim of the Tewodros Campaign starting in the last week of February was to sweep the Dergue troops right out of the two provinces in a twin offensive, one driving towards Gondar city in the north and the other to Bahr-Dar and Debre Markos, the provincial capital, a little to the south. When the heat turned on Bahr-Dar, the fighters' northern arm was clearing the road to Gondar from where they could effectively block any effort by Dergue troops to come south to the aid of their beleaguered brigades around Lake Tana.

My main interest at the front was not to be in the thick of battle, but to observe the Front's approach to handling civilians and to stabilizing its new territories. However, I was discovering it was impossible to separate military from social policies, one of which was to avoid putting civilians (or fighters for that matter) into unnecessary danger of death or injury and therefore never to fight in towns. I can't remember a single battle fought in a town and in 1988, when they took control of Adwa and Axum, they vacated them again when their presence brought down MiG bombardments on the heads of the people. A year later, they were able to reoccupy them without the same risks to the population. The struggle for hearts and minds underpins all their strategies and on several occasions their strategists have expressed their amazement to me at the lack of concern for public well-being and local opinion, the easy resort to terror as a mode of control, shown in some countries.

Three battles were involved in the liberation of Bahr-Dar.[2] The first was at Hamusit, the debris of which we had observed at the end of our journey here; the second was the capture of Tisabai power station; the third was the destruction of the 603rd Army Corps. All of them took place outside the town. The power station on the Blue Nile near the famous Tisissat Falls supplied the electricity for most of Gojjam and Gondar. The Front, learning the lesson of the Dergue sabotage of power supplies when they evacuated Mekelle two years before, saw the continuation of basic facilities as a fundamental part of their strategy to win the support of the population. The peasants in the countryside could be won over by land reform, by elected councils, by freedom from the Dergue's crippling pricing and marketing policies for agricultural produce. It was not so simple to win over the towns; it was better to alienate them as little as possible in the first place. Unable to gauge how many of those in positions of responsibility had heard their broadcasts and would respond positively, the Front could not take the risk and secured the power station and reassured its workers in a swift and effective military operation, before the local garrisons knew what was happening.

The next day, Aklilu and I set out for the hour's drive to the falls of the Blue Nile (or Abai, as it is called here), which flows south out of Lake Tana and weaves its circuitous course to its junction with the White Nile in the Sudan. Beyond the breathtaking falls, the hydro-electric plant was concealed from casual view deep inside the gorges of the river and we had to climb down several flights of steps to reach it. The river was at its lowest at this season, although it still boiled away below us between the confining cliffs. The power station had been installed by the Yugoslavians and the technology was now outdated, but it was adequate for the supply of power to all the little towns in this region. The young intelligent electrician in charge spoke good English and gave me a thorough tour of the plant. It had three generators, each supplying four megawatts, but only one was functioning because of the low water.

I had already talked to Zewdu Ayelew, the woman Commander responsible for the operation, which had secured the plant and, although the visit did not teach me anything new (except about the generation of electricity) it made her account come alive. She had been a fighter for eleven years and maybe these experiences accounted for the fact she seemed much older than her twenty-five years. Zewdu was one of a dozen or more divisional commanders (a division is made up of five regiments), the highest rank a woman has achieved so far in the EPRDF army.

A Woman Commander

I have always been a combat fighter. For the first three years, I was simply in the rank and file and then I trained first as a barefoot doctor for the army and then as a junior nurse. After four years in the medical personnel, I changed to a combat role when I became a Force Commissar, then a Regiment Commissar three years ago. After one year, I became Head of Organization of a Division and then I became Division Commissar a year ago. I have been in all the major offensives.

Our Division had several tasks to fulfil in the taking of Bahr-Dar. The decisive part was played by four regiments. The mechanized division was concentrated on Hamusit where the Dergue mechanized divisions were stationed, so we called that the "center of gravity." That's where the main battle took place. After that, the bridge across the Blue Nile was bombarded by the enemy.

On Sunday, February 24, the first objective was to capture Tisabai, where there is a hydro-electric generating plant. It is a very big station, supplying electicity to the whole of Gondar and Gojjam up to Debre Tabor. The 150th Brigade was stationed there, so first we had to destroy this enemy as fast as possible to secure the safety of the hydro-electric power. Speed was all-important so as not to give them time to reorganize.

We waded the Nile on foot. The water came up to our chests and we were holding our guns above the water. As we started the crossing, the enemy ran away towards the center of Tisabai and we crossed almost without opposition. Our first target was to take control of the Hydro-Electric station. The EPRDF had guaranteed the workers' salaries and in fact the power from the hydro-electric station was interrupted for only a short time. Since then, everything has proceeded as normal.

The next day, on Monday 25th, our second mission was to attack the headquarters of the 603rd Army Corps near the lake, not far from the airport. When we finished at Tisabai, there was intensive bombardment of the airport and their camp. The enemy began to retreat, so the mission was changed. Because tanks were bombarding the headquarters, we changed direction with the movement of the enemy. We cut across country to the Addis road, thus cutting off their line of retreat, and annihilated the enemy.

Our tactics are first of all to organize ourselves in echelons. The first echelon dislocates the enemy by taking the center of gravity, where the core command is situated, and the second echelon attacks the disorganized enemy. Then the first echelon is ready for the next mission. So, they work in concert. You have to identify the main direction of blow. Battle is a combination of movement and fire. It is a rolling gait; each echelon is a leg. You make battle by moving and firing. When one is moving, the other gives cover.

The battle is a combination of arms, human beings, and military science. For us, the decisive element is the human beings, not the arms. We know the enemy has superior arms and technology, but no matter how much the latest technology is in the hands of the enemy, the decisive factor is the human beings. Our army knows its objective. A fighter knows he will benefit from this revolution. It will fulfil his class interest. He has chosen to join the army in an unimaginable heroic spirit, fired by the love of the people, determined to fight to the finish. The enemy soldiers are conscripted by force; they don't believe in it; they don't know why they are fighting. This is one of the reasons we capture in thousands. In the last two or three weeks, we have captured between seventy and eighty thousand prisoners. The reason is the enemy army has no dedication, no belief in their aim. Here lies the secret of why we won very big battles. The crucial difference is our political objective and, second, the relationship between the rank and file and the commanders in our army. It is very spiritual, based on a comradeship, a love for one another. You cannot get this kind of relationship in the Ethiopian army. There, the relationship is that of master and slave.

Our army's politicization starts in the village in the youth association and the peasant association. Then, at the training center he learns extensively and intensively the aims of the revolution, both his individual and his class interest. Who is his enemy? Who are his allies? For fighters, the direction of political work for every action goes like this—how does it suit his class interest or how does it harm his class interest? In offensives in an area we agitate what will be gained by destroying this army—to his class, his farm, himself? If we don't, what is the loss to his class, his farm, himself? It is not theoretical because we adjust it with the ground.

When you start training, you agitate that the fighter will not die, that you won't lose a lot of human life; training means making it less costly in terms of loss of life and injuries. Struggle preserves his life; we make clear what it means to the revolution and to himself. We therefore agitate the importance of the battle area to the whole revolution. So, in this battle, what can we do to minimize the costs? This emphasis is not just during the preparation, but even in the middle of the battle itself. The achievements are communicated from one unit to another—"We have captured this mountain"—so the army fights gallantly and heroically because news passes from force to force, from regiment to regiment.

We agitate before, during, and after the battle. This is all the job of the political commissar. First, after the plan was made by the organization, the divisional commanders met from the different divisions participating in this operation. There was intensive discussion of the first draft of the plan, evaluating the whole situation, including the enemy, the people around Gojjam and Gondar, our own organizational strength, the enemy's weakness and strength, the people's desires and expectations. We made an intensive evaluation of the whole situation and the whole area.

From this evaluation, we decided why it was necessary, what was its urgency, what was the likelihood of victory, why would we win, what problems we faced. All this was discussed thoroughly, also by the rank and file. After this we had different meetings, based on our specific task. We had one discussion with Regional Command specifically on Tisabai Hydro-Electric Power Station. What would the capture of this facility mean to the people of this area? What was the importance of capturing it without destruction or damage to the installation? We had to be very selective and very careful.

The discussions were first general, then specific to each task. For every battle, it was the same. Hamusit, for example. I must stress, during all this period, everything is very secret. The information is related at different times to the rank and file, but in the discussion of Operation Tewodros, the rank and file are agitated only in a general way, until a day or two before departure, when they learn the specifics of time and place. They are used to this way of doing things anyway, from their experience.

In the area to which our regiment was assigned, we were very mobile. It took us more than three days to walk across the area. We had not worked there before, so we didn't involve the people, but there were some villages whose people spontaneously gave us support all the same, carrying mate-

rials and food. In the Hamusit and Woreta area, because they were on the main road, the whole preparation with the people—for stretchers, food, wounded, PoWs—was very intense and marvellous, but because we had to walk for four days, in this case, it was not practicable for us.

There are always casualties—among ourselves, among the people around, among the enemy themselves. The enemy soldiers are brought here by force and are dying here against their interest. We know that. We know they are opposing the Dergue, that they are our class allies from poor families. So, we say we should capture them safely, but not kill them and this has been proved by our experience. Many of them join the EPRDF, or if they go home they never fight us. If you capture them safely and educate them, they will join the revolution or become farmers. As Dergue soldiers they don't benefit from this war. They are all against the state, but because they have no means of opposition we think of ways of saving them, not killing them. They are our brothers. They are poor peasants; they have no political interest in the battle. We have captured in thousands. Tens of thousands have joined the TPLF. Our direction of blow is mainly focused on the command, as part of the ruling class. So when we fight we concentrate on capturing the officers, not the rank and file.[3]

The next day, we make a tour of the battle areas. We are joined by Getachew, one of the technical munitions experts for the Front. First, he takes us to the airport, one of the few international airports in Ethiopia. Firing from the other side of the lake, the Front scored a direct hit on the airport building, now just a blackened and semi-demolished skeleton of steel girders and fragments of concrete. In piles, at one end of the runway, are bombs in their wooden casings ready for loading onto MiGs. There are others stacked or scattered apparently at random in the surrounding grassland, cluster bombs and shells. They lie there in the grass as innocent as sheep and the long dry gleaming grasses blow back and forth in the indifferent wind.

From there, we drive to the headquarters of the 603rd Army Corps, a couple of miles away on the same side of the lake. As we approach the perimeter, the only signs of battle are stretches of scorched and blackened grassland. The camp itself appears to be untouched. It has been until recently a large and well-ordered base for one of the crack corps of the Dergue Army. Lines of huge semi-circular galvanized structures stand in double rows. Getachew has keys to every storehouse and bunker, although doors to some are wide open and flapping in the wind. Some are filled with bunks for accommodating the troops; some are stores and are still filled with sacks of grain and chili pepper and boxes of tinned foods. Furthest from the perimeter are the munitions stores, emptied by the EPRDF of all light and immediately useful weapons, but crates of mine detectors are still here and wooden boxes of bullets of all sizes, Belgian *nata* guns, anti-tank missiles, boxes of TNT and some sophisticated electronic weaponry that Getachew does not fully understand. In a secure underground concrete bunker, several hundred yards away are stored the more volatile mines of all kinds, anti-personnel mines, anti-tank mines, time bombs, with mine detectors and fuses. The light from the doorway does not penetrate the darkness and we feel our way with our toes between the deadly stacks with the help of one pencil torch.

It is hard to believe that little more than a week ago this deserted installation, now abandoned to the waving grasses and the birds, was a thriving military complex. For the first time, I absorb the hideous reality of the vast fortune invested by this government for use against Ethiopian civilians. Every rocket at the airport would have been dropped on villages or towns, as so many have been before; many of these mines would soon have been in place in several concentric rings around garrison towns. In Tigray, two years ago, I photographed in the battered hospitals of Adigrat and Mekelle many shepherd boys maimed by mines in the fields around the towns. Many more had been killed outright, along with their oxen, sheep, and goats.

At the same time, there is an ironic contrast between all this highly organized and equipped war machine and the guerrilla fighters who seem to run rings round the Dergue army. There are several pairs of guards evident at intervals around the camp, scruffy in their motley uniforms and long hair, but they are humorous and gentle when I stop to talk to them, curiously innocent as well as delightedly curious at the chance to talk to a *firenji*. These are EPDM fighters and Amharic-speaking, so I need Aklilu's help. In this heartland of Amhara culture, it is they who play the major role, as far as their numbers allow. The coalition Front does not want to give the impression that Tigrayans are trying to dominate the Amharas. They have been dominated too long themselves not to be sensitive about probable misinterpretation. However, these young fighters look identical to the ones I am living with back at the house on the shores of the lake, who when they are off-duty cook for themselves, scrub their bodies in the lake, play volleyball or football like ten-year-olds and, in the evening, love to dance and to listen to songs of the revolution. It is hard to believe they are part of the efficient force that has been so consistently successful against the largest army in Africa.

The Gulf War has ended. I am glued to my radio at both ends of the day, but my experiences here give me a different perspective. I find myself speculating on the feelings of the soldiers in the thick of it and on the thousands of Iraqui civilian casualties so curiously invisible. I am impervious to the propaganda of the USA.

Most days, Aklilu and I go down into Bahr-Dar, either to find something to eat or on our way somewhere else. Despite the assurances of the Front that they have been warmly welcomed, the mood of the town does not feel good. Not only are hundreds of Dergue cadres, according to Aklilu, demanding salaries on an equal basis with government employees like teachers or workers in the power station or oil refinery (to whom the EPRDF has promised continuation of salary), but thousands of soldiers have returned here in civilian clothes so they are difficult to identify. AK47s are changing hands at knockdown prices. For such a positive person, Aklilu sounds discouraged.

"There are so many problems," he says, as we are driving around one day, looking for a late lunch, "so many hundreds of people demanding money. The Workers Party of Ethiopia are still here in force and are agitating the people against us."

Aklilu's work has brought him close to the center, but he is not a policy maker and has no special responsibility here apart from me. I realize he is on the outside looking in almost as much as I am. It must have been like this in Woldia and Debre Tabor, only liberated a year ago, I remind him, yet now the people are organizing democratic elections there and supporting the Front.

"And it's only a few days since the EPRDF took control here." I add, conscious of the irony of my giving rather than receiving reassurance.

He slows down to ask a couple of young women walking along the pavement if they can tell us where we can find food, but they turn their backs on him, puffing out their lips in a rude grimace. He shrugs it off.

"They are only prostitutes. They do not like us because they know we don't use prostitutes. Their income depends on the garrisons and when we defeat them they have no money."

A boy directs us to a small hotel. The front bar is filled with men drinking tea, but we go into the empty dining room at the back where the owner brings us *injera* and sits down to talk. He and Aklilu have a long debate in Amharic, which I find hard to follow, but as they occasionally break into English I at least follow the main lines of discussion. Under Haile Selassie, this man was, at one time, a member of the *Shengo* or Parliament; now he hates the Dergue. His main motive is excessive taxation, but his twin hatred is socialism.

"Never mention socialism to me or anyone else in this town," he says, his hands cutting slices through the air.

When Aklilu expounds, with his pleasant manner, the Front's democratic line, the hotel owner reveals that his main anxiety is "the unity issue." His argument follows the lines of Dergue propaganda and, either from prejudice or ignorance, he ignores the coalition of nationalities in the Front, referring to it as a Tigrayan movement interested only in Tigrayan domination of Ethiopia.

"The TPLF are for breaking up Ethiopia," he cries passionately.[4] "Eritrea is demanding independence, but what will Ethiopia do without access to a port?"

After the end of the war, Aklilu points out, because they have cooperated to get rid of the brutal dictator, Eritrea and Ethiopia will have a better relationship than at any time during thirty years of war and, in any case, Ethiopia will be Eritrea's best customer so there will be important economic reasons for good relations. But, the local defeat of the Dergue forces is too recent for the hotel owner to absorb arguments, which contradict old habits of thinking. He seems to have a vision of an Ethiopia in which every province will irrationally choose to secede, against all its economic interests. Nevertheless, Aklilu is charming, the exchange is good-humored and they part smiling. I suspect that the motive force behind the conversation is largely entrepreneurial. Aklilu is selling the Front and our host is encouraging custom, in which case he is in the stronger position because before we leave he extracts a promise from us to return the following day for a lunch of Lake Tana fish.

It is difficult to generalize about the mood of the town. The population is in no sense homogeneous and factors like class and ideology influence the response to the EPRDF. Both workers in the few industries and the mass of townsfolk who live off some form of trade are natives of the town. Random conversations suggest there is some evidence for the Front's assertion that these groups either support them in broad terms because they hate the Dergue or at least are not overtly hostile and want to safeguard their longterm interests in the town. In another category are the professionals, lecturers, teachers, and industrial managers, who are not natives but outside appointees paid by the government. These are the intellectuals or more educated class who are very skeptical about this movement of scruffy guerrillas from the north, which is sweeping southwards. They believe the propaganda that the intruders are secessionist, socialist, and a danger to the integrity of the country. It is this group that seems to be raising problems. Although the Front wants the higher education colleges to continue teaching, the staff are deeply suspicious of them, fearful of losing their salaries, yet reluctant to do anything which would look like collaboration if the Dergue should return. The students are anxious lest a qualification gained in the new liberated area will be invalid in Addis Ababa, where, almost without exception, they locate their future interests. The Front is frustrated because its method is to work through discussion and persuasion, but they are unable to assemble these people together to discuss anything at all because the Dergue's cadres have advised them not to attend meetings. Understandably, it is beyond anybody's comprehension that these rebels might win the war.

It is also early days.

Here, as in other newly liberated towns, some groups took immediate advantage of the Front's early announcement of freedom of expression and assembly and, about four days after their entry into the town, a few hundred people took to the streets in a demonstration against them. This would have been an invitation to summary arrest or death under both Haile Selassie and the Dergue. According to Tadesse Kassa, the new EPDM administrator for the Front, the event was organized by the Dergue Party and attended mostly by students and teenagers carrying hostile slogans. I missed the demonstration, but the principle emotion admitted by onlookers I questioned afterwards was fear that the youngsters would be shot and astonishment that, although stones were thrown at the fighters, not a single shot was fired back. The fighters followed the demonstrators at a distance and called them to a meeting in the stadium. No one came, of course, and so far there has not been a counter demonstration on behalf of the Front, but there is little doubt that this practical demonstration of democratic rights made a deep impression on the people. Many people began to criticize the gathering, saying "We support the EPRDF" or "This is the day of our liberation." This can be explained away as fear or an attempt at ingratiation with those they see as their new masters, but one woman says to me with evident sincerity, "This is the first time we saw an armed man hit by a stone who did not fire back and kill innocent people."

Tadesse Kassa, the Front's Administrator for the military zone of Gojjam and Gondar, an Amhara and a member of the EPDM, has set up a temporary office in another vacated house of a Dergue official.[5] In the room where I wait to see him, I find Mulugeta waiting too. In a war zone, people are rarely in command of their movements or their schedule; they are subject to the urgency of the moment. They come together for a time and then the patterns of the dance whirl them away in different directions, never to meet again. So, we are delighted to have this chance. He tells me he has come to help in the negotiations with the higher education staff; I give a nutshell account of my latest experiences. Then the door opens, I am invited into Tadesse's office and I have not seen Mulugeta since.

Tadesse is an interesting man who looks too young and slight for the responsibilities of his position. I am surprised he has time to see me, but, although he asks me to keep my questions to a minimum because of the pressures on his time, he answers each one so thoroughly that I am still there two hours later. We talk over the Front's strategy for maintaining essential services and employment by guaranteeing salaries. Power supplies were interrupted for only two days; water is now available, but not everywhere (not in the house where I am living, for example). In Tigray and Wello all the professionals left with the Dergue when the Front took over. Although they have not been exactly cooperative and the two higher education colleges are closed, at least they are still here.

"If their salary is guaranteed," says Tadesse, "we believe they will stay here. The one thing they ask is security. Also, unlike under the Dergue, they get their salary without deductions."

One of the main problems has been the threat of civil disorder from armed soldiers and WPE members, as well as from thieves and looters. Malcontents have nowhere to go because, not only is the surrounding countryside under the control of the Front, but the peasants have for some time been supporting them against the Dergue and becoming fighters for EPDM.

Tadesse sees the challenges of stabilizing Bahr-Dar within the context of the surrounding area and the overall struggle for power. The crucial mistake of the Dergue, he says, is to have forfeited the support of the "powerful and strategic class, the peasants' by never carrying out a proper land reform in their interest.[6]

"You cannot solve the question of land in isolation from the question of power. You need the power before you can democratically distribute power. The peasants have to have the power themselves. Now, we have a proper democratic reform. We have liberated this area from the junta so now we can distribute the land in the interest of the mass of the peasants. The peasants have got the land because they fought for it. But, it is not enough to have land distribution and land rights—you have to make it productive. Therefore, the decisive path is to go forward and fight to destroy the Dergue because the decisive thing is to take power. If the power is in the hands of the people then you can have unrestricted democratic peace. If the people are to live together in peace, they must play a decisive part in destroying the enemy. We are fighting now in Gondar and Gojjam. We must keep the momentum of this revolution and this can only be achieved by the destruction of the junta."

Aklilu is worried about keeping the Hagere Selam vehicle for too long. He wants to replace it with one of the many government Toyotas, which have become available to the Front with the capture of Bahr-Dar. Negotiating for

Abai's approval seems to take all day, while I stay "at home" in the general's bungalow.

Most of the time I sit on the rocks by the lake bringing my diaries and notebooks up to date. I sit out of the sun under a fig tree as big as a church, cooled by the breeze coming off the water. Hornbills, black and white and orange, fly in and out of the branches and birds with long streamers for tails and smaller birds with magnificent crests, which I think may be hoopoos. I swim in the lake most mornings soon after sunrise, but sometimes the water is so full of weed clutching at my legs and chest it is difficult to enjoy it. At that time of day the lake is as still as glass and dotted with lone fishermen in their papyrus canoes, identical to my eyes with those I have seen in reproductions of Egyptian pyramid paintings. Later in the day, the wind whips the water into small waves so there is a constant sea beat in the garden, in the house, in my sleep.

I'm getting to know the fighters based here. I have had to negotiate the loan of a pan and a share of a stove to make my porridge at breakfast time. Three days of porridge have done great things for my morale. The women fighters who do the cooking in the unit camped nearest to the house have taken personal responsibility for my happiness. We communicate in a mixture of English, Tigrinya, and Italian. This morning, they did a coffee ceremony for me on a mat of flowers and leaves with plumes of incense perfuming the air. Then, they decided to make me some special "European" pancakes, but they had been unable to find eggs ("material here— *non c'e*!") and the flour and water batter stuck to the pan in blackish patches. They were very apologetic. The other fighters picked off the charred bits, but I thought them rather tasty.

The following morning, I have arranged to talk to Dergue prisoners of war, but Aklilu drives up in the new landcruiser, saying Hurry, hurry hurry— he's just discovered the EPRDF cultural troupe are doing a show at the textile factory, so we go there instead. Communications seem rather inefficient because we arrive for the last song. There is a big crowd of workers there, but when I do a count I realize they are only a handful of the workforce of three thousand. Apparently, they too are afraid of being seen collaborating with the enemies of the Dergue and are all convinced the return of Dergue control in Gojjam is only a matter of time. I find it hard to reconcile the poor turn-out with Tadesse's assertion of workers' support, but they could be biding their time before demonstrating it in public. The concert is part of a policy of reassurance and so the program emphasizes Amhara and Oromo dances and Amharic songs. Nevertheless, the performers include one or two

Tigrayans, including Atsede with her base guitar, whose story I included in my book.[7] By chance, I have on me the photograph I took of her and her guitar which, I meant to give to Roman or Iyassu to pass on to her. Now, I can give it in person.

The next day, we return to the textile factory to witness the first payout of wages promised to the workers by the Front. The deal is that wages are guaranteed as long as the workforce cooperates in keeping the factory going. In fact, this factory is still closed. It produces cotton cloth and clothing, but it is now cut off from its old source of raw materials in government territory in the Awash valley to the south. The workforce is willing to work and has no other means of life, so the EPRDF has undertaken to pay them until alternative supplies can be negotiated.

Understandably enough, on this occasion there is a crowd of at least three thousand waiting patiently for their wages as the sun climbs up the sky. Some are milling around; most are sitting quietly on the ground. In the middle where the crowd is thickest, is a pickup. I see Abai standing in the back, leaning on the cab and watching the crowd in a relaxed sort of way. With him is Mulu, a senior woman fighter who lives in my house, holding a satchel. She is responsible for the pay-out. There are two or three others and a couple of guards. Like Aklilu, Abai has a pistol on his hip. The rank and file are never without their Kalashnikovs; senior fighters always carry pistols.

Aklilu brings the factory manager to talk to me. He is obviously reluctant, but reluctant also to antagonize these unfamiliar bosses. He, like everyone else I have talked to here, is so deeply scarred by fear and the daily expectation of repression, that spying, suspicion, reprisals, and unremitting attention to saving one's skin have assumed the appearance of normality and seem as inevitable as human nature. He refuses to give his name and looks scarcely reassured when I put away my pad and pen. In fact, the information I ask for and which he gives is banal and not at all compromising, but then I haven't internalized the rules of a paranoid dictatorship like he has. The factory was established under Haile Selassie twenty-nine years ago, the workforce is three thousand, the wages, excluding the management, come to seven hundred thousand birr a month paid fortnightly, today's payout will be financed eventually by the sale of existing stock, ten to fourteen tons of raw cotton per day are needed, he and the Front are negotiating an alternative supply from the Sudan through Metema, and so on. I want to ask if he is a member of the WPE (of course he is), what proportion of the workforce are party members and what part they have played in the daily functioning of the factory, but I know it would be a waste of breath. In six months time, I might be able to get some answers. The Front seem to know most of it already. Tadesse told me there are Party members in the textile industry, but this does not necessarily indicate heartfelt opposition.

"It's a matter of labels," he said, "just titles, and the workers don't even know them. They're inactive. We only arrest the notorious ones who are working not only against us, but also against their fellow workers and against the people."

Abai is going to address the crowd so Aklilu and I squeeze among them into the shade of a tree. I quickly note down the information from the factory manager before I forget it, while the sun moves around and burns down on my head again. Abai talks through a loud hailer for what seems a long time. Perhaps, it's because I don't understand the Amharic; perhaps it's the sun. Aklilu whispers the bare bones of the address: "This factory does not belong to the EPRDF; it belongs to you. It is for you to make a success of it through your own work. You must guard it and look after it. We stand for democracy and workers' rights. Only the party members have reason to fear and then only if they still stand with the Dergue and are engaged in sabotage. We will have no mercy on them or on those who accommodate them. You must expose them." Afterwards, between three and four hundred Party members come forward and own up of their own accord.[8]

It is now a fortnight since the battle of Hamusit. One morning, I wake to the news that the city of Gondar is captured and the whole province of Gondar, as well as Gojjam is now under EPRDF control.[9] Aklilu tells me this will make a profound difference to the process of stabilizing Bahr-Dar through reassuring the people that the Dergue is even less likely to re-establish its power here. I learn, for the first time, that over the last few days the government has launched a series of simultaneous offensives in an effort to reclaim territory and distract the momentum of Campaign Tewodros. Troops from Asmara, in Eritrea, attacked north Tigray around Adwa[10]; troops from Addis pushed into north Shewa and more brigades moved from Shewa into south Gojjam in an effort to recapture Dejen. All were repulsed.

Later in the day, we go to the hospital to interview wounded prisoners of war. There are no guards on the gate. We just walk in. No one asks for our papers or challenges our presence there. I presume war casualties are not considered a security risk, but, inside, I am surprised by how many patients are on their feet and walking around. I am also surprised by how many patients there are. It is a small hospital, completely given over to the Dergue army. Injured fighters are being treated in a Front field hospital somewhere in the countryside. The wards are packed to bursting. Patients on their pallets are ranged along the corridors, along the external covered walkways, in rows against the outside walls, along the sides of the quadrangles between buildings, which in any case are filled with huge emergency hoop tents for those in need of intensive care. Between the pallets, the less serious patients mill around in groups.

"Why is the security so lax?" Aklilu says. He sounds annoyed. "It is scarcely guarded. There is nothing to stop the mobile patients from walking out or Party agitators from walking in."

Aklilu wants to register our presence in the proper manner and ask permission to talk to the patients. No one appears to be in charge. After a few minutes, we track down the head nurse, a man called Getane.[11]

He is a young man with a gentle manner and gives straightforward answers to all my questions. This is the biggest hospital in Bahr-Dar, he says. It is a government hospital and has been a military hospital with military personnel for a year. Civilian patients are admitted only if it is not needed for military purposes. The military personnel all left when the EPRDF entered the town.

"What about the civilian patients now?"

"They have all been discharged. Now there are only soldiers here, wounded and medical cases."

The patients started arriving the first day of Campaign Tewodros and the next day there was a wholesale evacuation from Bahr-Dar.

"All the staff left the hospital for two days and the civilian staff came back on Thursday. During this time, the Red Cross were the only staff."

"Did you say the Red Cross?"

"Yes, the International Committee of the Red Cross have a team here."

But I thought the ICRC were forbidden by their charter to staff military hospitals![12] The ICRC team is made up of a Swedish surgeon and three nurses.

We ask to see the surgeon, but Getane says the Red Cross team are all off-duty.

The first casualties arrived before the EPRDF entered the town. There was no security and during this period, when most of the staff were absent, medical instruments and supplies were looted from the hospital. They have had to cope without them and without the military personnel who were seven percent of the total of over two hundred staff. Food supplies are still a problem.

"Before, food was supplied by the Ministry of Defense; now it is supplied by the EPRDF. In between, there was a food shortage and there still is. We need liquid food and there are not enough infusions. Some sorts of wounds preclude normal food. The EPRDF has promised to bring it. Their doctor, with overall responsibility, has an appointment with me. We have already received supplies of *teff* for *injera* and *wat* (*injera* sauce)."

" How do the staff feel about the changes?"

"The present staff are all civilians and they don't have responsibility for recording the numbers. They are OK because they have been promised their salaries. Payment day was over a week ago."

Getane says we can go ahead and select patients to interview. Avoiding the patients who are very sick and those whose mobility suggests light injuries, I choose at random an alert, pugnacious-looking young man lying on a mattress against an outside wall. Immediately, a large crowd of mobile prisoners closes round us. His name, he says, is Adisu Kebede, aged twenty. He was with the Fourth Mechanized Division at Hamusit, part of the crew of a tank, when he was shot in the knee so he couldn't escape. I ask what he knew about the Front before the battle.

"I didn't know they were fighters. I thought they were just bandits. We were not properly prepared because we didn't know the actual power of the EPRDF. It was out of our imagination."

"Can you explain why you were defeated?"

"What do you mean—defeated? We weren't defeated!"

A laugh goes up from the audience. A smart alec. He hasn't the courage to refuse to answer, but plays to the audience when he can.

"Then why were you captured?"

"I can't explain it. I don't understand it."

"As a prisoner of war, how are you being treated?"

"Of course we are being treated well. This is not a prison. It's a military hospital. I knew all these nurses before. They are treating us. We are not prisoners of war."

The crowd laughs.

"What about the future? Would you go on fighting on the side of the Dergue if you could."

"Yes. The Dergue is coming back to Bahr-Dar this week."

This conversation is getting too surreal to pursue. The trouble is, it *doesn't* feel like a prisoner of war camp. And there are no guards on the gate.

I am crouching down to talk to him. Aklilu is standing behind me, translating. Suddenly, another prisoner starts shouting at him aggressively. It sounds like invective. Aklilu tries to break in. He goes on shouting, with gestures in my direction. Aklilu's hand goes to his pistol. The large crowd moves closer. Other voices join in. We cannot get out even if we try.

We are saved (perhaps) by an equally belligerent voice rasping "Good afternoon!" A white woman is standing there, her expression even more hostile than the soldiers."

"May I ask what you are doing here in my hospital?"

It is the Swedish surgeon. I explain we had asked to see her, but had been told she was off-duty (somebody has fallen over himself to break the news of our presence).

"Oh *hello!* You must be the surgeon we've heard about." My hand goes out to shake hers and the crowd parts. I speak with the overwhelming charm I reserve for charmless white expatriates in authority in Africa. She cannot stand against it and invites us to come and talk when we have finished interviewing.

Aklilu has decided to make important modifications in our interviewing technique—like changing the balance of power in our favor. We walk out of there without hurrying, but without letting too much space grow between us and the surgeon's receding stocky form. With hindsight, it does seem to me that we walked like a couple of kids into the lion's den. We'd even left Fekre, our guard, guarding the *car,* for God's sake!

"So what happened back there, Aklilu? What was he saying?"

"He was throwing at me all the Dergue propaganda. He said they hadn't been defeated. He said they are winning in Gondar and are coming to overwhelm the EPRDF."

He looks seriously annoyed. I don't know whether it's because of the jibes or because he is regretting his casualness about our security.

"Every word he spoke was the latest Dergue line. He even seemed to know about the campaigns over the last few days like the one into Adwa. We only heard about those this morning. I think the WPE is regularly coming into this hospital to agitate them. I'll speak to Abai about it."

He adds, "But he doesn't seem to have heard the Dergue brigades were all wiped out."

"What was he saying about me?"

He laughs suddenly.

"The Dergue's propaganda is always accusing us of being in the pockets of the Arabs, of selling out Ethiopia to the Arab states in return for money and arms." He shouted at me, 'Why do you bring this Arab here?' I laugh at that, but at the same time it makes me feel more endangered. One of my weaknesses is that I rarely feel scared, but *can they be that irrational?*

"If I didn't have a strong sense of identity," I reply, "I'd be in a bit of a crisis. In the Sudan, they called me an Israeli, in Adwa an Italian, in Mekelle a Cuban, everywhere else a *firenji*—and now I'm an Arab!"

After this, I insist that we interview prisoners on their own. We sit inside the Toyota. By chance perhaps, but without exception, they are all infantry soldiers, uneducated and from a peasant background. Most of them seem to hate the Dergue. Adam Ali is a typical example.[13] He was captured at Tisabai. His unit had no forewarning of the arrival of the Front and they were drinking tea when the first shot was fired (most of their stories included farcical little details like this). His wound in the chest is nearly healed.

"I was recruited by force three years ago. I was newly married. I was plowing my land and building my house. I didn't know the Dergue was in the area. Two soldiers came with guns and called me over. I was suspicious. "Why?" I said. They said there was nothing to worry about, but they cheated me. I had to go with them and at the place where we went there were many gathered together and they said I had to go and fight for the motherland. I had three months training."

Some of them want to go home and see their families; some of them offer to fight with the Front, although they seem only to have the vaguest idea of what it stands for. "They just fight for the people" seems to be the level of information of this group, but their distrust of the government is not at all hazy and seems to have made them impervious to Dergue propaganda.

The Swedish surgeon is called Asa Molde and she has been working here for three months. With her in the ICRC house are an Australian physiotherapist and two nurses, one French and one German. I was wrong about the invitation to tea, including Aklilu. The absence of a distinction in English between the singular and plural forms of *you* can be a problem. She meets us at the door.

"Would you just wait out there!" she says nastily to Aklilu, waving him away.

He looks disconcerted. So do I. My charm becomes a bit thin lipped, but I sit down anyway and no doubt they will be less suspicious if I am on my own. Most expatriates assume a comradeship of white people (which most of the time is surprisingly true) and an agreement on basic values (which is not). The overriding response of these four women to my presence is wonder at my presence. They seem to think I've dropped from the sky.

"But *how* did you get here?" asks the Australian physio.

They don't seem able to believe it when I say I've travelled from the north with the Front. They keep repeating incredulously the last words I've uttered.

"You've travelled from the *north*?

"With the *guerrillas*?"

They too have absorbed the propaganda of the Dergue. In the absence of any counter information, it would be more surprising, I suppose, if they had not. But the sensationalism of their expectations in the light of the reality of my day-to-day experience, makes me want to laugh. It turns out they are petrified at being in a war zone and are expecting death (or worse?) from the terrible rebels. They are concerned that their families may be frantic for their safety. I am surprised, in my turn, because I always thought the ICRC a rather gung ho organization whose personnel jumped at the chance of being in a war zone. We all spend a few minutes modifying our uncritical assumptions. In the conversation that follows, they reveal not only their misinformation about the Front, which is understandable, but also complete ignorance about the political situation in Ethiopia and the nature of the Dergue. Such ignorance, it seems to me, working as they are in a military hospital on the side of a brutal dictatorship, flies in the face of their declared neutrality and is tantamount to an act of political affiliation.

19

GONDAR

In the house by the lake, my backpack has been packed since dawn, ready to leave for Gondar. We return briefly to pick up our things only to hear that Abai has changed his mind about my going so soon after its capture. He is having serious doubts about my security again. The Dergue forces in the battle for the town exceeded thirty thousand, many of whom are now scattered over the countryside. In addition, there are thousands of *shemek* on the loose, the trained and brutal Dergue contra-guerrillas, as well as countless members of the WPE. No one knows how they will read the situation. No one knows which way they will jump. It is too early for anything to be under control.

I want to go. I insist on going, but even I know it is meaningless bluster. Fortunately, Aklilu wants to go too. He holds out. For nearly an hour we wait for two more Toyotas to make up a convoy. Then, by four thirty in the afternoon, we are on our way.

Transport is too scarce to waste any space and as usual, the Toyota is full. The young guard, Fekre, shares the front passenger seat with Aklilu, next to the open window, his gun barrel resting on the sill. Perhaps he is admiring the landscape; perhaps he is scanning every thorn bush for a *shemek*. I am told to sit in the back between two men. It's a four-hour journey of a hundred and eighty kilometers.

Stories pass the time. Sometimes, they are stories we exchange; sometimes they are in our heads. Sometimes, they are mini-epics, the one-liners, which balloon with unexpressed significance, filled in with imagination. Next to me on the right is Mohammed, the secretary of the Officers Democratic Movement (EDORM), now one of the organizations in the Front, whose members have transferred their allegiance from the Dergue to the EPRDF.

"I was a pilot in the airforce," he says.

On my left is a middle-aged man called Tadesse, who looks familiar. He keeps his AK47 between his knees and leans his chin on the barrel, cushioned by a folded shawl. He is a militia from Sheraro with a large family and I once stayed in his house. He is a long way from home.

"He is a brave and loyal friend of the revolution," Aklilu says.

Tadesse says, "Five of my children are fighters."

As we drive northwards up the eastern side of Lake Tana, I am surprised to see so many "villagized" settlements dotting the undulating plain. I thought they were all in the south. They are unmistakable. Real Ethiopian villages, like villages anywhere, are human-shaped, rounded by little bulges to accommodate human needs, their structures anomalous in size, round or square, substantial or flimsy to serve different purposes. These look more like army camps. The tin-roofed identical dwellings made of concrete blocks are all equidistant from one another in straight lines. This, along with forced resettlement, has been one of Mengistu's experiments in social engineering. Either to demoralize dissident areas or to make space for collectivization on fertile soil, whole communities have been uprooted from their traditional land. So many of them. The stories I've been told of removal and dispossession start to clamor in my head. At least it is the clamor of survivors. From the others—the thousands who died of disease and hunger, who perished in floods trying to escape, who were killed by wild animals, who wasted away with misery and homesickness, who just disappeared—there is only silence.

Evening becomes dark night. North of the lake, the road climbs over a dramatic range of mountains, their crests barely discernible against the stars.

"Seven years ago," Aklilu tells us, "I took part in an operation here. I was part of a guerrilla force staging an ambush."

I peer out into the darkness. I can't see a thing.

"It was in 1985.[1] It was the time of the famine. The Dergue took advantage of the situation and started a whole series of very dangerous offensives into the rural area of Tigray. We were distracted. The TPLF was helping the people to survive. Our fighters were accompanying people to the Sudan and so on. We had to devise a tactic to divert the purpose of the enemy."

Aklilu was part of a five-person committee, three from the Tigrayan and two from the Amhara liberation fronts. Even then the two movements worked in close cooperation, although they had not yet formed a united front. Moving at night, they managed to penetrate deep into Gondar to this mountain ridge. Here, they staged a raid to alert the Dergue to their presence, so that the army sent troops from Bahr-Dar northwards and from Gondar southwards. Both contingents stopped short of the rocky gorges where the TPLF were supposed to be operating and then they sent one vehicle in each direction to investigate the danger. Aklilu and his companions lay low and let them through. When each vehicle reached the other side, the Dergue force assumed it was safe and sent in the entire convoy.

"We ambushed and destroyed them and also captured some small towns in the area," finished Aklilu. "Almost at once, troops began to be diverted from Tigray to Gondar."

One story grows out of another. In one of these towns the guerrillas temporarily occupied, Aklilu found in the prison a prisoner under the sentence of death. He was on his way from Gondar, where he had been sentenced, to Bahr-Dar where he was to be hanged. He had killed a WPE cadre who had assaulted him, so, as far as his rescuers were concerned, he was a political prisoner of a sort.

"If you let me go," he cried, "I will work for you forever. Only give me a gun!"

He wanted to go to Tigray as a fighter, but they said he would be more valuable as a militia and underground worker in the province of Gondar, working with the EPDM and biding his time until they moved south in force.

"He is still with us," says Aklilu. "He is still working locally and now Gondar has been completely liberated!"

Even in the dark last night, it was clear that Gondar, like Rome, is built on hills. I saw Fasiladas' castle briefly outlined against the night sky. Then, while Aklilu dashed into the Commissariat to find out what they should do with me, a long crocodile of men and women, ghostly wrapped in their white shawls, wound up the hill, past the car, and into the darkness. There must have been hundreds of them, accompanied by a few armed fighters. So far, I've seen nothing else.

I am staying in a hotel called the Quara on one side of the main square. It's almost empty, which is hardly surprising. But, where are all those intrepid journalists who pack into the battle zones to bring us news of the Gulf War, Liberia, Somalia, the Balkans? The truth is they like to fly into capitals and stay in Hilton Hotels; they don't like lengthy, dangerous, and uncomfortable night convoys over the Sudanese border and no hot showers. This is a hidden war, a secret revolution. But, the absence of observers does leave the field wide open to disinformation. Last night, before I slept, I heard an item about the capture of Gondar on the World Service news. An Ethiopia "expert" called Patrick Gilkes was declaring that Ethiopian rebels were hanging people in the main square in Gondar. My God, that's just outside my window! I keep looking through the curtains to make sure, but it all looks very peaceful to me.

Aklilu went out early to case the area and came back a short time later to take me to breakfast, as this hotel does not supply food. With Aklilu at the wheel and Fekre as a guard, we only drove a few yards across the square to a little cafe crowded with townspeople snatching breakfast. Now we're here, Aklilu seems manic about my safety. The Dergue has portrayed the Front in its propaganda as puppets of foreign powers, especially the Arabs. These were the allegations fired at us by the Bahr-Dar prisoners of war. Abai is worried I'll be a special target for a WPE bullet. It's true I stick out a bit, that I feel about as conspicuous as "a tarantula on a slice of angel food cake," in Raymond Chandler's words, and often feel like wearing a veil, but when I catch sight of myself in the cafe window I just can't imagine this small unimposing figure being mistaken for an important agent of a foreign power.

"Why are you laughing?" asks Aklilu.

"It's no good. I can't seem to feel scared."

He's just heard that hundreds of party members are responding to the Front's hard-line declaration against the WPE by voluntarily coming forward to admit their membership and hand over their weapons. Perhaps that was the long procession I saw last night in the dark.

"Well then, there are fewer left to take a potshot at me."

"You are not being serious," says Aklilu. "I bear a very heavy responsibility."

The subtext of this conversation is my bid for more freedom; the result is that I sit in the hotel room waiting for Aklilu to come back and tell me what I'm allowed to do. In fact, the town feels peaceful, almost desultory, waiting. I am waiting; long lines of water pots wait with women for the water tanker to come; WPE members are waiting in the enclosures set aside for them; soldiers rounded up in the countryside are waiting in the square in columns to be sent to a prisoner of war camp; the townsfolk are waiting as if holding their breath in case the Dergue comes back.

The Front sees the Tewodros Campaign as the first stage of "the battle for Addis," in Mulugeta's words. Aklilu too refers to the *strategic* importance of gaining control of Gondar and Gojjam. How can two provinces on the western borders of Ethiopia, apparently far from Addis Ababa, be so significant? Aklilu says that *strategic* action means planning which is not wholly military, but also engages the people's participation in some way.

"It is essential to work with the people in each area and increase the mass base as a support for further military moves."

This was certainly what dictated the pace in Tigray and Wello. I remembered Meles saying, several years ago, that it was counter-productive to *impose* changes on the people and that things could only progress at the rate at which they could absorb and accommodate them. But this strategic way of working has been characteristic of the whole process of revolution here and one of the explanations of the pace—sixteen years already; it doesn't tell us what is specially significant about these two provinces.

One reason, of course, is that the people of Gojjam and Gondar, as well as those of Wello and North Shewa (already liberated), are the heartland of Amhara support for the Addis Ababa (Amhara-dominated) government. At least, to deprive the Dergue of the support and resources of this region would be a blow against its power; to gain the people's support as well would be to increase the multi-nationality strength of the Front and therefore help to qualify it by degrees to solve the problems of a multi-nationality state in the future.

I sit cross-legged on the floor with the map spread out in front of me and other strategic points become immediately obvious. The Front could not have by-passed Gondar and Gojjam without leaving large Dergue garrisons behind them. They cannot risk being squeezed between different sets of government forces and must avoid leaving troops available to come to the aid of the Dergue at a later stage. The Front now has a corridor to the province of Wellega and from there to the southern half of the country, where it can connect up with the Oromo wing of their coalition, the Oromo People's Democratic Organization (OPDO). My guess is that from here their next move will be Wellega, due south of Gojjam and due west of Addis Ababa, and from there, they will move on the capital.

In the afternoon, I ask Kinfe about the battle for Gondar.[2] He is the overall commander of the coalition Front's forces here and also a member of Central Committee. Some of his points I find particularly interesting. One is his assertion that this battle can only be seen in the context of the victories at Bahr-Dar.

"The center of gravity is like a chain—Hamusit, Bahr-Dar, Gondar. In Hamusit, the 605th Army Corps was the center of gravity. The 25th Infantry Division we faced here was a part of it. The mechanized corps in Hamusit was smashed and that was the command center for the 25th Division. So, although it was huge, it could not exist alone. That was why the battle of Hamusit for Bahr-Dar was done first—for the center of gravity was there."

The battle for Gondar was over in six hours and was very low on casualties.

"What were they?"

They don't usually tell their casualties, but in this case he makes an exception because they were so low.

"We only had two wounded and one martyred—although, in fact, there were many more casualties because of landmines and so on, but it was minimal compared to other battles. The Dergue casualties were between one and two hundred wounded and not more than two hundred dead. The main concern will be the prisoners of war. If you say about these slight casualties no one will believe you. Even the fighters did not believe it. In fact, we were shocked!"

The battle began at seven in the morning and went on until one pm. There were the usual unpredictable, even farcical, departures from the plan. The Dergue forces at Azozo and Losa Mariam crumbled so much more quickly than expected there was no time to block their flight.

"Instead, we were forced to chase them. The command escaped first, before the army, with heavy artillery and tanks, right through Gondar."

It must have been a funny sight, the tanks and vehicles of the Dergue lumbering through the center of the town with the Front's forces in hot pursuit, waved on by the populace. This is confirmed by shopkeepers I talk to later.

"They were running away through the center of the town," says one. "We were all standing on the side, watching them."

"Usually, the military don't want to fight," comments another. "These people were very good. They never fired at them when they were chasing them. They never fired unnecessarily. That's why few people were killed."

They caught up with them ten kilometers to the north of Gondar, where the Dergue soldiers were trying to make the tanks unusable by burning them and tipping them into gullies.

Dergue tanks were not the only procession through the town that Friday morning. Gezai Werki, the First Secretary of the WPE in North Gondar, had already driven into the center, announcing victory and rallying the people through a loud hailer from the back of a military pick-up. The night before, he had ordered the summary execution of one hundred and twenty people from the prison. The next morning, a further hundred and fifty were supposed to be shot, but there wasn't time. Instead, hearing the news of the imminent arrival of the EPRDF, Gezai Werki paraded ostentatiously through the town and then, without stopping, took off into the countryside north of Gondar in a desperate bid to save his skin. The bid failed. A day or two later, peasants in the area captured and killed him, along with Brigadier General Wegahu Turra, an army commander, and Colonel Tadesse Sillatu, Gondar's chief of security. The Front claim they were resisting arrest. All this is told to me by an ancient Fitaurary, a governor of Gondar under Haile Selassie, who comes to see me in the hotel, clutching signed photographs of the Queen and Princess Anne, as if they are a passport to my attention.

Two days later, we drive into the hills north of Gondar to a place called Tikil Dingay to view the abandoned tanks. Out of twelve, only one is burned out and useless; the others flounder at odd angles at the bottom of ravines and steep slopes, but the Front's mechanics assure me they are still in working order. Huge diggers have scooped dirt roads out of the slopes in great shallow loops to reach them and bring them out. One is already at the top and a mechanic obligingly starts it up to demonstrate its abilities with a cloud of diesel smoke and a roar that seems likely to bring boulders from above tumbling on our heads.

"Look—we can see Tigray from here," says Aklilu, to whom tanks are not a novelty, "and over there is Kaza and the mountains of Dejenna."

We are very high. Every way I look I see an undifferentiated landscape of brown mountain crags reaching to the horizon. The mountain stronghold, where several years ago I first met the Front's leadership, was in Dejenna. But, every peak seems as similar as waves in the sea and I cannot pick out a single distinguishing landmark. Somewhere out there, is the spot where peasants have taken rough vengeance on Gezai, the killer king of Gondar. I cannot find it in my heart to blame them.

A curious thing happened a week or so after this—after we had left Gondar, in fact—but the story belongs here, so here I will tell it.

Aklilu and I were back in Woldia. We had been talking to farmers in the villages all the morning and had come back ravenously hungry. One restaurant had stopped serving, so we had to go to another further up the road. We coincided there with a man who, but for his greying hair, I would have described as a young man. He was the only other customer and so we got into conversation.

His name was Dawit Berhane, from Tigray.[3] He started off his story smiling and cool, but grew first serious and then passionate. He had been a truck driver until one day he was arrested and sent for three years to Gondar prison. He had been arrested on some trumped-up charge like a faulty driving license, in effect for being Tigrayan. He was released the day the Front took the town. The prisoners had done a count, for the three years he was there, of those executed. There were three thousand, four hundred and fifty-three.

"There were only about three hundred from nationalities other than Tigrayan or Eritrean. Some of them were shoe-shine boys, people like that. Some were arrested for singing songs, which mentioned the EPRDF! Others for being in a restaurant and asking for Tigrinya music, not revolutionary songs, just love songs produced in Addis. This was what it was like!"

On the Thursday, the day before Gondar was captured, he was among nineteen people taken from his cell to be shot. All but two were Tigrayans. The total from all the cells, he thought, was nearer to three hundred than the hundred and twenty the Fitaurary had told me. The prison authorities were always meticulous about the paper work, perhaps because promotion in the party was often based on the numbers of "counter-revolutionaries" a member exposed and "put out of action." His name, as I said, was Dawit Berhane, but the paper authorizing execution was made out in the name of Dawit Berhe. He was sent back to his cell until the clerical error was rectified and the execution was postponed until six in the evening, the following day. At four in the afternoon, he was freed by the Front.

We finished lunch and went on to a bar to drink tea. Aklilu bought Dawit a whisky. It was now ten days since his release, but he still could not believe he was free; he slept badly and was plagued by nightmares. He showed us arms scarred by torture and described the scars all over his body.

"If you don't believe me, ask other drivers who were with me there. They even tied me to a car and pulled me along the ground."

He had family in Addis Ababa, Asmara, and the Sudan. Two of his children were with his mother in Asmara and two in Addis with his wife. I asked if he would join them. He looked at me for a moment and said to Aklilu:

"How could she think I would go back there? I am reborn like a baby. I am not only saved from prison; I am saved from the grave. EPRDF have saved my life, so my life belongs to them. I will fight for them. I was to die for nothing, for no reason whatever. If I work with the EPRDF to destroy this regime, I don't mind even if I get killed. My death will have purpose."

Now he was working as a driver for the Front.

After Dawit left us, we stayed a few minutes longer, finishing our drinks. Aklilu seemed touchy and didn't want to talk. Then, suddenly words burst from him. He said that in Tigray every family knew these things. Mothers sent off their children to fight; they didn't want their children to die, but they knew it was necessary to fight this regime.

You know, when I went off to fight I was especially close to my mother. She felt ve

family—and I felt for her too. When I went to the field, she was crying for a long time, so much that one of my brothers said he would go and find me and

lantly and not be diverted from what I had to do. She and my father died three years before we liberated Axum. I was Commander of that front. I

the neighbors came out and were crying. Even now, I hardly ever go to Axum."

He stood up abruptly.

"Let's go," he said.

When we were in the car, he said, equally abruptly:

"You know, I don't like to hear these stories. I find them very irritating!"

Diary: Tuesday, March 13

The front moves south.

News from the front —a battle for the bridge across the Blue Nile between Gojjam and Wellega. The Front annihilates the 31st Division. 21,000 captives, 3,000 killed and wounded. Weapons captured: one tank, heavy artillery (120 mm.), 31,000 light guns. Fighting continues against the 201st Airborne Division.

It is impossible, in Gondar, to separate the present moment from the past. Its six great castles loom proudly over the town. Gondar's history is part of the history of feudal Ethiopia. It was the seat of Prince Kassa, who became Emperor Tewodros, who first tried to bring the Abyssinian fiefdoms into some sort of unity, whose name has been given to this campaign. I can't claim to know this history well, despite reading a few books, but even in my own investigations the name of Gondar has come up again and again. When I look at its buildings now and wander its streets, the present moment is just the top layer in a fat historical sandwich. Its inhabitants are also locked into the past. Below this visible world, they hear the murmur of past times and past experience and, most of all, past voices.

This must, in part, explain the welcome given by the people when they first saw the Front's forces.

"When we entered, the women were ululating," Kinfe said, "the youngsters playing, people shaking our hands and kissing us."

Helawe Dagmawe, the new administrator, says much the same thing.[4] Almost at once, the Front held a reception in Castle Square to explain their policies and program, which was attended by about twenty-five thousand people. He claims the majority were sympathetic. As the days go by, it seems to me also that the people here, despite shortages of water and power, are much more supportive of the Front than in Bahr-Dar and the atmosphere more positive and peaceful. Their past experience of terror, at the hands of the Dergue, must have much to do with this sense of release, of liberation—at least in the short term.

"It's convincing the people that is the first priority," says Helawe. "Our basic principle is that the people are a mighty force, that if they use their initiative and creativity and if they feel a sense of freedom they can solve their problems for themselves."

He refers to the massacres of the Red Terror. The hated Party chief, so recently despatched, had an even more murderous predecessor called Melaku Tefera, whose real name translates as "Angel of Fear," but is more commonly remembered as the Butcher of Gondar. During his nine years as Party chief here, he was renowned for the range of tortures and numbers of brutal deaths he ordered.

Once, in Khartoum, I met Lisane Yohannes, the older brother of Harnet (the woman fighter whom I met in the Propaganda Bureau on my first visit). He told me of his experiences in Gondar, where he had been a teacher before the start of the Dergue or the Tigrayan revolution. He joined the Front as an underground member in Gondar and his experiences were enlightening both for the Front's early methods of organizing clandestine support in the towns and for his memories of Melaku Tefera, before the Butcher even got into his stride.

Underground in Gondar

I was a teacher in Gondar. In September 1975, I became a member of the TPLF. I was assigned to recruit as many members as possible, basically introducing the existence of the TPLF and popularizing the revolution. I went to Bahr-Dar to talk to Tigrayan businessmen and teachers, to Adi Arkai and to Seraba in Western Gondar, mostly to talk to teachers. We used codes, usually figures, and whenever I wanted to pass a message or record something we used a very secretive method that nobody would understand. For example, I went to a bar where lots of people played billiards. I would play with the person concerned and communicate through playing the game. We would camouflage ourselves in this way or, if we were playing cards, through discussing the points. Another tactic was to be as carefree as possible, never indicating you were interested in youth or politics, in national issues or government affairs, making people think you are a beer-swiller, joking with the women in the bars, joking and sounding like a playboy.

In fact, the TPLF code of discipline was strong. You were not supposed to drink. You were not supposed to womanize. I remember when one of our members did get drunk and nearly exposed himself in a quarrel, and we said if he went on like that he would have to go to the field. I deliberately mixed with Amhara colleagues, especially one friend, going to his house, having him to mine, always avoiding political discussions—in fact, if he ever heard later that I had gone to the field it must have been a big surprise!

That year was a good year. No one knew we existed as a clandestine group and we managed to recruit and to grow. The other opposition group, the EPRP, was much more established. They were also very strong that year. Anyone against the government was regarded as EPRP. Most of the teachers were in the EPRP, except Tigrayans and Eritreans, but the government never suspected us, mostly through ignorance.

The next year, things changed. The government was strengthening itself. It was trying to liquidate opposition groups, especially the EPRP and I am a witness myself to what happened in Gondar. The students demonstrated against the Dergue. The slogans demanded democratic rights for the people, for the restoration of civilian government and so on. The Dergue officials ordered their forces to disperse the demonstrators and the students were attacked from three directions. The Rapid Deployment Force of the Dergue with semi-automatic bren guns started shooting students in daylight. There was nowhere for the students to run away and escape. I saw corpses of my own students. I managed to count four or five, as I was very near the shootings. Later, I discovered that twelve died immediately and more died in the hospital (about twenty-six altogether) and many more were wounded. It was very tragic.

From that incident onwards, things changed. The EPRP started killing Dergue officials and it was a routine of the day to hear of shootings, deaths, imprisonment, torture—life was terrible. Students boycotted classes. There was nothing to do. Then students were forced to attend; teachers were forced to teach. I was beaten by a Dergue official right in front of my students.

Every morning, the Party head, Melaku Tefera, or his deputy, Lieutenant Gebre-Igziabher, came to the school to check attendance. One fine morning I was wearing my lab gown and waiting for the students to come for a lab period. This lieutenant asked what I was doing standing in front of the door. I replied I was waiting for students to come.

He said, "Wait in the classroom!"

I said, "OK, let them come."

With a stick, he started beating me and went on until I reached my desk.

"This is where you should wait for them, bloody bastard! We know who is guiding the students not to study. We know who is behind it all! It is you!"

But, I was not imprisoned, although I was beaten badly. When I told my colleagues I was beaten, they said, "You were lucky. Don't complain. They could have shot you or taken you to prison."

There wasn't any teacher who was not beaten or imprisoned or tortured. On their side, the EPRP was killing also. Despite this, we were meet-

ing at least once a week. We exchanged information, we collected contributions, we received papers from the Front, we read and distributed them and in that year we twice sent the Chairman of the Committee to Endeselassie to bring us updates and also to take our contribution to the Front.

Now, it was different from before. We had difficulty moving from place-to-place. We had to have a permit from the authorities and there was a lack of transport because of the petrol shortage. Despite these difficulties, we were able to continue our clandestine work. I managed to go to Bahr-Dar once. There was still little known about the TPLF.

We went on doing our work and suddenly one of our committee members was imprisoned. His name was Gebrehiwet Kebedow. He was arrested as a suspected EPRP member, as he had EPRP members as friends. It was a big blow for us because he was one of the strong, staunch members of our committee. This guy was in prison and we were all ready to leave Gondar, not only because he might break under torture, but they searched his house and all the codes, the names, the money was in his house. He put it above the ceiling. He was very relaxed and welcomed their search and they never found it or I wouldn't be here now. Another member was living with him and immediately grabbed everything and hid it in another place.

I had a telephone call and was told to get ready to leave. We went to see Kidane, our member, and played cards in his hotel and we all agreed that Gebrehiwet would not let us down. We decided to give it two or three days. As we foretold, Gebrehiwet remained silent, never admitting either membership of the EPRP or of the new movement, the TPLF. The prison was full of prisoners. They only allowed you to see the prisoners on Sundays. We went in turns to provide him with cigarettes and food. We weren't allowed to go all at once. I think he spent only three months in prison and then he was killed. One Sunday, we were given all his clothes and his belongings.

After that, someone we knew was released and told us of all the torture Gebrehiwet faced and of his strength. He was so determined. He never uttered a single word. His family was in Gondar. He had two brothers he was taking care of. He was not married. He sacrificed his life so that the TPLF could continue.[5]

I must find out more about the Red Terror. Young people were slaughtered in thousands and apparently Gondar was the site of some of the worst massacres.

"We will ask Kinfe," says Aklilu. "He comes from Gondar and through his contacts he will put you in touch with the right people."

Kinfe invites us to coffee at his house. I know he was brought up in Gondar so I am expecting to meet his parents, but it is his relatives who greet us at the door and make us welcome. Family ties are so close in Ethiopia that it is often difficult and irrelevant to judge the degree of relationship, especially as—in English anyway—people refer to cousins as sisters and brothers and responsibility for even distant relatives from less well off branches of the family is assumed without question. We also meet old family friends there and a stream of people who have just heard that Kinfe is in Gondar, turn up to embrace him.

It is a highly charged occasion, full of reunions, tears, and expressions of joy. Our hostess sits on her little stool to make the coffee, surrounded by a mat of fresh leaves and flowers. I think she is Kinfe's aunt. She is very nice, very elderly, and very fat.

"She was young when I saw her last," says Kinfe, smiling at her.

He joined the struggle fifteen years ago straight from Addis after three years at the university, so it is at least eighteen years since he saw his family here.

"It's having twelve boys and no girl to help me that's made me old," she says, nodding sagely and shaking the coffee roasting shovel under our noses so we can appreciate the aroma.

"Coffee" turns out to include *injera* with lenten bean sauce, *himbasha* and boiled sweets. As we tuck in, Kinfe begins telling me about the Red Terror. He had already left for the field, but hardly a school friend of his has survived in the town. He knew particularly well the family of his best friend.

"They lost two sons, my friend and his younger brother. I used to be there all the time. I was sleeping there, eating there. Now, I cannot go there any more. They cannot bear to see me."

He nevertheless seems confident of arranging meetings for me, but at that moment his cousin comes in. When Kinfe last saw him, he was ten or eleven; now he is a mechanic with his own garage. Then, a man arrives of about Kinfe's age. They greet each other and talk quietly, perhaps exchanging eighteen years of news, clasping each other's hands the whole time. This is not the moment to talk about the Red Terror.

It is never the right moment to talk about the Red Terror, in Gondar, not on this visit anyway. For all Kinfe's efforts, no one wants to talk to me. On one morning a day or two later, someone is finally persuaded to meet me, but he does not turn up for his appointment. This town saw a whole generation massacred and no one will talk to me about it. They are either so terrified of the Party or so fearful of the Dergue's return or else totally programmed in fear and silence. Ironically, this conveys more to me of the nature of this government than a whole line of witnesses queuing up to be interviewed. I already know that after the killings the bodies remained for a time on the streets. Parents were threatened with reprisals if they were seen to mourn. They had to buy the bodies back for burial for the price of the bullet that killed them. Most people could not afford it.

Present and past begin to overlap when Aklilu decides I should see around the castles of Gondar. They are all together in a huge compound within a crenellated wall with half a dozen gates, a castle complex at one end of town, built by successive Lords of Gondar to represent their might and security. Only the castles remain, as a monument to hubris and the evanescence of power. Six castles of six kings. They out-castle all other castles I have seen. To this day, their massive walls, towers, domed turrets, and soaring flights of stone stairways are still for me the *essence* of castle. Constructed in red-brown stone, they glow in an afternoon sun, which turns into gold the brown grass parkland. Yet, it is a curiously unsatisfactory experience. Aklilu does not seem much better-informed than I am. We are cast for a couple of hours into tourists, but tourists without a guide, who do not know how to make sense of their experience and need help to explicate the meanings of what they see. In the end, I come away full of admiration for Ethiopian masons, a reverence begun in Tigray for domestic architecture and reinforced in the highlands further south. The lords and paymasters may have passed away but these mammoth constructions in perfect condition remain a silent testimony, not to the riches that bought them, but to the ingenuity and skills of the men whose hands raised them to the sky.

Near the entrance is a fusty moth-eaten lion. The smell guides us to his cage. This symbol of feudal empire, of Haile Selassie, the Lion of Judah, of an Abyssinian might long on symbols and short on substance, is looking decidedly long in the tooth, worn out, just an unhappy lion in fact. Let's hope the system he represents, the source of so much misery and injustice, is also decayed beyond hope of resuscitation.

In Haile Selassie's time, one of these castles was a museum of artifacts and furnishings of the feudal era. He stayed here when he visited Gondar. Under the Dergue, Melaku Tefara and his successors converted it to a house of torture. The lower floors are a jumble of rubbish and dirt, rags and shabby desks and chairs, offices littered with balls of paper and cigarette stubs. We look around for evidence of torture, but all we find are a few inconclusive thongs and lashes. Yet, apparently torture routinely took place here.

Most of the shutters are closed. I sit down in a dim dirty office for a few moments, while Aklilu pokes around in another room, and wonder what has happened here. Why is it, when we hear tales of brutal inhumanity, full of everyday weakness and rare heroism, we identify with the spots of noble resistance, when the opposite is much more likely? Hannah Arendt's phrase comes back to me, *the banality of evil*. I was brought up among saints and martyrs, but sitting on a rickety chair in this dirty silent gloom, the difficulty of retaining idealism comes home to me for the first time, the rarity of holding out against the mundanity of rolls of dirt, torn paper, and fag-ends.

We emerge into the late afternoon sunshine. In Castle Square, there is another long column of prisoners of war rounded up from the countryside. Later, we pass the queue for the Front's amnesty office. It winds down the street and round the corner. More party workers are taking advantage of the amnesty to give up their weapons. I have already taken photographs of rooms stuffed with Kalashnikovs and rifles and bren guns, guarded around the clock by fighters. So enthusiastic has been the response to the amnesty, that storage space is already a problem.

We have transferred to the Fogera Hotel, one of the four state tourist hotels. One reason is that it has kitchen staff and our presence helps to give them work; another is that the Hotel manager, Kidane Assegahegne, has been for years an underground member of the Front. In the early seventies, he had built up the Quara Hotel (from where we have just moved) from almost nothing to a successful establishment, until it was forcibly requisitioned by the Dergue. Later, Kidane was imprisoned and tortured for seven years in Addis Ababa, where, by coincidence, he was a close friend of Aklilu's brother who was there for nine years. Until only last week, the Fogera was filled with Party members and Dergue officials. Little did they suspect that Kidane was also providing a refuge for agents of the Front in disguise. Presumably, it would have been an excellent source of information for someone with his ears open.

The restaurant and main facilities are in the main house of the hotel, but we stay in one of several thatched two-room chalets in a beautiful garden full of shady pines, flowering hibiscus and other shrubs and trees. The rooms are very pleasant, painted white, and decorated with traditional Ethiopian designs and fabrics. The thatch keeps them cool and projects over a veranda, where I can write and work. It is very pleasant, but if this is the Ethiopia tourists see, they won't understand anything of the politics and oppression that have forced the people into poverty and starvation or the insufferable pressures that have driven them to armed struggle. On the other hand, the alternative tour I could devise of the *real* Ethiopia would not attract many takers. All a poor country can hope for from tourists, no matter what the government of the day, is their foreign currency.

There are no tourists now and the hotel is virtually empty. Fighters don't stay in hotels, although, as my guide, Aklilu is staying in the room next door. Two of the staff, Solomon, a Tigrinya-speaker from Asmara, and Mohammed, an Amhara, take turns in bringing meals to my little veranda. They are trained in servility and don't respond to friendly overtures. After throwing away the lumpy porridge the cook makes me from our stores, I go to the kitchen the next morning to make it myself.

In the basement, under the main hotel building is the largest cooking range I have ever seen, about fifteen feet long and five wide. When I walk in, the round lids have been removed and Mohammed is stuffing wood into it through the top—a dangerous business as tongues of flame leap out towards the ceiling. Just to cook my porridge. But, the process of measuring and stirring and explaining and laughing while my face grows beetroot red in the heat also thaws the ice. After this, they lose some of their formality and, when Aklilu goes off to make contact with relatives in the town, they come to talk to me about their fears for the future. They are terrified of being laid off, terrified of losing their salaries, and suspicious of the Front. This suspicion has nothing to do with ideology. Their only sense of responsibility is to their families. They too hate the Dergue, but work is work and they would rather serve its fascist representatives than struggle for survival while testing out promises of the Front, which, in the light of all their experience of authority, can only seem vague and unreal. "Democracy" is only a word, barely an idea. *Does it put money in your pocket?*

Aklilu is much absorbed by his newly-found relatives. He finds he is a great uncle, although only thirty-four, of a tiny child not yet five, but full of vitality and brightness. Her name is Eden, but they call her Minya. He loves to carry her around, take her with us in the car and give her little treats. One evening, Aklilu's brother's wife's sister invites us and other friends for a meal. For the first time, I meet the whole family, but the center of attention is Minya. The next day, I am more or less confined to the hotel writing an article, so he brings her to the garden to play. Work is forgotten. Soon, we are running round the paths, chasing her and being chased, catching her while she jumps off walls, giving her rides. Solomon and Mohammed join in, chucking their training to the winds. The garden echoes with shrieks of laughter. Even the fighters on the gate come to see what's happening. I have a feeling that these games do more to break down suspicion than a thousand worthy words.

But, most of the time the hotel is secluded behind walls designed to keep tourists and their property safe from beggars and thieves, to keep poverty at a proper distance. I have never stayed in such a hotel before—in Europe, let alone Ethiopia—and I feel cut off from life. I recall, with nostalgia, the comradely bustle on the shores of Lake Tana of fighters washing, singing, trying out their English, dancing in the evenings to the *krar*. All that must be going on somewhere here too. I recall the absence of privacy in the villages with something like longing, the unshooable children peering round the door frame or following in a column when I go for a pee. Worth a few fleas and bedbugs anytime. Nevertheless, a lot of the time I am out and, when I'm not, the quiet garden is a good place to work and also to talk to people who appreciate discretion.

I spend several wasted hours going to or waiting for interviews that never happen, mostly on the Red Terror, because people are fearful and in the end they vote with their feet. Sometimes, on the other hand, people seek me out, perhaps because they think I might put in a word for them with the new authorities. After all, graft has been the order of the day. I think this is why the ex-governor came, royal photographs in hand, although in the end he never asked me anything and told me quite a lot. An Indian businessman wants to get a message of reassurance through to his parents who, temporarily visiting other family in Addis, now cannot get back across the lines. No one wants to give his name.

It's refreshing, therefore, to hear Kidane's story.[6] He comes one day and sits under the thatch on my little veranda and starts to talk. He does not seem to have any doubts about the permanence of the Front's hold on Gondar and Gojjam. He is proud to give his name, happy to come out of the shadows at last. I won't reproduce his story here in full. Most of it is about his years in prison and if I passed into these pages, the full weight and number of the prison experiences I've heard in this country, your hearts would fail under the sorrow of it. But, every story I hear contains unique details or common facts uniquely expressed. With Kidane, it is the way he speaks about his family.

Kidane became an underground agent for the Front, in Gondar, soon after the start of the revolution. His motivation was his personal experience of what they call "national oppression." He had come from Adwa when he was fourteen to live with relatives and from earning a bare living as a small trader, he worked hard to establish himself in the hotel business. He is forty-seven, no longer a young man.

"I was not feeling as if Gondar was my birthplace or my homeland. We Tigrayans were annihilated, dehumanized, like second-class citizens. You can't imagine. I had a hotel. The Ethiopian Hotel was opposite. If they were asked to pay one hundred birr in tax, I would be asked to pay one thousand. When I heard my people were engaged in struggle, I decided I must support this struggle. I had no rest. I was always disturbed. I had no good times. My feelings were always tortured and I was never easy, so I didn't mind about my family. The one way I could fight the oppression was to join the struggle. Also, I knew the way my people were living in Tigray."

I ask him what he meant by not minding about his family.

"I just imagined that one day, if something happened, I could be exposed and I knew my family, my children, would then have a problem, but I accepted that this sacrifice must be paid. Then, someone who was living in Addis was arrested and gave my name under torture."

He is quiet for a moment. He has been so visibly happy the last few days, it's hard to imagine what it must be like recalling those times.

"I know what happened to my family when I was in prison. They were like skeletons. They had to go from one family to another to get help. But, I took it as a price for the revolution."

"Did they accept it too?"

"My wife is Tigrayan."

"Did she stay in Gondar?"

"Yes. She was going to come to Addis. They were all scattered to different relatives, looking for help. My home was dismantled. I sent messages not to come to Addis. "The money you'd use for transport, use for food for the children," I told her. "Try to look after the kids. There are other relatives in Addis. I am OK." There were some very bad people here, especially supporters of the Dergue Party, who used to tell my children, "Your father is killed. He is dead," and they would cry."

He is blind in one eye. His head was badly kicked in prison and his injured eye formed a cataract.

"They pulled out my toenails," he says. "Here is one of them."

And he pulls out of his pocket a horny curl of nail.

On his release, he reported to his previous office and, through the intervention of a sympathetic Oromo who remembered him, Kidane was assigned to a hotel in Woreta. When Woreta came under the control of the Front, he was shifted back to Gondar.

"In Woreta I was alone, but we were reunited in Gondar. My last daughter was born about the time I went into prison. When I came out I didn't know her and she didn't know me."

Later, the same day, I am surprised when a man called Geramo actually does turn up to talk about the Red Terror.[7] I suspect it's not his real name. He is a small neat man, a teacher, with a very precise manner of speaking. He reads his information into the microphone from a prepared sheet of paper, like a very boring school-room lecture from a past age:

"The Red Terror took place from 1978 to 1980. I was an elementary school teacher. The reasons for the Red Terror are mainly the involvement of oneself in any democratic movement, such as EPRP, TPLF, ELF, and what have you for that matter. Or, it might be in any ordinary business, like selling goods more than the price they were supposed to be sold or if someone was found stealing. The opposition was basically to the Dergue and to the opportunists in it who were blind to see the mass suffering by the privileges they extracted by being bureaucrats and higher officials...."

I remind myself that pedantry is not an indicator of inaccuracy and as usual, there are some interesting details, especially when I break into the monologue and he starts speaking off the cuff. For the first time, I hear about Free Action, a sort of free-for-all killing jamboree.

"There was an action called Free Action, which meant the soldiers could kill anyone they saw on the street for several days in January and February 1978. They took Free Action when students and teachers came out of the schools. They arrested any citizen without trial. A teacher, called Wondumu, was going home after work when he was shot down with some high school students."

He pauses for a moment and shuffles his papers, as if undecided whether to go back to reading or to continue ad lib.

"I remember one occasion here," he goes on. "One day they killed as many people as possible and they laid them right from the gate of the prison to the airport, which is fifteen kilometers away from Gondar."

"What did you say about the airport?"

"The airport is fifteen kilometers away. Yes, madam."

"And you actually saw all the bodies—they were laid head to toe, were they—from the prison to the airport? Or were they laid side by side?"

My questions are grotesque and tasteless, but I need to get an idea of numbers.

"At intervals."

"This morning, Kidane spoke of mothers being forced to dance on their children's bodies. What did he mean by that?"

"No, that is an exaggeration. He was speaking figuratively. I don't want to give you anything that is not perfect. Of course, say, a mother wants to see whether her son or daughter is killed or not. Well, and imagine she found her son's body lying there in the street. She was not allowed to cry. No, she was not allowed to cry."

"What did they do, if they saw her crying?"

"Well, they may take her to prison or they may beat her. This is a true story."

"What about—were the parents allowed to come and take their children away, those children?"

"No. No. It was impossible."

"Why?"

"Because the Dergue wanted to bury them in one hole. People were killed; they dug a hole and put them there."

"Do people know where their children are buried?"

"At least they know the area."

"They did it secretly then, did they?"

"Of course. They did it secretly. The work was done by the prisoners themselves and it was in Azozo, about twelve kilometers away from this town, near the airport."

I am silenced. I cannot ask another question. But, he goes on anyway. He is talking fast now and what he says is not entirely coherent. His voice is full of suppressed—anger, sadness?

"And I remember one occasion, because I had been in prison for two years without any trial and the occasion that I remember—a wife and a husband were killed together. They laid their dead bodies as if they were embracing each other and that lady was pregnant, madam. She was pregnant. She told this to Major Melaku and he said, he said, "I'm sorry, I can't help you." She told him she was pregnant and he could not excuse it."

The woman's name was Amawayish Fente from Dabat, he says. He gives me other names, all teachers. He won't say whether they were his colleagues or not. He is still afraid of being identified.

A year after this visit to Gondar, a mass grave, apparently one of many, is exhumed near Gondar airport, uncovering more than a thousand bodies.

That evening I eat supper alone. Aklilu has gone off to join his family. Then Kinfe comes to invite me to join some of them in the hotel restaurant. It is at the top of the hotel in an open gallery under the roof, accessible up a picturesque outside staircase. Kidane is there and Helawe, the new administrator, also the top Commander for EPDM (I forget his name) and others of the leadership in the Tewodros Campaign, some of whom I recognize—about a dozen altogether. Later, we are joined by Aklilu. There are bottles of Scotch on the table, provided by Kidane. They talk quietly to each other, sometimes to me. They don't need to exchange information, yet it is a kind of sharing. It is very quiet and low key, yet, of all the celebrations in my life this is the most vivid. They sit there, talking desultorily, occasionally refilling glasses, and their faces are shining. How can I describe it? Shining.

If I needed convincing of the strategic nature of these victories, then this is the moment.

20

Amhara Country

A few days after this celebration, we left Gondar for the return journey to Wello and Tigray.

Aklilu wanted to go straight back to Hagere Salam. He was uneasy about how much time he had spent away from his work at headquarters; I on the other hand was reluctant to return to Tigray at once. This was my first opportunity to gather information in the Amhara liberated area. I felt I had not given due weight to their contribution. In the future, it seemed to me, it would be the participation of these Amhara, their stand against the discriminations and injustices of the largely Amhara regime, which would swing the balance of perception from the Front as a Tigrayan elite replacing an Amhara elite to the Front as a multi-national democratic coalition replacing a uni-national dictatorship. Even more significant would be the support of the Oromo people, the largest nationality in Ethiopia and the most historically oppressed.

"So what do you want to know?" asked Aklilu. "What is your program?"

As East Gojjam has been considered the stronghold of support for the Amhara right to rule, I wanted to know how they felt now, after a year under the EPRDF. Then, in Wello, they had just completed land reform. How had that been done? What did that mean to the peasants in practical terms? To find out I had to go into the villages and talk to the farmers themselves.

"What about Mersa?" says Aklilu. "It's not far from Woldia. It is a paradise. You can get fruits, sugar cane, coffee. But it also suffered very much from the Dergue."

"Right. Mersa too."

"And then we'll go at once to Hagere Salam."

So we set off—on the same road, but less interested in the landscape than on our journey out, more interested in stopping in the little villages and farms. This was not an investigation in depth; it was, at best, an impression. Aklilu speaks Amharic well; it is a qualification for coming into these provinces, but presumably it is obvious that he is not an Amhara native. I could not measure how much the candor of our informants was affected by their knowledge that my companions belong to the Front or the proportion of expediency in their replies.

In Debre Tabor, the landcruiser broke down and our driver, Haile, after all his strategems had failed, had to hitch a lift on a truck back to Bahr-Dar to get a new battery. Holed up in the fleapit hotel for a few days, I came down with a cold and I felt feverish and ill just when I was stuck with a bed I would rather not lie on. The first night, the fleas were leaping about like fountains in the light of my torch. In the end, I sprayed the whole room including the inside of my sleeping bag, and nearly died of fumes. The next night, the rats kept waking me up. I blocked the large rathole in the corner with a four gallon water carrier Aklilu had parked in my room. What sounded like a small army turned up, scrabbling behind the walls and over the ceiling, squeaky and indignant. I thought I had grown used to rats, but I stayed awake most of the night as if under siege by monsters, expecting them to chew through the ceiling and land on my face.

The hotel seemed to be looked after by two young men. I saw one of them once sweep the veranda, but I never saw a woman there or any real cleaning being done, whereas in other hotels I've stayed in the lines are full of washing every day and women cleaners wage perpetual war against the flying dust. One morning, left alone with Fekre to keep an eye on me, I struck up a conversation with the younger one and then with his older nineteen year old brother, Joseph. I asked them what they thought of the Front. Joseph's reply was similar to the views of hotel staff in Gondar, anxious, uninformed, swayed by a narrow but understandable self-interest and shot through with prejudice against non-Amhara nationalities. It went something like this.

"I liked the Dergue better than the EPRDF because my personal situation meant that I could live better then. Look at the town now—no electricity, no communications, the schools shut down because there's no one to pay the teachers' salaries. This town has such severe problems now. I was in an orphanage run by a German relief organization, but since the Dergue was pushed out of this area they haven't been able to get my money to me. The bank stopped operating when the Dergue left.

"There were some problems before, but now it's terrible. There was no democracy under the Dergue and I think the EPRDF program sounds very nice, but unless they get power in the whole country they won't be able to change anything. In the meantime, how do I live? It will take years for them to capture Addis Ababa. The only reason for their success so far is that the

Dergue army is made up of so many nationalities. The people in the south of the country, like the Oromo people, are fearful at the sound of a bullet. There are many Oromo in the army and they'd rather surrender. But, round Addis and Asmara are the strongest sections of the army and they won't be able to defeat them."

Halfway through this conversation Fekre came over and tried to get them to go away. "Leave it," I said. "It's OK." He left us reluctantly, worried by Joseph's flailing arms and raised voice. His duty was to guard me, whether I wanted to be guarded or not. I wondered whether it kept me isolated from general opinion; on the other hand, members of the Front have been open about who were likely to be hostile to them. Helawe, in Gondar, had referred to those "attached to the government or the old ruling class, people benefiting from those regimes."[1]

Later the same day, Aklilu brought the chairman of the new *shengo* or local council to talk to me. As you would expect, he gave me a different view.[2]

It had taken a year to prepare for the first elections they had ever had. A draft of the proposed laws of the *shengo* had been circulated for discussion to every area. An assembly of the people had argued them out and eventually a majority had approved the equal rights of women to property and land, new marriage laws, equality of Muslims and Christians and so on, but they had made some mistakes. Against the recommendations of the participating fighters, "undemocratic elements" (in other words feudal remnants and Dergue Party members) had been elected to positions of authority. When the time came to discuss land reform some months later, these individuals, of course, argued against it. They were voted off and replaced.

For much of the time in Debre Tabor, I am left to my own devices. At about four in the afternoon, Aklilu turns up and suggests a walk. The "walk" turns out to be a visit to two hospitals. I should have known he would not mean a casual stroll. From the way he is greeted I guess this is how he has been spending his time since we got here. It has slipped my mind that he was a former head of the TPLF Health Department and that health concerns top his list of priorities.

The hospital is pleasantly and spaciously designed with a number of single-story buildings laid out among grass and trees. A gentle young man shows us round and answers my questions. He tells us that all the qualified medical staff abandoned the hospital when the Front captured the area a year ago. At the moment, he is in charge although he is only a senior nurse trained by the Front. The only other staff are a number of "barefoot doctors," who are all fighters recruited from the peasants with minimal but intensive training in some basic principles and simple diagnostic skills.

There is a chronic water shortage in Debre Tabor. Inside the buildings, the wards, clinics, and offices are so filthy it would be hard to believe we were in a hospital at all but for the numbers of ragged moaning patients, some crowded two to a fetid mattress on the rickety bedsteads. How can you maintain standards of hygiene without water? As in most African countries, patients' families here provide food and non-medical care. This is a practice borne of necessity and it is the disadvantages of the system that are most evident to the visitor. As well as swirls of dirt on walls and floor, food remains under the beds attract flies and the air is thick with the smell of urine and feces.

The main problems here are malaria and venereal diseases, particularly AIDS. This is the case in most Ethiopian towns, especially where large numbers of prostitutes have accumulated to serve army garrisons. These are the problems of poverty. This is what *underdevelopment* means. Too many problems, too few resources. Poverty, poor water, malnutrition, no health education, and minimal health care, all lower the immune system and bring early death. Yet, he goes on talking in his gentle voice; Aklilu's face is calm. This is their everyday experience. Do they ever feel overwhelmed? The fighters in these civilian hospitals just seem to get on with it, patiently, without lamentation, without fuss.

I try to express some of this to Aklilu as we walk down the road afterwards to the second hospital. He says that emotional responses are no help.

"But, there has to be a solution," he adds. "For us, it is the armed struggle."

It is only a short walk to the Front's field hospital, which was set up here because of Debre Tabor's closeness to the front line over the last year. It is temporarily housed on the fringe of the town in huts and cottages vacated by Dergue Party members or rented from peasants. Gebre Livanos, a surgeon and old colleague of Aklilu's, comes to greet us and show me around. My responses are completely attuned by now to this environment, but our visit to the civilian hospital and the very word "hospital" itself raises the ghost of Western judgements. By those standards, these peasant houses are no more than hovels with crumbling walls, packed mud floors and no running water, but they are swept as clean as possible and meticulously tidy compared to either the civilian hospital or the hotel. Compared with ordinary hospitals, this field hospital is set up to be mobile, Gebre Livanos tells me, but it functions in partnership with the even more mobile surgical and medical teams, which work on the battlefield itself. They provide emergency treatment on the spot and are responsible for bringing the wounded here to the field hospital.

Genet, the Battlefield Nurse

I am nineteen. I come from a family of three boys and four girls. I am in the middle, second from top. I am from Mekony, in Raya. It is a town in a beautiful district, a center of trade in a big plain, fertile, and rich.

It was in 1988, three years ago, that I became a fighter. The problems of people in Tigray and also my personal problems made me want to fight. I was an eighth grade student. I had many brothers. One went to foreign countries seven years ago, three completed high school and had no job, one was a fighter. So, I knew there was no way to solve any problems without fighting and getting rid of this government.

Before 1988, Mahony and Korem were under the government and then they were liberated for the first time. So, I went up to the fighters and asked them to join, but they wouldn't accept me. They said I was too young—I was very small then—in these two years I've grown up so much. I told them, "When the enemy recaptures this town they will kill me for supporting you, so you have to take me." So, they gave in. I tried to make my family understand why I wanted to be a fighter.

I went to Wolqait for three months to be trained. Then I did a political course for seven months, so it was nearly a year altogether. I was very happy. There was a lot of education for me. I was dark before and became clear, a free person. I had an idea of everything. I was free to be a soldier. Before, I had never seen a woman fighter. I was completely changed to an independent person. In previous times, we women were oppressed and no one believed we could do what men do. When I am fighting with my comrades I feel very special.

Before our training, they took our personal details and recorded my father's connection with medicine. When we finished our course, there was a demand from the medical department, so I was assigned to them and I trained as a barefoot doctor for a further three months. There were thousands of wounded prisoners of war and as a part of our training and as part of our service all of our batch worked in the POW center. The prisoners were our enemies, yet, when we treated them they didn't feel like our enemies at all. That was new for me. I never thought I'd have that feeling.

When there was continuous fighting on the front in Wello, I was assigned to this fighters' hospital in Woldia. In February, a year ago the Dergue was trying to push us out of Woldia. There were many many wounded fighters. Then, there was one team assigned to the Gondar front and I was with that team. In every regiment or force there are special fighter assistants to transport the wounded immediately from the field of battle and take them to the surgical team, about an hour behind the front line. Its location depends on local conditions like bombardment or topography. Then, another team takes them from the surgical team back to the hospital. From Debre Tabor's capture till now I was with the Corps surgical team and particularly involved with transporting the wounded from the frontline back to the hospital and seeing to all their needs on the way, giving injections, dressings, tablets prescribed by the nurse.

Now, I'll be working in the surgical department, doing things like patient care, dressing wounds, nursing, generally helping. If I get an opportunity for further training I'd like to be a lab technician.[3]

In one house, there are two operating theaters. Both rooms are small, constrained by the proportions of the average dwelling. One is for major surgery, and in the circumstances is extraordinarily professional and hygienic. The walls are lined with clean sheeting and on a length of linoleum unrolled on the floor stand the (folding) operating table, the theater lights and anesthetic equipment. The second theater, for minor operations, is just a normal scruffy room, although swept and tidy, of course. This one is occupied by a fighters' surgical team in the early stages of preparing for an operation. On the operating table, a wounded fighter is receiving blood before a leg amputation. A bullet wound in the thigh has cut the arteries. Sometimes, minor arteries take over the job of circulation, Gebre Livanos explains, so, hoping to save the leg, they have delayed operating. This time it hasn't paid off. The leg has turned gangrenous.

Intellectual knowledge of battlefield casualties is not at all the same as confronting, in real life, a man awaiting amputation. No wonder he looks glum. I feel glum too, complicated by a sense of self-indulgence, as I am not the one lying on the bed. A woman surgeon, called Gurges, is overseeing the transfusion and she will later be carrying out the operation. The members of the team, as well as Gebre Livanos and Aklilu, are cheery and chatting all around the patient. Perhaps, it is a deliberate psychological technique—certainly a studied gloom would not be helpful. No one moderates his voice if someone is sleeping here, so I wouldn't be surprised if it's the same if a person is critically ill. Maybe, if that is the cultural habit, you don't need peace and quiet, even if you're dying. Maybe, visited by the spectral quiet and reverence accorded such situations in the West, an Ethiopian would be frightened into the next world in one jump. Maybe this poor guy on the bed has seen such terrible things on the field of battle that he is grateful to be alive with or without a leg. But, I remember when I had malaria the general level of noise in the Green Hotel, especially strident cassettes played at top volume, bit into my brain more than the bugs and made me pray for an electricity cut.

Here in the field hospital, this little room resonates with the loud voices of fighters and the high chirps of the children they seem to be surrounded by these days. Gurges, an old friend of Aklilu's, is talking about this case to him in Tigrinya, to me in English.

"When will he be transferred to the major operating theater?" I ask

Everyone laughs.

"Oh no, he will stay here," says Aklilu. "An amputation is not a "major" operation. Major means an abdominal wound—something like that."

Aklilu seems so at home here. For ten years he was first a medical worker, then a field surgeon, and finally overall head of the Health Department. Gebre Livanos is the chief surgeon as Saba was in Gondar. All these field surgeons have been trained up on the spot over the last sixteen years from the most promising personnel available. Trainees begin as barefoot doctors (as Aklilu did) and then their training is gradually intensified to include anatomy and physiology and the practical skills of battlefield surgery.

Soon after breakfast the next morning, Gurges turns up at the hotel with another woman fighter in the medical corps, Roman. She is on her way to another field hospital between here and Woldia to teach a refresher course to nurses. When our landcruiser is on the road again, we will give her a lift. The young fighter I saw yesterday, they tell me, has had a successful amputation (a strange concept) and is recovering well. They spend the morning with me and take me back to Gurges's house for lunch. It always touches me that, wherever I go, women assume that I need the company of women and search me out to carry me off somewhere. It is not an idea we are used to articulating in the West, but I find it is true and I always come back feeling refreshed. Gurges and her husband, Kasai, a doctor who teaches medicine, are renting a room from a peasant family. In the next room, the mother of the house is weaving strands of dried grasses into a basket. I go to greet her and watch for a while, unable to communicate in Amharic and making do with nods and smiles, until the smell of roasting coffee summons me back to the others. To go with the coffee, Gurges has made delicious little cakes of fried dough with a filling of peppery lentils; then she serves *injera* with *ergo* or curds. Gurges is in the early stages of a pregnancy and gets very tired. Later, she comes back to the hotel with me and we share the flearidden bed for a couple of hours' nap.

Aklilu wakes us up at the end of the afternoon. Haile has come back by bus with a battery. The delay was not getting hold of a new battery but in getting back with it. Within half an hour we have said goodbye to Gurges, Roman jumps in with me in the back seat, and at long last we set off in the direction of Woldia.

I wake up, in Woldia, to a morning like a Scottish summer. At this time of year at an altitude of about two thousand meters, it is cool and frequently rainy. The town crouches under steep hillsides furred with bushes and small trees. Until the end of the morning, thick mist swirls halfway up their sides. I keep confusing intermittent thunder with distant artillery fire or approaching MiGs. I don't take my sweater off all day.

It is strange to be back here after weeks spent in the heightened atmosphere and constant insecurity of Bahr-Dar and Gondar. It seems so peaceful. While messages are going to and fro to set up my land reform program, I pay a visit to the site of a recent MiG bombing raid, a food relief depot on the edge of the town where many of the poor were killed as they patiently queued for their ration. Woldia still seems peaceful. Yet, nearly every day MiGs rumble in the sky like distant thunder. On the day of the celebrations to mark the completion of the new land reform, the start of the ceremony is repeatedly delayed until late in the afternoon and even then the peasants massing in the arena to watch the plays and listen to the speeches keep glancing nervously at the sky as if expecting a MiG to sweep down on them out of the blue haze. Yet, Woldia still feels peaceful to me. It is the difference between danger from the air and insecurity on the ground. This feels more like Tigray—the enemy above, but comrades beneath. The EPDM, the Amhara branch of the Front, has been working in the area since 1981 and, even though the Dergue was not expelled until a year ago, the rural peasants have long supported them. In Bahr-Dar and Gondar, on the other hand, we never knew when the anonymous innocent-seeming bystander in the road would turn into a WPE member with a gun.

This is where the people demonstrated democracy by demonstrating against the Front. They stoned the fighters (who retreated to a safe distance) before some of them realized that Dergue troops would have shot them long before. So eighteen months ago the town was neither peaceful nor friendly. In any case, towns always lag behind the countryside in supporting the rebels because the Dergue garrisons, administrators and Party members are concentrated in the towns. The townspeople are not only first in the queue for reprisals if they step out of line, but also for Dergue propaganda against the "bandits."

"When the Dergue was here," a woman called Desta tells me, "he was teaching us the EPRDF were not human beings, that they were cannibals, dirty and ignorant—bandits coming to loot the property of the town. Some believed the propaganda; some didn't know what to think."[4]

The ostensible cause of the demonstration was the circulation by Party members of "information" that all the town property had been taken to Tigray —from the hospitals, the generating station, the schools. Three-quarters of the town turned out on the streets in militant mood. The slogans on the banners demanded that Eritrea remain a part of Ethiopia and that looted property be restored. Ma'aza, who ironically is now an administrator in the new elected council or *shengo,* was one of them.

"The demonstrators beat and kicked the fighters and even destroyed one of their cars with stones. They threw stones at the fighters—but the fighters did nothing. This kind of experience is unknown in Ethiopian history. No demonstration was possible under the Dergue and any attempt would have been suppressed by the police. So, the people were astonished and thought this must be democracy."

The fighters suggested that the people elect a committee to investigate the allegations of looting. "The committee went to the specified places," says Desta, who is vice-head of the Women's Association, "and found that the property had not been looted at all, so the people called a meeting and took self-criticism. 'The demonstration we had was based on false information,' they said, and they exposed the agitation of the feudals and of the WPE."

The following day, the people held another demonstration in support of the Front.

Woldia seems a thriving town, if numbers on the streets at any one time are anything to go by. Its wide main street, lined with small hotels, restaurants and bars, is always crowded with pedestrians, peasants laden with bundles, donkeys laden with firewood, merchants' trucks and carts drawn by skeletal horses with flanks rubbed by harnesses into open, fly-blown wounds. Goats and sheep nibble in corners at any time of day, and in the morning and evening, oxen and cows amble through the streets with their minders in tow.

Three times a day, we push through the crowd to find a meal in some little restaurant and in between we make our way through the maze of muddy back lanes to hear the views of different groups of men and women about the time under the Dergue, the coming of the Front and the founding of the first democratic *shengo*.

"But, there was an elected *shengo* here under the Dergue, wasn't there? What is the difference between that and this one under the Front?"

I am talking to Admassu, a member of the present *shengo* and a judge.[5]

"Under the Dergue," he replies, "the representatives were only nominally elected. The WPE decided who would be nominated. The people didn't oppose him because of the consequences. In some cases, we were told to elect even a person we had never seen before. We were told to elect a person with a certain emblem. There were electoral boxes and we were told to put a card in a certain box."

I hear similar tales of corruption everywhere. The old beneficiaries of Haile Selassie's regime had been displaced by a new class of beneficiaries, the Party members of the Dergue. Their catalog of crimes are repeated endlessly—the selling of relief food, the escalation of bribery to facilitate the most routine activity, even the number of deaths and aborted babies from forcing pregnant women and the old to work for relief food in planting trees and building roads. Can all this be true? About bribery, I am given details of sums involved and the circumstances. The worst offenses and the most deeply felt concern rights to land.

So a few days later, we drive out into the countryside to find out from the peasants in the countryside about land. I have already attended the completed land reform celebrations with thousands of jubilant landholders at the arena at one end of town. I have witnessed their enthusiasm for a grisly burning of Mengistu in effigy. I have talked to people in Woldia about the differences between Mengistu's land reform in the late seventies and the present one. I already know that the Front's policies for setting up democratic councils, which would themselves be responsible for dividing the land according to democratic criteria, have gained them widespread support. But, I feel a need to see for myself this *land* they toss about in conversation. I want to pace about on it, to understand through my own eyes the difference between fertile land and medium land, to feel with my own feet the stony dust of the lowest category of *poor soil.*

We end up in a rural *kebelle* called Mahal Macherey 025. It is a hot dry day, although recent rain has softened the ground enough for plowing to begin. The dry gold of the fields is here and there interrupted by black rectangles of newly turned soil and, although we have made an early start, farmers are there before us, already guiding their slow-paced oxen back and forth. As we climb out of the landcruiser, we can see a plow team at work several fields away. Yet, the crack of the whip can be clearly heard over the quiet air, even its hum as he whirls it over his head and the curious warbling whistles that highland plowmen use to their oxen.

Four men are waiting to meet us.[6] They have all been elected by the local community to take particular responsibility for implementing land distribution. The Chairman of the Peasants' Association is an elderly man of sixty-three, his face worn by work and sun, but of the others, the Association Secretary, the Chairman of the *shengo* and the head of the Land Redistribution Committee, the oldest is only thirty-six. First of all, we sit round a table in the *shengo* building for some questions and answers. These men too want to tell me about the time under the Dergue and the differences between then and the present situation. They use the personal experiences of themselves and their neighbors as examples. Mengesha, now thirty, expresses himself vividly on forced conscription. When he was only a teenager, he ran away to live in the bush to avoid military service. When the authorities caught and imprisoned him, he tried to avoid it again by signing up for one of the new collective farms.

"That was even worse. When I joined the collective, all the people were mixed up together with their oxen and their land. That was the worst tentacle. After six months in the association, I escaped and came here. When I went to drink *talla* in the town they grabbed me anyway, so I became a soldier."

He was posted to Tigray. I have collected so many accounts from the Tigrayan side about Dergue garrisons, especially in Shire, and especially in Shire about the Battle of Endeselassie in 1988, which was a turning point of the civil war. Now Mengesha, who resisted conscription so hard, tells what it felt like from the other side.

"When the 17th division was destroyed in 1988, in Shire, I was wounded in the battle and I managed to escape to Tekezze—losing blood, walking to Gondar. We were retreating through Tekezze, but there were five or six ambushes and finally only two cars got through over the border. Very few officers and soldiers managed to escape and everything was captured. The general managed to escape to Gondar with two cars. I started walking on foot, but after five days I was picked up and taken to Gondar, where I stayed in the hospital for my wound. Then, they referred me to Addis. In Addis, I complained on the grounds of health and I got out of the army."

The main emphasis of his companions is on the Dergue resettlement policy, by which farmers were forced off their land to make way for cooperatives and into "villagized" government settlements. About this, the peasants are voluble and bitter. Wele, the old man, was taken by force with his seven children to Wellega.

"My land was taken for collectivization. Those who were farming my land were given means of production and fertilizers. They took my land and my plants. Four of my neighbors died in Wellega. After five years, my oldest daughter came from Addis to Wellega and brought me back to my village. But, I was accused of being an outlaw. I was not allowed to live in this village. So, I lived in Woldia, homeless and without the means of life with seven of my sons and daughters for a year."

"How did you get your land back?"

"The EPRDF arrived in October. I went to see the fighters. 'Fighters! Fighters! Where is the responsible fighter?' I told him my story. He said, 'Where is your village?' I showed him and he said, 'Go, stay in your village. Make a shelter and stay there—your house will be returned.'"

I was surprised. I had assumed that the resettlement policy was largely a weapon of war to demoralize Tigrayan dissidents; I had not realized the extent to which it had also been applied south of Tigray among the Amhara people, assumed to be the heartland of support for an Amhara-dominated government. It confirmed the Front's contention that a new ruling class had taken the place of the old Imperial one, but that the peasants everywhere were the losing class. Wele Yomar, head of the Peasants' Association, summed it up.

"The Dergue had already kicked out the bureaucrats and feudals. That's true. He nationalized the land. But, the best houses in the village were not for us still. New bureaucrats were set up. The people were forced to settle in far places or in one place like a concentration camp. We suffered diseases, poverty. The crops were taken. These buildings were grain stores. We produced the grain but they took the produce. A new class took the place of the old and still the peasants had nothing. Some went to Safawa, in the Sudan, and others to these 'villages,' destroying our beautiful houses with axes."

They were eloquent on the hated Grain Production and Marketing Corporation set up by the Dergue to buy quotas from the peasants, cheaply, which were then sold at a high price. Thirteen months ago the Dergue, faced with rebellions in almost every part of Ethiopia, abolished the organization —but too late to resuscitate opinion or popularity.

"How do you know the EPRDF won't let you down in the same way?"

"The fighters teach us our rights," Mengesha joined in, "and we also tell them our problems under Haile Selassie and the junta. We tell them we want peace, we want land. They tell us, they say they are also fighting for these things. This is a promise—we still haven't seen the results, but we already have the land, so we are hoping we will get the produce of our labor. It's a promise."

They clearly believe the promise will be kept, not least because, in typical Front fashion, the fighters' role has been restricted to advice and to overseeing a process in which villagers themselves have taken the measurements and made the decisions, all of which have been amended and ratified by an assembly of the people. The size and type of land shares are specific to each area, according to the soil standard, topography and size of population, but here, as elsewhere, there are common elements. Provision has been made for a common cattle pasture, for roads and paths, and for a meeting-place for villagers; felling of trees is forbidden on certain hillsides to allow regeneration of forest cover. Differences to be taken into account are not only those of fertility, but of distance. The anomaly in this district is that more of the available land is near the village than at a distance. Of the far land, there is only fertile or poor and therefore, by agreement, those who farm poor land have twice the share of those who have fertile plots.

They give me precise figures of the agreed numbers of square meters for an individual, for a married couple, and for numbers of children of both near and distant land and the dates of the preparatory work, the congress of the people, and the beginning and end of actual land distribution. The only real problem is the lack of a natural spring. There are several artesian wells, but during the Dergue, thieves stole the generator, which worked the water pump of the village well. Although fighters tracked it down and restored it to the village, it is still awaiting repair. This conversation gives an insight into the undercurrents of village politics. Spare parts have to be purchased for the repair of the generator.

"There is now a problem of money, until time passes and we get the fruits of the new system," says Yassin, the head of the land distribution committee.

He is saying they have no money until the first post land-distribution harvest is sold.

"Spare parts are a problem," he goes on, "the biggest problem in this *kebelle.* We want know-how from the EPRDF. There are good wells but they need something more to make them work."

By "know-how" he means cash assistance towards spare parts. When I question one of the local fighters, however, the story is slightly different.

"We believe the people have to learn how to solve these problems for themselves. We think they could find the resources for the spare parts if they really wanted to, but they prefer to wait."

"How far do they have to walk to find water?"

"About three hours each way."

"And of course it is the women who fetch the water and the men who decide not to repair the generator."

He smiles.

"Exactly."

Yes, it would be a different story if the men had to walk three hours from a distant spring with a heavy water jar on their backs.

We spend a pleasant couple of hours walking over the fields, pacing out the plots of individual villagers and inspecting the non-functioning wells. It is now the hottest time of the day and they invite us into a shady hut for a gourd of *talla,* as the local beer is called in Amharic. One or two other villagers join us. As gourds are emptied, they are refilled by Wele's wife. She hovers discreetly in the background just as she hovered, unmentioned and silent, in the margins of her husband's story of exile in Wellega. He said so often *I was taken by force* and *I went there with my sons and daughters* that I had assumed his wife was dead. When I asked him, he looked surprised. "Oh no, my wife was with me," he said.

This whole area is boiling with animosity against the government. Perhaps it is true of the whole country, but I can only speak of where I have been. The contact here in Wello between the people and the Dergue, their experience of injustice and corruption, has been so direct compared with the people in Tigray where the hegemony of the Front, at least in the countryside, has long broken the cycle of oppression except from the air. Here, the time of slow-burn is over. The lid is off. The freedom to speak, at last, has released a torrent of hatred.

It is the same story wherever I go, but nowhere is it more evident than in Mersa. Yet, it would be easy to miss it, if you were passing through, if you did not give time to questions, to talk. On the surface, people are quiet. The unruffled bustle of the town has not changed. People go about their business as they must have done under the Emperor, under the Dergue. Now, it is the time of the Front. I can imagine a casual visitor or a tourist, if such exotic creatures existed at this time, thinking with a touch of complacent sophistication, "What difference does it make—to them? Life goes on! The struggle for survival!" and so on and so forth. They would be wrong.

Yet, the men and women who talk to me, never shout or scream, rail or lament. They talk in low voices with a kind of deadly determination, which is more chilling than clamor. Their words look more sensational written down than they ever sound to the ear.

"For the last fifteen years, this enemy has eaten our flesh and drunk our blood," Negusse Mekonnen says quietly.

Mohammed Said sees the current slaughter on the battlefield as a continuation of the earlier slaughter of young people in the Red Terror.

"In our tradition, if you avenge, you are honored," he says. "If you don't, if someone kills your brother, it is a shame if you take no action. *Demelash* is an avenger. The EPRDF is our avenger. So, we have decided to fight."

Is it significant, is it mere chance, or is it expediency that every Amhara peasant I have spoken to blames the Dergue, not the EPRDF, for Amhara deaths in the war?

Mersa is a small town not very far from Woldia. It was the site of a terrible atrocity by the retreating Dergue forces as the Front's fighters closed on them a year ago. They retreated to a safe distance and then they turned their heavy BM rocket launchers onto the defenseless town.

We drove here lightheartedly in daylight, even though overflying aircraft delayed our departure.

"They are not interested in us," Aklilu said confidently. "They are on their way to more strategic areas."

I was glad of an opportunity to see more of the local countryside. Wello is also a drought-prone area, but to me it couldn't look more different from the brown stony landscapes I have been used to in Tigray. It is the time of the small rains here, of course, but nevertheless, it seemed green and fertile compared to further north. The villages we passed through on the way here were green not only with the usual dusty eucalyptus trees, but with sugar cane, banana trees, and other crops that won't grow in more arid lands. Aklilu has been longing to come to Mersa. I suspect it was the prospect of this trip that persuaded him to delay returning to Hagere Salam.

"Mersa has been a paradise for the Dergue," he said. "It is famous for its fruits, for its coffee. It is famous for its juices."

Certainly, as we approached, the landscape took on the look of a garden. Where the road curved or narrowed to cross a bridge, bands of youths were waiting to sell us lengths of sugar cane and bunches of bananas, as well as the usual cigarettes and chewing gum. Nevertheless, the town looked pretty much like other towns as we drove through it—a wide dusty crowded main street dividing into two halves a huddle of dwellings in a maze of lanes. It was getting hotter as the sun climbed the sky and a brief stop at a bar for a glass of rosy papaya juice thick enough to eat with a spoon convinced me that Mersa was everything it was cracked up to be.

Our destination was a peasants' meeting on the edge of town. The hall, in a grove of eucalyptus, was packed with about three hundred men and women representatives from surrounding districts, who had come in answer to the Front's call to arms. As we went in, two fighters seated at a table on the stage were giving a briefing on the recent campaign in Gojjam and Gondar and the latest situation further south at the new front in Wellega. It was so dark after the brightness outside that it took me a minute of two to realize we were creating such a stir, such a diversion from the business of the meeting, that we felt bound to go out again.

And here, we are waiting in the shade outside until the next break. I am filling in the time as usual by writing my diary, while restless Aklilu cruises the compound, talking to peasants taking time out from the discussions in the hall.

The catalog of resentments I hear when peasants eventually come to talk to me in the break are no different from elsewhere: deprivation of land, forced villagization, forced recruitment into the army, forced resettlement.[7]

Everywhere, the bitterness of compulsion, the reprisals, and recriminations for those who refuse to comply quietly.

"They took us to a strange far place," an older woman called Zemzem Nuriya tells me. "It was terrible how we survived, just roasting beans. They presented these places as paradise, but when we went, it was just us and we were told to build everything ourselves. They took away the strong ones. Some of us escaped to the Sudan; many died on the way and then, over a year ago, the EPRDF brought us back to Maichew, in southern Tigray. We couldn't come back here until it was liberated. That's why we have bitter hatred for the enemy."

"I escaped and came back here," Admassu adds, "but the government declared we were not Ethiopian and that our neighbors could not give us fire. We were told if we wanted to eat, we had to go back. We were forbidden to marry the villagers. They were forbidden to attend our funerals. We had no rights. They tried to isolate us and force us to return to those areas. We were the most hated and isolated in our village."

Many people I talk to, not just those attending this meeting, inveigh against forced recruitment into the Dergue army, although they are encouraging their children or intending themselves to join the Front's forces. They talk in terms of protecting and maintaining the power they have gained, which, when I ask them, they define as land and the *shengo.* Tefera Kebede has come to Mersa to sign up as a fighter:

"We have our land. We established our *shengo.* Democracy is for everyone. We have the power. We are convinced that we are the beneficiaries of this revolution. That's why I am here. We must fight to get rid of this government once and for all."

There is a Muslim merchant, in the town, who played an important role during the Dergue bombardment. Aklilu tracks him down, but he refuses to talk to me. I don't know what, if any, pressure is applied—I never offer money inducements—but, just as we are about to leave, a message arrives that he has changed his mind. Nevertheless, when we meet, in the back room of a little cafe, his manner is hostile.

"Why can't they share the information, these journalists?" he says to Aklilu, ignoring me completely, "Why can't they share the information I've given already? I don't want to talk to them!"

His eyes are hidden behind sunglasses. He has a curious expressionless face, as if carved from polished wood, with high cheekbones. Yet, once he begins to speak, he is not only articulate and concise, but impassioned. He not only talks about the bombardments, but, as so many others have done, he sets them in a context of a range of Dergue misdeeds and gives precise figures (which I have omitted here) of comparative taxation under Haile Selassie and the Dergue.

The Testimony of Sheikh Hassen Ali

You can't finish describing the crimes of this junta in a short discussion. It's too big, it's too wide. But, in a few words, the people were forced to pay different kinds of taxation and fees. The working community was giving everything to officials, different tithes with different names, the Motherland Call, the Campaigns. The second point was that the peasants produced for a fixed price. If they didn't have enough they had to buy more in the market to make up the quota and give it for nothing. Conscription by force was done with great brutality. Our sons were taken by force. If they ran away, the father and mother would be imprisoned. The whole story was of imprisonment and punishment.

The atrocities of this government is not this only. One of its features, one of the crimes committed against this people, is resettlement. People who had food to eat, oxen for plowing, were forced to go to a place they didn't know. It was a way of punishment if there was a dispute against an official. Thousands were taken from this area, Wello; thousands were eaten by wild animals. It would be more reasonable if they had nothing to eat and no property, but why were those people forced against their interest and their will?

In different villages around ... I'll give one example from around Wichale —one village was ordered to dismantle the next village, and that one a third village, and so on. Then, they were taken to a valley and ordered to build a small hut near a river. Except for a few, one day most of the people were taken by the flood and drowned. This everyone knows. There is a rift valley where there are bad floods—in Chefa in Wello. More than two thousand peasants were swept away.

The traders, because of the variety of taxes, preferred dying to living. You just worked to give the money. The difference from Haile Selassie's time is like the difference between the sky and the earth. Now, Ethiopians are in prison, the whole nation under this government, and every day taxation multiplies and takes new forms. The people of Mersa were the slaves of the government. They gave everything they had. The officials liked Mersa. It was their heaven.

On January 5th 1990, a Sunday night, the officers, administrators and officials retreated from Woldia. They came here with more than two hundred vehicles, BM heavy artillery, tanks, and thousands of soldiers.

"What happened?" we asked.

"Nothing. Everything is fine."

Then they left for Dessie.

The next morning fighters from the EPRDF arrived. We received them warmly. The Dergue had left Mersa on its own and we had to receive the newcomers. Why should we fight them? The Dergue had taken himself off and left us alone. The people of Woldia demonstrated against the EPRDF and there were a few people who wanted to mobilize the people of Mersa to do a demonstration here, but we refused.

"What have the EPRDF done against Mersa? So, why should we demonstrate against them?"

So we absolutely refused.

The people of Mersa have done nothing, nothing against the state to be sentenced to such a bombardment. The Dergue even left of their own will. In my opinion, the reasons for the bombardment of Mersa were three. First, we received the fighters warmly; second, because we didn't do the same demonstration as in Woldia; third, because the Dergue doesn't care about the people and so could completely destroy the town, like a donkey. If they can't have it, then this "paradise" must be destroyed.

It was the end of January. They fired a multiple rocket launcher from Wichale and attacked us early in the morning when the people were still asleep. They attacked in three directions, the west, the east, and the center of the town. More than thirty-five houses were completely destroyed, not burned; four houses were burned to ashes. More than thirty-two people were killed. I was a member of security, elected under the EPRDF transitional administration, so I was carrying the wounded to the clinic—thirty-three wounded. Ten cattle were killed. The shells were continuous and after eleven a.m., the people of Mersa scattered out of the town—mothers with some children in one direction, fathers in another, other children elsewhere. It was total chaos. They ran to the west to nearby villages. No one knew where the mothers, fathers, and children were. In a matter of hours this became a ghost town. Nobody was left. It was completely deserted. No one could control anything—just fled to save their lives, people not looking for husbands, not looking for sons, or taking property. It continued until five p.m. Only after three days did mothers meet their children. Only then could families be reunited. There were a few pregnant women who died in the area they fled to. Better not to speak of those things—it is very upsetting.

After five or six hours, I was all alone in the town. All the houses were open for looting and robbery, but there were no looters. I was the only person left. Then, after five or six hours, I got a few men together and we collected all the bits of bodies in sacks and buried five or six at a time in graves we dug. You cannot bear to think of it—all these bodies just cut to pieces. Very tragic. The whole town, all the houses were open. No one took food, clothing, anything, with them. The town was completely changed.

For three or four days, five days, two weeks, everyone tried to find out what was happening in order to come back.

When this story started to leak out, I couldn't eat. I became very nervous. When did such a government commit such crimes, like bandits? I have never seen a government commit such genocidal crimes against its people. I was protecting the bodies against dogs until they were buried. I feel upset when people ask me about it—everything comes back and it is as if I am experiencing it all over again. I can't imagine a state could finish off his own people who never committed anything bad against it—old men, children, and finishing them with missiles. What crime had they committed? In my life, I can never forget this distress.

The reason I refuse when journalists come to speak to me is I feel sick and too upset. I feel very bad. I feel shocked, nervous, and emotional. It's not because I don't want to speak about this atrocity.[8]

Sheikh Hassen gets upset. I get upset. Aklilu gets upset. If Aklilu, with all the bitterness he has known, all the sights he has seen, has not managed to grow a thicker skin, then what hope is there for me?

We drive back to Woldia in silence. The next morning we set off for the long trek northwards. Back to Tigray.

21

Conversations with Leaders

We have come to the last chapter of my last expedition before the end of the war.

It is already April. The war is nearly over. The pace is quickening. I can feel it in the air. I catch it lightly in exchanges overheard in the street. In Alamata, in Korem, in Maichew, in Mekelle. It is heavy, obvious, in the intensity with which fighters listen to the radio.

The campaign for the province of Wellega is over. The Front's forces are fast closing in on Addis Ababa from the north and west. Industrial unrest has broken out in Addis Ababa, where most industry is concentrated. There are sporadic strikes. The situation is beginning to resemble the last months of Haile Selassie's reign, when his overthrow was preceded by instability and unrest. Is this coincidental? I am convinced they could finish it quickly if they wished, but military goals are not the only priorities. I wonder what the strategies are for peaceful takeover, for reassuring international opinion, for political alliances, for stabilizing the country after the economic destruction of the last sixteen years. That is what I am going to Hagere Salam to find out.

I started off this expedition by talking to the leadership in the caves of Hagere Salam and it looks as if that is how I shall end it. After that, the long homeward trek to the Sudanese border. In their different ways, Meles and Tamrat and Kuma, in the conversations that follow, accumulate into a manual of revolution the wisdom and experience of two decades of struggle, the key to one of the very few successful revolutions the world had known.

We pause in Mekelle long enough for Aklilu to send a message to Hagere Salam to say we are back. We only have to wait a day for the reply, which instructs us to come at once, and we leave at eight the next morning. It is only sixty or seventy kilometers, but it takes three hours because of the state of the road.

As before, I am shown to a simple room in the cave for guests and spend the afternoon outside on the cliff path, writing. There is no one about. The only sound is birds. The stillness of the caves, their lofty situation and the sense of space, with the landscape stretching out and below me until the far haze melts into the huge bowl of sky, make all tensions fall away and leave the mind quiet. Meles comes at the end of the afternoon. He shows none of the stresses of responsibility to be expected at this final stage of struggle and appears as relaxed and peaceful as the landscape.[1]

For today's discussion I have two contrary drives. There are important gaps I need to fill about earlier phases of the revolution, gaps shown up by all the work I have done since we last met. On the other hand, my recent experiences further south have thrown up questions about future strategies for ending the war and winning the peace. It doesn't matter, Meles says. If there is too much to talk about this evening, he will make some time before I leave. So, although we start off by chatting about my experiences at the front in Bahr-Dar and Gondar (he wants to know what I have seen, how I reacted, especially what impression I formed of the support or hostility of local people) we decide to leave the future until later and adopt a chronological solution by going back to the early years of the struggle.

Sixteen years have passed since the first fighters went to Dedebit with heroic ideas of changing the world. It has been a long process. So much has changed on the way. They started out as youthful idealists inspired, on the one hand, by the radical aspirations to democracy and equality of the Ethiopian student movement in the sixties and seventies and, on the other, by the situation in Tigray itself, where poverty and maladministration were raising the bitterness of the peasantry to new levels. But, this was no different from the aspirations of failed revolutionaries in many parts of the world. I need to sharpen my understanding of the evolution of ideas, which has underpinned the growth of the organization to its present powerful position. Its strength is based on the support of the peasants and therefore I always pay particular attention to what Meles has to say about the peasants. I am back to the same question. How did these relatively privileged individuals develop the rare ability to communicate across cultural and class barriers and first win, and then retain, the respect of this apparently subjected, but often intransigent, majority? Somewhere, sometime, idealistic theory was transformed into effective practice. It is on this crack, in this space between theory and practice, that I want to press my first questions.

Meles is thoughtful, remembering. He is also generous with his time. He goes back to the first years of the revolution, sixteen years ago. Their ideas and ideals, he says, were influenced by Maoism and with the idea that heroic individuals like Che Guevara could transform society, that they could change everything through intensive political work as in China.

"Those idealist approaches were never to be fully realized. We changed all that."

"Why? How were they inadequate?"

"The first thing the intellectual has to learn is that even the best ideas are never fully correct. Once you start talking to the peasants about their problems and how to change them, you begin to learn that the brain of the people has some fundamentally correct and wise and courageous ideas in it. You begin to learn to appreciate not only their hardships but their resilience and their desire for change and improvement."

He speaks slowly, pausing sometimes to gaze beyond me into his thoughts.

"To see us as givers in the revolution is to have a totally false picture. We received training from them in how to survive in the forest, which wild plants are edible and useful and which are not. They showed us how to hunt meat, how to find cool water, how to identify the different animals—how to identify a cheetah from the sound it makes on the dry grass at night, because if you pull a gun on a cheetah it will spring, but if you light a flame it will go away."

He describes some of their experiences in the first year, including his own near death from typhoid.

"In our country, there is a tremendous feeling of neglect and contempt for the peasants and workers. It sometimes makes me mad. Education is also responsible. They think the mind is a blank until it is overlaid by education. The peasants do have undoubted ignorance in many respects and this is all the intellectuals see, not the wisdom that comes from experience, from life itself. We expected from the very beginning the peasants' will to fight and change their lot, which reinforced our respect for them. This was the first major influence."

"A successful outcome must have seemed so remote. How did you persuade them to join a long struggle?"

"We came to understand very fast that if you have to remold their opinions, you have to start from where they are. You have to sharpen and elaborate the instincts for freedom they already have. If you try to instil new theories you don't proceed far. You must start and widen and deepen what they already have and in the process the two things get fused and changed at the same time. Their opinions become more developed and the theories become green and lively. We came to realize you can only put basic targets in theory. The rest has to be filled in by the experience of the peasants through practice."

I recall all my conversations with peasants in Agame and more recently in Wello about land reform, how the Front had set the general targets for dividing the land, but the people had elected committees of those they trusted to work out the details. Hiwot Ayele, the chair of Mekelle Women's Asociation, told me about the struggle women had during the formation of the *baito* to argue their case for women's rights. The Front had inspired them with aims, but they had to fight for their rights themselves.

"They must be given the chance to make mistakes and learn from them," Meles is saying. "It must not be the relationship of a child with his guardian, but of equals, even though some might be more enlightened. The group as a whole, must benefit so you share the privileges of education and enlightenment, therefore you have to take your time, not rush things. You have to convince the people through practice that this is in their interest. It never turns out that you have all the answers. The original approach is never all the proper one, sometimes only the core of it remains. It will have been transformed and enriched and developed in the process."

I go on running through my memory practical examples of the general propositions he is making about the need to reconcile leadership and guidance with a political philosophy, which allows people the freedom to make mistakes and learn from them. In both Debre Tabor and Mekelle, they had ignored the Front's advice and elected to the *baito* "undemocratic elements" like WPE members or remnants of the old feudal landowning class, only to have to replace them later when they were revealed as implacably opposed to land reform.

But, Meles is also referring to the leadership, to the Front also making mistakes.

"We had to develop our concepts again in this process, a continuous process of learning and relearning."

He gives two examples. First, the early fighters lacked consistency on the national question and "slipped into narrow nationalism." This was a relatively short phase. I reflect that it can be a fine line between narrow nationalism and recognizing that the nationality issue in Ethiopia is a primary question. It has never ceased to confuse international commentators who fail to see the difference between self-determination and independence and have continued to brand the Front as "secessionist" years after they abandoned that position. Their more subtle line, since then, has been to espouse a right to self-determination "up to and including secession" for all the nationalities in Ethiopia, in other words a multi-nationality state whose unity is voluntary and based on mutual respect, but whose common interests bind them together.

Meles's second example refers to a loss of direction in the mid-eighties. The Front had grown so fast in terms of numbers that it outgrew the early ideas and strategies and a period of stagnation set in. They had developed a huge army, for which small mobile units fighting an essentially guerrilla war were no longer appropriate. There were few victories against the sophisticated mechanized army of the Dergue and the effort to survive the great famine after 1984 put social and political developments on hold.

"How did you recover?"

"There were some fierce debates in the organization—around 1984 to 1985. The overwhelming majority accepted that we had not succeeded in keeping up with the situation, projecting possible events in the future and preparing ourselves for them. We had to reorganize, redirect everything, and that took time and engagements were very minimal because we were concentrating on internal reorganization and redirection. At that time, there were a lot of discussions, when a thousand or more delegates would discuss things for more than a month. We retrained our army. We raised our experience into clearly-formulated theoretical approaches and then tried to explain this down to the village level. You can describe that period as a period of discussions, about everything. These discussions took a long time, but when they materialized, the change was so sudden that many people couldn't see what had changed."

"So what were these new directions?"

"In terms of a political philosophy, for example, letting the people learn from their experience and what this means for an organization that tries to lead the people. It changed from condition to condition. If it was the *baitos*, it was focusing on some of the problems of the *baitos*. After these changes, we pushed the decision-making levels downwards as much as possible to the hamlet level. Things were developing in a direction that would alienate people who could not travel for four days to county *(wereda)* meetings. These were mainly women and also people who were not, in a sense, professionally engaged in a political process."

"So the energy began to be at the bottom?"

"Yes."

The new strategies sought to democratize not only decision-making, but to involve the peasants in every area of struggle. The turning-point, militarily, was the battle of Shire in February 1989. A few weeks afterwards—that year before last which now seems so much longer ago—Meles had explained the tactics to me how they had pierced deep into the Dergue regular army to dismantle the command and control structures, scattering the mass of the soldiers to be mopped up by local militia and women.

"They were ordinary unarmed people, including unarmed women. It was truly a people's war and it had a lasting impact on everybody including the regular army. After that, the army felt incapacitated if it didn't have this kind of backing."

"Yes, I've talked to Aregash as well about your awareness of the dangers of the army becoming separated as an elite group from the people."

"Yes, there's more than just a single lesson to be learned from one particular experience. It may have many ramifications. That experience gave many lessons to many different sectors of the people organized in the armed struggle. To the regular army, it showed it its proper place—that it's not decisive in the armed struggle. It's only an element of the people, armed in a certain way, organized in a certain way, but nonetheless a part of the overall strength of the fighting people. It had a very important lesson for the regular army. It had important lessons for everybody in different ways."

He comes back again and again to process, but any old process will not do. The task of the leaders is to direct the political struggle by setting guidelines:

"You have a target in the sense of certain conclusions that you want to pass to someone or some sector; then you devise a proper tactic for how you want the people to learn a proper conclusion through their practice. In the process you usually develop the conclusion itself. It never turns out to be fully correct; the practice itself modifies and enriches it. At the same time, you get across your conclusion faster and the whole struggle is accelerated without leaving the masses way behind or leaving the leading organization way ahead."

"So, each time you put this tactic into practice again it is further modified, so that it's a constantly evolving process."

"And a constantly improving process," adds Meles.

We turn away from the political philosophies of the past to the difficulties ahead. I can see that in the liberated areas, where they have had years to perfect their methods of working with the people, they have been able to create strong support. But, how can they put these methods into practice in the newly-liberated areas and in the west and south of the country, especially at the speed they are going?

Meles acknowledges there may be problems, but is on the whole optimistic. He outlines two stages. The first will be the transitional period, a period of stabilization, of defining federal boundaries, working out a new constitution and a new state structure, setting up a new democratic political system. The second stage will begin after the EPRDF has received a mandate in the first democratic elections to put into practice its revolutionary democratic program.

"We hope this will in a very long-drawn out process lead to a more equitable and just social system too, the end of exploitation and so on, but at this moment it is not possible to see how things will work out exactly, except in the sense that it should be very original and that it should be a very protracted process. It should be a democratic transformation. One should not have to abandon democracy in order to achieve socialism, because we are now convinced more than at any time before that if socialism is not democratic then it is not going to be socialism at all."

"I don't think you'd care to be called pragmatic, but if they could hear this conversation in the West they would probably level this accusation at you or even praise you for it."

Meles gazes in his thoughtful way into the middle distance before he answers.

"Pragmatism, as I understand it," he says at last, "is different from what we are trying to achieve. Pragmatism is going after what is achievable, not what is desirable. We are going after the desirable, but to us the desirable is desirable because it is achievable. We have clear, broad targets. We don't have a clear blueprint; the blueprint will have to be worked out in the process. And it will develop. It will not be the same clear picture that you had in the initial period. So, we are trying to marry the desirable with the achievable. To pragmatists, politics is the art of the possible; to us politics is the marriage of the possible with the desirable and I think this is a difference. We are not saying, like the Dergue, Let's see what comes out of it—we have some aims we are trying to achieve. Avoiding imposing these things, either through deceit or through force, is to allow the people to work out their own solutions, at the same times as trying to guide this process towards a certain ultimate goal."

A fighter has come in with a flask of hot water and we pause while he prepares tea for us. Then he continues.

"When you talk about "participatory democracy," it has evolved a lot. Even the initial periods of the *baito* were not as rich as what we are trying to achieve now, so you can only set up participatory democracy as the overall target; not democracy for bigwigs only, but democracy for the housewife, democracy for the shepherd, democracy for the ordinary peasant—involvement of these sectors in deciding their own destiny, starting at the level of issues raised in the village and rising right up to national issues."

The aim, he says, is to get the people permanently involved. It is important not to rush things. Democratic practice takes time. It doesn't work to impose political lines. Ultimately, the criterion is practice and you have to allow ideas to be developed and enriched through practice.

"I think a leader who has made himself indispensable is a leader who has completely failed. This applies equally to any organization. You have to allow practice to determine whether your ideas are correct or not. If they are not correct or they are not fully correct, you have to keep your ideas open to see and to correct these things. This is to us a fundamental change of direction in terms of the ideas we had about socialism, communism, and revolution in our student days."

We have been talking for several hours. Through the open door, it is pitch dark. Beyond the rim of the cliff path there is no flicker of lamps to point up the landscape. In the countryside, if there is no moon, the end of day is the end of light. Our talk has been punctuated by fighters bringing tea, bringing the usual dishes of army camp pasta, more tea. I am suddenly tired; Meles looks fresh and springy and, presumably, will continue with his night's work. I look at my watch and exclaim when I discover it is after midnight. Meles is apologetic. I laugh and say no, it's not that. Only now, it's my birthday. Ethiopians do not share our culture of the birthday, but Meles went to an English school in Addis so we exchange the usual pleasantries and say goodnight.

Back in my room, I stand on the bed to unscrew the light bulb and then collapse. But, a few moments later my slide into oblivion is halted by a light knock at the door. When I open it a young fighter proffers me half a bottle of gin. With it is a note wishing me a happy birthday, adding "I have managed to dig out some gin to cheer up your otherwise dreary birthday—Meles." I am touched. I can also do with some alcohol. I notice the label—England type, Dry Gin, Made in Ethiopia. In my backpack is a small hard Tigrayan lemon and a penknife.

So here I am, quaffing gin and water with a squeeze of lemon, all alone, sitting up in my sleeping bag in my ascetic cell in a cave halfway up a mountain, feeling not at all dreary. Happy Birthday!

Next morning I wake early. Outside on the cliff path, the air is sharp. The sun rises behind the mountain, casting the path and the escarpment into shadow but illuminating the brown plateau and fields below with a warm gold. Behind and above me in the sun on the cliff top, an invisible sentry is singing softly to himself. It is too cold to be still and I walk to the end of the path and ramble about among the rocks until the day warms up.

Most of the day, I sit on the rock outside my cave. Twice, I run inside when I hear the distant rumble of MiGs, but nothing is to be seen in the span of sky visible from this rock face. Young fighters occasionally drop by in ones and twos to have a chat. They are intrigued to have this white visitor and in their innocent and friendly way they want to check me out for themselves. In between, I tell myself I am working when much of the time I am mesmerized by the view. Far below and across the valley more and more fields are changing to a ribbed dark brown as they are plowed. Tiny teams of oxen crawl across the landscape like flies. I can hear with strange clarity all the sounds of the plateau. Its saucer shape must magnify and project them. From distant fields, I can hear the whistles of the farmers to encourage the oxen as they plow. On the far edge of the plateau, before it plunges down to the next level, I can just see tiny specks moving in a brown field, yet from the same direction I can hear loud shouts, the crack of rock hitting rock, the clang of pick and shovel, as if a hundred yards away. A village group must be terracing the hillside. Below me, a huge bird of prey, a buzzard or an eagle, is sweeping around in great effortless glides, his magnified shadow keeping sinister pace over the thatched roofs, neat compounds and tilled plots. Every time his shadow slides over the compound at the foot of the escarpment, a cockerel gives a loud squawk.

Yesterday evening, when the formal session was over, we began to talk about the local villagers, both here below and in the area surrounding the little town of Hagere Salam. Meles talked with great respect of the atrocities they endured when the town was occupied by Dergue garrisons, of their unswerving loyalty. He feels most secure and at ease among the peasants and he respects particularly their independence and self-reliance. "To us, they are our old fathers and our old mothers," he said to me. "They call us their sons and their daughters." His words about the survival training given by peasants to the first fighters are still vivid in my mind. They also gave important lessons in peasant culture. Opinions about peasants have usually come from the pens of the educated and the urban who have never shared their way of life and who have described them as conservative, backward-looking, and anti-revolutionary. How can it be as simple as that? How can the labels and categories of urban life be appropriate to the different stresses of rural survival?

Gazing down now on the neat rounds of thatch and ovular haystacks, I see the survivors in a culture of survival. I see them treading a narrow path beset by risks and dangers, between a series of ambushes, which can trip them into hunger and starvation—rains, which come too early or too late, the ox that mysteriously sickens and dies, hailstorms battering the young crop, army worm and locusts—all the unpredictable elements in the unchanging cycles of changing seasons. Traditionally, they have been forced to feed others before themselves. They have been subject to the constantly evolving demands of those who extract a "surplus" from what in fact is scarcely enough to feed themselves. These peasants experience a world that never meets their needs, in which their best hope is mutual support in combating scarcity and a just sharing of the produce of their work. Resisting transformations which will separate them from the land and cause them no longer to be peasants, they aspire rather to justice within a world in which work is the condition for equality. They hunger after justice. They support this revolution because it promises justice. Will it be able to deliver its promise?

Yet, the time for land distributions is passed. There is no longer enough land to go around. In the highlands of Tigray, the plots are too small to be divided further. But, what is the alternative? The tenacity with which peasants here cling to the land is itself a sign of the impoverishment and underdevelopment of the Ethiopian economy. The industrial sector is still too undeveloped to support those the land cannot feed, but what will happen as it expands? Will the trickle of young people from the land turn into a flood? Will the shanty towns, which already surround the cities, engulf them, as they have done elsewhere? The experience and skills of thousands of fighters, young men and women who were born and brought up in peasant villages, have already alienated many of them from a future on the land. To meet their needs they will be looking to the industrial expansion the Front has promised.

The following morning I wake just as early, but tired. There seemed to be a lot of activity in the night and at some point fighters were talking loudly in the cubicle next door. I wake myself up by climbing the mountain and by nine I am more than ready for breakfast. Usually, an attentive fighter comes along with tea. But no one comes. The path outside the caves is deserted. On the rocky slopes beyond, over which I have rambled for two hours and in which camouflaged dwellings are concealed behind slits in the rock, there is no one to be seen. (Oh, why didn't I shovel down more of that pasta last night?) When it is past eleven, parched, and hungry, I wander along the path again to Meles's place, marked by a shawl-draped satellite dish. Sitting outside is an unknown but leaderly looking fighter (comely, urbane—that sort of thing), who sure enough, when I croak, "Tea, tea! Any chance of breakfast?," my knees giving way, replies in perfect English. He is charming and apologetic, explaining that important discussions kept everyone awake all night and now they are asleep, but that he will get someone to attend to me at once. Feeling demanding and unfighterly, I wish I had been forewarned.

Later in the afternoon, a fighter comes to take me to Tamrat, the head of the Ethiopian Peoples Democratic Movement.[2] The western sun is still hot and strong and beating into the mouths of the cave dwellings, so we retreat into a cool shadowy room away from the cave mouth.

"I will try very frankly to tell you everything you want to know about the EPDM and the EPRDF," he says, in his soft-spoken and charming manner, as I sit down and sort out my recording equipment. Although I have had sporadic contact with groups of Amhara fighters since my first visit, I still feel very vague about the history of the EPDM and of its relations with the Tigrayan front, so this is where we start.

His movement, Tamrat tells me, began as a splinter group of the EPRP, the main revolutionary movement founded by students at Addis Ababa university in the early seventies. The EPRP's membership was predominantly Amhara, educated, and urban. Later in the decade, perhaps under the stresses of constant persecution by the Dergue and the wholesale flight or capitulation of so many of its members, it became increasingly undemocratic in its internal organization, until finally those members with democratic principles broke away and formed the EPDM. The founding congress, in 1981, not only adopted a democratic political program, but also formally acknowledged the oppression by the Amhara of the other subjugated nationalities in Ethiopia and accepted as the solution to ethnic conflict self-determination for all nationalities on the basis of equality. In fact, many of the EPDM's early members were drawn from the Agew people around Sekota and the Lasta district in North Wello, where they established their first liberated area.

It sounds from Tamrat's account as if the Front's basic solution to the nationalities question, which I have so long identified with the TPLF—unity paradoxically achieved through recognition of and respect for difference—was first thought out by the EPDM. Certainly, according to Tamrat, it was the TPLF's early secessionist ideas that divided the organizations until the mid-eighties, when the Tigrayans also decided to adopt a policy of self-determination instead of outright secession. I find it extraordinarily interesting that this policy, later to be distorted by Amhara opposition groups into allegations of fragmentation of Ethiopia, originated within an Amhara-based movement. Tamrat describes vividly what they are up against.

"The whole history of Ethiopia, as they say, is the history of the Amhara, the whole life-blood, from the early days—Menelik, Haile Selassie and now the Dergue; the blood-life, the so-called tradition of the central region of Ethiopia is, they say, the Amhara."

"It's contradictory then, isn't it, that they talk about unity all the time and then in a civil war work to set Amhara against Tigrayan, Amhara against Oromo?"

"For them, unity is the domination of the Amhara ruling class; for them, what unity means is that history, the history of the Amhara ruling class. The EPDM became opposed to this."

"Do you think opposition from an Amhara-based organization is more powerful, then, than from the other nationalities?"

"Especially at this time. The Dergue says that the EPDM is a puppet organization of the TPLF, but we cooperate with the TPLF because of our principles. We are an independent organization with its own programs and policies, our own method and leadership and our own nature, which is multi-national. The EPDM is the only organization in Ethiopia who supports the struggle of nationalities as a whole and the struggle of the Tigrayan people in particular and the Dergue knows this struggle of the TPLF is a very dangerous thing for its power. The Dergue knows this very well. Any organization that supports this struggle is also very dangerous, especially when it comes from a multi-national Amhara organization like the EPDM."

So Tamrat's organization has been working in the Amhara heartland where the government would expect to find its traditional support. This makes it a very powerful opposition organization. No wonder the Dergue and the Addis Ababa elite have been ignoring its existence and representing the "rebels" as narrow nationalist Tigrayans seeking their own power at the expense of the Amhara and of Ethiopian cohesiveness.

"In these central areas, the experience of the Dergue's atrocities, oppression, villagization, the war—these things were very hated, so the EPRDF going to any corner of this country got a lot of support. The question of land is there, the question of Dergue economic policies, which the people didn't accept, have never accepted. Our policies are very democratic and are accepted in the rural areas, especially."

I ask if there have been any problem areas since these provinces were liberated by the Front.

"There were problem areas. One was around Debre Tabor. It's an Amhara area and they are the most Amhara of Amharas."

"When I was there recently, I heard there are still feudal landlords in place there, that the Dergue land reform did not oust them all. Is this so?"

This is an extremely important question because many Ethiopian scholars contend that the early years of the Dergue had their good aspects and that the Dergue land reform policy was among them, in that it finally put paid to feudal power.

"They are still in place," Tamrat replies, "but at this time there is land reform. So, that will root them out economically. There is one thing about these areas of Gondar and Gojjam—the feudals and the peasants are all Amhara. The link is there between the feudals and the Amharas, but there is another question that cannot be linked, another difference between the feudals and the peasants. The land is in the hands of the feudals. In this, there is a contradiction, a very fierce contradiction that helps us. The feudals wanted to rally the peasants with Amhara propaganda: "The Tigrayans are coming. They want to rule us Amharas, and so on. We simply emphasize the question of the land. "This is the problem. There must be land reform. You must get the pure land. Then the peasantry sides with us."

"How do you do it? Do you arm the peasants and then they fight the feudals?"

"When we go into a new area, we go to the poor peasants and we arm them. The first shot of the peasants will be against the bureaucratic administrative apparatus of the Dergue, because that is the very spot that oppresses the peasants. So, after that, we raise the question of land. Then will come the contradiction. Then the armed peasants will go and fight."

"So, what stage have you reached in that process? Let's take Debre Tabor as the example."

"This time, it's going OK. Before the land reform, there was a question of people's support. There is a *shengo*, an elected council, in Debre Tabor also. That *shengo* is a weapon for launching land reform, a very strong weapon."

"So what stage has land reform reached in the Debre Tabor area?"

"It is complete. At this time, the land has already been taken from the feudals. They can live like private citizens if they like or they can go to the Dergue, or they can go away altogether. But if they like, they can live like anyone else; they can have their share of the land for as many children as they have in their family—just like anyone else. Exactly the same share as any peasant."

"The feudal sentiments in the peasants go so deep."

"Yes, culturally. But the first thing we pursue is land reform. This is the main weapon that rallies the peasants around us and their using the free market for their goods. The Dergue's Agricultural Marketing Organization was felt to be very oppressive. When we raised this question about price control and so on, it seemed an economic question, not a political question, but it's also a political question and a matter of life and death to the peasantry. We promised a free market. The peasantry can take his product freely and take it to the market and sell it. This moves the whole people."

"Have they had experience yet of even one harvest?"

"Yes, they have. One harvest—and one before land distribution, so you can say two harvests. This by itself makes the political consciousness very sharp and the support for the EPRDF very strong."

So even in the Debre Tabor area, the Amhara heartland, the Front has rural support, because of the land reform and the free market and also because of the *shengo.*

"We have strong support," Tamrat adds, "among the broad masses, the lowest people."

"So where do the problems in these problem areas lie exactly?"

"The problem exactly lies here. The feudals are stronger here than in other areas, more strong in their economic potential. Their land has been taken, but they have all the other things. They have got more money, more experienced administrative capacities than the feudals in Wello. They have got a far greater influence culturally than the feudals in Wello. They have got more contacts with the bureaucrats of the Dergue."

"Can you do anything about them?"

"There is no special mechanism for controlling them, other than the normal ones—making people more conscious of them, implementing democratic rights, learning from their own experiences. This all takes time."

"Are the feudals excluded from elections to the *shengo*? I know they are in some areas."

"Yes, they are in some areas. We want them to be excluded, but the final decision is from the people themselves. There have been some examples of people refusing our opinion and not excluding feudals from elections. And, in Southern Wello there is a place where during the elections the EPRDF gave as its opinion that bureaucrats of the Dergue and feudal remnants should not be elected. The people rejected this. In some places, the people rejected it wholly; in some places they argued for the election of individual bureaucrats and feudals. 'We know this person; we'll elect this person,' they said. We had our opinion, we described it, we explained. 'No,' they said. 'We know them; we'll elect them.' We said, 'OK, the final decision is yours.' After some months, the people found those people sabotaging land reform, those feudal remnants round Kobo, Alamata. And, they dismissed them from the leadership of the *shengo*. They dismissed two people and re-elected others. 'The EPRDF told us and we didn't listen. We have learned from this,' they said. There's also another example in Gaient. The Gaient representative is still in the *shengo.* Anyway, he has learned from the Northern Wello case and is being very cautious."

It is late in the evening by the time Tamrat and I say goodnight. Only then do I discover that all this time Fissaha Garedew from the Ethiopian Democratic Officers Revolutionary Movement has been waiting to talk to me. This group of Dergue officers, politicized in the prisoner of war camps, is an independent organization within the Front and is a striking example of the success of their enlightened policy, especially towards prisoners of war, of converting enemies into allies wherever possible. So, instead of falling prostrate on my bed, I stay up talking for a further three hours until two o'clock in the morning. It is obvious that the whole of the camp, not only Meles, runs on the night work principle. My questions to Fesseha are intended to find out about the founding of the EDORM and its functioning as an organization within the EPRDF, but I find far more compelling his account of being an officer in the Dergue Army. Except for that interview with the lieutenant at Bahr-Dar hospital, where I failed so ignominiously to penetrate his subterfuges, so far I have only talked to reluctant involuntary recruits.

A View from the Other Side

I was from a trading family in Dessie. I completed high school with honors in 1979, and then I had to find a job. The next year there was a program for a scholarship abroad. The criteria were participation in the Youth Association and not being a member of EPRP. We were nominated to go to Cuba for nearly three years. We had no idea it was for military training until we were taken to an army camp. This caused a crisis among us, so they sent a message to Mengistu, who replied that we had been nominated to be military cadets. Some nominees went mad. First, we attended a language session, then military training in different fields. Mine was intelligence, collecting information in the field.

I was eighteen when I went to Cuba; now I'm thirty. If you refused you would be killed. In fact, we were terrorized and that was one of the reasons some people went mad. This is the thing we always used to talk about when members of our batch got together—that we too were forced recruits. We were trained for three months, back in Ethiopia to be airborne. I jumped five times from an airplane. We had special wings and a parachute symbol to wear on our uniform. The Third Division symbol was a lion. I began serving as an officer in Eritrea. I was on the staff of the Second Revolutionary Army, not in a particular division. I changed to the 605th Corps and was transferred to Wello. Nine months later, in 1988, I was captured.

One of the important points about the army is that everyone hates this war. We were all against this war and wanted an immediate ceasefire, but we didn't know the solution. Everyone was exhausted and frustrated, everyone wanted peace—and therefore, we gave attention to the broadcasts. We blamed the war on the EPRDF, not the state, because we were on the other side. They told us the state was taking all possible means to solve the situation peacefully and that the EPRDF was rejecting their proposals, and therefore, the fighting was forced to continue. When things went wrong, we just took it as the sabotage of individuals distorting the policies of the state, not as the state itself.

The important focuses of dissatisfaction are forced recruitment and low pay. Everybody fights, but they are paid at different rates. The National Service recruits are paid almost nothing and the regular army a bit more, but in any case they just drank it. The officers have a bit better salary, but even the officers, not enough. The regular soldiers were paid ninety dollars a month, occasionally a bit more for long service. National Service recruits had pocket money of about twenty dollars a month, the same for militias—but everyone died the same. Soldiers had no personal rights. A soldier didn't get to see his family. He was denied annual leave. If he was sent to Eritrea, he never came back—it was taken for granted that he was a dead man.

While I was in the army, my impression of the EPRDF, was that it was an army of bandits. I was working as an intelligence officer, so I had the opportunity of monitoring their radio station. I was disturbed by the broadcasts, especially the way they said prisoners of war were being handled. I didn't really believe what they were saying, but it did start to raise doubts about the bandit propaganda. I was not an active supporter of the state. In fact I hated the state, but I did not have any clear idea about how it could be solved. In the radio programs they were exposing the junta and many points I took as correct, because they were correct. I suspected they were secessionists. Gradually, there were developments, especially the founding of the EPRDF. I felt these people had left their wrong line and this would make them attractive to many young people in Ethiopia, but I thought they had adopted it as a manipulative tactic. On one side, we took it for granted the EPRDF were the ones against peace, but without analyzing it, I did have certain doubts. "Why—if they are really bandits, if they are not supported by the people, how are they getting bigger and stronger?" One of the main reasons for the war is that no one understands the propaganda of either the democratic nature of the EPRDF or the nature of the state itself. This keeps the state in power longer. It was only after I joined the EPRDF that I came to know the nature of the state.

Most of the recruits had prepared civilian clothes and identity cards to escape. Therefore, the officers had no morale left for winning battles. The soldiers' whole impetus was to hide and escape. Sometimes, the Military Security in the army caught and killed them. Therefore, the rank and file completely distrusted the officers and the officers completely distrusted the soldiers. Everyone was thinking how to save his life. Among the officers, generally everybody wanted to put himself on the safe side, so he would never speak officially about political things. Occasionally, with very close friends, one or two, you would discuss the situation, but never openly.

After our army, in Tigray, had been destroyed, I was in the mountains near Maichew. After hiding in the mountains around Korem, I was searching for someone to take me to Alamata (the next garrison). It was eight p.m. I asked a peasant to show me the way. At first, I was received with insults. Then, I asked where the fighters were and told them I was an officer. I met a peasant and asked where I could find them. He showed me a house. I knocked at a door, but when I called for the person who lived there, the fighters came and said, "Don't you know fighters are here?" So, I sat down with them, like chatting among friends. They said, "Our organization shows mercy to all prisoners of war. We will give you teaching. You can fight with us or go to the Sudan or home. We give salvation to the oppressed." These were their first words. So, I decided to test whether the words were true.

I observed very closely on my way to the POW center, the conditions of the fighters, their relations with each other, with the prisoners, with the people, and this gradually changed my mind. I was very much interested in the way these bandits were treating the community. I took them as cheaters and wanted to know the specific ways of cheating the community and persuading the youngsters to join the army. At the center, they didn't start political discussions immediately. Even when they did start, I still had the same stance as when I was an officer. I hadn't changed. I didn't shed all my opinions. I wasn't sure they were genuine. I was curious how they were manipulating and misdirecting the Tigrayan community. This was the most important point for me.

When we started political education at the POW center, I was gradually persuaded. There were panels, open discussions, classes, on different political issues. Gradually I began to condemn my position in the army. Even finally, I had a very deep regret for being an army officer. If I had been killed in battle, it would have been for nothing—not for the people or anything. I came to want to fight for the organization. When the moment of choice came, I had already decided beforehand to join. I even tried to persuade my friends to join and to convince them. I was actively working by writing poems, organizing dramas, literature, condemning the army and motivating others to fight. Those who came over to the EPRDF increased every day. Of course, there were different positions between the officers. First, there were those who decided to fight against the enemy with the EPRDF to consolidate the nation; some wanted to go to the Sudan; others wanted to just stay in the liberated area. These choices were pre-

sented to us by the EPRDF. Those who decided to stay in the liberated area, later tended to join the EPRDF army. Those who at first inclined to rejoin the junta, after a while decided to stay in the liberated area.

The Officers Movement was founded on April 23, 1990 by officers who had been captured and politicized by the EPRDF in the POW center. This organization was important in that the officers in the Ethiopian army had their own problems of oppression, therefore, it was better to organize separately than to join any of the other organizations as individuals. It's more important, especially in relation to the task of the army. We analyzed, based on class analysis, why most officers who joined were junior officers. We categorized the junior officers as an oppressed class in direct relation with the rank and file and also that they themselves were victims of the ruling class. We categorized the officers into three groups, first, the lower officers from sub-lieutenant to captain. The second group, majors, lieutenant-colonels and colonels we saw as vacillating, in as much as they want to change to the ruling class, but they can join the lower officers too. An individual in this group can go in either direction. He goes with the ebb and flow of the revolution. The third category, the generals, are part of the ruling class and can never side with the revolution.

The mainstay of EDORM are the lower officers like captains and lieutenants, although there are a few colonels and majors. These officers are very important because they are the link between the rank and file and the upper officers who are part of the ruling class. We are working to paralyze the army through influencing the majority of officers. First we convince him that the EPRDF is working for the people. Those who don't want to join us, we paralyze by making them neutral and passive. We have formed cells; we write letters to individuals; we broadcast; we make contact either to win support or at least minimize support for the state.

Therefore our organization is no longer just prisoners of war—only the founders. We are now an organization of hundreds and we expect shortly to be an organization of thousands. Many officers are escaping from the state. There is a very organized tentacle of the spy network within the army called Military Security, therefore, it is very hard to escape and join EDORM, but many do. Some join by deserting. Some captured officers later go back to the Ethiopian army. These people know all about the EPRDF, but for certain personal reasons they choose to go back. In battle, they never fight, but just go over to the EPRDF.

The EDORM broadcasts, three times a week, are very popular in the Ethiopian army. They focus on their real problems. One program called "Who should speak?" has different interviews with officers who really analyze the situation, life in the army, the problems. Those who join usually follow the news programs, then get hold of pamphlets. They get a vacation and go to their home area. They study a route and escape. The other way is in battle, through being taken prisoner.

Our other method is to paralyze the personnel. One way of paralyzing is to make contact with old mates, writing, and exchanging letters. Some don't want to join because of their personal problems, therefore we recruit them as agents. We agitate on the radio and isolate them from the state and they become passive. Our propaganda is by radio or pamphlet, or by personal contact. We agitate that the state is against the people and that they are dying for nothing.

We also train members of the EPRDF in different branches with differents skills, in the mechanized units, for example, communications, intelligence, engineering, or maintenance. Not all our skills are relevant for this army. The officers transfer the necessary points demanded by the EPRDF for its needs. We adapt to the EPRDF's special military science. We provide a vital and crucial contribution in training in the effective use of guns. The EPRDF captures many modern weapons and is usually without the skills to use them. Therefore, they sit in the stores and are of no use. Many officers are well-trained in their use. So, the organization of the mechanized units is especially important. Before, the EPRDF was trying to destroy the enemy with very unequal technological capacity; now they have a very strong mechanized unit. Members go to the front line, especially for the maintenance of tanks, artillery, and vehicles. If necessary, we fight like any combatant.

This army is not an army like the present Ethiopian army. The relation between the rank and file and the officers is based on comradeship. It is not a tool or a machine; a politicized army knows its objective and the interests of society and its political life is interrelated with the condition of the people.[3]

Just before I go to sleep, Aklilu sends a message to say that Kuma Demeksa, Chairman of the OPDO, the Oromo organization within the coalition, will be ready to talk to me at nine in the morning. The Oromo people are the largest ethnic group in Ethiopia and, according to Tigrayan informants, have suffered the most at the hands of successive dictatorships. Their traditional lands in the southern half of the country were conquered and annexed by Emperor Menelik II at the end of the nineteenth century. He rewarded his warrior lords, the *neftegna,* with huge tracts of Oromo land on which the people were reduced to serfs. Since the days of Haile Selassie, the Oromo Liberation Front (OLF) has been demanding the independence of Oromia.

Whether they are as elitest and undemocratic as I have been told they are, I have been unable to confirm, but they certainly don't seem to have consolidated their position and their support among the Oromo masses. Now this new democratic Oromo branch of the EPRDF has been founded. Still a fledgling movement, it will be interesting to see if they make headway in the south. In the future, "after victory," hazy to me but not at all to these leaders, it will be their effectiveness in gaining support among the many nationalities in the southern half of the country which will make or break this movement in the long term.

After a very short night, Aklilu calls for me as I am gathering my equipment together and we make our way along the cliff path just before nine. Sitting and smiling on the same rock outside Meles's place, is the urbane fighter who rescued me with breakfast yesterday morning. It is Kuma.[4]

"No, no, we are already good friends," he says, waving away Aklilu's introduction.

Although the OPDO was only founded a year ago, Kuma and his co-founders were not newcomers to political dissidence and the struggle for liberation. Rejecting the OLF as undemocratic and secessionist, they had been fighting with the Amhara EPDM for years before they decided to form a separate Oromo organization within the coalition front. He is eloquent also on the long resistance of the Oromo people over the last hundred years to subjugation by the Amhara.

"Our fathers and our grandfathers, starting with Menelik's taking of our land, have been fighting continuously until now, even though they have not necessarily been been fighting scientifically or effectively. This situation is still continuing in revolts everywhere against the central government. Therefore the founding of the OPDO, its special and new role in Oromo history is that it is democratic and can coordinate the resistance, but the resistance is not something new. It has been in existence for years."

Aklilu breaks in to confirm from his own experience the resistance of the Bale people he witnessed when he was a student in the south. I am conscious of my ignorance. I have never been to any of the areas they are talking about. I know little of these rich and diverse cultures from the southern half of Ethiopia and will have no chance to explore them until after the end of the war. My experience of this country has scarcely scratched the surface and I get a sudden sense of the difficulties that lie ahead for the Front, even after the victory of which they are so confident, in welding together into any kind of unity so many nationalities for whom multiple oppressions and the impositions of cardboard "unity" may have exacerbated difference into an unyielding enmity.

As if hearing my unspoken thoughts, Kuma refers to attitudes to the Amhara as a key issue.

"Our difference with the OLF on this point is that they take every member of the Amhara as an enemy and even other nationalities also. This approach is not based on class analysis and we evaluate it as wrong. It was the ruling class and not the nationalities of Ethiopia who were the enemies of the Oromo people. Therefore, it is a very wrong stand."

"Nevertheless, it may be a stand that has an appeal for your people."

"Yes. Especially the Oromo of the east and south, Harar, Arsi, and Bale —because the atrocities committed by the *neftegna* were so great, the Oromo of these areas tend to hate every Amharic-speaking individual as a cruel and murderous creature. Therefore, our primary task is to fight narrow nationalism. They never dream of living with other Ethiopians. It will take a long time and be very hard work to convince them because it's so inculcated that highlanders are their enemies. Because these areas are areas of intense resistance, Menelik captured them with very great bloodshed, killing thousands. Thirty thousand were killed in Arsi alone. Therefore, there is an historical and fortified hatred to *habesha,* or highland Abyssinians. By channelling their strong national feeling, it is a very good area for struggle."

"Doesn't this make problems for you?"

"That is one problem area. There is also the opposite sort of problem among those who are living around the center of the country who are highly disseminated among the Amharas. We have to fight their inferiority complex. They accept, as a rule, that they are not equal to the Amharas, who are their predestined rulers. So, especially around Shewa and Addis, we have to fight to raise their national identity and consciousness. They must be proud and not hide it. In north Shewa, which is the center of Amhara chauvinism, after agitation, the Oromo went from one extreme to the other and became very aggressive against the Amharas. "They treat us like domestic animals," they said. "This was a stage in political consciousness."

A young fighter has come in with tea things. We pause briefly to hand round cups, stir in sugar, and take a sip or two. Aklilu is silent. We wait while Kuma seems to meditate, stirring his tea. Then he continues:

"This narrow nationalism extends even to our fighters. When they see our EPRDF fighters fighting together, the Oromo nationality says it's good, but still they have doubts and suspicions—especially among the mass, but also a little among the fighters. They remember the words of the junta when it came to power. They also said they were 'for the people' and look what happened! You cannot trust Amharas."

I find myself responding to this thoughtful man. He is sharing with me their genuine difficulties in building a multinational state. He is not fobbing me off with easy ideals and superficial optimisms.

"Empirically, you see Oromo who sympathize with other nationalities, especially with the oppressed people of Tigray, so they are not worried about Tigrayans and take them as their own, but they are especially doubtful of Amharas. They have a saying: "Like parasites in the gut, no matter how much you wash them, the Amharas you can never make clean."

"So how do you handle these nationalist feelings?"

"To have such a narrow nationalist sentiment in Oromia is a condition to motivate an organization to fight against national oppression, but it can never make you strong. Different factors help to make you strong. Unless you work with the class interest of the people you will never be strong—listening to their problems, working for the interest of the mass of the people. They must get something very practical from their own struggle or it will never be enough. The people join us because they understand what it is about, because they get something out of it. Otherwise, you are not representing them and you never get stronger. The problem with the OLF is that they are not working with the mass. They have been existing for years and years without showing any strength or growth. Strength is not in slogans—practice is essential to make people claim their own struggle."

"What is your attitude towards minority nationalities within the traditional Oromo territory?"

"Our attitude to these minorities is directly emerging from our own position. Because we accept our own right to self-determination we also accept theirs. They are not a sub-group of the Oromo. They are mostly completely independent. Although they are within the bounds of the big Oromo land, we have never claimed them as Oromo or under Oromo. This is one of the crucial points where the OPDO differs from other Oromo organizations. For us, we accept the legitimate right of the minority nationalities to decide their own fate, without any pressure. As equally as we argue for our own right, they must be free to do the same. For example, the Beni Shangul movement in Western Wellega on the border with the Sudan are fighting for their own autonomy. The OPDO supports their struggle and accepts the legitimacy of their organization and wants no restrictions on their struggle against oppression. The same with the Gambela People's Liberation Front. They have asked to join the Front. The OLF, however, wants them to fight under the umbrella of the OLF and don't accept their right of self-determination. They say they are a branch of the OLF because they are within OLF territory. We say even if a minority is few in number, their equality stems from a principle of democratic right."

"How do you argue against Oromia as a separate state?"

"There is no problem about the viability of Oromia as a separate state, because its economic potential is very great. It forms the largest proportion of human and material resources of the present state. However, as far as our choice goes as an organization (although of course the people of Oromia will decide), we see the greater advantage of a big nation—in speedy development, strong defense, a big pool of skills. The OPDO's choice is a democratic Ethiopia. Unity is preferred and we teach this, not because Oromia as a nation cannot stand alone, but because a united and democratic Ethiopia is in the interest of the Oromos, as long as equality is achieved. It will bring more benefits to them. But, in an organization accepting the right of self-determination, the people must decide. This principle cannot be violated."

I feel disappointed when Aklilu lets me know there will be a car ready to take us to Mekelle at the end of the afternoon. I don't see how there will be time for the update on the current situation and future policies I had been hoping for. The sense of peace and timelessness of this mountain citadel I realize is largely illusory. This is the control center for a revolutionary war that is nearing its end and the commmunications, strategic planning and decisions that emanate from these quiet caves must produce stresses of all kinds as well as acute pressure on time. I have been treated generously and I feel in a weak position to put in any more requests. Then, a note arrives from Meles suggesting a meeting after lunch. He adds that his wife and daughter have arrived and we will all meet later.

The weeks at the Gondar and Gojjam fronts gave me a sense of knowing what was going on. I had gone there, not as a war reporter out to capture the sensationalism and the carnage of the battlefield, but to investigate the Front's methods of conflict resolution and stabilization of a probably hostile and suspicious local population in the immediate aftermath of war. Nevertheless, I found myself fascinated by military strategy and by the Front's curious combining of remorseless and sophisticated battlefield tactics with humanitarian concern for the "canon fodder" of the Dergue army. I felt close to the military center for the first time. I could talk easily to both rank and file fighters and top commanders, who were always ready to answer questions after an operation. It is not an easy habit to get out of. Since then, I have felt out of touch, so I welcome Meles's update, which is a fairly detailed account of the location of the remnants of the four armies of the Dergue, the extent of their destruction and the threat they still pose. It adds up to a strategy, already far advanced, of the systematic elimination of Dergue forces wherever they are and the further from Addis Ababa the better.

"The liberation of Bahr-Dar and Gondar," says Meles, "could be considered a dress rehearsal for the task of liberating the major cities, for the final push for country-wide victory. The experience we have gained in stabilizing the newly-liberated towns will be carefully analyzed, processed, and used in stabilizing Addis Ababa. As a matter of fact, practically all the leadership are still in Bahr-dar and Gondar, trying to analyze the experience. We do not have a complete blueprint now, but we can talk about the broad outlines."[5]

On the BBC World Service, as the Front's forces approach nearer to the capital from the north, west, and east, the tone of the reporting has been getting ever more hysterical. Various informants, mostly from Addis, predict a *bloodbath* and describe the rebel forces in terms that must make Addis citizens shiver in their beds. Yet, no exhortations by Mengistu or calling up of older and younger recruits seems able to halt the inexorable progress of encirclement. So, I am interested when Meles categorically denies the likelihood of a bloodbath.

"As a general principle, we will try to minimize the disruption. It's only a development of the experience of Bahr-Dar and Gondar, especially to try and maintain the schools and productive sectors and retain the skilled manpower. We will go about it in a process involving the people."

Absence of disruption to the functioning of the capital will depend, he says, on two principles, the elimination of all the military concentrations of the Dergue outside the capital and the demoralization of Dergue remnants, also outside the capital, through a propaganda and organizational offensive.

"A part of this will be to encourage mass insurrections and mass movements inside the town, the types of strikes that we now have."

For his part, Mengistu is apparently completing the sabotage of the Ethiopian economy so effectively achieved by the war. Meles refers to the rumors that the dictator's wife and children have already left for a farm in Zimbabwe and that he has transported there cars and whatever portable wealth he has been able to amass.

I am well enough acquainted by now with the leadership's emphasis on strategic planning to know that they must have mapped out a program of action for "after victory" and so our conversation turns to the future. The plan, as Meles outlines it, is to call a national conference as soon as possible of all political groups to decide the formation and program of a transitional government. He predicts an internationally-supervised ceasefire, followed by a period of stabilization, including a referendum in Eritrea to establish the people's desire for independence or not.

"Then, we'll call elections for a constituent assembly to draft the constitution of the country. And after such a constitution has been drafted and endorsed by the people, we'll have internationally-supervised elections for a new government. That will be the end of the transitional period."

We discuss the various political groups who might want to be involved and those organizations like the OLF and the EPRP who would be less likely to play a constructive role in an EPRDF-brokered new Ethiopia. What about the small, educated elite, mostly Amhara, who have been running the country under the successive dictatorships? They have no power base among the people and would have little to gain from a democratic system.

"Do you plan to keep the present bureaucracy in place," I ask, "to ensure the smooth-running of the capital?"

"We will differentiate between the different elements of the bureaucracy. There is the bureaucracy that is mainly concerned with repression—the army, the security services, and so on. These will probably disintegrate in any case. Then you have the civilian bureaucracy and that we want to keep intact for the time being. They cannot be replaced overnight; they can only be transformed. In the long run, we will still need skilled manpower, still need some sort of state apparatus. The worst thing you can do is to disrupt things without preparing replacements, and we don't have ready-made replacements. Replacements will have to come out in the process, by empowering the people, and that will be a gradual process."

Our remaining discussion sets out in greater detail Meles's general formulations as I have indicated them here. It is interrupted by the sound of voices out on the cliff path and his little daughter, Samhal, trots through the door, closely followed by her mother. She is a fighter whom I first met four years ago on my first trip to Tigray, but this is my first meeting with Samhal. She is two years old. Beaming, Meles takes her on his knee. A fighter comes in with tea. Our discussion is over.

When the sun is low in the sky, I leave with Samhal and her mother. They will be dropped off at her place of work, the Press Department, in some camouflaged ravine in the Tembien lowlands; Aklilu and I go on by a roundabout route to Mekelle. There is nothing now between me and departure, but transport delays and the constraints of night travel, difficult terrain and the convoy over the Sudanese border mean that it will be a departure both long-drawn-out and unpredictable.

There is a welcome delay in Mekelle. The knowledge that I'm on my way home revives my emotions for my family, blessedly asleep for the past few weeks, but the huge leviathan of the journey and the Sudan lies across my path and deprives my homecoming of any sense of reality. I feel torn by the imminence of farewells. Not only have I been here for several months, but it is a few months that can be never be repeated. This long struggle for survival is nearing its end and these people are forcing into being an Ethiopia, which will be never be the same again. *After victory*. They tell me that it will be a new and the most difficult period of struggle, to introduce democracy and human rights into a country that has never known either. But it will be a period of struggle very different from this one. What does it hold? Some of it will resemble the old struggle—negotiations, interminable meetings, conferences—but at least they will be out in the open at last. No more night travel, no more caves, no more camouflage. Then the paraphernalia of the modern state will be upon them—elections, bureaucracy, international relations, diplomacy, the World Bank, and the I.M.F?

Aklilu is looking out for a landcruiser to get me to Adwa. He will keep me company that far. He thinks I should have little trouble finding transport through REST from there to the convoy pick-up point. Meanwhile, there are always more questions to ask, more gaps to fill, and in the evenings I spend time with Roman or Aregash or Mebrat or Gebru or other friends and I know that never again will I find them so easy and accessible and all together in Mekelle. In the new Ethiopia, they will be scattered widely, their new responsibilities spreading them thinly across the map and weighing them with obligations as yet only to be guessed.

A landcruiser is found. Roman and Mebrat come to my room and give me a beautiful embroidered Tigrayan dress and we say an emotional farewell. Early the next morning, the yard of the Green Hotel is deserted in the half light before sunrise. The baggage is piled into the back and I set off for the last time on the long trek to the border with the Sudan.

Next time I come to Ethiopia, I will be flying like any other foreign visitor into Addis Ababa.

Part Four

The Last Act of the Drama

May 1991

22

The Taking of Addis Ababa

The informants, in order of speaking

Tsadkan Gebretensai, Tigrayan, male, Deputy Commander of the EPRDF forces.

Habtom Andemariam, 27, Amhara, male, electrician, Addis Ababa.

Mekebib Woldeyohannes, 25, Amhara, male, student, Addis Ababa.

Merkab Bishew, 50, Amhara, female, nurse, Addis Ababa.

"Kawita" Teklit Gebremariam, 35, EPRDF fighter since 1981. His field name means "the one who makes big holes in the ground." Peasant family from Adwa district, Tigray. Commissar of a brigade (800-1,000 fighters). Wounded three times. Married with one child.

Getachew Belai, 34, male, from Mekelle, Tigray. Prisoner for eight years in Mekelle and Addis Ababa prisons.

Ghirmai Berhe, 38, male, from Mekelle, Tigray. Prisoner for eight years in Addis Ababa prison.

"Oromo" Letai Mesfin, 28, EPRDF woman fighter since 1980. Peasant from Adwa area, Tigray. Commander of a division (three to four brigades or four to five thousand fighters). Wounded twice. Married with one son.

"Manjus" Haile Tesfay, 31, EPRDF fighter since 1981. Peasant from Tembien, Tigray. Field name means "youth." Brigade Commander. Never wounded. Married, one son.

Ghooish Ghirmai, 32, EPRDF fighter since 1980. Peasant from Axum area, Tigray. Brigade commander. Wounded once. Married with a son and a daughter.

Mulu Kidane, about 32, female, civil engineer, from Addis Ababa.

"Bandit" Shewainesh, 29, EPRDF woman fighter since about 1977. Peasant from Shire, Tigray. Brigade commander. Wounded three times. Married at nine years old, captured by a bandit one year later. After four years, bandits surrounded by the TPLF. Husband fled to the Dergue and was executed; "Bandit" joined the TPLF.

"Wodiraya" Berhe Beraki, 29, EPRDF fighter since 1982. Peasant from Raya Azebo, Tigray. Field name means "son of Raya." Deputy Brigade-Commander. Wounded four times. Married with one son.

Zewdi Kiros, 28, EPRDF woman fighter since 1980. Peasant from Tembien, Tigray. Deputy commander of a division. Never wounded. Married with one son.

Alemtsehai, 46, secretary at American Embassy, Addis Ababa.

Lama, late thirties, from Tigray, fled as refugee to Manitoba, Canada, in 1977; returned in June 1991.

The action

Tsadkan When we talk about the strategy for the taking of Addis Ababa, we have to go back three or four years to during the armed struggle and see events leading up to this take-over.

Habtom At that time, I was a private electrician working in the *kebelles.* Under the Dergue regime, the Dergue called the EPRDF *weyane* or *gotegna* (person who brings divisions), all savage or destructive people according to Dergue propaganda. *Weyane* means killer, a brutal or inhuman bandit.

Mekebib I was a part-time student at Addis Ababa University at the time. I am from a poor family, so I joined the evening extension program. On the campus, there were so many political attitudes from students and teachers, lecturers and professors and there were explosive pressures from every corner of the country. For three decades, there had been so many political questions. The Dergue was separated from the people. The Dergue was compelling the people by force—so many writers, so many people from the lower classes with grievances—and he forced all these to keep their mouths shut, not to disagree. There was no dissent.

Tsadkan After we totally defeated the 604th Corps in Endeselassie, in February 1989, which led to the Dergue evacuation of Mekelle, it was clear from that day to the whole public, especially in Tigray, that the defeat of the Dergue was only a matter of time. Organizing a clear strategy from that time on was the priority. The plan was to move down to the central highlands of Ethiopia from where we could be in close touch with the indigenous Amhara population and organize and arm them, but militarily it was a good strategic posture from which to threaten the most vital areas of the Dergue—from which to attack the road to Addis Ababa, Addis itself, and the military movements from Addis Ababa to Dessie, Gondar and Bahr-dar. Therefore, it was a very important area for us.

After evacuating Mekelle, the Dergue was planning another campaign to retake it. We began preparations in Southern Tigray and North Wello and defeated a big enemy force, so the gate was open to the central highlands of Ethiopia, South Wello and North Shewa and Gondar.

Merkab During the last seventeen years, I was working as a volunteer in the *kebelles* as a public health nurse, elected by the people, and involved in literacy campaigns and social development committees. During these times, of course we did not expect the EPRDF ever to take over the government because I knew very little about it. I was very much frightened to hear about the *weyane.* In case it was told to the officials, the only people I spoke to were my servant and children. I didn't even turn on the radio or listen to tapes. There was terror on us.

Tsadkan We formed a clear strategy to finish the war *outside* Addis Ababa. Once we were in those central areas, we knew that it meant continuous battles, because we wanted to stay in these areas as a springboard for the final offensive. When it became clear that the Dergue could not push us back, we planned a strategic offensive. The strategy was to draw the Dergue out of Addis Ababa and annihilate the whole army if possible, so that there would be no force after the end of the war to make problems. To this end, there were a series of operations: Campaign Tewodros cleared enemy units in Gondar and Gojjam and cut them off completely from Addis Ababa.

From there, we went south to Wellega, where we forced the enemy to spread out its forces. We forced a hasty assembly of forces in Ambo, just west of the capital. When we reached Ambo, there was almost panic in the enemy camp.

Habtom After that Tewodros campaign, they started a campaign in Wellega and from there went to Ambo, North Shewa and South Shewa. The Dergue were propagandizing Addis Ababa people to defend themselves and take arms from the *kebelles* and other places to stand by to fight the invaders. People were disturbed and very terrified. We thought we had to die and the people would have terrible suffering.

Mekebib By the time the EPRDF was in every corner of the country, people did not know very much about their aims and neither did I. Everything was concentrated in Addis. It was like the head office of the country, because political groups and social movements carried on in Addis. So many national questions had been arising for so many years. Some nationalities were treated like like strangers in the country and their human, political, and democratic rights were not respected by the government. We were being told that the EPRDF's policies were like apartheid.

ETHIOPIAN PRESIDENT IS FORCED TO FLEE COUNTRY

President Mengistu Haile Mariam of Ethiopia has resigned and fled the country after pressure from the Soviet Union, the US and the rebels against his 14-year-old regime.

Julian Ozanne
Financial Times, London, May 22, 1991

Tsadkan From Dessie, we went to Debre Berhan and the forces of the Tewodros campaign went to Ambo and crushed the enemy troops and put the capital under pressure from all sides. Then, Mengistu fled from Addis Ababa because really there was no use fighting.

After this operation, our forces spread out and captured all the main roads —the roads to Gimma, Wellega, Gojjam, Assab, Debre Zeit, and the army camp were all captured—and then went to the east and southern areas and wiped out units of the Dergue. So, literally, the remaining forces in

Addis Ababa were totally cut off from the surrounding country. Then, most of our forces camped around Addis Ababa until we knew the outcome of the London Conference. When we knew the peace conference had failed, we were given orders to go in to Addis Ababa.

Meanwhile, we had heard there was some anarchy in Addis. It had no units to protect it. From the outset, we expected some fighting there, so we trained some two thousand fighters in commando units for fighting in towns, but by the time we went in we knew this was unlikely.

Kawita As you know, we had been told what to expect. Addis Ababa is a very big city with many people and the enemy was very destructive. They might start shooting from different buildings, from industrial areas, from everything that makes a city a city. They might pull us in two and the city would be destroyed. The enemy would be as vicious as possible. We were oriented to expect all this. We were instructed to save the people as much as possible from being killed, also the buildings and industrial areas from being destroyed, that there should not be a big price in life.

The military aspect was to concentrate and focus only on small arms, not to use bombs and heavy guns. As for the enemy, our first priority was to capture them; if that was not possible, then to shoot with small arms—to save both life and infrastructure. We, as commanders, were oriented by the EPRDF how we were to do it and then we prepared those under our command—to spare life and infrastructure. Right from the top leadership down to the leaders of the smallest units, the leaders had to ensure strictly that directives were observed.

ADVANCING REBELS PUT SQUEEZE ON THE CAPITAL

...In the capital yesterday, workers took a jack hammer to "Johnnie Walker"—a 30 ft. statue of Lenin, frozen in full stride, a stone's throw from the Imperial Palace.

Children, old people, and armed policemen looked on, laughing and singing "Mengistu ran away," as workers began uprooting the bronze statue.

Marxist ex-President Mengistu Haile Mariam fled to Zimbabwe on Tuesday.

The joke in the capital during the later stages of Colonel Mengistu's 14 years of rule, was that Lenin was walk-

ing to the airport with the wealth of Ethiopia in his pocket. He gained his "Johnnie Walker" nickname because his pose was like that of the "toff" used to advertise whisky.

The new Ethiopian leader, acting President Lt-Gen Tesfaye Gebrekidan, released more than 180 political prisoners yesterday, most of them detained for alleged involvement in the abortive May 1989 coup.

But Ethiopians gathered in the sunshine to watch the removal of Lenin appeared unimpressed. "Sorry to say, we don't accept Tesfaye," said a young man. "We want democratic rights and a leader elected by the people."

They might not want the rebels either, he said, but it was well beyond the government's ability to stop them entering Addis Ababa.

Catherine Bond
Daily Telegraph, London, May 24, 1991

Getachew General Tesfay Gebrekidane—he claimed to bring unity and peace to the country by having negotiated with opposition forces and he promised to give hard results by taking certain political measures. So, as political prisoners in Addis Ababa, we were confident of being released, but he released members of the army who were alleged to be involved in the failed coup d'etat, only in prison for two years, and some involved Oromo. As for other kinds of political prisoners, especially Tigrinya speakers, these were left out. We felt very angry and we were ever expecting the worst.

Ghirmai When Mengistu fled, there was a special condition in the prison. Everyone was happy—murderers, the life-sentenced. Tesfay Gebrekidane released Amhara prisoners, including two EPRP members. Not only me, but every political prisoner from Tigray thought we were to die.

"If they take twenty of us with two guards, we have to be ready. Let's at least try something."

We couldn't sleep. We concealed knives, or anything we could use as a weapon. We heard reports about war in Debre Berhan and what happened next in Ambo and, finally, on Sunday evening, the shortwave radios were no longer hidden. Forty or fifty prisoners were listening to the BBC or to the EPRDF news. When the EPRDF took Debre Zeit, a stronghold of the Ethiopian airforce, I remember I said *Dihri selefa intay terefa*—there's no stopping them now. We thought it was all over. "Let them kill us now," some prisoners said.

Oromo We entered Dessie the day Mengistu and his crowd ran away. This guy, Tesfay Gebrekidan, was announcing all sorts of reforms, but we knew everything would stay the same. We knew the army was collapsing. Soldiers were looting and had started to kill each other. The city was falling apart in a horrible way and we didn't want Addis Ababa to be destroyed on the eve of a peaceful Ethiopia. The soldiers running towards the city were plundering on the way and we knew we had no choice but to enter Addis.

Manjus We knew the morale of the enemy was very low and they would therefore fight in a very destructive way. The preparation was very important, because although there had been fighting in some towns, there had never been fighting in a place like Addis Ababa, where there were so many people and where the infrastructure and houses were so much intermingled. The problem was different from the rural area. It was a big job to extract the enemy from among the people. It had to be done with very few fighters, but very effectively because the low morale of the enemy would be destructive and irresponsible. When a soldier loses hope he goes berserk in war. Therefore, in my mind I was thinking women and children and the civilian population, in general, should be spared at any cost. So we were oriented in a new way. Each soldier had to be clear. The goal was the well-being of the people and the infrastructure.

Merkab We were hearing rumors all the time—and we heard they were nearer to Gondar, Wello, Tigray, and Mekelle. So the first thing I knew was the direct radio announcement on Monday, May 27. It was the EPRDF who announced it. Everything was closed in Addis. Addis felt like a football stadium—people just sitting there, no way out, imprisoned, only allowed to watch the play. The EPRDF were closing in from every direction, from Ambo, from Dessie side, from Debre Zeit. Even the day before, I was in the *kebelle* office and we were called to take machine guns to keep ourselves free from thieves. I didn't, but some people did. That made me very much frightened that there would be more killing—even in Addis Ababa, because if I have a gun I can even shoot at my neighbor. And on the day they came people were buying Kalashnikovs for twenty dollars because they were stolen and up for sale.

Habtom Everyone prepared by storing food and taking money out of the bank, because when the EPRDF came, according to the Dergue, no one would be able to live or work or survive at all. Until the moment we were to die, we collected food and money. Everyone went to the market to get food and to the bank to collect money and to the *kebelles* to collect guns and ammunition.

Merkab My *kebelle* is on the Debre Zeit road and on Monday I watched Dergue soldiers coming in a single line. They were retreating before the EPRDF. Then we knew the EPRDF would be coming soon. Most of the people were not properly following their message from their radio. We knew nothing about the *weyanes,* but we wanted to see them, to know who they were, what they looked like, what they wore. On the day they were coming we were preparing food, taking money from the bank because we were expecting the EPRDF to rob the bank, so people, on Monday, were queueing up at the bank on the road to Debre Zeit near our *kebelle*—a very long queue to collect the money. On Tuesday, there was a curfew for two days, but people were so curious they wanted to see the soldiers of the EPRDF, but they weren't a bit what we were expecting.

CHAOS AS ADDIS FORCES COLLAPSE, NAVY FLEES AND AIR FORCE SURRENDERS AS REBELS ENCIRCLE ETHIOPIAN CAPITAL ON EVE OF PEACE TALKS * FOREIGNERS SCRAMBLE TO LEAVE

There were chaotic scenes at Addis Ababa airport yesterday, as thousands of foreign nationals tried to leave the country.

The rebels last night warned the government and airlines against using either the city's international airport or military airport. They said they had both covered by heavy artillery. The crackle of semi-automatic and other fire broke out across the city as darkness fell and continued into the night. The sky was lit by red tracer flashes.

The gunfire was heavy at times in the hills around the presidential palace, but it did not appear to be a coordinated battle and it was not immediately clear who was responsible for the shooting.

Peter Biles
The Guardian, London, May 27, 1991

Ghooish We realized, since it was known that military depots were in Addis Ababa, that these must be very carefully handled, that if they started to explode there would be great destruction of civilian life. Therefore, extra care was taken to avoid all depots and military installations in the city. This was very important. The instruction for this, knowing there were these huge places, was that before each bullet was fired the enemy must be give a chance to give himself up, but if not, that every bullet fired must land on target, never on the civilian population. Right down to the rank and file, each soldier was responsible for executing this plan.

Mulu When Addis was surrounded by the EPRDF, the people were so scared. We thought there would be civil war on the streets. In the last week or two before the EPRDF entered the city, hundreds, maybe thousands, of Dergue soldiers fled into Addis from the surrounding countryside. They were not organized. They seemed like individuals. The city was full of them. They looked humble and frightened and tried to use bullets to pay for food. Before that, we were always afraid of soldiers because of the terrible things that they did, especially to women. We had been listening to the EPRDF radio. We weren't scared of the EPRDF in themselves, but of what the Dergue soldiers would do when they came into the city. There were so many guns, so many bullets in the city.

Getachew We were released on Monday May 27, the day of the London Conference. It was the first time in history that Addis Ababa prison was without guards. They locked the doors and fled during the night. There were certain conditions, that day after the breakdown of the Debre Berhan force, the soldiers demanded three months salary and they were very frightened about being taken, therefore, they were suddenly kind to the political prisoners at that moment. They even told us they would let us free. They tried to equip themselves with any available arms. There was a rumor from the prison guards that they would set prisoners free, so we spent our time trying to collect our baggage. On Sunday, we sent our belongings to our relations, but most people carried their mattresses.

At one p.m., people started to line themselves along the doors, pleading for the doors to be open. But, there was disagreement among the guards, some saying yes and some saying no. Others were saying they could not send them through the gate and be responsible for their escape. After a few minutes, certain guards started firing arms, leading prisoners to escape through the west part of the prison near the fence to the OAU headquarters. It was miraculous. There was a roar of gunfire and we fled. So, people were forced to carry their belongings and jump the two fences. There was even a boggy area, but we were forced to go that way. I held back from the first wave because I was afraid I'd be shot escaping, but then, I joined the group, carrying two cases, one full of books and the other of clothing. I was forced to throw my bags over the wall. I kept throwing them over the fence and picking them up on the other side.

Ghirmai Monday morning was very different because the guards started disobeying and refused to take some prisoners to court and early in the afternoon they started to loot the prison—typewriters, the co-op shop (which was supposed to be for prisoners, but was totally for the officers). The criminals came first, bursting from the cells to the gates. We were too fearful to be first; in fact, they were shooting up in the air. Most of the prisoners were carrying their mattresses, which were useless. Every car was sounding its horn in sympathy with us. I found my cousin Alem, weeping on the fence of the prison. She came, at once, when she heard shots and because I was a bit late she was weeping.

ETHIOPIA'S NEW LEADERS GIVE COMMITMENT TO DEMOCRACY

The United States-brokered peace talks on Ethiopia came to a swift and successful end yesterday with the main insurgent groups proclaiming themselves committed to a pluralist democracy. They also agreed that Eritrea should be allowed to determine its own future, including independence if it wished.

The rebel groups have given assurances that the famine relief routes will immediately be reopened, with the Eritrean ports of Massawa and Assab fully operational.

The prime minister of the defunct government, Tesfaye Dinka, boycotted yesterday's talks, but his absence scarcely caused a ripple. The toppled regime is now irrelevant, and the rebel victory is complete.

Hella Pick
The Guardian, London, May 29, 1991

Tsadkan We went in on the night of May 27. Our forces entered Addis Ababa all night, slowly, and early in the morning we were all over the city. We knew there would be no serious fighting, but we wanted to avoid small skirmishes, so we planned to capture the big centers first and then spread out to other areas after the big centers had been consolidated. This strategic plan was on the assumption that there might be WPE members or police or undercover security agents ready to make trouble. The special brigade for Mengistu's protection was still there, so there was the possibility of a fight with these people.

We divided the city into thirteen major sections. Every section had its center of attention, like the area of Siddis Kilo, Arat Kilo, Bole, and the airport, the Ministry of Defense, the Palace, the embassies. So, attention was paid first to taking these areas, consolidating them and then spreading out to other areas for units to clean the area assigned to them. We managed to collect some people from the city, from the Sendafa area and Debre Zeit to guide us, because our army was primarily a peasant army who had no knowledge of Addis Ababa.

Oromo I was in command of the brigade entering the city from the north flank. The first brigade went to the palace; the third brigade went to the airport; the fourth brigade went to the National Palace; the second brigade was used as a defense in the rear. No tanks or big stuff to be used.

Kawita We were waiting in Sendafa for the result of the peace talks in London when we received news through the people of Sendafa and from our command that the city was in a bad way, that soldiers coming from all directions were vandalizing, robbing, plundering. We were given instructions to start about midnight. When we were approaching Bole airport, I will never forget the lights of Addis. An old Amhara man of sixty-five promised to show us the way, but we told him there would be some danger. We met soldiers on the Asmara road. We told them to be calm and not lose their lives. There were not too many, but we did not return their fire. We entered Bole Airport about five-thirty. We opened a door and found some cooks. They showed us where the Dergue soldiers were hiding. Eight hundred and forty-five soldiers surrendered before daybreak.

Bandit I came from the direction of Dessie. We started walking to Addis Ababa at twelve midnight, forty-one kilometers from Sendafa. There was a radio broadcast continuously repeating what was happening on all the fronts. We knew the hour had arrived. We had been fighting for so many years. We were very hungry to meet the people of Addis Ababa. We had all our soldiers, horses, arms, ready to move. We had reports from the international news and every soldier was oriented about this news coverage and we felt the eyes of the world upon us and how important it was to go in and carry out our role with great care. We all felt very conscious. The first shots were carried out at five o'clock in the morning.

Wodiraya We entered Addis Ababa in trucks. The heavy weapons and tanks stayed behind, because our first priority was to spare lives and property and infrastructure. Therefore, we got into trucks and dropped off at

Arat Kilo. There were soldiers there. We said hello to them and went on to the palace.

Tsadkan There was some resistance around the palace where the special brigade of Mengistu was deployed. It was a small area, but they had about sixty Russian-made T62 tanks. We attacked from two positions—from the road that comes directly from Meskel Square and from the Parliament Building. These two groups had eight tanks. We managed to burn four tanks and kill the soldiers and then captured all the rest of the tanks. The battle took from forty-five minutes to an hour. Apart from that, there was small sporadic gunfire in the city, but no organized meaningful resistance except around the palace and about ten a.m. Addis Ababa was totally under our control.

Oromo Yes, we faced stiff resistance in the Palace. They were trusted forces who believed in the regime and we did pay quite a price there. We entered the palace at five-thirty and at a quarter to eight, the last shots were fired.

Wodiraya They fired the first shots and we called to them not to fight, not to lose their lives. But, they continued and then we started to shoot back. We went into the palace and they refused to listen so we had to deal with that. By six o'clock, people came to talk to us and we told them we were the EPRDF, that we had to end this war. People came up and provided us with food and water. They also told us where the Dergue's hidden weapons were. We captured Dergue soldiers; we did not execute any. We tried to explain our line, our aims. There were demonstrators supporting us in some places. This is what we were expecting.

Manjus We took the Asmara road to Meskel Square and linked with the palace. We were only twenty minutes from the enemy when they started to fire from their tanks. My first memory was of ululating women in their homes. Some who dared come out gave us lots of kisses and hugs. Some started to climb on the Dergue tanks themselves and were crying out peace. The EPRDF leadership had told us the people of Addis were waiting for us. A few hours earlier, we had heard that the city was collapsing and we had to avert carnage, but I never expected to see it like that. As soon as they saw women fighters, they ignored us men—they were so happy to see women fighters.

"We have waited so long," one said. "I am so proud of the female comrades because I can see what they symbolize."

Merkab We heard on the radio they were coming. They came and there was no shooting until that moment, but it was not big shooting like taking over a government. But, we were used to such shooting among the Dergue, even a bit longer.

Habtom EPRDF was saying over their radio that they were trying to bring peace and democracy and to destroy the Dergue, this fascist government. Anyway, at this time, the Dergue administration had been disarmed and retreated through the airport and by car and many went into exile in Zimbabwe. Within a week, the EPRDF took over in Addis. They came in the middle of the night and we only heard there was some fighting. When we came out in the morning, on every corner there were groups of fighters in shorts and wrapped in shawls. In groups of three or four, they stopped on corners, separately. We were expecting them to be like bandits or savages, but they were very human and very confident. They talked with people smoothly. They mostly spoke Tigrinya. They tried to speak Amharic. We asked them things in Amharic and they tried to explain in Amharic what the EPRDF is, what was their aim, how they passed their struggle.

Merkab They were not big as we thought, but very small, very short. Their hair, their clothes—we had never seen anything like it before. When we saw this we thought, "These people can't be taking over the government." We thought some foreign government must be backing them. They were small in size, very thin, with very curious eyes, hair long and in locks, and their clothing was... Everyone had a cloth over one shoulder and over the other, a gun. We thought they'd fight, insult, but their calmness made the people calm, their calmness reflected on others. They were not even in a line, just walking in twos or fours and standing on the road.

When I saw the women fighters, I felt very soft-hearted for that woman because I know that women do not want to fight, but I knew they had no chance to live a peaceful life, no belongings, but had to go to the front. I was thinking of their menstrual periods and what difficulties they must have. In towns, we keep our distance from men, but I think they lived like comrades and brothers, not sexually.

Habtom The Dergue soldiers had gathered in the city and formed thieves' gangs and took to stealing and violence. But, the EPRDF arrived and they were sociable and reasonable. Shortly after that, when they tried to stabilize the people without any disturbance people went on with their life and work. There was no harassment of women. They were disciplined. They were dispersed throughout the city on the streets.

Kawita At seven a.m. at Bole airport, we heard on the radio that Addis Ababa had fallen. Then, we came across a plane on the runway full of Dergue and Soviet officials. They refused to come out and talk. Then Tsadkan and others came out to talk to them. The people came and offered us their shoes. It was a joyous experience. They took the youngest fighters on their backs.

At the airport, they offered us food and we accepted and ate together with the people who offered it to us because they offered in such a spirit we couldn't refuse. At the military camp, we were offered lots of *injera* but we were suspicious of it so we didn't eat it. There were people who cried when they saw us cooking our food in very difficult situations and they asked, "Is this how you passed this life in the bush?" People would have tears in their eyes. But after a minute, we were very fed up with this Dergue food. We washed it down with tea and whenever we couldn't find any other food, we dissolved sugar in water and that kept us going.

Tsadkan When I was near the periphery of Addis Ababa, I expected some hostilities, not big, but skirmishes. I was towards Sendafa on a hilltop, which could help me view the whole city at nine a.m. on May 28. The battle for Addis was over and I had to enter the city. A little later, I was in my landcruiser. I saw a lot of people standing together. I was very curious to see who they were. Some were clapping, some were raising their fists in salute and trying to say things to us. All the way from Kotebe to Bole to the Palace, people were shouting, hailing, clapping, and so on. I stayed for some hours in Bole and then went to the center in the afternoon.

In the afternoon, the whole population was on the streets looking at the fighters. There was clapping and jubilation and also some relief. This scene of our entering Addis Ababa is something I will never forget. It was beyond my expectations. It was beyond my expectations, not because I thought people would hate us, but because I thought they would be hiding in their houses while we flushed out small units and chased opponents. I didn't expect people to express their relief on that day. That is something I will always remember.

Mekebib: I was asleep at home on the 28th. At dawn, I heard shots from the National Palace. Every family was disturbed. By the next morning, all the people thought we were in danger. We came from our huts to see what's going on on the streets and found the soldiers in small units with guns on their shoulders and just waiting—very watchfully—in case of some disturbance from any direction. They thought some Dergue soldiers might be hiding in corners. But, there was no disturbance. We thought they would be like wild animals or frightening like a *chirac*, a monster to scare children. Most of the people came out to see and showed their pleasure in their faces. We tried to speak to them, ask them where they came from and what they wanted. There were some problems to communicate because there are many nationalities in our country and, because starting their struggle from their homeland, they have moved from there to places of different languages.

Merkab So the people went out to see them and on the day they came, in the afternoon, there was some looting of the offices by the townsfolk. Everyone was free and wandering about and looting. I stayed at home. Then, they set the curfew. That night, there was some fighting—we heard some shooting from the Palace.

Mekebib On Tuesday lunchtime, at one o'clock, they made many announcements on the radio. They were declaring their take-over and the overthrow of the Dergue: "After so many years of struggle, we are here and we've come to save the people; we are on the side of the oppressed people and prepare the way for peace and stability." They told us to stay indoors for twenty-four hours. They repeated this many times on the day. People did not believe the radio words. "Even the Dergue spoke to us like this at first," they said. There was a lot of suspicion.

Merkab Yes, I remember when I was a nurse in Gondar, twenty-five years ago. I was part of a team going for health development. The people were suspicious of our intentions.

"It was this way," they said, "when the Italians came to our country, they said they wanted to develop health clinics, but they took our land."

"But, we are Ethiopians."

"So, were they guided by Ethiopians."

"The Ethiopian Government also takes our land," said another.

So, we had to gather the elders and talk to them for a long time in the church before we could go ahead.

Zewdi The task of our division was not to go to Addis Ababa, but to Dire Dawa. From Dessie, we went to Bati, to the Afar lowlands, to Awash and from there to Dire Dawa. We were in trucks. All the way, people were lining up to greet us. When we started the journey, Debre Zeit and Addis Ababa had already fallen, so we were moving during the day. Oromos came out to clap and ululate. They were offering food and competing whose food would be accepted. There were even soldiers joining in. We met hundreds of soldiers in a very bad way, with hunger and thirst. We gave them our water and biscuits. These soldiers were completely stranded, cut off from their comrades. The people were asking us, "Why are you leaving us? What if the enemy comes again?" They always showed us where the soldiers were. This was such an important day in my life. Addis fell on Tuesday. So, this was one or two days after that—on Wednesday or Thursday.

In the Eastern Command, we got the same orientation as for Addis Ababa, although Addis Ababa was much larger than Harar or Dire Dawa. Dire Dawa was the first one to fall. As Addis was already taken, the morale of the enemy was at its lowest. We took two things into consideration: to enter the cities in this area as peacefully as we possibly could and, second, the WPE presence in this area. We made contact with the generals. We told them, "The capital has fallen, don't lose your lives." We waited and waited for them to surrender. The generals of Dire Dawa and our generals met together, fully armed to discuss the procedures of surrender. They also discussed how weapons should be given up and also the presence of many WPE members in the area, who we knew would not give up easily. Also, the security forces would make it very difficult for the generals to give themselves up easily. Eventually, they all surrendered and then the EPRDF and the generals had a party together.

This area has a different quality. The culture is different; the language is different. They had never met on so new a ground in a way. Therefore we had prepared for this. Oromos and Somalis were there. There were even language difficulties. But the people had heard about the EPRDF and knew we were liberating them from a terrible enemy. We knew they were appreciating us.

Habtom They were not savage killers, but reasonable people, most of them in their twenties or thirties or youngsters. There were some women too, but they were not the same as Dergue women soldiers. These were also wearing shorts and shawls and plastic sandals and carrying guns, just like boys. They were indifferent to everything except their mission. Their food was mostly sugar and water or they mixed jam and water and drank it. They had very little food with them, and anyway, there was very little left in Addis. During the capture, there was a new dawn of hope because we had imagined them as killers.

Mekebib I tried to appreciate them and was eager to hear what they were trying to tell us. It was very difficult, but after the first day, we were getting used to them, acquainted. Then we began to realize they were friendly and very democratic. In my locality, the youngsters especially hated them because of the radio propaganda of their badness. But, afterwards, they became acquainted with fighters and group leaders. Boys were opposing their ideas: "You are not fit to govern Ethiopia," "You are from only one nation" and so on. But, their answer was very democratic, not arguing, but explaining their aim. The Dergue soldiers were very different, especially at the gate of the prisons—very rough and tough. Everyone avoided them because they were afraid. They beat people, tore their clothes.

Oromo We were already prepared for life on the streets, because we had brought our dried food for ourselves, enough for a month. As fighters, we are never allowed to ask the people for food and we couldn't go to the restaurants because we had no money, and we wouldn't do that anyway. We had dry biscuits we had made ourselves from wheat and then we had tinned vegetables and we mixed them and ate that. We were frequently offered food. A month later, we were allowed to use people's kitchens and utensils. We had taken our position, our place, and we stayed there. The month of that food was very hard.

Tsadkan Our army was scattered throughout the town and even if provocation was very high, they had to respond with discussion and not to rise—only in extreme conditions. These were the instructions against provocation. Their discussion, patience, and vigilance had a very strong impact on the population that peace and order had been established in the town. Some notices, everyday, were coming on TV and radio. There was reassurance in propaganda leaflets, government announcements, everyday addressing the people directly and telling them peace and order were being established. People were fed up with the Dergue and wanted some change and welcomed change. They welcomed the EPRDF because they brought this change and they heard it was a democratic organization and the maturity of the Ethiopian people and the people in Addis Ababa not to panic, but be sober and responsible, was one factor that contributed to a very smooth and fast stabilization of the city.

Merkab On Revolution Square [now renamed Meskel Square], they were going up and down in groups, but they were posted at the emigration office and they were cooking and washing on the street. They were posted to particular offices at the Ministry of Defense, residing on the asphalt and cooking and looking after themselves.

Alemtsehai They came as a fighting force, as conquerors, but when we saw their behavior, it was completely out of character. It was very difficult to believe it at the beginning. It grew even stranger, as it did not change. They came to this compound—about twenty people were below in the yard of our apartment block. But what struck me was—the first day they arrived one of them asked one of the residents for a match. She threw a box to them, but he replied, "I am called to a briefing, so I don't need it after all." She said, "Keep it," but he refused. They never take anything anyone offers. In fact, *they* ask us to eat and drink with *them.* We noticed they were very disciplined and knew their objectives. The ones we talked to were not interested in Addis Ababa. They wanted to go back and help their mothers and fathers in Tigray.

Mekebib There were some robbers stealing from the houses and running very fast. When the EPRDF fighters saw, they immediately took action. This was not very often, but there were some incidents.

Merkab I heard that near Mexico Square, near the Technical School and Wabe Shebelle, there were two men trying to throw grenades. Some EPRDF fighters were in a car moving around and a young fighter shot first and killed one.

Mulu The EPRDF came up from the direction of Debre Zeit. We live on the Debre Zeit road. Everyone hid in their houses. If they had a pistol they waited, quiet, listening to everything outside, with their pistol in their hand, ready to defend themslves. But, everything stayed quiet and the EPRDF entered and took control of the city and it was quiet and peaceful. After a few days, we began to talk to the EPRDF fighters. They were very thin and seemed very tired, maybe from walking so many kilometers. They seemed too tired even to talk.

The only thing that happened—maybe one or two nights later—an ammunition store exploded. It was quite near to our house, about four a.m. in the morning. They say it was Dergue soldiers who didn't want the ammunition to go to the EPRDF—but I don't know. The explosion blew our front door away and all the windows and light fittings were smashed to bits.

For years, I was living with the Dergue. I hate politics.

Merkab From the time Mengistu went, me and my family were very worried about the future and for the last two weeks before he left there was registration in the *kebelles*, masked by saying that those who already had identity cards must have new ones and those outside who were displaced over the last year must come to Addis Ababa, because the EPRDF were approaching. Anyway, I knew a family, nearby, living near the Debre Zeit road. One of them was a friend, unmarried, a university graduate who started to work for six hundred birr. Her mother, three brothers, one sister, two other relatives, and one soldier who was injured (therefore eleven people) were all living in that house—none of them registered. Therefore, she had to buy sugar at four or five dollars a kilo (instead of one birr from the *kebelle*). Also, they couldn't be registered because they had no letter from the area they came from. They just walked and that was illegal. Therefore, I was trying to buy for her from the *kebelle* on my ration card. But, by the time the EPRDF arrived, they called for registration and she gave all eleven names and got registered.

But, in the next few days after the EPRDF arrived, we heard rumors that registration was for organizing killing, starting off with those who are displaced and therefore newly registered, because they would cause less disturbance than long-term residents. So, we thought this was going to happen under the EPRDF, that these new soldiers were arriving to kill, therefore, there was terror for the first week. So, this terror caused tension and then, one week later, the ammunition depot exploded and we thought it was this new war. My house was only two hundred meters from the depot and all my windows were broken, all my lights. So, then we thought everyone was going to be killed according to the list. Our door smashed open wide, everything was broken. We thought a bomb had been thrown into the house and we went to hide under the beds because "they might throw another if they hear us talking." But, when we went to the bedroom side there was a huge fire blazing and turning the sky to yellow and orange and people running about, shouting and screaming.

Alemtsehai Once things had settled down, we went to a local meeting for our *kebelle*. The whole family, we all went. A woman sitting behind us—she was a leader of the Dergue cooperative shop—kept muttering and talking all the time. She was saying that the EPRDF were taking all the camels and donkeys and sending them to Tigray, that their democracy was a lie. In fact democracy had become a mockery here. I turned round and said, "democracy is not lying; democracy is truth."

Tsadkan After we captured Addis Ababa, we immediately established a temporary committee to administer the city and got control of the TV station. We were meeting all the time, gathering information. We sent out some notices on television. We opened an office where all the big government officials should report. In the first two or three days, almost all the government ministers and officers came to the Ministry of Defense to report and they were put in custody—all except those who took refuge in the Italian Embassy. This was aired and publicized to the public, which gave some reassurance that we had the situation under control. We gathered government functionaries and told them to continue working normally. We couldn't answer all their questions, but we chatted and to some extent they were reassured.

Merkab After two or three days, there was no curfew. Then, we began to say these people are pleasant. They didn't get angry even when we abused them. Now, there is a division among the people. Once they came to know that the fighters were going to be the government, then the old oppressing classes wanted to keep their power, but the oppressed class wanted to accept the new peace and the new policies of self-reliance.

Lama I have been living in Manitoba for years, but I came back just after Addis was liberated. I felt guilty about running away to Canada to lead a soft life while people were suffering here. I nearly didn't come. I thought they would look at my nice clothes and be thinking, "He is an intruder. Who is this traitor?" I thought I would meet my old school friends without arms or legs. I wasn't sure I could handle it. I talked to other Ethiopians there and they want to come and see later on, but I knew I must come now.

The other day, in Addis, I saw a line of young fighters, all so young and all carrying guns. Those fighters, I thought, were perhaps hardly born when I left the country. They were so quiet, so disciplined. Before, it was impossible to get near the palace of Mengistu, where Meles has his office now. It was ringed with guards and you could not get within a hundred meters. Now, there is one guard and you can go right up to the gate. He asked me what I wanted and I mentioned someone I know. He called someone else to ask if he knew the name, put his arm on my shoulder and said, "Is it your brother?" I couldn't believe it.

They have not criticized me. It has all been within me. When I look at them I think, "How is this possible? Have they really defeated the Dergue army?"

Postscript

The defeat of the military dictator, Mengistu, and the entry of EPRDF into Addis Ababa on May 28, 1991 brought the long civil war to an end. Although it also brings this story to an end, at the same time, it was the beginning of another, perhaps longer, struggle to establish a democratic Ethiopia.

On May 27 and 28, Meles Zenawi, Chairman of the Ethiopian People's Revolutionary Democratic Front, and Isaias Afwerki, head of the Eritrean People's Liberation Front, met in London for peace talks, chaired by the US Assistant Secretary of State for African Affairs, Herman Cohen. It was also attended by Tesfaye Dinka, Prime Minister of the defeated regime, who boycotted the second day of talks after it was agreed that EPRDF forces should go into Addis Ababa to stabilize the capital and to form an interim government.

This EPRDF government stayed in power for only one month, until a five-day National Conference met on July 1 to discuss how they could share power in a more democratic transitional government. It was attended by representatives from twenty Ethiopian political and nationality organizations and observers from sixteen governments and international organizations. The conference undertook to establish a multi-party electoral system through which it would hand over power to an elected government. One of its most significant achievements was the acceptance of a Charter, which would be the supreme law of the land during the transitional period. The Charter expressed a broad commitment to democratic rights, including the rights of the different nations in Ethiopia to self-determination "up to and including secession" and the creation of a governing Council drawn from different nationalities. It promised the development of a new federal administrative structure, reflecting national and local interests, the drafting of a new constitution, which would enshrine a range of civil and human rights, including the outlawing of discrimination on the grounds of gender or religion, the creation of an independent judiciary, and a commitment to relief and reconstruction of war-affected areas. Later in the month, the Council of

Representatives elected Meles Zenawi President of the Transitional Government and Tamrat Layne Prime Minister.

All the promised developments are now in place or in process. In the first two years, provincial boundary changes facilitated semi-autonomous regional administration. During the early months of 1994, there was extensive discussion down to village level about the alternative possibilities for the new constitution. In April, I attended consultative conferences in Addis Ababa with representatives of women, elders, and Muslims about how their interests could be safeguarded constitutionally. In December 1994, a Constituent Assembly of elected representatives from every area debated and ratified the new Constitution.

In June 1995, regional and national democratic elections took place throughout Ethiopia, supervised by international observers. The EPRDF won these elections and formed the first democratically elected government in Ethiopia's history. Some opposition parties, particularly the Oromo Liberation Front (OLF) and those formed by Amhara elite fearing displacement, boycotted the elections. The Founding Congress of the Federal Democratic Republic of Ethiopia was held in August 1995. Under the new constitution, the highest executive post was that of Prime Minister, to which Meles Zenawi was elected, with Tamrat Layne as deputy. Finally, in March 1996, elections were held at district and village levels.

The struggle is not over, however. It is no easy task to introduce a democratic culture into a country that has only known dictatorships, in which absence of civil rights has meant that the path to advancement was through nepotism, personal influence, and manipulation. Elites, who gained power under past dictatorial regimes, are resisting a democratic system from which they personally cannot benefit. EPRDF itself has had its own problems. In October 1996 Tamrat Layne was demoted from office for corruption and ejected from his party, the Amhara National Democratic Movement (the new name for EPDM), and from EPRDF.

Ethiopia is still beset with economic difficulties, but the present government has diverged from the economic policies of its predecessors by making security of land tenure and development support for the subsistence farmers who make up eighty-five percent of the population central to its first agricultural five-year plan. In 1996 Ethiopia exported maize and sorghum for the first time in its history. But that is another story.

Notes

Chapter 1

1. "Torch of the revolution" (Tigrinya *shig weyanit*.f.) a peasant activist.
2. Berhane Aberra, field name "Meley" (apple), TPLF Commander, interviewed in Tigrinya, January 30, 1987.

Chapter 2

1. Gedaref, a town south east of Khartoum near the Ethiopian border.
2. The Tigray People's Liberation Front was founded on February 18, 1975, by a group of dissident Tigrayans, most of them students, who had left Addis Ababa to avoid arrest by the military government.
3. The Convoy, as it was called, was started by REST after 1978 but greatly expanded between 1983 amd 1986, when REST's transport fleet increased from 20 to 285 trucks. A consortium of aid agencies, dismayed at the displacement and loss of life of the Tigrayan population, founded the Tigray Transport and Agriculture Consortium (TTAC), to tackle the problems of relief distribution. The convoy travelled several times a week, at night, from the REST garage outside Gedaref and was a life-line for the survival of the Tigrayan population during the 1975-1991 civil war and therefore for the liberation struggle of the TPLF.
4. REST was founded in 1978 by members of the TPLF, as a humanitarian organization through which aid agencies could channel relief aid and essential medical supplies from the West to the villages of Tigray.
5. The *Dergue* refers to the military government which came to power in September 1974, after the deposition of Emperor Haile Selassie. *Dergue* was originally the name for a committee of a group of officers elected by their brigades. At first the army did not demand the overthrow of Haile Selassie, but better conditions, incorporating vague demands for greater democracy taken over from urban political movements. Fearful of feudal reaction, the army officers siezed power, but to stabilize its hold on power, it had to destroy the feudal class and bring the radicalized middle class under

its control. After 1977, they were supported by the USSR who armed them against dissident movements.

6. *Banda* is the Tigrinya term for groups of Dergue-trained counter-revolutionaries who regularly infiltrated Tigray to commit atrocities, blaming it on the TPLF. See Aklilu's definition in Chapter 15.

Chapter 3

1. Major Mengistu Haile Mariam was among the group of junior officers who in the early months of 1974 came to represent the widespread dissatisfaction felt by the Ethiopian army, which itself was reflecting the popular discontent at the social and administrative chaos of the imperial regime. After the formal deposition of Haile Selassie in September, he became the leader of the Provisional Military Administrative Council (PMAC), or the Dergue, and initiated a series of brutal purges of rival leaders, opposition groups and of the Dergue itself.

Chapter 4

1. Agazi was born in Wukro, a town north of Mekelle in eastern Tigray, but received his later education in Asmara, Eritrea, where he was influenced by the revolutionary ideas of the armed struggle for independence which had begun in 1962. From there he went to University of Addis Ababa, where he was active in the radical student movement which was a major force in the toppling of Haile Selassie. In February 1975 he was one of the eleven or so members of the Tigray National organisation (TNO) who went off to Dedebit in western Tigray to start the TPLF.

Chapter 5

1. There is a distinction between a "base area" and a "base camp". In the early years of the armed struggle, the TPLF had a series of base areas, such as Dedebit in the west, Sheraro in the north west, Agame in the north east. These were at first operational areas in which the small numbers of TPLF fighters would seek to build a relationship with the people of that area, but later became those parts of the liberated area where the TPLF training establishments, military, educational and medical/surgical, were sited. As more and more of the rural area of Tigray came under their control during the eighties, "base camps" became the headquarters of the Central Committee and of the de facto government in a series of inaccessible locations for security.

2. Kudusan Nega coincided with me on this occasion in Dejenna (see later in the chapter). Years after this in 1997 in Mekelle, she described to me her astonishment to see garlic and onions in the camp as the fighters had a very restricted diet and had not seen vegetables for a long time. 'They are not for us; they are for the *ferenji*,' she was told.
3. Another example of this code was the edict not to kill the enemy in battle if it was avoidable; it was preferable to take him prisoner. It is difficult to assess how far such codes were implemented, but enlightened self-interest no doubt played a part. Certainly the TPLF (and later the EPRDF) took huge numbers of prisoners and laid on extensive programs of political education in the P.O.W. camps. Two of the first organizations in the new EPRDF in 1989, the Oromo Peoples' Democratic Organization (OPDO) and the Ethiopian Democratic Officers' Revolutionary Movement (EDORM), originated in the prisoner of war camps.
4. *Shifta,* "bandits," needs clarification in the Ethiopian context. In this case it has the conventional meaning of a roving band of robbers who harass and live off the people. It was also used to denote those who were outlawed for political reasons, sometimes from the noble class, sometimes for standing against the noble class. These were sometimes called *weyane* (rebels) in Tigray, as were the TPLF by the Dergue.
5. Sebhat Nega, a founder member of TPLF and former chairman.
6. This narrative is drawn from the accounts of several founder fighters of the TPLF, but mostly from Asgede Gebreselassie, interviewed in Tigrinya in Endaselassie on April 16, 1991, and Meles Zenawi, interviewed in English on March 27/28, 1991.
7. Meles Zenawi, interviewed in English at the Dejenna base camp, January 5, 1987.
8. This was one of the points of political difference from the EPLF. Eritrea had been colonized since the end of the 19th century by Italy and the EPLF interpreted their political contradiction as a "colonial question." The TPLF, on the other hand, considered the primary contradiction for Ethiopia to be the oppression by the central ruling elite of the non-Amhara nationalities and saw their predicament as a "national question." These differences of history and political analysis underlay the divergent aims of their respective struggles. Whereas the EPLF fought for independence from Ethiopia, the TPLF fought for self-determination for the different nationalities as one aspect of a democratic Ethiopia.
9. Bissrat Asfaw, interviewed in English in London, April 4, 1985. This interview was published as "Besserat Asfaw, a Woman Fighter" in *Dying for Profit: The Causes of Famine in Africa* Third World First, 1985.

10. The USSR began to give economic and military support to the Dergue in 1977. The USA, who had supported the Haile Selassie government, was still in the throes of a policy dilemma about whether to continue or break off this support to the successor regime, when Somalia invaded the contested Ogaden region. The Soviet Union and Cuba, who had been supporting Somalia, then changed sides and went to the aid of Ethiopia. The USA followed suit by tranferring its support to Somalia.
11. Lemlem Gesesse, interviewed in Tigrinya in London, July 1988. Lemlem was the daughter of one of the founder fighters of the TPLF, Gesesse Ayele, field name "Suhul". He was a respected member of the Parliament (*shengo*) under Haile Selassie, a campaigner for development for Tigray and equal rights for Tigrayans, but he was distrusted and persecuted as a Tigrayan nationalist by both Haile Selassie and the Dergue. The founders of the TPLF left for the field from his house in Endaselassie in Shire on February 18, 1975. Harassment of the family by the authorities led to Lemlem also fleeing to the field in 1976. She was one of the first women fighters.
12. Tigray was organized by the TPLF into three administrative regions. Region One was the west, Region Two the central highlands, and Region Three, the east, including the Afar lowlands. "Region Four" signified the Tigrayans in the rest of the world, who were also organized into associations their adoptive countries. Each region in Tigray was further divided into zones. There were twelve zones altogether during the civil war and the chief administrator of each was the zone secretary. There are now four zones in Tigray.

Chapter 6

1. The Departments were started in 1978 and began to pull together in a more formal way, organizing work that had already begun in the rural area, such as the "Mass Bureau" or 08. This was the largest and possibly the most important department, responsible for organizing the people. It had several subsections, such as a branch responsible for organizing and training the cadres (*shig weyenti*), one for administration of baitos, one of the Women's Association, for organizing clandestine agitation in the Dergue towns and so on. Other departments were Education, Health, Agriculture and Transport.
2. The Red Star Campaign in 1982 was an effort by the Dergue to annihilate the EPLF in Eritrea. The Dergue had by that time recruited an army of an estimated 245,000 men. Half of these were used against the EPLF in their base area in Sahelian Eritrea. The TPLF sent several brigades of fighters to fight alongside the EPLF.

3. Shire was a district (*awraja*) in western Tigray of which the main town is Endaselassie, but the county name 'Shire' is commonly used as the name of the town, as here.
4. Yemane Kidane (fieldname "Jamaica"), interviewed in English in Mekelle, March 25, 1991; Asgede Gebreselassie, interviewed in Tigrinya in Endaselassie, April 16, 1991; Aklilu Tekemte, interviewed in English in Mekelle, February 6, 1991.
5. The TPLF practice was to carry out land reform in each area as they slowly gained control of the countryside in the late 1970s and early 1980s. This was the second land reform program they carried out in 1987. The aim of the first was to destroy the feudal stranglehold on land; the aim of the second was to increase production in support of the war.
6. *Zar:* a spirit which is thought to take possession of certain individuals who thereby gain special powers, especially of spiritual and bodily healing. The TPLF have worked hard to discourage superstitious beliefs and practices in the countryside, where these were most powerful. Although they have no doubt diminished with increased development of the economy and education, they are unlikely to have been eliminated.
7. *Debtera:* previously a highly educated class of the priesthood of the Ethiopian Orthodox Church, particularly skilled in the interpretation of sacred texts, and usually trained in elite monasteries in Gondar and Gojjam. Allegedly because they abused their knowledge or their position or because their special powers were perceived as arcane knowledge, their links with the Church have been severed. They make a living as fortune-tellers and, within the superstitious rural culture of Tigray, they are often regarded as sorcerers.
8. *Owlia:* the name given to a powerful spirit which is believed to take possession of certain people who then have special powers to heal all kinds of sickness.
9. The *Fukuras,* highly educated in the Muslim religion, were thought to possess special powers and practice sorcery, often involving *anderebi,* a kind of poltergeist.
10. *Kitab*: a little bag, usually of cloth, containing appropriate charms and worn around the neck.
11. Meskel, the Cross, also means the religious feast day which celebrates the cross of Christ in early September and is therefore associated with the Ethiopian new year, 1 September. The important moment of the religious rituals is the lighting of a bonfire. In Addis Ababa, the square where these annual celebrations take place is called Meskel Square.
12. Tekebach Murubi, interviewed In Tigrinya in Ruba Lemin, April 1991.

13. EDU: Ethiopian Democratic Union, the political party of "the feudals" and their followers and beneficiaries, led by Ras Mengesha Seyoum, the hereditary prince of Tigray.
14. In fact, the highest level congress was the TPLF Congress held every three or four years and composed of roughly equal numbers of elected representatives from TPLF fighters and from the mass associations. This was the congress which discussed and voted on policy presented by the executive, the Central Committee, and which elected the executive for the next term. There were standing councils (*baitos)* of the people at the district (*wereda*) and village (*tabia*) levels, but at the zone level at this time Tigray was administered by the TPLF and congresses were convened for special purposes, such as this one on land redistribution, to which representatives were elected from district and village councils.
15. It has been customary to divide the peasants into three grades according to their wealth, rich, middle and poor. The level of income and expertise of the middle peasant was adopted as the development objective for all peasants. This was the policy known as "standardization."

Chapter 7

1. There is a reference here to James Fenton's news correspondents in *The Snap Revolution*, Granta 18 Spring 1986 p38.
2. The Dergue's *Zemacha* sent some 30-50,000 university and secondary school students to the rural areas to take the revolution to the peasants, particularly the program of land reform. According to TPLF in the 1980s, the Dergue land reform had serious flaws, as did the Dergue peasant associations, created in the rural areas to build a popular basis for its rule in the guise of decentralizing authority and to administer land reform. The officials of the PAs (and their counterparts in the towns, the *kebelles*) became the long arm of authoritarian rule.
3. Berhanu Abadi, interviewed in English in Dejenna, February 23, 1987.
4. Mebratu told this story in Mai Hanse on January 21, 1997. I discovered later that this was the version of the Axum Bank story which was told to young fighters in the training camp. A more factual version is given in Chapter 16.

Chapter 8

1. Also see Peter Niggli *Ethiopia: Deportations and Forced-Labour Camps* Berliner Missionswerk, 1986, a translation of an original German report published in May 1985.

2. According to Lemlem Hagos, this was the River Barro.
3. Lemlem Hagos identified these people as "the Anuak, a river people who live by hunting and fishing".
4. During most of the 1980s, the Oromo Liberation Front (OLF) was one of the movements cooperating with the TPLF in the armed struggle against the military dictatorship, the Dergue. Their aim was, and still is, secession for the parts of Ethiopia they identify as Oromia. After the TPLF encouraged the foundation of the Oromo Peoples' Democratic Organization (OPDO) in 1989 as a member of the coalition of the EPRDF, relations between TPLF and OLF soured.
5. Lemlem Hagos, interviewed in Tigrinya in August 1989 in Khartoum.
6. The Irob nationality is one of the minority nationalities in Tigray. Their homeland is in Agame in north-east Tigray around the town of Alitena on the Eritrean border.

Chapter 9

1. Aregash left the EPRP for the TNO. The Ethiopian Peoples' Revolutionary Party (EPRP) grew out of the radical student opposition to the Haile Selassie regime which gathered momentum in the late 1960s and early 1970s. In the mid-1970s it was the most important and powerful of the dissident parties. Its political analysts identified class as the primary contradiction, whereas the Tigrayan National Organization (TNO), which in February 1975 was to become the TPLF, thought that oppression on the grounds of nationality took precedence over class oppression.
2. Hiwot Negash, fieldname "Laflaf," woman fighter, interviewed in Tigrinya in Wukro, 11 April 1991.
3. Later in the 1980s the dictator, Mengistu Haile Mariam, struck a deal with the Israeli government to exchange the *Falashas* for arms. The majority of the Falasha people were taken to Israel in a series of flights at first secret, later exposed in the press.
4. Tsehaitu Fekadu, interviewed in Tigrinya in Sheraro on January 12, 1987 and April 18, 1991.

Chapter 10

1. International Women's Day, March 8, is still celebrated in many countries on the date chosen by Clara Zetkin, a German Marxist, at the Second International in 1910, to commemorate a woman garment workers' strike in the USA.

2. Kebbedesh Haile, woman fighter, interviewed in Tigrinya at Marta School, February 13, 1987.
3. The *Kebelle* Youth Association was a part of the authoritarian structure of the State under the Dergue. Its officers exercised considerable powers of coer-cion and punishment.
4. Genet Negash, woman fighter, interviewed in Tigrinya at Marta School on February 13, 1987.
5. Drar Gebreyesus, field name "Anbassa" (lion) and Berhane Aberra, field name "Meley" (apple), interviewed in Tigrinya in Mai Humer, January 30, 1987.
6. Saba, woman fighter and Director of Marta School, interviewed in English at Marta School, February 11, 1987.
7. Greenham Common was a US Airforce nuclear base in Berkshire in England where cruise missiles were sited until the end of the Cold War. From 1983 it was encircled by women's peace camps and became the model of protest by women anti-nuclear activists all over the world.

Chapter 11

1. The situation has now changed. The five nationalities in Tigray at this time were the Tigrinya-speakers (the majority), the Afar, the Kunama, the Agew and the Saho-speaking Irob. Since the institution of a federal structure in 1993, based on self-determination for the nationalities, the policy of the government has been to give as much autonomous status to minority nationalities as their numbers permit. Thus the Afar-speaking eastern lowlands have become part of a separate Afar state, Region Two, and the Agew speakers in the south have been hived off as part of the Agew-speaking zone *(zoba)* of Sekota in Amhara or Region Three. Smaller minorities have their local government as a zone (county) or wereda (district), according to the population.
2. Eysa Mohammed, Afar woman fighter, interviewed in Tigrinya at Marta School, February 13, 1987.
3. The Ethiopian Peoples' Democratic Movement (EPDM), founded in 1981, was a splinter movement from the Ethiopian Peoples' Revolutionary Party (EPRP). Both groups were predominantly Amhara, but the EPDM founders differed from the EPRP on the nationality issue. EPDM considered national oppression a primary contradiction in Ethiopia, thus approximating more closely to the TPLF. A more detailed history will be found in Chapter 21.
4. Tartarow Sebeho, fighter and musician, interviewed in Tigrinya at the Music Department in Kaza, February 15, 1987.
5. Iyassu Berhe, fighter and head of the TPLF Cultural Department, interviewed in English at the Music Department in Kaza, February 15, 1987.

Chapter 12

1. Berhan Gebremikael, laundry woman, interviewed in Tigrinya in Endaselassie, June 16, 1989.
2. Yomar and Rahma, prostitutes, interviewed in Tigrinya in Endaselassie, June 4, 1989.
3. Abrahet Teklemuze, prostitute, interviewed in Tigrinya in Endaselassie, June 15, 1989.
4. Askale Yohannes, former bank employee, interviewed in English/Tigrinya in Mekelle, June 8, 1989. Soon after this Askale became a fighter. She died in the last stages of the war.
5. Tadelle, administrator of Mekelle, in 1989, interviewed in Tigrinya in Mekelle, June 10, 1989.
6. Genet Negash, woman fighter. This conversation in Tigrinya took place in Mekelle, June 10, 1989.
7. Meles Zenawi, interviewed in English near Samre, 9 June 1989.
8. Aregash Adane, woman fighter, Central Committee member, interviewed in English near Samre, June 9, 1989.
9. Both quotations from Geday Legesse, peasant, interviewed in English at a Sudan border post, May 31, 1989.
10. These two quotations from Liknesh Tekle, field name "Lichy", woman fighter, interviewed in Tigrinya in Endaselassie, June 16, 1989.
11. Werknesh, woman fighter and squad commander, interviewed in Tigrinya in the TPLF garrison at Mugolat, June 11, 1989.
12. Berihu Deres, farmer, interviewed in Tigrinya with others in Hausien, June 11, 1989.

Chapter 13

1. EPRDF Congress Report, *Documents from the First National Congress of the Ethiopian Revolutionary Democratic Front*, January 1991.
2. The Ethiopian Democratic Officers' Revolutionary Movement (EDORM) was started in prisoner of war camps by officers of the Dergue forces captured by TPLF. The TPLF assessment of the brutal nature of the dictatorship of the Dergue assumed that middle-ranking officers and ordinary people, given the chance to espouse a viable democratic alternative, would be a source of valuable recruits to the resistance struggle. This assumption underpinned their preference for taking prisoners and re-educating them in the camps.
3. The Marxist-Leninist League of Tigray (MLLT) was founded in 1985. Its main thrust seemed to be to argue for much greater consultation and peasant

participation than before, at all levels of political and, interestingly, military practice. The first battles in which these principles were tried out were the Battle of Dejenna in 1988 and the Battle of Endaselassie in February 1989. Both were victories and turned the tide against the Dergue. I have been told by the TPLF leadership that MLLT has been dissolved since 1991.

4. Much has been made, especially by Western journalists, of the alleged espousal by the TPLF of the "Albanian model". My own assessment is that this is largely mythical. The TPLF grew out of the Marxist-oriented student movement against the Haile Selassie regime in Addis Ababa and there is no doubt that Marxist and Marxist-Leninist explanations for the subjection and poverty of the mass of the Ethiopian population had validity for the TPLF. They investigated intensively a range of revolutionary precedents in China, the Soviet Union, Albania and elsewhere, including the writings of African leaders prominent in the struggle against colonialism. They discriminated betweem them on the grounds of practice and the attention they paid to the welfare of the poorest sectors. Albania was among these. Early in 1991 Meles Zenawi, in answer to my questions, paid tribute to these studies of revolutionary practice as having contributed to the political maturation of the TPLF, but denied that they had ever adopted Albania or any other country as a "model." Although the allegations have been rife in the West, where Albania existed more as a symbolic political "other" than as a coherently analysed set of political practices and popular responses, I have yet to see any substantiated evidence of TPLF political practice which justifies the association with Albanian Communism.
5. The TPLF was a party whose minimum common programme, anti-feudalism and anti-imperialism, had wide appeal in Tigray. MLLT was of much narrower appeal to the small educated minority and it is doubtful whether the mass of the people could distinguish its principles. Nevertheless, it was widely accepted by association with the TPLF, so intensely popular with the people as the source of the benefits of land redistribution and the baito. The rest of Ethiopia identified Marxism-Leninism with the brutal impositions of the Dergue and rejected it.
6. Meles Zenawi, interviewed in English in Hagere Selam, February 3-4, 1991.

Chapter 14

1. Iyassu Berhe, head of the TPLF Cultural Department, interviewed in English in Addis Ababa, October 4, 1991.
2. Blatta Haile Mariam Redda has since died.

3. Balambarass Mulaw Wores and Desta Abuy, farmers, interviewed in Tigrinya in Quiha, February 10, 1991.
4. Asrat, merchant, interviewed in Tigrinya in Mekelle, February 19, 1991.
5. See Glossary.
6. Alberto Sbacchi *Ethiopia under Mussolini: Fascism and the Colonial Experience*, Zed Press 1985.
7. I am indebted to Iyassu Berhe for sharing his researches with me. These poems I first heard in Asrega on and after June 18, 1989.
8. Kiros Aberra, Assefa Gebremariam and Kindaya Natu, farmers, interviewed in Tigrinya in Mekelle, February 11, 1991.
9. Yemane Kidane ("Jamaica"), founder member of the TPLF, interviewed in English in Mekelle, March 25, 1991.

Chapter 15

1. Tamrat Bezab, farmer from Subaha Sarsit, interviewed in Tigrinya in Adigrat, April 5, 1991.
2. Halefom Tekelu, farmer from Marwa district, interviewed in Tigrinya in Adigrat, April 5, 1991.
3. Sebhat Nega, interviewed in English in Mekelle, 4 April 1991.
4. Yemane Kidane ("Jamaica"), interviewed in English in Mekelle, March 25, 1991.
5. Iyassu Berhe, interviewed in English at Ruba Lemin, 31 March 1991; Sebhat Nega, interviewed in Mekelle, April 4, 1991.
6. Mebratu Adhanom, farmer, interviewed in Tigrinya in Sobeya, April 5, 1991.
7. Keshi Beraki Woldu, priest and farmer from Marwa, interviewed in Tigrinya, April 5, 1991.
8. Halefom Tekelu, farmer from Marwa, interviewed in Tigrinya, 5 April 1991.
9. Desta Kidane, farmer from Sobeya, interviewed in Tigrinya in Adigrat, April 5, 1991.
10. These religious groups or *mahber* are an important part of community life. They usually have as many members as there are months in the year and observe a particuar saint's day every month with special prayers, taking it in turns to host the gathering.
11. Halefom Tekelu, farmer from Marwa, interviewed in Tigrinya, April 5, 1991.

Chapter 16

1. Dahab Tesfay, peasant activist, interviewed in Tigrinya in Adi Nebried, April 17, 1991.

2. Roman Ayenew, peasant activist, interviewed in Tigrinya in Adi Nebried, April 17, 1991.
3. Asgede Gebreselassie, founder member of the TPLF, interviewed in Tigrinya in Endaselassie, April 16, 1991.

Chapter 18

1. Seyoum Gezai, Gebrehiwot Kiros and Tadesse Ayele, farmers, interviewed in Tigrinya in Adi Gudom, February 24, 1991.
2. The Battle of Hamusit, Saturday February 23; the capture of Tisabai power station, Sunday February 24; the defeat of the 603rd Army Corps, Monday February 25, 1991.
3. Zewdu Ayelew, Division Commander, interviewed in Tigrinya in Woldia, March 4, 1991.
4. His words reflect Dergue propaganda. The Dergue refused to recognize the existence of the coalition Front, EPRDF. It had only recently admitted the existence of the TPLF. Even now, since the end of the war, opposition groups refer to the EPRDF government as "the TPLF," possibly hoping to exploit old narrow nationalist rivalries between Tigray and Amhara.
5. Tadesse Kassa, EPDM, EPRDF Administrator in Bahr-Dar, interviewed in English in Bahr-Dar, March 6, 1991.
6. The TPLF/EPRDF have always denied the validity of the Dergue land reform in 1976. They say, on the one hand, that it facilitated, through the peasant associations set up for the purpose, an extension of social and political control, as well as the collection of unpopular taxes; on the other, that it was only a partial redistribution of land in that the Dergue kept feudal landlords in place when it suited its plans.
7. Atsede Teklai, woman fighter and bass player in TPLF and EPRDF cultural groups, interviewed in Tigrinya in Asrega on June 18, 1989. See Jenny Hammond, *Sweeter Than Honey: Testimonies of Tigrayan Women*, New Jersey, Red Sea Press 1990.
8. Bahr-Dar Textile Factory, March 9, 1991.
9. Battle of Gondar, Friday, March 7, 1991.
10. This incursion north of Adwa took place, curiously enough, on March 1, 1991, the anniversary of the Battle of Adwa in 1896, and so was referred to at the time as "the second Battle of Adwa".
11. Getane, head nurse, interviewed in Amharic, in Bahr-Dar Hospital, March 8, 1991.
12. By a curious coincidence, two months after this, I was travelling in Tigray with a Norwegian government official responsible for disaster relief. In the

course of conversation and exchange of experiences I described my time at the front. He was even more interested in this snippet than I was. Apparently his department was responsible for funding the Bahr-Dar hospital and the ICRC team, but as a civilian hospital.

13. Adam Ali, 26, farmer and Dergue prisoner of war, from Metekel in Gojjam, interviewed in Amharic in Bahr-Dar Hospital on March 8, 1991.

Chapter 19

1. The inconsistency in dating (seven years from 1985 would make it 1992) is probably an effect of translation from the Ethiopian calendar, which begins in September.
2. Kinfe Gebremedhin, Commander of EPRDF forces, interviewed in Tigrinya in Gondar, March 12, 1991.
3. Dawit Berhane, truck driver. This conversation in Tigrinya took place in Woldia, March 19, 1991.
4. Helawe Dagmawe, EPDM Administrator of Gondar, interviewed in English in Gondar, March 12, 1991.
5. Lisane Yohannes, teacher, member of the TPLF "underground", interviewed in English in Khartoum, May 9, 1991.
6. Kidane Asegahegn, hotel manager and member of the TPLF "underground", interviewed in Tigrinya in Gondar, March 15, 1991.
7. Geramo, teacher, interviewed in English in Gondar, March 15, 1991.

Chapter 20

1. Helawe Dagmawe, EPDM, EPRDF administrator of Gondar, interviewed in English in Gondar, March 12, 1991.
2. Hawudtu Ambiu, chairman of Debre Tabor *shengo*, interviewed in Amharic in Debre Tabor, March 16, 1991.
3. Genet Araya, woman fighter in battlefield medical team, interviewed in Tigrinya in Debre Tabor, March 16, 1991.
4. Desta Abraha, Vice-chairperson of the Women's Association of Woldia and representative to the *shengo* congress, interviewed in Amharic in Woldia, March 21, 1991.
5. Admassu Tilahun, member of woreda and Woldia *shengo,* a judge and member of the Justice Committee, interviewed in Amharic in Woldia, March 21, 1991.

6. Wele Yomar, chairman of peasants' association, Mengesha Asmamew, secretary of peasants' association, Yassin Gumata, responsible for redistribution of land, and Welku Meles, chairman of the *shengo*, interviewed in Amharic in *kebelle* Mahal Macherey 025, March 21, 1991.
7. Zemzem Nuriya, woman peasant and victim of resettlement, Admassu Teshame, farmer and victim of resettlement, Teferi Kebede, farmer, interviewed in Amharic in Mersa at EPRDF recruitment centre.
8. Sheikh Hassen Ali, merchant, interviewed in Amharic in Mersa, March 20, 1991.

Chapter 21

1. Meles Zenawi, Chairman of TPLF and EPRDF, interviewed in English in Hagere Selam, March 27/28, 1991.
2. Tamrat Layne, Chairman of EPDM, interviewed in English in Hagere Selam, March 29, 1991.
3. Fissaha Garedew, member of Central Committee staff of EDORM, interviewed in Amharic in Hagere Selam, March 29, 1991.
4. Kuma Demeksa, Chairman of OPDO, interviewed in Hagere Selam, March 30, 1991.
5. Meles Zenawi, Chairman of TPLF and EPRDF, interviewed in English in Hagere Selam, March 30, 1991.

INDEX